To Oppose Any Foe

TO OPPOSE ANY FOE

The Legacy of
U.S. Intervention in Vietnam

Edited by

Ross A. Fisher
John Norton Moore
Robert F. Turner

CAROLINA ACADEMIC PRESS

Durham, North Carolina

ISBN 1-59460-206-9
LCCN 2005937561

Carolina Academic Press
700 Kent St.
Durham, NC 27701
Telephone (919) 489-7486
Fax (919) 493-5668
www.cap-press.com

Printed in the United States of America

To Ambassador Frederick "Fritz" Nolting,
who served his country with distinction.

"Let every nation know, whether it wishes us well or ill, that we shall pay any price, bear any burden, meet any hardship, support any friend, oppose any foe, to assure the survival and success of liberty."

— President John F. Kennedy
Inaugural Address
January 20, 1961

Contents

Preface

Three decades have passed since the last American helicopter lifted off from Saigon, but the Vietnam War still lives in the American memory. Political candidates tout their combat experience in the conflict, while journalists and voters question the lack of participation by others. American battles overseas are certain to draw at least some comparisons to the Vietnam War, whether it be from those who criticize the intervention in the first place or those who find fault with the military execution.

Public opinion is still deeply split on the morality and wisdom of the conflict. The Vietnam War was so costly and divisive that the controversy surrounding it continues to this day, and perhaps no history of the war approaching objectivity will be possible until several more generations of historians have passed. It will be their task to wade through the polarized views of the conflict in search of a version that most resembles the truth.

Perhaps the only thing that all can agree on is that the effects of the Vietnam War on the course of American history and that of Southeast Asia have been profound. The war's legacy has influenced historical trends, policy ideas, political alignments, and legal ideas both in the United States and in the rest of the world. This book is a compilation of work by some very able University of Virginia law students exploring that legacy.

All but two of the essays in this book were products of a seminar on "Legal and Policy Issues of the Indochina War," which for the past fifteen years has been taught by Professors John Norton Moore and Robert F. Turner, who in 1981 co-founded the University of Virginia's Center for National Security Law. Two of the essays in this compilation, Michael Charles Rakower's "The Khmer Rouge: An Analysis of One of the World's Most Brutal Regimes" and Benjamin

Kringer's "The Third Indochina War: A Case Study on the Vietnamese Invasion of Cambodia," were written in another seminar taught by Professor Moore entitled "The Rule of Law: Controlling Government." They were selected because they are germane to the themes of this book. These essays represent work of sufficient quality that we felt they should be shared with a broader audience.

The essays were chosen as well because they explore themes that have not been fully explored by other scholars in the field and express views that make an original contribution to the Vietnam debate. Many of these views have been expressed in some form by others, but the writers of these essays have each added something of value to think about for those interested in examining the Vietnam War in another light. The broad theme of the book is a multifaceted analysis of the legacy of America's involvement in Vietnam, a commitment that the United States undertook many years before the first Marines landed on its shores and the name of the country became a household word in American living rooms.

The title is drawn from President John F. Kennedy's inaugural address in January 1961, in which he promised that America would "pay any price, bear any burden, meet any hardship, support any friend, oppose any foe, to assure the survival and success of liberty" around the world. This pledge, which reinforced a commitment made with but a single dissent by the U.S. Senate when it consented to the ratification of the SEATO Treaty in 1955, ultimately led to America's long and arduous struggle in Indochina. As editors, we will not pass judgment on whether this commitment was imprudent or the promise too sweeping. Indeed, we hold differing views on the subject and want to emphasize that the authors of these essays argue on behalf of their individual views alone.

Yet, we have agreed that each of these essays makes a contribution toward achieving a better understanding of the causes and consequences of the Vietnam conflict. Moreover, they have been chosen with an eye toward those who have best profited from the use of primary sources in the formulation of their arguments, for with a subject as controversial as the Vietnam War, it is especially important to step back from the overheated rhetoric and look to the raw facts to draw conclusions. Excessive reliance on secondary sources, though sometimes necessary in historical research, can have egregiously unfortunate results when opinion on a topic is so split. Heroes become villains, incompetents become geniuses, victories become defeats, and sometimes even right becomes wrong, all depending on one's personal views of the issue being studied. For instance, the 1968 Tet Offensive was a devastating political defeat for the United States, but in fact it was a smashing military victory because the Viet Cong ranks were repulsed and decimated in the encounter. For each American or South Vietnamese soldier killed during the Tet Offensive, Hanoi or the Viet Cong lost ten. Certainly, the repulse was costly, but perhaps that is the crux of the matter. One's view of whether the incident was a victory or a defeat depends on personal opinions regarding the broader conflict and whether the struggle was worth the cost.

Thus can broader historiographical trends be influenced by the spirit of the time period in which the author is writing as well as his or her personal opinions. History is full of such examples. Historians' views of Reconstruction, for instance, have undergone a dramatic revision in the last few decades, completely overturning the dim view of the era that had reigned since the late nineteenth century. Earlier views of the radical Republicans as vindictive conquerors have been replaced by an image of them as munificent apostles of a biracial democracy whose opinions were ahead of their time. President Andrew Johnson has been transformed in historical accounts from a champion of moderation and reconciliation into a petulant and egotistical racist. Which version is right? One has to look to the original sources and judge for oneself, and the values of the historian inevitably enter into the equation. With time, a similar phenomenon may occur with regard to the Vietnam War.

It is too soon to say what direction that shift may take. The bulk of present-day Vietnam War chroniclers, taking their cue from a string of prizewinning journalistic accounts, still regard the Vietnam War as a tragic mistake and portray its perpetrators as hubristic and arrogant Cold Warriors. "Vietnam" has thus entered the American political lexicon as a synonym for "foreign policy failure." That account may have some merit, but it is being challenged by a new breed of scholars and historians who contend that the cause in Vietnam was noble and the objectives important. And that view is strengthened by the realities that followed the American withdrawal and the Communist conquest of South Vietnam, Laos, and Cambodia—including the slaughter of an estimated three million human beings by the new Communist regimes, more lives than had been lost in the previous fourteen years of combat. Now is a good time for scholars to explore other possibilities aside from the caricatures that have emerged from authors on both sides whose bitterness diminishes the value of their work.

This book is divided into three sections, each representing a different aspect of the Vietnam legacy: historical, legal, and contemporary. The first section deals with the historical legacy of the war and begins with an analysis of the U.S. commitment to support President Ngo Dinh Diem in his fight to stave off Ho Chi Minh's attempts to conquer South Vietnam. Many contend that it was the seminal event of Diem's overthrow that triggered the decision in 1965 to escalate the conflict, and thus it sets the scene for the other essays. Subsequent essays in this section deal with the consequences and logic behind U.S. intervention in the Vietnam conflict. The book then turns to the aftermath of U.S. withdrawal with regard to the fate of Vietnam and the broader region of Southeast Asia. The slaughter of Cambodians at the hands of Pol Pot's Communist regime and the deaths of tens of thousands of South Vietnamese represent serious consequences of U.S. withdrawal that have not drawn the amount of attention they deserve. The second section analyzes the effect of the Vietnam War on legal developments, a variegated subject because so many controversies involving international and constitutional law have arisen as a result of the conflict. Legal issues with regard to the legitimate use of force, naval warfare, intelligence gathering, and human rights have all witnessed developments as a result of the Vietnam controversy. Finally, the book concludes with essays on the influence that the Vietnam War exerts on contemporary policy issues like the U.S. mission in Somalia, the proper advisory role of the Joint Chiefs of Staff, the ongoing war in Iraq, and international terrorism.

President Kennedy's words hold renewed meaning at a time when America is so broadly engaged overseas in defense of its liberty, values, and security. Terrorism rather than Communism is now our principal global adversary in a different "long, twilight struggle." In a sense, the lessons are similar. We have learned since September 11, 2001, that even after the end of the Cold War, our cause remains inextricably tied to the success of freedom throughout the world. Yet, differences remain. The invasion of Iraq, for instance, has drawn intense controversy with regard to whether it was a proper front in the war on terror, just as Americans still argue over whether Vietnam was the right place for engagement in the battle against Communism. Continuing the debate about the best way to advance the cause of freedom and listening with an open mind to differing views on that subject is a fitting tribute to the liberty for which America fights.

Ross A. Fisher
John Norton Moore
Robert F. Turner

Acknowledgments

Special thanks goes to the authors of these essays for graciously agreeing to the publication of their papers in this book. Each one has something valuable to say, and we hope that their arguments will compel readers to think on this subject from fresh perspectives.

Equally valuable are the speakers who have visited the seminar from which these essays originated. They consist of scholars and authors, former government officials, veterans, and, in some cases, all of the above, and they all share a passion for learning from the experiences of the Vietnam War and educating others about it. Some are still living and others have passed away, but all have made an immeasurable contribution to the understanding of the authors who wrote the essays in this compilation. Distinguished speakers who have addressed the seminar include: Dr. Norman Graebner, Professor Robert O'Neil, Dr. Lewis Sorley, Dr. H. R. McMaster, Colonel Harry Summers, the Honorable James Schlesinger (former Director of Central Intelligence and Secretary of Defense during the final days of the war), General Al Grey (former Commandant, U.S. Marine Corps), Admiral Thomas Moorer (former Chairman, Joint Chiefs of Staff), Commander Paul Galanti (USN, retired, and POW during the Vietnam War), Dr. Robert E. Morris, Dr. Marin Strmecki (who assisted President Nixon in writing *No More Vietnams*), Professor W. Hays Parks, Dr. Jeffrey Addicott, Dr. Gary Solis, and the Honorable William E. Colby (former Director of Central Intelligence and CIA Station Chief in Saigon before the war).

We also appreciate the assistance of the administrative staff of the Center for National Security Law, Donna Ganoe, Kay Wood, Kathy Wood, and Elyse Hunter, on this project. In addition, we would especially like to thank Joanna Murdick, a valued member of the Center's staff who for many years helped organize and coordinate this and other seminars, for taking on the task of copyediting, formatting, and indexing the volume. Lastly, we would like to thank the donors to the Center for National Security Law whose contributions helped fund this publication.

The following publishers have kindly granted permission to reprint lengthy quotations:

- In chapter 1, Frederick Nolting, *From Trust to Tragedy: The Political Memoirs of Frederick Nolting, Kennedy's Ambassador to Diem's Vietnam* © 1988. Reproduced with permission of Greenwood Publishing Group, Inc., Westport, CT.
- In chapter 4, Serge Thion, "The Cambodian Idea of Revolution," *in Revolution and Its Aftermath in Kampuchea* (David P. Chandler & Ben Kiernan eds., 1983) (Yale Southeast Asia Studies Monograph Series). Reprinted by permission of Yale University Southeast Asia Studies.
- In chapter 5, Karl D. Jackson, *Cambodia, 1975-1978* © 1989 Princeton University Press. Reprinted by permission of Princeton University Press; and Kenneth Quinn, "Explaining the Terror," *in Cambodia 1975-1978* (Karl Jackson ed., 1989). Reprinted by permission of Princeton University Press.
- And in chapter 11, James L. Woods, "U.S. Government Decisionmaking Processes During Humanitarian Operations in Somalia," *in Learning from Somalia* (Walter Clarke & Jeffrey Herbst eds., 1997). Reprinted by permission of Westview Press, a member of Perseus Books, L.L.C.

About the Editors

Ross A. Fisher is from Great Falls, Virginia. He attended Princeton University and graduated *summa cum laude* in 1999 with an A.B. degree in history. While writing his senior thesis, he worked extensively with the papers of George W. Ball, the under secretary of state for Presidents John F. Kennedy and Lyndon Johnson. Mr. Fisher attended the University of Virginia School of Law, where he received a J.D. and a Masters Degree in History in 2004. He is now an attorney at the law firm of Kaye Scholer LLP in Washington, D.C., and lives in Arlington, Virginia.

John Norton Moore is the Walter L. Brown Professor of Law at the University of Virginia School of Law, where he serves as Director of the Center for National Security Law, which he founded in 1981. For more than two decades he also served as Director of the Graduate Law Program at the University of Virginia. A former four-term chairman of the American Bar Association's prestigious Standing Committee on Law and National Security, he is the author or editor of 27 books and more than 160 scholarly articles. He has held seven presidential appointments in government, including serving two terms from 1986 to 1991 as the first Chairman of the Board of Directors of the United States Institute of Peace. He has also served as Counselor on International Law to the Department of State, Ambassador to the Third United Nations Conference on the Law of the Sea, and Chairman of the National Security Council Interagency Task Force on the Law of the Sea. He has served twice as a member of U.S. legal teams arguing cases before the International Court of Justice. He served for two decades on the editorial board of the *American Journal of International Law*, and contributed numerous articles to the *Journal* and other legal periodicals on various aspects of the Indo-China conflict. He is a member of the Council on Foreign Relations, the Order of the Coif, Phi Beta Kappa, and many other professional and honorary organizations. He also served as the Legal Advisor to the Kuwait Representative to the United Nations Iraq-Kuwait Boundary Demarcation Commission. With respect to the Indochina War, Professor Moore has been actively involved with the legal issues of the conflict for more than three decades and was the principal co-author of the lengthy legal brief on the conflict approved by the American Bar Association in 1966 and placed in the *Congressional Record* by Senator Jacob Javits. Professor Moore worked on the legal issues while Counselor on International Law to the Department of State, met with congressional leaders on the issues, wrote the book *Law and the Indo-China War*, which won the Phi Beta Kappa Award at the University of Virginia, was a principal figure in the national legal debate on the war, and, more recently, edited *The Vietnam Debate: A Fresh Look at the Arguments* (1990) and *The* Real *Lessons of the Vietnam War: Reflections Twenty-Five Years After the Fall of Saigon* (2002).

Robert F. Turner holds both professional and academic doctorates from the University of Virginia School of Law. He co-founded the Center for National Security Law in 1981 and has continued to serve as its Associate Director since then, except for absences for government service. During 1994-95, he occupied the Charles H. Stockton Chair of International Law at the U.S. Naval War College in Newport, Rhode Island, where he taught a seminar on "The Lessons of Vietnam." He has also taught a popular undergraduate seminar on Vietnam at Virginia and for many years has co-taught a postgraduate interdisciplinary Vietnam seminar at the Law School with Professor Moore, from which most of the chapters in this volume emerged. A former three-term chairman of both the ABA Standing Committee on Law and National Security and the Committee on Executive-Congressional Relations of the ABA Section of International Law and Practice, he served extensively in Indochina between 1968 and the final evacuation in 1975—first as a journalist, then twice as an Army officer on detail to the American Embassy in Saigon, and finally while serving as national security adviser to a member of the U.S. Senate Committee on Foreign

Relations. In addition to traveling through Laos and Cambodia, he visited 42 of South Vietnam's 44 provinces. His highly-acclaimed 1975 book, *Vietnamese Communism: Its Origins and Development*, was one of about two dozen books on Vietnam recommended in the *Washington Post Book World* in April 1985, and one of about a dozen books mentioned in an author's postscript to President Nixon's *No More Vietnams*. Professor Turner has served as Special Assistant to the Under Secretary of Defense for Policy in the Pentagon, as Counsel to the President's Intelligence Oversight Board at the White House, as Principal Deputy Assistant Secretary of State for Legislative and Intergovernmental Affairs, and as the first President of the U.S. Institute of Peace. Author or editor of more than a dozen books or monographs and many articles, he has testified before more than a dozen committees of Congress on various issues of international and constitutional law and is a member of the Council on Foreign Relations, the Academy of Political Science, the Committee on the Present Danger, and other professional organizations.

About the Contributors

Captain Jane G. Dalton, JAGC, USN, is the Navy's Assistant Judge Advocate General for Civil Law. She manages a 75-person legal team that advises the Secretary of the Navy, the Chief of Naval Operations, the Judge Advocate General, and Navy commanders world-wide in the areas of international and operational law, admiralty law, environmental law, administrative law, claims and tort litigation, other general Navy litigation, immigration and legal assistance, and national security and intelligence oversight law. Previous positions include the Legal Counsel to the Chairman of the Joint Chiefs of Staff (2000-2003) and Commanding Officer, Naval Legal Service Office, North Central (1998-2000). A 28-year career naval officer, CAPT Dalton joined the Navy as a line officer and qualified as a Surface Warfare Officer before being accepted into the Navy's Law Education Program and transferring to the Judge Advocate General's Corps.

Ross A. Fisher. See "About the Editors."

Mark H. Hamer is a partner in the San Diego, California, office of DLA Piper Rudnick Gray Cary U.S. LLP, where he specializes in antitrust and securities class action litigation. He graduated from the University of Virginia in 1988 with a B.A. in History, with High Distinction. As an undergraduate, he was a member of the Distinguished Majors Program in History. In 1991, he graduated from the University of Virginia School of Law, where he served on the *Virginia Law Review*. He is a native of Memphis, Tennessee.

Major Brian Allan Hughes is in the Judge Advocate General's Corps of the United States Army. He is presently assigned as the Chief of Military Justice, United States Army Southern European Task Force (Airborne), Vicenza, Italy. He received his J.D. from the University of Virginia School of Law in 2000, where he was recognized as a member of the Order of the Coif. He received an M.B.A. from Troy State University as a Truman Scholar in 1997. He received a B.A. from Claremont McKenna College, where he graduated *summa cum laude* as a Distinguished Military Graduate and Arthur Adams Strategic Studies Fellow in 1992. Previous assignments include Chief of Operational Law, 173d Airborne Brigade, Operation Iraqi Freedom (Bronze Star, Combat Jump Star); Chief of Operational Law, United States Army Southern European Task Force (Airborne), Vicenza, Italy; Chief of Operational Law, 2d Infantry Division, Uijongbu, Korea; Assistant Operations Officer, 3d U.S. Infantry Regiment (The Old Guard), Washington, DC; Commander, Presidential Salute Gun Battery; and Platoon Leader, 1st Battalion, 503d Parachute Infantry Regiment, Tongduchon, Korea.

Benjamin E. Kringer is currently an associate in the Washington D.C. office of Baker Botts LLP. Licensed to practice law in Virginia and Washington, Mr. Kringer represents both domestic and international clients in a variety of civil and criminal matters, including allegations of RICO violations, antitrust and breach of contract. Mr. Kringer attended college at William & Mary, receiving a B.A. in economics, and earned his law degree from the University of Virginia in Charlottesville, Virginia.

Gary R. Lawson, II, from Coronado, California, is a 1997 graduate of the United States Naval Academy and a former Marine infantryman. He is currently pursuing graduate degrees in law and business administration from the University of Virginia.

Michael A. McCann is an assistant professor of law at Mississippi College School of Law. He received an LL.M. from Harvard Law School, a J.D. from the University of Virginia School of Law, where he was a Hardy Cross Dillard Fellow, and a B.A., *magna cum laude*, from Georgetown University. He has also published articles in law reviews affiliated with Yale Law School, the University of Virginia School of Law, and the University of Wisconsin Law School.

Hiren P. Patel was born in Nairobi, Kenya, but grew up in Columbus, Georgia. He received a B.A. from Rice University in Houston, Texas, in 2000, *cum laude*, in political science and policy studies. He received a J.D. from the University of Virginia School of Law in 2003. While in law school he was Managing Editor of the *Virginia Tax Review*, Chief Justice of the Moot Court Board, and part of the University of Virginia's national champion and international semifinalist team at the Philip C. Jessup Moot Court Competition in 2001. He currently practices law in San Diego, California, at the law firm of DLA Piper Rudnick Gray Cary U.S. LLP.

Michael Charles Rakower obtained his B.A., *cum laude*, from the University of Pennsylvania in 1993. He received his J.D. in 1999 from the University of Virginia School of Law, where he served on the Managing Board of the *Virginia Journal of International Law*. Following graduation, he joined Latham & Watkins LLP as an associate in their New York office, regularly leading securities offerings valued in the hundreds of millions of dollars for issuers and underwriters and frequently providing M&A counseling to investment banks. Mr. Rakower also counseled businesses devastated by the attack on the World Trade Center and obtained political asylum for refugees. After leaving Latham & Watkins LLP, Mr. Rakower served in the Prosecutor's Office of the United Nations International Criminal Tribunal for Rwanda (ICTR), assisting in the prosecution of Rwandan military leaders for their role in the 1994 genocide. Following his work at the ICTR, Mr. Rakower represented a prison inmate in a federal lawsuit against the City of New York that resulted in a six-figure settlement and was featured on the front page of the *New York Law Journal*. Mr. Rakower recently completed a clerkship with the Honorable Richard C. Wesley of the United States Court of Appeals for the Second Circuit and has returned to private practice as a solo practitioner. Mr. Rakower sits on the Board of Directors of the American Friends for the Kigali Public Library, a non-profit organization committed to building Rwanda's first public library, and on the Board of Acelero Learning Plainfield, an organization designed to administer a federal Head Start program to low-income families in New Jersey. Mr. Rakower is married to Sali Rakower, a fellow 1999 graduate of the University of Virginia School of Law.

John H. Raleigh graduated, *magna cum laude*, from the University of Notre Dame with a B.A. in English Literature in 1992, and received a J.D. from the University of Virginia in 1995. From 1995 through 1999, he worked for the international law firm, Squire, Sanders & Dempsey LLP, specializing in corporate and international law. He is currently a Vice President in the Legal Department of International Management Group, an international sports marketing and management group.

Lieutenant Colonel Ronald R. Ratton is a member of the USAF JAG Corps. He was commissioned through the United States Air Force Academy in 1985 where he received a B.S. in International Affairs. After completing Signals Intelligence Officer Technical Training, he served as an intelligence officer in North Carolina and Texas. From 1990 to 1993, Lt Col Ratton attended Notre Dame Law School in South Bend, Indiana, where he graduated *cum laude* in 1993. In 1993, he was assigned as a JAG to the 12th Flying Training Wing, Randolph AFB, Texas. In July 1996, he was assigned as the Staff Judge Advocate for the 424th Air Base Squadron, RAF Fairford, England, where he served until August 1998. Next, he attended the University of Virginia School of Law, earning a Master of Laws in International Law in 1999. In June 1999, he was assigned to the U.S. Embassy in Rome, Italy, where he served as Deputy Officer in Charge, U.S. Sending State Office for Italy. From July to September 2000, Lt Col Ratton deployed to HQ SFOR, Camp Butmir, Sarajevo, Bosnia-Herzegovina, where he served as an assistant legal advisor. In July 2002, he was assigned as the Staff Judge Advocate, 374th Airlift Wing, Yokota Air Base, Japan. Lt Col Ratton is a member of the Indiana Bar.

Historical

I

The Kennedy Administration and the Overthrow of Ngo Dinh Diem: What Happened, Why Did It Happen, and Was It a Good Idea?

Ross A. Fisher

INTRODUCTION

The role that President John F. Kennedy's administration played in the coup that ousted South Vietnamese leader Ngo Dinh Diem was one of the most controversial foreign policy episodes of the Vietnam War. Diem's relationship with the U.S. government traversed several rocky periods dating from the late 1950s,[1] but his 1963 clashes with the Buddhists and what many perceived to be his "authoritarian" nature were the most significant factors leading to his overthrow.[2] The perception, unfortunately for Diem, was more critical than the reality. Several influential American newsmen loathed him, and they had the ear of Henry Cabot Lodge, who was appointed ambassador to Vietnam just as Diem's troops raided the Xa Loi and other major Buddhist pagodas in August of 1963.[3] The news reports on Diem's alleged Buddhist repression also heavily influenced American public opinion and many officials in the U.S. government.[4] Diem had a large contingent of

---

[1] WILLIAM COLBY & JAMES MCCARGAR, LOST VICTORY: A FIRSTHAND ACCOUNT OF AMERICA'S SIXTEEN-YEAR INVOLVEMENT IN VIETNAM 74-75 (1989).

[2] *Id.* at 29-30.

[3] NEIL SHEEHAN, A BRIGHT SHINING LIE: JOHN PAUL VANN AND AMERICA IN VIETNAM 359-60 (1988).

[4] GEORGE BALL, THE PAST HAS ANOTHER PATTERN: MEMOIRS 370 (1982).

admirers as well as critics within the Kennedy administration, making the American role in his overthrow an episode over which, as Robert Kennedy later put it, "the government split in two."[5]

Diem's harshest critics in the Kennedy administration and those largely responsible for his overthrow were those who, generally speaking, had the most doubts about the war. Foremost among them were Averell Harriman, Roger Hilsman, and George Ball of the State Department, as well as Michael Forrestal, a Vietnam specialist working in the White House.[6] Diem's relationship with Harriman, the assistant secretary of state for Far Eastern affairs, soured when Diem protested Harriman's negotiated neutralization of Laos, which further opened South Vietnam's Laotian border to North Vietnamese infiltration.[7] The U.S. ambassador to India, John Kenneth Galbraith, urged the Kennedy administration not to tie its support to Diem and helped convince his good friend Ball, the under secretary of state, that Diem was a liability.[8] Yet, neither Ball nor Secretary of State Dean Rusk was heavily engaged on the Vietnam issue at that time. Ball was deeply involved with U.S. policy toward Western Europe,[9] while Rusk was preoccupied with Cold War issues involving Berlin and the Soviet Union.[10] This situation gave a great deal of autonomy to Far East specialists like Hilsman, Harriman, and Forrestal, who took advantage of the power vacuum on this issue to press their anti-

---

[5] EVAN THOMAS & WALTER ISAACSON, THE WISE MEN: SIX FRIENDS AND THE WORLD THEY MADE 639 (1986).

[6] *Id.* at 635-39.

[7] FREDERICK NOLTING, FROM TRUST TO TRAGEDY: THE POLITICAL MEMOIRS OF FREDERICK NOLTING, KENNEDY'S AMBASSADOR TO DIEM'S VIETNAM 83 (1988). Harriman later became under secretary of state for political affairs, the third-ranking official at the State Department, in 1963. Hilsman, who before Harriman's promotion had been director of the State Department Bureau of Intelligence and Research, then became assistant secretary of state for Far Eastern affairs. ELLEN J. HAMMER, A DEATH IN NOVEMBER: AMERICA IN VIETNAM, 1963, at 31, 39 (1987).

[8] BALL, *supra* note 4, at 370.

[9] *See, e.g., id.* at 208-22.

[10] NOLTING, *supra* note 7, at 129.

Diem agenda when the Buddhist crisis exploded.[11] They argued that Diem's crackdown was turning the Vietnamese population against the government, which was making it impossible to win the war against the Viet Cong.[12] Rusk and Ball, the first- and second-ranking officials at the State Department, respectively, approved the telegrams of the anti-Diem cabal with little protest and largely delegated the Diem issue to the Vietnam and Southeast Asia specialists within the administration.[13] This confluence of factors led to the sending of the August 24, 1963, cable that unleashed the chain of events culminating in Diem's overthrow.[14]

Yet, Diem had his supporters within the administration, who were led by Frederick Nolting, Lodge's predecessor as ambassador to Saigon, and were concentrated among the U.S. military and intelligence community.[15] Nolting, General Maxwell Taylor of the Joint Chiefs of Staff, General Paul Harkins of the Military Assistance Command in Vietnam, William Colby and John McCone of the Central Intelligence Agency, and several others strongly opposed undermining Diem.[16] To counter the critics' contentions that the war was unwinnable under Diem, they pointed to progress that Diem had made against the Viet Cong in spite of the Buddhist protests.[17] They believed that Diem was the strongest

---

[11] *See* Memorandum from Michael V. Forrestal of the National Security Council Staff to President John F. Kennedy (July 3, 1963), *in* 3 FOREIGN RELATIONS OF THE UNITED STATES, 1961-1963: VIETNAM 448 (John P. Glennon, Edward Keefer & Louis J. Smith eds., 1991) [hereinafter 3 FRUS: VIETNAM].

[12] Memorandum of a Conference with the President, White House, Washington (Aug. 28, 1963), *in* 4 FOREIGN RELATIONS OF THE UNITED STATES, 1961-1963: VIETNAM 2-6 (John P. Glennon & Edward C. Keefer eds., 1991) [hereinafter 4 FRUS: VIETNAM]; BALL, *supra* note 4, at 372.

[13] BALL, *supra* note 4, at 371-72.

[14] Telegram from the Department of State to the Embassy in Vietnam (Aug. 24, 1963), *in* 3 FRUS: VIETNAM, at 628.

[15] MAXWELL D. TAYLOR, SWORDS AND PLOWSHARES 290 (1972).

[16] COLBY & MCCARGAR, *supra* note 1, at 138-39.

[17] *Id.* at 142-43.

man to lead the South Vietnamese and that he was without peer as a leader in comparison to his rivals.[18]

Although the Vietnamese coup leaders initially backed off their plans at the end of August, Lodge kept up a steady drumbeat of support for a potential coup.[19] The plotting generals kept in touch with the Embassy and CIA field agents in South Vietnam regarding their plans while Lodge secured approval from Washington for a policy "not to thwart" a coup.[20] When it was clear in late October that the dissident generals would soon launch their coup, a fierce new debate took place within the Kennedy administration between Diem's supporters and opponents, but by then it was too late to change the course of events.[21] Diem was overthrown and brutally killed, an unanticipated development that shocked President Kennedy and several others within the administration.[22]

Critics within the administration argued that Diem was a dictator who oppressed and alienated the Buddhist majority and that the United States could therefore not win the war with him in command.[23] The facts, however, belie the underlying elements of these arguments. Diem, it is true, had a poor touch for public relations, especially toward the world outside of Vietnam.[24] Nor did he maintain the same level of adherence to civil liberties as that which existed in the United States.[25] However, he was a democratically elected leader who was facing in the Buddhist

---

[18] Memorandum of a Conference with the President, White House, Washington (Aug. 28, 1963), *supra* note 12, at 2-6; TAYLOR, *supra* note 15, at 290, 295.

[19] Telegram From the Embassy in Vietnam by Ambassador Henry Cabot Lodge to the Department of State (Sept. 5, 1963), *in* 4 FRUS: VIETNAM, at 110.

[20] Telegram From the Embassy in Vietnam by Ambassador Henry Cabot Lodge to the Department of State (Oct. 5, 1963), *in* 4 FRUS: VIETNAM, at 367.

[21] Memorandum of a Conference with the President, White House, Washington (Oct. 29, 1963), *in* 4 FRUS: VIETNAM, at 470.

[22] TAYLOR, *supra* note 15, at 301.

[23] BALL, *supra* note 4, at 370.

[24] Telegram From the Embassy in Vietnam by Ambassador Henry Cabot Lodge to the Department of State (Aug. 30, 1963), *in* 4 FRUS: VIETNAM, at 58.

[25] MARGUERITE HIGGINS, OUR VIETNAM NIGHTMARE 167 (1965).

protesters a group committed to subverting his government[26] and, as history later showed, heavily influenced by the Communists.[27] While Diem was most unpopular in the cities where the protests were erupting, his popularity in the countryside, where the bulk of the Vietnamese lived, remained solid.[28] Moreover, the progress of the war made under Diem in 1963 showed that his conflicts with the Buddhists had not undermined the war effort as his critics contended.[29] This situation was similar to the one faced by the United States involving South Korean leader Syngman Rhee in the Korean War, yet America did not support a coup against him.[30] Subsequent events exposed the weaknesses of the arguments employed by Diem's critics as the South Vietnamese position rapidly deteriorated upon his downfall.[31] Moreover, the coup sent a message to other leaders in the region that it was dangerous to be a U.S. ally.[32] Therefore, support for the Diem coup was the most serious error that the Kennedy administration made in its policy toward Vietnam.

---

[26] Senator Thomas Dodd, Speech to the United States Senate and Information Introduced Into the Record with the Speech (Feb. 23, 1965) (on file with the CREST Cold War History Project at the National Archives in College Park, Maryland) (citing Marguerite Higgins, *The Buddhist Militants: Isn't It Time to Face the Truth*, WASH. STAR (Jan. 23, 1965)).

[27] TAYLOR, *supra* note 15, at 368.

[28] Memorandum of a Conversation, White House, Washington (Sept. 10, 1963), *in* 4 FRUS: VIETNAM, at 161.

[29] *Id.*

[30] *See, e.g.,* QUEE-YOUNG KIM, THE FALL OF SYNGMAN RHEE 16 (1983); *see also* RICHARD C. ALLEN, KOREA'S SYNGMAN RHEE: AN UNAUTHORIZED PORTRAIT 138-51 (1960).

[31] LYNDON JOHNSON, THE VANTAGE POINT: PERSPECTIVES ON THE PRESIDENCY, 1963-1969, at 43-44 (1971).

[32] RICHARD M. NIXON, RN: THE MEMOIRS OF RICHARD NIXON 256-57 (1990).

DIEM'S ASCENT TO POWER AND UNLIKELY SURVIVAL

"The Miracle of Diem": A Prelude to Invasion

Despite the controversy that later engulfed Diem, even his critics conceded that his tenure as president of Vietnam started auspiciously.[33] He garnered a reputation among both Americans and Vietnamese as a patriot of great integrity after refusing to cooperate with the French colonialists before World War II and subsequently spurning Ho Chi Minh's offer for a position in his Cabinet.[34] When Ho Chi Minh asked Diem to join him in 1946, Diem responded,

> You and I want totally different futures for Vietnam. Can you guarantee you will not try and impose a dictatorship of the proletariat here? . . . I have seen your agents at work . . . . They act like criminals . . . . Your agents have the blood of many honest nationalists on their hands.[35]

After fleeing South Vietnam for fear of his life, he returned following the withdrawal of the French and the partition of Vietnam.[36] Senator Mike Mansfield, a later critic of Diem, hailed him at the time for his "nationalism, his personal incorruptibility and courage, and his idealistic determination."[37] Diem was supported by the U.S. government and overwhelmingly elected by

---

[33] *See, e.g.,* ROGER HILSMAN, TO MOVE A NATION: THE POLITICS OF FOREIGN POLICY IN THE ADMINISTRATION OF JOHN F. KENNEDY 417 (1967).

[34] HIGGINS, *supra* note 25, at 157-58.

[35] Higgins drew her account from Diem and information from a French diplomat to whom Ho Chi Minh had described the conversation. *Id.*

[36] *Id.*

[37] ARTHUR M. SCHLESINGER, JR., A THOUSAND DAYS 300 (1965). When John F. Kennedy was a congressman in the early 1950s, he was invited to meet Diem by Justice William O. Douglas along with Mike Mansfield. According to Ellen Hammer, "They were impressed by the confidence and depth of feeling revealed by this normally shy man when he spoke of his country and his self-appointed mission to win freedom for Vietnam." HAMMER, *supra* note 7, at 47.

the South Vietnamese people over the opposition of Bao Dai following the withdrawal of the French from Vietnam.[38]

Yet, even his greatest supporters doubted Diem's ability to fend off the North Vietnamese Communists and still unify South Vietnam, which was riven by feuding sects.[39] When Secretary of State John Foster Dulles pressed French Prime Minister Pierre Mendès-France to support Diem on October 3, 1954, Mendès-France, "after reiterating French misgivings as to Diem's ability, told Secretary Dulles he would give [Diem a] . . . 'good try.'"[40] The U.S. top secret report on the negotiations conceded to the National Security Council that "Diem's opponents may simmer for [the] time being, but he still faces [a] protracted fight to ensure control" because "[h]e can't count on real loyalty of any of [the] existing politico-military groups."[41] It added that the government in South Vietnam was "unable to get on its feet."[42] Another recently declassified top secret National Security Council briefing regarding South Vietnam given on October 25, 1954, was riddled with pessimism. "Our army attache estimates that present trends will result by late 1955 in Communist-dominated coalition government in the south or a complete Communist takeover," the report stated, "except possibly of major population centers."[43] Moreover, the report stated, "army morale is low" and "[d]isunity in South [Vietnam] puts Diem in [a] weak position in forthcoming discussions with [the] Viet Minh on national elections."[44] The next day, the NSC was informed that the South Vietnamese

---

[38] COLBY & MCCARGAR, *supra* note 1, at 112.

[39] *Id.* at 128.

[40] National Security Council Briefing on the Situation in South Vietnam (Oct. 5, 1954) (unpublished and recently declassified top secret briefing) (on file with the CREST Cold War History Project at the National Archives in College Park, Maryland).

[41] *Id.*

[42] *Id.*

[43] National Security Council Briefing on the Situation in South Vietnam (Oct. 25, 1954) (unpublished and recently declassified top secret briefing) (on file with the CREST Cold War History Project at the National Archives in College Park, Maryland).

[44] *Id.*

"[g]overnment paralysis continues," and "Diem stays in [power] only because [the] opposition fear[s] to remove him physically."[45] Observers viewed the situation with concern. Vice President Richard Nixon discussed the situation at the time with the high commissioner of Malaysia, Sir Gerald Templer. "We talked about the situation in Indochina," Nixon remembered, "and Templer shook his head sadly. 'I hate to admit this because he's a real SOB, but what they need there is a Rhee,'" Templer said in reference to Syngman Rhee, South Korea's authoritarian anti-Communist leader at the time.[46] This drastic proposal was evidence of the chaos into which Diem stepped, a situation contemporary observers believed only the strongest of leaders could tame.

Yet, Diem unified South Vietnam against all odds. Even Roger Hilsman, who was later one of the chief supporters of Diem's overthrow, wrote that "[n]o one who knew the situation in Vietnam gave Diem more than a very slight chance of coming out alive, much less of bringing the country under his control. But somehow he did it . . . ."[47] The economic revival and progress of South Vietnam during the 1950s was dubbed by many as "the miracle of Diem."[48] He methodically brought the rival sects under his control, which stabilized the country and laid the foundations for economic growth.[49] From 1955 to 1961, production in the South Vietnamese economy improved across a broad swath of sectors. Rice production increased from 2.8 to 4.6 million metric tons, rubber production increased from 66,000 to 79,000 metric tons, and commercial catches of fish increased from 100,000 to 250,000 tons.[50] With U.S. aid, fifty-one factories were built in South Vietnam, which Ambassador Frederick Nolting described as "the

---

[45] National Security Council Briefing on the Situation in South Vietnam (Oct. 26, 1954) (unpublished and recently declassified top secret briefing) (on file with the CREST Cold War History Project at the National Archives in College Park, Maryland).

[46] NIXON, *supra* note 32, at 122.

[47] HILSMAN, *supra* note 33, at 417.

[48] NOLTING, *supra* note 7, at 7.

[49] DEAN RUSK & RICHARD RUSK, AS I SAW IT 436 (Daniel S. Rapp ed., 1990).

[50] NOLTING, *supra* note 7, at 7.

beginning of an industrial base in a country which until then had no industrial base whatsoever."[51]

Diem also instituted programs to improve transportation, communications, rural health, and education across South Vietnam.[52] Under his leadership, South Vietnam launched an ambitious anti-malaria campaign in the countryside,[53] established two new universities, and four new vocational schools.[54] Hilsman later credited him for his dramatic improvement of the South Vietnamese educational system, noting that "the number of elementary students doubled; the number of secondary-school students trebled; and the number of university students quadrupled."[55] Diem's achievements were all the more impressive because he accomplished them in spite of South Vietnam's absorption of 900,000 refugees fleeing from persecution in North Vietnam.[56] Dean Rusk, who was later to become secretary of state, met Diem in 1957 when he was president of the Rockefeller Foundation. As Rusk remembered the occasion,

> Diem had inquired about agricultural assistance. We did not fund his project, but I was impressed with him. He seemed to be a genuine nationalist, an experienced and successful leader, and dedicated to his country. Diem helped reconcile dissident sects within South Vietnam and presided over growing economic prosperity. He impressed me as a doughty fighter, committed to the independence and security of South Vietnam. We appreciated his staunchness.[57]

---

[51] *Id.*

[52] *Id.* at 8.

[53] COLBY & McCARGAR, *supra* note 1, at 69.

[54] NOLTING, *supra* note 7, at 8.

[55] HILSMAN, *supra* note 33, at 418.

[56] JOHNSON, *supra* note 31, at 50.

[57] RUSK & RUSK, *supra* note 49, at 436.

North Vietnamese Infiltration and the Increased Volume of Diem Criticism

The situation took a turn for the worse, however, upon the formation of the Communist National Liberation Front in South Vietnam, which sought through guerrilla and terrorist tactics to overthrow the South Vietnamese government.[58] In the last four months of 1959, the Viet Cong assassinated 119 local government leaders and began systematically killing members of the South Vietnamese anti-malaria eradication teams to sow discord among the population.[59] Theodore Sorenson, a Kennedy aide who was deeply ambivalent about Diem, wrote that

> [i]n 1961 all the evidence was not yet in on the extent to which the antigovernment forces in the South were the creatures of the Communist North. But it was reasonably clear that many of them were trained in the North, armed and supplied by the North, and infiltrated from the North through the Laotian corridors, across the densely wooded frontier and by sea. The North supplied them with backing, brains, and a considerable degree of coordination and control. Their food and shelter were largely provided at night by South Vietnamese villagers, who were sometimes wooed, with promises of land, unification and an end to political corruption, repression and foreign troops, and sometimes terrorized, with demonstrations of kidnaping, murder, and plunder, before the guerrillas vanished back into the jungle at daybreak.[60]

The Diem government reeled in the face of this onslaught, but clung tenaciously to its position. It instituted the strategic hamlet program to help the villagers in the countryside protect themselves, frustrating the North Vietnamese Communists in their attempt to conquer the country.[61] By early 1963, Diem's forces, with

---

[58] THEODORE SORENSON, KENNEDY 650 (1965).

[59] COLBY & MCCARGAR, *supra* note 1, at 69.

[60] SORENSON, *supra* note 58, at 650-51.

[61] COLBY & MCCARGAR, *supra* note 1, at 100.

American financial and advisory assistance, had fought the Communists to a stalemate. That year, Wilfred Burchett, a Communist Australian sympathizer with the Viet Cong, conceded that "1962 must be largely credited to Saigon."[62] As military historian Lewis Sorley put it, the reason the Vietnamese Communists were later glad to see Diem overthrown was that "he was cleaning their clocks, big time."[63]

Yet, there was another side to this struggle that brought harsh criticism to Diem from many in America and the rest of the world. His supporters and critics agreed that he was "authoritarian" in his methods and stubbornly refused to adhere to outside advice.[64] Diem conceded in an interview with Marguerite Higgins that civil liberties, such as freedom of speech and habeas corpus, were not high on his list of priorities as long as his government was fighting for its survival.[65] Some, like Hilsman, later accused the regime of using "fiendish torture," although the nature and extent of it and whether the reports were true are hard to verify.[66] Nonetheless, all agreed that the Diem regime was quick to arrest those who were suspected of being a threat to the regime and was not inclined to allow mass demonstrations that criticized it.[67] Diem's supporters,

---

[62] *Id.* at 102.

[63] Discussion with Lewis Sorley, Vietnam War historian, Charlottesville, Virginia (Nov. 13, 2002).

[64] Colby wrote that many

> critics of Diem focused on the differences between the democratic regime outlined in the 1956 Constitution and the reality of Diem's authoritarian rulings from the Palace on all important matters.
>
> Since these critics were particularly prevalent among the more sophisticated intellectual circles of Saigon, their views were readily available to Americans.

COLBY & MCCARGAR, *supra* note 1, at 29-30. "Ngo Dinh Diem was a stubborn man," Nolting added. NOLTING, *supra* note 7, at 81. "He did not deny ruling his country with an authoritarian hand," wrote Higgins. HIGGINS, *supra* note 25, at 171.

[65] "[T]his country," he told her, "is in a life-and-death struggle. Even Western democracies suspend civil liberties during war emergencies." *Id.* at 167.

[66] HILSMAN, *supra* note 33, at 521.

[67] HIGGINS, *supra* note 25, at 167.

however, were sympathetic with his predicament on the grounds that it was unrealistic to expect a leader of a country in such perilous circumstances to adhere to American standards of civil liberties. As James Schlesinger, who later became secretary of defense under Presidents Nixon and Ford, put it,

> Diem had offended much of the press in this country, partly for the right reasons and partly for the traditional American view that people should behave with great restraint when they are engaged in a mortal combat. As one of my colleagues once said, there was South Vietnam down on the ground with the North Vietnamese on top of them, and we kept coming in and saying, 'Are you behaving with circumspection, are you behaving with democratic restraint to the South Vietnamese?' When you're engaged in mortal combat, particularly when it is a civilization other than our own, you cannot impose American standards on them without doing damage to the country that you are attempting to protect.[68]

Besides, Schlesinger noted, "the real question for the United States was not whether Diem was behaving as a Jeffersonian democrat. The real question for the United States at that stage was, 'Would replacing Diem improve the situation in South Vietnam, or would the situation deteriorate?'"[69] To most of those in the U.S. military and intelligence community, the answer was perfectly clear. Diem, with the limited resources at his disposal, had up to that point fought the Viet Cong to a standstill.[70] As a political leader, he had major shortcomings, but history would show that he was the most competent person in South Vietnam to combat the Viet Cong in the military arena.

Diem was also criticized for those with whom he surrounded himself. Diem became increasingly dependent on his brother, Ngo Dinh Nhu, whose tactics in suppressing dissent were often ruthless,

---

[68] Discussion with James Schlesinger, former secretary of defense of the United States, Charlottesville, Virginia (Oct. 16, 2002).

[69] *Id.*

[70] COLBY & McCARGAR, *supra* note 1, at 102.

a fact that was seized upon by the press as well as critics of the U.S. commitment in South Vietnam.[71] Although Diem himself was considered incorruptible even by his antagonists,[72] those surrounding him were not. His brother Nhu and especially his brother Ngo Dinh Can, who Nguyen Cao Ky later called "the uncrowned king of Annam, [and] the supreme fixer," took bribes in return for access to and favors from the regime.[73] Furthermore, Diem's relationship with U.S. Ambassador Elbridge Durbrow became damaged when Durbrow pressured Diem for more political and land reforms and was dissatisfied with the results.[74] Durbrow advised Diem to banish Nhu from his government, but Diem bristled at this advice.[75] "It was pretty damn tough on him," Durbrow remembered. "He didn't like a . . . damned word I said."[76]

Those who assailed Diem thus considered him incompetent, repressive, and out of touch with his people. Ironically, the criticism that Diem had "lost contact with the people" was voiced in a 1962 report by Senator Mansfield, who had so profusely praised Diem in the 1950s.[77] One early and persistent critic of Diem was President Kennedy's ambassador to India, John Kenneth Galbraith. He fretted that U.S. Ambassador Frederick Nolting, who

---

[71] *See, e.g.,* BALL, *supra* note 4, at 370.

[72] "An ascetic Catholic steeped in Confucian tradition, a mixture of monk and mandarin, he was honest, courageous, and fervent in his fidelity to Vietnam's national cause; even Ho Chi Minh respected his patriotism," wrote journalist and historian Stanley Karnow. STANLEY KARNOW, VIETNAM: A HISTORY 213 (1983). Ho Chi Minh said that Ngo Dinh Diem was "a patriot in his way," and asked an Indian diplomat in 1963 to "[s]hake hands with him for me if you see him." HAMMER, *supra* note 7, at 222.

[73] NGUYEN CAO KY & MARVIN J. WOLF, BUDDHA'S CHILD: MY FIGHT TO SAVE VIETNAM 72 (2002).

[74] COLBY & MCCARGAR, *supra* note 1, at 74-75.

[75] WILLIAM J. RUST & THE EDITORS OF U.S. NEWS BOOKS, KENNEDY IN VIETNAM 10-11 (1985).

[76] *Id.* at 11.

[77] NOLTING, *supra* note 7, at 86.

had replaced Durbrow in 1961,[78] did not "appear to put any real pressure on Diem. I worry more about South Vietnam than Berlin."[79] He was mystified by America's continued support of Diem and wrote in his diary that "everything is complicated by Diem's fear of getting thrown out. The soldiers of his army get almost no pay, no leave, their relations starve and they spend a lot of their time guarding the politicians . . . . It sounds like a Christ-awful mess."[80]

Ambassador Galbraith, who was a close friend of fellow Diem critics Averell Harriman and George Ball,[81] wrote to President Kennedy in March 1962 that, from his personal observations in Vietnam, "any alternative to Diem is bound to be an improvement."[82] He wrote again in a memorandum to the president a month later that "[i]t must be recognized that our long-run position cannot involve an unconditional commitment to Diem."[83] It is unclear how much of an impact these opinions had on the president, but they clearly influenced those who later supported Diem's overthrow. George Ball, who had great doubts from the beginning about the U.S. commitment in South Vietnam[84] and later

---

[78] John M. Newman gives a detailed account on the replacement of Durbrow by Nolting. John M. Newman, JFK and Vietnam: Deception, Intrigue, and the Struggle for Power 34 (1992).

[79] John Kenneth Galbraith, Ambassador's Journal: A Personal Account of the Kennedy Years 206 (1969).

[80] Id. at 236.

[81] Galbraith later wrote that "[t]hree of my closest friends in public life were Chester Bowles, George Ball and Averell Harriman." Whenever he came to Washington, he would stay with the Harrimans. "For many years I needed no Washington hotel," wrote Galbraith. "I had lodging as a matter of course with the Harrimans, as more than occasionally did my wife, at their handsome house in Georgetown, closely adjacent to official Washington, the State Department and Foggy Bottom." John Kenneth Galbraith, Name-Dropping: From FDR On 157, 159 (1999).

[82] Galbraith, supra note 79, at 281.

[83] Memorandum from the Ambassador to India, John Kenneth Galbraith, to President John F. Kennedy, in 2 Foreign Relations of the United States, 1961-1963: Vietnam 298 (John P. Glennon, David Baehler & Charles S. Sampson eds., 1990) [hereinafter 2 FRUS: Vietnam].

[84] Karnow, supra note 72, at 266.

supported Diem's overthrow,[85] wrote in his memoirs that Galbraith "told me in unambiguous terms that Diem was an insurmountable obstacle to success, and I had had the same word from some of my press friends."[86] Averell Harriman, the U.S. assistant secretary of state for Far Eastern affairs who also later supported the Diem coup,[87] concluded by 1962 after reading Galbraith's memoranda that Diem was "a losing horse in the long run."[88]

Harriman did not need much convincing, for his relations with Diem soured during the 1962 negotiations over the neutralization of Laos. Diem angrily complained to Harriman that the agreement would contain no effective policing provisions to prevent the North Vietnamese Communists from further infiltrating South Vietnam through the Laotian border.[89] Nolting, who was perhaps the staunchest American supporter of the South Vietnamese leader, later wrote that Diem harangued Harriman at length on the history of North Vietnamese broken promises and "treachery," starting with the Viet Cong murder of his older brother.[90] Harriman, according to Nolting,

> turned off his hearing aid and closed his eyes. He appeared to be asleep. Diem noticed this with some annoyance but continued his monologue. . . . Finally Harriman snapped, 'I have a fingertips feeling, Mr. President, that the Russians will police this agreement and make the others live up to it. We cannot give you any guarantees, but one thing is clear: if you

---

[85] BALL, *supra* note 4, at 371.

[86] *Id.* at 370.

[87] *Id.* at 371.

[88] At that time, however, Harriman added that "we should not work against him." THOMAS & ISAACSON, *supra* note 5, at 635.

[89] NOLTING, *supra* note 7, at 83. Some date the beginning of friction between Harriman and Diem even further back in time. "They took a violent dislike to each other from their first meeting in 1961," remembered Nguyen Dinh Thuan, who served in Diem's government as secretary of the presidency. "It was very unfortunate. Diem did not understand Harriman's role in the Democratic Party and Harriman did not understand Diem." HAMMER, *supra* note 7, at 20, 31.

[90] NOLTING, *supra* note 7, at 83.

do not sign this treaty, you will lose American support. You have to choose.'

. . . Diem finally signed the accords. That proved to be a costly mistake, and I came to regret having urged him to do so. It soon became apparent that the Communist signatories, specifically North Vietnam, ignored the treaty's provisions from the beginning . . . . Harriman's 'fingertips feeling' about Russian 'policing' was not borne out by the facts. The Ho Chi Minh Trail, protected by the treaty from interdiction by our allies, was enlarged and developed by North Vietnam into a major route of infiltration into Laos, South Vietnam, Cambodia, and Thailand. Some called it the 'Harriman Memorial Highway.' Later, when the United States entered the war in force, our country became engaged in trying to knock out by bombing, at the sacrifice of many American lives, what was given away by negotiation.[91]

Word of the sharp disagreement between Nolting and Diem on the one hand and Harriman on the other over the Laos issue leaked to the press in June of 1962. One columnist reported that Nolting, upon stating that he had difficulty squaring the Laos agreement with his conscience, had been told by Harriman, "You are working for the Kennedy administration and not God."[92] Although both men played down the reports and denied at the time there was tension between them,[93] Nolting's memoirs and subsequent

---

[91] *Id.*

[92] A copy of this column by Robert S. Alley was included in a letter from Fitzgerald Bemiss to Frederick Nolting. Letter from Fitzgerald Bemiss to Frederick Nolting (June 11, 1962), (unpublished letter) (on file with the Frederick Nolting Papers at the University of Virginia Alderman Library).

[93] Nolting wrote to an inquiring friend at the time that "there are many complex factors in almost any foreign policy decision, and everyone must give his honest views from where he sits . . . . There is no friction between Mr. Harriman and me that I know of and I have no reason to doubt his statement that the report that he was demanding my reassignment is entirely without foundation." Letter from Frederick Nolting to Fitzgerald Bemiss (July 2, 1962) (unpublished letter) (on file with the Frederick Nolting papers at the University of Virginia Alderman Library).

developments indicated otherwise.[94] More importantly, this was the beginning of a steadily increasing antagonism by Harriman against Diem that would only augment over the next year. "It became an emotional matter . . . ," Robert Kennedy remembered of Harriman's animus toward Diem, "and in fact, his advice was wrong . . . . [Harriman] started us down a road which was quite dangerous."[95]

Diem's problems were compounded by the fact that his relations with the American press in Saigon during the early 1960s were surly at best. General Maxwell Taylor observed that "[b]y the time of my visit" to South Vietnam in 1962, "many newsmen were committed to a full-scale vendetta against Diem and his government which they pursued tirelessly until his overthrow a year later."[96] Homer Bigart of the *New York Times*, who reported from Vietnam until he left the country in the summer of 1962, was deeply antagonistic toward the Saigon regime and penned the phrase "Sink or Swim with Diem" to describe his view of American policy in South Vietnam.[97] Relations only deteriorated upon Bigart's replacement by David Halberstam, and they were worsened by the continued critical reporting by Neil Sheehan of the United Press International and Malcolm Browne of the Associated Press. These reporters detested Diem, and they made no secret of it.[98] President Kennedy's press secretary, Pierre

---

[94] Contrast the above view with the statement from Nolting's memoirs:

Despite his long and distinguished service to our country in other fields, Harriman's judgment and direction of policy toward Southeast Asia were, in my opinion, disastrous. His attempt to "neutralize" Laos was a dismal failure, and his growing hostility to President Diem and his family became a major factor in Diem's overthrow. Harriman's prestige and political influence in Washington, however, were so great as to become decisive in the crucial actions our government took in 1963.

NOLTING, *supra* note 7, at xiv.

[95] HAMMER, *supra* note 7, at 32.

[96] TAYLOR, *supra* note 15, at 258-59.

[97] NOLTING, *supra* note 7, at 87.

[98] PIERRE SALINGER, WITH KENNEDY 325 (1966); SHEEHAN, *supra* note 3, at 359-60.

Salinger, wrote that "the Diems reserved their special hatred for three young American correspondents," Halberstam, Sheehan, and Browne. "Their dislike was reciprocated fully by the reporters, who came to the joint or independent conclusion that there was never going to be any real progress in the war in Vietnam until the Diem government fell and was replaced by one with a real understanding of the needs of the Vietnamese people."[99] Nolting referred to these reporters as the "get Diem" crowd.[100] As Salinger wrote,

> Whether they intended it or not, their articles reflected the bitter hatred they had for the Diem government and their avowed purpose (stated to a number of reporters in Saigon) to bring down the Diem government. It is a deep question of reportorial ethics whether the destruction of a government is within the legitimate framework of journalistic enterprise.[101]

Nor did the reporters deny that their goal was to bring down Diem, for Halberstam and Sheehan went so far as to urge the U.S. ambassador that he be replaced.[102] They said they were doing it for the good of the war effort in South Vietnam, as Sheehan later wrote in *A Bright Shining Lie*,[103] but this sort of overt official advisory role is usually frowned upon as a compromise of the impartiality that reporters claim to seek. General Taylor wrote that Diem "never seemed to realize the disastrous effects for his government that a hostile press could create."[104] American officials in Saigon attempted to mend Diem's relations with the U.S. press corps on his behalf, but these efforts were largely unsuccessful.[105]

---

[99] SALINGER, *supra* note 98.

[100] NOLTING, *supra* note 7, at 88.

[101] SALINGER, *supra* note 98, at 325-26.

[102] SHEEHAN, *supra* note 3, at 359.

[103] *Id.*

[104] TAYLOR, *supra* note 15, at 257.

[105] *Id.*

THE FIRST PHASE OF THE DIEM COUP

The Buddhist Crisis and the Split between City and Countryside

As rocky as Diem's tenure was, U.S. government support remained steady until the "Buddhist crisis" erupted, leading to a chain of events that would culminate in his death. Diem encountered the most serious threat to his regime following the May 8, 1963, Buddhist national holiday, when South Vietnamese troops, for reasons that are disputed, opened fire on a crowd of protesting Buddhists outside a radio station in Hue.[106] Nine were killed and several more were injured.[107] The purported reason for the protest was that Diem would not allow the Buddhist flag to be flown above the Vietnamese one.[108] Diem claimed there was an explosion in the middle of the crowd caused by a Viet Cong grenade,[109] sowing confusion that led the crowd to make a furious attempt to take over the radio station.[110] It was only after this happened, Diem and his defenders argued, that the troops opened fire on the crowd to restore order.[111] For proof of this version of the story, the South Vietnamese government stated that the explosion was caused by a plastic bomb of the sort used by the Viet Cong.[112]

Diem was roundly condemned by his critics both among Buddhist leaders and the Western press for his lack of contrition following the incident.[113] To them, it was another sign that his

---

[106] HILSMAN, *supra* note 33, at 468.

[107] *Id.*

[108] *The Overthrow of Ngo Dinh Diem, May-November, 1963, in* 2 THE PENTAGON PAPERS: THE DEFENSE DEPARTMENT HISTORY OF UNITED STATES DECISIONMAKING ON VIETNAM 226 (Senator Gravel ed., 1971) [hereinafter PENTAGON PAPERS].

[109] Telegram From the Embassy in Vietnam by Ambassador Frederick Nolting to the Department of State (May 22, 1963), *in* 3 FRUS: VIETNAM, at 314.

[110] NOLTING, *supra* note 7, at 106.

[111] *Id.*

[112] HIGGINS, *supra* note 25, at 167.

[113] BALL, *supra* note 4, at 370.

regime was a dictatorship that was out of touch with its people.[114] The situation further deteriorated with the onset of mass demonstrations and riots in Saigon and Hue by Buddhists and students who claimed that they were victims of government-sponsored persecution.[115] In the media highlight of these protests, a Buddhist monk named Trich Quang Duc immolated himself in front a group of Western reporters and Vietnamese onlookers in an intersection in Saigon on June 11, 1963. The incident, which many viewed as a protest against alleged government mistreatment of Buddhists,[116] had a dramatically negative effect on U.S. and world opinion toward Diem.[117] Madame Nhu, Diem's sister-in-law, only made the situation worse when she publicly cheered the Buddhist "bonze barbecue."[118]

The crisis led U.S. policy makers, especially within the State Department and among the middle echelons of the U.S. Embassy in Saigon, to explore alternatives to the Diem regime.[119] The refrain that Diem's critics employed ceaselessly was that "we can't win with Diem."[120] This argument was based on the premise that Diem was alienating the South Vietnamese people from his regime, which would inevitably hurt army morale and increase support for the Viet Cong.[121] Secretary of State Dean Rusk, who was more preoccupied with Berlin and the Soviet Union, largely referred the question to subordinates.[122] They convinced him, as he wrote in his memoirs, that "in the early 1960s, Diem lost touch with his people," but Rusk did not heavily engage the issue.[123] George Ball, whose attention was more focused on European issues,[124] deferred heavily to the advice of the Far East specialists

---

[114] Id.

[115] SHEEHAN, supra note 3, at 357; HILSMAN, supra note 33, at 471-72.

[116] MARILYN B. YOUNG, THE VIETNAM WARS, 1945-1990, at 96 (1991).

[117] Schlesinger, supra note 68.

[118] BALL, supra note 4, at 370.

[119] Id.

[120] TAYLOR, supra note 15, at 290.

[121] BALL, supra note 4, at 370.

[122] NOLTING, supra note 7, at 129.

[123] RUSK & RUSK, supra note 49, at 436.

[124] See BALL, supra note 4, at 208-22.

in the State Department like Averell Harriman and Roger Hilsman, who were increasingly angered by Diem's intransigence in the face of the mounting Buddhist protests.[125] Ball, Hilsman, Harriman, and Michael Forrestal in the White House came to the conclusion that Diem was a liability.[126] "Now, beginning with Diem's treatment of the Buddhist problem toward the middle of 1963," Ball wrote, "I became increasingly convinced that we had tied our nation's fortunes to a weak, third-rate bigot with little support in the countryside and not much even in Saigon."[127]

The premise of Ball's conclusion is hard to analyze, but it is probably not correct. Diem had always been most unpopular in the cities while holding onto strong support, or at least acquiescence, in the countryside. As Colby noted, Diem won reelection in 1961 with less than half the votes in Saigon, but with 89 percent of the overall vote.[128] If these figures are even remotely accurate and the election was fairly held, it shows a stark cleavage between South Vietnamese public opinion in the cities as opposed to the rural areas. R. G. K. Thompson, the head of the British Advisory Mission in South Vietnam, told President Kennedy in April of 1963 that Diem had "much support in the country[,] where it count[s]," while he had "written off the Saigon intelligentsia."[129] Thompson added that "if Diem disappeared there would be a risk of losing the war within six months since there [is] no other leader of his caliber available."[130] While there was discontent with his regime in Saigon and Hue, which had already been the hotbeds of his critics, there is very little evidence that Diem was losing support in the countryside beyond the conclusory assumptions of critics who surmised that the villagers must have been offended because the majority of them were Buddhist. In fact, it is not even clear that the premise of this assumption is accurate. A major study

---

[125] *Id.* at 371-72.

[126] *Id.* at 371.

[127] *Id.* at 370.

[128] COLBY & MCCARGAR, *supra* note 1, at 112.

[129] Memorandum of a Conversation, White House, Washington (Apr. 4, 1963), *in* 3 FRUS: VIETNAM, at 198.

[130] *Id.*

of Buddhism in Vietnam completed in 1965 concluded that only 30 percent of South Vietnamese were practicing Buddhists, while the rest of the population consisted mostly of ancestor worshippers and a minority of Catholics.[131] Moreover, even of the group that was Buddhist, a report by the United Nations concluded that Diem had not oppressed them at all.[132] One member of the UN fact-finding team stated following the investigation that allegations of systematic repression of Buddhists were unsubstantiated "hearsay," and other members of the team affirmed his conclusion.[133]

Furthermore, the self-proclaimed leader of the Buddhist movement against Diem, Thich Tri Quang, was later found to have had Communist ties. He had been arrested twice by the French for aiding the Communists and, according to Higgins, had been meeting secretly with the National Liberation Front.[134] She called him "Machiavelli with incense."[135] In retrospect, Ambassador Nolting was convinced that the whole crisis was a Communist

---

[131] Senator Thomas Dodd, Speech to the United States Senate and Information Introduced Into the Record with the Speech, *supra* note 26 (citing a report by Dr. Mai Tho Truyen that there were about four million Buddhists in South Vietnam).

[132] Senator Thomas Dodd quoted Ambassador Fernando Volio Jiminez of Costa Rica, a member of the investigation team, as stating:

> It is my personal feeling that there was no policy of discrimination, oppression, or persecution against the Buddhists on the basis of religion. Testimony to this effect was usually hearsay, and was expressed in vague or general terms.
>
> When a witness tried to give some concrete proof to the Mission, the incident he cited came down to individual or personal actions. On the basis of the evidence, there was not a governmental policy against the Buddhists on religious grounds.

Senator Thomas J. Dodd, *Letter of Introduction, in* REPORT OF THE UNITED NATIONS FACT-FINDING MISSION TO SOUTH VIET-NAM, at v (1964).

[133] *Id.* at vi.

[134] Senator Thomas Dodd, Speech to the United States Senate and Information Introduced Into the Record with the Speech (Feb. 23, 1965), *supra* note 26.

[135] HIGGINS, *supra* note 25, at 25.

plot.[136] General Paul Harkins, head of the Military Assistance Command in Vietnam, wrote that Tri Quang "admitted . . . that he had been planning to go full out against [the] Diem regime prior to May 8."[137] Harkins, like Nolting, considered the Buddhist crisis to be "a well organized covertly led Communist trick."[138] Whether this was true remains unclear, but it is clear that Tri Quang represented an extreme faction whose views were not shared by the South Vietnamese population as a whole.[139] General Maxwell Taylor considered Tri Quang "unscrupulous"[140] and believed him to be "a dangerous conspirator, who, if not actually controlled by the Hanoi leaders, often conducted himself in strict conformity with their interests."[141] He wrote that "[s]ubsequently, the evidence became pretty clear that at least some of these immolations were contrived by Tri Quang and his henchmen to discredit Diem . . . ."[142] Tri Quang told Higgins that "[w]e cannot get an arrangement with the north until we get rid of Diem and Nhu."[143]

Indeed, military observers whom the United States sent into the countryside to investigate army morale did not find the atmosphere nearly as politically charged against Diem as it was in the cities.[144] This is the likely explanation for the episode that occurred in the midst of the Buddhist crisis, when President Kennedy sent Joseph Mendenhall and General Victor Krulak to Vietnam to give independent reports on Vietnam. Krulak reported after visiting military units throughout each region of South Vietnam that the war was progressing well and that the impact of the Buddhist crisis

---

[136] NOLTING, *supra* note 7, at 115.

[137] Telegram From the Commander, Military Assistance Command, Vietnam, General Paul Harkins, to the Joint Chiefs of Staff's Special Assistant for Counterinsurgency and Special Activities, General Victor Krulak (Sept. 12, 1963), *in* 4 FRUS: VIETNAM, at 194.

[138] *Id.*

[139] Dodd, *supra* note 26 (citing information that the protesters comprised at most 50,000 people out of a South Vietnamese population of about 14 million).

[140] TAYLOR, *supra* note 15, at 290-91.

[141] *Id.* at 368.

[142] *Id.* at 290-91.

[143] Dodd, *supra* note 132, at vii.

[144] Memorandum of a Conversation, White House, Washington (Sept. 10, 1963), *supra* note 28.

on army morale was minimal.[145] He reported that there was some dissatisfaction with Nhu among the South Vietnamese military but that there was overwhelming respect for Diem and a general desire to put the political problems aside in favor of moving on with the war.[146] Mendenhall gave a bearish view based primarily on his conversations with South Vietnamese in Saigon and Hue that Diem's repression was alienating the population in such a way that a Viet Cong victory was inevitable.[147] The country, he reported, was on the verge of a religious civil war between Catholics and Buddhists because of Diem's policies.[148]

After listening to these diametrically opposing views of the progress of the war, Kennedy asked, "The two of you did visit the same country, didn't you?"[149] Krulak offered what was likely the correct explanation by stating that Mendenhall was "reporting on the metropolitan and urban attitudes," while he was "reporting on 'national' attitudes."[150] This split was further evidence of a misconception of overwhelming national hostility towards Diem, when in fact the public relations crisis was largely confined to the cities. This is important to note because the cities comprised only 15 percent of Vietnam's population.[151] In the countryside and in the army, where the war was mostly being fought, the Buddhist crisis had an impact, but not to the extent that it was perceived in much of the Western media. As James Schlesinger put it, the conflict with the Buddhists "certainly had an adverse effect" on public opinion toward Diem among the South Vietnamese, but the episode was "more shocking to American opinion than it was in country."[152]

---

[145] Id.

[146] Id.

[147] Id. at 162.

[148] Id.

[149] Id.

[150] Id.

[151] Memorandum of a Conversation, Department of State, Washington (Aug. 31, 1963), in 4 FRUS: VIETNAM, at 74 (quoting a statement made in the meeting by Frederick Nolting).

[152] Schlesinger, supra note 68.

The American Anti-Diem "Cabal"[153]

Nonetheless, Diem's antagonists in the U.S. government began quietly exploring possible alternatives to him during the summer of 1963. When Ambassador Nolting took a vacation to Greece in mid-June, he was temporarily replaced by his deputy, William Trueheart, who viewed Diem with disfavor and immediately pushed for a hard line against the South Vietnamese leader on the Buddhist issue.[154] Knowing Trueheart was a more favorable audience than Nolting,[155] Diem's critics in the State Department sent cables floating the possibility of supporting a coup to oust Diem. On June 14, 1963, a cable to Trueheart drafted by Chalmers Wood and cleared by Hilsman and Harriman advised the acting ambassador to "increase covert and overt contacts with non-supporters of GVN. In [the] present situation this should only be done if you feel our (overt or covert) contacts with those who might play major roles in [the] event of [a] coup are now inadequate."[156]

On July 1, Michael Forrestal wrote to National Security Advisor McGeorge Bundy that "[w]e all believe one more burning bonze will cause [a] domestic U.S. reaction that will require a strong public statement despite [the] danger that this might precipitate [a] coup in Saigon."[157] Forrestal then pressed his case on President Kennedy for a harder line against Diem and warned

---

[153] I am borrowing the term "cabal" from a description of the anti-Diem group by James Schlesinger. *Id.*

[154] Telegram from William Trueheart at the Embassy in Vietnam to the Department of State (June 9, 1963), *in* 3 FRUS: VIETNAM, at 368-69; *see also* Telegram From William Trueheart at the Embassy in Vietnam to the Department of State (June 12, 1963), *in id.*, at 383-84.

[155] They undoubtedly surmised this from the unfavorable cables Trueheart was sending back to Washington. *Id.*

[156] Telegram Drafted by Chalmers Wood at Department of State to the Embassy in Vietnam (June 14, 1963), *in* 3 FRUS: VIETNAM, at 394.

[157] Telegram From Michael V. Forrestal of the National Security Council Staff to McGeorge Bundy, the President's Special Assistant for National Security Affairs (July 1, 1963), *in* 3 FRUS: VIETNAM, at 432.

him of the possibility of Diem's ouster. In a memorandum on July 3, he wrote:

> *Secretary Ball, Governor Harriman, Roger Hilsman and I* feel that the political problem has come to such a point in the United States that we could not avoid public comment in the face of another bonze suicide, and that therefore we *should leave no stone unturned* to persuade Diem to change his attitude. Everyone recognizes that Diem's position in South Vietnam has now become as critical as it has ever been, and that the United States may have to grope its way through government upheaval in Saigon.[158]

Thus, several weeks before the cable that would lead to Diem's overthrow, the four senders of it, Ball, Harriman, Hilsman, and Forrestal, had already started preparing the groundwork for Diem's ouster. Ironically, in that same memo, Forrestal wrote that "despite the political turmoil in South Vietnam, the war against the Viet Cong seems to be progressing surprisingly well."[159] This in a nutshell captures the logical inconsistency of support for the Diem coup. Those advocating Diem's overthrow were so convinced that the war was unwinnable under him that they were nonplussed by facts to the contrary, which indicated that the shooting war was unaffected by the political situation. They held, in short, a theory vainly in search of facts to support it.

This group of Diem critics relentlessly pressed their view on the president that Diem's actions were making a coup inevitable and that this possibility would not be so bad. Hilsman, in a meeting with the president, Ball, Harriman, Forrestal, and Bundy stated on July 4, "Our estimate is that no matter what Diem did there will be coup attempts over the next four months," and that

---

[158] Memorandum from Michael V. Forrestal of the National Security Council Staff to President John F. Kennedy (July 3, 1963), *supra* note 11, at 448 (italics added).

[159] *Id.*

everyone agreed that the chances of chaos in the wake of a coup are considerably less than they were a year ago. An encouraging sign relative to this point is that the war between the Vietnamese forces and the Viet Cong has been pursued throughout the Buddhist crisis without noticeable let-up.[160]

This statement showed the same internal inconsistency that Forrestal's had shown. Even Diem's opponents conceded that *the military war against the VC was still going well,* so why did they insist that they could not win with Diem? Perhaps the answer was that they viewed Diem's ouster as an acceptable military sacrifice that was necessary from a public relations perspective. Moreover, all four of the main U.S. government supporters of the Diem coup were skeptics of the war.[161] It could be that the military success that even they believed Diem was achieving was not as high of a priority as their goal of disassociating the United States from what they perceived to be a repressive regime.

The next day, Ball asked Nolting "what would happen if there were a change in government."[162] Nolting replied that "if a revolution occurred in Viet-nam which grew out of the Buddhist situation, the country would be split between feuding factions and . . . the country might be lost to the Communists."[163] Nolting concluded that "if we repudiated Diem on this issue his government would fall."[164] Ball continued this line of questioning nonetheless, asking Nolting "whether there was any one person around whom conflicting groups in Viet-Nam might coalesce in the event of Diem's disappearance from the scene."[165] In that event, Nolting suggested that "Vice President Tho . . . would be the best person, although he would be opposed by Nhu."[166] One can

---

[160] Memorandum of a Conversation, White House, Washington (July 4, 1963), *in* 3 FRUS: VIETNAM, at 452.

[161] THOMAS & ISAACSON, *supra* note 5, at 635-39.

[162] Memorandum of a Conversation, Department of State, Washington (July 5, 1963), *in* 3 FRUS: VIETNAM, at 466.

[163] *Id.*

[164] *Id.*

[165] *Id.* at 467.

[166] *Id.*

see in Ball's line of questioning of the unsuspecting Nolting that the possibility of supporting Diem's ouster was on his mind.

When Nolting returned to Saigon from his vacation, he was angered to learn of the hard line that Trueheart had taken toward Diem.[167] Although he knew he was soon scheduled to return to the United States, he used the few weeks he had left to try to repair the relationship between Diem and the U.S. Embassy.[168] Meanwhile, the anti-Diem contingent continued to send cables regarding plans in the event of a possible coup. On July 23, Hilsman cleared a cable from the Department of State to Nolting stating that "in light [of the] growing crop of reports on coup plans, we judge [the] odds favor [an] attempted coup within [the] next few months if not weeks," and that the United States should "hold to the posture of watchful waiting" rather than opposing such a coup.[169] Assistant Secretary of State for Public Affairs Robert Manning reported in late July that one group who almost universally supported Diem's replacement was the press. "The correspondents," he wrote,

> reflect unanimous bitterness toward, and contempt for, the Diem government. They unanimously maintain that the Vietnamese program cannot succeed unless the Diem regime (cum family) is replaced; this conviction, though it does not always appear in their copy, underlies all the reports and analyses of the correspondents.[170]

The anti-Diem faction within the State Department agreed wholeheartedly with the press's view of Diem and grew incensed with Nolting for his defense of the regime. In a telephone conversation on August 1, Harriman told Hilsman that he was

---

[167] COLBY & MCCARGAR, *supra* note 1, at 134; SCHLESINGER, *supra* note 37, at 902.

[168] NOLTING, *supra* note 7, at 117.

[169] Telegram From the Department of State Drafted by Theodore Heavner & Paul Kattenburg to the Embassy in Vietnam (July 23, 1963), *in* 3 FRUS: VIETNAM, at 524.

[170] Report From the Assistant Secretary of State for Public Affairs, Robert J. Manning, to President John F. Kennedy (between July 21 and July 31, 1963), *in* 3 FRUS: VIETNAM, at 532.

"disturbed" by Nolting's statement that Diem had not been persecuting the Buddhists and that Nolting "ought to be recalled at once," upon which Hilsman said that he "couldn't agree more."[171] On August 6, Hilsman sent a memo to Ball stating that "the chances of an attempted coup in the next few weeks" were "50-50," and that "*[i]f Diem is overthrown, the risks of the interregnum period are great but they are probably less great than they were a year ago.*" He added:

> *If Diem is not overthrown, it is becoming increasingly likely that he will ultimately try to resolve the Buddhist problem by means of repression.*
>
> If so, it is quite possible that his popular support will be so reduced that he could no longer hope to defeat the Viet Cong.[172]

Memoranda such as these, which favorably analyzed the results of a possible Diem overthrow, left no doubt that a solid group had formed who supported Diem's ouster. General Harkins observed, "It looks like the State Department thinks Diem is the enemy, rather than the Viet Cong."[173] Ambassador Nolting, who had asked to be replaced six months before for "personal reasons,"[174] requested an extension to mend U.S.-South Vietnamese relations in light of the crisis. His superiors in Washington rejected his request.[175]

---

[171] Hilsman added, however, that "in [Nolting's] defense he ought to say that [Nolting's statement] was distorted and taken out of context." Memorandum of a Telephone Conversation Between the Under Secretary of State for Political Affairs, Averell Harriman, and the Assistant Secretary of State for Far Eastern Affairs, Roger Hilsman, Washington (Aug. 1, 1963), *in* 3 FRUS: VIETNAM, at 550.

[172] Memorandum From the Assistant Secretary of State for Far Eastern Affairs, Roger Hilsman, to the Acting Secretary of State (Aug. 6, 1963), *in* 3 FRUS: VIETNAM, at 555 (italics in original).

[173] NOLTING, *supra* note 7, at 116.

[174] SCHLESINGER, *supra* note 37, at 901.

[175] NOLTING, *supra* note 7, at 119.

Henry Cabot Lodge's Arrival in Saigon and the August 24 Cable

Diem's fortunes took a major turn for the worse when Henry Cabot Lodge replaced Frederick Nolting as U.S. ambassador to Saigon in late August of 1963. Shortly before Lodge's arrival, on August 21, 1963, Diem's and Nhu's police forces raided the Buddhist pagodas at Xa Loi and elsewhere throughout the country, arresting thousands.[176] Diem explained his actions by stating his belief that the Buddhist pagodas were infiltrated by the Viet Cong and that they were using the pagodas as places to stash weapons.[177] Diem's critics nonetheless seized on the episode as evidence that he had become too reliant on Nhu and that he needed to be replaced.[178] The incident aroused a fierce reaction from Diem's critics within the administration and from Lodge, who was asked by South Vietnamese army generals what the attitude of the United States would be toward a possible replacement of the Diem government.[179] The generals were unhappy about the pagoda raids and considered it a slander upon them that many believed that the army, and not Nhu's police, had carried them out.[180] Moreover, upon arriving in Saigon, Lodge invited Halberstam, Sheehan, and Browne to have lunch with him to hear their "advice."[181] Sheehan, according to his later account, did not know of the plotting generals' request, but

> told him, in sum, that the Ngo Dinhs were so mad and hated that they were incapable of governing . . . and that if Diem and his family stayed in power the war was certain to be lost. If

---

[176] Voice of America Broadcast, Saigon (Aug. 26, 1963), *in* 3 FRUS: VIETNAM, at 636.

[177] NOLTING, *supra* note 7, at 121.

[178] BALL, *supra* note 4, at 370.

[179] KARNOW, *supra* note 72, at 284; HILSMAN, *supra* note 33, at 484.

[180] "The name of the army had been sullied by this operation and those of us who had not participated in the attack . . . had to accept the recriminations and complaints of the public," wrote General Tran Van Don. TRAN VAN DON, OUR ENDLESS WAR: INSIDE VIETNAM 91 (1978).

[181] SHEEHAN, *supra* note 3, at 359.

they were replaced by a military regime there was no guarantee that a junta of generals would do better, but there was hope that they might. With the Ngo Dinhs one could look forward only to defeat.[182]

When Sheehan asked what Lodge's "impression" was at the end of their lunch, the new ambassador "smiled. 'About the same as yours,' he said."[183]

Lodge sent a cable summarizing the generals' request to Harriman and Hilsman in the State Department, who received it on Saturday, August 24, 1963.[184] They found Ball at the ninth hole of a Washington golf course, where they told him of Lodge's cable and said that the generals needed a quick response.[185] Hilsman and Harriman had already drafted a cable responding to Lodge, for which they needed approval from Ball, who was acting secretary of state due to Rusk's absence from Washington.[186] The cable stated to Lodge that the

> U.S. Government cannot tolerate [a] situation in which power lies in Nhu's hands. Diem must be given [a] chance to rid himself of Nhu and his coterie and replace them with [the] best military and political personalities available.
>
> If, in spite of all your efforts, Diem remains obdurate and refuses, then we must face the possibility that Diem himself cannot be preserved.[187]

On routine matters, Ball, as under secretary of state, had the authority to clear cables on his own, but the importance of the cable led him to seek Rusk's approval as well as that of the leading U.S. military and intelligence figures.[188] The problem, however,

---

[182] *Id.*

[183] *Id.* at 360.

[184] BALL, *supra* note 4, at 371.

[185] *Id.* at 372.

[186] *Id.* at 371.

[187] Telegram from the Department of State to the Embassy in Vietnam (Aug. 24, 1963), *supra* note 14.

[188] BALL, *supra* note 4, at 371-72.

was that they were all out of town, as was the president.[189] Rusk was at a UN conference in New York,[190] Secretary of Defense Robert McNamara was hiking in the Grand Tetons,[191] CIA head John McCone was on vacation in California,[192] President Kennedy was at Hyannisport,[193] and General Maxwell Taylor, the head of the Joint Chiefs of Staff, was at a Washington restaurant.[194] Of these, the group reached only Rusk and Kennedy before they sent the cable.[195] Kennedy said he would sign off on it only if the secretaries of defense and state agreed.[196] According to Rusk,

> George Ball called me on an open phone and in rather guarded tones read me the cable. I thought George told me Kennedy agreed with this cable. I later learned that Kennedy had said, "I will approve it if Rusk and McNamara approve it." But at the time, thinking Kennedy's approval restricted my own freedom of action, especially in dealing with such a sensitive matter on an unclassified phone, I gave my concurrence.[197]

McNamara, McCone, and Taylor could not be reached before the cable was sent later that day.[198] Ball later said he obtained the approval of Roswell Gilpatric, McNamara's deputy, Richard Helms, the deputy director of the CIA, and General Victor Krulak, Taylor's subordinate,[199] although Taylor strongly disputed this version of events in his memoirs.[200]

---

[189] Schlesinger, *supra* note 68.

[190] KARNOW, *supra* note 72, at 287.

[191] THOMAS & ISAACSON, *supra* note 5, at 639.

[192] COLBY & MCCARGAR, *supra* note 1, at 138.

[193] HAMMER, *supra* note 7, at 179.

[194] BALL, *supra* note 4, at 372.

[195] *Id.* at 371-72.

[196] *Id.* at 371.

[197] RUSK & RUSK, *supra* note 49, at 437-38.

[198] BALL, *supra* note 4, at 372.

[199] *Id.*

[200] TAYLOR, *supra* note 15, at 292.

Those who had not been consulted about the cable that weekend were furious on Monday that it had been sent.[201] Even Rusk, who had been consulted, said that he, McNamara, and Kennedy "looked at the cable and realized that it went further than we wanted to go."[202] Taylor and McCone in particular were very angry.[203] Colby remembered,

When I showed McCone the text and explained that no one at the staff levels of the various departments had been consulted before it was sent, he was furious. He was, as always, outwardly calm, but his calm was now exceptionally icy. His brief vacation was abandoned. "I'll return to Washington with you tonight," he said.[204]

"As if some of the conspiracy-laden atmosphere of Saigon had found its way back to Washington," Taylor later wrote,

a small group of anti-Diem activists picked this time to perpetrate an egregious "end run" in dispatching a cable of the utmost importance to Saigon without obtaining normal departmental concurrences, an action which created extremely hard feeling among President Kennedy's advisers at a time when he badly needed their harmonious cooperation.[205]

McNamara later confirmed that the cable "shocked" Taylor, for

Max knew it represented a major change in our Vietnam policy; what is more, it was totally at variance with what he believed was the proper course . . . .
I do not share Max's view that the cable represented an egregious end run. We all knew that Hilsman sometimes went

---

[201] COLBY & McCARGAR, *supra* note 1, at 137-39.

[202] RUSK & RUSK, *supra* note 49, at 438.

[203] COLBY & McCARGAR, *supra* note 1, at 138; TAYLOR, *supra* note 15, at 292.

[204] COLBY & McCARGAR, *supra* note 1, at 138.

[205] TAYLOR, *supra* note 15, at 292.

outside official channels to increase the chances his views
would prevail. The fault lay as much with those who failed to
rein him in as it did with Hilsman himself. But it shocks and
saddens me today to realize that action which eventually led to
the overthrow and murder of Diem began while U.S. officials
in both Washington and Saigon remained deeply divided over
the wisdom of his removal; no careful examination and
evaluation of alternatives to Diem had been made by me or
others . . . . We never did give it the consideration it
deserved.[206]

Colby, in contrast to McNamara, considered Harriman rather than
Hilsman to be the ringleader.[207] Nolting, whom the coup
supporters had not even attempted to consult[208] and who had
clashed with Harriman before, was livid. He later wrote, "I was
appalled that our government would encourage a group of
dissident generals to overthrow their elected government."[209]
Robert Kennedy said a year later that the president had regretted
allowing the cable to clear and that he had "passed it off too
quickly over the weekend at the Cape, he thought it was cleared by
McNamara and Taylor and everyone at State. In fact, it was
Harriman, Hilsman, and Mike Forrestal at the White House and
they were the ones who were strongly for a coup."[210]

Debate raged throughout the next week at the White House
about the wisdom of continuing to support Diem.[211] President
Kennedy opened the meetings by saying that

Mr. Halberstam of the *New York Times* is actually running a
political campaign [to oust Diem]; . . . he is wholly
unobjective, reminiscent of Mr. [Herbert] Matthews in the

---

[206] ROBERT S. MCNAMARA & BRIAN VANDEMARK, IN RETROSPECT: THE
TRAGEDY AND LESSONS OF VIETNAM 55 (1995).

[207] COLBY & MCCARGAR, *supra* note 1, at 138-39.

[208] NOLTING, *supra* note 7, at 124.

[209] *Id.* at 125.

[210] MCNAMARA & VANDEMARK, *supra* note 206, at 54-55.

[211] THOMAS & ISAACSON, *supra* note 5, at 638-39.

[Fidel] Castro days . . . . [I]t [is] essential that we not permit Halberstam unduly to influence our actions. . . . Diem and his brother, however repugnant in some respects, have done a great deal along the lines that we desire and, when we move to eliminate this government, it should not be as a result of *New York Times* pressure.[212]

Hilsman interjected that appeasing the press was not the driving force behind the policy, upon which Taylor said that "there are many military difficulties involved in executing the plan embodied in the . . . [August 24] cable; . . . Diem is truly the focus and . . . we should put our first effort on him."[213] Ball and Hilsman countered that Nhu was the real issue; he was controlling the Buddhist policy and dominating Diem.[214] President Kennedy then asked them what would happen "if we find we are faced with having to live with Diem and Nhu," upon which Hilsman answered that "this would be too horrible to contemplate because of Nhu's grave emotional instability."[215] President Kennedy, clearly annoyed at the entire situation and skeptical about the cable, called for another meeting to more fully discuss the issue.[216] General Taylor proposed inviting Nolting to the meeting, to which Kennedy agreed.[217] Hilsman

---

[212] Memorandum for the Record of a Meeting at the White House, Washington (Aug. 26, 1963), *in* 3 FRUS: VIETNAM, at 638. President Kennedy was comparing Halberstam's lack of objectivity toward Diem to the favorable news stories written about Fidel Castro by *New York Times* journalist Herbert Matthews prior to Castro's 1959 overthrow of Cuban General Fulgencio Batista. Matthews was later criticized for romanticizing Castro and contributing to the success of his rebellion. "Castro has strong ideas of liberty, democracy, social justice, the need to restore the Constitution, [and] to hold elections," Matthews wrote in a 1957 statement brimming with irony in light of later events. One historian later wrote that these articles "electrified the world and caused a sensation inside Cuba," thus giving a boost to Castro. GEORGIE ANNE GEYER, GUERRILLA PRINCE: THE UNTOLD STORY OF FIDEL CASTRO 167-69 (1991).

[213] Memorandum for the Record of a Meeting at the White House, Washington (Aug. 26, 1963), *supra* note 212, at 639.

[214] *Id.*

[215] *Id.* at 641.

[216] *Id.*

[217] *Id.*

objected that "Nolting's views are colored, in that he is
emotionally involved in the situation." Kennedy replied, "Maybe
properly."[218]

Over the next two days, a flurry of cables passed between
Washington and Saigon as government and military officials
gathered information.[219] Meanwhile, the debate intensified. "My
God," Kennedy complained to his friend Charles Bartlett as his
advisors exchanged recriminations over the cable, "my government
is coming apart."[220] On August 28, Taylor sent Harkins a cable
stating that the August 24 cable was "prepared without DOD
[Department of Defense] or JCS [Joint Chiefs of Staff]
participation. Authorities are now having second thoughts."[221] The
stage was set for one of the most contentious meetings of the
Kennedy administration.

The August 28 Meeting and the "We Can't Win with Diem" Argument

At noon on August 28, less than two hours after Taylor cabled
Harkins, President Kennedy convened a major meeting at the
White House that included the heads of the CIA, the Defense
Department, the four who had sent the August 24 telegram,
Ambassador Nolting, the attorney general, and several others.[222]
Ball argued on behalf of the coup supporters that "it would be
difficult if not impossible for us to live with a situation in which
Nhu is ascendant in South Vietnam." Therefore, he concluded, "we
[have] . . . no option but to back a coup. We are already beyond the

---

[218] *Id.*

[219] COLBY & MCCARGAR, *supra* note 1, at 141; *see, e.g.,* Telegram From the Chairman of the Joint Chiefs of Staff, General Maxwell Taylor, to the Commander, Military Assistance Command, Vietnam, General Paul Harkins (Aug. 26, 1963), *in* 3 FRUS: VIETNAM, at 648.

[220] THOMAS & ISAACSON, *supra* note 5, at 639.

[221] Telegram From the Chairman of the Joint Chiefs of Staff, General Maxwell Taylor, to the Commander, Military Assistance Command, Vietnam, General Paul Harkins (Aug. 28, 1963), *in* 3 FRUS: VIETNAM, at 675.

[222] Memorandum of a Conference with the President, White House, Washington (Aug. 28, 1963), *supra* note 12, at 1.

point of no return. The question is how do we make this coup successful."[223] President Kennedy responded that he did "not believe we should take the position that we have to go ahead because we have gone so far already. If a coup is not in the cards, we should unload."[224] Nolting said that he had "grave reservations about proceeding against Diem. The good faith of the U.S. is involved." Moreover, Nolting said he

> had given personal commitments to Diem . . . . We should not support a coup in the expectation that we can get another government which we can deal with and a base on which we can win the war against the Viet Cong. Supporting a coup is bad in principle and sets a bad precedent.[225]

This aroused a strong reaction from Ball, who said that Diem had "broken promises he had made to us. The actions [Diem and Nhu] are taking are in violation of good faith."[226] Ball was "not sympathetic to the allegation that we were breaking commitments" and said that "Diem and his followers are taking anti-American actions."[227] He saw three alternative scenarios:

> 1. We can't win the war against the Communists with Diem in control. The U.S. position in the eyes of the world is being badly damaged. Hence, we can't back off from our all-out opposition to Diem and Nhu.
> 2. If we merely let the generals proceed and then, if they fail to overthrow Diem, we have lost as well. This outcome is half-baked and no good.
> 3. We decide to do the job right. There is no other acceptable alternative. We must decide now to go through to a successful overthrow of Diem.[228]

---

[223] *Id.* at 2.
[224] *Id.* at 3.
[225] *Id.*
[226] *Id.* at 4.
[227] *Id.*
[228] *Id.*

Harriman echoed Ball's argument on the allegedly certain defeat that the United States would face with Diem, stating that "we have lost Vietnam if the coup fails."[229] He added, "We cannot win the war with the Nhus. We have lost the fight in Vietnam and must withdraw if a coup does not take place. We put Diem in power and he has doublecrossed us. Diem and his followers have betrayed us."[230] He supported "removing Nhu" and said "that it was a mistake that we had not acted a long time ago. We had made a mistake in working with Nhu on the strategic hamlet plan."[231] Hilsman chimed in that "we can't stop the generals now," and "they must go forward or die."[232] Like Harriman and Ball, he argued that "we cannot win the war unless Diem is removed."[233] Nolting interrupted to say that "only Diem could hold this fragmented country together."[234] Ball vehemently disagreed with Nolting, stating that his approach "spelled nothing but disaster."[235] Harriman then lit into Nolting, angrily stating that he had "disagreed with Mr. Nolting from the beginning" when he first became assistant secretary of state and that Nolting was "profoundly wrong." He was "sorry," continued Harriman, "to have to be so blunt about saying this."[236] Harriman added, "The political situation in Vietnam will blow up sometime. We have in Vietnam a situation similar to that which existed in Korea under Syngman Rhee. The political forces in Vietnam will rally quickly against Diem."[237]

At this meeting, the "we can't win with Diem" critique was fully articulated by Harriman, Ball, and Hilsman. These figures

---

[229] *Id.* at 5.

[230] *Id.*

[231] *Id.*

[232] *Id.*

[233] *Id.*

[234] *Id.* at 6.

[235] Glennon & Keefer, *Editorial Note, in* 4 FRUS: VIETNAM, at 8 (quoting Roger Hilsman's notes on the Aug. 28, 1963, meeting).

[236] *Id.* at 9.

[237] Memorandum of a Conference with the President, White House, Washington (Aug. 28, 1963), *supra* note 12, at 6.

essentially saw the war as more of a political than a military struggle, which they believed that Diem was losing because his actions against the Buddhist protesters were turning Vietnamese public opinion against them.[238] Ball later wrote that Diem was "more a Tammany tiger than a disciple of Thomas Jefferson."[239] Furthermore, Ball wrote that he considered Madame Nhu to be "vicious and vindictive" and believed that "we could not retain our self-respect as a nation so long as we supinely accepted the Nhus' noxious activities."[240] Yet, here again and in the notes of the August 28 meeting, the logical inconsistencies of their argument showed through. It was true, as Harriman stated, that Diem was far from perfect and that the United States faced the same situation with him that it had faced with Rhee in South Korea. Yet, no one in the U.S. government had supported a coup against Rhee because the alternative, losing South Korea to North Korean Communist Kim Il Sung, would have been worse. If anything, Diem was less of a dictator than Rhee, for at least Diem allowed free elections, whereas Rhee curtailed all semblance of constitutional democracy when his political position was threatened in 1952.[241] In fact, the issue that Harriman raised regarding Rhee was one of the strongest arguments *against* carrying out the coup. Diem, like Rhee, was a figure with authoritarian propensities who was better equipped than the rest of his countrymen to fight the war against Communists who were invading his nation.

President Kennedy remained skeptical after the August 28 debate about the merits of overthrowing Diem.[242] Robert Kennedy later recalled that his brother subsequently "always said that" approving the August 24 cable "was a major mistake on his

---

[238] BALL, *supra* note 4, at 370.

[239] *Id.*

[240] *Id.*

[241] "Any signs of an independent buildup of power [Rhee] crushed with efficiency and ruthlessness," wrote Quee-Young Kim. QUEE-YOUNG KIM, THE FALL OF SYNGMAN RHEE 16 (1983); *see also* RICHARD C. ALLEN, KOREA'S SYNGMAN RHEE: AN UNAUTHORIZED PORTRAIT 138-51 (1960).

[242] ARTHUR M. SCHLESINGER, JR., ROBERT KENNEDY AND HIS TIMES 713 (1978).

part."[243] President Kennedy was also unhappy about the hasty manner in which the cable was sent. He said shortly before his death in a Dictabelt recording that the cable was "badly drafted" and "should never have been sent on a Saturday."[244] He added in retrospect that he should not have agreed to it "without a roundtable conference at which McNamara and Taylor could have presented their views."[245] Despite President Kennedy's subsequent uneasiness with the cable, however, the effects of it could not be easily reversed. McNamara later considered it "one of the truly pivotal decisions concerning Vietnam made during the Kennedy and Johnson administrations."[246] The fury with which Kennedy's advisors debated this issue reflected their understanding of how significant the cable was, and, to some degree, resentment over the tactics that the pro-coup faction had used to get the cable approved. "I frankly thought it was an end run," said Gilpatric in agreeing with Taylor's assessment of the cable drafters' methods.

> I didn't see why it had to be done Saturday night with the President away, with Rusk away, with McNamara away, [and National Security Advisor McGeorge] Bundy away. I was suspicious of the circumstances in which it was being done . . . . In other words[,] the Defense and military were brought in sort of after the fact.[247]

Taylor felt as though the anti-Diem faction had presented the rest of Kennedy's advisors who had not approved the cable with a *fait accompli*.[248]

Moreover, many observers at the August 28 meeting were stunned at the vehemence with which Harriman attacked Nolting.

---

[243] *Id.*

[244] President Kennedy made the recording two days after Diem's death. SALLY BEDELL SMITH, GRACE AND POWER: THE PRIVATE WORLD OF THE KENNEDY WHITE HOUSE 421 (2005).

[245] *Id.*

[246] *Id.* at 403.

[247] HERBERT S. PARMET, JFK: THE PRESIDENCY OF JOHN F. KENNEDY 331 (1983).

[248] *Id.*

Gilpatric said later that he could not recall a time when someone in a president's presence "took the tongue-lashing that Nolting did from Harriman. And I don't think it would have been tolerated by the President from anyone else."[249] Nolting and Colby, however, were not surprised. "[T]he incident was vintage Harriman," Colby later wrote, "totally devoted to his view of what would benefit the President and the United States, and riding roughshod over anyone who dared to challenge him."[250] Nolting agreed that this behavior was typical of Harriman's style. "Shut up! We've heard from you before!" Nolting remembered Harriman shouting at him at a National Security Council meeting on one occasion. Nolting remembered that "President Kennedy intervened to say that he wanted to hear what I was saying. Harriman's rudeness did not surprise me."[251]

Harriman, a longtime luminary within the Democratic Party and in diplomatic circles, was a blunt-spoken man who had earned the nickname "the Crocodile."[252] He had impressed President Kennedy and others in the past with his previous diplomatic achievements and deep knowledge of foreign leaders.[253] Even so, the president's patience with him was rapidly wearing thin. Robert Kennedy later remembered that the president became "very unhappy" with Harriman following this episode, "so much so that Robert, noting that Harriman 'put on about ten years during that period . . . because he was so discouraged,' asked his brother 'if he couldn't rehabilitate him by just being nice to him . . . because he's a valuable figure.'"[254] Despite President Kennedy's skepticism of

---

[249] SCHLESINGER, *supra* note 242, at 713.

[250] COLBY & McCARGAR, *supra* note 1, at 138.

[251] NOLTING, *supra* note 7, at 128.

[252] "Plodding yet at times strikingly bold, detached yet also intense, he earned the nickname 'the Crocodile' by affecting a drowsy manner that would suddenly give way to a snap of action," two journalists wrote later. THOMAS & ISAACSON, *supra* note 5, at 20.

[253] HAMMER, *supra* note 7, at 29, 31.

[254] SCHLESINGER, *supra* note 242, at 713. Robert Kennedy also said that President Kennedy had "lost confidence" in Hilsman by time of the president's death in late November of 1963. The quoted words in this footnote are a

Harriman's arguments, however, he opted not to make a firm policy decision regarding a coup,[255] a move that would prove costly as the events that his subordinates helped set in motion slipped steadily out of his control.

The Aborted Coup and Lodge's Campaign to Overthrow Diem

Lodge responded the next day to the doubts emanating from Washington about the coup. He wrote:

> We are launched on a course from which there is no respectable turning back: The overthrow of the Diem government. There is no turning back in part because U.S. prestige is already publicly committed to this end in large measure and will become more so as facts leak out. In a more fundamental sense, there is no turning back because there is no possibility . . . that the war can be won under a Diem administration, still less that Diem or any member of the family can govern the country in a way to gain the support of the people who count, i.e., the educated class in and out of government service, civil and military, not to mention the American people. In the last few months (and especially days), they have alienated these people to an incalculable degree.[256]

Lodge therefore agreed with those who thought the war could not be won with Diem. He advocated a proactive stance toward the coup, writing that "[w]e should proceed to make [an] all-out effort to get the Generals to move promptly."[257] He said that the generals were hesitating because they "doubt we have the will power, courage, and determination to see this thing through. They are haunted by the idea that we will run out on them even though we

---

paraphrase of Robert Kennedy's words. Thomas C. Reeves, A Question of Character: A Life of John F. Kennedy 409 (1992).

[255] Colby & McCargar, *supra* note 1, at 138.

[256] Telegram From the Embassy in Vietnam by Henry Cabot Lodge to the Department of State (Aug. 29, 1963), *in* 4 FRUS: Vietnam, at 21.

[257] *Id.*

have told them pursuant to instructions, that the game had started."[258]

The coup doubters in Washington, however, were slowly winning the upper hand. McNamara told Kennedy that day that he "recommended that we disassociate ourselves from efforts to bring about a coup" and that there was "no valid alternative to the Diem regime."[259] The solution in his view and that of most of Kennedy's advisors was to rid Diem of Nhu's influence.[260] To this, Lodge responded on August 30 that he agreed "that getting the Nhus out is the prime objective," but the "best chance of doing it is by the Generals taking over the government lock, stock and barrel."[261] For the moment, however, he was frustrated because "[m]y greatest single difficulty in carrying out the instructions . . . is inertia. The days come and go and nothing happens . . . . There is not yet enough to show for the hours which we have all put in."[262] There was no point, said Lodge, in asking Diem to get rid of Nhu, for "[h]e wishes he had more Nhus, not less."[263] A coup to oust Diem was therefore, in his opinion, the only way to get rid of Nhu.

That same day, Lodge paid a visit to Roger Lalouette, the French ambassador to Saigon, who had been in Vietnam for five years.[264] Based on his experience and that of the French, Lalouette strongly advised Lodge not to overthrow Diem.[265] Lalouette told Lodge that

> Diem has a steadfastness and determination which is rare in Asia and is valuable. In many ways he is the best Chief of State

---

[258] *Id.*

[259] Memorandum of a Conference with the President, White House, Washington (Aug. 29, 1963), *in* 4 FRUS: VIETNAM, at 27.

[260] *Id.*

[261] Telegram From the Embassy in Vietnam by Ambassador Henry Cabot Lodge to the Department of State (Aug. 30, 1963), *supra* note 24, at 38.

[262] *Id.*

[263] *Id.*

[264] Telegram From the Embassy in Vietnam by Ambassador Henry Cabot Lodge to the Department of State (Aug. 30, 1963), *supra* note 24, at 58.

[265] *Id.* at 59.

in Southeast Asia. His weakness is that he is not a political leader, cannot make speeches, [or] cultivate the press . . . .

He is much better off with Nhu than without him. Nhu is efficient and intelligent. The war against the Viet Cong can be won with [the] Diem administration in office.[266]

Lalouette continued that the "present situation is largely the work of the press, helped greatly by Vietnamese ineptness."[267] He added, "In the days of French administration, suicides of Buddhists were very common and had no effect whatever on the population. They create much more excitement abroad than they do in Vietnam."[268]

Two points should be gathered from these statements. First, the fact that Ambassador Lalouette discussed the possibility of an American-sponsored coup to Lodge showed how little of a secret it was and that Diem was certainly aware of the American machinations against him. Second, Lalouette's views conform to James Schlesinger's opinion that the public relations crisis stemming from the Buddhist imbroglio was far more acute outside Vietnam than within it. The Buddhist immolations, based on the French experience, had been commonplace and did not impact public opinion within South Vietnam in the manner perceived by the American press. The assumption that they were turning the population against Diem was therefore highly questionable. The "crisis," in Lalouette's view, was predominantly media-created and rested more within American than Vietnamese public opinion. Lalouette added that, based on French intelligence, the "Viet Cong are very discouraged and morale is very low in North Vietnam."[269] In other words, *Diem was winning the war against the North*. Lalouette's believed that "[i]n a year or two the guerrilla danger might be ended."[270] At the end of the meeting, he told Lodge, "Let

---

[266] *Id.* at 58.
[267] *Id.*
[268] *Id.*
[269] *Id.* at 59.
[270] *Id.*

me say two things, first, try to calm American opinion[,] and, second, no coups."[271]

Lalouette's words fell on deaf ears, but at the time, it did not seem to matter, for the next day, the CIA received word from its sources that "[t]his particular coup is finished."[272] The generals had lost their nerve, and it appeared that Diem was the only foreseeable alternative in sight.[273] Lodge had no regrets, for "[w]e used every asset we had," and "we have shown our willingness to put ourselves on the line."[274] Yet, the aborted overthrow made things difficult for Lodge, for he sensed that "the government suspects us of trying to engineer a coup."[275] The relationship between Lodge and Diem had gotten off to a terrible start, and it was only going to get worse.

THE SECOND PHASE OF THE DIEM COUP

The Resuscitation of the Coup and the Renewed Diem Debate

For the next three months, Lodge kept up a steady drumbeat of criticism of Diem and support for a coup.[276] By pursuing this course, he went against the advice of most of the military and intelligence establishment, former Ambassador Nolting, and Vice President Lyndon Johnson, who believed that "[w]e must reestablish ourselves and stop playing cops and robbers."[277] Lodge, however, considered the Diem regime incapable of the reform he

---

[271] *Id.*

[272] Telegram From the Central Intelligence Agency Station in Saigon to the CIA in Washington (Aug. 31, 1963), *in* 4 FRUS: VIETNAM, at 64.

[273] COLBY & MCCARGAR, *supra* note 1, at 141-42.

[274] Telegram From the Embassy in Vietnam by Ambassador Henry Cabot Lodge to the Department of State (Aug. 31, 1963), *in* 4 FRUS: VIETNAM, at 67.

[275] *Id.*

[276] COLBY & MCCARGAR, *supra* note 1, at 143; *see, e.g.,* Telegram From the Embassy in Vietnam by Ambassador Henry Cabot Lodge to the Department of State (Sept. 11, 1963), *in* 4 FRUS: VIETNAM, at 172.

[277] Memorandum of a Conversation, Department of State, Washington (Aug. 31, 1963), *supra* note 151, at 74.

thought it would need to win over the South Vietnamese people. He referred to Diem on September 5 as the ruler of

> a medieval, Oriental despotism of the classic family type, who understands few, if any, of the arts of popular government. [Diem and Nhu] cannot talk to the people; they cannot cultivate the press; they cannot delegate authority or inspire trust; they cannot comprehend the idea of government as servant of the people.[278]

He wrote a few days later that he was

> struck by [the] fear which pervades Saigon, Hue, and Da Nang. These cities have been living under a reign of terror which continues . . . . Most families of government officials have felt [the] government's oppressive hands on their children, with results in attitude that can be expected. [There is a g]rowing number of students . . . talking of [the] Viet Cong being [the] preferred alternative to [the] existing government (I have been told this in both Saigon and Hue).[279]

From these cables, it seems that Lodge was making the same conceptual error that other critics of Diem had made; he spoke mainly with those in the cities, where Diem was most unpopular, and took what he heard as an automatic affirmation of his view that the war could not be won under the regime. He wrote on September 11 that "the elite is filled with hostility towards the Gov[ernmen]t of Viet Nam" and "hate the government for good reason."[280] He thought that "the government is obviously cut off from reality . . . and privately thumbing its nose at the US."[281] In

---

[278] Telegram From the Embassy in Vietnam by Ambassador Henry Cabot Lodge to the Department of State (Sept. 5, 1963), *supra* note 19.

[279] Telegram From the Embassy in Vietnam by Ambassador Henry Cabot Lodge to the Department of State (Sept. 9, 1963), *in* 4 FRUS: VIETNAM, at 144.

[280] Telegram From the Embassy in Vietnam by Ambassador Henry Cabot Lodge to the Department of State (Sept. 11, 1963), *supra* note 276, at 172.

[281] *Id.*

the absence of a coup on the horizon, Lodge proposed casting about for ways to cause Diem's downfall. He believed that "the time has arrived for the U.S. to use what effective sanctions it has to bring about the fall of the existing government and the installation of another."[282] He recommended that "[r]enewed efforts should be made to activate by whatever positive inducements we can offer the man who would take over the government, Big [Duong Van] Minh or whoever we might suggest."[283] In his mind, almost any alternative leadership was therefore superior to Diem.

Lodge's September 11 cable caused a major stir among Washington policy makers. Many, like Taylor and Rusk, were skeptical of Lodge's allegations that Diem was a tyrant and urged that the situation be kept in perspective.[284] Rusk remembered in a meeting the night after receiving the cable that Chiang Kai-Shek in China had been similarly criticized.[285] He noted "similarities in the Vietnamese situation" and stated that "we must not yield to the temptation of despairing of Diem and act in a way which would result in the Communists taking Vietnam."[286] Taylor also urged his fellow policy makers to "look at what is happening in a historical perspective," and he did not believe "that Lincoln, during the Civil War, would have acted in a way to meet the protests of a religious, political movement."[287] Taylor moreover suspected "that there ha[s] been some penetration by the Viet Cong of the Buddhists."[288] Rusk believed that Lodge needed to focus on the objective of winning the war rather than on Diem's shortcomings and observed that

> this was not the first time the US Government has been confronted with far-reaching issues affecting vital interests in a

---

[282] *Id.* at 171.

[283] *Id.* at 173.

[284] Memorandum of a Conversation, White House, Washington (Sept. 11, 1963), *in* 4 FRUS: VIETNAM, at 186.

[285] *Id.*

[286] *Id.*

[287] *Id.*

[288] *Id.* at 187.

country whose leadership stubbornly resists measures which we consider necessary to achieve desired results. One thinks of Chiang Kai-Shek on the mainland, Syngman Rhee, [Norodom] Sihanouk, [Gamel Abdel] Nasser, [Mohammed] Mossadegh and others.[289]

He recommended negotiating with Diem rather than actively undermining him.[290]

Yet, Lodge continued his campaign for Diem's removal.[291] Normally, such a course would have been impermissible to an ambassador, but Lodge was a special case.[292] Colby wrote that President Kennedy treated Lodge with "kid gloves" for political reasons.[293] Kennedy knew that it would be helpful to have a Republican to share the blame if things went wrong in Vietnam.[294] After Rusk had initially surprised Kennedy by recommending Lodge's appointment, the president even "joked" to his advisors that "the idea of getting Lodge," an old political rival whom he did not particularly like on a personal level, "mixed up in such a hopeless mess as Vietnam was irresistible."[295] Earlier in his political career, he had defeated Lodge in his 1952 campaign for the U.S. Senate. Lodge was also Richard Nixon's vice presidential running mate "on the Republican ticket that Kennedy had defeated in 1960."[296] Moreover, members of his staff who had worked with

---

[289] Draft Telegram from the Department of State by Dean Rusk to the Embassy in Vietnam (Sept. 12, 1963), *in* 4 FRUS: VIETNAM, at 196.

[290] *Id.* at 197-98. Rusk apparently changed his position quite often during the Diem debate. As Robert Kennedy later put it, Rusk "was for a coup and then he was against it. He was all over the lot." REEVES, *supra* note 254, at 409.

[291] *See, e.g.,* Telegram From the Embassy in Vietnam by Ambassador Henry Cabot Lodge to the Department of State (Sept. 19, 1963), *in* 4 FRUS: VIETNAM, at 261.

[292] COLBY & MCCARGAR, *supra* note 1, at 135.

[293] *Id.*

[294] *Id.* Arthur Schlesinger wrote that "the thought of implicating a leading Republican in the Vietnam mess appealed to his instinct for politics." SCHLESINGER, *supra* note 37, at 902.

[295] KENNETH O'DONNELL, DAVID POWERS & JOE MCCARTHY, "JOHNNY, WE HARDLY KNEW YE" 15-16 (1972). HAMMER, *supra* note 7, at 169.

[296] *Id.*

Kennedy since his early days in Boston politics later implied that the president considered Lodge to be a snob.[297] "The President had an Irish distaste for the aloof North Shore Yankee Republican . . . ," wrote Kennedy Special Assistant Kenneth O'Donnell. "When we were watching Lodge on television at the Republican convention the night he accepted the Vice-Presidential nomination, Kennedy said to us, 'That's the last Nixon will see of Lodge. If Nixon ever tries to visit the Lodges at Beverly, they won't let him in the front door.'"[298] The idea of enmeshing Lodge in such a difficult diplomatic situation had thus amused Kennedy for many reasons, but, if this thought was indeed part of the original motivation for nominating him, it was a ruse that backfired badly on the president.

According to Robert Kennedy, the president regretted the Lodge appointment within weeks but could not figure out an acceptable way to remove him.[299] Robert Kennedy, who had warned his brother prior to the appointment that he would "have a lot of difficulties with Lodge," later reminded President Kennedy of his words.[300] The president responded, Robert Kennedy remembered, by saying "it was terrible about me 'cause I always could remember when I was right."[301] Lodge "wouldn't communicate . . . ," Robert Kennedy said later. "You'd send out a message and ask a lot of questions and he'd send back a message of one line: 'Your message both concerned and amused me. Signed Henry Cabot Lodge.'"[302]

Lodge was, as Madame Nhu put it, not an ambassador, but a "proconsul."[303] Pursuant to this role, he bucked advice he received from Washington and refused to negotiate with Diem. "Visiting

---

[297] O'DONNELL, POWERS & MCCARTHY, *supra* note 295, at 15-16.

[298] *Id.*

[299] HAMMER, *supra* note 7, at 170.

[300] The words in quotations are Hammer's description of Robert Kennedy's warning. *Id.* Robert Kennedy was not alone in his unfavorable opinion of Lodge. James Schlesinger later opined that Lodge was "not the sharpest tool in the box." Schlesinger, *supra* note 68.

[301] HAMMER, *supra* note 7, at 170.

[302] *Id.* at 246.

[303] *Id.*

Diem is an extremely time-consuming procedure," he wrote, "and it seems to me there are many better ways in which I can use my waking hours."[304] He did not believe Rusk's recommendations would "bring about the removal of the Nhus unless they are geared to a Vietnamese coup d'etat which is well organized around one man."[305] Lodge added on September 19, in direct contradiction of Rusk's and Taylor's advice, that "whatever sanctions" we use against Diem to force him to change "should be directly tied to a promising coup d'etat and should not be applied without such a coup being in prospect."[306] This was not a passive approach to a potential coup. Rather, Lodge was actively promoting a coup in order to use the threat as leverage against the Diem government.

Lodge even proposed using the Voice of America as a means to sow discontent against the Diem regime. He recommended that the VOA broadcast

> a series of utterances . . . of basic American ideals such as free speech, free press, habeas corpus, due process, dignity of the individual, pursuit of happiness, all men created equal, government is the servant of the people, etc. At present virtually all these principles are being flagrantly violated in Viet-Nam . . . .
>
> [The p]urpose of this proposal should be to arouse [the] Vietnamese people to a point which would worry Diem and Nhu . . . .[307]

Encouraged by American support through their CIA contact, Lucius Conein, the coup leaders, led primarily by South Vietnamese generals Duong Van Minh and Tran Van Don, revived

---

[304] Telegram From the Embassy in Vietnam by Henry Cabot Lodge to the Department of State (Sept. 13, 1963), *in* 4 FRUS: VIETNAM, at 203.

[305] *Id.*

[306] Telegram From the Embassy in Vietnam by Ambassador Henry Cabot Lodge to the Department of State (Sept. 19, 1963), *supra* note 291, at 261.

[307] Telegram From the Embassy in Vietnam by Ambassador Henry Cabot Lodge to the Department of State (Sept. 27, 1963), *in* 4 FRUS: VIETNAM, at 300.

their plans for Diem's overthrow.[308] Don told Conein on October 3 that they had formulated a specific plan for a coup but refused to provide details.[309] Lodge was pleased with this turn of events and urged on October 5 that Washington adopt a policy "not to . . . thwart" a coup while keeping in touch with the coup leaders regarding their plans.[310] Meanwhile, Hilsman cabled Lodge that day to encourage this course of action, writing to him that "Diem's regime has trappings of democracy, but in reality it has been evolving into [an] authoritarian government maintained by police terrorist methods."[311] President Kennedy, through McGeorge Bundy, approved of a "covert effort . . . to build contacts with possible alternative leadership," but emphasized that "no initiative should now be taken to give any covert encouragement to a coup."[312] Lodge happily obeyed the first part of the president's instructions and disregarded the second. Lodge's well-advertised disdain for Diem was the only encouragement that the coup leaders needed.[313] Kennedy's options in dealing with Lodge were limited, however. He was going to run for reelection in 1964, and a Lodge resignation in protest would have been a major political headache.[314]

Coup rumors intensified in late October. Colonel Nguyen Khong told his CIA contact that "[a] small, powerful group [of]

---

[308] It is unclear whether Conein was answering to Lodge or to the CIA headquarters. It seems odd that Conein would act against the wishes of his superiors like McCone in Washington, who opposed a coup. Yet, according to Don, Conein was an ally of Lodge. Don later wrote that "Ambassador Henry Cabot Lodge and Conein were definitely backing us, feeling that a change in leadership was long overdue." DON, *supra* note 180, at 97.

[309] Telegram From the Central Intelligence Agency Station in Saigon to the CIA in Washington (Oct. 3, 1963), *in* 4 FRUS: VIETNAM, at 354-55.

[310] Telegram From the Embassy in Vietnam by Ambassador Henry Cabot Lodge to the Department of State (Oct. 5, 1963), *supra* note 20.

[311] Telegram From the Department of State Drafted by Hilsman to the Embassy in Vietnam (Oct. 5, 1963), *in* 4 FRUS: VIETNAM, at 374.

[312] Telegram From the President's Special Assistant for National Security Affairs, McGeorge Bundy, to Ambassador Henry Cabot Lodge in Vietnam (Oct. 5, 1963), *in* 4 FRUS: VIETNAM, at 379.

[313] DON, *supra* note 180, at 97-98.

[314] COLBY & MCCARGAR, *supra* note 1, at 135.

military officers who can control sufficient forces are prepared to launch a coup against the Diem government. He outlined how they can assassinate Diem almost at will . . . ."[315] Kennedy had made it clear that any U.S. support for a coup would be on the condition that Diem not be killed.[316] Yet, given the information U.S. intelligence was receiving from the coup plotters, it seems strange that Diem's murder would turn out to be such a surprise. Moreover, as Hilsman later noted, the need to kill rather than wound a king was an Asian as well as a Western saying.[317]

The generals, in their belief that the United States supported the coup, approached General Harkins with their plans. He rebuffed them, stating that "coups were not my business though I [have] heard rumors of many."[318] Nolting remembered that Harkins believed a coup was "crazy."[319] General Don, fearing that this meant that the United States was changing its policy toward a coup, again requested and received assurances from Lodge and Conein that this was not the case.[320] Don later wrote that the conspirators were certain by the time they were about to launch their coup that Conein and Lodge supported Diem's overthrow; Conein, Don wrote, had even offered material assistance, which the generals refused.[321] If the generals did not believe the United States supported them, their fear of betrayal would likely have prevented or at least delayed the execution of their plans.[322]

---

[315] Telegram From the Army Attaché in Vietnam, Raymond Jones, to the Assistant Chief of Staff (Intelligence), Department of the Army (Oct. 22, 1963), *in* 4 FRUS: VIETNAM, at 420.

[316] TAYLOR, *supra* note 15, at 301.

[317] HILSMAN, *supra* note 33, at 521.

[318] Telegram from the Commander, Military Assistance Command, Vietnam, General Paul Harkins, to the Chairman of the Joint Chiefs of Staff, General Maxwell Taylor (Oct. 24, 1963), *in* 4 FRUS: VIETNAM, at 433.

[319] NOLTING, *supra* note 7, at 131.

[320] DON, *supra* note 180, at 98-99.

[321] *Id.*; *see also* Telegram From Ambassador Henry Cabot Lodge at the Embassy in Vietnam to the Department of State (Oct. 28, 1963), *in* 4 FRUS: VIETNAM, at 452 n.5.

[322] DON, *supra* note 180, at 98.

In the last few days of October, it was clear to top U.S. officials in both Washington and Saigon that a coup was near.[323] Lodge continued to assail Diem in his cables, while a vigorous debate recommenced in Washington on the merits of replacing the South Vietnamese leader.[324] Diem's supporters in Washington gained unexpected support from a fact-finding mission to Vietnam led by Representative Clement Zablocki.[325] Zablocki told General Krulak afterwards that the group he had led

> included several members who left the US with a preconception that the Diem regime must be liquidated, while others went to Vietnam with an open mind. *All returned, however, with the same convictions . . . that Diem, with all his faults, his autocracy, his tolerance of venality and brutality, is durable, and has been winning . . . .* There is no visible substitute for Diem, at least none which guarantees improvement; *thus actions by US representatives to join with coup plotters . . . is harmful.*[326]

This conclusion is remarkable, for even those within the delegation who had been opponents of Diem came back convinced that he was the only man to lead the country because, for all his faults, *he was winning the war.* Moreover, they believed that the "conduct of the resident US press is a grave reflection upon their entire profession. They are arrogant, emotional, unobjective and ill-informed."[327] Every single member, then, came to the conclusion that Lalouette had pressed upon Lodge in late August. Moreover,

---

[323] COLBY & MCCARGAR, *supra* note 1, at 150-51.

[324] On October 28, Lodge wrote that although Diem was "likable," he was "cut off from [the] present, . . . living in the past, . . . truly indifferent to people as such . . . and is unbelievably stubborn." Telegram From Ambassador Henry Cabot Lodge at the Embassy in Vietnam to the Department of State (Oct. 28, 1963), *supra* note 321, at 442.

[325] Memorandum for the Record by the Joint Chiefs of Staff's Special Assistant for Counterinsurgency and Special Activities, General Victor Krulak (Oct. 28, 1963), *in* 4 FRUS: VIETNAM, at 446.

[326] *Id.* (italics added).

[327] *Id.*

the report, like Lalouette's unsolicited condemnation of a potential U.S.-sponsored coup, showed that U.S. complicity in Diem's overthrow was one of the worst kept secrets in Saigon. Diem told Higgins shortly before his death that he knew certain Americans were plotting against him, which, he said, was a major mistake because he saw "no George Washingtons" in his military who could lead the country in his place.[328]

Diem's supporters in the military and intelligence community mounted an eleventh hour counterattack to try to prevent the coup.[329] On October 29, the president convened a meeting to discuss the likely outcome of the emerging revolt.[330] Colby estimated that the pro-Diem and anti-Diem forces were evenly matched, upon which the advisors launched into a debate on whether the coup was likely to prevail.[331] At this point, Robert Kennedy interjected to say that, even though he had not read all the cables,

> the present situation makes no sense on the face of it . . . . To support a coup would be putting the future of Vietnam and in fact all of Southeast Asia in the hands of one man not now known to us. Diem will not run from a fight or quit under pressure.[332]

---

[328] HIGGINS, *supra* note 25, at 169.

[329] *See* Memorandum of a Conference with the President, White House, Washington (Oct. 29, 1963), *supra* note 21, at 470.

[330] *Id.* at 468.

[331] *Id.* at 468-70.

[332] *Id.* at 470. It should be noted that Robert Kennedy had an ambivalent attitude toward Diem, but that opinion did not stop him from believing that a coup would be profoundly unwise. "Diem was corrupt and a bad leader and it would have been better if we didn't have him," he said several months later.

> But we inherited him. He came with the job. So what do you do? . . . It's better if you don't have him but you have to have somebody that can win the war, and who is that? . . . It's bad policy to get into for us to run a coup out there and replace somebody we don't like with somebody we do because it would just make every other country nervous as can be that we were running coups in and out.

Taylor agreed with the attorney general, saying that "even a successful coup would slow down the war effort because the new central government would be inexperienced. In addition, all of the province chiefs appointed by Diem would probably be replaced by a new government."[333] McCone concurred, stating that "[t]he failure of a coup would be a disaster and a successful coup would have a harmful effect on the war effort."[334]

Harkins added his angry objections from Saigon that Lodge had made several key decisions involving the military without consulting him, and that overthrowing Diem would harm the war effort.[335] He and Ambassador Lodge, wrote Harkins, "are currently in touch with each other[,] but whether the communications between us are effective is something else . . . . Fritz [Nolting] would always clear messages concerning the military with me or my staff prior to dispatch . . . . This is not true today."[336] As Harkins put it to Taylor, "When I said last week I was out of the coup business I did not realize I was going to be out of touch."[337] Harkins wrote that he was "shocked" to see the messages that Lodge had sent to Washington without his consultation.[338] Harkins believed that Lodge's course of action was a woeful mistake because the United States did not know if Diem's replacement would be any better.[339] "I'm not opposed to a change in government, no indeed," he wrote,

---

SCHLESINGER, *supra* note 242, at 715.

[333] Memorandum of a Conference with the President, White House, Washington (Oct. 29, 1963), *supra* note 21, at 470.

[334] *Id.*

[335] Telegram From the Commander, Military Assistance Command, Vietnam, General Paul Harkins, to the Chairman of the Joint Chiefs of Staff, General Maxwell Taylor (Oct. 30, 1963), *in* 4 FRUS: VIETNAM, at 480-82.

[336] *Id.*

[337] Telegram From the Commander, Military Assistance Command, Vietnam, General Paul Harkins, to the Chairman of the Joint Chiefs of Staff, General Maxwell Taylor (Oct. 30, 1963), *in* 4 FRUS: VIETNAM, at 499.

[338] *Id.*

[339] Telegram from the Commander, Military Assistance Command, Vietnam, General Paul Harkins, to the Chairman of the Joint Chiefs of Staff, General Maxwell Taylor (Oct. 30, 1963), *supra* note 335, at 481-82.

but I'm inclined to feel that at this time the change should be in methods of governing rather than [a] complete change of personnel. I have seen no batting order proposed by any of the coup groups. I think we should take a hard look at any proposed list before we make any decisions. In my contacts here I have seen no one with the strength of character of Diem, at least in fighting communists . . . . I am not a Diem man per se. I certainly see the faults in his character . . . . Most of the Generals I have talked to agree they can go along with Diem, all say it's the Nhu family they are opposed to.

I would suggest we not try to change horses too quickly . . . . After all, rightly or wrongly, we have backed Diem for eight long hard years. To me it seems incongruous now to get him down, kick him around, and get rid of him.[340]

Harkins added that a coup against an ally would create a terrible precedent, for "leaders of other under-developed countries will take a dim view of our assistance if they too were led to believe the same fate lies in store for them."[341] Lodge responded to these concerns by cabling to Washington that he did not think the United States had "the power to delay or discourage a coup."[342] However, he then contradicted himself by stating, "It is theoretically possible for us to turn over the information which has been given to us in confidence to Diem[, but] . . . this would undoubtedly stop the coup and make traitors out of us."[343]

Yet, it is worth asking who the traitor was. By promoting Diem's overthrow with assurances of confidentiality to the plotting generals, Lodge had placed the United States in the position of betrayal in any circumstance. By supporting the coup, Lodge was betraying Diem, who was a U.S. ally. However, it would have been

---

[340] *Id.*

[341] *Id.* at 482.

[342] Telegram From Ambassador Henry Cabot Lodge at the Embassy in Vietnam to the Department of State (Oct. 30, 1963), *in* 4 FRUS: VIETNAM, at 484.

[343] *Id.* at 484-85.

a betrayal of the generals to expose their plans to Diem. Either way, Lodge's assurances to the generals had tarnished U.S. credibility.

The Coup and the Aftermath of Diem's Murder

On November 1, the generals launched the coup.[344] Their forces surrounded the presidential palace, upon which Diem called Lodge to ask about the U.S. attitude toward the coup.[345] Lodge was noncommittal but offered to provide a safe exit for Diem should he accept the generals' request that he step down.[346] Diem refused, stating, "I am trying to re-establish order," before hanging up.[347] Diem and Nhu tried to escape, but they were arrested that night and executed in an army personnel carrier by Minh's assistants, Colonel Duong Huu Nghia and Captain Nguyen Van Nhung, on Minh's orders.[348] Don later wrote that "Colonel Nghia shot point blank at them with his submachine gun, while Captain Nhung, who was inside the same vehicle, sprayed them with bullets before using a knife on them."[349] Don wrote later that he was furious that they had done this, for he, like other generals, had respected Diem's accomplishments and had joined the coup upon the belief that Diem would not be killed.[350] Nguyen Cao Ky, who played a lesser role in the coup, also wrote that he was "shocked and angry" to hear of the assassinations and that "if I had known that murder had been on the conspirators' agenda, I might have reconsidered my participation . . . . With these killings I lost what little respect I once had for the generals."[351]

Don said that Minh later tried to deny his role in the executions,[352] but according to McNamara, Minh told an American

---

[344] COLBY & MCCARGAR, *supra* note 1, at 152-53.
[345] *Id.* at 153.
[346] *Id.*
[347] *Id.* at 154; KARNOW, *supra* note 72, at 307.
[348] DON, *supra* note 180, at 112.
[349] *Id.*
[350] *Id.*
[351] CAO KY, *supra* note 73, at 97.
[352] DON, *supra* note 180, at 113

a few months later, "We had no alternative. They had to be killed. Diem could not be allowed to live because he was too much respected among simple, gullible people in the countryside."[353] This remarkable statement was further evidence that Diem was still quite popular in the rural areas where most South Vietnamese lived and that he had managed the war well. McNamara noted that even Tran Van Huong, who had been jailed for criticizing Diem, said,

> The top generals who decided to murder Diem and his brother were scared to death. The generals knew very well that having no talent, no moral virtues, and no political support whatsoever, they could not prevent a spectacular comeback of the president and Mr. Nhu if they were alive.[354]

It was significant that Diem retained the respect of even those who opposed him.

Kennedy first heard about Diem's death when he and his advisors were meeting the next morning to discuss the ongoing events.[355] McNamara remembered that in the middle of the discussion, Michael Forrestal "burst into the room with a flash message from the Situation Room" that Diem and Nhu were dead.[356] "When the President received the news," McNamara wrote, "he literally blanched. I had never seen him so moved."[357] Taylor confirmed this recollection, writing that

> Kennedy leaped to his feet and rushed from the room with a look of shock and dismay on his face that I had never seen before. He had always insisted that Diem must never suffer more than exile and had been led to believe or had persuaded himself that a change in government could be carried out without bloodshed.[358]

---

[353] MCNAMARA & VANDEMARK, *supra* note 206, at 84.
[354] *Id.*
[355] TAYLOR, *supra* note 15, at 301.
[356] MCNAMARA & VANDEMARK, *supra* note 206, at 83.
[357] *Id.* at 84.
[358] TAYLOR, *supra* note 15, at 301.

Kennedy's advisors and friends, ranging from Diem's staunchest supporters to his most caustic critics, recalled that the president was profoundly stunned and upset upon hearing the news. "I saw the President soon after he heard that Diem and Nhu were dead," wrote Diem critic Arthur Schlesinger. "He was somber and shaken. I had not seen him so depressed since the Bay of Pigs."[359] O'Donnell, who bitterly criticized Diem in his memoir,[360] wrote that "the brutal killings of Diem and Nhu . . . shocked and depressed" Kennedy.[361] Sorenson, who was more ambivalent about Diem, wrote that Kennedy "was shaken that Diem should come to such an end after his long devotion to his country, whatever his other deficiencies, remarking that Diem's bitterest foes, the Communists, had never gone that far."[362] Another friend who saw Kennedy in the White House looking "pale and nervous" after the coup tried to console him by saying that Diem and Nhu were "tyrants." Kennedy replied, "No. They were in a difficult position. They did the best for their country."[363]

Unlike Kennedy, the Americans who had helped bring down Diem had no apologies and no regrets. Higgins called Hilsman and began, "Congratulations, Roger. How does it feel to have blood on your hands?"[364] Hilsman responded, "Oh, come on now, Maggie. Revolutions are rough. People get hurt."[365] Lodge was ecstatic.[366] He cabled to President Kennedy a few days later that "[t]he

---

[359] SCHLESINGER, *supra* note 37, at 909.

[360] He referred to the Diem regime as a "police state" that was, in his view, guilty of "persecution of religious and political minorities." O'DONNELL, POWERS & McCARTHY, *supra* note 295, at 16-17.

[361] *Id.* at 17.

[362] SORENSON, *supra* note 58, at 660.

[363] PETER COLLIER & DAVID HOROWITZ, THE KENNEDYS: AN AMERICAN DRAMA 309, 351 (1984). Collier and Horowitz obtained this quote in an interview with Mary Gimbel, although they do not indicate whether Gimbel was the person to whom Kennedy made the statement. This quote also appeared in COLBY & McCARGAR, *supra* note 1, at 157.

[364] A.J. LANGGUTH, OUR VIETNAM: THE WAR 1954-1975, at 258 (2000).

[365] *Id.*

[366] COLBY & McCARGAR, *supra* note 1, at 156.

prospects now are for a shorter war."[367] Inhabitants of Saigon, where Diem haters were in abundance, rioted in celebration[368] and burned down the pro-Diem *Times of Vietnam.*[369]

Yet, why did Diem's American antagonists exult that the United States had helped overthrow a democratically elected ally and install a military junta? The coup backers recognized the public relations difficulty of squaring their support for Diem's overthrow with American traditions of supporting democracies. Ball wrote in retrospect that "[e]ncouraging coups, of course, ran counter to the grain of America's principles but Diem's legitimacy was dubious at best; we had in effect created him in the first place."[370] Hilsman immediately drafted and sent a circular telegram that was approved by Rusk giving talking points to U.S. embassies around the world.[371] He wrote,

All missions, especially in [the] Western Hemisphere, should be prepared to give [a] full explanation of this decision and [the] *sharp distinction between its basis and [U.S. Government] . . . opposition to military coups against democratic regimes elsewhere.* Elements of difference are these:

(1) [The] Diem regime had become [an] instrument of [the] complete personal authority of one family.

(2) [The] Diem regime was deeply opposed not merely by [the] mass of people but increasingly by its own senior officials, civilian and military.

---

[367] KARNOW, *supra* note 72, at 311.

[368] *Id.* According to Robert Kennedy, President Kennedy had decided at some time before his death to replace the ambassador. "We were going to try to get rid of Henry Cabot Lodge," Robert Kennedy recalled later. REEVES, *supra* note 254, at 409.

[369] HILSMAN, *supra* note 33, at 521.

[370] BALL, *supra* note 4, at 371.

[371] Circular Telegram From the Department of State Drafted by Roger Hilsman and Sent to All Diplomatic Posts (Nov. 2, 1963), *in* 4 FRUS: VIETNAM, at 536.

(3) [The r]egime was increasingly incapable of giving effective direction to [the] national effort against Communist subversion and aggression.[372]

These contentions about Diem, however, contained major inaccuracies. Diem had made his reputation for integrity among the bulk of the South Vietnamese people by refusing to bow to the French and opposing the Communists.[373] The United States threw its support to Diem in 1954 because Diem had become popular in his own right. Diem was elected in 1955 and reelected in 1961 by large margins,[374] and yet the United States overthrew him to install an unelected military dictatorship in his place. Hilsman's contention about Diem's failure to fight Communist aggression was wholly inaccurate, especially in comparison to his successors, as subsequent military events showed. The damage control efforts of the American coup supporters did little to reassure allies of the United States. The event sent shockwaves through the leadership in non-Communist Asia, for they were disturbed by the precedent that America would overthrow an ally. As Pakistani leader Ayub Khan told Richard Nixon,

> I cannot say, perhaps you should never have supported Diem in the first place. But you did support him for a long time, and everyone in Asia knew it . . . . And then, suddenly, you didn't support him anymore, and Diem was dead . . . . Diem's murder meant three things to many Asian leaders: that it is dangerous to be a friend of the United States; that it pays to be neutral; and that sometimes it helps to be an enemy! Trust is like a thin thread, and when it is broken it is very hard to put together again.[375]

Proof that Diem's supporters had been right in opposing the coup surfaced almost immediately, as the Viet Cong increased

---

[372] *Id.* (italics added).
[373] HIGGINS, *supra* note 25, at 156-57.
[374] COLBY & MCCARGAR, *supra* note 1, at 112.
[375] NIXON, *supra* note 32, at 256-57.

their attacks and the South Vietnamese military position rapidly deteriorated.[376] Although John Mecklin of the U.S. Information Service and Hilsman, two of Diem's antagonists, later claimed that the deterioration had occurred before the coup and that military reports had covered this up,[377] the weight of the evidence is heavily against this argument. The South Vietnamese military position disintegrated precipitously within just a few weeks of Diem's overthrow.[378] President Lyndon Johnson received his first major exposure to this catastrophe when he met with McCone and Lodge two days after he took office in late November of 1963. "Lodge was optimistic," Johnson remembered.

> He believed the recent change of government in Saigon was an improvement. He was hopeful and expected the new military leaders to speed up their war efforts. He stated that our government had put pressure on the regime of Ngo Dinh Diem to change course. Those pressures, he admitted, had encouraged the military leaders who carried out the coup on November 1, 1963 . . . .
>
> I turned to John McCone and asked what his reports from Saigon in recent days indicated. The CIA Director replied that his estimate was much less encouraging. There had been an increase in VC activity since the coup, including more VC attacks. He had information that the enemy was preparing to exert even more severe pressure. He said the Vietnamese

---

[376] "In the months that followed," wrote John Mecklin of the U.S. Embassy, "there was relentless deterioration everywhere, confirming in dreary succession all the black predictions of those who had opposed the coup." JOHN MECKLIN, MISSION IN TORMENT: AN INTIMATE ACCOUNT OF THE U.S. ROLE IN VIETNAM 282 (1965).

[377] *Id.* at 282-83; HILSMAN, *supra* note 33, at 522.

[378] "The overthrow of the constitutional government in Vietnam created a political vacuum there," Nolting later wrote. "Throughout the country the situation deteriorated rapidly. The Viet Cong and Hanoi immediately seized their opportunity. The strategic hamlets were attacked and began to be wiped out. The civilian government officials, including the province chiefs, did not know what to do, with everybody getting crossed signals from the military junta." NOLTING, *supra* note 7, at 133.

military leaders who carried out the coup were having difficulties organizing their government and were receiving little help from civilian leaders. McCone concluded that he could see no basis for an optimistic forecast of the future.

I told Lodge and the others I had serious misgivings. Many people were criticizing the removal of Diem and were shocked by his murder . . . . I thought we had been mistaken in our failure to support Diem.[379]

Given this intelligence and his previous inclination to support Diem, Johnson "believed the assassination of President Diem had created more problems for the Vietnamese than it had solved."[380] He "saw little evidence that men of experience and ability were available in Vietnam, ready to help lead their country" and was "concerned that worse turmoil might lie ahead in Saigon."[381]

President Johnson removed Harriman and Hilsman from their posts at the State Department shortly after he took office. "When I became president," Johnson later said, "the first man I instructed to be fired was Hilsman . . . . It took three-four months, but it was one of the first things I did."[382] As for Harriman, President Johnson blamed him especially for the August 24 coup telegram and said that he "would not trust Harriman 'to take out my garbage.'"[383] Johnson transferred him to the African affairs section of the State Department so that Harriman would no longer be involved in Vietnam policy.[384] The damage Hilsman and Harriman had inflicted by undermining Diem became ever more apparent after their departure.

The most compelling evidence that the ouster of Diem had inflicted major damage on the military effort against North Vietnam comes from the words of the Communists themselves. Truong Nhu Tang recalled in his *Journal of a Vietcong* that

---

[379] JOHNSON, *supra* note 31, at 43-44.
[380] *Id.* at 45.
[381] *Id.*
[382] HAMMER, *supra* note 7, at 314.
[383] THOMAS & ISAACSON, *supra* note 5, at 641.
[384] *Id.*

although the coup succeeded, the events that followed did nothing to fulfill the Americans' cherished hopes. To their immense frustration, Don's government proved to be . . . less effective than Diem's. An atmosphere of relief and relaxation had replaced the previous tension, but the ruling Military Council seemed lethargic and without direction. Before many months had passed, drift was to give way to outright confusion.[385]

Viet Cong and other Communist leaders around the world were thrilled to see Diem gone.[386] They had respected him deeply; a Vietnamese Communist representative in Paris said shortly thereafter that Diem had been their most formidable opponent.[387] Nguyen Huu Tho, the head of the National Liberation Front, said the coup was a "gift from Heaven for us."[388] Nolting wrote that another Viet Cong leader said, "We could not believe the Americans would be so stupid as to undermine Diem."[389] Bui Cuong Tuong, the Viet Cong chief of education, culture, and training in Ben Tre province at the time, echoed this sentiment.[390] Taylor later wrote that *Izvestia*, an official Soviet newspaper, "expressed satisfaction with this turn of events."[391] Mao Tse-Tung also doubted the wisdom of undermining Diem. "After all," he told Edgar Snow, "following his assassination, was everything between Heaven and Earth more peaceful?"[392]

Clearly, to ask the question was to answer it. The situation had not become more peaceful following Diem's murder. In the words of the official history of the war by the Vietnamese Communists,

---

[385] TRUONG NHU TANG, JOURNAL OF A VIETCONG 89 (1985).

[386] Sorley, *supra* note 63.

[387] COLBY & MCCARGAR, *supra* note 1, at 158.

[388] *Id.*

[389] NOLTING, *supra* note 7, at 133-34.

[390] Discussion with Robert F. Turner, Professor at the University of Virginia School of Law, Charlottesville, Virginia (Nov. 20, 2002).

[391] TAYLOR, *supra* note 15, at 302.

[392] MCNAMARA & VANDEMARK, *supra* note 206, at 84-85.

> Ngo Dinh Diem and his brother, Ngo Dinh Nhu, were
> murdered by lackeys of the Americans. The Saigon regime . . .
> collapsed into a state of continual crisis from which it could not
> recover. Taking advantage of the convulsions and
> contradictions within the puppet army and the puppet regime,
> all our battlefields increased their operations.[393]

The Viet Cong destroyed 424 strategic hamlets and 219 mountain
hamlets in November 1963 alone.[394] The Vietnamese Communist
official history considered Diem's downfall to be a tremendous
boon to the North, quoting a memorandum from McNamara to
President Johnson stating that after the coup, "revolutionary forces
made very rapid progress . . .[,] controlling a very large percentage
of the population in a number of key provinces."[395]

The legacy of Diem's overthrow became even clearer the next
year when the United States was forced to choose between
accepting the fall of South Vietnam or entering with a large
number of ground troops.[396] Up to the point of Diem's death, only
seventy-eight Americans had been killed in South Vietnam.[397]
With U.S. monetary and advisory assistance, Diem had fought off
the North Vietnamese without the help of substantial American
ground forces.[398] Yet, his successors were not equal to the task,
and successive South Vietnamese leaders were toppled, one after
another, in successive coups.[399] The Diem assassination and the

---

[393] VICTORY IN VIETNAM: THE OFFICIAL HISTORY OF THE PEOPLE'S ARMY OF
VIETNAM, 1954-1975, at 121 (Merle L. Pribbenow trans., 2002).

[394] *Id.* at 121-22, 460n.1.

[395] *Id.* at 123.

[396] NOLTING, *supra* note 7, at 135.

[397] MCNAMARA & VANDEMARK, *supra* note 206, at 321.

[398] NOLTING, *supra* note 7, at 139. Robert Shaplen, who had spent twenty
years in Vietnam, wrote after Diem's death, "Those who knew Diem best tell
that neither he nor Nhu would ever have invited or allowed 550,000 American
soldiers to fight in their country and to permit the devastation caused by air
attacks." As Arthur Schlesinger later put it, "The Ngo brothers were, in their
own anachronistic fashion, authentic nationalists. They were reluctant about
American troops and resistant to American interference." SCHLESINGER, *supra*
note 242, at 717-18.

[399] THOMAS & ISAACSON, *supra* note 5, at 646-47.

resulting military deterioration made South Vietnam a U.S. responsibility,[400] and led to American intervention in what Nolting and others later deemed to be the "most unnecessary war in American history."[401] As Nolting put it in a letter to Robert Kennedy in 1967,

> Regarding Vietnam, it seems to me that no Western government dealing with that situation has been consistently right or successful over an extended period of time during the last 22 years. The Kennedy administration, I think, was on the right track, until its change of attitude towards the Diem regime in 1963. Then a tragic error was committed, blurring the moral issues and leading to direct heavy U.S. involvement. I keep thinking it might help clear the air, both at home and in Vietnam, to admit that basic mistake.[402]

CONCLUSION

In conclusion, the United States originally supported Diem because he had gained a reputation as a courageous and honest patriot by advocating independence from France and spurning the Communists.[403] When he assumed leadership in South Vietnam following the French withdrawal in 1954, almost no one believed that he was capable of unifying the country,[404] which had been devastated by years of war and splintered by feuding factions.[405] However, under Diem's leadership, the South Vietnamese political situation stabilized and the economy grew rapidly.[406] His most serious difficulties began in the late 1950s when North Vietnamese cadres began to infiltrate the South and undermine his government

---

[400] NOLTING, *supra* note 7, at 137-38; Schlesinger, *supra* note 68.

[401] NOLTING, *supra* note 7, at 124.

[402] Letter from Frederick Nolting to Robert F. Kennedy (Apr. 25, 1967), (unpublished letter) (on file with the Frederick Nolting papers at the University of Virginia Alderman Library).

[403] HIGGINS, *supra* note 25, at 157-58.

[404] HILSMAN, *supra* note 33, at 417.

[405] RUSK & RUSK, *supra* note 49, at 436.

[406] NOLTING, *supra* note 7, at 7.

through terrorist tactics.[407] Yet, with American advisory and financial assistance, he fought the Communists to a stalemate by the beginning of 1963.[408]

However, by the early 1960s, criticism of Diem, even from some former American supporters, began to mount.[409] His American critics in the press and diplomatic corps accused him of not respecting civil liberties,[410] refusing to reform his government,[411] and tolerating corruption.[412] Ambassador John Kenneth Galbraith in India helped convince George Ball and Averell Harriman in Washington that Diem was a liability.[413] Harriman's relationship with Diem worsened dramatically following the treaty neutralizing Laos, which Diem opposed because it further opened the South Vietnamese border to North Vietnamese Communist infiltration.[414] Many American reporters in Saigon also despised Diem, and this feeling colored their news reports to the United States.[415]

Yet, Diem's government remained relatively stable until the Buddhist crisis began in May 1963, which led to the first phase of American support for the Diem coup.[416] As the crisis persisted throughout the summer, Diem's antagonists in Washington, led by Averell Harriman, Roger Hilsman, George Ball, and Michael Forrestal, began entertaining the possibility of facilitating Diem's removal.[417] They were convinced that Diem was persecuting the Buddhist majority, which was turning the South Vietnamese population against the government and creating a public relations

---

[407] SORENSON, *supra* note 58, at 650.

[408] COLBY & MCCARGAR, *supra* note 1, at 102.

[409] NOLTING, *supra* note 7, at 86.

[410] BALL, *supra* note 4, at 370.

[411] COLBY & MCCARGAR, *supra* note 1, at 74-75.

[412] CAO KY, *supra* note 73, at 72.

[413] BALL, *supra* note 4, at 370.

[414] NOLTING, *supra* note 7, at 83.

[415] SALINGER, *supra* note 98, at 325; Report From the Assistant Secretary of State for Public Affairs, Robert J. Manning, to President John F. Kennedy (between July 21 and July 31, 1963), *supra* note 170.

[416] PENTAGON PAPERS, *supra* note 108, at 226.

[417] Telegram Drafted by Chalmers Wood at Department of State to the Embassy in Vietnam (June 14, 1963), *supra* note 156.

fiasco for the United States.[418] The assumptions underlying this
theory were questionable, however. The Buddhists' self-anointed
leader, Thich Tri Quang, had Communist ties and openly
supported coming to terms with the North,[419] and it later became
clear that he was a perennial troublemaker with no loyalty to the
South Vietnamese government.[420] His faction, moreover, did not
represent the opinions of the population at large,[421] for the
countryside, where Diem was most popular, remained largely calm
during the urban unrest in Saigon and Hue. Military observers in
the countryside reported that the shooting war against the Viet
Cong was proceeding well.[422]

Ambassador Frederick Nolting in Saigon was a staunch
supporter of Diem, but when his deputy, William Trueheart,
became the acting ambassador while Nolting was on vacation,
Diem's opponents within the U.S. Embassy and the State
Department pressed for a tougher negotiating stance with the South
Vietnamese regime.[423] Ambassador Nolting tried to fix the
relationship between the United States and the Diem government
when he returned to Saigon, but much damage had already been
done.[424] Support for Diem's ouster had grown within the secondary
levels of the U.S. State Department and diplomatic corps.[425] The
situation worsened when South Vietnamese police raided several
Buddhist pagodas just before Ambassador Henry Cabot Lodge
replaced Nolting,[426] spurring Lodge to send word back to
Washington that South Vietnamese generals wished to know if the
United States would support a coup against Diem.[427] Harriman,

---

[418] BALL, *supra* note 4, at 370-71.

[419] Dodd, *supra* note 132, at vii.

[420] TAYLOR, *supra* note 15, at 290-91.

[421] Dodd, *supra* note 26.

[422] Memorandum of a Conversation, White House, Washington (Sept. 10, 1963), *supra* note 28.

[423] Telegram from William Trueheart at the Embassy in Vietnam to the Department of State (June 9, 1963), *supra* note 154.

[424] NOLTING, *supra* note 7, at 117.

[425] TAYLOR, *supra* note 15, at 290.

[426] Voice of America Broadcast, Saigon (Aug. 6, 1963), *supra* note 176.

[427] KARNOW, *supra* note 72, at 284; HILSMAN, *supra* note 33, at 484.

Hilsman, Ball, and Forrestal sent a vaguely worded cable in response on Saturday, August 24, 1963, indicating that they supported a change in South Vietnam's leadership.[428] Diem's supporters, upon returning to Washington a few days later, were furious that the cable had been sent without their approval.[429]

Although the coup fizzled a week later,[430] it marked the beginning of the second phase of U.S. support for undermining Diem. Lodge mounted a campaign of relentless criticism of the Diem regime through his cables, in which he energetically supported a coup.[431] Although President Kennedy and several in the defense and military establishment were unhappy with Lodge's course of action,[432] the president treated Lodge with leniency for political reasons.[433] He believed he could not afford to have his Republican ambassador resign in protest just before his 1964 reelection campaign.[434] When the plotting generals approached their American contacts with renewed plans for a coup, Lodge made it clear that he was pleased and that he strongly desired Diem's overthrow.[435] Lodge urged skeptics of the coup in Washington to allow the coup plotters to proceed unabated and ignored all advice to the contrary.[436] The dissident South Vietnamese generals launched their coup on November 1, and Diem was murdered on the orders of General Duong Van Minh.[437] Kennedy was horrified at the outcome, for he had always

---

[428] Telegram from the Department of State to the Embassy in Vietnam (Aug. 24, 1963), *supra* note 14; NOLTING, *supra* note 7, at 124.

[429] COLBY & MCCARGAR, *supra* note 1, at 138.

[430] Telegram from the Central Intelligence Agency Station in Saigon to the CIA in Washington, *supra* note 267.

[431] *See, e.g.,* Telegram From the Embassy in Vietnam by Ambassador Henry Cabot Lodge to the Department of State (Sept. 5, 1963), *supra* note 19.

[432] HAMMER, *supra* note 7, at 170.

[433] COLBY & MCCARGAR, *supra* note 1, at 135.

[434] *Id.*

[435] DON, *supra* note 180, at 97-99.

[436] Telegram From the Embassy in Vietnam by Ambassador Henry Cabot Lodge to the Department of State (Oct. 5, 1963), *supra* note 20.

[437] DON, *supra* note 180, at 112.

conditioned any U.S. support for a coup on Diem remaining unharmed.[438]

Kennedy himself was murdered three weeks later, which left his successor, President Lyndon Johnson, to face the consequences of Diem's overthrow.[439] The military situation worsened dramatically as a result of the chaos that ensued following Diem's death.[440] The Viet Cong expanded their attacks on the South Vietnamese, whose position crumbled throughout the country.[441] President Johnson faced the choice of whether to abandon South Vietnam to the Viet Cong or introduce substantial American ground forces.[442] He chose the latter option, thus embarking on a course that would cost 58,000 American lives over the next ten years.[443] Johnson faced this dilemma as a direct result of America's role in Diem's assassination,[444] a course of action largely initiated by Diem antagonists within the secondary levels of the U.S. government who through skillful bureaucratic maneuvering thwarted the wishes of their superiors.[445] Had Diem lived, President Johnson would likely have never had to make this unpalatable decision at all, for American machinations had helped deprive South Vietnam of the one leader who was capable of fending off the North Vietnamese Communists.[446] Thus, supporting the Diem coup was the gravest error that the Kennedy administration made in its policy toward Vietnam.

---

[438] TAYLOR, *supra* note 15, at 301.

[439] JOHNSON, *supra* note 31, at 43-44.

[440] MCNAMARA & VANDEMARK, *supra* note 206, at 321.

[441] NOLTING, *supra* note 7, at 133.

[442] *Id.* at 135.

[443] MCNAMARA & VANDEMARK, *supra* note 206, at 321.

[444] In Nolting's words, "The link between the overthrow of the Diem government of South Vietnam in 1963 and the 'American' war that followed is now, I think, clear to most people." NOLTING, *supra* note 7, at 139.

[445] TAYLOR, *supra* note 15, at 290-93.

[446] As Nolting put it, "only Diem can hold this fragmented country together." Memorandum of a Conference with the President, White House, Washington (Aug. 28, 1963), *supra* note 12, at 6.

BIBLIOGRAPHY

Primary Sources

Published Documents

Dodd, Thomas. Letter of Introduction. *Report of United Nations Fact-Finding Mission to South Vietnam.* Washington: United States Senate Committee on the Judiciary, and the Subcommittee to Investigate the Administration of the Internal Security Act and Other Internal Security Laws, 1964.

————. Speech to the U.S. Senate and Information Introduced into the Record with the Speech, February 23, 1965. Washington, D.C.

Foreign Relations of the United States, 1961-1963, Volume II: Vietnam, 1962, edited by John P. Glennon, David M. Baehler, and Charles S. Sampson. Washington: United States Government Printing Office, 1990.

Foreign Relations of the United States, 1961-1963, Volume III: Vietnam, January-August 1963, edited by John P. Glennon, Edward C. Keefer, and Louis J. Smith. Washington: United States Government Printing Office, 1991.

Foreign Relations of the United States, 1961-1963, Volume IV: Vietnam, August-December 1963, edited by John P. Glennon and Edward C. Keefer. Washington: United States Government Printing Office, 1991.

Report of United Nations Fact-Finding Mission to South Vietnam. Washington: United States Senate Committee on the Judiciary, and the Subcommittee to Investigate the Administration of the Internal Security Act and Other Internal Security Laws, 1964.

The Pentagon Papers: The Defense Department History of United States Decisionmaking on Vietnam (Senator Gravel Edition), Volume II. Boston: Beacon Press, 1971.

Unpublished Documents

Declassified Military and Intelligence Documents from the CREST Cold War History Project, National Archives, College Park, Maryland.

The Frederick Nolting Papers, University of Virginia Alderman Library, Charlottesville, Virginia.

Memoirs

Ball, George W. *The Past Has Another Pattern: Memoirs.* New York: W.W. Norton & Company, 1982.

Cao Ky, Nguyen, with Marvin J. Wolf. *Buddha's Child: My Fight to Save Vietnam.* New York: St. Martin's Press, 2002.

Colby, William, with James McCargar. *Lost Victory: A Firsthand Account of America's Sixteen-Year Involvement in Vietnam.* New York: Contemporary Books, 1989.

Don, Tran Van. *Our Endless War: Inside Vietnam.* San Rafael, California: Presidio Press, 1978.

Galbraith, John Kenneth. *Ambassador's Journal: A Personal Account of the Kennedy Years.* New York: Signet, 1970.

———. *Name-Dropping: From FDR On.* New York: Houghton Mifflin Company, 1999.

Hilsman, Roger. *To Move a Nation: The Politics of Foreign Policy in the Administration of John F. Kennedy.* Garden City, New York: Doubleday & Company, 1967.

Johnson, Lyndon B. *The Vantage Point: Perspectives of the Presidency, 1963-1969.* New York: Holt, Rinehart and Winston, 1971.

McNamara, Robert S., with Brian VanDeMark. *In Retrospect: The Tragedy and Lessons of Vietnam.* New York: Random House, 1995.

Nixon, Richard M. *RN: The Memoirs of Richard Nixon.* New York: Touchstone, 1990.

Nolting, Frederick. *From Trust to Tragedy: The Political Memoirs of Frederick Nolting, Kennedy's Ambassador to Diem's Vietnam.* New York: Praeger, 1988.

O'Donnell, Kenneth P., and David F. Powers with Joe McCarthy. *"Johnny, We Hardly Knew Ye."* Boston: Little, Brown & Company, 1972.

Rusk, Dean, as told to Richard Rusk. *As I Saw It*, edited by Daniel S. Papp. New York: W.W. Norton & Company, 1990.

Salinger, Pierre. *With Kennedy.* Garden City, New York: Doubleday & Company, 1966.

Schlesinger, Arthur M., Jr. *A Thousand Days: John F. Kennedy in the White House.* Greenwich, Connecticut: Fawcett Crest, 1965.

Sheehan, Neil. *A Bright Shining Lie: John Paul Vann and America in Vietnam.* New York: Random House, 1988.[447]

Sorenson, Theodore C. *Kennedy.* New York: Harper & Row, 1965.

Tang, Truong Nhu. *Journal of a Vietcong.* London: Jonathan Cape, 1985.

Taylor, Maxwell D. *Swords and Plowshares.* New York: W.W. Norton & Company, 1972.

Discussions with the Author

Schlesinger, James. Discussion with the author. October 16, 2002. Charlottesville, Virginia.

Sorley, Lewis. Discussion with the author. November 13, 2002. Charlottesville, Virginia.

Turner, Robert F. Discussion with the author. November 20, 2002. Charlottesville, Virginia.

Secondary Sources

Books

Allen, Richard C. *Korea's Syngman Rhee: An Unauthorized Portrait.* Rutland, Vermont: Charles E. Tuttle Company, 1960.

Collier, Peter, and David Horowitz. *The Kennedys: An American Drama.* New York: Sutton Books, 1984.

---

[447] I am listing this book as a primary source because the chapter draws almost exclusively from Sheehan's recollections of his own actions.

Geyer, Georgie Anne. *Guerrilla Prince: The Untold Story of Fidel Castro.* Boston: Little Brown and Company, 1991.

Hammer, Ellen J. *A Death in November: America in Vietnam, 1963.* New York: E.P. Dutton, 1987.

Higgins, Marguerite. *Our Vietnam Nightmare.* New York: Harper & Row, 1965.

Karnow, Stanley. *Vietnam: A History.* New York: The Viking Press, 1983.

Kim, Quee-Young. *The Fall of Syngman Rhee.* Berkeley, California: Institute of East Asian Studies of the University of California, 1983.

Langguth, A. J. *Our Vietnam: The War 1954-1975.* New York: Simon & Schuster, 2000.

Newman, John M. *JFK and Vietnam: Deception, Intrigue, and the Struggle for Power.* New York: Warner Books, 1992.

Parmet, Herbert S. *JFK: The Presidency of John F. Kennedy.* Norwalk, Connecticut: The Eastern Press, 1983.

Reeves, Thomas C. *A Question of Character: A Life of John F. Kennedy.* Rocklin, California: Prima Publishing, 1992.

Rust, William J. *Kennedy in Vietnam.* New York: Charles Scribner's Sons, 1985.

Schlesinger, Arthur M. *Robert Kennedy and His Times.* Boston: Houghton Mifflin, 1978.

Smith, Sally Bedell. *Grace and Power: The Private World of the Kennedy White House.* New York: Random House, 2005.

Thomas, Evan, and Walter Isaacson. *The Wise Men: Six Friends and the World they Made.* New York: Simon & Schuster, 1986.

Victory in Vietnam: The Official History of the People's Army in Vietnam, 1954-1975, translated by Merle L. Pribbenow. Lawrence, Kansas: University of Kansas Press, 2002.

Young, Marilyn B. *The Vietnam Wars, 1945-1990.* New York: HarperCollins, 1991.

II

A War Worth Fighting: How the United States Military Presence in Indochina From 1965 to 1975 Preserved Global Democratic Security

Michael A. McCann

"They came home without a victory not because they were defeated, but because they were denied a chance to win."
— Ronald Reagan, February 24, 1981.[1]

INTRODUCTORY OVERVIEW OF THE COMMUNIST EMPIRE IN 1965: HOW THE SOVIET UNION AND CHINA SIMULTANEOUSLY COMPETED WITH ONE ANOTHER AND THREATENED THE UNITED STATES

For the United States, 1965 presented a global landscape that appeared favorable to Communist expansion. Not only were internal Communist movements present in many nations, but neutral and allied nations were beginning to seek accord with both the Soviet Union and China. Equally significant, the Soviet Union and China were providing both munitions and financial assistance

* This paper was written during the fall of 2000, when I was a second-year law student at the University of Virginia School of Law. I wish to thank my father, Major (ret.) William P. McCann, M.D., who served in the United States Army during the Vietnam War, for sharing his experiences and wisdom. I also wish to thank John Norton Moore and Robert F. Turner, Director and Associate Director, respectively, of the Center for National Security Law at the University of Virginia School of Law, for their insight and guidance.

[1] Daniel F. Gilmore, *Vietnam Veteran awarded Medal of Honor*, U.P.I., Feb. 25, 1981.

to numerous nations and insurgent groups. In fact, the Soviet Union announced at the start of 1965, "Let this year be a year of further strengthening of the fraternal friendship of the countries of Socialism, a year of strengthening of the unity of the international communist movement."[2] It is from this initial analysis, as well as from subsequent examination, that we can predict that an American departure from Vietnam in 1965 would have produced negative effects on both American national security and global stability.

Europe

As the American war effort in Vietnam proceeded without resolution, and as the American military was roundly criticized for its use of chemical weapons against the North Vietnamese, several European nations began to improve their relations with the Soviet Union. For instance, in April of 1965, French President Charles de Gaulle declared that France "would cooperate with the Soviet Union . . . to attain peace and progress," adding further that the two nations were "fundamentally in accord [without] any national differences between them."[3] Significantly, the *New York Times* assessed de Gaulle's welcoming of the Soviet Union as "deepen[ing] allied diplomatic misgivings over the aims of the new French-Soviet friendship."[4] Perhaps even more troubling, de Gaulle spoke fondly of the "national affinity of the two peoples," which signaled to the United States "a new advance in France's movement away from the United States and the Western alliance toward stronger ties with Eastern Europe."[5]

France was not alone in cultivating a friendship with the Soviet Union in 1965. In fact, less than a week after de Gaulle spoke of the "time-honored sympathy" between French and Soviet citizens,

---

[2] Theodore Shabad, *Moscow "Wishes" Peace for 1965*, N.Y. TIMES, Jan. 3, 1965, at A24.

[3] Drew Middleton, *De Gaulle Gives Pledge to Soviet*, N.Y. TIMES, Apr. 4, 1965, at A12.

[4] *Id.*

[5] *Id.*

the leadership of Cyprus acknowledged that it had entered into a comprehensive arms agreement with the Soviets.[6] Specifically, Archbishop Makarios, the president of Cyprus, revealed that Soviet anti-aircraft missile equipment had been dispatched to the island.[7]

Austria's political wanderings also vexed the United States in 1965. Although Austria declared itself "committed to permanent neutrality," its foreign minister was a Socialist with Communist ties, and international observers regarded Austria as "still trying to figure out where to fit into Europe."[8] While "neutrality" may not have set off an alarm, Austria's critical strategic position within Europe had constituted a vital component in the North American Treaty Organization's over-arching ambition, which was to prevent the westward spread of Communism. Therefore, Austria's political ambivalence in 1965, coupled with the apparent courtship of France by the Soviet Union, may have encouraged other European nations to open political dialogue with the Soviet Union. Moreover, it stands to reason that such dialogue would have become more prevalent had the United States retreated from its fight with a "fourth-rate" North Vietnamese army in 1965.

Africa

Both the Soviet Union and China targeted Africa as a developing continent ripe for Communist ideology. In particular, the Communists surmised that as many African nations struggled with the transition from colonized states to nation states, they would seek both political and financial support from external sources. For instance, in 1965, the Soviet Union provided $500 million dollars of aid to Egypt to help modernize its army and improve its social programs.[9] Also in 1965, the Soviet Union

---

[6] W. Granger Blair, *Makarios Says Cyprus Has Russian Equipment*, N.Y. TIMES, Mar. 30, 1965, at A4.

[7] *Id.*

[8] Richard E. Mooney, *Austrians Ponder Position in Europe*, N.Y. TIMES, Mar. 29, 1965, at A4.

[9] Hendrick Smith, *Red Aid to Cairo is at $500 Million*, N.Y. TIMES, Jan. 4, 1965, at A3.

pledged to encourage "national liberation struggle" in Angola, Mozambique, Aden, and the Congo.[10]

Importantly, political leaders within Africa had begun to develop close relationships with Communist officials by 1965. In Kenya, for example, Vice President Oginga Odinga not only engaged in "spirited public defenses of Communism," but he also enjoyed "close connections with the Chinese and Russians."[11] Moreover, Kenyan President Jomo Kenyatta warned of an impending Communist threat: "It represents no less a threat to the freedom of Africans than did imperialism in its heyday . . . it is naïve to think that there is no danger of imperialism from the East."[12] Interestingly, in fact, President Kenyatta removed Vice President Odinga from his Cabinet, an act further illustrating the seriousness of which African leaders regarded the Communist threat.[13]

Tanzania offers a telling illustration of the relentless competition between the Soviet Union and China for influence in Africa. By June of 1965, the Soviet Union had delivered 1,142 tons of arms, ammunition, and military vehicles, while, in comparison, China had delivered 1,025 tons of arms and ammunition.[14] Chinese Premier Chou En-lai visited Tanzania in June, prompting one observer to muse, "Mr. Chou's portrait is everywhere [in Tanzania], reflecting the success of China's efforts here."[15] Yet, only three months earlier, the Chinese Communist Party had denounced the Soviet Union for allegedly seeking "subordination of smaller nations and employment of policies to divide the Communist world."[16] Though the massive inflow of Soviet aid to Tanzania confirmed the Chinese charge, a similarly massive inflow

---

[10] Shabad, *supra* note 2.

[11] Lawrence Fellows, *Kenya Cabinet Ministers Scores Vice President*, N.Y. TIMES, June 1, 1965, at A13.

[12] *Kenyatta Excludes a Red Role in Kenya*, N.Y. TIMES, June 2, 1965, at A5.

[13] *Odinga Removed from Delegation*, N.Y. TIMES, June 4, 1965, at A7.

[14] Lawrence Fellows, *Tanzania to Greet Chou Today; Her Capital is in Festive Array*, N.Y. TIMES, June 4, 1965, at A8.

[15] *Id.*

[16] Seymour Topping, *China to Intensify Drive*, N.Y. TIMES, Mar. 23, 1965, at A13.

of Chinese aid confirmed the Soviet Union's corresponding charge that China had sought "an open split in the international Communist movement."[17] Of perhaps greatest importance, the considerable Communist aid in 1965 reflected the surging influence of the Soviet Union and China in Africa. Thus, an American departure from Vietnam in 1965 might have triggered doubts in Africa as to whether the United States could challenge the seemingly ubiquitous Soviet and Chinese presence.

Asia

While sharply rebuking the Soviet Union for its use of foreign aid as a tool of external influence, China demonstrated its own expansionist tendencies by signing long-term economic and cultural agreements with Afghanistan in May of 1965. Specifically, the agreements included Chinese financial assistance to the Afghanistan government.[18]

Likewise, later that month, China's military aid to Vietnam increased dramatically, prompting one American official to find China "demonstrating that its commitment to the Vietcong is greater than that of Moscow."[19] Aside from supplying Vietnam with substantial aid, China also signaled its "unwavering support for Vietnam" by having Chinese Foreign Minister Chen Yi declare that "If the United States crossed the 17th Parallel to attack North Vietnam and if the Government of Vietnam asks for aid, our help will be assured."[20]

Similarly, China provided both substantial aid and moral support to the Indonesian Communist Party in 1965, even to the point of collaborating on a short-lived coup d'état of the democratically elected Indonesian government. This topic will be discussed in greater detail in the section "Southeast Asia: Falling Dominoes."

---

[17] *Id.*

[18] *Chen Yi Visits Afghanistan*, N.Y. TIMES, Mar. 23, 1965, at A11.

[19] Charles Mohr, *President Hints at Help for Asia*, N.Y. TIMES, Mar. 26, 1965, at A1.

[20] *Warning by Chen to U.S. Reported*, N.Y. TIMES, Mar. 22, 1965, at A10.

By June of 1965, the Soviet Union had responded to these Chinese advances by pledging military aid to the North Korean government. The significance of such Soviet aid was not lost on China, for North Korea had served as one of China's closest ideological allies, and, to the aggravation of China in June of 1965, North Korea had been a welcome recipient of enormous Chinese assistance during the Korean War.[21] At the same time, China observed an improvement of relations between Pakistan and the Soviet Union. Indeed, in early June, Pakistani leadership visited Moscow, which, to international observers, "underscored the improvement in relations between the Soviet Union and Pakistan."[22]

The Soviet and Chinese competition for influence in Asia in 1965 peaked in June when the Soviet Union decided to attend the annual Asian-African conference in Indonesia for the very first time. In response, Chinese officials protested that the Soviet Union had no place at the conference, stating that "the Soviet Union is a European and not an Asian power." However, according to a "Soviet informant," the Soviet Union attended only to counter surging Chinese influence in Vietnam, which had resulted in the "Russians feeling they have a stake in Asia that did not exist before."[23] As the two Communist powers jockeyed for influence in Asia, it appears again that a United States departure from Vietnam in 1965 would have painted the American resolve against Communist expansion as a weakened caricature of its former self, particularly when juxtaposed with an aggressive Communist movement to recruit allies.

---

[21] *North Koreans in Moscow Get Pledge of Military Aid*, N.Y. TIMES, June 1, 1965, at A7.

[22] *High Soviet Aide to Make Four-Day Visit to Pakistan*, N.Y. TIMES, June 1, 1965, at A13.

[23] Peter Grose, *Soviet Challenge to Red China Seen*, N.Y. TIMES, June 5, 1965, at 1.

THE DOMESTIC SYMBOLIC IMPORTANCE OF A U.S. RETREAT FROM VIETNAM IN 1965

Domestic Support for the War Effort

Although many today recall the Vietnam War as an unpopular military engagement, many Americans had ardently supported the active prevention of Communist expansion into other Southeast Asian countries. Likewise, many Americans expressed a willingness to maintain American troops in Vietnam until the conflict could be resolved satisfactorily. To illustrate these points, in a 1969 CBS News Poll, 71 percent of respondents were "willing to keep troops there" in response to the question: "Suppose you really knew that our presence in Vietnam for several more years would prevent Communist take-overs in other countries of Southeast Asia. Would you be willing or not to keep our troops there?"[24]

Not only were many Americans supportive of both the war effort and the deterrence of Communist expansion, but many influential Republicans and Democrats in Congress similarly endorsed an activist approach. For instance, Senate Minority Leader Everett Dirksen (R-IL) and House Minority Leader Gerald R. Ford (R-MI) issued a joint statement on February 17, 1965, highlighting the need for persistent military activity in Vietnam.[25] Moreover, in its 1994 report on *The U.S. Government and the Vietnam War*, the United States Senate Committee on Foreign Relations concluded that "most of the Democratic leaders [in 1965] urged the President to escalate the war."[26] Specifically, the

---

[24] STAFF OF SENATE COMM. ON FOREIGN RELATIONS, 103D CONG., THE U.S. GOVERNMENT AND THE VIETNAM WAR: EXECUTIVE AND LEGISLATIVE ROLES AND RELATIONSHIPS 147 (Comm. Print 1994) (citing CBS News Poll conducted by telephone between Nov. 23 and 25, 1969).

[25] 1965 CONGRESSIONAL QUARTERLY ALMANAC, 89TH CONG. 456.

[26] STAFF OF SENATE COMM. ON FOREIGN RELATIONS, 103D CONG., *supra* note 24. As to specific reasons for Democratic support, at an NSC meeting on Feb. 6, 1965, "John W. McCormack (D/Mass.), Speaker of the House . . . agreed that the U.S. should respond [to the North Vietnamese attack on the U.S. base at Pleiku]

Committee on Foreign Relations listed the following congressional leaders as supportive of heightening the war effort in 1965: Speaker John W. McCormack (D-MA), House Majority Leader Carl Albert (D-OK), House Majority Whip Hale Boggs (D-LA), Senate Majority Whip Russell Long (D-LA), House Foreign Affairs Committee Chairman Thomas E. Morgan (D-PA), House Armed Services Committee Chairman L. Mendel Rivers (D-SC), House Appropriations Committee Chairman George Mahon (D-TX), and Senate Appropriations Committee Chairman Carl Hayden (D-AZ).[27] Moreover, the war effort received greater legitimacy on August 18, 1965, when former President Dwight D. Eisenhower declared that preservation of American national security required "the Communists . . . be stopped in Vietnam," even if American forces were needed.[28]

On the other hand, some American leaders expressed doubt in 1965 as to the viability of military activity in Vietnam. For instance, Henry Cabot Lodge, ambassador to South Vietnam, cabled President Johnson in late September and expressed that "There is clearly a limit to our ability to meet force with force. If we send troops to enough places, we—not the Communists—will be contained."[29] Likewise, other top officials, while recognizing the appropriateness of the war effort, believed that any escalation of fighting into the North could trigger a more expansive war. For instance, in a memorandum dated January 20, 1966, to President Johnson, Undersecretary of State George Ball asserted that increased bombing of North Vietnam would lead to a greater North Vietnamese dependence on both China and the Soviet Union, "who in turn could increase their pressure on North Vietnam. It could also lead to a direct confrontation between the U.S. and China and

---

by a retaliatory airstrike on North Vietnam." The need to bomb the North was best illustrated in early June 1965 when General Westmoreland concluded that "there was imminent danger of a Communist victory." *Id.*

[27] *Id.*

[28] *Id.*

[29] *Id.* at 59 (quoting Cable from Henry Cabot Lodge, U.S. Ambassador to South Vietnam, to President Johnson (Sept. 27, 1965)).

possibly the Soviet Union."[30] Like Ball, both Secretary of State Dean Rusk and Secretary of Defense Robert McNamara believed that avoiding war with China was imperative, though, according to the Committee on Foreign Relations, Rusk also maintained that the "measured action" of the Johnson administration "was ultimately less likely to provoke a nuclear war than either of the major alternatives of either abandoning Vietnam or a major escalation on our part."[31]

In general, however, support for the U.S. war effort in Indochina appeared strong. Indeed, a majority of Americans endorsed the engagement. Likewise, many Democratic and Republican leaders believed that neither President John F. Kennedy nor President Lyndon Baines Johnson had fully enabled the American military to defeat the North Vietnamese, although some officials certainly expressed resistance toward the prospect of escalation. Importantly, therefore, a departure from Vietnam in 1965 would likely have been regarded as an unpopular action, both in Congress and in the American public. Not only would it have appeared counterintuitive to abandon a fight against an inferior army, but, as Professor Pamela Sodhy, Chair of Southeast Asian Studies at Georgetown University, points out, "there was too much national ego" on the line.[32] Indeed, Professor Sodhy doubts that the U.S. public would have approved the retreat of 125,000 American troops from a conflict with what, at the time, was widely-regarded as a "fourth-rate army."[33]

National Ego at Risk in Indochina

Many top Cabinet officials maintained that a retreat by the United States in 1965 would have damaged American prestige,

---

[30] *Id.* at 151 (citing Memorandum from George Ball, Undersecretary of State, to President Johnson (Jan. 20, 1966)).

[31] *Id.* at 144.

[32] Interview with Pamela Sodhy, Chair of the Southeast Asian Studies Department, Georgetown University, in Washington, D.C. (Nov. 5, 2000).

[33] It is possible that much of the national mood could be characterized by Professor Sodhy's comment: "We are not the French." *Id.*

perhaps irreparably. For example, Secretary of State Rusk, in a memorandum to President Johnson dated July 1, 1965, clearly urged the president to remain in Indochina. Indeed, Rusk feared the far-reaching, international consequences that a departure would have posed to the United States' global reputation as *the* bastion of democracy.

> The integrity of the U.S. commitment is the principal pillar of peace throughout the world. If that commitment becomes unreliable, the communists would draw conclusions that would lead to our ruin and almost certainly to a catastrophic war. So long as the South Vietnamese are prepared to fight for themselves, we cannot abandon them without disaster to peace and to our interests throughout the world.[34]

Similarly, *NSAM 288*, issued in March of 1964, starkly enunciated the emblematic significance of U.S. involvement in Vietnam: "The RVN [Republic of Vietnam] is a politico/military keystone in Southeast Asia and is symbolic of U.S. determination in Asia as Berlin is in Europe—to prevent Communist expansion. U.S. national prestige, credibility, and the honor with respect to world-wide pledges, and declared national policy are at stake."[35] Further, *NSAM 288* maintained that "it is incumbent upon the United States at this stage to invalidate the Communist 'wars of national liberation.'"[36]

In the same way, other official government documents reveal a widely-shared internal belief that U.S. self-respect was at stake in Vietnam. For example, JCSM-652-65, issued on August 27, 1965, to the secretary of defense, made clear that "The war in Vietnam is the single most critical international problem facing the United States today, and it portends the most serious immediate threat to

---

[34] STAFF OF SENATE COMM. ON FOREIGN RELATIONS, 103D CONG., *supra* note 24, at 144 (quoting Memorandum from Dean Rusk, Secretary of State, to President Johnson (July 1, 1965)).

[35] *Id.* at 45 (quoting NSAM 288 (March 1964)).

[36] *Id.*

continued U.S. world leadership and national security."[37]
Similarly, a 1967 memo to President Johnson from Director of
Central Intelligence Richard Helms unambiguously highlighted the
profound ramifications of an American defeat in Vietnam:

> The worst potential damage would be of the self-inflicted kind:
> internal dissension which would limit our future ability to use
> our power and resources wisely and to full effect, *and lead to a
> loss of confidence by others in the American capacity for
> leadership.*[38]

Likewise, American leaders' proclamations reaffirmed
institutional backing for the war effort. Most significantly, in his
State of the Union Address on January 12, 1966, President Johnson
plainly stated the symbolic magnitude of preserving freedom in
Vietnam:

> We will stay because in Asia and around the world are
> countries whose independence rests, in large measure, on
> confidence in America's word and in America's protection. To
> yield to force in Vietnam would weaken that confidence, would
> undermine the independence of many lands, and would whet
> the appetite of aggression. We would have to fight in one land,
> and then we would have to fight in another—or abandon much
> of Asia to the domination of Communists. And we do not
> intend to abandon Asia to conquest.[39]

Like President Johnson, Senator Stuart Symington (D-MO), a
member of both the Foreign Relations and the Armed Services
Committees, emphasized the geopolitical significance of defending
Vietnam against Communist aggression. Indeed, Senator

---

[37] *Id.* at 47 (quoting JCSM-652-65 (Aug. 27, 1965)).

[38] W.W. Rostow, *McNamara's Vietnam War Reconsidered*, SOC'Y MAG., Nov.
1, 1998, at 78 (emphasis added).

[39] STAFF OF SENATE COMM. ON FOREIGN RELATIONS, 103D CONG., *supra* note
24, at 141 (quoting President Johnson, State of the Union Address (Jan. 12,
1966)).

Symington had maintained that an American defeat or retreat would harm American prestige and increase the probability that Vietnam's neighbors would likewise fall to Communism. In fact, upon return from a trip to Southeast Asia on January 25, 1966, Senator Symington conveyed these points when addressing the Senate:

> If South Vietnam is not the right place to defend the free world against totalitarian aggression, we should retire from that country on the best terms possible. This would probably result in a Communist takeover of additional countries and would damage seriously the world position and status of the United States.[40]

Even opponents of the war effort acknowledged the exorbitant political costs of failing in Vietnam. For instance, on the August 1, 1965, broadcast of *Face the Nation*, Senator Richard B. Russell (D-GA), chairman of the Armed Services Committee, declared that a defeat in Vietnam "would be a worse blow to our world prestige and to our reputation for keeping our word under all conditions than it would be from either a strategic or a tactical or an economic standpoint."[41] More poignantly, Russell dramatically avowed America's pride: "Our flag is committed, our national honor is committed, our prestige is committed, and our whole power for the maintenance of world peace and avoidance of a nuclear war is laid squarely on the line in Vietnam."[42]

Therefore, from across the political spectrum, an abandonment of Vietnam in 1965 would have proved incompatible with the United States' role as a superpower. It appears that few American leaders would have tolerated an American departure, for doing so would have greatly jeopardized American prestige. Moreover, U.S. credibility as a believable deterrent to the spread of Communism would have been cast in doubt, thus emboldening Communist groups and corroborating that the "paper-tiger," as Chairman Mao

---

[40] *Id.* at 142.

[41] *Id.* at 23 (citing *Face the Nation* (CBS television broadcast, Aug. 1, 1965)).

[42] *Id.*

liked to call the United States, could not quell insurrection movements. This outcome seems particularly plausible given that, as shall be discussed later in sections "Southeast Asia After the American Departure in 1975" and "Worldwide Developments: How the U.S. Withdrawal from Indochina Emboldened Communism," foreign leaders openly expressed skepticism regarding the American capacity to defeat Communism following its withdrawal from Indochina in 1975.

INTERNATIONAL SUPPORT FOR U.S. INVOLVEMENT IN VIETNAM IN 1965

In order to engender greater international legitimacy for the American efforts in Vietnam, President Johnson and Secretary of State Rusk traveled to Iran in April of 1965 and held war discussions with leaders from both the Middle East and Europe. President Johnson hoped the discussions would enlarge support for the war, including from nations not directly threatened by Communist advancements in Indochina.

From the perspective of the Johnson administration, the trip appeared successful. For instance, Secretary Rusk hailed the "tremendous response" from European and Middle Eastern leaders. Furthermore, the Johnson administration seemed convinced that numerous nations embraced the deterrence of Communist expansion as an essential component to global stability. Indeed, as Secretary Rusk remarked, the destabilization of Germany illustrated this very point: "When you look at recent events in Berlin, you understand that things can change very quickly without notice."[43]

On the other hand, few European and Middle Eastern nations publicly endorsed the United States and its efforts in Vietnam. The silence exhibited by many nations partly surprised onlookers, given that, as one British observer maintained, Vietnam reflected a global war disguised in regional clothing. "Vietnam's . . . importance lies in the fact that it is a theatre in which the

---

[43] *Soviet Ridicules Johnson Speech on Asia as "Nosy Propaganda,"* N.Y. TIMES, Apr. 11, 1965, at A1.

Americans and other nations are actively fighting a war against an enemy backed by Russia, China, and the satellite countries."[44] However, many nations harbored grave misgivings over certain military strategies employed by the United States. For instance, Dr. Marin J. Strmecki notes that both Presidents Kennedy and Johnson refrained from utilizing naval power in order to stop arms shipments from both the Soviet Union and China.[45] At the start of 1965, Great Britain enunciated the consequences of this same criticism: "British officials believe that the use of seapower in the Indian Ocean by Britain and the United States can be more effective than the use of land forces to guarantee the independence of Thailand and Burma or even the neutrality of Vietnam."[46] Therefore, inadequate naval power severely disadvantaged ground troops in their attempt to quell the Communist threat, thus making America's allies warier of becoming involved with such an operation.

Clearly, nations that neighbored Indochina, and therefore most directly feared Communist expansion, had the greatest stake in seeing the United States prevail. Not surprisingly, these nations often expressed the most enthusiastic support for the American war effort in Vietnam. In 1965, Australia most ardently advocated the United States staying and winning. On the opposite end of the spectrum, Japan appeared far more reticent in its support. In fact, Japan sought to improve relations with China in 1965, perhaps reflecting a preemptive response to the American military struggles in Vietnam. The specific actions and declarations of Australia and Japan in 1965 will be analyzed below.

---

[44] ALAN GLYN, WITNESS TO VIETNAM 276 (1968).

[45] Dr. Marin J. Strmecki, Vice President, Director of Programs, Smith Richardson Foundation, Address at the University of Virginia School of Law (Nov. 15, 2000).

[46] Sydney Gruson, *U.S. Allies Oppose Wider Asian War*, N.Y. TIMES, Jan. 1, 1965, at A2.

Australia

Perhaps more so than any other nation, Australia passionately defended the United States throughout 1965. For instance, on March 23, Australian Minister for External Affairs Paul Hasluck addressed the Australian Parliament and fervently endorsed U.S. military activities.[47] This address proved notable not only because it contrasted with the reluctance exhibited by many other nations, but because at around this time, many nations had condemned the United States for employing a limited amount of chemical weapons against North Vietnamese soldiers. In 1965, however, Australian officials were far more concerned that "the war in South Vietnam is being lost to the Communists." Indeed, Australian officials worried aloud that as the United States struggled to defeat the North Vietnamese, political support for the war effort within the United States would eventually suffer, thus making more likely "a diplomatic settlement leading to an eventual communist takeover of South Vietnam with Communist China becoming, in time, the dominant power in Southeast Asia."[48]

Australia had good reason to fear Communist expansion, for its military forces were incapable of thwarting off a substantial military invasion. To illustrate this point, the January 2, 1965, edition of the *New York Times* revealed that "Australia at present is ill-equipped to deal with any major challenge—small army, navy, and air force . . . it will be two years before Australia has enough military strength to command respect from her Asian neighbors."[49] This military inadequacy was particularly meaningful since the Australian government "feared . . . a step-up of the Malaysian-Indonesian conflict could result in Indonesian efforts to stir up trouble for Australia in the Australian-governed eastern half of New Guinea."[50]

---

[47] *Australia Supports U.S.*, N.Y. TIMES, Mar. 24, 1965, at A5.

[48] Tillman Durdin, *Australia Disturbed by Sukarno's Moves in a Warlike Policy*, N.Y. TIMES, Jan. 4, 1965, at A6.

[49] *Id.*

[50] *Id.*

Australian concerns over the spread of Communism extended beyond worries of an invasion. Specifically, in fact, internal Communist tensions were becoming increasingly apparent by 1965. For instance, on March 20, a sizable labor strike orchestrated by the Australian Communist Party appeared to "represent the persistent effort of a Communist-backed group of labor leaders to gain dominance over the first major step in a broad plan to control the work force in other big new mining and mineral processing enterprises in the fast-developing state of Queensland."[51]

While the internal Communist movements in Australia never seriously threatened the government in 1965, it is clear that Australia harbored grave misgivings that Communism was spreading, particularly in the form of Indonesian Communists. Therefore, a U.S. departure from Indochina in 1965 could have diminished Australia's confidence in its ability to repel the spread of Communism into its borders. It is not surprising that Australia so forthrightly advocated the United States' efforts in Vietnam.

Japan

Like Australian leaders, Japanese officials were particularly wary of the Communist threat from Indochina. For instance, on January 3, 1965, the *New York Times* reported that "Japanese officials believe that a possible fall of Southeast Asia to Communism is of far more importance to Japan's future than Communist China's recent emergence as a prospective nuclear power."[52] Moreover, like the Australians, the Japanese were troubled that a U.S. failure in Vietnam would embolden China in its expansionist activities. Along those lines, when Japanese Premier Eisaku Sato sought to improve relations with China at the conclusion of 1964, Japan may have been acting preemptively. On December 31, 1964, Premier Sato "voiced confidence that he will find in Washington complete understanding of his desire to expand

---

[51] Tillman Durdin, *Australian Reds an Issue in Strike*, N.Y. TIMES, Mar. 21, 1965, at A38.

[52] Robert Trumbull, *Japan Sees 1965 As Decisive Year*, N.Y. TIMES, Jan. 3, 1965, at A28.

relations between Japan and Communist China."[53] At the same time, Sato recognized that China's struggles with Taiwan had significant implications for the future of Japan: "Japan and the United States will be the two countries most affected by whatever result may come out of the question of Communist China and Nationalist China."[54]

The unpopularity of the United States in Japan also troubled Japanese officials. Indeed, a number of Japanese groups regarded the United States' use of chemical weapons against North Vietnamese soldiers as an attack on all Asian people. This "race" argument led to a Tokyo rally featuring 5,000 activists demanding the withdrawal of U.S. troops from South Vietnam. In fact, the activists claimed that "Asians are being used as 'guinea pigs' for new types of gases."[55] In all likelihood, such protest activity invigorated the Japanese Communist Party, as evidenced by the Party's aid to the Indonesian Communists in the Gestapu Coup attempt later that year.[56] Furthermore, had anti-American sentiment become more violent, the United States may have decreased its military presence in Japan, a development that would have, "from the point of view of world peace . . . been very dangerous."[57]

From the U.S. perspective, neither a Japan sympathetic to Communist China nor one in social turmoil would have been desirable. As Christopher Layne wrote in *Foreign Policy*, "By constraining Japan, America 'reassured' Japan's neighbors that [Japan] would remain peaceful and thereby assuaged the neighbor's fears of . . . Japanese economic determination."[58]

---

[53] Robert Trumbull, *Sato Hopeful of U.S. Sympathy on Japan's Chinese Dealings*, N.Y. TIMES, Jan. 1, 1965, at A2.

[54] *Id.*

[55] *5,000 in Tokyo Bid U.S. Quit Vietnam*, N.Y. TIMES, Mar. 28, 1965, at A3.

[56] JUSTUS M. VAN DER KROEF, COMMUNISM IN SOUTHEAST ASIA 34 (1980).

[57] GLYN, *supra* note 44, at 258.

[58] Christopher Layne, *American hegemony—without an enemy*, FOREIGN POL'Y, Sept. 22, 1993; *see also* Layne (quoting Melvyn Leffler, historian, ("neither an integrated Europe nor a united Germany nor an independent Japan must be permitted to emerge as a third force")); *see also* Benjamin Schwarz, *Why America thinks it has to run the world*, ATLANTIC MONTHLY, June 1996, at 92,

Similarly, Secretary of State Dean Acheson insisted on the need for an economically successful Japan, for such a Japanese state of affairs would "help immunize the region against Communist expansion."[59]

Importantly, in 1970, Undersecretary of State Eugene Rostow bluntly described how an American departure from Vietnam would have encouraged Japan to become more hawkish. Rostow argued that such an occurrence would have left Japan little choice but to develop nuclear weapons:

> I think the Japanese will draw certain conclusions [from an abrupt American departure from Indochina]. And I think their policy will take on a much more nationalistic cast. I think the first thing that would happen would be that they wouldn't ratify the nuclear-non-proliferation treaty. They would feel compelled to become a nuclear power.[60]

Military expert Aaron Freidberg concluded that if Japan were to become a nuclear power today, it might "cause China to accelerate and expand its nuclear programs, which could then have an impact on the defense policies of Taiwan, India (and through it, Pakistan) and Russia."[61] While it remains unclear whether the same national security reverberations would have been felt in the late 1960s, it is nevertheless certain that a Japanese nuclear arsenal would have destabilized the region and perhaps even accelerated a regional race for nuclear arms. Therefore, from the perspective of both Japanese stability and global and regional security, an American departure from Vietnam in 1965 would have likely produced negative effects.

---

available at LEXIS, News Library, Atlantic Monthly File ("the 'adult supervision' role of United States foreign policy following WWII was to protect nations from themselves").

[59] Schwarz, *supra* note 58, at 92.

[60] *Id.*

[61] *Id.*

SOUTHEAST ASIA: FALLING DOMINOES

In 1963, President Kennedy seemed to validate the fear that many Southeast Asians harbored toward Communist expansion. Specifically, when asked by David Brinkley of NBC News if he doubted the "Domino Theory" in Southeast Asia, President Kennedy replied:

> No, I believe it. I believe it. I think that the struggle is close enough. China is so large, looms so high just beyond the frontiers, that if South Vietnam went, it would not only give them an improved geographic position for a guerrilla assault on Malaya, but would also give the impression that the wave of the future in Southeast Asia was China and the communists. So I believe it.[62]

The "wave of the future" that President Kennedy referred to in 1963 seemed quite plausible in 1965. In fact, upon closer observation of Vietnam's neighboring nations, the Communist threat appeared resolute and the "dominoes" were beginning to wobble. Domestic political chaos, economic turmoil, and the distrust of neighboring nations all helped to cultivate Communism in Indonesia, the Philippines, Malaysia, and Thailand. The Communist threat in each of these nations will now be addressed.

Indonesia

By 1954, less than a year after the Federation of Indonesia had gained independence, the Communist Party of Indonesia (PKI) had attained a membership of 200,000 along with 2,000,000 additional "sympathizers." In 1956, the first Indonesian elections were held and the PKI received 20 percent of the national vote, thus securing 39 of the 257 seats and emerging as one of the country's four largest political parties. The PKI continued to make political in-

---

[62] Rostow, *supra* note 38.

roads in 1957. In that year's election, the PKI won an absolute majority in twelve constituencies in Java, including the provincial capital of Semarang, which "shocked" the Nationalist Party, the largest political party in Indonesia.[63]

As the 1950s came to a close, the PKI's growing foothold in Indonesian politics proved readily detectable and, consequently, the PKI would increasingly thereafter impact both domestic and foreign policy. In fact, in order to engender broader support, General Suharto, commander of the Army Strategic Reserve and arguably the second most powerful Indonesian politician after his rival President Sukarno, allied himself with the burgeoning PKI. In turn, however, resistance to the PKI became persistent and even violent. In 1958, for instance, a group composed of dissident army officers and leaders of the Islamic Masyumi Party created "the Revolutionary Government of the Republic of Indonesia (PRRI)." The PRRI was based in West Sumatra and its aim was not to dissolve Indonesia but rather to "oppose [General] Suharto's policy of allying himself with the powerful PKI."[64] By the start of the 1960s, the PKI had clearly become a critical participant in Indonesian politics.

An essential subtext to the rise of the PKI rested in the personal rivalry between General Suharto and President Sukarno. In essence, each leader vied for greater control of the national political spotlight and each viewed the PKI as either an asset or a liability, depending on the year in question. Take, for instance, General Suharto's alliance with the PKI in the late 1950s, followed by President Sukarno's decision to solicit support from both the Soviet Union and China as a way to appeal to the PKI.

In acquiring both financial and military aid from the superpowers, President Sukarno proved particularly adept at playing the United States against both the Soviet Union and China. An illustration of this point was the Indonesian economic crisis of the early 1960s and how, "by playing off East against West,

---

[63] J.H. Brimmell, Communism in Southeast Asia 339 (1959).

[64] Bertil Linter, *Centrifugal forces stir in Indonesia*, Jane's Intelligence Rev. (June 1, 2000), *available at* LEXIS, News Library, Jane's Defence Publications File.

[President Sukarno] had managed to obtain more than $1.7 billion dollars from both the West and the Communist bloc."[65] Interestingly, President Sukarno, on a visit to the United States in 1961, told President Kennedy, "You are against Communism, then give me your support, for I am the best bulwark in Indonesia against Communism."[66] President Kennedy, believing this pledge, dispatched millions of dollars in aid in order to "shore up President Sukarno's dictatorship or 'guided democracy' as he prefers to call it." President Kennedy also acquiesced to President Sukarno's successful campaign to strong-arm the Netherlands into ceding New Guinea to Indonesia.[67]

At the same time the United States sought alliance with Indonesia, however, President Sukarno convinced both the Soviet Union and China that he could serve as a strong ally for their own interests. In fact, noted one observer, "although he sometimes quoted Jefferson approvingly in the presence of the Americans, the Indonesian leader reserved his highest admiration for the Soviet Union and Communist China."[68] In turn, those nations, like the United States, contributed millions of dollars in aid. President Sukarno's rather dexterous political machinations even prompted one Yugoslavian diplomat to remark, "Sukarno rides East against West, his Communists against his army, even Moscow against Peking. He's a miracle."[69]

By 1965, President Sukarno had clearly played his cards in favor of the Communists, particularly China; his political "two-step" had come to an end. Until that point, however, not only had he received domestic political capital for harshly criticizing the Vietnam War, but the PKI had grown precipitously since 1954. In fact, by the start of 1965, the PKI's membership had swelled to 2.5 million people—a startling increase of 1,250 percent from 1954.[70]

---

[65] *Indonesia's Boss*, N.Y. TIMES, Jan. 2, 1965, at A2.
[66] *Id.*
[67] *Id.*
[68] *Id.*
[69] *Id.*
[70] *Sukarno's Motive Seen as Plan for Rival to U.N.*, N.Y. TIMES, Jan. 4, 1965, at A1.

With the largest Communist party in the non-Communist world,[71] one PKI official boasted, "We are getting bigger all the time."[72] In addition, the PKI widened its domestic affiliations, such as those with farmers and associations for women and youth.[73]

The growth of Communist party affiliation was particularly evident among Java's poor farm villagers, many of whom PKI officials had persuaded to become Communist partisans. They claimed that the Communists were converting "quiet Javanese villages" into "party strongholds" and "indoctrinating the peasants in Communist ideology."[74] The appeal of the Communists was readily apparent, as one villager explained: "The Communists are the only people who have ever offered to help us."[75] In largely parroting the appeal of Communism in North Vietnam, Indonesian Communist propaganda centered on "Crushing the imperialists and the so-called village devils—among them the larger landowners, corrupt village officials and moneylenders."[76]

Likewise, the PKI adroitly exploited the increasingly poor reputation of the United States in Indonesia. For instance, on January 1, 1965, some three hundred Communist-led Indonesian, anti-American demonstrators encouraged Indonesian airport workers to refrain from servicing U.S. Embassy planes, since its pilots were "spying."[77] Furthermore, on March 23, President Sukarno ordered the seizure of all American-owned oil companies and rubber estates, and he closed down the U.S. Information Service center in Indonesia as well. At the same time, President Sukarno expelled several American Peace Corps officers as "agents of the CIA."[78] Furthermore, he facilitated the PKI in

---

[71] *U.S. Sending Bunker on Jakarta Mission*, N.Y. TIMES, Mar. 23, 1965, at A1.

[72] Neil Sheehan, *Reds, Pressing Reforms, Win Wide Peasant Support in Java*, N.Y. TIMES, Mar. 27, 1965, at A3.

[73] *Id.*

[74] Neil Sheehan, *Village in Java a Case Study in Red Tactics*, N.Y. TIMES, Mar. 28, 1965, at A3.

[75] *Id.*

[76] *Id.*

[77] *Demonstrators Assail U.S.*, N.Y. TIMES, Jan. 2, 1965, at A4.

[78] Neil Sheehan, *Java Reds Harry Peace Corpsmen*, N.Y. TIMES, Apr. 11, 1965, at A2.

barring mail to the U.S. Embassy, an act that, to some, symbolized "the latest move in the anti-American campaign being waged by the Indonesian Communist party."[79] Finally, Communist-affiliated unions "freely moved against Government orders and seized a Goodyear plant in Western Java."[80]

These acts of Communist aggression against American interests, coupled with both the surging appeal of Communist ideology among poor farmers and President Sukarno's notable acquiescence—if not tacit approval—of Communist aggression, suggested that by April 1965 Indonesia was well on its way to becoming a Communist nation. Likewise, it appeared equally clear that "President Sukarno [was] unable/unwilling to prevent a virtual take-over of his government."[81]

Significantly, many observers believed that by 1965 Indonesia had "moved further away from 'neutrality'" and developed a "close association with Communist China,"[82] thus signifying that "President Sukarno had decided that the time had come for active joint planning and operation with the Chinese."[83] In fact, this close association prompted one top American official to predict "the emergence of a 'Peking-Jakarta axis' to sponsor and coordinate revolutionary moves."[84] Perhaps not coincidentally, while President Sukarno was cultivating a relationship with China, General Suharto, who at this point in time had become an ardent *opponent* of Communism, was encountering steep difficulty in his own ranks. "Indonesia's military leaders, who are anti-Communist, are said to have quarreled among themselves while Communists have shown growing strength."[85] With the military in disarray and with China becoming a close ally, the opening for a Communist takeover in Indonesia appeared uniquely ripe.

---

[79] Neil Sheehan, *U.S. Embassy's Mail is Cut Off by a Red Union in Indonesia*, N.Y. TIMES, Mar. 24, 1965, at A1.

[80] *Workers Seize Goodyear Plant*, N.Y. TIMES, Mar. 21, 1965, at A8.

[81] *U.S. Sending Bunker on Jakarta Mission, supra* note 71.

[82] *Id.*

[83] Tad Szulc, *Washington Cites China*, N.Y. TIMES, Jan. 4, 1965, at A5.

[84] *Id.*

[85] *U.S. Sending Bunker on Jakarta Mission, supra* note 71.

The worsening of relations between Indonesia and Malaysia further illuminated the budding axis between Indonesia and China. In late 1964, President Sukarno pledged to "crush Malaysia before the cock crows on New Year's Day." Indeed, President Sukarno's hostility had becoming increasingly volatile since September 1953, when Malaysia had gained independence—an occurrence which he considered "part of a British plot to encircle his country."[86] In fact, by early 1965, President Sukarno, acting in accordance with the enthusiastic support of the PKI,[87] withdrew Indonesia from the United Nations as a form of protest to Malaysia's membership on the Security Council[88] and then ordered a series of military raids on the Malayan coast.[89] Moreover, he vowed to wage war against Great Britain, which had previously dispatched over 1,000 troops to defend Malaysia. In response to President Sukarno's threat, the United States halted its information activities and closed its remaining economic and military assistance offices.[90] This final act by the United States exhibited that, under no pretense, could Indonesia have been considered an ally, even if it had not already become an enemy.

Some argue, however, that President Sukarno's decision to quit the United Nations related far less to his rhetorical disgust over Malaysia's ascension to the Security Council[91] than to two more important motives: 1) symbolizing "Indonesia's growing ties with China";[92] and 2) illustrating his "need to win greater support from Indonesia's Communist Party, which is in accord with the Chinese

---

[86] *U.N. General Assembly's Action*, N.Y. TIMES, Mar. 23, 1965, at A4.

[87] *Sukarno's Motive Seen as Plan for Rival to U.N.*, *supra* note 70.

[88] *Sukarno Threatens U.N. Bolt if Council takes in Malaysia*, N.Y. TIMES, Jan. 1, 1965, at A1.

[89] *Indonesia Tells U.N. She Will End Her Membership*, N.Y. TIMES, Jan. 2, 1965, at A1.

[90] *U.S. Sending Bunker on Jakarta Mission*, *supra* note 71.

[91] *Indonesia Tells U.N. She Will End Her Membership*, *supra* note 89 (President Sukarno, in telling his nation that UN membership harms the independence of Indonesia, proclaimed, "The crown of independence is standing on your own feet.").

[92] *U.S. Sending Bunker on Jakarta Mission*, *supra* note 71.

line."[93] Therefore, Indonesia's choice to leave the United Nations supplied credible evidence of its burgeoning Communist identity, and when coupled with China's vast military assistance,[94] Indonesia was transforming into an external threat as well.

The U.S. government appeared to concur with this sentiment. In fact, in 1965, one "high ranking" American official predicted that "Peking and Jakarta would seek to form a Communist-oriented Asian arrangement outside the UN, drawing into it North Vietnam and North Korea, and possibly Cambodia."[95] To validate this point, North Korean Prime Minister Kim Il Sung visited Indonesia in April, an engagement which symbolized to many "Indonesia's growing cooperation with Communist China and Peking's Asian allies and the leftward development of Indonesia's political structure."[96] Significantly, then, this rapidly developing "axis" likely reflected both a falling Indonesian "domino" as well as a globally disuniting China, particularly since China had lost interest in its UN membership and sought instead to align the interests of nearby Communist nations.

On September 30, 1965, the "Jakarta-Beijing" axis reached its dramatic climax. In what was seen as the final piece in China's "attempt to turn Indonesia into a communist client state," an abortive coup attempt—a.k.a. the "Gestapu Affair"—was carried out by Chinese-funded elements of the PKI. The coup attempt sought to overthrow a powerless administration and install a Chinese-backed Communist regime.[97] However, the coup was poorly organized and it provided a fortuitous opportunity for General Suharto to mobilize the military and defeat the PKI. As a result, the leader of the PKI, Diap Nusantara Aidit, was executed and over 150,000 suspected Communists were imprisoned.

---

[93] Szulc, *supra* note 83.

[94] *Id.*

[95] *Id.*

[96] *Sukarno Welcomes North Korean Chief*, N.Y. TIMES, Apr. 11, 1965, at A3.

[97] Ian James Storey, *Indonesia's China Policy in the New Order and Beyond: Problems and Prospects*, CONTEMP. SE. ASIA (Apr. 1, 2000), at 145, *available at* 2000 WL 22308632; *see also* KROEF, *supra* note 56, at 34-35.

By March of 1966, General Suharto had become the de facto Chief Executive (a role he would retain for over thirty years) and had established the New Order regime with himself as president. At the same time, President Sukarno was discredited, Communism was outlawed, Chinese Indonesians began to endure what would become many years of ethnic discrimination, and, in retaliation for Beijing's role in the coup, Indonesia suspended all diplomatic relations with the PRC for the next twenty years. Particularly in the context of China's aid to North Vietnam, many observers viewed the coup as emblematic of "Communist China's ultimate ambition to assert hegemony over Southeast Asia by supporting regional communist insurgency movements, or through overt military action."[98]

Although General Suharto had successfully eradicated the Communist threat to most of Indonesia by 1966, violence persisted on some of the smaller Indonesian islands for years to come. Most notably, turmoil arose on the 1,000 islands of the Moluccas in 1966 following General Suharto's decision to execute one of the founders of the independent "Republik Maluku Selatan (RMS)." In response, riots ensued, and the RMS destroyed the Indonesian Embassy in the Netherlands.[99]

Clearly, the year 1965 was one of enormous turbulence for Indonesia. Moreover, Indonesia's increasing affinity for Communism and its emerging nexus with China suggested its vulnerability to Communism. This appears especially true when considering the relationship between events in Indonesia and those in Vietnam. Indeed, this point is best expressed by an Australian official who, in early 1965, predicted that "The chances that Indonesia would become Communist would greatly increase if the Vietcong triumph."[100] Therefore, had the Gestapu Affair been executed more effectively, Indonesia may have very well become a Communist nation, and one with access to vital natural resources as well as one strategically positioned within the Indian Ocean. Along those lines, had the United States left Indochina in 1965, it

---

[98] *Id.*

[99] Linter, *supra* note 64.

[100] Durdin, *supra* note 48.

is clearly possible that China might have shifted its focus to Indonesia, thus enhancing the probability that Indonesia would have become a Communist nation.

The Philippines

Communism also developed in the Philippines, though its threat, unlike the early PKI and its participation in Indonesia's elections, focused more on armed conflict than on the political process. Moreover, the Filipino Communist Party suffered from internal division that prevented a more successful effort. By the end of 1956, however, it featured a "Liberation Army" of 860 persons, 560 of whom were armed. The Party itself contained a relatively modest "membership" of 21,000 "sympathizers"; actual "member" figures proved elusive.[101] Furthermore, by the close of the 1950s, experts had concluded, "the likely future of the Communist movement in the Philippines is obscure in the extreme" due to its internal dissent. On the other hand, noted one reporter, while "there is at present very little anti-Americanism in the Philippines, the seeds are there, and in the soil of economic distress they could grow."[102]

By the early 1960s, some of those seeds began to germinate. Not only did the Filipino economy stagnate and its leadership often prove inept, but the American presence in the Indochina conflict enabled the Communist Party to denounce the "imperialist" Americans. Indeed, as Justus M. van der Kroef writes, the combination of "Communist-infiltrated youth, labor, and farmers' organizations laid the agitational and proselytizing foundation from which the Maoist Philippine Communist Party and its New People's Army could later develop."[103]

As the 1960s progressed, economic problems continued to plague the Philippines. For instance, between 1965 and 1970, $378 million of direct foreign investment evaporated, largely due to

---

[101] BRIMMELL, *supra* note 63, at 343-44.
[102] *Id.*
[103] KROEF, *supra* note 56, at 181.

international skepticism over the country's political stability.[104] In fact, in May of 1965, many of those economic concerns became international headlines when a frantic labor strike arose at the Manila Caltex plant. [105]

However, despite the development of political protest movements and the years of intense economic turbulence, the Communist Party failed to capitalize. Three primary reasons explain this failure and why the Communist Party did not enjoy greater success in the Philippines until 1968.

First, as mentioned earlier, the Party suffered from internal dissension and organizational flaws. Second, the Moscow-Peking Axis had been deterred by the Filipino government's participation in the Southeast Asia Treaty Organization (SEATO) and SEATO's de facto successor, the Association of Southeast Asian Nations (ASEAN).[106] Consequently, neither the Soviet Union nor China displayed much interest and thus they largely resisted aiding the Communist Party. Third, many Filipino citizens were upset by the apparent infiltration of Communist Indonesian troops in early 1965 and were likewise alarmed by its striking similarity to North Vietnamese aggression against South Vietnam. Consequently, the Filipino government harshly responded to quell any Indonesian overtures. As a matter of fact, the *New York Times* reported on March 28, 1965, that, according to one Filipino official, "Authorities suspect that among ordinary immigrants are Indonesian agents and spies . . . and ranking officers of the Indonesian Army."[107] Significantly, this suspicion caused relations to deteriorate between Indonesia and the Philippines and heightened the Filipino effort to prevent a Communist invasion. In fact, the Philippines prepared to spend $50 million dollars against "infiltration or possible invasion."[108] Likewise, on June 1, 1965, the Filipino National Security Council "unanimously agreed that

---

[104] *Id.* at 91.

[105] *Manila Caltex Strike Ends*, N.Y. TIMES, June 1, 1965, at A16.

[106] BRIMMELL, *supra* note 63, at 343; See section "The Stabilizing Effect of SEATO and ASEAN from 1965-1975" for more details.

[107] *Indonesia Threat is Seen in Manila*, N.Y. TIMES, Mar. 28, 1965, at A3.

[108] *Id.*

the Philippines should send 'additional aid' [of 2,000 army personnel] to South Vietnam."[109]

By the end of 1968, however, the Filipino Communist Party had become better organized and more violent. Most notably, when it met from December 26, 1968, to January 7, 1969, in Luzon, the Southern Tarlac province, it organized the new "Communist Party of the Philippines."[110] Subsequently, on March 29, 1969, the "Conference of Red Commanders and Soldiers of the People" or the "New People's Army" was created as a Communist military force.[111] Significantly, this military force contributed to the raid of the presidential palace "Malacanang" in Manila on January 30, 1970, which was described as "one of the country's worst political riots."[112] Similarly, the Communist military force engaged in a series of guerrilla attacks on President Ferdinand Marcos' government.

The New People's Army continued to terrorize President Marcos' government from 1969 to 1972. However, despite suggestions that President Marcos "overplayed" the Communist threat in order to seize greater power, his declaration of martial law in 1972 helped stabilize the Filipino political structure. Moreover, President Marcos engendered greater military loyalty by raising all military salaries by 300 percent. In turn, these actions helped to deter the Communist movement.[113]

Therefore, the Communist threat in the Philippines was far less disruptive or menacing than was the PKI in Indonesia. However, as was the case in evaluating the PKI's threat to Indonesia, the Philippines' position within the global context must also be considered. First, the Philippines represented a strong ally of the United States, from which it received both military and financial assistance. Had the United States abandoned Indochina in 1965, it is far less certain whether the Philippines would have had the

---

[109] *Manila Backs More Vietnam Aid*, N.Y. TIMES, June 1, 1965, at A6.
[110] KROEF, *supra* note 56, at 88.
[111] *Id.*
[112] *Id.*
[113] *Id.* at 95.

independent strength to repel a Communist Indonesian invasion that same year.

Additionally, both the Soviet Union and China were dissuaded by the Philippines' commitment to the United States, but if the United States had departed Indochina in 1965, would that commitment have been as strong? This is a particularly important question given that President Marcos had failed to achieve stable political support until he became a de facto dictator in 1972; between 1968 and 1972, President Marcos navigated his country through great turbulence. It is therefore possible that President Marcos, in order to hold on to power, may have been willing to accept Communist aid in return for acquiescing to Communist influence—just as President Sukarno had done in Indonesia from 1960 to 1965.

Finally, assuming the United States had departed Indochina in 1965, the Communist Party of the Philippines would have become emboldened by the apparent success of the Vietnamese "people's movement." Therefore, the Party may have more actively encouraged strikes and labor groups—the very activities that, to many Filipinos suffering from the economic crisis, would have probably seemed quite reasonable, if not desirable.

Granted, these scenarios are speculative, though a weakened American resolve to stop the spread of Communism in Southeast Asia would have clearly modified the variables in the Philippines and likely increased the probability of Communist ascension.

Malaysia

The Malaysian Communist Party, like the early PKI in Indonesia, sought relatively legitimate means to political ascension. Indeed, in 1959, the Party attempted to "construct a broad United Front which will make its victory possible in future elections."[114] Moreover, as one onlooker from the Royal Institute of International Affairs predicted in 1959, "The Malaysian Communist Party will clearly enjoy a fine field of opportunity in

---

[114] BRIMMELL, *supra* note 63, at 339.

the multiple problems which face the Government—economic, racial, and other others. It is by the skilful—and entirely legal—exploitation of these problems [that the party will succeed]."[115]

Perhaps most threatening to the Malaysian government was the following sentiment: "The Communists can always appeal to anti-Westernism as an overriding emotional factor, a line of approach not open to a Government which is well aware of Malaysia's dependence on international capital and the commodity market for its precarious prosperity."[116] In fact, because of Malaysia's economic dependence on Western nations, "the fate of Malaysia, more than any other country in the region, probably depends on the tact and farsightedness of the West."[117]

The greatest Communist threat to Malaysia, however, was not internal. Rather, repeated attempts by Indonesian raiders to claim territory in Malaysia presented the most worrisome Communist activity. Significantly, by the start of 1965, Malaysia had begun preparation for a Communist invasion. Motivation for such preparation arose not only after experiencing continuous confrontations with Indonesian raiders, but also after listening to the inflammatory rhetoric of both the PKI and President Sukarno concerning Malaysia's increased influence in the United Nations. As a matter of fact, not only did Indonesia threaten to abandon the United Nations, but it also threatened to attack Malaysia (e.g., President Sukarno vowed to "crush" Malaysia).

An interesting quotation illustrates just how close these nations were to extensive warfare when, on January 1, 1965—the deadline by which President Sukarno had promised to have crushed Malaysia—Yang Di-Pertuan Agong, king of Malaysia, recognized that war had begun and declared, "Indonesia's confrontation policy [had failed] to dent our unity or break our spirit."[118] Only one day later, the rhetoric escalated when Prince Abdul Rahman, prime minister of Malaysia, remarked, "no one would shed any tears" if Indonesia withdrew from the United Nations—"good riddance . . .

---

[115] *Id.*

[116] *Id.*

[117] *Id.*

[118] *Malaysian Sees War On*, N.Y. TIMES, Jan. 2, 1965, at A1.

[It is] only another example of Indonesia's defiance of world opinion . . . [and] a decisive defeat for President Sukarno."[119]

By the end of January, the nations had positioned armies on the Indonesian island of Borneo and the Malaysian states of Sarawak and Sabah. In addition, the probability of a broader conflict rose when Great Britain dispatched 1,000 troops to buttress its 12,000 soldiers already stationed in Malaysia.[120] Notably, Professor Sodhy points out that as Malaysia pressed both Great Britain and the United States for aid, "Indonesia laughed at Malaysia when it solicited help, particularly from the United States. There were domestic political costs of 'giving in to the white man.'"[121] Importantly, such "capitulation" to Western aid served only to galvanize public sympathy among the Malaysian people for the domestic Communist movement.

By March 20, the conflict with Indonesia had intensified as Malaysian officials, citing Indonesian "terrorist operations," discovered a cache of arms, ammunition, and explosives off the northwest coast of Malaysia.[122] Subsequently, on June 1, Malaysian aircraft defended against a second Indonesian raiding army.[123] Two days later, fourteen Indonesian raiders who had earlier landed on the southeastern portion of Malaysia were captured.[124]

To make matters worse, while Malaysia repelled attacks from Indonesia, domestic troubles continued to plague the Malaysian government. Specifically, race riots between Malays and Chinese erupted in both Singapore and Malaysia, two technically distinct political states conjoined under one murky federation. Indeed, in 1965, Malaysia faced not only a military threat from Indonesia, but also vilifying, anti-Malaysian rhetoric from Singapore Prime Minister Lee Kuan Yew. Specifically, Prime Minister Lee

---

[119] *"No one would shed tears,"* N.Y. TIMES, Jan. 3, 1965, at A4.

[120] *Id.*

[121] Interview with Pamela Sodhy, *supra* note 32.

[122] *Curfew Set in Malaya Area*, N.Y. TIMES, June 1, 1965, at A16.

[123] *Malaysian Force Searching for New Indonesian Band*, N.Y. TIMES, June 2, 1965, at A9.

[124] *14 Indonesians are Captured*, N.Y. TIMES, June 4, 1965, at A2.

lambasted the Malaysian government for allegedly treating its Chinese population as "worker ants" under the rule of the Muslim Malaysians.[125] Likewise, Prime Minister Lee refused to reconcile with a Malaysia that "will always be dominated by Malays."[126]

However, the Indonesian Communist threat mostly dissipated once the Gestapu Affair failed miserably in early 1966. Although Indonesia and Malaysia continued to have poor relations thereafter, the threat of military invasion diminished, particularly when both became members of ASEAN in 1967. Correspondingly, the Communist Party of Malaysia endured a backlash of anti-Communism among the Malaysian people, even though the Party had maintained its separation from the Indonesian Communist movement.[127]

Moreover, Singapore gained complete autonomy by August 1965, thus diffusing some of the conflict between it and Malaysia. However, tensions between the two nations persisted over the next few years. In fact, on May 13, 1969, violence in Malaysia peaked when a series of riots erupted, killing more than 2,000 people.[128]

In 1965, therefore, the Communist threat to Malaysia was most acute. By absorbing the continued aggression of Indonesian Communist troops, Malaysia experienced constant duress throughout the entire year. Equally significant, Malaysia contended with an internal Communist group, though research indicates that the group was neither affiliated with the Indonesian Communists nor did it pose a viable threat to the Malaysian government. However, when evaluating the Indonesian Communist threat in the context of race riots and heightened rhetoric from Singapore Prime Minister Lee, it is clear that 1965 reflected a tumultuous time for Malaysia.

---

[125] Seth S. King, *Threat of Partition Raised in Malaysia Dispute*, N.Y. TIMES, June 2, 1965, at A15.

[126] *Id.*

[127] However, Professor Sodhy, a native of Malaysia, contends that China had provided aid to the Malaysian Communist Party; *see* interview with Pamela Sodhy, *supra* note 32.

[128] Andrew T.H. Tan, *Singapore's Defence: Capabilities, Trends, and Implications*, CONTEMP. SE. ASIA (Dec. 1, 1999), at 451, *available at* 1999 WL 1999 WL 28043977.

Therefore, a U.S. departure from Indochina in 1965 would have likely only exacerbated Malaysian turmoil. A number of observations corroborate this deduction. First, Malaysia and China were long-standing enemies, and if China had no longer needed to counter the presence of American troops in Vietnam, it could have (and probably would have) provided greater aid to Indonesia. Importantly, this aid would have increased the likelihood of a successful Communist take-over in Indonesia and would have therefore emboldened Indonesia in its war against Malaysia. In that sense, an American departure would have made the Malaysian "domino" more likely to fall. To further complicate matters, however, had Indonesia formally declared war against Malaysia, the Anzus Treaty, which had provided for the common defense of Australia and New Zealand, would have enabled either Australia or New Zealand to request the presence of American forces in Malaysia.[129] Therefore, if the United States had abandoned Vietnam, and such action precipitated further conflict in Malaysia, then the United States would have, at least technically, been obliged to return to the region.

Second, an American departure would have supplied China with a greater opportunity to improve relations with Singapore. While Prime Minister Lee expressed opposition to Communism, the offer of assistance to help defeat Malaysia—a common enemy of both Singapore and China—may have been too tempting for him to reject. Though even improved relations with China would not have likely given rise to a Communist Singapore, it is clear that a tightening nexus between China and Singapore would have worked to the disadvantage of the United States in its quest to stop the dominoes from falling.

Thailand

Fears of Communist expansion into Thailand were apparent as early as 1950. In fact, in NSC Directive 64, President Harry S. Truman was warned that Thailand could easily fall to

---

[129] Szulc, *supra* note 83.

Communism: "The neighboring countries Thailand and Burma could be expected to fall under Communist domination if Indochina were controlled by a Communist-dominated government. The balance of Southeast Asia would then be in grave danger."[130]

Although the fears expressed in NSC Directive 64 never fully materialized over the next fourteen years, the Communist Party of Thailand (CPT) continued to grow nonetheless. Indeed, by December of 1964, the CPT, on the advice of the Chinese government, fully committed itself to a "movement" or active strategy of absorbing Communism into Thai society. At the same time, the Thailand Independence Movement emerged in Beijing, calling for, among other objectives, "the expulsion of US imperialists from Thai territory."[131] Clearly, China observed an opening in Thailand and hoped that stimulating anti-American activities would help spur Communist expansion. Along these lines, JCSM-652-65 demonstrates that, by August of 1964, the United States had recognized the opening that China saw in Thailand: "Included within the basic U.S. military strategy must be a buildup in Thailand to ensure attainment of the proper U.S.-Thai posture to deter CHICOM aggression and to facilitate placing U.S. forces in an advantageous logistic position if such aggression occurs."[132]

Equally significant, by May of 1965, Thailand, and particularly its farming industry, was mired in poverty. In response to these circumstances, a group of Communist-leaning, anti-American organizations spawned. For instance, the Thailand Federation of Patriotic Workers was established with the primary intention of "overthrow[ing] the US imperialist-oriented regime in Thailand."[133] This trend continued into 1966, as the Thai Patriotic Youth Organization, the Thai Patriotic Teachers and Professors

---

[130] STAFF OF SENATE COMM. ON FOREIGN RELATIONS, 103D CONG., *supra* note 24, at 2 (quoting NSC Directive 64 (1950)).

[131] KROEF, *supra* note 56, at 195.

[132] STAFF OF SENATE COMM. ON FOREIGN RELATIONS, 103D CONG., *supra* note 24, at 144 (quoting JSCM-652-65 (Aug. 27, 1964)).

[133] KROEF, *supra* note 56, at 196.

Group, the Poor People's Federation, the Self-Liberated Farmers, and the Planters' Association all were established with similar intentions. In fact, by 1968, the rhetoric escalated and some of these organizations published "various press releases on the primacy of guerrilla struggle and on the need for a military solution to Thailand's problems."[134]

Not only was Thailand threatened by both internal Communist movements and by Chinese persuasions, but Laotian and Cambodian Communists increasingly crossed the Thai border, a phenomenon especially evident following the 1965 discovery of "a steady infiltration of Communists taking place both from Laos and Cambodia, into what was known as the North Eastern Provinces."[135] These mini-invasions would continue through 1968.

As demonstrated by NSC Directive 64 and by JCSM-652-65, the U.S. government felt great trepidation over the spread of Communism into Thailand. Not only would Thailand have represented another fallen domino, but a Communist Thailand would have symbolized a stunning blow to democracy, for Bangkok had served as SEATO's Headquarters. Therefore, noted one observer, "If Thailand were to fall victim to Communist aggression, this would represent the greatest single factor in the complete collapse of all efforts to resist Communism in Southeast Asia."[136]

In response to both the Communist incursions and the farming crisis, the United States provided substantial aid to Thai farmers, including industrial advice and contributions of modern agricultural machinery and tractors. Importantly, stressed Dr. Alan Glyn at the time, this kind of "practical aid forms the best defence against Communism in these areas."[137]

Consequently, the Communist threat, both internal and external, appeared readily apparent in Thailand by 1965. Thus, if the United States had departed from Indochina that same year, would Thailand have been more or less likely to fall? The evidence

---

[134] *Id.*

[135] GLYN, *supra* note 44, at 227.

[136] *Id.* at 228.

[137] *Id.* at 227.

seems abundantly clear: Thailand was mired in a state of economic crisis throughout the 1960s, and this crisis provided feeding ground for a proliferation of Communist organizations. Had the United States abandoned Indochina, those organizations would have almost certainly generated greater appeal from the Thai people, particularly its farmers. Equally troubling, China had taken a special interest in Thailand, both due to its geographic position and its role as the host nation for SEATO, an organization symbolic of regional democratic unity. Finally, Communist forces from both Laos and Cambodia raided Northeastern Thailand on repeated occasions. Collectively, these factors suggest that if the United States had abandoned Indochina in 1965, Thailand might have readily fallen to Communism, either due to emboldened internal Communist organizations or the invasion by some combination of Chinese, Laotian, or Cambodian forces.

LATIN AMERICA, SOUTH AMERICA, AND THE CARIBBEAN: TREMBLING DOMINOES

Though the Communist threat endangered Southeast Asia more than any other part of the world in 1965, it extended well beyond that region. Indeed, it is likewise important to consider the Communist threat in both Latin America and South America, particularly that posed by Fidel Castro and Cuba. Unquestionably, all evidence indicates that Cuba exported a dangerous mixture of Communism and terrorism, even sending troops to Vietnam in late March of 1965 in order to "demonstrate Cuba's solidarity with the Vietcong."[138] At the same time, the Soviet Union pledged to encourage worker strikes in Latin America, specifically citing potential opportunities with "Colombian teachers, Chilean miners, and Uruguayan civil service employees."[139]

However, Cuba posed a far greater immediate threat to its neighboring nations in Latin America and the Caribbean. With "the

---

[138] *Token Cuban Force Possible*, N.Y. TIMES, Mar. 25, 1965, at A4.

[139] Shabad, *supra* note 2.

most efficient military instrument in all of Latin America,"[140] Cuba
represented a continuing menace to such nations as El Salvador,
Nicaragua, Guatemala, Bolivia, and Peru. In addition to Cuban
impositions, the Dominican Republic endured myriad internal
Communist insurrections. Moreover, because these nations were
mired in economic poverty, they exhibited vulnerability to
Communist takeovers. Indeed, Castro was well aware of this
phenomenon and, in January of 1966, called the first "Afro-Asian-
Latin American Peoples' Solidarity Conference" in Havana, where
the Soviet Union openly pledged to "support armed subversive
movements . . . bringing about the overthrow of existing
governments and establishing Communist governments dependent
upon extra-continental Communist powers."[141]

Central America and South America

By March of 1965, the president of El Salvador had accused
Castro of dispatching Cuban raiders into his nation.[142] Also, while
repelling those raiders, El Salvador suffered from inadequate food
output and largely ineffective economic and social policies.[143]
Therefore, El Salvador presented an enticing target for Communist
expansion. President Kennedy, in fact, regarded the Communist
threat to El Salvador as extremely viable, particularly since he was
"convinced that the Communist threat would come mainly in the
underdeveloped regions."[144]

The unease expressed by President Kennedy only reflected
recent events, for three years earlier, the Communist threat visibly
emerged in El Salvador. In fact, in early 1962, a provisional

---

[140] Paul Hofmann, *Cuban Red Party Canvassing Army*, N.Y. TIMES, Mar. 21,
1965, at A1.
[141] WASHINGTON INSTITUTE FOR VALUES IN PUBLIC POLICY, CENTRAL
AMERICA IN CRISIS 8 (1989) (quoting *The Economic Impact of the Caribbean
Basin Initiative*, Senate Comm. on Foreign Relations, 97th Cong. (Mar. 21,
1982) (statement of Richard E. Feinberg and Richard S. Newfarmer)).
[142] *El Salvador Accuses Cuba*, N.Y. TIMES, Mar. 23, 1965, at A5.
[143] Tad Szulc, *Latin Lands Gain is Found Limited*, N.Y. TIMES, Mar. 21, 1965,
at A8.
[144] Rostow, *supra* note 38.

military junta narrowly defeated a challenge by the Revolutionary Party of April and May (PRAM)—a group "politically of a pro-Castro orientation."[145] Moreover, during the 1970s, Cuban-backed Marxist groups in Nicaragua would continue to fund the Communist effort to overthrow El Salvador's democratically elected government. During that time, in fact, "the Government of Nicaragua engaged in a substantial and continuing attempt . . . to destabilize and overthrow the Government of El Salvador."[146]

Nicaragua also served as a target for Castro. For instance, in 1959, Castro orchestrated an unsuccessful invasion of Nicaragua from Costa Rica, and the invasion was timed to coincide with a Socialist-organized strike of workers from various industries.[147] Similarly, in 1961, the Sandinista National Liberation Front (FSLN), an organization determined to overthrow the Nicaraguan leadership, was founded in Havana with the aid of Castro.[148]

The Communist surge in Nicaragua continued as Castro supplied both arms and training to FSLN forces, thus expanding his influence over the region.[149] By 1979, the FSLN, with American support, had overthrown the Somoza dynasty, which had ruled Nicaragua since 1936.[150] Soon thereafter, however, the FSLN abandoned any guise of democratic reforms and, in spite of American aid, invited hundreds of Cuban "advisors" to assist in economic and political planning.[151]

Guatemala presented another illustration of political instability that had been precipitated by economic poverty and governmental corruption. Such political turbulence was worrisome, particularly

---

[145] WASHINGTON INSTITUTE FOR VALUES IN PUBLIC POLICY, *supra* note 141, at 11.

[146] JOHN NORTON MOORE, THE SECRET WAR IN CENTRAL AMERICA 10 (1987) (quoting ROBERT F. TURNER, NICARAGUA V. UNITED STATES: A LAWYER LOOKS AT THE FACTS (1986)).

[147] NICOLAS RIVERO, CASTRO'S CUBA 111 (1962).

[148] PAMELA FALK, UNITED STATES, SOVIET UNION, CUBA AND SOUTH AFRICA ON ANGOLA: NEGOTIATOR'S NIGHTMARE (1988).

[149] MOORE, *supra* note 146, at 10.

[150] WASHINGTON INSTITUTE FOR VALUES IN PUBLIC POLICY, *supra* note 141, at 8.

[151] *Id.* at 103.

given the nation's Communist history, as Communist President Jacobo Arbenz had ruled Guatemala from 1951-54.[152] While the Communist threat was less prevalent in Guatemala than in Nicaragua in 1965, the Guatemalan government had proven unable to fully embrace democratic reforms. In fact, by early 1965, the military government (also described as the "state of siege") had been imposed after a series of bombings, and according to its leader, Colonel Enrique Peralata Azurdia, the military rule "[would] not be lifted until the situation has been stabilized."[153]

Turmoil would continue to plague Guatemala as the 1960s came to a close and the 1970s began. Importantly, one of the joint goals of the FSLN-Cuban alliance was to incite "revolutionary internationalism" in the other Central American countries, and Guatemala served as a key target for this guerrilla-warfare style operation.[154] Likewise, the FSLN-Cuban alliance unabashedly pledged support for "[a] struggle for a 'true union of the Central American peoples within one country', beginning with support for national liberation movements in neighboring states."[155] Sadly, such activity only served to endanger the citizens of Guatemala: "From the early 1960s on, leftist guerrilla activities . . . have added uncertainty to an already deteriorated political situation."[156] Moreover, Cuba provided substantial aid to the Guatemalan Armed Forces, a Communist organization dedicated to overthrowing the government. By all accounts, Guatemala was in a state of political turmoil by 1965, and Communist aid contributed greatly to that turmoil.

Castro also targeted Bolivia as a vulnerable target for Communist growth. Specifically, Bolivia harbored dangerous elements of Castro's attempt to export Communism. To illustrate this point, a plan crafted at the Cuban Embassy in 1961 plotted

---

[152] Washington Institute for Values in Public Policy, *supra* note 141, at 17.

[153] *Guatemala Sets Rule by Charter*, *supra* note 141.

[154] Moore, *supra* note 146, at 22.

[155] *Id.* (quoting FSLN, Tricontinental No. 17: Program of the Sandinista Front of National Liberation (Mar-Apr. 1970), at 61-68).

[156] Washington Institute for Values in Public Policy, *supra* note 141, at 17.

numerous Communist-sympathizing marches on the nation's capital; Cuba had hoped such marches would encourage civil unrest. Although these marches failed to precipitate a larger revolution, Castro nevertheless successfully cultivated friendships in the Bolivian government. In particular, Castro convinced his friend Feldman Veladre, the Bolivian minister of education, to participate in anti-American demonstrations and help smuggle Cuban arms into Bolivia. Moreover, the national revolutionary movement of President Paz Estenssoro embodied a number of Cuban-style reforms, including both land and farming reform.[157]

By June of 1965, some American officials believed that "a Communist plot was afoot" in Bolivia. In particular, evidence suggests that the Italian Communist Party sought to subvert the government.[158] Likewise, political instability was rampant, as Bolivia's military junta, which had succeeded Estenssoro, "press[ed] for wide economic and military help from the United States to complement its measures to reorganize the nationalized mining industry and overcome a violent, Communist-dominated strike."[159] Although the strength of the Communist threat in Bolivia did not appear overwhelming, it nonetheless triggered enough concern for the Bolivian Government to solicit American insight in thwarting Communist takeovers.

Peru also caught the eye of Castro. In fact, by 1960, he had successfully disseminated subversive propaganda, aided the Peruvian Communist Party, and developed friendships with Peruvian military leaders.[160] Likewise, by 1965, anti-American activities were readily detectable. For instance, on June 3, a group of American Peace Corps volunteers were expelled because of the U.S. intervention in the Dominican Republic, a nation that, as will soon be discussed, dealt with its own Communist insurrections.[161]

---

[157] RIVERO, *supra* note 147, at 127.

[158] Henry Raymont, *Bolivia's Regime Tightens Control*, N.Y. TIMES, June 1, 1965, at A3.

[159] Henry Raymont, *Bolivia Pressing for Wide U.S. Aid*, N.Y. TIMES, June 4, 1965, at A9.

[160] RIVERO, *supra* note 147, at 116.

[161] *Americans Reported Ousted From Faculty Posts in Peru*, N.Y. TIMES, June 3, 1965, at A5.

Consequently, both unprovoked aggression against Americans living in the region and Castro's overtures to the Peruvian military evinced a Communist threat to Peru.

Stability in Central America, South America, and the Caribbean was vital to the United States and its allies for both national security and economic reasons. Years later, in fact, President Ronald Reagan would clearly articulate the overall strategic importance of the region: "Two-thirds of all our foreign trade and petroleum pass through the Panama Canal and the Caribbean. In a European crisis, at least half of our supplies for NATO would go through these areas by sea . . . because of its importance, the Caribbean Basin is a magnet for adventurism."[162] Moreover, the region's economic hardship alarmed the United States. Interestingly, in 1961, then-Vice President Johnson declared that Communism was most likely to arise in those poor nations ignored by the United States: "The greatest danger Southeast Asia offers to nations like the United States is not the momentary threat of communism itself, rather the danger that stems from hunger, ignorance, poverty, and disease."[163] By extrapolation, then, the United States' neighbors to the south, with their extreme poverty, were also vulnerable to Communist expansion.

Therefore, a U.S. departure from Vietnam in 1965 could have generated negative reverberations far closer to home. Significantly, in fact, Professor Samuel P. Huntington of Harvard University has noted that when the United States departed from Indochina in 1975, that departure, in conjunction with declining American influence abroad, signaled to South and Latin America that the United States may not have been as reliable in sustaining democratic growth as had been previously perceived.[164]

In the same way, one might argue, had the United States withdrawn from Vietnam ten years earlier, similar doubts about the American resolve to cultivate democracies would have arisen,

---

[162] Layne, *supra* note 58.
[163] Rostow, *supra* note 38.
[164] *Is Democracy Dying?*, U.S. News & World Report, Mar. 8, 1976, at 50.

thereby opening the door for Communism. For instance, Bolivia might have resorted to violence, rather than peaceful intervention, to defeat its internal Communist threat. Alternatively, El Salvador could have endured heightened insecurity in its quest to defeat Cuban invaders, for if the powerful U.S. military had to retreat from battle with a vastly inferior North Vietnamese military, it is unlikely that the El Salvadorians would have placed much trust in American assistance, particularly if Cuba had escalated its attack. Then again, the FSLN and its Cuban "advisors" could have seized control from the Somoza family earlier, thus paving the way for Castro to expand his influence throughout Latin America, and perhaps even into Mexico. Finally, an American retreat from Indochina and its battle with the "fourth rate" Vietcong army in 1965 would have emboldened similar anti-American activists in such nations as Peru and Guatemala. These deductions, while all exploratory, lead to the conclusion that an American departure from Indochina in 1965 would have disadvantaged American interests in South and Latin America. As the discussion in the section "Worldwide Developments" will note, this conclusion is only strengthened when viewed in the context of 1970s domestic American politics, where weakened American leadership failed to deter Communist expansion.

The Dominican Republic

Cuba also made significant progress in exporting Communism to the Dominican Republic. In the early 1960s, Cuban agents positioned inside the Dominican Republic distributed propaganda that criticized the United States' presence on the island as "preventing a real people's revolution" and urged Dominican citizens to take arms against American military personnel.[165] At the same time, those agents aided subversive movements to overthrow the Dominican government, prompting one Dominican observer to conclude, "There is always the threat that Communists from Cuba

---

[165] RIVERO, *supra* note 147, at 138.

will move in."[166] Importantly, this persistent threat served only to decrease political stability and diminish governmental legitimacy.

By 1965, political violence had become commonplace in the Dominican Republic. For instance, in early June, a violent clash arose between the police/junta-controlled military forces and the leftist-leaning demonstrators. By this point, President Johnson had announced that some 4,200 marines were prepared to join 16,000 American military personnel already stationed in the Dominican Republic.[167] Specifically, the forces were dispatched to both prevent violent clashes and, more importantly, to deter a viable Communist force in the Dominican Republic, as such a Communist force would have rendered impossible a movement to unify the region against Cuban expansion. Indeed, as the *New York Times* reported in 1965, "Suspected Communists were among the serious obstacles to Washington's earlier plan to form a 'broadly based' coalition."[168]

Not surprisingly, President Johnson expressed grave apprehension of Communism spreading into the Dominican Republic. In fact, when discussing the possibility of sending additional troops to the island, he highlighted the success American forces had already achieved in reducing the Communist threat, and thus defended the wisdom of dispatching more troops: "The threat was greater before 21,000 Americans arrived there . . . [the Communists] joined the revolution, and they participated in it, [and] they were in charge of it."[169] Moreover, President Johnson advocated the fundamental principle of preventing the spread of Communism into the American hemisphere: "I think it is a well-known and well-advertised doctrine of the hemisphere that the principles of Communism are incompatible with the principles of our inter-American system."[170] In addition, Morris Leibman, a

---

[166] *Id.*

[167] Juan de Onis, *2 Dominicans Die in Clash Inland*, N.Y. TIMES, June 1, 1965, at A1.

[168] Max Frankel, *U.S. Now Favors Dominican Vote in 2 or 3 Months*, N.Y. TIMES, June 3, 1965, at A1.

[169] *Transcript of the President's News Conference on Foreign and Domestic Affairs*, N.Y. TIMES, June 2, 1965, at A16.

[170] Tom Wicker, *Johnson Defends Moves*, N.Y. TIMES, June 2, 1965, at A1.

Chicago attorney and member of President Johnson's "Wise Men," an informal group of foreign policy advisors, acknowledged the eerie parallel between the Communist threat in Vietnam and the one found in the Dominican Republic, as well as the recognition that failing to contain either one of them could lead to "2 or 3 Vietnams or Dominican Republics at once."[171]

Clearly, the United States had perceived a viable Communist threat in the Dominican Republic in 1965. However, had the United States departed from Indochina that same year, it is possible that American forces stationed in the Dominican Republic would have come under greater attack by inspired Communist rebels. In turn, had the Nicaraguan Marxists and Cuban Communists witnessed an American retreat from Indochina, aid from either Nicaragua and Cuba could have come sooner. Correspondingly, while the Communist rebels in the Dominican Republic would have become more confident with an American retreat from Indochina, the American forces in the Dominican Republic could have lost faith in their—and their leaders'—ability to defeat a group of rebels. Alternatively, the United States, having retreated from Indochina, could have concluded that a second defeat to a "fourth-rate" Communist army—this time in the Dominican Republic—would have proven disastrous, thereby encouraging a far larger, more dangerous conflict in the region. Neither possibility would have seemed favorable to the United States.

THE STABILIZING EFFECT OF SEATO AND ASEAN FROM 1965-1975

While the United States continued its fight in Vietnam, meaningful relationships between Southeast Asian nations arose. Importantly, cultivating such relationships enhanced regional unity and, along with stimulating improved economic trade, engendered invaluable cultural understanding as well as a greater common defense against outside aggression. Consequently, these nations

---

[171] STAFF OF SENATE COMM. ON FOREIGN RELATIONS, 103D CONG., *supra* note 24, at 50.

experienced enhanced institutional strength, thus helping to diminish the prospects for internal Communist insurrection and external Communist invasion.

The Southeast Asia Treaty Organization (SEATO)

As stated as an official purpose upon its ratification in 1955,[172] SEATO reflected the shared fear among Southeast Asian nations of the creeping expansion of Communist ideology: "In a world threatened by Communism, SEATO is a necessary bulwark of security, and an instrument of peaceful progress."[173] Equally significant, SEATO desired an improved and dependable system of common defense. To illustrate this latter goal, Article III of the Southeast Asia Collective Defence Treaty laid out that "each member, through co-operation and the sharing of experience, has increased its defensive strength. The combined power of the alliance . . . [is] recognized as a stabilizing factor in Southeast Asia."[174] On the other hand, SEATO lacked the organizational strength of an alliance like NATO, since there were no "SEATO forces" like those found in NATO. Rather, the members of SEATO subscribed "towards what is essentially an Insurance Policy against any one of its members being threatened by attack from Communism."[175]

Therefore, despite its laudable intentions, SEATO provided no collective defense against Communist aggression. Although proponents like Senator Hugh Scott (R-PN) regarded SEATO as useful in "blocking further Communist aggression in South Vietnam,"[176] many critics found SEATO as worth little more than the paper it was written on. For instance, when Communist raiders from both Cambodia and Laos repeatedly attacked Thai border

---

[172] Signatories included Australia, France, New Zealand, Pakistan, the Philippines, Thailand, Great Britain, and the United States.

[173] GLYN, *supra* note 44, at 275 (quoting "Story of SEATO," Public Information Office, SEATO Headquarters, Bangkok, Thailand).

[174] The Southeast Asia Collective Defence Treaty, Art. III (1955).

[175] GLYN, *supra* note 44, at 274.

[176] *Scott Asks SEATO Parley to Back U.S. Stand in Asia*, N.Y. TIMES, Mar. 3, 1965, at A3.

villages in 1965,[177] there was no "collective response" from the SEATO nations.[178] In stark comparison, had an Eastern bloc nation repeatedly invaded the geographic territory of a NATO nation, it was both politically assumed and legally established that NATO would immediately act to stop such aggression. Hence, no such activity arose in Europe during the Cold War, while Thailand, without external assistance, repeatedly repelled Communist attackers during the 1960s.

On balance, SEATO proved only marginally effective in deterring Communist expansion. Most significantly, the organization's greatest flaw rested in its inability to encourage member nations to defend one another. However, as Senator Scott noted, any organization that united the non-Communist nations in Southeast Asia was likely better than no organization at all. Moreover, by simply being in such an alliance, the member nations likely improved their communication channels and began to view themselves as a region—or a "theater"—as opposed to isolated states. This development, perhaps more so than any other, provided the foundation for the creation of the Association of Southeast Asian Nations (ASEAN), a far more important organization in the quest to stop the spread of Communism.

The Association of Southeast Asian Nations (ASEAN)

Between 1965 and 1967, SEATO continued to prove ineffective in deterring Communist attacks, and the United States continued to prove ineffective in defeating the North Vietnamese Communists. In response, several nations[179] within SEATO determined the need for firmer unity in deterring Communist aggression. To illustrate this conclusion, in 1966, Prime Minister Lee of Singapore characterized U.S. involvement in Vietnam as only "buying time" for Southeast Asia to unite against Communism: "If we just sit down and believe people are going to

---

[177] See *infra* at section "Southeast Asia: Falling Dominoes."

[178] GLYN, *supra* note 44, at 279.

[179] Indonesia, Malaysia, the Philippines, Singapore, and Thailand.

buy time forever after for us, then we deserve to perish."[180]
Perhaps realizing that the American force in 1967 could not defeat
the North Vietnamese, and therefore the "time bought" was
running out, SEATO member nations disbanded and then founded
ASEAN, an organization that, unlike SEATO, featured provisions
for common defense.

Although it began as only a "loose economic grouping,"[181]
ASEAN essentially "provided a way to bring together the
ideological orientations and security policies of maritime Southeast
Asia (i.e. Indonesia, Malaysia, the Philippines, and Singapore) and
Thailand, the mainland state with a similar disposition."[182] Most
interestingly, ASEAN's core states—Indonesia, Malaysia, and
Singapore—had harbored long-standing reservations toward one
other, particularly given their history of warfare. Remarkably
however, despite mutual distrust, Indonesia, Malaysia, and
Singapore aligned, thus signifying how past bitter enemies worried
more about Communist expansion in 1967 than about traditional
ethnic or cultural rivalries, even though such rivalries had spanned
centuries. Equally significant, the very "residual anxieties" of long-
standing disputes among those three nations were "gradually
resolved over time" following the creation of ASEAN,[183] thus
suggesting that common participation in anti-Communist alliances
may have offered the incidental effect of reducing historical
distrust.

Importantly, ASEAN's success extended far beyond unifying
Indonesia, Malaysia, and Singapore in the fight against
Communism. This was most notably detected in Thailand, a nation
that had been left to own self-defense under SEATO, yet while
under ASEAN, received critical military support to help expel
Communists infiltrating Northeast Thailand. In addition, when
Vietnam invaded Cambodia in 1979, ASEAN instantly grappled
with the attack's regional implications: "Vietnam had significantly

---

[180] Rostow, *supra* note 38.

[181] *It's that Price Again*, ECONOMIST, Dec. 1, 1979.

[182] N. Ganesan, *ASEAN's Relations with Major External Powers*, CONTEMP.
SE ASIA 258 (Aug. 1, 2000), *available at* 2000 WL 22308632.

[183] *Id.*

eroded Thailand's national security, turning it into a 'frontline state', in direct confrontation with Vietnam."[184] In response, Thailand, with assistance from ASEAN, augmented forces on its Eastern border and repelled further Communist aggression westward. In light of these developments, Admiral Robert L. J. Long, former Commander of U.S. forces in the Pacific, highlighted the symbolic victory achieved by ASEAN and the Free World: "ASEAN is one of the true success stories [of the Vietnam War]."[185] Likewise, as observed by Marvin Stone of *U.S. News & World Report*, ASEAN's success in Thailand may have halted the domino effect.[186]

Equally significant, ASEAN also exuded fortitude by deterring Communist aid to Communist organizations within each ASEAN nation. For instance, by the mid-1970s, China, "in an effort to gain ASEAN's support for its anti-Soviet policies," had halted its assistance to regional movements.[187] ASEAN's progress continued into the 1970s. In fact, by 1979, "ASEAN had become much more cohesive and politically determined since the Vietnamese marched into Cambodia."[188]

Just as meaningful, ASEAN sought an alliance with the United States and, not surprisingly, that overture was well-received. Indeed, this development evinced a viable counter-measure to the rabid anti-American sentiment embraced by various Asian factions, particularly those that had characterized the Vietnam War as "American soldiers" versus "Asian soldiers." In fact, from 1967 to 1975, the United States "had an overwhelming influence on the ASEAN states . . . and [helped] ASEAN [overcome] institutional lethargy [in its early stages]."[189] Furthermore, even after Congress terminated the Vietnam War effort (as well as reneging on the American pledge to defend Southeast Asia against Communism) in

---

[184] *Id.*

[185] Marvin Stone, *Southeast Asia Revisited*, U.S. NEWS & WORLD REPORT, Oct. 12, 1981, at 90.

[186] *Id.*

[187] Storey, *supra* note 97, at 245.

[188] *It's that Price Again*, *supra* note 181.

[189] Ganesan, *supra* note 182.

late 1974, Prime Minister Lee of Singapore repeatedly maintained, "the need for U.S. presence in Asia."[190]

Another meaningful by-product of ASEAN's institutional strength was Malaysia's improved relations with fellow member Indonesia, an occurrence that perhaps best illustrated ASEAN's effectiveness in enhancing relationships. For this very reason, upon recollecting the importance of ASEAN years later, the foreign minister of Malaysia hailed the American presence in Vietnam—even in defeat—as greatly beneficial to every nation in Southeast Asia, for, by 1975, ASEAN nations could cooperatively repel further Communist expansion. Indeed, the foreign minister unequivocally worded his contention:

[In 1975] the United States withdrew their last soldiers from Vietnam and the worst of ASEAN's fears . . . came to pass. *But ASEAN by then had seven solid years of living in neighborly cooperation.* Call it foresight, or what you will, the fact remains that with ASEAN solidarity there were no falling dominoes in Southeast Asia following the fall of Saigon to the communists, and the United States withdrawal from Southeast Asia.[191]

However, had the United States departed Vietnam in 1965, would ASEAN have even been formed in 1967? Thailand thrived precisely because of ASEAN, and, as discussed earlier, an American departure would have likely increased Communist activity in and around Thailand. Indeed, in Richard Helms' 1967 memorandum to President Johnson, he concluded that a U.S. loss in Vietnam by 1967 would have "the most direct and immediate implications . . . in the region of Southeast Asia itself. The key country would prove to be Thailand, where the situation would be perilous and complicated."[192] The very strength of the Philippines in fighting off Communism also illuminates this point. Likewise, as J. H. Brimmell notes, the Moscow-Peking Axis failed to

---

[190] *Id.*

[191] Rostow, *supra* note 38 (emphasis added).

[192] *Id.*

generate much interest in the Philippines partly because of its membership in ASEAN.[193] Would, by 1980, the Filipino Communist Party have been described as "tiny" if ASEAN had never been formed?[194] Moreover, would Malaysia and Indonesia have united to fight Communism without the prodding of other ASEAN members to do so? These are important questions when evaluating the benefits and costs of abandoning Vietnam in 1965.

SOUTHEAST ASIA AFTER THE AMERICAN DEPARTURE IN 1975

Once the United States departed Vietnam in 1975, ASEAN fears of Communist expansion from the preceding decade became prophetic. In fact, despite assurances from President Gerald Ford in late 1975 that "no area of the world is more important to us than Asia," as well as solemn declarations by Secretary of State Henry Kissinger that "we have learned at a painful cost, that equilibrium in Asia is essential to our own peace and safety," Soviet-backed aggression in Southeast Asia escalated following the American withdrawal.[195] More specifically, as numerous congressional leaders largely acquiesced to Soviet aggrandizement, Vietnamese forces, supported heavily by the Soviet Union, invaded Cambodia in 1978, prompting Prime Minister Lee of Singapore to lament, "The fighting in Cambodia might spill over into the rest of Southeast Asia, and the Soviet Union, in supporting Vietnam, will be able to extend its area of influence still wider."[196]

The Tightening of Relations Between the Soviet Union and Vietnam and the Vietnamese Invasion of Cambodia in 1978

As Vietnam rebuilt its infrastructure from the remnants of warfare, its relationship with the Soviet Union improved. In fact, in

---

[193] BRIMMELL, *supra* note 63, at 344-45.

[194] KROEF, *supra* note 56, at 137.

[195] *One More Try by U.S. for a Stable Asia*, U.S. NEWS & WORLD REPORT, Dec. 22, 1975, at 26.

[196] *It's That Price Again, supra* note 181.

1978, the "Treaty of Friendship and Cooperation" between the Soviet Union and Vietnam was enacted, an agreement procuring extensive Soviet aid to the Vietnamese government. To many observers, the Treaty also symbolized the "most concrete expression" of enhanced relations between these two Communist nations.[197] Not coincidentally, less than a month after the Treaty's enactment, Vietnam, considerably buttressed by Soviet weaponry, invaded and occupied Cambodia. In fact, by 1979, the Soviet Union was spending $6 million a day to support the 200,000 Vietnamese troops in Cambodia.[198] By 1981, one observer alarmingly surmised, "The Soviets are all over Asia. In the north, they have perhaps 50 divisions facing China. They are supporting the Vietnamese in Cambodia. They are upgrading their Pacific air forces with modern Backfire bombers."[199]

Not surprisingly, official Vietnamese statements concerning the Cambodian invasion struck defensive and largely propagandistic tones. For instance, Vietnam championed its rescue of Cambodian citizens from hands of the genocidal Khmer Rouge: "Kampuchea became a hell on Earth—3,000,000 of the 7,000,000 Kampucheans were killed off during those three years. That was a disaster brought about by the most horrible regime of genocide in human history." Moreover, in deriding the Khmer Rouge's "guise of communism," Vietnam disparaged Pol Pot and his followers as false messengers of the Communist ideology. Lastly, Vietnam alleged that Cambodia had "launched an aggressive war against Vietnam and conducted armed provocations against Laos and Thailand," thereby necessitating Vietnamese intervention.[200]

Perhaps most notably, the Vietnamese invasion of Cambodia persuaded nearby nations to suddenly reconsider the value of having American troops stationed in Indochina. Indeed, several of these nations had previously criticized the U.S. "abandonment" of the South Vietnamese people and, likewise, doubted the American

---

[197] Ganesan, *supra* note 182.

[198] Stone, *supra* note 185.

[199] *Id.*

[200] BBC Summary of World Broadcasts (citing comments made by Truong Chinh made in the Hanoi Press, Nov. 28, 1979).

willingness to preserve democracy abroad. Yet, as the Communist threat neared, these nations began to warmly welcome the prospect of American intervention once again.

Thailand perhaps best demonstrates this sudden change in disposition, as it dramatically reversed its relations with the United States from 1975 to 1981. To vividly illustrate this point, first consider that by 1975, history had confirmed Richard Helms' previously discussed prediction in 1967 that an American withdrawal from Vietnam would have gravely damaged the American image in Southeast Asia, particularly in Thailand, where the American capacity to defeat Communism was openly questioned. In fact, in the summer of 1975, Thai Prime Minister Kukrit Pramoj reacted to the American loss in Indochina by requesting the removal of 42,000 American troops stationed in Thailand.[201] However, as the American presence gradually withdrew from Thailand, the Soviets gradually increased their naval operations around Thailand and supported a Vietnamese invasion of neighboring Cambodia as well. Therefore, perhaps it should come as no surprise that in October of 1981, Prime Minister Pramoj—the man who had vowed to "throw the Americans out of Thailand" six years earlier—suddenly decreed, "the American image has been restored in Thailand. Even the leftist press reflects no animosity . . . [and is willing to] stand up to the Russians everywhere. We take heart from that."[202] Apparently, not only did time heal wounds, but so did the ubiquity of Soviet troops.

Vietnamese leader General Vo Nguyen Giap, however, attempted to assuage the concerns of Thailand and other nations that feared an expansionist Vietnam. For instance, on October 30, 1979, General Giap delivered a national address in which he noted, "The provocateurs and reactionary elements of some countries in Southeast Asia . . . are shouting about a Vietnamese threat, but such a thing does not exist." Along these lines, General Giap insisted that Vietnam's invasion of Cambodia pertained solely to Vietnam's "long time fight for its independence," and that Vietnam would continue to "respect the independence and sovereignty of

---

[201] *One more try by U.S. for a Stable Asia, supra* note 195.
[202] Stone, *supra* note 185.

other countries irrespective of the intentions of the USA, China or other sovereignty forces."[203] Unconvinced, one Malaysian official characterized the Giap statement and similar proclamations as "statements made by Kremlin and Hanoi chieftains [that are] nothing but a mean trick to weaken the will of the people of Thailand and other countries in this region."[204]

Clearly, despite official Vietnamese propaganda, Vietnam, under the guiding hand of the Soviet Union, was becoming more expansionist as the 1970s came to a close. In fact, by 1985, Vietnam had invaded and occupied Cambodia, had partial occupation of Laos, and had troops performing offensive activities on both the Laotian-Thai and the Cambodian-Thai borders. [205]

Soviet Naval Expansion in Southeast Asia

Perhaps even more meaningful than the Soviet-backed Vietnamese invasion of Cambodia was the dramatically expanding Soviet naval presence in both the Indian and Pacific Oceans following the American withdrawal. Indeed, by the early 1980s, the Soviet Union had established numerous bases in Vietnam for both for its air and naval forces.[206] To many observers, this rapid Soviet expansion in Southeast Asia posed troubling strategic implications for global security.

Most alarmingly, the Soviet naval force grew swiftly in the early 1980s, as unmistakably evidenced in comments made by then Seventh Fleet Commander, Vice Admiral M. Staser Holcomb:

Three years ago, [the Soviets] had virtually nothing in Cam Ranh Bay. A few weeks ago, we had a high-water mark in which Soviet naval presence got above 20 ships. That's a

---

[203] *General Giap on Relations with China and Southeast Asia* (BBC Summary of World Broadcasts, Nov. 2, 1979).

[204] *Voice of the Malayan Revolution* (BBC Summary of World Broadcasts, Dec. 15, 1979).

[205] Robert J. Caldwell, *We seem to be winning in Vietnam*, Copley News Service, Jan. 19, 1998.

[206] *Id.*

significant presence, looking on South China Sea lines of communications on which the whole region depends. Clearly, the Socialist Republic of Vietnam gets strong encouragement from the Soviets' being there as a kind of guarantor of maritime power.[207]

To make matters worse, the Soviet naval expansion flauntingly exploited previous American investments. To illustrate, consider remarks made at the time by military expert Martin J. Lasater: "You find Soviet naval ports at two bases the U.S. spent hundreds of millions of dollars to establish—at Da Nang and Cam Ranh Bay in South Vietnam."[208] Equally significant, the scope of Soviet naval dominance only widened following the American withdrawal from Vietnam. For instance, Lasater maintained that "for the first time, the Soviet Navy has broken out of the northern Pacific port of Vladivostok, free to range over thousands of miles of Asian waters."[209] Likewise, according to Lasater, the Soviet Union had only begun its quest for naval dominance: "Moscow's aim is . . . to sit astride the key sea-lanes of the Far East."[210] Perhaps most alarmingly, the Soviets had appeared to gain the regional upper hand in a theoretical naval battle with the United States: "Given the present force levels available to the U.S. and U.S.S.R. in the Indian and Pacific oceans, a favorable outcome of that struggle would be in doubt, especially if it were initiated by a Soviet surprise attack against our surface fleet."[211]

Further complicating matters for the United States, according to Admiral Holcomb, were the woefully-equipped ASEAN naval fleets: "I don't think the countries in the region want the U.S. to keep land-based forces there . . . None of the navies [of ASEAN nations] are in a position to deal with the Soviets at sea—the 'blue

---

[207] *U.S. Navy v. Soviet Fleet—How They Stack Up*, U.S. NEWS & WORLD REPORT, Apr. 4, 1983, at 56.

[208] Stone, *supra* note 185.

[209] *Id.*

[210] *Id.*

[211] Stone, *supra* note 185.

water threat.' The Seventh Fleet is."[212] As a result, the corresponding need for a sufficient American naval presence garnered the attention of ASEAN leaders. For instance, in 1981, Singapore Prime Minister Lee declared, "The naval balance must be a rough U.S. equivalent to Soviet naval power in the area. There must be sufficient American forces to influence the thinking of governments."[213] Similarly, Australian Prime Minister Malcolm Fraser expressed concern over the "growing Russian naval strength in the Indian Ocean" while, at the same time, advocating "a strong American presence, including construction of U.S. bases, to counter the Russian threat."[214] Even leaders from distant parts of the world anxiously ruminated over the emerging Soviet naval threat. For instance, South African Prime Minister John Vorster openly feared that American naval forces were falling behind their Soviet counterparts: "I think the United States should take special note of what is happening in the Indian Ocean, where there is an alarming build-up of Communist military power. I see a vital need for an Allied naval presence that will match that build-up."[215]

By the early 1980s, the Soviet navy, emboldened by the American failure in Vietnam, unambiguously threatened Southeast Asian security. However, the threat extended beyond Southeast Asia. Indeed, as the Soviet navy grew, the danger posed to all democratic nations likewise grew. Thus, in 1976, the Supreme Allied Commander of Europe, General Alexander Haig, held that the Soviet navy had been transformed into "a global force . . . [and was] part of the Kremlin's strategy for worldwide imperialism."[216]

---

[212] *U.S. Navy v. Soviet Fleet—How They Stack Up, supra* note 207.

[213] Stone, *supra* note 185.

[214] *U.S. Losing Respect of Allies?*, U.S. NEWS & WORLD REPORT, Apr. 26, 1976, at 31.

[215] *Id.*

[216] *Edge of Disaster*, NEWSWEEK, Feb. 9, 1976, at 35.

Three-Pronged Regional Approach to Deterring Communist Expansion: "Self-Reliance"; Solidarity through ASEAN; and Sustained Economic Growth

Another consequence of the American withdrawal from Indochina was the increasingly hawkish behavior of Southeast Asian nations in countering Communist expansion. In fact, fearing the "specter of communist invasion through Thailand and Malaysia down to Singapore," a dangerous regional arms race ensued, particularly since "with Thailand rushing to arm itself, Malaysia could not fall behind, and in turn, neither could Singapore."[217]

The potential spread of Communism also proved worrisome to Indonesia, especially with regard to the "leftist leanings of East Timor [which] worried General Suharto . . . who in 1975 had seen allies in Indochina fall to Communism." Like his counterparts in nearby nations, General Suharto responded to the American withdrawal by quickly bolstering Indonesia's defense and national security programs. By December 1975, in fact, General Suharto had trumpeted his enhanced military force as the primary deterrent to regional Communist expansion. And, to vividly illustrate his military's newfound strength, General Suharto commanded a violent invasion of East Timor.[218]

Therefore, the American departure from Indochina in 1975 precipitated great anxiety among Southeast Asian leaders. Likewise, the resulting vacuum provided these leaders with meaningful incentives to expand their military programs. In fact, the departure may have even encouraged them to employ aggression rather than diplomacy in attempting to resolve matters of national security.

On the other hand, this arms race was conducted in the context of burgeoning ASEAN cooperation. To illustrate this very point, in February of 1980, Indonesia and Malaysia, two nations with a history of mutual aggression, jointly issued the "Kuantan

---

[217] Tan, *supra* note 128, at 451.

[218] Linter, *supra* note 64, at 3.

Declaration," an unprecedented proclamation of shared suspicions of the Chinese.[219]

Equally important, this arms race began in 1975. By that year, as already discussed, ASEAN had become a unifying force and had reduced regional distrust. However, if the United States had departed Vietnam in 1965, would an arms race at that time have proved as melodious? Three reasons suggest no. In fact, an ensuing arms build-up in 1965 may have even triggered a massive regional conflict.

First, by 1965, Malaysia, Indonesia, and Singapore had all been at war with one another, while each, at the same time, had consistently fended off internal Communist aggression—a challenge shared by Thailand and the Philippines. Therefore, the Southeast Asian political climate was already ripe for conflict. In contrast, by 1975, domestic Communist movements within Southeast Asia had largely splintered following the rupture of Soviet-style and Chinese-style Communism, thus weakening their collective strength. For example, by the early 1970s, the Communist Party of Malaysia had divided into three factions, a development which likely diminished the overall Communist threat to Malaysia.[220] This suggests, therefore, that had the United States withdrawn from Vietnam in 1965, a united Malaysian Communist movement would have possessed a greater capacity to destabilize the Malaysian political structure at that time than it did as an undivided movement in 1975. To illustrate this point, consider how in 1979, a pro-Chinese faction of the Malaysian Communist Party openly denounced another Malaysian Communist faction that had been allied with the Soviet Union: "We must never harbor any illusion about Soviet social-

---

[219] Ganesan, *supra* note 182.

[220] KROEF, *supra* note 56, at 203, 207; *see also* KROEF, *supra* note 56, at 206 (On the other hand, the "Malayan National Patriotic Youth and Student Movement" was founded by the Malaysian Communist Party in 1975, gaining popular support among young people and, at the time it "appear[ed] similarly persuaded of the necessity of the path of violence."). Therefore, it is possible, though unlikely, that the Communist threat in Malaysia was actually *stronger* in 1975 than in 1965.

imperialism and Vietnamese expansionism. Everyone knows that the Soviet Union is . . . ambitious to dominate the world."[221]

Second, consider that in 1965, Southeast Asian nations suffered from massive economic hardship, thus enhancing the appeal of Communist propaganda. Consequently, had the United States departed Vietnam that year, rapid militarization might have intrigued regional leaders as a method of enhancing national security. Likewise, such activity might have also proved an attractive ruse to those leaders for prolonging their political careers. That is, borrowing from the customary Soviet practice of parading nuclear arms through the streets of Moscow, Southeast Asian leaders may have employed an arms race in part to shift public attention away from poverty and hunger and toward apparent, if deluding, national strength. Moreover, considering the ineffectiveness of SEATO in engendering trust among member nations, had an arms race ensued in 1965, it would have posed substantial danger to the region.

A third and related point suggests that the absence of Southeast Asian unity in 1965 may have offered Vietnam a viable opportunity to invade neighboring nations. Indeed, in part because it had not yet suffered the extensive military losses it subsequently suffered from 1965 to 1975, the North Vietnamese army possessed great strength at that time. This notion is corroborated by Professor Sodhy, who maintains that had the United States withdrawn in 1965, the North Vietnamese would have, in all likelihood, immediately invaded South Vietnam.[222] Equally troubling, the North Vietnamese army would have encountered little resistance at that time, thereby sending a terrifying message to the rest of the region.[223] And in 1965, such a message would have seemed especially worrisome given the lack of unity among Southeast Asian nations.

---

[221] *Voice of the Malayan Revolution, supra* note 204.

[222] Interview with Pamela Sodhy, *supra* note 32.

[223] *Id.*

The Strengthened Partnership Between ASEAN and China

An additional consequence of both the American withdrawal
from Indochina in 1975 and the Soviet-backed Vietnamese
invasion of Cambodia in 1978 was the increased reliance by
ASEAN member nations on China for protection. Indeed, ASEAN
member nations, perhaps believing that the United States,
constrained by a domestically powerful yet internationally timid
Congress, no longer possessed the will to defend Southeast Asia
against Soviet expansion, and therefore believed that China
provided the next best alternative. Thus, one foreign policy expert
characterized Thailand's gravitation toward China as the "high
point of diminishing U.S. influence" in Southeast Asia.[224] A Thai
official commented in late 1981 on the Thai-Sino mutual necessity
to deter Soviet expansion that "[o]ur national interests now
coincide with China—they fear the Soviets and so do we."[225]
Moreover, American military diplomats recognized Thai officials'
renewed fears of Communist expansion, and how those fears
highlighted the Sino-Soviet split and the burgeoning alliance
between Thailand and China: "To the Thais, the grave threat today
is not from the ancient antagonist, China, but the nearby
Vietnamese and their Soviet backers."[226] Similarly, an American
diplomat noted that "Singapore also regards the Soviets and Hanoi
as Enemy No. 1."[227]

Equally significant, China perceived an alliance with ASEAN
as beneficial to its own self-interests, for it would serve "as part of
a broader strategy to balance growing Soviet influence in
Indochina."[228] Of particular concern to China was Vietnam's 1978
invasion of Cambodia, a close ally of China, for it further damaged
Sino-Siam relations. Specifically, China not only regarded the
invasion as aggression against one of its allies, but, more
importantly, "China realized that Russia was now supporting the

---

[224] Ganesan, *supra* note 182.

[225] Stone, *supra* note 185, at 90.

[226] *Id.*

[227] *Id.*

[228] Ganesan, *supra* note 182.

Vietnamese occupation of Cambodia, [thereby] increasing its encirclement of the mainland."[229]

On the other side of the 4,500-mile Sino-Soviet border, Soviet officials increasingly voiced concern over China's growing ties with ASEAN member nations. Indeed, one expert characterized the Soviet-Sino relationship in the following terms: "The Soviets don't understand the Chinese. They don't know what they're up to. They suffer from a grand paranoia [regarding Chinese activities]."[230] In addition, improved U.S.-Sino relations following President Richard Nixon's trip to China in 1972 only heightened Soviet anxiety, particularly given the diplomatic nexus between ASEAN and the United States.

However, not every ASEAN member nation was receptive to China's overtures. In fact, both Indonesia and Malaysia valued "the utility of Vietnam in containing China's hegemonic ambitions towards Southeast Asia."[231] Despite these assessments by Indonesia and Malaysia, China's previous alliance with Vietnam had clearly been eviscerated, and as America entered the 1980s, the Vietnamese-Soviet threat was looming large in Southeast Asia.

WORLDWIDE DEVELOPMENTS: HOW THE U.S. WITHDRAWAL FROM INDOCHINA EMBOLDENED COMMUNISM

On a return visit to Vietnam in 1991, former U.S. Senator and Vietnam veteran Bob Kerrey (D-NE) encountered a gentleman who had served in the South Vietnamese parliament before the Vietnam War. At the conclusion of an otherwise pleasant conversation, the gentleman gravely reminded Senator Kerrey of an American promise that had gone painfully unfilled: "We believed you. We didn't think you would leave. We thought you

---

[229] Stone, *supra* note 185, at 90.

[230] *Breakup of Communist World?*, U.S. News & World Report, Aug. 9, 1976.

[231] Ganesan, *supra* note 182.

would stay to the end."[232] The sentiment expressed by that former South Vietnamese parliament member dated back to 1975, when numerous global leaders wondered aloud whether the United States had left the battlefield against Communism and whether it no longer possessed the will to see democracy prevail.

For some, the signs gave little hope: A Soviet military machine growing to epic proportions; a recalcitrant American Congress weary of any active foreign policy; and an American president unwilling to deploy troops onto the battlefield. To make matters worse, the Soviet Union sponsored nearly unabated advances in both Angola and Afghanistan. In short, by the end of the 1970s, many foreign leaders had begun to doubt whether the United States could win the Cold War.

The Soviet Union's Increased Military Spending

Following the American withdrawal from Indochina in 1975, the Soviet Union rapidly accelerated its military industrial complex, particularly in regards to offensive weaponry. Such behavior deeply troubled American military officials. For example, in February of 1976, General Haig ominously declared "the explosion of Soviet military capabilities . . . far exceeds the requirements of a purely defensive posture . . . [T]he enemy is moving."[233] Indeed, in Europe alone, the Soviet front stationed on the Eastern Bloc-NATO border increased by 100,000 troops following the American withdrawal from Indochina.[234]

Equally worrisome, the Soviet Union began to outpace American defense spending by significant margins. For example, in 1975, the Soviet Union spent 85 percent more on military equipment, and 66 percent more on research and development than did the United States.[235]

---

[232] C. David Kotok, *Contrasting Lessons Learned: The Final Hours*, Omaha World-Herald, Apr. 3, 2000, at 6a.

[233] *Edge of Disaster*, *supra* note 216.

[234] *Id.*

[235] 1976 Republican Party Platform, Aug. 21, 1976.

Not surprisingly, American allies anxiously contemplated the military spending discrepancy. Some, like South African Prime Minister John Vorster, openly questioned whether the American nuclear arsenal alone would provide adequate deterrence against conventional Communist forces:

> I am genuinely afraid that the United States may be staring themselves blind against the threat of an A-bomb war when, in reality, the Russians are preparing for a conventional war. The Soviets are outstripping the free world in the manufacture of every conceivable weapon of conventional war: warships, tanks, guns, bombers, and fighters—everything. [236]

Such criticism seemed particularly persuasive in 1976, as the United States had only one year earlier abandoned a conventional war effort against a Soviet-sponsored campaign in Vietnam.

The "Confused" American Political Leadership

The Soviet Union rapidly accelerated its military spending in 1975 in part because it regarded American leadership as "confused." This perception was augmented by a Congress seemingly obsessed with truncating presidential foreign affairs powers and one willing to employ both legislative means (i.e., enactment of the Wars Powers Act) and political maneuvers (i.e., reduction of defense and national security spending) to achieve that very goal. As a result, the Soviet Union shrewdly discerned that it could exploit an American political landscape "unwilling to compete in a continuing contest for global leadership."[237]

More specifically, the Soviet Union sought to capitalize on the paucity of American initiatives designed to deter Communist advancements. Indeed, not only did congressional reluctance largely preclude victory in Vietnam, it also prevented adequate funding for the Angolan resistance fighters who battled and were

---

[236] *As Cape Town Sees It: Why the Communists have their eyes on Africa*, U.S. NEWS & WORLD REPORT, June 14, 1976, at 59.

[237] *Breakup of Communist World?*, *supra* note 230.

ultimately defeated by Soviet-backed forces. As a result, the Soviet Union soon decided to hasten its efforts to export Soviet ideology and thus listened closely for additional "targets of opportunity— more Angolas—where the Kremlin may feel it can make gains without provoking a reaction from Washington."[238]

American allies also detected a weakened American resolve to fight Communism and an increasingly obstinate Congress. At the time, one French official even lamented, "The problem is not whether the U.S. is ready to face up to Soviet intimidation, or capable of it, but whether it wants to."[239] Likewise, the French official sensed NATO's disenchantment by the "continuing fight between the White House and Congress over which has the responsibility for U.S. foreign policy."[240] More bluntly, he found the United States "psychologically unable to act, and Angola is proof of this."[241]

Similarly, high-ranking Italian officials appeared skeptical of the American resolve. Indeed, one such official observed, "The United States . . . is a weakened giant. Vietnam appears to have taken [its] toll."[242] Likewise, Canadian officials were astonished by the "willingness of a powerful country like the U.S. to confess so openly its frustrations with minor powers like Cuba . . . [it] is bewildering."[243]

Taken together, while Congress may have achieved institutional strength at the expense of the president, the strength of the nation only deflated. Moreover, by emasculating efforts to intervene on behalf of endangered democracies, Congress would only reaffirm America's post-Vietnam War reputation as a diminished superpower, one inhibited by its aversion to conventional warfare. As a result, Mao's "paper tiger" characterization from years earlier appeared distressingly prophetic.

---

[238] *Id.*

[239] *U.S. Losing Respect of Allies?*, *supra* note 214.

[240] *Id.*

[241] *Id.*

[242] *Id.*

[243] *Id.*

The Growing European Dissatisfaction with Capitalism and the Increased Acceptance of Communism Among Western European Nations

While the United States seemed incapable of deterring the spread of Communism, several European nations began to improve their relations with the Communist Party. In fact, according to one European onlooker in 1976, "Today, over U.S. objections, some Europeans no longer view Communism as a threat and are moving toward acceptance of Communists in Alliance governments."[244] As a result, ominous predictions regarding the fate of NATO began to emerge: "In the past, NATO's strength was based on Alliance-wide opposition to Communism. Britain fears that the [welcoming of Communism] could one day alienate America and tear the Atlantic Alliance apart."[245]

Within Western Europe, the political systems of Italy and France experienced perhaps the greatest surge in Communist ideology following the American exit from Vietnam. Revealingly, in 1976, University of Chicago Professor Fredrich A. Hayek predicted, "Italy is inching towards a Communist takeover" as evidenced by Communist gains in the Italian parliament and in public opinion polls.[246] While the Italian Communist Party remained a distinct political entity from the Kremlin, Michael J. Crozier, a professor at the Paris "Centre de Sociologie des Organisations" in 1976, concluded that its success "constitutes a real and growing threat to Western Democracy as we know it."[247] Furthermore, the very "threat" described by Professor Crozier appears more conceivable when considering Italy's massive economic hardship in the late 1970s: "If the situation goes on too long in Italy where productivity has dropped dramatically, the Communists will provide the only [hope]."[248]

---

[244] *Id.*

[245] *Id.*

[246] *Is Democracy Dying?*, U.S. NEWS & WORLD REPORT, Mar. 8, 1976, at 50.

[247] *Id.*

[248] *Id.*

European observers likewise expressed concern regarding the precipitous growth of the French Communist Party, particularly when, as one observer noted, "If you imagine a France vulnerable for economic, political and military reasons, with the Soviet next door, the situation could bring a tremendous change in the equilibrium of the whole world."[249] Though overly dire, such a scenario appeared slightly more credible when viewed in the context of French skepticism toward free markets and capitalistic values. This disenchantment was particularly evident when many French citizens viewed soaring energy prices as illustrative of defects in free markets.[250]

American officials were also troubled by these developments in Europe. In fact, Daniel Patrick Moynihan, who, in 1976, served as the U.S. ambassador to the United Nations, detected growing discontent with the Western style of government: "Democracies are becoming a recessive form of government, like monarchies used to be—something the world is moving from rather than to."[251] In contrast, the Soviet Union appeared confident, if not authoritative, particularly when compared to its rival—the United States—which seemed distracted by institutional power struggles and political indecisiveness unbecoming of a superpower. Likewise, at the time, some placed value in the perception that the Soviets "don't see complexities. They simply make decisions."[252]

Rising Soviet and Cuban Involvement in Angola

The continent of Africa, endowed with prized natural resources, served as another target for Communist expansion. In particular, the Soviet Union, along with the aid of Cuba, sought to expand the Soviet empire into oil-rich Angola. In turn, they would seek to envelop Mozambique, Rhodesia, and even South Africa.

Indeed, evincing a striking juxtaposition of the two superpowers, while the last group of American troops stationed in

---

[249] *Id.*
[250] *Id.*
[251] *Id.*
[252] *Id.*

Vietnam set to depart in 1975, 50,000 Soviet-sponsored Cuban soldiers invaded Angola and imposed a Communist dictatorship upon its people.[253] Moreover, in unison with the "Movimento Popular de Libertação de Angola" or the MPLA Marxist party, Cuban Communists had, through ruthless aggression, gained complete control of the country by early 1976. And by that time, much of the European population had fled, taking with them business expertise and advanced medical training. Consequently, Angola fell into severe economic crisis, thereby increasing poverty and diminishing national health standards.[254]

Remarkably, the United States Congress responded to the invasion of Angola by passing the Clark Amendment, legislation that prohibited American aid to the Angolan resistance fighters of the "União Nacional para a Independência Total de Angola" or UNITA party.[255] In fact, Congress embraced this measure in spite of advice shared by expert American military personnel, who projected Angola as "The latest manifestation . . . of the propulsion of Soviet geopolitical power at a relentless pace."[256] In essence, the decision to refrain from aiding Angolan resistance fighters was grounded on the instantly apparent, though largely misleading fear that Angola would represent "another Vietnam." Although the U.S. delegation to the United Nations ultimately blocked Angola's admission into the United Nations, it was only after Congress had acquiesced to the Soviet-backed invasion.

Though their words fell on mostly deaf congressional ears, African leaders harshly criticized the failure of congressional leaders to act. For instance, Prime Minister Vorster of South Africa lambasted them: "It is well known that the White House wanted to take certain initiatives in Angola but was stopped by Congress

---

[253] 1976 REPUBLICAN PARTY PLATFORM, supra note 235.

[254] Pamela S. Falk, *Cuba in Africa*, FOREIGN AFFAIRS 1077 (Summer 1987), *available at* 1987 WL 22308632.

[255] Walt Vanderbush & Patrick J. Haney, *Policy Toward Cuba in the Clinton Administration*, PUB. OPINION Q. (Sept. 1, 1999), *available at* 1999 WL 18360245.

[256] *Edge of Disaster, supra* note 216 (quoting General Alexander Haig).

from doing so . . . [A]s a result, the opportunity to stop [the spread of communism] is lost."[257]

Back home, many American observers were equally dismayed by the congressional failure to respond. Still smarting from Congress's decision to walk away from Vietnam, critics feared that failing to thwart the Soviets in Africa would only exacerbate a deteriorating American reputation abroad: "Resistance to the Soviet-sponsored Cuban intervention in Angola must not be allowed to become the subject of partisan debate . . . lest our credibility and deterrent strength be greatly diminished."[258] Other commentators, such as famed economist Milton Friedman, worried that a Soviet victory in Angola would lead only to further Soviet expansion into South Africa, a troubling prospect that would have adversely impacted both America's national security and economic well being. Specifically, according to Professor Friedman, "Soviet control of South Africa might enable domination of OPEC. Command of South Africa's Simonstown naval base would enable the Soviet Union to stop or at least seriously hamper that traffic at will."[259]

The ever-widening Communist threat in Africa likewise included Soviet and Cuban aid to Rhodesian terrorists who, while operating from Mozambique, conducted several brutal raids on villages that were unresponsive to overtures.[260] And, as with Angola, the United States refrained from responding. These raids deeply troubled those nations neighboring Rhodesia, particularly as the raids grew more frequent and more violent. For that reason, African leaders, such as Kenyan President Kenneth Zaunda, chastised the United States for "failing to help to extend a hand of friendship to help Rhodesia . . . and the result is that one of the worst fears of the Western powers, as well as ourselves has come

---

[257] *As Cape Town Sees It: Why the Communists have their eyes on Africa,* *supra* note 236.

[258] 1976 REPUBLICAN PARTY PLATFORM, supra note 235.

[259] Milton Friedman, *South Africa and the Soviet Union,* NEWSWEEK, May 24, 1976, at 78.

[260] *Black v. White in Africa—Rhodesia's Side of the Story,* U.S. NEWS & WORLD REPORT, May 24, 1976, at 31.

true—Communism [is viable in Africa]."[261] Along these lines, President Zaunda reflected ominously, "I see the infiltration of Communism as a threat to African unity."[262]

Like his colleague President Zaunda, South African Prime Minister Vorster feared the Soviet's expansionist pursuits in Africa: "The Communist takeovers in Angola and Mozambique have destabilized all of Africa."[263] Moreover, as discussed above, Communist expansion into South Africa would have proved most damaging to the United States. Not only would the Soviet Union have gained access to OPEC exports, but it would have controlled 25 percent of the continent's total mineral output, for South Africa was relatively abundant in critical resources, such as uranium and gems. Perhaps most importantly, the Soviets would have obtained vital naval bases on the southernmost tip of Africa, thus providing them a critical advantage in the event of any regional warfare.[264]

Astutely, Professor Friedman, in explaining his disappointment with Congress, asked a simple, yet central question in 1976: "Have we learned nothing from either Vietnam or Angola?"[265] Apparently, the answer was no. The United States largely ignored pleas from African leaders to help quell the spread of Communism throughout southern Africa, instead myopically surmising that "another Vietnam" would have emerged. By refraining from assistance, the United States essentially acquiesced to Soviet foreign policy. Indeed, Soviet troops would remain in Africa until the end of the Cold War.

The Soviet Invasion of Afghanistan

Perhaps the seminal example of America's post-Vietnam unwillingness to deter Soviet expansion occurred between 1978

---

[261] *A Black African speaks his mind*, U.S. NEWS & WORLD REPORT, May 3, 1976, at 30.

[262] *Id.*

[263] *As Cape Town Sees It: Why the Communists have their eyes on Africa*, *supra* note 236.

[264] *Id.*

[265] Friedman, *supra* note 259.

and 1979, when the Afghan Communist Party, buttressed by 30,000 Soviet troops, overthrew the mainline Afghanistan government and crushed anti-Communist groups. Consequently, Afghanistan became a "client state" of the Soviet Union, adopting Communist policies and establishing Soviet-run military bases.[266] Moreover, the Soviet Union supplied substantial military, political, and economic support to ensure the sustainability of the new regime. Unquestionably, the Soviet takeover imposed its most heavy burden on the Afghan people. Indeed, as the Communist regime gained control, 300,000 Afghan refugees flooded into the treacherous mountains on Pakistani-Afghan border, while many other Afghans perished in the fighting.[267]

Consistent with the Angolan invasion, the American response to the Afghanistan invasion was limited to words, not actions. And, as with Angola, the Soviets seized upon their rival's diffidence and, in the process, demonstrated little respect for American leadership. To illustrate this point, only days after President Jimmy Carter informed Premier Leonid I. Brezhnev that the Soviet-led coup represented "a grave threat to peace" and a violation of "basic principles of U.S.-Soviet relations [embraced by the 1972 détente agreement where the two nations pledged to avoid military confrontations]," the Soviet Union tripled the size of its force from 10,000 soldiers to 30,000 and began to accelerate its airlift program to supply their combatants.[268]

Not surprisingly, President Carter's ineffective handling of the Afghanistan crisis prompted sharp rebuke from foreign leaders. For instance, according to a 1979 *Newsweek* article, "It is now commonplace that neither French Giscard d'Estaing nor German Helmut Schmidt respects the President."[269] More demonstrably, other leaders criticized President Carter for failing to "threaten the

---

[266] Zalmay Khalilzad, *Anarchy in Afghanistan*, J. Int'l Affairs (June 22, 1997), *available at* 1997 WL 11003861.

[267] Don Oberdorfer, *Soviets Answer Carter's Plea by Tripling Their Forces in Afghanistan*, Wash. Post., Dec. 30, 1979, at A1.

[268] *Id.*

[269] Russell Watson & Fred Coleman, *Has the U.S. Lost Its Clout?*, Newsweek, Nov. 26, 1979, at 46.

stick when offering the carrot." For example, David Watt, director of Britain's Royal Institute for International Affairs, noted, "You can't run a government on the basis of 'Let a hundred flowers bloom.'"[270]

Perhaps even worse, President Carter's reluctance to deter Soviet expansion engendered sympathy for the United States, a phenomenon seemingly unbecoming of a "superpower." To bluntly illustrate this point, consider remarks by a spokesman for Chancellor Schmidt: "Nobody here gloats over U.S. misfortunes. Rather, we feel pity about them."[271] Even the Soviet Union appeared perplexed by the actions—or inactions—of the United States: "A Soviet military official who was outlining the strategic situation said that much depended on Moscow's evaluation 'of current American policy—whatever it is.'"[272]

Nevertheless, President Carter expressed "uncertainty, bordering on puzzlement" as to why the Kremlin would ignore his requests, and he remained convinced that American forces would prove unnecessary.[273] Rather, in his view, "deeply religious, highly motivated Afghan tribesmen will continue to present severe problems for a Soviet-dominated regime in Afghanistan."[274] While the Soviet Union did indeed leave Afghanistan by 1989, thus lending credence to President Carter's prediction, the Afghan people would not soon forget the ruthless Communist regime from 1979-89. Moreover, after ten years of brutal Soviet rule, Afghanistan was in ruins by 1989, and though it would gain independence from Soviet control, it has become one of the world's poorest, most anarchic countries. On a larger level, then, as the 1970s came to a close, the continued American refusal to deter Soviet expansion served only to diminish U.S. standing among world leaders and reaffirm its legacy of failure from the Vietnam War.

---

[270] *Id.*

[271] *Id.*

[272] *Id.*

[273] Oberdorfer, *supra* note 267.

[274] *Id.*

CONCLUSIONS: A WAR WORTH FIGHTING AND A WAR WORTH *WINNING*

Beyond debate, the American military experience in Indochina came with substantial costs, both human and political. Perhaps most harrowingly, more than 55,000 American soldiers lost their lives, more than 300,000 suffered injuries, and many others returned home with emotional wounds that, for some, time would not heal. Moreover, on an institutional level, by failing to defeat the North Vietnamese, the U.S. government became divided, highlighted by an unprecedented congressional attempt to usurp foreign powers from the presidency—a development leading to regrettable foreign policy choices grounded more on institutional dominion than on national interests. Indeed, such divisiveness, coupled with a retreat from battle, deeply wounded the United States' reputation as a viable safeguard to the Soviet Union and its expansionist tendencies. To make matters worse, political acquiescence to Soviet advancements in southern Africa and, most notably, Afghanistan, only exacerbated concerns about America's willingness to most effectively fight the Cold War.

Despite these negative outcomes, however, the Vietnam War proved to be an engagement of far greater benefit than cost. As evidenced in this analysis, by continuing the fight in Indochina between 1965 and 1975, the American military presence deterred the spread of Communism, particularly in Southeast Asia and Latin America. That is, while the United States remained in Vietnam after 1965, other Southeast Asian nations were able to overcome old rivalries and create meaningful partnerships. *This* legacy of the American involvement in Vietnam is one that Southeast Asia most celebrates today for improving economic conditions, frustrating internal Communist movements, and providing individualistic incentives to create a potent system for regional security. As a result, when the United States ultimately departed Indochina in 1975, Southeast Asia proved far better equipped to repel the spread of Communism.

Equally significant, the American presence in Indochina between 1965 and 1975 facilitated the deterioration of relations between the Soviet Union and China. Specifically, as Vietnamese leaders grew increasingly reliant upon Soviet assistance to help combat American troops, and as Soviet-backed Vietnamese forces invaded Cambodia—one of China's closest and most ancient allies—China renewed its deep-rooted enmity with Vietnam. At the same time, China compromised Sino-Soviet relations by establishing rapport with ASEAN, an organization composed of democratic Southeast Asian states seeking to deter Soviet-sponsored advancements. Perhaps most significantly, improved relations between the United States and China sealed the irreparable Sino-Soviet split.

Alternatively, what geopolitical consequences would have emerged if the United States had departed Indochina in 1965, rather than in 1975? For one, data suggests that such an action would have been met with scorn by most American citizens and political leaders, as, at that time, efforts to constrain Soviet advancements in Southeast Asia received strong public approval. More importantly, Communism would have likely spread throughout Southeast Asia and, although less likely, perhaps into Australia, Japan, and Central and South America as well. This is true not only because internal Southeast Asian Communist movements enjoyed far greater strength and unity in 1965 than they did in 1975, but also because dire economic conditions made Communist expansion ripe at that time. Simultaneously, across the Pacific Ocean, Cuban troops and "advisors" were positioned throughout Latin and South America, serving to improve relations between Castro and regional leaders.

An American retreat in 1965 would have also emboldened internal Communist movements in Southeast Asia, as well as vitalized Fidel Castro's various machinations south of the U.S. border. More sharply put, if the United States possessed neither the political will nor the conventional military capacity to fight a "fourth-rate" North Vietnamese military, then Mao's "paper-tiger" charge would have been confirmed: Any battle against the United States where it would not deploy nuclear weapons is a battle that the United States could not win. Certainly, insurgent (though Soviet and Cuban backed) domestic Communist movements—

under their thinly-veiled guise of "national liberation fronts"—in nations such as Thailand, Malaysia, Guatemala, and Nicaragua would not likely have warranted the use of American nuclear weapons under any circumstances. However, if the dominoes kept falling, global security would have been endangered and the United States might have been forced to turn to extraordinary measures in order to defend its own national security.

In truth, the Vietnam War was not only worth fighting, it was worth winning. As discussed in this chapter, the United States sacrificed a great deal of prestige, both abroad and at home, by retreating. Along those lines, the American superpower status suffered immeasurably as allies began to doubt and commiserate over America's international floundering. Some even found the United States unsuitable to play such a lead role in the Cold War, especially as the Soviet Union's quest for global domination encountered such minimal resistance. In fact, as evidenced by unabated Communist advancements in Angola and Afghanistan, the Soviet Union simply no longer feared the consequences of angering American politicians.

On a more human level, though, the Vietnam War was worth winning because it would have prevented the millions of deaths that ensued in Southeast Asia following the American retreat. From the tragedy of the South Vietnamese "boat people," to the equally horrific Vietnamese "re-education" camps, to the most tragic—the Killing Fields in Cambodia—the American retreat triggered consequences far beyond those affecting political dynamics. Indeed, years after he objected to the war effort, Senator Kerrey acknowledged his own regrets: "Our withdrawal from Southeast Asia in April 1975 allowed Pol Pot to bring the killing fields to Cambodia [and] 3 million Cambodians were killed through executions and forced labor . . . ," he said. "[M]y own objection to the war was somewhat misguided."[275]

Therefore, the legacy of the American withdrawal from Indochina in 1975 should not rest solely upon its negative repercussions. Rather, any honest analysis of the Vietnam War

---

[275] Kotok, *supra* note 232.

must also take into account how the American presence in Indochina between 1965 and 1975 deterred the spread of Communism. At the same time, however, we should ask "what if" —What if we stayed and fought until we were victorious? Would Afghanistan, Mozambique, and Angola have been invaded? Would the Cuban-backed FSLN have taken over Nicaragua? Would the United States have maintained its previously untarnished record in warfare? We will never know these answers, for once Ronald Reagan was sworn in as our nation's 40th president in 1981, the tide soon turned and, by 1991, the United States had won the Cold War. But, if instead, had the United States retreated from Indochina in 1965, *would* we have been so fortunate?

BIBLIOGRAPHY

Ball, George. *Memorandum to President Johnson.* January 20, 1966.

BBC Summary of World Broadcasts. *From comments by Truong Chinh made in the Hanoi Press.* November 28, 1979.

————. *General Giap on Relations with China and Southeast Asia.* November 2, 1979.

————. *Voice of the Malayan Revolution.* December 15, 1979.

Brimmell, J. H. *Communism in Southeast Asia.* Oxford University Press, 1959, at 339, 343-45.

Caldwell, Robert J. "We seem to be winning in Vietnam." *Copley News Service*, January 19, 1998.

CBS Network. Transcript from "Face the Nation." August 1, 1965.

CBS News Poll. Conducted by telephone between November 23 and 25, 1969. From the Roper Center at University of Connecticut (1996).

Congressional Quarterly Almanac, 89th Congress (1965).

Economist. "It's that Price Again." December 1, 1979.

Falk, Pamela. *Cuban Foreign Policy: Caribbean Tempest.* 1986, at 21.

Falk, Pamela S. "Cuba in Africa." *Foreign Affairs* (Number 5, Volume 65), Summer 1987, 1077-80.

Feinberg, Richard E., and Richard S. Newfarmer. *The Economic Impact of the Caribbean Basin Initiative,* prepared statement before the Committee of Foreign Relations of the U.S. Senate, March 21, 1982.

Friedman, Milton. "South Africa and the Soviet Union." *Newsweek.* May 24, 1976, at 78.

FSLN "Program of the Sandinista Front of National Liberation." *Tricontinental No. 17* (March-April 1970), at 61-68.

Ganesan, N. "ASEAN's Relations with Major External Powers." *Contemporary Southeast Asia* (Number 2, Volume 22). August 1, 2000, at 258-59.

Glyn, Alan. *Witness to Vietnam.* London: Johnson Publishing, 1968, at 227-28, 258, 274-76, 279.

JCSM-652-65. *A Memorandum for the Secretary of Defense.* August 27, 1965.

Johnson, Lyndon Baines. State of the Union Message, January 12, 1966.

Khalizad, Zalmay. "Anarchy in Afghanistan." *Journal of International Affairs.* June 1, 1997.

Kotok, C. David. "Contrasting Lessons Learned: The Final Hours." *Omaha World-Herald.* April 3, 2000, at 6a.

Kroef, Justus M. van der. *Communism in Southeast Asia.* Berkeley: University of California Press, 1980, at 34-35, 88, 95, 137, 181, 195-96, 203, 207.

Layne, Christopher. "American hegemony—without an enemy." *Foreign Policy.* September 22, 1993, at 5.

Linter, Bertil. "Centrifugal forces stir in Indonesia." *Jane's Intelligence Review* (Number 6, Volume 12). June 1, 2000, at 3, 7-8.

Lodge, Henry Cabot. Cable to President Johnson. September 27, 1965.

McNamara, Robert S. *In Retrospect: The Tragedy and Lessons of Vietnam.* New York: Random House, 1995.

Moore, John Norton. *The Secret War in Central America: Sandinista Assault on World Order.* Frederick, Maryland: University Publications of America, Inc., 1987, at 10, 22.

Newsweek. *Edge of Disaster.* February 9, 1976 at 35.

New York Times. "Americans Reported Ousted From Faculty Posts in Peru." June 4, 1965, at 10.

———. "Australia Disturbed by Sukarno's Moves in a Warlike Policy." January 3, 1965, at 1.

———. "Australia Supports U.S." March 24, 1965, at 5.

———. "Australian Reds an Issue in Strike." March 21, 1965, at 22.

———. "Austrians Ponder Position in Europe." March 29, 1965, at 4.

———. "Bolivia Pressing for Wide U.S. Aid." June 4, 1965, at 1.

———. "Bolivia's Regime Tightens Control." June 1, 1965, at 1.

———. "Chen Yi Visits Afghanistan." March 23, 1965, at 12.

———. "China to Intensify Drive." March 23, 1965, at 13.

————. "Cuban Red Party Canvassing Army." March 21, 1965, at 1.

————. "Curfew Set in Malaya Area." March 21, 1965, at 5.

————. "De Gaulle Gives Pledge to Soviet." April 4, 1965, at 12.

————. "De Gaulle Gives Pledge to Soviet." April 11, 1965, at 12.

————. "Demonstrators Assail U.S." January 2, 1965, at 4.

————. "El Salvador Accuses Cuba." March 23, 1965, at 2.

————. "Guatemala Sets Rule by Charter." June 3, 1965, at 2.

————. "High Soviet Aide to Make Four-Day Visit to Pakistan." June 1, 1965, at 4.

————. "Indonesia Tells U.N. She Will End Her Membership." January 2, 1965, at 1.

————. "Indonesia Threat is Seen in Manila." March 28, 1965, at 3.

————. "Indonesia's Boss." January 2, 1965, at 2.

————. "Interview with President Johnson." June 2, 1965, at 1.

————. "Japan Sees 1965 As Decisive Year." January 3, 1965, at 2.

————. "Java Reds Harry Peace Corpsmen." April 11, 1965, at 2.

————. "Johnson Defends Moves." June 2, 1965, at 1.

————. "Kenya Cabinet Ministers Scores Vice President." June 1, 1965, at 10.

————. "Kenyatta Excludes a Red Role in Kenya." June 2, 1965, at 8.

————. "Latin Lands Gain is Found Limited." March 21, 1965, at 3.

————. "Makarios Says Cyprus Has Russian Equipment." March 30, 1965, at 14.

————. "Malaysian Force Searching for New Indonesian Band." June 2, 1965, at 2.

————. "Malaysian Sees War On." January 2, 1965, at 1.

————. "Manila Backs More Vietnam Aid." June 1, 1965, at 10.

————. "Manila Caltex Strike Ends." June 1, 1965, at 15.

————. "Moscow 'Wishes' Peace for 1965." January 3, 1965, at 10.

————. "No one would shed tears." January 3, 1965, at 10.

————. "North Koreans in Moscow Get Pledge of Military Aid." June 1, 1965, at 14.

————. "Odinga Removed from Delegation." June 3, 1965, at 8.

————. "President Hints at Help for Asia." March 26, 1965, at 3.

————. "Red Aid to Cairo is at $500 Million." January 3, 1965, at 5.

————. "Reds, Pressing Reforms, Win Wide Peasant Support in Java." March 27, 1965, at 5.

————. "Sato Hopeful of U.S. Sympathy on Japan's Chinese Dealings." January 1, 1965, at 2.

————. "Scot Asks SEATO Parley to Back U.S. Stand in Asia." March 29, 1965, at 3.

————. "Soviet Challenge to Red China Seen." June 4, 1965, at 1, 8.

————. "Soviet Ridicules Johnson Speech on Asia as 'Nosy Propaganda.'" April 11, 1965, at 4.

————. "Sukarno Threatens U.N. Bolt if Council takes in Malaysia." January 1, 1965, at 1-2.

————. "Sukarno Welcomes North Korean Chief." April 11, 1965, at 5.

————. "Sukarno's Plan is Said to Be a Group to Rival U.N." January 4, 1965, at 1-2.

————. "Tanzania to Greet Chou Today; Her Capital is in Festive Array." June 4, 1965, at 4.

————. "Threat of Partition Raised in Malaysia Dispute." June 2, 1965, at 5.

————. "Token Cuban Force Possible." March 25, 1965, at 15.

————. "U.N. General Assembly's Action." January 2, 1965, at 1.

————. "U.S. Allies Oppose Wider Asian War." January 1, 1965, at 2.

————. "U.S. Embassy's Mail is Cut Off by a Red Union in Indonesia." March 24, 1965, at 1.

————. "U.S. Now Favors Dominican Vote in 2 or 3 Months." June 3, 1965, at 1.

————. "U.S. Sending Bunker on Jakarta Mission." March 23, 1965, at 1, 5.

————. "Village in Java a Case Study in Red Tactics." March 28, 1965, at 3.

————. "Warning by Chen to U.S. Reported." March 23, 1965, at 12.

————. "Washington Cites China." January 4, 1965, at 2.

————. "Workers Seize Goodyear Plant." March 21, 1965, at 1.

————. "2 Dominicans Die in Clash Inland." June 1, 1965, at 1.

————. "14 Indonesians are Captured." June 14, 1965, at 2.

————. "5,000 in Tokyo Bid U.S. Quit Vietnam." March 28, 1965, at 3.

NSAM 288. Issued in March 1964.

NSC Directive 64. Issued in 1950.

Oberdorfer, Don. "Soviets Answer Carter's Plea by Tripling Their Forces in Afghanistan." *The Washington Post*. December 30, 1979, at A1.

Republican Party Platform (1976). August 21, 1976, at A1.

Rivero, Nicolas. *Castro's Cuba*. Washington D.C.: Luce, 1962, at 111, 116, 127, 138.

Rostow, W. W. "McNamara's Vietnam War reconsidered." *Society Magazine* (Number 6, Volume 35). November 1, 1998, at 78.

Rusk, Dean. Memorandum from Secretary Rusk to President Johnson on deployment of forces, July 1, 1965.

Schwarz, Benjamin. "Why America thinks it has to run the world." *The Atlantic Monthly* (Volume 277, Number 6). June 1996, at 92.

SEATO Public Information Office, *Story of SEATO*. Bangkok: Thailand, 1967.

SEATO Public Information Office, *Article III of The Southeast Asia Collective Defence Treaty* (ratified in 1955).

Sodhy, Pamela. Chair of the Southeast Asian Studies Department, Georgetown University. Personal interview conducted in her office at Georgetown University, November 5, 2000.

Stone, Marvin. "Southeast Asia Revisited." *U.S. News & World Report*. October 12, 1981, at 90.

Storey, Ian James. "Indonesia's China Policy in the New Order and Beyond: Problems and Prospects." *Contemporary Southeast Asia* (Number 1, Volume 22). April 1, 2000, at 145-47, 245.

Strmecki, Marin J. Vice President, Director of Programs, Smith Richardson Foundation. Discussion on November 15, 2000.

Tan, Andrew T. H. "Singapore's Defence: Capabilities, Trends, and Implications." *Contemporary Southeast Asia* (No. 3, Vol. 21). December 1, 1999, at 451.

Turner, Robert F. *Nicaragua v. United States: A Lawyer looks at the Facts.* 1986.

United States Senate Committee on Foreign Relations. 103rd Congress. *The U.S. Government and the Vietnam War.* June 1994, at 23, 45, 47, 50, 141-42, 144, 147.

U.S. News & World Report. "A Black African speaks his mind." May 3, 1976, at 30.

———. "As Cape Town Sees It: Why the Communists have their eyes on Africa." June 14, 1976, at 59.

———. "Black v. White in Africa—Rhodesia's Side of the Story." May 24, 1976, at 31.

———. "Breakup of Communist World?" August 9, 1976.

———. "Is Democracy Dying?" March 8, 1976, at 50.

———. "It won't be easy—dealing with allies on one hand, old battlefield enemies on the other." December 22, 1975, at 26.

———. "U.S. Losing Respect of Allies?" April 26, 1976, at 31.

———. "U.S. Navy v. Soviet Fleet—How They Stack Up." April 4, 1983, at 56.

Vanderbrush, Walt, and Patrick J. Haney. "Policy Toward Cuba in the Clinton Administration." *Political Science Quarterly.* September 1, 1999.

Washington Institute for Values in Public Policy. *Central America in Crisis* (1989), at 8, 11, 17, 103.

Watson, Russell, and Fred Coleman. "Has the U.S. lost its Clout?" *Newsweek.* November 26, 1979, at 46.

III

The Debate Over Cease-Fire Violations in Vietnam, 1973-1975: Congress and the Myth That Nixon and Thieu Sabotaged the Paris Agreement

Mark H. Hamer

On January 27, 1973, after four years of diplomacy between the United States and North Vietnam (Democratic Republic of Vietnam, or DRV), Henry Kissinger and Le Duc Tho finally presented the world with an "Agreement on Ending the War and Restoring Peace in Vietnam." The Paris Peace Accords marked the end of American involvement in the second Indochina War and purportedly set the stage for the peaceful resolution of the conflict in South Vietnam. It called for a cease-fire by all parties, an immediate withdrawal of U.S. forces, and an exchange of prisoners. It also included the guarantee of political freedoms by both parties in the South, so that a free election could be held to determine the future of Vietnam. By all appearances, the two parties in South Vietnam—President Nguyen Van Thieu's Republic of Vietnam (RVN) and the Communist Provisional Revolutionary Government (PRG)—could now settle their differences without bloodshed.

Instead, the two years that followed the Paris Peace Agreement were marked by violent military confrontation. In fact, the fighting actually escalated in the weeks immediately following the signing of the cease-fire on January 27, 1973. This "cease-fire war" raged on until North Vietnamese tanks rolled into Saigon in April 1975. Indochina's renewed military struggle was supplemented by a propaganda war, in which Hanoi and Washington publicly accused each other of violating the Paris Peace Agreement. Each side also presented evidence of its own obedience to the terms of the Accords to emphasize that its adversary was responsible for the collapse of the peace.

In the end, the debate over who was sabotaging the cease-fire was a decisive factor in the outcome of the third Indochina War (1973-75). This debate had a substantial impact on Congress' decision to sever support for the Thieu government, which in turn had a decisive impact on the outcome of Thieu's war with the DRV. The fall of Saigon might have been avoided, or at least postponed, if the debate over the cease-fire violations had been resolved differently.

From 1973 to 1975, Congress made critical decisions to deny further aid to Saigon and to prohibit any military retaliation for North Vietnam's continued aggression. After spending millions of dollars and losing 50,000 lives to support its ally South Vietnam, the United States refused even to deliver the minimal aid necessary to remedy fuel and ammunition shortages as the DRV divisions marched toward Saigon. Congress' actions at best hastened, and at worst caused, the DRV victory in 1975. In this time frame, many in Congress embraced the assumption that Thieu and Nixon, not Hanoi, were the stumbling blocks to peace. This assumption served as a key rationale for the congressional abandonment of South Vietnam.

Yet this assumption is flawed. While all three Vietnamese parties violated the cease-fire to some extent, the RVN substantially complied with the Agreement. In contrast, the DRV and PRG had no intention of complying, and regarded the Agreement as an opportunity to prepare for the final military conquest of the South. First, no persuasive argument can be made that the United States failed to fulfill its obligations under the Paris Peace Accords. The Nixon administration promptly carried out its promises to North Vietnam—in particular the withdrawal of U.S. forces. Second, while it is correct to say that Saigon violated some parts of the Agreement, those violations were typically in response to DRV offensive actions or were political obligations contingent upon effective implementation of the cease-fire provisions. Third, the assumption that the North Vietnamese desired peace and had abandoned their military ambitions to invade Saigon is false. The North viewed the Paris Peace Agreement as an opportunity to lick wounds and prepare for the final assault in the South. Virtually every provision of the Accords was massively and flagrantly violated by North Vietnam. In fact, the documented violations by Hanoi dwarf even the most exaggerated allegations of U.S. and RVN noncompliance. Congress' conclusion that Nixon and Thieu were violating the Accords while Hanoi earnestly strove for peace was a fundamentally erroneous analysis of the situation.

This chapter will begin with a brief summary in the section entitled "The Paris Peace Agreement" of the key provisions of the Paris Peace Accords, which are divided generally into military and political provisions. Next, "The Debate Over Violations of the Military Provisions of the Paris Peace Accords" will examine the debate over violations of the military provisions of the Agreement, focusing on (1) the obligations of the RVN and the PRG, (2) the obligations of the United States and DRV, and (3) the mutual withdrawal from Laos and Cambodia. "The Debate Over Violations of the Political Provisions of the Paris Peace Agreement" will explore the debate over alleged violations of the political provisions, with emphasis on the political prisoner question. Finally, the "Conclusion" will note (1) that North Vietnam was primarily responsible for the collapse of the Agreement, and (2) that Congress' contrary conclusion—that South Vietnam and Nixon sabotaged the Agreement—contributed to key congressional decisions that led to Saigon's conquest.

THE PARIS PEACE AGREEMENT

The triumphant signing of the Paris Accords on January 27, 1973, broke the diplomatic deadlock that had plagued U.S. negotiators for years. The United States had insisted upon mutual withdrawal of troops from the South as the bottom line for any negotiated settlement. Similarly, Le Duc Tho's delegation refused to accept any agreement that recognized Nguyen Van Thieu as the legitimate ruler of South Vietnam.[1] The breakthrough occurred in the fall of 1972 when the United States conceded that DRV troops could remain in place in the South, and Hanoi conceded that Thieu could remain in power, pending a political resolution over the fate of Vietnam.[2] The result was an ambiguous "standstill cease-fire" in which each party in South Vietnam—the PRG and the RVN— would retain control over the territories it occupied as of the date of the Agreement. This solution left South Vietnam divided into "leopard spots" controlled by either side, inviting future conflict to solidify the borders.

The backbone of the Agreement was a series of military provisions designed to terminate the hostilities. First, all parties in South Vietnam were required to observe a cease-fire at midnight on January 27.[3] At the same time, the United States was required to cease its bombing of the North and to remove all mines in DRV waters.[4] The United States promised to withdraw its troops within sixty days—even though the 145,000 North Vietnamese troops[5] were allowed to remain in place in the South.[6] As a security measure, the Agreement prohibited the introduction of new military troops or equipment to the South.[7] However, it permitted the United States and North Vietnam to send war materiel on a "piece-for-piece" basis to replace destroyed, damaged, or expended munitions.[8] Both sides were required to exchange prisoners of war immediately and to provide information and assistance in locating any soldiers missing in action.[9] Finally, both the DRV and the United States were required to withdraw from the

---

[1] A. Goodman, The Search for a Negotiated Settlement of the Vietnam War 59 (1986).

[2] Id. at 82.

[3] Agreement on Ending the War and Restoring Peace in Vietnam, January 27, 1973, 24 U.S.T. 5, art. 2.

[4] Id.

[5] Can the U.S. Make the Truce Stick?, U.S. News & World Report (Feb. 12, 1973), at 18.

[6] 24 U.S.T., art. 5, at 6.

[7] Id., art. 7, at 7.

[8] Id.

[9] Id., art. 8, at 8.

wars in Cambodia and Laos and to cease all military activities there.[10]

In addition to the military provisions, the Agreement included political provisions to pave the way for a peaceful solution to the future of Vietnam. The two South Vietnamese parties agreed to settle all conflicts by negotiation rather than by force[11] and agreed to ensure specific democratic liberties of the people.[12] A National Council of Reconciliation and Concord would be set up to plan for eventual elections to determine the political control of South Vietnam.[13] Furthermore, the unification of Vietnam would be implemented by negotiation between North and South Vietnam, without "coercion or annexation."[14] Until such reunification, both sides were required to respect the integrity of the "provisional" border between the two nations, and to respect the demilitarized zone.[15]

THE DEBATE OVER VIOLATIONS OF THE MILITARY PROVISIONS OF THE PARIS PEACE ACCORDS

Military Obligations of the RVN and the PRG

The foundation of the Paris Agreement is Article 2. As of midnight on January 27, all parties were required to halt military actions in South Vietnam. Any future disagreements between the Republic of Vietnam and the Provisional Revolutionary Government had to be resolved by negotiation, not by force of arms. The parties were required to create a Joint Military Commission to implement the cease-fire.[16] The Agreement also created an International Commission of Control and Supervision (ICCS) to monitor the cease-fire and to handle any claims of

---

[10] *Id.*, art. 20, at 20.
[11] *Id.*, art. 10, at 9.
[12] *Id.*, art. 11, at 9.
[13] *Id.*, art. 12, at 10.
[14] *Id.*, art. 15, at 11.
[15] *Id.*
[16] *Id.*, arts. 16-17, at 12-15.

violations by either side.[17] The four national delegations that composed the ICCS—Poland, Hungary, Canada, and Indonesia—were required to agree unanimously that a violation had occurred prior to making a report.

Despite these explicit provisions, the war in Indochina raged on. Over 120,000 casualties were reported by January 27, 1974, the first anniversary of the truce.[18] And by April 1973—less than three months after the cease-fire—the two parties had submitted over 90,000 reports of alleged violations to the ICCS.[19] As Congress explored the causes of the continued bloodshed, they concluded that President Thieu—and his friends in the White House—bore the responsibility.

In May 1973, the Senate Foreign Relations Committee heard testimony regarding a military aid package to South Vietnam. Two key witnesses before the Committee were Elliot Richardson, outgoing secretary of defense, and Gareth Porter, Cornell University professor and director of the Indo-China Resources Center, a nongovernmental organization that was accumulating data about the cease-fire violations in Vietnam.

Porter told the Committee that "evidence from independent sources clearly indicates that it is the Thieu government and not the [PRG] which has systematically violated the cease-fire."[20] He noted that the South Vietnamese "launched major military operations which continued for extended periods" to seize "territory held by the Communists at the time of the cease-fire."[21] In contrast, "a survey of the reports by foreign correspondents who witnessed such attacks fails to turn up a single case in which the hamlet had been entered by Communist forces after the cease-fire deadline."[22] This analysis was backed up with numerous

---

[17] *Id.*, art. 18, at 15.

[18] *In a Year of Vietnam Truce: 120,000 Casualties*, U.S. NEWS & WORLD REPORT (Feb. 4, 1974), at 45.

[19] *Non-Policing a Non-Truce*, TIME, April 16, 1973, at 26.

[20] *Foreign Military Sales and Assistance Act: Hearings on S. 1443 Before the Senate Comm. on Foreign Relations*, 93d Cong., 1st Sess. 268 (1973) (statement of D. Gareth Porter, Cornell University) [hereinafter *Foreign Sales Hearing*].

[21] *Id.* at 450.

[22] *Id.* at 449.

documented descriptions of specific violations of Article 2 by the RVN.

The real situation was not quite that simple. Technically, most of the attacks in the weeks immediately following the deadline were launched by the RVN. However, the Communists had initiated a last-minute land grab in the days immediately preceding the cease-fire date. An estimated 300 non-Communist hamlets were overrun by PRG troops just before the deadline.[23] In fact, twenty-eight hamlets had been seized on the very day of the cease-fire,[24] and fifty-two had actually come into Communist hands *after* the deadline.[25] As Graham Martin, U.S. ambassador to South Vietnam, told the Congress in July 1974, the evidence then available clearly indicated that "most of those that have been taken back [by the RVN] are the ones which had been held by the Government of South Vietnam at the time of the initiating of the Agreement, immediately before the cease-fire itself actually took place."[26]

Furthermore, Thieu was quite open about his intentions. At the time of the cease-fire, Thieu told *Le Monde*: "If Communists dare put a foot in our zones, we will kill them."[27] On January 29, an RVN spokesman disclosed information about the PRG land-grab offensive, called it a clear violation of the cease-fire, and announced the RVN's intention to recover the hamlets that had been seized.[28] The U.S. Embassy then informed Thieu that it considered it "perfectly legitimate for his government to take back

---

[23] A. GOODMAN, THE LOST PEACE 169 (1978).

[24] Nash, *Dissolution of Paris Peace Accords*, NAT'L REV. (Oct. 24, 1975), at 1169.

[25] PORTER, A PEACE DENIED: THE UNITED STATES, VIETNAM, AND THE PARIS AGREEMENT 189 (1975). Porter lends little credence to the accusation of fifty-two post-deadline takeovers by the PRG, since this figure comes from Thieu's observers—not from independent witnesses on the scene.

[26] *Report on the Situation in the Republic of Vietnam: Hearing Before the Subcomm. on Asian and Pacific Affairs of the House Comm. on Foreign Affairs*, 93d Cong., 2d Sess. 31 (1974) (statement of Hon. Graham Martin, U.S. Ambassador to the Republic of Vietnam) [hereinafter *Report on South Vietnam*].

[27] LARRY BERMAN, NO PEACE, NO HONOR 243 (2001).

[28] PORTER, *supra* note 25, at 189-90.

all the territory it had lost before the cease-fire took effect," because the Communist's "pre-cease-fire offensive had given them an unfair advantage."[29] Secretary of Defense Richardson publicly described the Saigon actions as "a process of oscillation back to a posture closer to what [existed] before these [last minute] surges took place."[30] Unlike the PRG, which engaged in a furtive land-grab offensive, the RVN engaged in an open counterattack, which it publicly announced as a proper response to the PRG seizures to restore the status quo at the time the Agreement was negotiated.

More importantly, not all post-deadline battles were initiated by the RVN. The PRG launched numerous offensives long after January 27 to grab hamlets that had always been in RVN hands. In March, American journalists reported that two villages—Rach Bap and Ton Le Chan—were overrun after heavy pummeling by PRG artillery fire.[31] In April, several more Communist-initiated battles were reported by non-RVN witnesses.[32] Also, the PRG made frequent overt attacks on RVN shipping along the Mekong.[33] Porter dismissed such incidents of PRG aggression, saying that these attacks "clearly were not the beginning of an offensive but were aimed at pressuring Saigon to move back towards a stable cease-fire."[34]

The aggression of the PRG was not limited to RVN hamlets and ships, however. The enforcement mechanisms of the cease-fire—the ICCS of Article 18 and the JMC of Article 16—were themselves the target of Communist attack. Each commission had the unenviable task of monitoring compliance with the cease-fire and reporting any violations. In the first four months of the Accords, the PRG fired upon ten helicopters that were clearly marked "ICCS."[35] One was shot down, killing the ten observers

---

[29] *Id.* at 191.

[30] *Id.* at 192.

[31] *Foreign Sales Hearing, supra* note 20, at 451.

[32] *Id.* at 452.

[33] PORTER, *supra* note 25, at 194.

[34] *Foreign Sales Hearing, supra* note 20, at 452.

[35] *As Vietnam Peace Hopes Fade—U.S. Tries Diplomacy Again*, U.S. NEWS & WORLD REPORT (May 28, 1973), at 82.

aboard.[36] In May, the PRG mortared the team headquarters of the ICCS at Tri Ton and Hong Ngu.[37] On numerous occasions, the Communists prevented ICCS teams from investigating reported violations, including the downing of an RVN helicopter, the PRG attack on Sa Huynh, and the installation of missiles at Khe Sanh.[38] This DRV violence persuaded Canada to withdraw from the ICCS because of danger to its delegates, and it was replaced by Iran.[39] The DRV refused even to pay their required share of ICCS expenses.[40] Even when the ICCS did examine RVN complaints of violations, the unanimity requirement enabled the Hungarian and Polish delegates to block a report on even the most egregious incidents perpetrated by their Vietnamese Communist comrades.[41]

Similarly, the Joint Military Commission (JMC) failed to monitor the cease-fire successfully because of PRG hostility. The PRG and Hanoi refused to even send their delegates to the JMC to examine violations alleged by the RVN.[42] The JMC ceased operating completely in 1974 when one unarmed U.S. observer, investigating a crash site with PRG permission, was shot dead as he got out of his helicopter.[43] Porter's assertion that the PRG eagerly desired implementation of the Agreement would suggest a warm cooperation with the ICCS and JMC. Instead, the PRG exploited the unanimity requirement to abort any reports on its own violations, and in some instances greeted official observers with gunfire.

Porter relied on a captured PRG document from October 1972, which called upon its cadres to engage in an "attack, uprising, and military proselytizing" offensive during the "decisive phase" immediately after the signing of the Agreement and before it

---

[36] *Id.*

[37] 68 DEP'T ST. BULL. 599, 600.

[38] *Id.* at 601.

[39] WASH. POST, July 22, 1973, at 19.

[40] ADMIRAL ULYSSES SHARP, STRATEGY FOR DEFEAT: VIETNAM IN RETROSPECT 261 (1978).

[41] *Non-Policing a Non-Truce, supra* note 19, at 26.

[42] *Foreign Sales Hearing, supra* note 20, at 448.

[43] GOODMAN, *supra* note 23, at 173.

became effective.[44] After January 27, however, the strategy would revert to a political struggle with the RVN, in which the people should "take to the streets to welcome peace" and "organize mass meetings."[45] Although this document is inconsistent with the PRG military operations after the deadline, it seems to lend credence to the argument that the Communists desired peace and were willing to lay down their arms after the cease-fire.

Another interpretation is more consistent with DRV thinking and with what actually transpired after the Accords. Hanoi had nothing to lose by pushing the PRG to seize as much territory as possible before the deadline. If Saigon did not retaliate, the "standstill cease-fire" arrangement of the Agreement would grant all of the captured territory to the PRG, as long as it was captured by 8:00 a.m. on January 28. If Saigon tried to regain the lost hamlets, it would have to do so after the deadline. This would give Hanoi an argument that Thieu was violating Article 2. Thus, the captured PRG document does not necessarily imply that the Communists had abandoned their military designs on Saigon or that they desired a permanent end to the war.

Other Communist documents not available in 1973 now indicate that the DRV had never abandoned its objective of conquering the RVN. In his 1982 autobiography, Communist General Tran Van Tra, leader of the PRG forces in the Mekong, revealed the expansionist thinking in Hanoi during the spring of 1973.[46]

First, Tra makes it clear that control of the South was the unflagging ambition of the Communists before, during, and after the Paris Accords. "By signing the Paris Agreement," Tra admits, Hanoi had "won a victory, but not a complete victory."[47] The ultimate goal was "our just liberation war"—in other words, the war to "liberate" South Vietnam from President Thieu and to

---

[44] *Foreign Sales Hearing, supra* note 20, at 452.

[45] *Id.*

[46] T. VAN TRA, VIETNAM: HISTORY OF THE BULWARK B-2 THEATRE, VOL. 5: CONCLUDING THE THIRTY YEARS' WAR (1982); *see also* P. DAVIDSON, VIETNAM AT WAR: THE HISTORY, 1946-1975, at 769 (1988).

[47] TRA, *supra* note 46, at 36.

replace him with the Hanoi politburo.[48] "The Agreement stipulated the ending of all U.S. military activities against the territory of the DRV by all forces" so that "the socialist North would have very good conditions to develop the great effectiveness of the base area . . . of the revolution in South Vietnam." With the Paris Peace Accords in hand, "if we had good position and strength in the South . . . it was certain that we would victoriously fulfill our glorious revolutionary enterprise, although we would have to overcome many difficulties."[49]

General Tra also confirmed that after a meeting in April 1973—only three months after the Paris Accords—the Hanoi Central Committee issued Resolution 21, which stated:

> the path of the revolution in the South is the path of revolutionary violence. Under all circumstances we must take advantage of the opportunity, maintain the line of strategic offensive, and provide flexible guidance in order to advance the revolution in the South . . . . At present the active, positive direction most beneficial to the revolutionary cause of the entire nation is always holding high the flag of peace and justice, and struggling politically, militarily, and diplomatically to force the enemy to carry out the Paris Agreement, in order to defeat the enemy.[50]

General Tra's account suggests that Hanoi had no intention of abandoning its plans to conquer Saigon. The Paris Agreement merely gave the Communists the opportunity to shift their offensive from the military to the political arena temporarily.

Another captured Communist document confirms Tra's description of Hanoi's real intentions. A PRG directive captured in

---

[48] *Id.* at 34.

[49] *Id.* at 38.

[50] *Id.* at 45. Tra dates the twenty-first plenary conference in April 1973, shortly after the Paris Agreement was signed. However, General Van Tien Dung, commander of all Communist forces, dates it in October 1973, after it was clear that the cease-fire was unworkable. V. TIEN DUNG, OUR GREAT SPRING VICTORY 10 (1977).

1974 disregarded the Paris Agreement—which Hanoi publicly embraced—as a political shroud for the war preparations then under way:

> We must not delude ourselves that we can negotiate peace or national reconciliation with the Thieu clique. We ought to struggle decisively to defeat the new colonialism of the American imperialist and . . . overthrow the Thieu clique. Only thus can national reconciliation and concord be achieved. Thus we have no other choice but to use violence, start the war to totally win the "Vietnamization" war of the enemy and to advance the Revolution. For that reason, to think of obtaining peace by negotiation is to entertain an illusion. We must be prepared for violence. We can only achieve peace by defeating the enemy through war . . . . Hence we must propagandize the people, especially the people in enemy controlled areas and enemy soldiers, that our slogan is peace . . . .[51]

The directive concluded that "a cease-fire is only a postponement; it is not the permanent peace longed for by our people."[52] Instead, "we must now master the concept of violence, above all the violence of war to defeat the enemy."[53]

It is hard to imagine stronger language indicating a contempt for the cease-fire. The DRV had not abandoned the military route; it had instead abandoned the overt and immediate military route. Porter was correct to assert that most of the battles in the weeks immediately following the cease-fire were initiated by the South. Thus, he is also correct to assert that the RVN attacks were violations of Article 2. But these violations were primarily in retaliation for PRG offensives in its last-minute land grab of January 1973. In contrast, many of the PRG cease-fire violations—including their attacks on the ICCS and JMC—cannot be explained away as defensive actions to counter RVN aggression. The RVN publicly stated that it would abide by the cease-fire once the PRG's

---

[51] Goodman, *supra* note 23, at 242.

[52] *Id.* at 243.

[53] *Id.*

land grab was neutralized; in contrast, the PRG and DRV welcomed the Agreement as a cloak for their military designs on Saigon.

When the U.S. negotiators agreed upon January 27 as the cease-fire date, they had intended to crystallize the status quo regarding the military borders. As Kissinger explained:

> I believed then, as I believe now, that the Agreement could have worked. It reflected a true equilibrium of forces on the ground. If the equilibrium were maintained, the Agreement could have been maintained. We believed that Saigon was strong enough to deal with guerilla war and low-level violations. The implicit threat of our retaliation would be likely to deter massive violations.[54]

The military equilibrium was a pillar of the Agreement. But the Paris Agreement froze the map at the time of the Agreement's effective date, not the time the Agreement was reached in principle. Thus, either side had a brief window of opportunity to press its military position forward and grab more land before the borders hardened on January 27 without technically violating the cease-fire provision. The PRG took advantage of this opportunity, forcing the RVN to choose between recapturing the lost territory by post-January 27 military action that violated the cease-fire, or accepting the new borders that changed the equilibrium on which the Agreement was premised. The RVN, with U.S. approval, chose to retaliate after the cease-fire, violating the Agreement and opening itself to charges by the DRV and others that the RVN caused the cease-fire's collapse.

Certainly, the United States had no illusions about the possibility that Thieu—a reluctant participant in the Paris Agreement—would violate the cease-fire by his own military aggression. But any military action by the RVN, other than correcting the PRG's last minute land-grab and defending against PRG attacks, would not have been tolerated by Nixon.

---

[54] H. KISSINGER, WHITE HOUSE YEARS 1470 (1979).

Ambassador Ellsworth Bunker told Thieu in February 1973 that "while it is clear that the other side has and is violating the cease-fire, we can't afford to have the Agreement threatened . . . by actions which are under our control."[55] As Norman Podhoretz acknowledged, the South Vietnamese "were also guilty of violations . . . [b]ut the difference between the two sets of violations was that those committed by the South Vietnamese were measures of self-defense, whereas those committed by the North Vietnamese were aimed at conquest."[56]

Gareth Porter correctly accused the RVN of violating Article 2 immediately following the cease-fire. But his conclusion that Thieu was thus responsible for sabotaging the peace and that his Communist opponents had a "real interest in compliance with the pact"[57] is a fundamentally wrong conclusion from the facts presently available.

Military Obligations of the United States and the DRV

The Paris Agreement included explicit promises by the United States to withdraw completely from the conflict in Vietnam. Article 2 required the United States to cease bombing the North and mining Northern waters; Article 4 prohibited it from intervening militarily in South Vietnam; and Article 5 mandated a total withdrawal of all U.S. forces within sixty days. Conspicuously absent was any provision calling for the withdrawal of North Vietnamese troops from the South. However, Article 7— the best substitute that the American negotiators could obtain from the DRV—prevented the introduction of any troops or war materiel into South Vietnam from any source. This would prohibit the North Vietnamese from moving more forces into the South or from resupplying troops already there. The one exception was the

---

[55] Bunker Cable for Kissinger, February 28, 1973, Backward Messages—1973—Vol. I [Part 2], Nixon Presidential Materials Project, *quoted in* P. Asselin, A Bitter Peace: Washington, Hanoi and the Making of the Paris Agreement 183 (2002).

[56] N. Podhoretz, Why We Were in Vietnam (1982).

[57] *Foreign Sales Hearing, supra* note 20, at 268.

"piece-for-piece" arrangement: each side in the South could seek the replacement of worn out or used equipment if the new items were "of the same characteristics and properties" as the old ones. Even with this loophole, Article 7 would make it difficult for the North Vietnamese to wage war in the South without violating the Agreement.

Other provisions seemed to put a leash on Hanoi's ambitions. Article 15 prohibited reunification of Vietnam by "coercion or annexation by either party," and Article 16 required the parties to respect the demilitarized zone. Finally, Article 20 explicitly prohibited North Vietnam from using the territory of Laos and Cambodia for military operations against the South—effectively shutting down the Ho Chi Minh Trail, at least on paper. Article 20 also required the United States and North Vietnam to "put an end to all military activities in Cambodia and Laos," to "totally withdraw from" these countries, and to "refrain from reintroducing" troops and war materiel into them.

Taken together, the U.S. obligations involved a total disengagement from Vietnam, while the DRV could remain in place, poised for a new offensive. Even so, the Paris Agreement prohibited any buildup in the South and forced the DRV to respect Laos, Cambodia, and the DMZ, its three routes of potential conquest. Any Communist offensive would require months of preparation, which would itself violate the Agreement. Thus, Nixon could accurately report that he had a document that would serve as a legal barrier to the fall of Saigon while permitting the United States to withdraw "honorably."

As the war raged on in 1973 and 1974, both the United States and the Democratic Republic of Vietnam accused each other of violating the Accords. At a press conference on March 15, 1973, President Nixon charged that the DRV was building up its forces in the South in violation of the Agreement.[58] A State Department Bulletin on May 14, 1973, backed up the president's claim with a long list of specific violations.[59] But the DRV had preempted the administration's charges by accusing the United States of

---

[58] *A Warning to Hanoi*, NEWSWEEK, Mar. 26, 1973, at 16.
[59] 68 DEP'T ST. BULL. 599.

violations in February. This put the United States on the defensive, even though it had ample evidence of DRV transgressions.

Central to Hanoi's claim was the charge that the United States had not really pulled out of Vietnam. Instead, the United States had left behind as many as 24,000 military advisors disguised as civilians.[60] Furthermore, Hanoi accused the United States of illegally supplying military equipment to the RVN.[61] The most publicized example of this was the transfer of 150 F-5E aircraft to the Saigon army well after January 27.[62] Lastly, the DRV accused the U.S. of continuing to bomb Cambodia in violation of Article 20 in February and March 1973.

Some in the American press were making the same arguments. David Shipler of the *New York Times* wrote a scathing portrayal of U.S. noncompliance with the Agreement.[63] He alleged that the U.S. aid to Saigon was encouraging Thieu to violate the Accords and that the United States was illegally managing the RVN war effort with thousands of disguised military advisors. He also implied that the United States was illegally supplying war items to Saigon, while the North Vietnamese were complying with the Agreement. Shipler's investigative report prompted a strongly worded rebuttal from U.S. Ambassador to South Vietnam Graham Martin, who cooperated with his investigation while Shipler was in Saigon. He said the article was filled with "inaccuracies and half-truths" and that it "deliberately omits" evidence of DRV violations and U.S. compliance, which was "pointed out repeatedly to Shipler."[64]

Another example of the charge of U.S. noncompliance came from Richard Falk, an antiwar spokesman, in a 1974 article

---

[60] DOES THE U.S. RESPECT ITS COMMITMENT TO END THE WAR IN VIETNAM? 5 (DRV Pamphlet, 1974) [hereinafter U.S. RESPECT].

[61] *Id.* at 17.

[62] *Id.* at 19.

[63] Shipler, *Vast Aid From U.S. Backs Saigon in Continuing War*, N.Y. TIMES (Feb. 25, 1974), at 21.

[64] *Vietnam—A Changing Crucible: Report of a Study Commission to South Vietnam for House Comm. on Foreign Affairs*, 93d Cong., 2d Sess. 35 (1974) [hereinafter *Crucible*].

marking the first anniversary of the Accords.[65] Falk stated that "in direct violation of the Paris Agreement[,] the United States is pouring military equipment into South Vietnam," while in contrast the "North Vietnamese and PRG official publications have continued to emphasize adherence to the Paris cease-fire . . . ." In short, "the United States has openly flouted a central feature of the Paris Agreement and has not been called to account."[66]

Long before these press accounts, Gareth Porter conveyed the same message to Congress in hearings on the administration's military aid request for South Vietnam. In May 1973, Porter found the Nixon administration's arguments lacking. He referred to the "massive buildup" of Saigon forces with U.S. aid and the transfer of U.S. equipment as violations of Article 7. While admitting the influx of North Vietnamese troops, he dismissed this development as a "response to the major new arms aid to President Thieu."[67] The administration's facts about the Communist buildup were not "reliable indicators of an imminent North Vietnamese offensive drive."[68] Instead, by accusing Hanoi of violating the truce, "the United States appears to be trying to establish a justification for later military intervention rather than trying to obtain compliance with the Agreement by all sides."[69]

The arguments that the United States was not complying with the withdrawal provisions are hard to support. Within sixty days of the cease-fire—as required in Article 5—the U.S. military had pulled its combat forces out of South Vietnam. Within the first week, 3,100 American troops left, and 20,000 came home over the next two months.[70] That first week also saw more than 40,000 tons of military equipment returned to the United States.[71] By May 1973, there were only 200 American military personnel remaining, all of whom either had supervisory functions under the JMC, were

---

[65] Falk, *Breaking Faith in Vietnam*, NATION (Jan. 12, 1974), at 38.

[66] *Id.* at 40.

[67] *Foreign Sales Hearing, supra* note 20, at 454.

[68] *Id.*

[69] *Id.* at 268.

[70] *No Calm After the Storm*, NEWSWEEK (Feb. 12, 1973), at 18.

[71] *Id.* at 18.

designated to help recover MIAs, or were associated with the Embassy security or the Defense Attaché Office.[72] The charge of 24,000 military advisors disguised as civilians is highly suspect: the Embassy records indicate the total number of official American personnel in all Vietnam was only 9,000.[73] Given the size and length of the American presence in Vietnam during the war, the speed and magnitude of the American pullout in early 1973 was remarkable.

Porter is correct to state that the United States transferred 1,300 fixed-wing aircraft, 800 helicopters, 1,500 howitzers, and 150 tanks to South Vietnam.[74] However, all of this equipment had been transferred to the RVN well before the January 27 deadline.[75] Thus, this war materiel was owned by the RVN and not the United States and was not subject to withdrawal under Article 5. In fact, all military equipment that had not been transferred to the RVN before January 27 was removed from Vietnam by March 28, 1973.[76] The evidence confirms substantial U.S. compliance with the withdrawal provisions.

The best evidence suggesting U.S. noncompliance was the widely publicized transfer of F-5E aircraft to the RVN. Article 7 permitted a "piece-by-piece" transfer of war materiel that was used up or damaged, if the new materiel was "of the same characteristics or properties." The RVN had numerous 1959 model F-5A fighter jets. The Department of Defense agreed to replace these fighters on a one-for-one basis with the 1972 model F-5Es, which were much faster and more maneuverable. The DRV charged that the United States was trying to "modernize the RVN air force" with a new brand of aircraft whose characteristics were "completely different."[77] This transfer was "a gross violation of Article 7."[78] However, the F-5As were "no longer available."[79] The

---

[72] 68 DEP'T ST. BULL., at 602.

[73] *Id.*

[74] *Foreign Sales Hearing, supra* note 20, at 454.

[75] 68 DEP'T ST. BULL., at 601.

[76] *Id.*

[77] U.S. RESPECT, *supra* note 60, at 18.

[78] *Id.* at 19.

[79] *Crucible, supra* note 64, at 34.

United States exchanged the F-5As for the only substitute that was available and viewed this exchange as a "piece-by-piece" transfer of the aircraft under Article 7. This transfer does not support an argument that the United States broke its promises at Paris.

In contrast, the evidence of flagrant and systematic North Vietnamese violations is staggering. It is now clear that Hanoi never ceased its preparations for war in the South. Despite Article 7's "piece-for-piece" limitation and Article 20's requirement of withdrawal from Laos and Cambodia, North Vietnam engaged in a massive infiltration of troops along the Ho Chi Minh Trail. Between January and March 1973, the DRV moved 40,000 men, 300 tanks, 150 heavy artillery pieces, 160 antiaircraft guns, and 300 trucks down the Trail.[80] In fact, the only change since January 27 was that "the North Vietnamese were driving southward in broad daylight, since they no longer were fearful of U.S. air strikes."[81] One observer stated that the Trail "looks like the New Jersey Turnpike during rush hour."[82] By April, only one month later, the DRV had added another 100 tanks and 150 heavy artillery pieces, for an estimated total of 27,000 tons of military equipment.[83] In addition to the massive violations along the Ho Chi Minh Trail in Laos and Cambodia, U.S. intelligence in May recorded 7,000 military crossings of the demilitarized zone dividing North and South Vietnam, in direct violation of Article 16.[84] In his autobiography, General Tra confirms that the DRV was funneling supplies to the South, recalling that the "weapons and equipment being supplied by the General Staff to B2 in 1973 were being received and transported efficiently."[85]

Because of the veto power of the Hungarian and Polish delegations, the ICCS proved incapable of policing these violations. In July, the Canadian delegation resigned from the ICCS in protest over the egregious DRV infiltration. The Canadian

---

[80] *A Trail Becomes a Turnpike*, TIME (Mar. 26, 1973), at 34.

[81] *Id.*

[82] *Id.*

[83] 68 DEP'T ST. BULL., at 599.

[84] *Id.*

[85] TRA, *supra* note 46, at 60.

team released a report detailing the Communist buildup and were resigning in part because the report "would never see the light of day" after it was voted on by the ICCS.[86] The report was "based on the testimony of captured North Vietnamese soldiers" whose statements "generally corroborated each other and fitted in with information from other sources."[87] These soldiers "left their own country about the time the Paris Agreement was signed" and "were instructed to keep coming."[88] The DRV troops had no contact with PRG soldiers, "except when they changed from North Vietnamese to Viet Cong uniforms at the border."[89] In conclusion, the Canadian team reported that "there has never been the slightest indication during the four and a half months of the cease-fire that the [DRV] has modified its infiltration policy," constituting a "deliberate violation of the Paris Truce Agreement."[90] In January 1973, there were 145,000 DRV troops in the South; by January 1975, their ranks had swelled to 300,000.[91]

Despite the evidence indicating U.S. compliance and DRV violations of the Agreement, the majority in the U.S. Congress shared the views of Gareth Porter, not Elliot Richardson. After Nixon vetoed a prohibition on combat operations by U.S. forces in Indochina, Congress sought to "tie" appropriations to such a ban.[92] On July 1, 1973, President Nixon reluctantly signed two appropriations bills that solidified America's surrender in Vietnam. The famous language attached to both bills was originally drafted by Senators Clifford Case (R-NJ) and Frank Church (D-ID). The Case-Church Amendment prohibited any expenditure of funds "directly or indirectly" for combat activities "in or over" or "off the shores of" Laos, Cambodia, North Vietnam, or South Vietnam

---

[86] *Canadians Say Hanoi Broke Pact*, WASH. POST (July 22, 1973), at 19.

[87] *Id.*

[88] *Id.*

[89] *Id.*

[90] *Id.*

[91] *Red's Big Drive in Vietnam: Will America Rush to the Rescue?*, U.S. NEWS & WORLD REPORT (Jan. 27, 1975), at 26.

[92] E. HALEY, CONGRESS AND THE FALL OF SOUTH VIETNAM AND CAMBODIA 42 (1982).

after August 16, 1973.[93] Nixon was no longer authorized to retaliate against the DRV anywhere in Indochina for its violations of the Paris Agreement. In October 1973, Congress further tied Nixon's hands with the War Powers Resolution. It prohibited the introduction of U.S. armed forces into "hostilities, or into situations where imminent involvement in hostilities is clearly indicated by the circumstances," without a congressional declaration of war, a congressional statutory authorization, or an emergency caused by an attack on the United States.[94]

Congress thus kicked aside a key buttress of the Agreement. As Kissinger told Nixon on January 9, 1973, Le Duc Tho had "repeatedly" told Kissinger that "[w]hat brought us to this point" in the negotiations was Nixon's "firmness and the North Vietnamese belief that [Nixon] will not be affected by either Congressional or public pressures."[95] "I knew," wrote Nixon, "that since Congress had removed the possibility of military action, I had only words with which to threaten. The Communists knew it too."[96] With these acts of Congress, it was obvious to Hanoi that "[t]he peace treaty could no longer be enforced" and "Hanoi now had a free hand."[97] Kissinger told reporters in 1975 that Congress caused the major North Vietnamese invasion by cutting aid to Thieu, and if he had known Congress would slash aid so drastically, he would never have negotiated the Paris Agreement.[98] In a letter to Congress, Nixon wanted the legislative branch "to be fully aware of the consequences of its actions."[99] He told them, "I can only hope the North Vietnamese will not draw the erroneous conclusion from this Congressional action that they are free to launch a military offensive in Indo-China."[100]

---

[93] L. FANNING, BETRAYAL IN VIETNAM 159 (1976).

[94] SHARP, *supra* note 40, at 263-64.

[95] KISSINGER, *supra* note 54, at 1464.

[96] R. NIXON, RN: THE MEMOIRS OF RICHARD NIXON 888 (1978); *quoted in* PODHORETZ, *supra* note 56, at 164.

[97] Sharp, *supra* note 40, at 263.

[98] WASHINGTON STAR (Mar. 20, 1975), *quoted in* HALEY, *supra* note 92, at 81.

[99] FANNING, *supra* note 93, at 159.

[100] *Id.*

The DRV drew precisely that conclusion. General Dung revealed that the potential for U.S. re-entry into the war was the critical factor in 1973-74 for deciding when to begin its military offensive.[101] DRV violations of the Agreement grew exponentially after Congress' votes. A January 1975 State Department report noted that North Vietnam had moved over 170,000 troops into South Vietnam—a direct violation of the Agreement.[102] The DRV had also brought an additional 400 tanks illegally into the South, which flagrantly violated the Agreement's "one-for-one" limitations on replacement of military equipment in the South. In contrast, Congress refused the administration's requests to replace the dilapidated RVN equipment in response, which would have complied with the Agreement.[103] When Thieu visited Washington in February 1975, he not only failed to win more support from Congress; Majority Leader Mike Mansfield and Minority Leader Hugh Scott refused even to meet his delegation.[104] With the United States out of the picture, the DRV launched a massive attack on the South, which ended with Americans and South Vietnamese clawing for space on U.S. evacuation helicopters in April 1975.

Nixon and Kissinger had signed the Paris Agreement under the assumption that the threat of a bombing retaliation in Hanoi plus firm U.S. support for Thieu would effectively deter any violations by the North. "We had no illusions about Hanoi's long-term goals," said Kissinger in retrospect, but "[w]e were determined to do our utmost to enable Saigon to grow in security and prosperity so that it could prevail in any political struggle."[105] Instead, Hanoi's violations of the Paris Agreement were rewarded by a congressional abandonment of Thieu and a very public restraint of Nixon's power to respond militarily.

While Nixon later blamed Watergate for his loss of executive power, Congress' resistance should have been foreseen. A Gallup poll on the day of the Agreement asked: "If North Vietnam does

[101] DUNG, *supra* note 50, at 19.

[102] SHARP, *supra* note 40, at 265.

[103] *Id.*

[104] *Id.* at 265.

[105] KISSINGER, *supra* note 54, at 1470.

try to take over South Vietnam again, do you think the U.S. should bomb North Vietnam, or not?" Seventy-one percent of Americans said "no."[106] Such strong antiwar sentiment, and an increasingly antiwar Congress, meant that congressional barriers to any retaliatory efforts by Nixon were inevitable after 1973.

The Wars in Laos and Cambodia

A bloody sideshow to the Vietnam War played out in the neighboring countries to the west. Both Laos and Cambodia were severed by the main North Vietnamese artery of military supply to South Vietnam, the Ho Chi Minh Trail. In addition, each neighbor had its own Communist insurgency that was supported by Hanoi. In Laos, the Communist Pathet Lao were engaged in a guerrilla war against non-Communist Prime Minister Souvanna Phouma. The Communist Khmer Rouge were seeking to oust the U.S.-supported Lon Nol from power in Cambodia. Article 20 of the Paris Agreement required both the United States and North Vietnam to:

> put an end to all military activities in Cambodia and Laos, totally withdraw from and refrain from reintroducing into these two countries troops, military advisers and military personnel, armaments, munitions, and war materiel.

While the United States complied with this provision, the North Vietnamese openly violated it from the very moment of the cease-fire.

The Laotian war was a comparatively minor problem. The North Vietnamese aided the Pathet Lao after the cease-fire in attacks on Pak Song on February 23 and on Tha Vieng on April 13.[107] Both of these incidents were clear violations of Article 20. In response, the United States announced that it would give military aid at the request of Prime Minister Phouma.[108] By

---

[106] BERMAN, *supra* note 27, at 262.

[107] 68 DEP'T ST. BULL., at 602.

[108] FANNING, *supra* note 93, at 146.

May, however, the Laotian parties had worked out a cease-fire of their own.[109] After May 1973, the only Article 20 violation by North Vietnam in Laos was the unrelenting infiltration of troops and equipment down the Ho Chi Minh Trail.

The Cambodian conflict was the source of much greater controversy. In his testimony before the Senate Foreign Relations Committee in May 1973, Gareth Porter accused the United States of violating Article 20 by bombing Cambodia after January 27. He argued that this action was clearly prohibited by the Agreement. A Cambodian cease-fire was contemplated by the Paris Agreement, but the United States was disregarding that document to pursue a military victory for Lon Nol.[110]

Secretary Richardson responded to these charges under the questioning of Senator Jacob Javits (R-NY).[111] Richardson explained that on January 29, two days after the Vietnam cease-fire, the Lon Nol government had unilaterally halted hostilities to seek a peaceful accommodation with the Khmer Rouge. U.S. air support for Lon Nol also ceased at that time. However, the Communists exploited the cease-fire by accelerating their offensive. At that time, there were no American troops in Cambodia, but there were 50,000 North Vietnamese troops there.[112] By February 7, the Lon Nol government had been forced to resume its military action. On February 8, at the request of Lon Nol, the United States also resumed its bombing campaign, citing the widespread North Vietnamese violations of Article 20 in Cambodia. At least 10,000 of the 50,000 DRV soldiers in Cambodia were fighting with the Khmer Rouge against Lon Nol.[113] The U.S. bombing raids were retaliatory strikes against DRV violations of Article 20 in Cambodia.

---

[109] 68 DEP'T ST. BULL., at 602.

[110] *Foreign Sales Hearing, supra* note 20, at 267.

[111] *Id.* at 297. Secretary of State William Rogers made similar arguments to the Senate Appropriations Committee in March 1973. *See Second Supplemental Appropriations for Fiscal Year 1973: Hearings before the Senate Comm. on Appropriations*, 93d Cong., 1st Sess. 2091 (1973).

[112] *Foreign Sales Hearing, supra* note 20, at 292.

[113] *Id.* at 293.

After the hearings in May 1973, a movement to pass anti-bombing legislation swept through Congress. An amendment was added to the 1973 Second Supplemental Appropriations Bill to prohibit the use of funds for military activity in Laos or Cambodia.[114] During the Senate debate, Majority Leader Mike Mansfield (D-MT) praised the amendment because it would "let these people decide their own destinies."[115] In response, Senator John Tower (R-TX) retorted: "Well, let us get the North Vietnamese out of there so they *can* work it out for themselves."[116] Senator Birch Bayh (D-IN) went on to chastise the United States for violating Article 20 and argued that North Vietnamese violations were no excuse for violating the Agreement ourselves.[117] This virtually guaranteed that DRV aggression would be encouraged, not deterred.[118] The Eagleton Amendment passed in the Senate 73-5 on May 31, 1973.[119] On June 13, 1973, the Case-Church Amendment extended that prohibition into the next year's budget. As a further blow, Nixon's aid request to Cambodia was slashed by $50 million in 1974.[120]

Congress' votes meant the death penalty for a free Cambodia. As Henry Kissinger explained:

Of all the countries in Indo-China, the Cambodians behaved most nobly and suffered for their patriotism in the most cruel fashion—not least at the hands of those in our country who professed to be outraged at our alleged violation of their neutrality and who then moved heaven and earth to prevent adequate support for them when North Vietnamese divisions

---

[114] HR 7447, Sec. 305, *quoted in* FANNING, *supra* note 93, at 149.

[115] CONG. REC., May 29, 1973, *quoted in* FANNING, *supra* note 93, at 150.

[116] *Id.*

[117] *Id.*

[118] Ironically, Senator Bayh had said years earlier: "There can be little question that if we are to turn tail and run, the entire South East Asia area . . . would come under Communist domination." CONG. REC., Mar. 16, 1965, *quoted in* PHAM KIM VINH, THE VIETNAMESE HOLOCAUST AND THE CONSCIENCE OF NATIONS 21 (1979).

[119] FANNING, *supra* note 93, at 151.

[120] *Id.* at 165.

and Khmer Rouge were despoiling that innocent country long after our troops had left.[121]

Without American backing, the Lon Nol government was doomed to destruction. The Khmer Rouge rebels took Phnom Phenh in early 1975, as Richardson had predicted. Within three years of the conquest, over a million Cambodians were slaughtered by their new Communist rulers.

THE DEBATE OVER VIOLATIONS OF THE POLITICAL PROVISIONS OF THE PARIS PEACE AGREEMENT

In addition to the provisions directing an end to the hostilities, the Paris Peace Agreement attempted to provide the framework for a political settlement in Vietnam. The political provisions were the subject of great controversy in America, where allegations of RVN violations had a direct impact on congressional aid to President Thieu.

In their many years of battle, both North and South Vietnam had accumulated a large number of prisoners. Article 8 of the Paris Peace Accords required the immediate exchange of prisoners of war and active cooperation in locating any soldiers missing in action.[122] The return of U.S. POWs had been a paramount concern of U.S. negotiators in Paris. Beyond this arrangement, Article 8 also required the return of "Vietnamese civilian personnel" imprisoned by the two South Vietnamese parties. This ambiguous term apparently referred to non-military political prisoners held by the PRG or RVN.

The Agreement also contemplated free elections in South Vietnam to determine its political control. Article 9 required "genuinely free and democratic general elections under international supervision."[123] To pave the way for these elections, the PRG and RVN were explicitly required to

---

[121] KISSINGER, *supra* note 54, at 1465.

[122] 24 U.S.T., art. 8, at 7.

[123] *Id.*, art. 9, at 8.

ensure the democratic liberties of the people: personal freedom, freedom of speech, freedom of the press, freedom of meeting, freedom of organization, freedom of political activities, freedom of belief, freedom of movement, freedom of residence, freedom of work, right to property ownership, and right to free enterprise.[124]

With such explicit guarantees, both sides would be forced to abandon repressive military conduct in the villages as well as on the battlefield. This would enable the South Vietnamese people to decide objectively whether Thieu or his Communist opponents would lead them in the future.

Although the DRV had decided to de-emphasize overt military warfare in early 1973, Articles 8 and 11 gave it potent weapons with which to assault the RVN by political warfare. The Communists engaged in a sustained propaganda barrage against Thieu by arguing that he was deliberately violating the political provisions of the Accords. Since Thieu was a repressive dictator, the argument went, he was refusing to loosen up his political controls lest he be ousted by the PRG in a peaceful political contest. Furthermore, the United States was propping up this oppressive regime through its aid to Thieu, much of which was used to abuse his own people.

Central to this claim was the allegation that Thieu was detaining thousands of political prisoners in violation of the Agreement. One DRV pamphlet in 1974 alleged that Thieu's police had herded over 1.6 million people into 160 concentration camps across South Vietnam.[125] The more celebrated figure was 200,000 political prisoners, which appeared in an official Hanoi press release in January 1974.[126] This figure was also presented by Father Chan Tin, a non-Communist South Vietnamese dissident, who tended to give the claim greater credibility in U.S. eyes. Pham Hong Linh, a DRV jurist, quoted the "treasured words" of Ho Chi

---

[124] *Id.*, art. 11, at 9.

[125] U.S. RESPECT, *supra* note 60, at 28.

[126] Press Release, Ministry of Foreign Affairs, DRV, Hanoi, Jan. 1974, *reprinted in* GOODMAN, *supra* note 23, at 220.

Minh that "nothing is more precious than independence and freedom," while noting that "Thieu has trampled under foot the 'rights and liberties of the citizens'" and "hundreds of thousands of people have been arbitrarily arrested, thrown into prison, and barbarously tortured because they demand peace."[127] He condemned the "Thieu administration's complete disregard for democratic liberties months after coming into force of the cease-fire prescribed by the Paris Agreement."[128]

The American press published many reports about the South Vietnamese prisons. *Newsweek* magazine reported that "nearly 45,000 South Vietnamese have been tried, convicted, and jailed for political offenses, and up to 100,000 others have been arrested and thrown into prisons everywhere . . . without trial."[129] Many of these prisoners were allegedly crammed into "tiger cages" for their political dissent. *Time* magazine said of the men in these cages: "It is not really proper to call them men any more." Instead, "shapes is a better word—grotesque sculptures of scarred flesh and gnarled limbs."[130] Far less frequent were reports of prison conditions in North Vietnam or the PRG territory beyond the view of Western journalists.

Hanoi's propaganda offensive on the political prisoner issue struck a receptive chord in many American hearts. In fact, many antiwar activists pursued their own investigation into the issue—without any comparable investigation into Communist prisons. Most prominent among these were Tom Hayden and his wife, actress Jane Fonda. As chairman of the "Indo-China Peace Campaign," Hayden made several expeditions to South Vietnam.[131] Under the sponsorship of Congressman Ronald Dellums, Hayden and Fonda were granted use of a House Judiciary Committee room to give a series of lectures in February 1974.[132]

---

[127] Pham Hong Linh, "Democratic Liberties in South Vietnam," *printed in* THE PARIS AGREEMENT ON VIETNAM: FUNDAMENTAL JURIDICIAL PROBLEMS 126-27 (July 1973).

[128] *Id.*

[129] NEWSWEEK (Dec. 8, 1972), *quoted in* GOODMAN, *supra* note 23, at 219.

[130] TIME (Mar. 19, 1973), *quoted in* GOODMAN, *supra* note 23, at 219.

[131] FANNING, *supra* note 93, at 168.

[132] *Id.*

The lectures, entitled "U.S. Relations With Southeast Asia," presented arguments identical to those being made in DRV propaganda pamphlets. Hayden told his audience that the struggle for democratic rights in North Vietnam had become a priority for the Hanoi government, although "it could not be carried out so well under all the bombing."[133] In contrast, the human rights record under Thieu was abysmal:

> I think you know very well what the struggle [by the PRG] for democratic rights consists of in the South. It consists essentially of the struggle to implement the Paris Agreement's political provisions. That the hundreds of thousands of political prisoners who should have been released, must be.[134]

Following these lectures, thirty-five congressional aides who had listened to Hayden formed the Capitol Hill Coordinating Committee, whose sole purpose was to sever all aid to South Vietnam.[135]

Just as visible was Congresswoman Bella Abzug of New York. Abzug also journeyed to South Vietnam, where she interviewed numerous prisoners and dissidents. In September 1973, and again in May 1974, the House Subcommittee on Asian and Pacific Affairs held hearings on the treatment of political prisoners in South Vietnamese jails. Abzug was a key witness in both hearings.

Abzug described the South Vietnamese prison situation as "one of the most compelling tragedies of our time—a spectacle of mass roundups, torture and mistreatment of tens of thousands of men and women and children which must be ended."[136] But the blood was not only on Thieu's hands:

---

[133] 31 Guild Prac. 99.

[134] *Id.*

[135] FANNING, *supra* note 93, at 168.

[136] *The Treatment of Political Prisoners in South Vietnam by the Government of the Republic of South Vietnam: Hearing Before the Subcomm. on Asian and Pacific Affairs of the House Comm. on Foreign Affairs*, 93d Cong., 1st Sess. 2 (1973) [hereinafter *Prisoner Treatment Hearing*].

U.S. aid to South Vietnam has been outrageously misrepresented as humanitarian aid to rebuild South Vietnam. In fact, most of it is military and police aid which is enabling the Thieu government to avoid observing the Paris Agreement. Its refusal to release its political prisoners, as called for in the Paris Agreement, is the most dramatic illustration of this misuse of American aid.[137]

As a representative example, Abzug referred to Madame Ngo Ba Thanh as "a leader in Vietnam of the women's peace movement and an outspoken advocate of civil rights."[138] She and the other prisoners were "being held in jail solely because they—or their friends or relatives—do not agree with President Thieu."[139] She agreed that Congress' "continued funding of the police and prison system" with its "massive numbers of political prisoners" was the stumbling block that made peace in South Vietnam impossible.[140] "If no political opposition is allowed," she told her fellow Congressmen, "opponents of Thieu can only turn to military solutions."[141] Accordingly, a slash in aid to South Vietnam was necessary to have peace in Indochina and to free its people from repression.

Identical arguments were espoused by Gareth Porter and Fred Branfman of the Indo-China Resources Center. Congressman Robert Nix of Pennsylvania, the acting chairman, shed some light on the charged political context of the hearings when he introduced the two expert witnesses. "The President is one of those rare individuals who has the capacity to use ambiguities to hide factual situations," Nix proclaimed as the Watergate scandal unraveled, "but we do not intend to have him fool us anymore."[142] Porter and

---

[137] *Id.*

[138] *Id.* at 4.

[139] *Political Prisoners in South Vietnam and the Philippines: Hearings Before the Subcomm. on Asian and Pacific Affairs of the House Comm. on Foreign Affairs*, 93d Cong., 2d Sess. 4 (1974) [hereinafter *Vietnam & Philippines Hearing*].

[140] *Prisoner Treatment Hearing, supra* note 136, at 8.

[141] *Id.*

[142] *Vietnam & Philippines Hearing, supra* note 139, at 38.

Branfman proceeded to illustrate just how Nixon was fooling the Congress. "There is substantial evidence of a willingness by the PRG and the North Vietnamese to abide by the terms of the Paris Agreement," Porter alleged, "if the U.S. will prevail upon Thieu to do the same."[143] However, Congress' "unconditional support for the Thieu regime," which disregards the political provisions of the Agreement, "leaves no option open for the other side—except another military onslaught."[144] Branfman echoed these concerns, warning that Congress's inaction in foreign affairs "has brought us to a near dictatorship in this country."[145] In short, "we think a suspension in aid, a Pause for Peace, is the fastest way to end this thing."[146]

The political prisoner debate was directly tied to congressional decisions about aid to Thieu, beginning at least with the McGovern Amendment to the Second Supplemental Appropriations Bill in 1973. Senator George McGovern (D-SD) demanded that the Congress "condition any further aid of any kind to South Vietnam on the release of all political prisoners," a condition that would be verified by the ICCS.[147] With the demonstrated partisanship of the Hungarian and Polish delegates to the ICCS, this restriction would guarantee that no aid would ever reach Thieu. McGovern's rider was defeated, only to be replaced on June 25 by an amendment outlawing any military activities in Cambodia or Laos.[148] This was the same Senator McGovern who, in 1965, said of Vietnam: "I would hope that we would be prepared to wage such a [prolonged] conflict rather than surrender the area to Communism."[149]

On December 17, 1973, McGovern's idea had greater success. The Foreign Assistance Act of 1973 authorized aid to South Vietnam under the condition that none of the money "will be used for support of police, or prison construction and administration."[150]

---

[143] *Id.* at 46.

[144] *Id.*

[145] *Id.* at 47.

[146] *Id.* at 48.

[147] FANNING, *supra* note 93, at 148.

[148] *Id.* at 153.

[149] CONG. REC., Jan. 15, 1965, *quoted in* VINH, *supra* note 118, at 20.

[150] FANNING, *supra* note 93, at 165.

Three days later, Senator William Fulbright (D-AR) wrote Kissinger, "The practice of political detention and of the maltreatment of prisoners by South Vietnamese authorities should weigh heavily on the conscience of all Americans . . . . I simply do not see how we can, in good conscience, deny any responsibility for the heinous acts of a government which owes its total existence to our support."[151]

In 1974, the Nixon administration tried desperately to push a supplemental aid package to South Vietnam through the Congress. Senator Edward M. Kennedy (D-MA) successfully attached an amendment that barred the emergency transfer of $266 million to South Vietnam.[152] This was the same Senator Kennedy who declared in 1965: "Do we want to defend freedom? We do, because it is our commitment, our heritage, our destiny."[153]

The aid package for 1975 met with even stiffer resistance. Nixon requested a relatively modest $1.4 billion for South Vietnam, warning that anything less would "affect their ability to defend their country against continuing Communist military pressure."[154] Congress allowed only $700 million—one-half of Nixon's request. After Watergate and Nixon's resignation, an even more antiwar and antiadministration Congress was elected in November 1974. In January 1975, President Ford was forced to sign a bill authorizing only $449 million for the next year.[155] The end result was that the United States, after billions of dollars and 50,000 lives invested in South Vietnam's survival, severed almost all support to its ally.[156] The statements of McGovern and others made it clear that the political prisoner issue was a key reason for slashing aid to Thieu.

The available prison data does not support the conclusion that Thieu systematically violated the political provisions of the

---

[151] BERMAN, *supra* note 27, at 254.

[152] FANNING, *supra* note 93, at 172.

[153] Nov. 1965, *quoted in* VINH, *supra* note 118, at 20.

[154] FANNING, *supra* note 93, at 175.

[155] *Id.* at 178.

[156] D. WALTON, THE MYTH OF THE INEVITABLE U.S. DEFEAT IN VIETNAM 143 (2002).

Agreement. President Thieu listed 5,081 prisoners in his jails as Communist political prisoners and promised they would be released as required in the Paris Agreement.[157] The remaining prisoners, he claimed, were convicted "common law" criminals. As promised, the RVN began releasing its political prisoners. By September 1973, 1,500 Communists had been set free by the South Vietnamese government.[158] Thieu also told a nationwide U.S. television audience on April 8, 1973, that anyone could visit his prisons to explore conditions there.[159] The visits of Hayden, Abzug, and others confirm that Thieu stood by his word.

Father Chan Tin's status as a non-Communist Catholic critic of Thieu and his prisons granted much credibility to his claim of 200,000 political prisoners in the South. First, Father Chan Tin's very presence as a visible and outspoken critic of Thieu should have indicated something about the relative political freedoms in the two regimes. Second, the total number of the *entire* prison population in South Vietnam was only 35,000.[160] This was a tiny fraction of the alleged community of political prisoners. The 35,000 figure included common criminals as well as the political dissenters. Even if one is skeptical of Thieu's figure of 5,081 political prisoners, it is impossible that the real number was anywhere close to 200,000, as was so frequently alleged. Instead, as Congressman Peter Frelinghuysen (R-NJ) noted, the figure was "exaggerated out of all proportion by those who are determined to discredit the Thieu government by any means at their disposal."[161]

Some of the dispute over the true figure was rooted in the ambiguity of the term "political prisoner." U.S. Ambassador to South Vietnam Graham Martin and his staff made a study of the issue prior to his report to the House Subcommittee on Asian and Pacific Affairs in July 1974. Martin's investigation confirmed that the total prison population of the RVN was 35,000, although it had

---

[157] *Prisoner Treatment Hearing, supra* note 136, at 3.
[158] *Id.* at 3.
[159] *Id.* at 7.
[160] *Crucible, supra* note 64, at 14.
[161] *Id.*

been reduced to 31,000 after Thieu's releases.[162] As for the allegations of detained political prisoners, Martin noted that the American definition of "political prisoner" was quite different from that used in Indochina. Martin defined the term as "someone who is in jail only because of his opposition to the regime."[163] In the South Vietnamese context, political prisoners are defined as "those who have used murder as an instrument of political argument"[164] or who "blow up installations."[165] To explain this, he cited an example used by Madame Ngo Ba Thanh, the celebrated dissident who, incidentally, was quite free to comment on such things. When asked if Sirhan Sirhan, the assassin of Robert Kennedy, would be considered a political prisoner, she said emphatically yes.[166] Using the American definition of political prisoner, Martin admitted that "I cannot say there are none in Vietnam."[167] However, Martin testified that he had "investigated every name given to me [by Thieu's critics] and we have yet to find one who would not be in jail for the same offenses if convicted in any country that you would care to name as an exemplar of democratic liberties in the world today."[168]

Most likely, Thieu was delaying release of prisoners until the DRV and PRG lived up to their obligations. It was his only leverage to pressure the Communists to comply with the Agreement. In fact, he may have reclassified some military prisoners as civilian prisoners in the sixty days before U.S. withdrawal to maximize this pressure.[169] Far from encouraging these tactics, the United States leaned on Thieu to open his prisons. In March 1973, Kissinger cabled Bunker reporting that Le Duc Tho had pressed him on Thieu's release of civilian prisoners. "I know you have taken this up with Thieu on several occasions, but absolutely nothing seems to have happened. Although Le Duc Tho

---

[162] *Report on South Vietnam, supra* note 26, at 8.

[163] *Id.* at 32.

[164] *Id.* at 8.

[165] *Id.* at 32.

[166] *Id.* at 8.

[167] *Id.* at 32.

[168] *Id.* at 32-33.

[169] Berman, *supra* note 27, at 253.

conveniently overstates the precision of our obligations, there is no question that we are committed to making a maximum effort with the [RVN] on this issue."[170]

Even if one accepted the most exaggerated allegations of RVN repression, Article 11 would not have been violated. The Agreement's list of "democratic liberties" were to be granted by the two South Vietnamese parties only after the cease-fire was implemented. However, there was never a cease-fire. President Thieu could hardly be expected to release thousands of Communist prisoners to sabotage his government from within while the PRG forces continued to assault his borders. Even so, under U.S. pressure, Thieu released 4,000 prisoners by the summer of 1974.[171]

Aside from the factual shakiness of the allegations of widespread violations of Articles 8 and 11 by Thieu, the fundamental premise of the argument was flawed. Logically, Thieu's motivation for violating the political provisions of the Accords must have been that he feared the result of a free political election in South Vietnam. Yet the evidence does not support this theory. Rather than rejecting the elections, President Thieu had "repeatedly called for definite dates for such elections" under international supervision.[172] The PRG had rejected these offers, claiming that there could be no free election under Thieu's regime. In a study of this issue on a month-long mission to South Vietnam, a congressional team led by Republican Peter Frelinghuysen of New Jersey concluded that the PRG was the barrier to elections.[173] Thieu desired elections because "under any impartial election—with adequate international controls and supervision—he would win overwhelmingly." Furthermore, "no informed diplomatic observer or intelligence analyst seriously questions this contention."[174] The mass migration of refugees fleeing from the North Vietnamese Communists after 1975 demonstrates

---

[170] *Id.* at 254.

[171] *Report on South Vietnam, supra* note 26, at 8.

[172] *Crucible, supra* note 64, at 12.

[173] *Id.*

[174] *Id.*

dramatically how large numbers of Vietnamese felt about the relative freedoms available under the two regimes.

Ironically, Thieu's position is confirmed by his nemesis, General Tran Van Tra of the DRV. Tra's autobiography refers to a captured RVN private policy directive, which outlined Thieu's objectives after the Paris Agreement. For the initial phase, Thieu intended to regain the territory lost to the PRG in a land-grab. Once this was accomplished, the second phase would be a time to "consolidate the gains" and "defend them solidly." Third, in a period coming "at latest" in 1975, Thieu said "there would be a political solution and a general elections to make things legal." By this time, "the war will wither away," and "the Viet Cong will only be an opposition party which engages exclusively in political struggle, nothing more and nothing less."[175] This document is consistent with the public statements made by President Thieu, and demonstrates his desire for free elections after the cease-fire was in place. Yet the underlying assumption of the political prisoner debate was that Thieu feared an electoral contest with the Communists.

Congress failed to explore the parallel issue on the Communist side. Thieu's official figure of 5,081 political prisoners was attacked as fraudulent; yet the figure simultaneously given by the PRG was a suspiciously low 637 non-Communist civilian detainees.[176] It is at the very least unlikely to assume that Thieu had captured seventy times as many prisoners as the PRG. As of 1969—before Vietnamization was under way—the RVN recorded 1,045 of its civilian personnel as abducted.[177] By 1973, that number had jumped to 67,500 South Vietnamese civilian detainees in PRG hands.[178]

Furthermore, the most egregious violations of Article 8 involved the military prisoners, not the civilian detainees. That provision required the immediate release of prisoners of war and aid in finding those soldiers missing in action. Hanoi initially

---

[175] TRA, *supra* note 46, at 57.

[176] PORTER, *supra* note 25, at 253.

[177] *Id.*

[178] FANNING, *supra* note 93, at 144.

complied with the POW release but suspended its cooperation on March 1, a violation of Article 8. The DRV resumed the releases only after Nixon halted mine-sweeping activities in Haiphong Harbor in retaliation. By March 29, 1973, Americans breathed a collective sigh of relief when Hanoi claimed to have released all of its American POWs, totaling 587.

However, the issue had not been resolved. The Department of Defense listed 53 Americans who were confirmed independently as North Vietnamese POWs, but who were not on the DRV's list of American captives.[179] For instance, Navy Lt. Ronald Dodge was shot down over Hanoi in 1967 and appeared in a photo in 1968 with his North Vietnamese captors. Yet Dodge was not on Hanoi's official POW list, and the DRV denied ever having held him as a prisoner.[180] These 53 "lost POWs" cast doubt on the DRV's claim that the 587 released prisoners were all that had been captured and suggested a violation of Article 8.

The idea of American POWs still languishing in Communist prisons gained some momentum in March 1977, when Marine PFC Robert Garwood emerged. Garwood had been captured in 1965 but was not released with the other Americans in 1973.[181] His appearance twelve years after his capture cast further doubt on the DRV's official 1973 list. Also, the mass exodus of refugees from the Socialist Republic of Vietnam (SRV) in the late 1970s brought numerous stories of live sightings of American POWs still in Communist prisons. Of the 460 documented reports of *living* POWs in Vietnam as of 1980, 280 were firsthand and 180 were hearsay reports.[182] Although there remains no confirmation of

---

[179] *American Prisoners of War and Missing in Action in Southeast Asia, 1973: Hearings Before the Subcomm. on National Security Policy of the House Comm. on Foreign Affairs*, 93d Cong., 1st Sess. 193 (1973).

[180] *Id.*

[181] *U.S. Aid to North Vietnam: Hearing Before the Subcomm. on Asian and Pacific Affairs of the House Comm. on International Relations*, 95th Cong., 1st Sess. vi (1977)

[182] *POW/MIA's: Oversight: Hearing Before the Subcomm. on Asian and Pacific Affairs of the House Comm. on Foreign Affairs*, 96th Cong., 2d Sess. 11 (1980) [hereinafter *1980 POW/MIA*].

living POWs, many believed that some U.S. prisoners may have remained in Indochina after March 1973.[183]

Stronger evidence exists for the conclusion that North Vietnam massively violated Article 8(c), which required aid in recovering the remains of soldiers missing in action. The official American list records 2,500 servicemen as MIAs.[184] As of 1981, North Vietnam had returned only seventy-two bodies and had consistently refused to cooperate with U.S. search teams that wished to examine crash sites.[185] In 1979, a Vietnamese mortician who escaped his country testified that he had personal knowledge of the remains of 400 U.S. prisoners.[186] When Colonel Stuart A. Herrington, a member of an MIA delegation to Hanoi in 1974, presented dozens of folders with information on MIAs, the DRV officials "adamantly refused to discuss these cases."[187] Privately, a DRV negotiator told Herrington:

> Of course we have information on many of your MIA personnel, and in some cases even the remains of pilots we shot down. And you must know we do not like to keep them. Their graves defile our ancestral soil. . . . But why should we give them to you for nothing?[188]

The DRV's record of compliance with Article 8 is abysmal. At worst, the evidence suggests that the DRV, and after 1975 the SRV, may have withheld U.S. POWs and the remains of MIAs. At best, the evidence indicates a consistent policy of exploiting the POW/MIA issue to exert diplomatic leverage on the United States

---

[183] *POW/MIA's: Oversight: Hearing Before the Subcomm. on Asian and Pacific Affairs of the House Comm. on Foreign Affairs*, 97th Cong., 1st Sess. 24 (1981) [hereinafter *1981 POW/MIA*] (statement of General Eugene Tighe of the DIA, relying in part on evidence presented in closed session, giving his personal conclusion that POWs are still alive in Vietnam).

[184] *Id.* at 11.

[185] *Id.*

[186] *1980 POW/MIA, supra* note 182, at 27.

[187] S. Herrington, Peace With Honor? An American Reports on Vietnam, 1973-75, at 54 (1983).

[188] *Id.* at 59.

by withholding information. Either way, their conduct is a violation of Article 8.

As for the "democratic liberties of the people" engraved in Article 11, it is hard to imagine a regime that has trampled them more thoroughly than the DRV or its more mature form, the SRV. In 1987, the SRV was ranked 80th of 89 countries cited for human rights violations.[189] The consistent picture painted by observers and refugees of the SRV is one of repression. After the conquest of Saigon in 1975, despite two years of Communist rhetoric about the lack of democratic freedoms under Thieu, the DRV proceeded to entrench a police state in the South.

Just three days after the last U.S. helicopter fled from Saigon, the Communist Military Management Section issued Order Number One—directing that the defeated report to and register with the new Communist regime.[190] Depending on their role in South Vietnam, specified groups were ordered to report to designated locations for "thought reform."[191] While many were released, at least 250,000 were removed to "reeducation camps" deep in the jungle, with no plan to return them to society until they posed no "threat" to the new SRV government.[192]

Despite Hanoi's public claims that there was "no bloodbath" in the South after 1975, forty-one public executions of "common criminals" were performed in the year following the conquest.[193] Not surprisingly, thirty-six of the executed "criminals" were soldiers in Thieu's army.[194] But this small official figure does not account for secret executions performed out of the eyesight of the world community. Of 800 refugees interviewed in 1983-85, 35 percent of them personally knew of at least one and often several persons executed for political reasons.[195] Nguyen Cong Hoan, a

---

[189] J. Desbarats, *Human Rights: Two Steps Forward and One Step Back, in* VIETNAM TODAY: ASSESSING THE NEW TRENDS 47 (T. Quang Trung ed., 1990).

[190] E. METZNER, H. VAN CHINH, ET AL., REEDUCATION IN POSTWAR VIETNAM: PERSONAL POSTSCRIPTS TO PEACE, at xii (2001).

[191] *Id.*

[192] *Id.* at xiii.

[193] Desbarats, *supra* note 189, at 62.

[194] *Id.*

[195] *Id.*

refugee who served as an opposition member of Thieu's assembly and later as a member of the SRV National Assembly, reports that 500 villagers were massacred by the Communists in the first days of the takeover.[196] One human rights organization estimates that 65,000 people were executed from 1975-85.[197] These reports, while proven only by hearsay and anecdotes, are consistent with the DRV's prior record, which included a massacre of the Nationalists in 1946 and the Hue bloodbath in 1968.[198]

Much lip service was given to the political prisoner issue by the DRV. After 1975, however, their true position on democratic freedoms was revealed. In 1983, SRV Foreign Minister Nguyen Co Thach admitted that "we had 1.5 million people in re-education camps" after the fall of Saigon, although he claimed only 10,000 were imprisoned by 1983.[199] Supporters of Thieu were branded as "traitors" and herded into concentration camps for propaganda indoctrination.[200] Private property was confiscated to facilitate the "collectivization" of the South.[201] Religious groups—both Catholics and Buddhists—were denied the freedom of worship that Thieu had respected, and all church property was confiscated by the state in 1975.[202] In Da Nang in 1985, 1,500 temples, churches, and pagodas were destroyed by government troops during the SRV's "stamp out superstition" campaign.[203]

Another casualty was freedom of speech. In the SRV, "disseminating propaganda against the state" became a criminal offense.[204] The state held a monopoly on the press, and any book or writing was censored and approved by the government before publication.[205] Even for politicians, criticism of the government was prohibited. Congressman Nguyen Cong Hoan revealed that "I

---

[196] N. VAN CANH, VIETNAM UNDER COMMUNISM, 1975-82, at 124 (1983).

[197] Desbarats, *supra* note 189, at 63.

[198] CANH, *supra* note 196, at 121.

[199] Desbarats, *supra* note 189, at 60.

[200] N. NGOC HUY, VIETNAM UNDER COMMUNIST RULE 9 (1982).

[201] CANH, *supra* note 196, at 23.

[202] HUY, *supra* note 200, at 9.

[203] Desbarats, *supra* note 189, at 49.

[204] *Id.* at 51.

[205] *Id.*

couldn't express my own opinion on the floor," and that "I couldn't refuse to read a prepared statement there if I was called on to do so."[206] The actual situation in the South under Hanoi's rule exceeded even the most exaggerated accounts of Thieu's oppression.

In short, the debate in America over violations of the political provisions of the Paris Accords seems one-sided in retrospect. McGovern, Hayden, Abzug, and the other critics of Thieu were probably correct to accuse him of holding Communists as political prisoners in 1973 and 1974 in violation of Articles 8 and 11. The evidence indicates, however, that the number was vastly smaller than the number alleged. Thieu's 4,000 releases indicate that he was reluctantly complying with the provisions, even though his compliance was expressly contingent upon a cease-fire that never occurred. Furthermore, the active and vocal dissent of domestic critics illustrates that Thieu's society compared to the DRV was relatively open—especially considering that it was engaged in a violent struggle for its own survival. To be sure, Thieu was not pleased with the Paris Agreement or its political provisions. Thieu's compliance with Articles 8 and 11 was not flawless. But to assign greater blame to Thieu than the PRG for the violation of the political provisions is not warranted by the evidence.

The hypocritical conduct of the DRV stands in sharp contrast to that of the RVN. While verbally attacking Thieu on the political prisoner issue, the DRV was intentionally violating its Article 8 obligations regarding POWs and MIAs. Also, the suspiciously low figure of 637 given by the PRG strongly suggests that their own violations of the political prisoner obligations of the Agreement were substantial. The Communists' true attitude toward political prisoners and basic human freedoms was revealed after 1975, when they either slaughtered or "re-educated" many potential dissenters and imposed a police state. In short, the Communist violations of Articles 8 and 11 far outstrip the worst conduct of President Thieu.

---

[206] CANH, *supra* note 196, at 150.

As Nixon told Kissinger presciently in September 1971, "When you come down to it, what's the alternative to Thieu? There's no other leader. The only alternative is a Communist government, and that would mean slaughtering the poor sons of bitches."[207] When Congress debated these issues in 1973 and 1974, they looked exclusively at President Thieu and found him lacking. Abzug and others pointed out the flaws of South Vietnam's implementation of the Paris Peace Agreement, including isolated and often exaggerated violations of Articles 8 and 11, as evidence that Thieu was the militaristic barrier to democratic liberties in Vietnam. But Congress ignored the alternative. By slashing aid to Thieu, Congress did not create peace in Vietnam. Instead, Congress handed over a comparatively free and open society—and a staunch U.S. ally—to a repressive Communist dictatorship with an abysmal human rights record.

CONCLUSION

Although the United States had terminated its direct participation in the Vietnam War with the Paris Peace Agreement in 1973, its role was still decisive in the final phase of the conflict. The third Indochina War was decided by the United States' loss of a political war, not merely by Saigon's loss of a military war.

Hanoi negotiated the Paris Agreement at a time when its military balance of power with the RVN and United States was discouraging. The 1972 offensive and the Christmas bombing of Hanoi had weakened the DRV's military hand. North Vietnam had only 145,000 troops in the South, while the RVN had over 300,000 regulars and U.S. financial backing.[208] In that environment, it was advantageous to shift to a political struggle to pursue its conquest of Saigon. Accordingly, Hanoi signed the Paris Peace Agreement, promising to abandon its military ambitions in South Vietnam, Laos, and Cambodia in return for total U.S. withdrawal. Yet the North Vietnamese troops remained in the South, and their covert

---

[207] White House Tape, Sept. 20, 1971, *quoted in* BERMAN, *supra* note 27, at 98.

[208] FANNING, *supra* note 93, at 164.

war preparations continued. The DRV pretended to support the Peace Agreement while secretly planning for a later military conquest after the departure of American forces.

Recently available documents confirm the North's intent. In January 1973, on the eve of final negotiations, Le Duc Tho visited China en route to Paris. Chou En Lai told his comrade to "adhere to principles but show the necessary flexibility" and "[l]et the Americans leave as quickly as possible. In half a year or one year the situation will change."[209] RVN Vice President Nguyen Cao Ky noted that "the Paris Agreement gave the world an entirely wrong impression. Though it was the end of the war for America, it was never regarded as the end of the war by Hanoi."[210]

Nixon and Kissinger were aware of Hanoi's attitude, but believed the Agreement was workable. With steadfast aid to President Thieu to bolster his defenses and with stern, credible warnings of bombing retaliations if Hanoi violated the Agreement, Nixon believed that South Vietnam could survive permanently, just like South Korea. "The biggest flaw of the Paris Agreement of 1973 was that the cease-fire provision allowed the North Vietnamese forces to stay in some South Vietnamese territory captured in the 1972 invasion," Nixon later reflected. "But at least we backed up that . . . damn treaty with power." When Congress severed aid, it caused the United States and Saigon to "lose the peace."[211] Kissinger similarly noted that "American troops have been in Europe for two generations" and "the armistice in Korea has been protected by American forces for over 40 years," but "only in Vietnam did the U.S., driven by internal dissent, agree to leave no residual forces; in the process, it deprived itself of any margin of safety when it came to protecting the Agreement. . . ."[212]

---

[209] 77 CONVERSATIONS BETWEEN CHINESE AND FOREIGN LEADERS ON THE WARS IN INDOCHINA, 1964-77 (D. Westad, et al. ed., 1998), *quoted in* BERMAN, *supra* note 27, at 2.

[210] N. KY, HOW WE LOST THE VIETNAM WAR (1978) *quoted in* BERMAN, *supra* note 27, at 246-77.

[211] Nixon, *quoted in* ASSELIN, *supra* note 55, at 188; and M. GONLEY, NIXON IN WINTER 256 (1998).

[212] H. KISSINGER, DIPLOMACY 691 (1994); also ASSELIN, *supra* note 55, at 188.

Without the shadow of the United States as a deterrent to Hanoi, the Agreement truly became a U.S. surrender document.

In contrast to the North Vietnamese, Thieu—while not thrilled with the Agreement—largely intended compliance. In a June 10, 1973 cable, Deputy Ambassador to South Vietnam Charles Whitehouse told Kissinger:

> the [RVN] believed when they signed that the Agreement would lead to a freezing of the military situation—and eventually to the attrition of [DRV] forces remaining in South Vietnam—and that this would set the stage for a political solution in South Vietnam . . . . They were also told that if there was a massive violation of the Paris Agreement, we would mete out dire punishment to the North Vietnamese. None of this has happened . . . .[213]

After the Paris Agreement, while maintaining its military position, Hanoi stressed the political front. The DRV initiated a propaganda offensive to accuse Thieu of violating the Agreement. Its primary targets were U.S. and RVN public opinion, to weaken support for Thieu in the two most important places. This would soften up his government for military conquest. Although the invasion was temporarily postponed, preparations for that conquest in violation of the Accords were incessant. Hanoi accelerated its activities in late 1973, when it became apparent that Congress was putting a leash on Nixon's flexibility to re-enter the war.

The propaganda offensive was having great success in the United States. Hanoi—and antiwar spokesmen in the United States—were accusing Thieu of massive violations of the Accords. South Vietnam was viewed as the obstacle to peace. The PRG wanted to run peacefully against Thieu in a free election, but Thieu wanted to destroy them. The Communists were peaceful reformers, and Thieu was a brutal totalitarian dictator. As Congress jumped on this bandwagon, the evidence of exaggerated claims against

---

[213] Whitehouse Cable for Kissinger, June 1973, *quoted in* BERMAN, *supra* note 27, at 252.

Thieu and of the DRV's real intentions were tossed aside. In 1973 and 1974, Congress severely reduced South Vietnamese aid, suffocating Thieu as he faced a growing number of invaders. Congress also explicitly told Nixon—and Hanoi—that there would be no American re-entry into the war, no matter what. In so doing, they kicked aside the two crutches that supported the Paris Peace Agreement.

Without question, Congress' actions to abandon Thieu were decisive. General Van Tien Dung, North Vietnam's Chief of Staff, later confirmed this fact. "The reduction of U.S. aid made it impossible for the puppet troops to carry out their combat plans and build up their forces. . . . Nguyen Van Thieu was then forced to fight a poor man's war. Enemy firepower had decreased by nearly 60 percent because of bomb and ammunition shortages."[214] For each step Hanoi took militarily toward the conquest of Saigon, Congress took its own step back from America's commitment to South Vietnam.

Thieu violated the cease-fire provision of the Agreement by militarily reclaiming the territory seized in the PRG's last-minute land grab, and Thieu most likely violated the political provision by withholding PRG political prisoners. The nature and extent of these violations were overestimated by the Hanoi propagandists and by Thieu's critics in the United States and South Vietnam. The PRG violated the Agreement by offensive military attacks after the cease-fire; by refusal to cooperate with the ICCS; and by retention of RVN political prisoners. The United States complied with its obligations, including a withdrawal of its troops from Vietnam and a limitation of its meager subsequent aid to a piece-by-piece replacement authorized by the Agreement. In contrast, the DRV violated the Agreement by its incessant infiltration of new troops and war materiel into the South, by its unrelenting aid to the Khmer Rouge in Cambodia, by its failure to cooperate with U.S. inquiries into the status of POWs and MIAs, by its conquest of Saigon through "coercion and annexation," and by its trampling of political freedoms in the South. While the RVN's compliance was

---

[214] Dung, *quoted in* PODHORETZ, *supra* note 56, at 165.

imperfect, the relative scale of the DRV and PRG violations undermines any conclusion that Thieu "sabotaged" the Paris Peace Agreement. Certainly, there is no persuasive evidence that Nixon did so.

In 1973 and 1974, many in Congress reached the opposite conclusion. Congress's resolution of the violations debate lies at the core of its decisions in the two years preceding Saigon's fall. Had Congress properly analyzed the situation, it would have bolstered aid to Thieu and given Nixon authorization to retaliate militarily if any violations occurred. This approach would have created a deterrent likely to coerce Hanoi to abide by the Agreement. If Congress had done this, South Vietnam might still be independent today—and the imperfections of Thieu's rule might have been erased peacefully with U.S. influence as the prospect of Communist invasion receded over time. Instead, Nguyen Van Thieu's flawed democracy was replaced by a brutal Communist regime imposed by its North Vietnamese invaders.

IV

The Khmer Rouge: An Analysis of One of the World's Most Brutal Regimes

Michael Charles Rakower

"Power gradually extirpates for the mind every human and gentle virtue."
— Edmund Burke, *A Vindication of Natural Society*

INTRODUCTION

The Khmer Rouge, the fanatical organization that spearheaded the Communist movement in Cambodia and reigned supreme in that land from 1975-79, is officially dead. But what is left of this regime that killed an estimated two million of its own people in a campaign of terror that stands near the top of a mountain of atrocities committed against humankind in the twentieth century? The world lost its best source of answers in 1998 when Pol Pot, the brutal and enigmatic leader of this barbarous group, died in disgrace, himself a captive of the guerrilla regime he led nearly from its inception. But the Khmer Rouge's downfall was not sudden. Weakened by a series of defections since its ousting from power and alienated by its international and domestic supporters, little was left of the Khmer Rouge when Pot died. However, memories of its genocidal rampage remain fresh in the minds of all Cambodians. Few believe that the world has seen the last of the Khmer Rouge. If history has taught them anything, it is that the Khmer Rouge will survive.

Despite the Communist rhetoric used to propel its leaders into power, few in the Khmer Rouge—perhaps not even Pol Pot—genuinely believed in the Communist movement. Maintaining secrecy over its agenda, the Khmer Rouge attracted followers unaware of its ultimate goal. Offering the least educated and poorest youths of the country sudden access to wealth and power, it developed a loyal following in those seeking pecuniary gain. Even inner-circle members, though aware of the movement's agenda, sought positions of power and prestige for themselves. As it gained force, the movement demanded absolute obedience on pain of death. By the time it took over the country in 1975, the Khmer Rouge had become a tyrannical dictatorship led by the genocidal Pol Pot. Soon after its overthrow in 1979, the Khmer Rouge changed course. Rather than returning to Communist ideology, Pol Pot set a new course for the guerrilla movement. This time his agenda was more pragmatic, though no less ruthless. Wedging himself between opposing forces, Pot attempted to lift the Khmer Rouge into established political circles. Using guerrilla warfare and propaganda, he continued this course until the day he died. In the meantime, Khmer Rouge forces slowly defected as the government promised them amnesty and a wealthy future.

So where is the Khmer Rouge now? It has merged with the government. Though ex-Khmer Rouge cadres have now professed their loyalty to the government, history has shown that they are truly loyal to only one thing: the pursuit of power.

A HISTORY OF POLITICAL APATHY

The political system and the basic culture made the concept of revolution wholly unthinkable in traditional terms.[1]

Modern day Cambodia stems from the kingdom of Angkor, which dominated Southeast Asia from the tenth to the fourteenth

---

[1] Serge Thion, *The Cambodian Idea of Revolution, in* Revolution and its Aftermath in Kampuchea 10, 12 (David P. Chandler & Ben Kiernan eds., 1983).

centuries.[2] As a testament to the wealth, power, and technological advancement of their empire, the kings of Angkor built a fantastic array of intricately carved stone temples during their reign. These temples, the most famous of which is called *Angkor Wat*, still stand today, symbolizing the glory of the once great Khmer (Cambodian) people. But since the fall of that empire, Cambodia faded in regional importance and regressed as a society. Ruled by an absolute monarchy until the French established a colonial protectorate there in 1863, Cambodia languished at just above subsistence levels.[3] Yet its people were content. They cared little about politics, their country's past, or personal economic growth. Eighty-five percent were land-owning peasants.[4] They accepted Buddhist teachings, believing that positions in life are preordained and that those in power deserve to be in power, as determined by good deeds in previous lives.[5]

Upon entering Cambodia and establishing its rule, the French immediately set out to change the face of the country. Reaping the benefits of Cambodia's cheap labor and natural resources, the French, in return, sought to educate the Cambodian citizenry, modernize its productive capabilities, and generally upgrade the country to a level on par with the rest of the industrialized world. French academics instilled in Cambodians a historical identity by teaching them about the greatness of both the Khmer empire and France, their new mother country.[6] As a testament to the glorious Khmer past, the French pointed to the temples of Angkor.[7] In admiration of modern France's humble beginnings, the French taught Cambodians to revere its 1789 peasant revolution.

---

[2] DAVID P. CHANDLER, THE TRAGEDY OF CAMBODIAN HISTORY 6 (1991).

[3] *Id.* at 3.

[4] R.A. BURGLER, THE EYES OF THE PINEAPPLE: REVOLUTIONARY INTELLECTUALS AND TERROR IN DEMOCRATIC KAMPUCHEA 8 (1990).

[5] CHANDLER, *supra* note 2, at 4.

[6] *Id.* at 6.

[7] *See* David Chandler, *From "Cambodge" To "Kampuchea": State and Revolution in Cambodia 1863-1979, in* THESIS ELEVEN 35, 37 (1997) ("The French, in other words, tinkered with Cambodian collective memory and thereby with its peoples' views of history and their identification with the State.").

Despite French influence, Cambodians lacked political
consciousness prior to World War II.[8] The concept of self-rule
eventually took root when the Japanese liberated Cambodia in
March 1945, instilling in the minds of educated Cambodians that
self-rule was indeed possible.[9] When the French later regained
control in October of that same year, they encountered an elite that
was both reluctant to relinquish power and skeptical of the
legitimacy of a monarchy.[10] Cambodians tasted a brief, tantalizing
dose of power and now they hungered for self-rule. In just seven
months, the Cambodian consciousness had been changed forever.

After a series of resistance movements, Cambodia achieved
independence in 1953.[11] Two years later, King Norodom Sihanouk
abdicated his throne, becoming Prince Sihanouk, and founded a
national political movement, which he dominated for the next
several years.[12] During his reign, revolutionary bells clamored in
neighboring countries. As Cambodia sought a policy of neutrality,
outside forces—Vietnam, Thailand, China, and the former Soviet
Union—saw the country as key to their own geopolitical agendas.
At this time, the largest crop of educated Cambodian youth the
country had ever seen entered a national economy incapable of
offering them the professional opportunities for which they had
been trained.

THE SEEDS OF TERROR

*In Cambodia, there are two sources for the idea of revolution,
namely the French school syllabus and the international
Communist movement. The two are not unrelated.*[13]

*The sheer strength of will, whatever the sacrifices, was to
overcome all material difficulties.*[14]

---

[8] Thion, *supra* note 1, at 15.
[9] CHANDLER, *supra* note 2, at 7.
[10] Thion, *supra* note 1, at 15.
[11] CHANDLER, *supra* note 2, at 8.
[12] *Id.*
[13] Thion, *supra* note 1, at 14.
[14] *Id.* at 21 (citing Maoist theory followed by the Khmer Rouge).

Saloth Sar, alias Pol Pot, was born to a peasant family in the province of Kompong Thom on May 18, 1925.[15] Initially educated in a Buddhist monastery, Saloth Sar attended technical school in Phnom Penh. After winning a scholarship to study radio electronics in Paris, Sar failed his exams three years in a row and returned to Cambodia. On his return from Paris, he found that the economy lacked opportunity for his skills. Although Prince Sihanouk had succeeded in improving educational opportunities for Cambodians both within the country and abroad, he had failed to stimulate the economy to support jobs for Cambodia's newest, most qualified class of jobseekers.[16] The frustrations felt by French-educated Cambodians resulting from this blocked ascendancy were exacerbated by their feelings of alienation.[17] They no longer felt connected to the illiterate peasant class from which they came, they had not yet reached middle-class status, and they were not members of the ruling elite.[18] As revolutionary pressures in neighboring countries reverberated throughout Southeast Asia, these well-educated youths united in the spirit of their French "brethren" in search of a solution similar to the revolution of 1789.[19]

Yet, these young idealists achieved little initial success. Adhering to Communist doctrine, they sought to develop a class consciousness among the peasants.[20] Patterning itself after Stalin, the Khmer Rouge canvassed the countryside asserting that the

---

[15] Nate Thayer, *Pol Pot Unmasked: He was obsessed with secrecy and total control*, FAR E. ECON. REV., Aug. 7, 1997 (pagination unavailable online). Like most details of Pol Pot's life, even his birthday is shrouded in mystery. Other sources suggest he was born on May 19, 1928. Sean Watson & David Le Sage, *Pol Pot: A Biographical Essay*, *available at* http://www.eliz.tased.edu.au/ ITStu97// olpot.htm.

[16] BURGLER, *supra* note 4, at 13.

[17] *Id.*

[18] *Id.*

[19] *See* Thion, *supra* note 1, at 14 (noting that French *lycees* instilled in Cambodians a reverence for revolution).

[20] Kate G. Frieson, *Revolution and Rural Response in Cambodia: 1970-1975*, *in* GENOCIDE AND DEMOCRACY IN CAMBODIA 10, 39 (Ben Kiernan ed., 1993).

landlords exploited the landless.[21] This theory was ill-suited to Cambodian realities and generally fell on deaf ears. Not only did the peasants feel unexploited, but a majority of them owned land.[22] To the extent exploitation existed, it occurred between the Chinese merchants and the Cambodian rice-harvesters. However, most peasants, content with their lot, remained unconcerned that the Chinese earned money from their labor.[23] Their Buddhist faith taught them passivity toward their socioeconomic status. This sentiment is aptly summarized by a cyclo driver, who remarked, "What can I do about it? I'm born into this life as a poor person and I can't have the opportunity to become educated like other people. I really pity myself."[24] So long as they had enough to eat and their way of life remained undisturbed, they remained content. Their respect for Prince Sihanouk, who they believed had earned his right to rule through good deeds in a previous life, was strong. In return for blind support, Sihanouk rarely interfered with the daily lives of the peasant populace.

In 1970, insurgent leader Lon Nol launched a coup against Prince Sihanouk that catapulted Cambodia into civil war and forced Sihanouk to flee for safety under the protection of the Chinese.[25] To protect Cambodia's newly-installed regime from North Vietnamese incursion, the United States and South Vietnam entered the fray.[26] Suddenly, the Cambodian countryside was transformed into a battlefield. Not only had Sihanouk lost his grip on Cambodia's rule, but he lost his struggle to maintain Cambodia's neutrality. Amidst this turmoil, the Khmer Rouge found its first opportunity to develop support. It implemented a two-pronged plan, again using hegemony as a tool: first, the

---

[21] BURGLER, *supra* note 4, at 15.

[22] Frieson, *supra* note 20, at 40.

[23] *See* BURGLER, *supra* note 4, at 9 ("From the peasants point of view, the local Chinese merchant provided him with commodities and with the opportunity to sell his harvest surplus. As the peasants were quite easily able to subsist on what was left them, they did not consider the price they had to pay for these services and goods unjust.").

[24] Frieson, *supra* note 20, at 43.

[25] *Id.*

[26] JOHN NORTON MOORE, LAW AND THE INDO-CHINA WAR 508 (1972)

Khmer Rouge built support for its Party with a "save Sihanouk" battle cry; and second, it actively concealed its true revolutionary goal.[27] This devious plan worked flawlessly. Regarding the efforts of Khmer Rouge members to conceal their true motives, one scholar notes:

> [R]evolution and the existence of a revolutionary party were not only played down in propaganda, they were completely hidden truths, revealed only to the enlightened few who could achieve senior positions in the apparatus. Revolution was not an asset but an ultimate goal, which had to be achieved by devious and clandestine means, since even the beneficiaries could not be led towards paradise.[28]

Implementing the Communist weapon of *conflict strategy*, the Khmer Rouge used anti-Lon Nol sentiment to build hatred against his foreign protectors—America and South Vietnam. Hammering into every citizen's mind the notion that Lon Nol was an American pawn and that the United States and South Vietnam sought to take away Cambodia's independence and oppress its people, the Khmer Rouge politicized the countryside. With every bomb, more and more Cambodians joined the ranks of the Khmer Rouge to fight the American "imperialists" and "aggressors"[29]:

> [A]rtillery shells and rockets rained down on the capital. People were killed while eating noodles, selling fish, standing around, nursing their children, and bicycling to work. They were defenseless. The war, if it had ever made sense to ordinary Khmer, made none in early 1974.[30]

As they watched friends and family die at the hands of "foreign aggressors" and as they hoped for an end to the bloodshed, many weary Cambodians found comfort in the ultra-nationalist hands of

---

[27] *Id.* at 35.

[28] Thion, *supra* note 1, at 23.

[29] Frieson, *supra* note 20, at 35.

[30] CHANDLER, *supra* note 2, at 230.

the Khmer Rouge, who promised an end to the conflict and a victory for the people. The courage of the Khmer Rouge soldiers, who fought under horrific conditions in a display of self-sacrifice and patriotism, impressed their Cambodian countrymen.[31] Even those who disagreed with Communist ideology began to believe that only the Khmer Rouge could provide a viable future for Cambodia.[32]

Having learned in the past that peasants did not understand such concepts as feudalism and capitalism, the Khmer Rouge launched a grass-roots campaign with a simple message: greater material wealth and a higher standard of living.[33] Members moved into the countryside, dressed and ate like commoners, and assisted village folk whenever possible.[34] They built trust by building homes and roads and providing medicine to the needy.[35] Slowly, they built a mass, loyal following that was totally unaware of the Party's master plan. Members joined either because they were well-educated students disillusioned with the current state of government or, more often, citizens resentful of Sihanouk's ouster and the ensuing devastation of the country at the hands of outside forces. Very few, however, possessed an inkling of the role they were to play in the forthcoming revolution. Indeed, the Party did not publicize its true leanings until late 1972, at which time many followers were shocked to learn of the movement's ultimate goals. One Khmer Rouge member who saw the Party's flag—complete with hammer and sickle on a red background—for the first time at a Party ceremony in September 1972 remarked, "It's as if I'd been stabbed in the chest with a knife."[36] By this time, it was too late to leave. Disloyalty against the Party was punishable by death.

By 1973, twenty-two years after the Communist movement began in Cambodia and just as Cambodians began to sense the Khmer Rouge's true objective, a new group of leaders emerged:

---

[31] BURGLER, *supra* note 4, at 51.

[32] CHANDLER, *supra* note 2, at 230.

[33] Frieson, *supra* note 20, at 40.

[34] BURGLER, *supra* note 4, at 35.

[35] *Id.*

[36] CHANDLER, *supra* note 2, at 219.

village children, aged thirteen and fourteen, indoctrinated by the Khmer Rouge soon after birth.[37] These children, the poorest and least educated, had been raised in Party and military cadre schools.[38] In the minds of Pol Pot and his inner-circle, these children, modeled after Mao's use of "poor and blank" youths— were the first pure crop of Khmer Rouge.[39] Trained in remote areas, free of "foreign propaganda," these children were trained to be killing machines, fully competent in the use of heavy artillery and fiercely loyal to the Party.[40] Condemning religion and rejecting parental control, they answered only to Angkar (the Party).[41] These poor, uneducated sons of peasants, separated from their family and bound only to the Party, were given the highest positions of command within the Khmer Rouge military.[42] Molded into obedient killing machines, psychologically controlled by the Party, and placed into positions of power for the first time in their young lives, these children displayed a level of brutality theretofore unseen.[43]

These new, devout followers assisted Pol Pot in ushering in a new era for the Khmer Rouge. With provinces in the countryside held securely under its domain, the Khmer Rouge waged a public campaign against Sihanouk, accusing him of hiding under the protection of the wealthy Chinese as his poor country suffered under the bombardment of American warplanes.[44] Exercising its control, it prohibited any showing of sympathy for Sihanouk's plight, on pain of death.[45] In only a few short years, the Khmer

---

[37] BURGLER, *supra* note 4, at 48.

[38] *Id.*

[39] CHANDLER, *supra* note 2, at 243.

[40] BURGLER, *supra* note 4, at 48.

[41] *Id.*

[42] *See* CHANDLER, *supra* note 2, at 243 ("Freed from family obligations, they displayed a loyalty to the Organization that was often absolute. . . . These boys and girls became the revolution's cutting edge.").

[43] *See* Chandler, *supra* note 7, at 46 ("Throughout the country, people were drawn towards the revolution by their supposition that they themselves, the perennially powerless segment of the population had been, or were soon to be, empowered.").

[44] BURGLER, *supra* note 4, at 47.

[45] *Id.*

Rouge had come full circle: after heavily supporting Sihanouk in order to develop its own base of followers, it later denounced him and murdered anyone suspected of siding with him.

On January 1, 1975, the Khmer Rouge began its assault on Phnom Penh.[46] On April 17, it claimed the city and the country. Most of the soldiers were between twelve and fifteen years old.[47]

YEAR O: GENOCIDE

[W]e have won total, definitive, and CLEAN victory, meaning that we have won it without any foreign connection or involvement. . . . We have waged our revolutionary struggle basically on the principles of independence, sovereignty and self-reliance . . . .[48]

For thousands of years the colonialists, the imperialists and reactionary feudalists have dragged us through the mud. Now with victory we have regained our honour, our dignity, now we smell good again.[49]

For the heroic Kampuchean people the 17th of April is a glorious victory of greater far reaching significance than the prestigious Angkor era.[50]

The Cambodian Revolutionary experience is unprecedented. What we are trying to bring about has never occurred before. That is why we are not following any model. . . .[51]

---

[46] CHANDLER, *supra* note 2, at 233.

[47] BURGLER, *supra* note 4, at 86.

[48] *Id.*, at 59 (quoting Pol Pot in a speech to the Khmer Rouge army).

[49] *Id.* at 58 (quoting radio broadcast by Khieu Samphan, Khmer Rouge inner-circle member).

[50] *Id.*, at 59.

[51] *Id.* (quoting Ieng Sary, Khmer Rouge inner-circle member).

Love Angkar,
Hate Angkar's Enemies:
Tell the Truth to Angkar.[52]

Once in power, the Khmer Rouge immediately set out to construct an agrarian utopia in the spirit of Mao, Lenin, and Jean-Jacques Rousseau.[53] Using any means necessary to achieve their objective and shrouded in secrecy, they implemented a plan of absolute control through subterfuge and force.[54] Every policy implemented had as its central aim to eliminate the individual by inculcating him into a mass collective.[55] Riding on a high from their surprising victory and fueled with ultra-nationalist pride, the Khmer Rouge attempted to achieve something that no other Communist revolution had ever dared: immediate societal reformation. Even Mao and Stalin, from whom much Khmer Rouge dogma derived, recognized that Socialism must be built over time.[56] But Pol Pot was convinced that Cambodia's greatness was unique, that it was capable of achieving things that no other nation could achieve. The French had instilled in the Cambodian consciousness the belief that their people had once been great. The

---

[52] Frieson, *supra* note 20, at 39.

[53] Although Pol Pot borrowed many social control techniques from Mao and Lenin, his overarching vision—a reversion to agrarian society—is so closely linked to Rousseau's back-to-nature philosophy that one cannot discount Rousseau's influence in forming Pot's vision. The following Khmer Rouge radio broadcast, in the true spirit of Rousseau, illustrates this point: "The young are learning their science from the workers and peasants, who are the sources of all knowledge. . . . And this science is possessed by the peasants and labourers alone." *See* Jonathan Sikes, *Pol Pot's New Wave of Killers*, SUNDAY TELEGRAPH, Jul. 22, 1990, (pagination unavailable online) (calling Khmer Rouge ideology a "mishmash" of Rousseauism and Maoism). *See also* CHANDLER, supra note 2, at 7 ("The Rousseauean notion of the essential innocence of the Cambodian People colored the thinking of all three leaders [Lon Nol, Norodom Sihanouk and Pol Pot].").

[54] It should be noted that the Khmer Rouge began imposing these mechanisms of social control over certain country provinces in 1973, though their efforts did not reach full-scale until 1975.

[55] *See* CHANDLER, *supra* note 2, at 244 ("The commands from the Revolutionary Organization covered every aspect of people's lives.").

[56] Thion, *supra* note 1, at 25.

Khmer Rouge's revolutionary success led its members to believe that Cambodia was returning to greatness. If China could achieve the Great Leap Forward in the 1950s, reasoned Pol Pot, Cambodia could achieve the Super Great Leap Forward in the 1970s.[57] Marking a new era in Khmer history, the Khmer Rouge renamed the country Democratic Kampuchea and called 1975 "Year 0." The belief that the Khmer Rouge could wipe away thousands of years of history was embodied by Pol Pot's declaration, "If our people can build Angkor, they can do anything."[58]

Immediately after conquering Phnom Penh and declaring victory, the Khmer Rouge set out to develop a new world order by razing society and starting anew. Pol Pot envisaged Democratic Kampuchea as an agrarian utopia, free from foreign influence and utterly devoted to its own ideals, which included the destruction of the individual in the name of the collective. Central to his plan was the element of secrecy. The identity of Party members and all future Party plans were kept strictly confidential. This served three main functions. First, it prevented anyone from mounting an attack against Party leaders, since they did not know who they were. Second, it gave the Party the appearance of a life of its own. Most organizations are controlled by a few central figures, but the Khmer Rouge seemed to guide itself. In fact, until as late as 1977, all Party decisions were deemed to have been made by the nameless, faceless Angkar.[59] Again, this technique shielded it from attack. Lastly, maintaining secrecy over future plans kept the populace in check, since what was permissible today might turn out to be impermissible, and punishable, tomorrow.

To achieve his great vision, Pol Pot attacked the pillars of modern Cambodian society—capitalism, Buddhism, kingship, hierarchical social relationships, and family—and replaced them with mechanisms intended to instill egalitarianism, collectivism,

---

[57] CHANDLER, *supra* note 2, at 245.

[58] Chandler, *supra* note 7, at 37.

[59] *Id.*

and self-reliance.[60] In one of its first moves upon attaining power, the Khmer Rouge forced the immediate evacuation of all cities, pushing every man, woman, and child into collectives in the countryside. This radical maneuver had three purposes, all of which were grounded in Angkar's need for total control of its citizenry. First, it was used to weed out the regime's greatest threat: city dwellers linked to foreign entities.[61] Anyone deemed to be linked to foreign forces was summarily executed.[62] This included members of the Lon Nol regime as well as all better-educated citizens trained to work as professionals in a capitalist economy. Those who were deemed not to have been so tainted as to necessitate murder were uprooted and sent to the countryside, thus dismantling their social connections and quelling any threat that they may have posed through organized rebellion.[63] Second, because Cambodia was to revert to an agrarian society, Angkar needed every able-bodied individual in the fields growing crops.[64] In theory, the revenue from agricultural production was to be used to build other industries within the country.[65] "When we have rice, we can have everything," became a popular motto.[66] Third, the evacuation dismantled Cambodia's market economy, choking off the influx of goods and currency. The only hand that was to feed the Khmer people was the hand of Angkar.

Demanding complete devotion to Angkar, the Khmer Rouge imposed a collectivist lifestyle on the people. Exercising its stranglehold over the population, it prohibited travel between collectives[67] and all trade (except for that conducted within a

---

[60] *Id.* at 38. It should be noted, however, that just as Pol Pot tore down the existing social framework, he built his own hierarchy, a far more rigid and extraordinarily violent system of control.

[61] Michael Vickery, *Democratic Kampuchea—Themes and Variations, in* REVOLUTION AND ITS AFTERMATH IN KAMPUCHEA 99, 101 (David P. Chandler & Ben Kiernan eds., 1983).

[62] *Id.*

[63] CHANDLER, *supra* note 2, at 247.

[64] *Id.*

[65] *Id.* at 245.

[66] BURGLER, *supra* note 4, at 60.

[67] *Id.* at 38.

cooperative).[68] It imposed a system of communal eating, carefully monitoring food rations.[69] The populace, accustomed to eating at home and alone with their families, especially disliked communal rationing.[70] But by centralizing the collection of goods and rationing food to the people, the Khmer Rouge imposed order even on those who would have been brave enough to withstand physical punishment.[71]

Another aspect of the Khmer Rouge war against individuality was its prohibition of religion. It defrocked all monks, forcing them to serve in the army and work in the fields as common people, and prohibited anyone from addressing them according to their honorific title.[72] In place of religious teachings, the Khmer Rouge forced individuals to attend village propaganda meetings twice a month and "lifestyle" meetings weekly.[73] The propaganda meetings included discussions of policies and programs furthering their collectivist agenda. Lifestyle meetings included self-criticism sessions modeled in the Marxist-Leninist tradition.[74] In these sessions, individuals were forced to admit their negative "trends" in front of a group of their peers in an effort to cleanse themselves and facilitate their humble servitude to Angkar.[75] Individuals were typically criticized for such things as not loving their work, looking sad, and failing to maximize their productive capacity.[76] As one cadre put it, "We had but one duty: think of the collective and purify ourselves."[77] Truth—as Angkar determined it—was demanded. *Nokorbal*, village spies, reported the slightest

---

[68] *Id.* at 49.

[69] Ben Kiernan, *Wild Chickens, Farm Chickens, And Cormorants: Kampuchea's Eastern Zone Under Pol Pot, in* REVOLUTION AND ITS AFTERMATH IN KAMPUCHEA 136, 142 (David P. Chandler & Ben Kiernan eds., 1983).

[70] *Id.*

[71] *Id.*

[72] BURGLER, *supra* note 4, at 49.

[73] *Id.* at 35.

[74] *Id.*

[75] Thion, *supra* note 1, at 29.

[76] BURGLER, *supra* note 4, at 83.

[77] *Id.* at 62.

transgressions left unmentioned.[78] Rewarded for uncovering anyone disloyal to the movement, these villagers often went to great lengths to inform on one another in hopes of ingratiating themselves with Angkar.[79]

In addition to imposing these structural changes on society, the revolution's tentacles reached less visible aspects of social life: Angkar imposed linguistic reforms, eliminating from the Cambodian vocabulary hierarchical pronouns conceding the country's capitalist past and foreign words reminding them of its colonized life;[80] it imposed uniform dress codes and prohibited all forms of vanity;[81] and it imposed strict sexual mores, prohibiting sexual activity outside marriage upon pain of death.[82] Marriages, when approved by Angkar, were conducted in mass ceremonies a few times per year.[83] David Chandler summarizes the situation well:

The flaws to be corrected in what the Khmer Rouge called the "old society" included social ranks, personal possession, wealth, consumerism, corrupt sexual mores, individualism, "family-ism," book learning, foreign ideas and "urban" society. . . . The leap that was to be made from visible authority figures, or patrons, to an invisible, unexplained, all-powerful body was impossible for most Cambodians, unaccustomed to such leaps of faith, but exhilarating for tens of thousands who were called on to administer Cambodia on Angkar's behalf.[84]

Any form of protest or dissention by villagers, such as an attempt to rally, prompted a violent—often deadly—response by one of the young, indoctrinated comrades.[85] Petrified of reprisal if

---

[78] *Id.* at 51.

[79] *See id.* at 88 (noting that children would creep under people's houses at night to eavesdrop).

[80] Chandler, *supra* note 7, at 47.

[81] *Id.* at 43.

[82] *Id.*

[83] BURGLER, *supra* note 4, at 81.

[84] Chandler, *supra* note 7, at 44.

[85] Frieson, *supra* note 20, at 44.

deemed a threat to the revolution, Cambodians were paralyzed with fear and resignation as the Party's ominous slogan reverberated in their heads: "One must trust completely in the Angkar because the Organization has as many eyes as a pineapple and cannot make mistakes."[86]

Thus, by controlling food distribution, psychologically manipulating the population, and controlling one's daily life through the use of terror, the Khmer Rouge set out to build a society of laborers in pursuit of its agrarian ideal. But its efforts soon devolved into a campaign to crush the spirit of mankind and warp its children into savage automatons fiercely loyal to a nameless, faceless organization that promised nothing to anyone other than the right to bask in its glory. Angkar killed two million people—approximately 15 percent of the Cambodian population.[87]

THE PEACE PROCESS

Four years after the Khmer Rouge took control of Cambodia and renamed it Democratic Kampuchea, the Vietnamese steamrolled into Phnom Penh in 1979, ousted the Khmer Rouge from power, renamed the country the People's Republic of Kampuchea (PRK), and installed its own brand of Communist rule.[88] The Khmer Rouge recoiled along the Thai-Cambodian border. In a shocking turn of events, it combined forces with Prince Sihanouk—the man they betrayed just a few years ago—and Son Sann, a former Lon Nol cohort who was instrumental in the coup against Sihanouk. Together, they formed the Coalition Government of Democratic Kampuchea (CGDK) to fight Vietnam's PRK.[89] This unlikely coalition, fearful of Vietnamese encroachment, garnered the support of the international community through the backing of China, Thailand, and the United States and

---

[86] BURGLER, *supra* note 4, at 38.

[87] R.J. RUMMEL, DEATH BY GOVERNMENT 193 (1994).

[88] TREVOR FINDLAY, CAMBODIA: THE LEGACY AND LESSONS OF UNTAC 1 (1995).

[89] *Id.*

occupied Cambodia's seat at the United Nations.[90] As Southeast Asia ailed from the devastations of protracted war, a stalemate ensued between the Vietnamese and the CGDK.

A breakthrough was reached in 1989 when Vietnam pulled out of Cambodia in order to soothe its relations with China. The Vietnamese left Hun Sen to govern Cambodia as its reigning strongman. To distance himself from Vietnam, Sen renamed the country Cambodia.[91] As foreign forces scaled back, all four factions—Hun Sen, Khmer Rouge, Prince Sihanouk, and Son Sann—spent the next two years, under the guidance of the United Nations, negotiating the Paris Peace Accords (the Accords), which were adopted on October 23, 1991.[92] The Accords committed all parties to a cease-fire and set a course for free and fair elections in 1993.[93] A crucial pre-condition of the elections was the agreement among the factions to disarm 70 percent of their military forces prior to electoral registration.[94] Demobilization of the remaining 30 percent was to occur after the election.[95]

The United Nations, via the United Nations Transitional Authority in Cambodia (UNTAC), oversaw implementation of this agenda.[96] The Supreme National Council (SNC), a coalition of the various political parties and led by Prince Sihanouk, was installed by the United Nations to administer governmental operations until the elections.[97] Hun Sen relinquished governmental control and acted as a "host party" for the SNC until elections.[98] The most ambitious and expensive operation in UN history (UNTAC cost $2.8 billion) was underway. In just two years, the United Nations

---

[90] *Id.* at 2.
[91] *Id.* at 4.
[92] *Id.* at 11.
[93] *Id.*
[94] *Id.*
[95] *Id.*
[96] *Id.* at 12.
[97] *Id.*
[98] FRANK FROST, THE PEACE PROCESS IN CAMBODIA: ISSUES AND PROSPECTS, at 12 (Centre for the Study of Australia-Asia Relations No. 69, 1993).

hoped to keep peace, make peace, and build peace between numerous factions in a nation scarred by decades of war.[99]

Not surprisingly, it did not take long for the Khmer Rouge to disrupt the peacemaking process. Concerned that free and fair elections would be its downfall, it refused to obey the conditions set by the Accords. Alleging that Vietnamese forces had not fully withdrawn from Cambodia, the Khmer Rouge refused to comply with the cantonment plans.[100] Claiming that Hun Sen had not relinquished control of state apparatus, it refused to submit to disarmament.[101]

Prior to elections, only 5 percent of Khmer Rouge forces had been cantoned. The United Nations was forced to suspend all cantonment efforts, lest the remaining factions be vulnerable to attack.[102] As the elections drew near, the Khmer Rouge engaged Hun Sen's forces in a series of skirmishes, the purpose of which was not so much to win as to scare the populace into electing it into office.[103] In the three months prior to the elections, politically-motivated murders skyrocketed. There were 200 politically-related deaths, 338 injuries, and 114 abductions.[104] Nonetheless, Cambodians were enthusiastic about the elections and would not be deterred. Having cowered in the past, they would not give in to Khmer Rouge bullying again. In mid-April, approximately five weeks before the elections, the Khmer Rouge formally withdrew from the peace process, citing frustration over Vietnamese occupiers and Hun Sen's links to them.[105] However, this was just a face-saving exit strategy used to de-legitimize the electoral process. By doing so, it hoped to form a "government of national

---

[99] Nate Thayer & Nayan Chanda, *Law of the Gun*, FAR E. ECON. REV., Jul. 17, 1997 (pagination unavailable online).

[100] FROST, *supra* note 98, at 13.

[101] Mats Berdal & Michael Keifer, *Cambodia, in* THE NEW INTERVENTIONISM: THE UNITED NATIONS EXPERIENCE IN CAMBODIA, YUGOSLAVIA AND SOMALIA 25, 43 (James Mayall ed., 1996).

[102] *See* FROST, *supra* note 98, at 17 ("We don't want to place the three factions that are cooperating with UNTAC . . . in an inferior position.").

[103] *Id.* at 16.

[104] Berdal & Keifer, *supra* note 101, at 54.

[105] *Id.*

reconciliation" in lieu of elections. The only surprising aspect of its tactic was the audacity it showed in admitting its intention to strong-arm a position in government:

> If the Western powers do not change their position, there is no other choice for the Cambodian people to show their anger at the Western powers. There will certainly be more incidents, such as the launching of hand grenades against the Vietnamese in Phnom Penh. We can foresee that the situation will get more unstable, more insecure, more confusing. The popular movement against the Vietnamese will increase. There will be more attacks. . . . If there are four Cambodian parties [in a future government] the DK [Democratic Kampuchea] party will be among them, and there will be peace in Cambodia.[106]

As a backup plan, the Khmer Rouge stockpiled weapons in anticipation of a new round of warfare and in complete disregard of the Accords.[107]

Yet, despite its attempts to subvert the elections, the Khmer Rouge was unable to stop an astounding 90 percent of registered voters from casting their ballots.[108] Yasushi Akashi, the UN secretary-general's special representative, jubilantly declared that the elections had been free and fair.[109] Out of 120 seats, fifty-eight seats were won by FUNCINPEC (the National United Front for a Neutral, Independent, Peaceful and Cooperative Cambodia), a party led by Prince Sihanouk's son, Prince Norodom Ranariddh; fifty-one seats were won by the CPP, led by Hun Sen; and the remaining few were won by various other parties.[110] The Khmer Rouge did not win a single seat. Sadly, the Khmer Rouge did not allow peace in Cambodia. As noted by the Centre for the Study of Australia-Asia Relations:

---

[106] Nate Thayer, *Bloody Agenda: Khmer Rouge set out to wreck planned elections*, FAR E. ECON. REV., Apr. 15, 1993 (pagination unavailable online).

[107] FROST, *supra* note 98, at 14.

[108] Berdal & Keifer, *supra* note 101, at 55.

[109] Rodney Tasker & Nate Thayer, *Difficult Birth*, FAR E. ECON. REV., Jun. 10, 1993 (pagination unavailable online).

[110] Frieson, *supra* note 20, at 25.

[T]he elections were a remarkable tribute to the organizational capacity of the UNTAC Electoral Component and to the courage and tenacity of the Cambodian people whose dedication to the process was unarguable. The high participation in the elections enhanced greatly the credibility of the U.N. involvement and of the peace process overall. The successful conduct of the elections, however, naturally did not stop the process of political conflict in Cambodia, which immediately entered a new phase at the end of May.[111]

Although the Khmer Rouge lost the elections in a humiliating defeat, its disgrace only served to make its members more dedicated, determined, and aggressive.[112] Rich from gem mining and timber operations on the Thai border and heavily armed with a weapons cache, the Khmer Rouge launched military and propaganda offenses soon after the new government was elected.[113] Its outlandish claims included, for example, an allegation that the CPP controlled 300,000 Vietnamese agents masquerading as civil servants, police, and soldiers, while FUNCINPEC led only 100 men.[114]

The legitimate political process, however, forged on. In an effort to build a more unified government, the Constituent Assembly ratified a new constitution on September 21, 1993.[115] The constitution provides for a constitutional monarchy, in which the king reigns but does not govern, and it vests governing responsibility in the hands of the prime minister. In another turn of events, Hun Sen used his own military strength to force an odd conclusion to the elections: both Prince Ranariddh and Hun Sen were named first and second prime ministers, respectively, and

---

[111] FROST, *supra* note 98, at 38.

[112] FINDLAY, *supra* note 88, at 106.

[113] FROST, *supra* note 98, at 41.

[114] *Id.*

[115] *Id.* at 57.

were charged with co-leading the country.[116] Prince Sihanouk was crowned king again.[117]

Through the initiation of the peace plan, free and fair elections, and the eventual compromise between the leading parties, the Khmer Rouge lost both its international and domestic support. Just as the world was ready to rejoice over the dissolution of this evil empire, the Khmer Rouge ominously declared, "Between the path for survival and the path for death, we choose the path for survival."[118] The Khmer Rouge would live to fight another day.

PHOENIX RISING?

We should have died in 1979. Our army was completely defeated and dismantled, but was rebuilt from the countryside. What's necessary for us is the countryside. . . .[119]

Following the elections, the Khmer Rouge retreated to its jungle strongholds to strengthen and fortify its troops and to mobilize a new war effort. Though many soldiers defected, leaving only about 15,000 troops (compared to more than 30,000 before the Accords), the Khmer Rouge still controlled 20 percent of the countryside.[120] Its new strategy ignored the election results and sought to force the parties in power to recognize the Khmer Rouge as a political force by stimulating unrest through carefully planned skirmishes.[121] Experts in protracted rebellion, heavily armed due to its recent weapons buildup, and in control of land rich in rice, gems, and timber, the Khmer Rouge could sustain itself indefinitely. The world community, under the impression that the combination of electoral defeat and military atrophy would spell the deathblow for the Khmer Rouge, was unprepared for the regime's new, more exacting attack. As one insider soon realized,

---

[116] *Id.*

[117] *Id.*

[118] Nate Thayer, *Survival Tactics: Khmer Rouge plans its post-poll strategy*, FAR E. ECON. REV., Jun. 10, 1993 (pagination unavailable online).

[119] *Id.* (quoting Pol Pot in a speech to Party cadres in 1992).

[120] *Id.*

[121] *Id.*

"If their objective was a military victory, OK [we could handle them], but their objective is political instability. For this they have enough troops."[122]

Consistent with its militaristic approach, the Khmer Rouge launched an offensive against government corruption and ineptitude. It seized upon every instance of bribery and failure to foster a sense of disillusionment and cynicism toward the governing powers.[123] As if calling upon old friends, it revived its racist and nationalist invective against the Vietnamese and foreign imperialists. But these familiar accusations did not garner the same level of support as before. Even the troops began to disbelieve charges of Vietnamese occupation. As noted by one Khmer Rouge defector, "When we went to fight, we did not see other nationalities."[124] Nor did Cambodians believe stories of foreign aggression:

> [V]illagers see millions of dollars coming in from abroad for development projects and health care. British and French aid groups are clearing thousands of land mines from roads and in villages. They are followed by UN-supported road-building crews, many of whom employ Khmer Rouge defectors and their families. After the roads are built, other aid workers enter to repair irrigation systems and provide veterinary health care.[125]

The people had finally concluded that the nation's true enemy was war itself. A new vision swept through the countryside. Symbolic of this new sentiment, the governor of Siem Reap—a town bordering on Khmer Rouge territory—announced to scores of drunken government officials, military officers and former Khmer

---

[122] *Id.*

[123] *See* Nate Thayer, *Theatre of the Absurd*, FAR E. ECON. REV., Sept. 1, 1994 (pagination unavailable online) ("It is this disenchantment, rather than policies of the murderous guerilla faction, that has planted the seeds for the survival of the Khmer Rouge.").

[124] Nate Thayer, *Rebels Without a Cause*, FAR E. ECON. REV., Apr. 27, 1995 (pagination unavailable online).

[125] *Id.*

Rouge cadres in celebration of the Cambodian new year, "With the Khmer Rouge and the government working together we will build roads, build schools, build happy places."[126] The crowd cheered wildly.

POLITICS MAKES STRANGE BEDFELLOWS

Crush! Crush! Crush! Pol Pot and his murderous clique![127]

The next few years after the elections were grim ones for the Khmer Rouge. Its troops were continually defecting to join government forces and reap the benefits of a brighter future.[128] The government grew adept at slowing the illicit timber trade. And the Khmer Rouge-controlled gem fields were drying up. Faced with declining revenue and abandonment by its troops, the Khmer Rouge's days appeared to be numbered. Just as it seemed that its existence was coming to a final and quiet end, the bitter feud between Hun Sen and Prince Ranariddh provided it with an opportunity to carry on.

Contemptuous of each other since their 1993 compromise, both men had been building personal support within the government military to strengthen their holds on power. Each extended offers to the Khmer Rouge to join their forces.[129] Pol Pot adamantly refused. Khmer Rouge cadres attempted to plan a mutiny whereby they would hand Pot over to the authorities and join FUNCINPEC's ranks. They met in secret with Ranarridh's emissaries. But Pot crushed their plans by ordering his most loyal

---

[126] *Id.*

[127] Nate Thayer, *Brother Number Zero*, FAR E. ECON. REV., Aug. 7, 1997 (pagination unavailable online) (quoting village chant during "people's tribunal").

[128] *See* Nate Thayer, *The Resurrected: The Khmer Rouge haven't disappeared*, FAR E. ECON. REV., Apr. 16, 1998 (pagination unavailable online) (noting that the government's promise that defectors could keep their territory, exploit gem and timber resources, and hold senior positions in its armed forces was quite persuasive).

[129] Nate Thayer, *The Deal That Died*, FAR E. ECON. REV., Aug. 21, 1997 (pagination unavailable online).

troops—a group of approximately 300—to ambush Ranariddh's men, executing ten and holding the remaining five captive. All talks ceased for three months, when in another attempt at peace, FUNCINPEC again opened covert negotiations with the Khmer Rouge. This time, the Khmer Rouge informed Pol Pot of its desire to negotiate. Disapproving, Pot attempted a murderous purge at the highest level. He ordered the execution of Sun Sen, the Khmer Rouge Defense Minister, and his family—fifteen people in all.[130] They were shot, dragged into the streets, and repeatedly run over by trucks. All-out war ensued.

Ailing and completely surrounded by his own men, Pol Pot surrendered on June 19, 1997. Ranariddh and the Khmer Rouge worked feverishly to develop a detailed plan of integration. Hun Sen, fearful of his future, condemned Ranariddh's contact with the Khmer Rouge as traitorous. Quickly and quietly, he prepared for war. On July 6, the Khmer Rouge planned to announce that it would formally recognize the Cambodian constitution, disband its governing body, and join the government forces.[131] The thirty-two-year reign of the Khmer Rouge would finally come to an end.

But peace was not to be had on that day. Instead, preempting the announcement of a Khmer Rouge dissolution, Hun Sen launched a coup on July 5, taking absolute control of the government, driving FUNCINPEC's Phnom Penh forces into the jungles and sending the deposed prince into exile.[132] Several months later, Hun Sen led a show trial against Ranariddh, still in exile, that convicted him for negotiating with the Khmer Rouge.[133] The court imposed a thirty-year prison sentence.[134] With no small sense of irony, Hun Sen was conducting secret negotiations with the Khmer Rouge on the day of Ranariddh's conviction.[135]

This jockeying for power revived the nearly defunct Khmer Rouge, which suddenly became a pivotal force in the race for

---

[130] Thayer, *supra* note 127.
[131] Thayer, *supra* note 129.
[132] *Id.*
[133] Thayer, *supra* note 128.
[134] *Id.*
[135] *Id.*

power. It attempted to curry favor with the international community by convicting Pol Pot in a "people's trial" in the middle of their jungle outpost and "shopping" him to anyone willing to "buy."[136] But before the world could act, Pol Pot, the leader of a thirty-eight-year armed rebellion responsible for the deaths of two million people in a reign of terror matched by the likes of Hitler and Stalin, passed away at the age of seventy-three on April 15, 1998, purportedly of a heart attack.[137]

Amidst this turmoil, a new round of elections was scheduled for just three months away. Ranariddh remained in exile, his influence weakened by his ousting and criminal conviction, while Hun Sen strengthened his power as he claimed credit for arranging peace with the Khmer Rouge and launched a brutal campaign of fear.[138] Allegations of electoral violations abounded, including, for example, that the CPP warned voters to choose Hun Sen and then took their thumb prints to track their votes.[139] These criticisms, along with the ongoing feud between Hun Sen and Prince Ranariddh, led to months of waiting as the parties negotiated a peaceful settlement. On November 26, 1998, both sides agreed to end the bloodshed.[140] Hun Sen was named the sole prime minister and Ranariddh, whose conviction was dropped, was named Speaker of the National Assembly.[141]

---

[136] Nate Thayer, *Nowhere to Hide*, FAR E. ECON. REV., Apr. 23, 1998 (pagination unavailable online).

[137] Nate Thayer, *Dying Breath: The inside story of Pol Pot's last days and the disintegration of the movement he created*, FAR E. ECON. REV., Apr. 30, 1998 (pagination unavailable online).

[138] Nate Thayer & Rodney Tasker, *"We Are Scared": But Cambodians still voted in droves*, FAR E. ECON. REV., Aug. 13, 1998 (pagination unavailable online).

[139] *Id.*

[140] Seth Mydans, *Familiar Rite, Familiar Politics in Cambodian Assembly*, N.Y. TIMES, Nov. 26, 1998, at A3.

[141] *Id.*

LEGACY OF THE KHMER ROUGE

The world community should stop talking now that Pol Pot is dead. It was all Pol Pot.[142]

Because of the realignment of forces over the last several years, the concept of a Khmer Rouge movement as we know it no longer has any meaning.[143]

[T]he point is, no one can afford to give the Khmer Rouge the benefit of the doubt. There can be no second chance. By the time we knew what they intended, it would be too late.[144]

What is left of the Khmer Rouge? Pol Pot is dead and the movement disbanded. But the bloodstains of Cambodian warfare—brother against brother—remain in the foreground of every Cambodian's memory. Ex-Khmer Rouge cadres inhabit every sector of the government and its military. Former low-level members, simple soldiers, were taught to place such little value on human life that their brutality against fellow Cambodians shocks the conscience. Yet, as soldiers in the government military, they are now charged with keeping the peace among Cambodia's citizenry.

Perhaps more threatening, however, are the high-level Khmer Rouge members who now sit in positions of power in the government. As Khmer Rouge, they were both barbarous and fanatical in pursuit of their political agenda. As high-ranking government officials, they may show strains of the same behavior, though it is unlikely that they will cling to any grand visions of a Communist overthrow. Indeed, it is questionable whether they ever truly believed in Communist ideology as a solution to government

---

[142] Thayer, *supra* note 137 (quoting Ta Mok, long-time member of the Khmer Rouge inner-circle and leader of the movement since he seized control from Pol Pot in July 1997).

[143] Thayer, *supra* note 127 (quoting Stephen Heder of the University of London's School of Advanced International Studies).

[144] James Pringle, *US challenges China over Khmer Rouge*, TIMES, Jul. 19, 1990 (pagination unavailable online) (quoting a Hong Kong based diplomat).

failure. Most of these men were opportunists at heart, Communism being just a convenient tool to mobilize a war effort. Even Pol Pot admitted in 1992 that the true source of Khmer Rouge power was its ardent following, not Communist ideology: "What's necessary for us is the countryside, not Communism."[145] But opportunism itself, where it preaches disregard for the rule of law, is devastating to any democratic movement.

CAMBODIAN POLITICS: A LESSON IN THE RULE OF FORCE

Killing and suppression are going on on a very large scale. Hun Sen is a murderous prime minister.[146]

As a lesson in democracy, the [1998] election's message to Cambodians may have been that real power does not yet come from the ballot box but from feudal chieftains.[147]

The notion of democracy in Cambodia is relatively young. Centuries ago, Cambodia was run by warlords intent on building their empire. After the fall of the Angkor Empire, Cambodia functioned peacefully under monarchical rule for centuries. The populace, mostly unconcerned with either politics or financial gain, simply existed. Even after the French occupied their country, forcing them to recognize France as their new mother country, most Cambodians remained apathetic toward politics. Cambodia did not become politicized until the 1960s, when foreign powers pulled the country into war and economic pressures mounted against Cambodia's educated youth. At that time, war cries echoed through the countryside, propaganda filled the air, bombs rained from the sky, all Cambodians drew sides, and the rule of law was replaced by the rule of force.

---

[145] Thayer, *supra* note 118 (quoting Pol Pot in speech to Party cadres in 1992).

[146] Nate Thayer, *Harrowing Tales: Hun Sen's forces torture and kill former allies*, FAR E. ECON. REV., Aug. 7, 1997 (pagination unavailable online).

[147] Mydans, *supra* note 140.

For a brief time, Lon Nol's forces reigned supreme. But the Khmer Rouge was fearless and intractable. Guided by strength of will and a ferocity rarely seen in the history of mankind, it soon overran Nol and took the country by storm. Yet, Pol Pot's troops lacked the strength of superior Vietnamese forces. A mere four years later, Vietnam took over Cambodia with relative ease. Again, the rule of force remained supreme.

Soon after, the political tenor of the region changed. Vietnam, Thailand, China, the former Soviet Union, and the United States turned toward negotiations and reconciliation rather than warfare. Vietnam relinquished control of Cambodia and the United Nations attempted to build a democratic infrastructure. Two years later, practically overnight, the United Nations achieved its goal of administering "free and fair" elections in Cambodia. The rule of law had been restored.

But these accomplishments were ephemeral. Hun Sen strong-armed his way into a co-prime ministership despite the fact that Prince Ranariddh had been duly elected. Hun Sen turned the world community's $2.7 billion effort at building a democratic movement in Cambodia on its end. The rule of law had been overcome once again.

Soon thereafter, the Cambodian government experienced internal, non-democratic clashes between Sen and Ranariddh. Each sought to build support against the other by forming alliances with military factions inside the government. Each sought deals with Khmer Rouge defectors. Eventually, Hun Sen won his battle with Ranariddh, taking control of the country in a bloody coup, brokering deals with Khmer Rouge defectors and sending Ranariddh into exile. During Ranariddh's forced absence, Hun Sen convicted him of traitorous activities and sentenced him to thirty years in prison. The rule of force took root.

Just three months later, the Hun Sen regime claimed an emphatic victory in what were deemed "free and fair" elections by the international community.[148] But the cursory review of the election process by foreign officials was so deficient that one provincial governor remarked, "the foreign observers just drove

---

[148] Thayer & Tasker, *supra* note 138.

along the road past the polling stations so fast that their tyres didn't touch the mud."[149] After further inquiry, the foreign community acknowledged that the elections were neither free nor fair.[150] In a fitting conclusion to the 1998 "democratic" elections, Hun Sen welcomed Ranariddh back into the political fold and formed an agreement that only loosely squared with the election results.[151] Currently, the rule of force remains firmly in place, though it is now masked by a rule of law veneer.

CONCLUSION: THE FUTURE OF DEMOCRACY IN CAMBODIA

Former Khmer Rouge cadres now in the government include Hun Sen himself, the defense minister, the interior minister, the finance minister, the head of the national assembly, and thousands of others in the provincial and local administrations.[152]

The UN dream of transforming Cambodian politics overnight from one of militaristic rule to one fully supportive of democratic values is dead. Though the Khmer Rouge may be defunct as a political entity, its motive—a voracious appetite for power and wealth—is alive and well in Cambodia. Nevertheless, despite the United Nations' inability to achieve its lofty goals, it did achieve a great deal of success: a democratic structure has been put in place and the populace enthusiastically supports electoral politics. But because the Cambodian government is operated by a large group of Khmer Rouge defectors, the United Nations must maintain pressure on this fragile, fledgling body to continue its reform. Future international efforts must force those in power to respect the democratic process. Otherwise, they will revert to their past behavior and bloody conflict will ensue. Democracy is possible in

---

[149] *Id.*

[150] Mydans, *supra* note 140 (noting that most foreign analysts now agree that the election was "badly flawed by the muscle and manipulation of Mr. Hun Sen's party.").

[151] *Id.* ("Its outcome was the result of post-election struggles as much as of the voting itself.")

[152] Thayer, *supra* note 128.

Cambodia, but it will require continued, steady pressure by outside forces for years to come.[153]

POSTSCRIPT

The story of the Khmer Rouge remains compelling not only as a horrifying fragment of Cambodian history, but also—and perhaps more importantly—as a case study in genocide. Fueled by an explosive combination of poverty, political isolation, demagoguery, and failed governance, genocide is a phenomenon of unabashed aggression that continues to repeat itself despite our assertions of "Never again!" Examining the factors leading to the Cambodian genocide will help diagnose (this author hopes) the symptoms that lead to such kinds of systematic collapse, with the goal of one day anticipating and stifling extremist movements before mass killings begin.

Michael Rakower, April 12, 2004

---

[153] This analysis was submitted in December 1999. Except for technical edits, nothing in it has been altered.

BIBLIOGRAPHY

Berdal, Mats, and Michael Keifer. "Cambodia." In *The New Interventionism: The United Nations Experience in Cambodia, Yugoslavia and Somalia*, edited by James Mayall, 1996.

Burgler, R. A. *The Eyes of the Pineapple: Revolutionary Intellectuals and Terror in Democratic Kampuchea*. 1990.

Chanda, Nayan, and Nate Thayer. "Law of the Gun." *Far Eastern Economic Review*, July 17, 1997.

Chandler, David P. *The Tragedy of Cambodian History*. 1991.

———. "From 'Cambodge' To 'Kampuchea': State and Revolution in Cambodia 1863-1979." In *Thesis Eleven*. 1997.

Findlay, Trevor. *Cambodia: The Legacy and Lessons of UNTAC*. 1995.

Frieson, Kate G. "Revolution and Rural Response in Cambodia: 1970-1975." In *Genocide and Democracy in Cambodia*, edited by Ben Kiernan, 1993.

Frost, Frank. *The Peace Process in Cambodia: Issues and Prospects*, Centre for the Study of Australia-Asia Relations Number 69, 1993.

Kiernan, Ben. "Wild Chickens, Farm Chickens, And Cormorants: Kampuchea's Eastern Zone Under Pol Pot." In *Revolution and Its Aftermath in Kampuchea*, edited by David P. Chandler and Ben Kiernan, 1983.

Le Sage, David, and Sean Watson. "Pol Pot: A Biographical Essay." Available at http://www.eliz.tased.edu.au/ITStu97//polpot.htm.

Moore, John Norton. *Law and the Indo-China War*. 1972.

Mydans, Seth. "Familiar Rite, Familiar Politics in Cambodian Assembly." *The New York Times*, November 26, 1998, at A3.

Pringle, James. "US challenges China over Khmer Rouge." *The Times*, July 19, 1990.

Rummel, R. J. *Death by Government*. 1994.

Sikes, Jonathan. "Pol Pot's New Wave of Killers." *The Sunday Telegraph*, July 22, 1990.

Tasker, Rodney, and Nate Thayer. "Difficult Birth." *Far Eastern Economic Review*, June 10, 1993.

―――――. "'We Are Scared': But Cambodians still voted in droves." *Far Eastern Economic Review*, August 13, 1998.

Thayer, Nate. "Pol Pot Unmasked: He was obsessed with secrecy and total control." *Far Eastern Economic Review*, August 7, 1997.

―――――. "Bloody Agenda: Khmer Rouge set out to wreck planned elections." *Far Eastern Economic Review*, April 15, 1993.

―――――. "Brother Number Zero." *Far Eastern Economic Review*, August 7, 1997.

―――――. "Dying Breath: The inside story of Pol Pot's last days and the disintegration of the movement he created." *Far Eastern Economic Review*, April 30, 1998.

―――――. "Harrowing Tales: Hun Sen's forces torture and kill former allies." *Far Eastern Economic Review*, August 7, 1997.

―――――. "Rebels Without a Cause." *Far Eastern Economic Review*, April 27, 1995.

―――――. "Survival Tactics: Khmer Rouge plans its post-poll strategy." *Far Eastern Economic Review*, June 10, 1993.

―――――. "The Resurrected: The Khmer Rouge haven't disappeared." *Far Eastern Economic Review*, April 16, 1998.

―――――. "Theatre of the Absurd." *Far Eastern Economic Review*, September 1, 1994.

―――――. "The Deal That Died." *Far Eastern Economic Review*, August 21, 1997.

Thion, Serge. "The Cambodian Idea of Revolution." In *Revolution and Its Aftermath in Kampuchea*, edited by David P. Chandler and Ben Kiernan, Yale Southeast Asia Studies Monograph Series, 1983.

Vickery, Michael. "Democratic Kampuchea—Themes and Variations." In *Revolution and Its Aftermath in Kampuchea*, edited by David P. Chandler and Ben Kiernan, 1983.

V

The Ideology of the Khmer Rouge: Intellectual Origins of the Kampuchean Revolution

John H. Raleigh

INTRODUCTION

On April 17, 1975, the Khmer Rouge captured the Cambodian capital of Phnom Penh from the faltering forces of Lon Nol's Khmer Republic. Forty-four months later, these same forces were driven from the capital by the Vietnamese invasion force. The intervening period may have witnessed the greatest per capita loss of life in a single nation in the twentieth century.[1] Of the 7.3 million Cambodians said to be alive on April 17, 1975, less than six million remained to greet the Vietnamese occupiers in 1978.[2] No one was entirely safe from this reign of terror.

---

[1] Karl D. Jackson, *The Ideology of Total Revolution, in* CAMBODIA 1975-1978: RENDEZVOUS WITH DEATH 37 (Karl Jackson ed., 1989) [hereinafter CAMBODIA 1975-1978].

[2] Estimates as to the total number of deaths in excess of the "normal" death rate during the Pol Pot regime vary considerably depending on the source. According to Hun Sen, the former Heng Samrin minister of foreign affairs, Cambodia had four million people left in 1979. However, most scholars believe this to be an exaggeration. The median hypothesis of a 1980 Central Intelligence Agency Study says that the Cambodian population dropped from 7.38 million in April 1975 to 5.85 million by January 1979. Ben Kiernan estimates that one million (1/8 of the population) Cambodians died during the Khmer Rouge reign. David Chandler has concurred with this figure. *See* R.A. BURGLER, 3 THE EYES OF THE PINEAPPLE: REVOLUTIONARY INTELLECTUALS AND TERROR IN DEMOCRATIC KAMPUCHEA 161-69 (1990).

Not only were the highest echelons of the Lon Nol bureaucracy and army quickly dispatched, but, in addition, the killing and the dying endured throughout the revolution's forty-four month tenure. As time passed, it devoured its own, especially at the infamous Tuol Sleng prison, where communist cadres and their families were being executed down to the last days of the Khmer Rouge rule as Pol Pot's regime purged and repurged itself in a fratricidal search for ideological purity and internal security.[3]

Given the immensity of the violence and suffering that characterized the Cambodian tragedy, inevitable questions arise as to what type of ideology could lead a government to such extremes. Pol Pot publicly revealed that Democratic Kampuchea (revolutionary Cambodia) was a Communist country in late September 1977,[4] and yet, repeatedly, Khmer Rouge leaders emphasized that the roots of their revolution followed no foreign model ideology.[5] They often claimed that there was, in fact, no "theory" behind their revolution.[6] Commentators outside Cambodia have added to the confusion. Recently, for example, many proponents of the global Communist philosophy have tried to deny the Khmer Rouge its Communist credentials by labeling Democratic Kampuchea as "rabidly fascist," practicing a form of "medieval barbarity."[7] Others have questioned whether the ideas of the leaders of the revolution had anything "to do with socialism or communism" and portrayed them as driven by extreme nationalism bordering on xenophobia.[8]

---

[3] Karl D. Jackson, *Introduction. The Khmer Rouge in Context, in* CAMBODIA 1975-1978, *supra* note 1, at 3.

[4] Kenneth Quinn, *Explaining the Terror, in* CAMBODIA 1975-1978, *supra* note 1, at 220.

[5] *See* BURGLER, *supra* note 2, at 58-60.

[6] *See* David P. Chandler, *A Revolution in Full Spate, in* THE CAMBODIAN AGONY 165 (David Ablin & Marlow Hood eds., 1987).

[7] *See* Karl D. Jackson, *Intellectual Origins of the Khmer Rouge, in* CAMBODIA 1975-1978, *supra* note 1, at 241.

[8] *Id.*

Were the Cambodian revolutionaries genuine Communists? If they were Communist, from where did their form of Communism derive—from Mao's China, Stalin's Russia, France of the late 1950s and early 1960s, or sources indigenous to Cambodia itself? Beyond this, what led the revolution to such extremes? This chapter will argue that the ideology of the revolutionary elite of the Khmer Rouge represented a unique and, in the end, dangerous amalgam of each of the influences listed above.[9] It was this dangerous mix that at least sanctioned, if not demanded, a resort to such extremes.

THE HISTORY AND PROGRESSION OF COMMUNIST THOUGHT

The philosophy and historical analysis of Karl Marx (1818-1883) is generally considered the origin of the line of thought that evolved into modern Communism. In his two seminal works, *The*

---

[9] The actions and politics of Yugoslavia's revolutionary Communist leader, Josip (Tito) Broz, undoubtedly influenced Pol Pot as well as these other sources. In 1950, at the height of the Stalinist attacks against Tito, Pol Pot (then Saloth Sar) traveled to Yugoslavia. He stayed for only one month as a student volunteer on a brigade that was building the highway from Zagreb to Belgrade, but later, he would exalt this visit, implicitly comparing the Yugoslavian revolution to Cambodia's own.

During his stay, Pol Pot was impressed by the small Communist country attempting to chart a separate course in spite of protests from its far more powerful Communist neighbor. He must also have been exposed to the massive mobilization of the country, as was his fellow Cambodian Leu Yang. "Everywhere," Yang wrote, "the People's Federal Republic of Yugoslavia resembles an enormous work site where factories, roads, railways and hydraulic centers are being built. This effort is also worthy of praise because of the strength of all of the people, united around their leaders, gives them the chance of gaining successive victories, knowing that it is a question of national survival." *See* DAVID P. CHANDLER, BROTHER NUMBER ONE: A POLITICAL BIOGRAPHY OF POL POT 30-31 (1992).

The parallels between Pol Pot and Tito are obvious. I have not discussed Tito's influence at length, however, because unlike Lenin, Stalin, Mao, Amin, and Fanon, Tito did not provide his own original, ideological contributions to Marxism. He, like Pol Pot, practiced an ideology that was primarily derived from nature.

Communist Manifesto and *Capital*, Marx argued that all history is the story of class struggle.[10] Therefore, it is in the analysis of class relations that the true answers to the great questions of politics and history are to be found.[11] Projecting what he saw as the current class dynamic, as developed in an increasingly industrialized society, to its logical extreme, Marx predicted that one day the masses of humanity (the proletariat) would cease to meekly carry out the self-interested dictates of the ruling class and would seize the levers of economic power (the means of production) and political authority for themselves.[12] When this occurred on a global scale, the natural harmony of the majority of humankind would prevail. Political competition for economic surplus would fade and, along with it, the vehicle of that struggle, the state, would wither and cease to exist.[13]

Vladimir Lenin (1870-1924), building on the works of Rudolf Hilferding, John A. Hobson, and others, extended Marx's work in a number of important ways. This extension has been characterized as a move from Marxian determinism to Leninist voluntarism. Lenin argued that the historical progression from primitive Communism to feudalism, through capitalism and socialism, and finally to Communism was not an objective necessity.[14] He argued that it is possible, under the right conditions, to skip a stage in the historical progression.[15]

Lenin also argued that it was not necessary for the proletariat to be the dominant force in society in order for the revolutionary transformation from capitalism to socialism to occur, as long as a properly motivated "vanguard party" existed to provide leadership and focus to the energy of the masses.[16] Lenin saw the role of the Communist party as a weapon of revolutionary struggle rather than a product of some slow societal evolution or spontaneous uprising

---

[10] *See* KARL MARX, THE COMMUNIST MANIFESTO 131 (H.L. Laski ed., 1967).

[11] *Id.* at 130-49.

[12] *Id.* at 148-49.

[13] *Id.* at 157-58.

[14] *See* ADAM WESTOBY, THE EVOLUTION OF COMMUNISM 174-75 (1989).

[15] *Id.*

[16] *See* ROY MEDVEDEV, LENINISM & WESTERN SOCIALISM 152-57 (1981).

of the working class.[17] Consequently, the full terrors of bourgeois development could be avoided by "stage-leaping" over the unpleasant period of capitalist accumulation and economic consolidation, directly into the period of the harmonious dominance of the many.[18] Joseph Stalin (1879-1953) was forced to deal with what he saw as the continuing ability of the capitalist nations to stave off their imminent collapse.[19] If the revolution failed to occur spontaneously on a global scale, then the Russian Revolution must be preserved to await such a global revolution.[20] Stalin's famous "socialism in one country" asserted that autonomous development of socialist forces in a single country would precede the emergence of a unified, global Communism.[21] This "socialism in one country" was counterpoised to Trotsky's alleged adventuristic internationalism, and had a strong nationalist connotation.[22] Another unique characteristic of Stalinism was the belief that the state must be greatly strengthened before it could be expected to wither away.[23] A third tenet of Stalinism, which like the second could be used to justify state repression and terror, was that class struggle must necessarily grow in intensity as socialism advanced.[24]

Mao Tse-tung (1893-1976) expanded the idea of Communism as developed by Marx and Lenin. One of the most striking developments introduced by Mao was his view of which groups constituted the revolutionary masses, his interpretation of the Marxian "proletariat." Mao expanded the traditional, Marxist-Leninist view of the proletariat as the urban working class with the conviction that the peasantry, the property-less of the countryside, must play an active role in building a socialist society.[25] Mao also

---

[17] Id.

[18] Id.

[19] See WESTOBY, supra note 14, at 173-74.

[20] Id. at 174-75.

[21] Id.

[22] See RAYA DUNAYEVSAYA, PHILOSOPHY AND REVOLUTION 140 (1973).

[23] See MEDVEDEV, supra note 16, at 192.

[24] Id.

[25] See LESZEK KOLAKOWSKI, MAIN CURRENTS OF COMMUNISM: ITS ORIGINS, GROWTH, AND DISSOLUTION 499 (1981).

introduced into the Marxist philosophy of history the idea that human change must accompany and support economic and technical progress.[26] This change could come about through a combination of study and revolutionary practice.

THE IDEOLOGICAL ORIGINS OF THE COMMUNISM OF THE KHMER ROUGE

Mao Tse-tung

Judging the amount of influence Maoist thought had on the development of Khmer Rouge ideology is complicated by the many contradictory statements made by the leaders of the Khmer Rouge. From 1977 on, Pol Pot frequently acknowledged the Cambodian revolutionaries' debt to the thought of Mao. At a press conference in Peking in late 1977, Pol Pot acknowledged the influence of Mao in the development of the Communist party platform of 1957:

We . . . learned from the experience of the world revolution and in particular Comrade Mao Tse-tung's works and the experience of the Chinese revolution played an important role at that time. After summing up the concrete experiences of the world revolution, particularly under the guidance of Comrade Mao Tse-tung's works, we have found a road conforming with concrete conditions and social conditions of our country.[27]

Pol Pot again acknowledged the influence of Mao while addressing a banquet hosted by the Central Committee of the Chinese Communist Party in the fall of 1977: "In the concrete revolutionary struggle of our country, we have creatively and

---

[26] See BURGLER, *supra* note 2, at 243; KOLAKOWSKI, *supra* note 25, at 151 (quoting Mao Tse-tung: ". . . the outstanding thing about China's 600 million people is that they are 'poor and blank.'. . . On a blank sheet of paper free from any mark, the most beautiful characters can be written . . . .").

[27] Quinn, *supra* note 4, at 219-20 (*citing* Foreign Broadcast Information Service, Springfield, VA, U.S. Department of Commerce, Oct. 3, 1977, at A20-21) [hereinafter FBIS].

successfully applied Mao Tse-tung's thought—from the time we had only empty hands to April 17, 1975."[28] And in his eulogy after Mao's death, Pol Pot described Mao as "the most eminent teacher. . . since Marx, Engels, Lenin, and Stalin."[29]

These acknowledgments by Pol Pot must be weighed against his contemporaneous statements that Cambodian Communism was unique and not a product of any foreign movement or influence.[30] Pol Pot consistently emphasized the need for indigenous goals and methods in the development of a revolutionary movement and a new society:

> Now that we have established that we need a line, what kind of line is it? A line copied from other people will do no good. This line should be based on the principles of independence, initiative, self-determination, and self-reliance, which means that we must rely primarily on our own people, our own army, our own revolution and on the actual revolutionary movement of the masses in our own country.[31]

The leaders of the Khmer Rouge also consistently dismissed the role theory played in the revolutionary movement of their country.[32] In 1976, for example, Ieng Sary emphasized this belief to a visitor from the Palestine Liberation Organization: "We did not act with the guidance of definite theories, but followed our feelings and carried out the struggle in a practical way. What is important is the determination and faith of the principal revolutionaries. We did not study in ideological schools, but practiced a struggle in the light of concrete situation."[33] In a speech commemorating the eighteenth anniversary of the founding of the Communist Party of Kampuchea (CPK), Pol Pot tempered Sary's denigration of theory, but still recognized the hegemony of

---

[28] *Id.* at 220 (*citing* FBIS I, Sept. 29, 1977, at A19).

[29] *Id.* at 221.

[30] *See* BURGLER, *supra* note 2, at 59.

[31] Jackson, *supra* note 1, at 40.

[32] *See* Chandler, *supra* note 6, at 165.

[33] *Id.*

practice, remarking that "theory helps practice, and practice helps theory, but practice remains the basis."[34]

Given these contradictory statements and the difficulty in deciphering which statements represent a genuine announcement of party beliefs and which are the result of mere political expediency, it is instructive to examine Khmer Rouge actions in light of these pronouncements. And in examining Khmer Rouge practices, it is striking the degree to which they can be explained by the beliefs and theories of Maoism.

The Critical Role Played By the Youth

Mao formed the Red Guard with masses of extremely young cadres and sent them to the universities, the government offices, the provinces, and the villages and hamlets to propagate and implement his programs. Similarly, Pol Pot's Communist revolution was run by extremely young cadres, often taken from the poorest sections of the country. For both of these leaders, extremely young peasants served as ideal revolutionaries because they (1) had no vested interest in continuing the old system, and (2) were the most effective targets of the Communist education programs, as they had not yet been corrupted by the old society.[35]

The Khmer Rouge focused on peasant youth (most often from the hill country) between the ages of twelve and sixteen. These children were given power and responsibility over whole villages and communes.[36] Prince Sihanouk described the recruitment and indoctrination of these cadres:

> Once they were enlisted in the revolutionary army, these children were separated from families, removed from their home villages to Pol Pot's indoctrination camps. They began their military careers at the age of twelve. Taken in hand so young, these *Youtheas* (youth) were convinced before long that

---

[34] *Id.*

[35] *See* Quinn, *supra* note 4, at 236.

[36] *See* DAVID P. CHANDLER, THE EARLY PHASES OF LIBERATION IN NORTHWEST CAMBODIA: CONVERSATIONS WITH PEANG SOPHI 9 (1976).

the Party was doing them the greatest of honors by naming them *Oppakar Phdach Kar Robas Pak*, literally, "the dictatorial instrument of the Party."[37]

Unlike Mao, however, Pol Pot apparently didn't use his education programs solely to indoctrinate these children in the Party ideology. Pol Pot took advantage of the impressionable youth to develop fierce soldiers and cadres.

Pol Pot and Ieng Sary quite rightly thought that if they trained their young recruits on cruel games, they would end up as soldiers with a love of killing and consequently war. During the three years I [Sihanouk] spent with the Khmer Rouge under guard I saw those guarding my "camp" constantly take pleasure in tormenting animals . . . the Khmer Rouge loved to make their victims suffer as much as possible.[38]

Prince Sihanouk described in greater detail the indoctrination and training methods of the revolutionaries:

Torture games became their principal training tool. Young recruits began "hardening their hearts and minds" by killing dogs, cats, and other edible animals with clubs or bayonets. Even after their April 17, 1975, victory, the Khmer Rouge kept in practice with a game consisting of throwing animals into "the fires of hell," since they had no human victims handy.[39]

Dith Pren, an employee of the *New York Times* in Cambodia who remained inside the country during the entire rule of Pol Pot, attested to the effectiveness of the Khmer Rouge's violent indoctrination of the youth.[40] He stated that he was always most afraid of those Khmer Rouge soldiers who were between the ages

---

[37] Quinn, *supra* note 4, at 237.
[38] *Id.*
[39] *Id.* at 238.
[40] *Id.* at 239.

of twelve and fifteen, because they seemed to be the most completely and savagely indoctrinated.

> [The Khmer Rouge] took them very young and taught them nothing but discipline. Just take orders, no need for a reason. Their minds have nothing inside except discipline. They do not believe any religion or tradition except Khmer Rouge orders. That's why they killed their own people, even babies, like we might kill a mosquito. I believe they did not have any feelings about human life because they were taught only discipline.[41]

Attacks on Vested Interests

In order to establish a truly classless society, a society ruled by the masses, the Khmer Rouge faced the problem of eliminating class divisions. The primary obstacle to this transformation was those individuals who benefited from the class system, who had a stake in society as it was structured.[42] In both recognizing and dealing with this problem, the Khmer Rouge followed the example set by Mao.

Following Mao's cry of "fight self-interest, establish the public interest,"[43] the Cultural Revolutionary Group directed its attack on four groups in China that it believed were opposed to the revolution and interested in maintaining the status quo:

(a.) the majority of rural cadres who had reached accommodations with the peasants or were afraid of losing their positions;

(b.) low-ranking officials whose loyalty was to their bosses;

(c.) ordinary peasants with kinship ties to village leaders, which gave them a favored position;

(d.) peasants with an economic stake in the status quo, such as the "rich peasants" who by 1962 were reemerging in the

---

[41] *Id.*

[42] *See* Quinn, *supra* note 4, at 227.

[43] *Id.*

villages as the government's emphasis turned to increased production.[44]

To uproot these opponents of the revolution, the Chinese again turned to young cadres from distant places, who were interjected into a commune, factory, or university.[45] With no stake in the status quo, they were uninhibited in their attacks on the institutional infrastructure.[46]

Likewise, as early as 1971, young cadres were showing up in villages in southwest Cambodia with a mission to purge local cadres, particularly those considered loyal to Hanoi, and then implement tough new Pol Pot programs.[47] Moreover, it was these outsiders who in June 1973 led the way in establishing new communes, which involved the systematic burning of all hamlets and villages and the forced relocation of thousands upon thousands of Khmer.[48] The new communes were patterned after those of the Great Leap. Similarly, the purges of the Party cadre and the elimination of intellectuals, students, and persons connected to the former government were rooted in the strategy of eliminating any group or individual with a possible vested interest in the old regime.

The Hatred of "Intellectuals"

Another similarity between the Cambodian and Chinese revolutions was a hatred of the intellectual elite. Mao revealed his great antipathy for, and fear of, the intellectual elite during the Great Leap. He believed that Chinese society was composed of essentially three elements: workers, peasants, and intellectuals.[49] Intellectuals, in this sense, were those in the Party and in society who were educated professionals or had technical training.[50] Mao

---

[44] *Id.*
[45] *Id.*
[46] *Id.*
[47] *Id.*
[48] *Id.*
[49] *See* BURGLER, *supra* note 2, at 251-52.
[50] *See* Quinn, *supra* note 4, at 228.

saw the "contradiction" between intellectuals and the peasants as one of the key stumbling blocks to the achievement of full socialism. Mao's great fear was that these "experts" were too conservative and too interested in maintaining their own elevated place in society.[51] The problem in China, as Mao saw it, was that this new elite (the intellectuals) emerged before the completion of the socialist transformation and thus had no stake in seeing the process completed. They were instead interested in maintaining the status quo.[52] Mao's attempt to eliminate this obstacle led to the Anti-Rightist Campaign of 1957:

> The Chinese anti-rightist campaign of 1957 was . . . aimed at jerking the intellectuals from their elite status and replacing them with peasants with greater political loyalty to the Party's ideology. In 1958, just as would occur later in the Cultural Revolution, administrators, managers, technicians were attacked for their lack of revolutionary zeal. Their punishment was to be sent to the countryside to be indoctrinated into the rigors of communal life. Their places were filled by peasants trained at "worker-peasant universities" and inculcated with the notion that they would master the intricacies of technology by virtue of their political ardor.[53]

The aim of Pol Pot's movement was to avoid a need to take this action by achieving complete socialist transformation prior to the emergence of this new elite; thus there was a need for speed and a total break from the past. Pol Pot waged an anti-intellectual campaign in 1976 and 1977 that extended throughout Khmer society and rivaled that of China.[54] Persons with any education or managerial background were singled out for harsh punishment or were subject to execution.[55] "In emulation of the Chinese, Pol Pot also allowed only 'poor,' usually semi-literate, peasants to

---

[51] *Id.*
[52] *Id.*
[53] *Id.*
[54] *Id.*
[55] *Id.*

participate in administrative and technological functions—a policy that greatly accelerated the crumbling of the Cambodian economy."[56]

Elimination of Individual Incentives

Still another similarity between Pol Pot's and Mao's revolutions was the attempt to eliminate individual incentives. Mao saw a contradiction in Chinese society between individualism and collectivism. He believed that individual incentives, favored by economic pragmatists like Deng Xiaoping and Zhen Yun, led to a "vested-interestedism" and, thus, away from socialism.[57] Social mobilization, Mao believed, could better motivate people to do work, and during the Great Leap Forward and the Cultural Revolution, there was a movement toward collective rewards.[58] In fact, in some areas in 1958, wages were done away with and workers were paid with part of their work product.[59] And later, the Cultural Revolution saw the initiation of the Ta Chai system in which collectives would accrue work points rather than monetary profits, as well as a system of red flag awards to communes making special economic achievements.[60]

Again emulating its ideological patrons, the Khmer Rouge leaders sought to eliminate all individual incentive in their economic system. Ith Sarin, one of the leaders of the Khmer Rouge, described this focus on the collective at the expense of the individual interest:

> The Organization continually guides them [the cadres] to try to get rid of "personal traits," individualistic aspects which they denounce as "reactionary traits," that in order to attain the highest, one must hold firm an "overall image" of the principle of "collectivity" and concentrate on the greater rather than on

---

[56] Id.

[57] Id. at 234.

[58] Id. at 229.

[59] Id.

[60] Id.

personal interest . . . . All of these traits are regarded as
opposed to the revolution as traits of the oppressor class, traits
of the reactionaries. [61]

The total destruction of the money economy, along with the
establishment of a completely communal work organization meant
that a Cambodian now had no way of accruing any type of material
wealth or even being rewarded for doing good or extra work.[62] The
Khmer Rouge saw this as a necessary step in the move to a
collective consciousness.

Anti-City Bias

One of the most striking and, for the Western world,
inexplicable similarities of the revolutions in China and Cambodia
was the emptying of the cities. In China, during the Great Leap
Forward and the Cultural Revolution, the revolutionaries enacted
programs to send millions of residents of the cities into the
countryside. Pol Pot and the Khmer Rouge took this bias to an
extreme never attempted by Mao. While Mao did relocate masses
of residents to the countryside, he never considered completely
emptying the major Chinese cities. Within days of the Cambodian
revolutionary victory, however, all of the cities in Cambodia had
been completely evacuated. Residents were forced into the
countryside where they could be placed in production brigades.[63]
Both Mao and Pol Pot saw the cities as the center of all of the
major obstacles to their country's transformation to complete
Communism. The cities were the site of the intellectuals, the
technicians, the bourgeois, the old regime, and the middle class. It
included those who had a vested interest in maintaining the old
society, the status quo. In the countryside, it would be easier to
maintain control over the Party's enemies—they would be isolated
from each other in small communes where they could be readily
controlled. Moreover, the cities had, in the past, proved

---

[61] *Id.* at 234.
[62] *Id.*

inhospitable to the communal process since they were structured on the basis of residence rather than production.[64]

Pol Pot, in fact, described many of his motivations in emptying the cities:

> One of the important factors of Cambodia's success after April 1975 is the evacuation of the city residents to the countryside. This was decided before victory was won, that is, in February 1975, because we knew that before smashing all sorts of enemy spy organizations, our strength was not strong enough to defend the revolutionary regime. Judging from the struggles waged from 1976 and 1977, the enemy's secret agent network lying low in our country was very massive and complicated. But when we crushed them, it was difficult for them to stage a comeback. Their forces were scattered in various cooperatives which are in our own grip.[65]

The Khmer Rouge had additional reasons to hate and fear the cities, which may explain the extremes to which they resorted once they won control of the country. The cities were seen by the revolutionaries as the center of foreign domination. They were dominated by very a large Vietnamese-Khmer and Sino-Khmer bureaucratic and commercial population. Moreover, the cities and their residents were the products of a system that the Communists blamed for destroying the traditional Khmer economy and nascent industrialization.[66] And these cities and their residents were hopelessly corrupted by the influences of international capitalism and the world market.

The Khmer Rouge hatred of and alienation from the Cambodian cities is evident in the official description of what they found when they captured Phnom Penh on April 17, 1975:

---

[63] *Id.* at 230.

[64] *See* Quinn, *supra* note 4, at 229.

[65] *See* Jackson, *supra* note 1, at 47.

[66] *See infra*, "Economic Expectations and Demands."

Upon entering Phnom Penh and other cities, the brother and sister combatants of the revolutionary army . . . sons and daughters of our workers and peasants . . . were taken aback by the overwhelming sight of long-haired men and youngsters wearing bizarre clothes making themselves indistinguishable from the fair sex. Our traditional mentality, mores, traditions, literature, and arts and culture and tradition were totally destroyed by U.S. imperialistic patterns. Our people's traditionally clean, sound characteristics and essence were completely absent and abandoned, replaced by imperialistic pornographic, shameless, perverted, and fanatic traits.[67]

Economic Expectations and Demands

In the same way that Mao, during the Great Leap, sought to move simultaneously to increase rice production, irrigation, and steel production, the Khmer Rouge vision of modernization emphasized extreme haste, the critical importance of rice, and the simultaneous pursuit of industrial advancement. What is striking, however, in both Mao's and Pol Pot's pursuit of these goals is their remarkably unrealistic expectations as to the pace and potential of economic advancement.

While the Communists of China and Cambodia despised the cities, Western influence, and intellectuals and technicians, they were not trying to transform their countries into the type of rural society that predated colonialism and capitalism. They were instead obsessed by a frantic drive toward modernization.[68] Mao's influence over Pol Pot in this respect is clear even in the choice of language Pol Pot uses in describing this move toward modernization.

In the agricultural field we are sure that we can achieve new progress by leaps and bounds. Regarding our future outlook, we should quickly change our beloved motherland from an underdeveloped agricultural country into a modern one and

---

[67] *See* Jackson, *supra* note 1, at 44.
[68] *Id.* at 59.

from a modern agricultural country into an industrial country, thus achieving the goal of a modern agricultural and industrial country.[69]

In his view of how this transformation of Cambodian society was to take place, Pol Pot again mimicked Mao in his radically optimistic and idealistic view of the way in which the acceptance of the correct ideology (Communism) could create a heroic labor, which would produce at a dizzying rate. Cambodia would achieve in a few years what took capitalist, imperialist societies generations. Haste was demanded as a consequence of this revolutionary optimism and required a flurry of activity at building sites all over Cambodia. As in the Great Leap Forward in China, massive amounts of labor were subtracted from rice cultivation for opening new land, increasing irrigation, and reopening factories, and this policy was pursued in the face of self-evident food shortages found throughout the country, especially in 1975-76.[70]

And yet, because of the steadfast nature of its belief in the potency of its new organizational forms, the regime constantly overstated its achievements even when the country was desperately short of grain.[71] Even as refugees attested to the desperate food shortages in the country, Radio Phnom Penh broadcast the following statement in 1975: "In our country there is no problem with famine, budgetary deficit, or the so-called deficit in the balance of payments. All of our seven million people have rice to eat and are joining our valiant revolutionary army to build a new Cambodia which is independent, democratic, nonaligned, gloriously flourishing."[72] Haste, revolutionary optimism, and the rhetoric of simultaneous agricultural and industrial modernization became the language of total revolution.

---

[69] *Id.*

[70] *Id.* at 62.

[71] *Id.* at 64.

[72] *Id.*

The Primacy of Willpower Over Weapons and Machines

The ideological pronouncements of the Khmer Rouge mirrored radical Maoism in its emphasis on the primacy of human willpower over weapons and machines, the superiority of the wisdom of the common people over academic learning, and the power of heroic labor to overcome all natural and material obstacles.[73] The Khmer Rouge, like their Chinese counterparts, believed they could replace machines and technical solutions with political militancy, thereby transcending normal developmental obstacles. Khieu Samphan provided an example of this belief in a speech delivered on April 15, 1977, in which he claimed that the production goals for 1977 would be reached by May:

> Have these achievements been made possible by machines? We have no machines. We do everything by mainly relying on the strength of our people. We work completely self-reliantly. This shows the overwhelming heroism of our people. This also shows the great force of our people. Though barehanded, they can do everything.[74]

Radio Phnom Penh's portrait of the armed struggle against Lon Nol emphasizes this same belief in the ability of heroism alone to triumph over technologically superior forces: "The great victory of the Cambodian revolution, based as it is on the stand of political conscience and revolutionary morals, is irrefutable proof that the human factor is the key and that the material factor is only secondary."[75]

For all the similarities between the Chinese and the Cambodian revolutions, there were significant differences. The Khmer Rouge leadership actually saw Mao's revolution as a failure; Mao's application of Communist thought, or his interpretation of it, did not in the end produce a classless society run by the masses. And the Khmer Rouge were determined to succeed where Mao failed.

---

[73] *Id.* at 74.
[74] *Id.*
[75] *Id.*

This determination survived despite warnings from experienced Chinese Communist leaders, as is evident in an event later related by Prince Norodom Sihanouk:

> In Peking in 1975, we visited Zhou Enlai—already seriously ill—in his hospital room. I heard him advise Khieu Samphan and Ieng Thirith not to try to achieve total communism in one giant step. The wise and perspicacious veteran of the Chinese revolution stressed the need to move "step by step" toward socialism. This would take years of patient work. Then and only then should they advance toward a communist society. Premier Zhou Enlai reiterated that China itself had experienced disastrous setbacks in the fairly recent past by trying to make a giant leap forward and move full speed ahead into pure communism. The great Chinese statesman counseled the Khmer Rouge leaders: "Don't follow the bad example of our great leap forward. Take things slowly: that is the best way to guide Kampuchea and its people to growth, prosperity, and happiness." By way of response to this splendid and moving piece of almost fatherly advice, Khieu Samphan and Ieng Thirith just smiled an incredulous and superior smile.
>
> Not long after we got back to Phnom Penh, Kieu Samphan and Son Sen told me that their Kampuchea was going to show the world that pure communism could indeed be achieved by one fell swoop. This was no doubt their indirect reply to Zhou Enlai. "Our country's place in history will be assured," they said. "We will be the first nation to create a completely communist society without wasting time on intermediate steps."[76]

And it was in its attempt to succeed where Mao failed that the Khmer Rouge became influenced by other strands of Marxist thought.

---

[76] *Id.* at 63.

The Cambodian Revolution and Stalinism

One of the weaknesses Pol Pot saw in the policies of Mao Tse-tung was his inability to eliminate the sources of resistance to his programs within his own country.[77] Mao faced continual resistance from key party members (Zhou Enlai and Deng Xiaoping), from peasants who opposed collectivization of land, the new "intellectual" class within the Party itself, and from families or members of the old ruling class.[78] Pol Pot faced similar opposition to his plan of transformation from nearly every level of Cambodian society: the Lon Nol government in Phnom Penh; non-Communist allies in his own coalition against Lon Nol; the Khmer Krom; the Vietnamese; Prince Sihanouk; urban dwellers; and, eventually, cadres from within his own party. In order to overcome these obstacles, Pol Pot devised a plan to eliminate every source of resistance, achieve the acquiescence of the peasantry, and completely change Cambodian society within the fastest time possible. Pol Pot believed he could succeed where the Cultural Revolution and the Great Leap Forward failed by taking two steps, which were absent in China: completely emptying the cities and the use of terror and violence on an unprecedented scale.[79] And it was in his use of violence that the Khmer Rouge paralleled Stalinism.

Although the Khmer Rouge acknowledged its relationship to Maoism, its leadership did not make specific references to the influence of Stalin.[80] Part of this may be explained by the geopolitical alignment of Communist countries during this period. For this was after the great Sino-Soviet split, an enormous division of mistrust and fear that had developed between China and the Soviet Union. This division directly affected the countries of Southeast Asia. These states were forced to choose between China and the Soviet Union; Vietnam chose the Soviet Union, while

---

[77] See BURGLER, *supra* note 2, at 260-61.
[78] *Id.* at 249.
[79] See Quinn, *supra* note 4, at 231.
[80] See Jackson, *supra* note 7, at 249.

Cambodia aligned itself with China.[81] Given this setting, it would have been natural for the Cambodian leadership to have been reluctant to acknowledge any debt to the Soviet Union.

It is clear, however, that the leaders of the Khmer Rouge were exposed to the ideas and methods of Stalin at a time when they were initially forming their own ideas of Communism. Virtually the entire top leadership of the Khmer Rouge came under the influence of the French Communist Party at a time when the Party was adhering to an extremely hard line.[82] Stalin was still the world Communist leader when Pol Pot arrived in France and when most of the Cambodian students were being inducted into the Communist-controlled Khmer Student Association in Paris. Pol Pot and his fellow students "learned their socialism from the French Communist Party in its most Stalinist period."[83]

While Pol Pot never specifically acknowledged any influence of Stalin in the formulation of policies for Democratic Kampuchea, there are significant similarities between Pol Pot's actions and those of the Soviet Union in the 1920s and 1930s. Pol Pot, like Stalin, moved with brutal swiftness in seeking to collectivize the rural agricultural sector, while at the same time promoting a program of heavy industrialization.

From 1929 to 1933, Stalin instituted what he labeled a "revolution from above," which was designed to lay the basis for the transformation of the Soviet Union.[84] This transformation was laid out in the Five Year Plan proposed by Stalin in 1929, which called for the immediate collectivization of Soviet agriculture, as well as an ambitious program of heavy industrialization.[85] Pol Pot began collectivizing the country just days after the Khmer Rouge victory over Lon Nol. The cities were emptied and communes

---

[81] See ELIZABETH BECKER, WHEN THE WAR WAS OVER 313, 348-49, 368 (1986); DUNAYEVSAYA, *supra* note 22, at 152-53.

[82] See Quinn, *supra* note 4, at 231.

[83] *Id.* at 234 (quoting W. Shawcross, *Paradise Lost*, N.Y. TIMES, Nov. 13, 1978).

[84] See Norman Pereira, *Stalin and the Communist Party in the 1920's*, HISTORY TODAY, Aug. 1992, at 22.

[85] *Id.*

were created throughout the countryside. A similar haste was established in promoting industrialization.

The most obvious similarity between the actions of the Khmer Rouge and those of Stalin is the level and scope of violence used as a tool for social transformation. Between 1929 and 1936 in the Soviet Union, the Kulaks were exterminated wholesale with their families; whole regions suffered famines caused by both nature and the government. Estimates of deaths have ranged from 29 to 65 million.[86] Similarly, the Khmer Rouge terminated its own people on a massive scale. Refugees described how individuals simply "disappeared" and how they quickly learned not to ask after them.[87] Victims were forced to describe their "network" of associates. "Networks" were a variation of the Stalinist purge system whereby friends, family, and like-minded colleagues were considered guilty by association with the accused. Networks were the equivalent of a political or sociological family tree—a chart with one's work colleagues, party cell members, boss, and family members listed together as if they represented one narrow political tendency or the cell of some subterranean political organization.[88]

A unique feature of Stalin's revolution, which was later imitated by Pol Pot, was the extent to which the purges affected the power elite. The Great Terror saw not only the elimination of millions of Soviet citizens, but also the elimination of most of the major figures in the revolutionary party.[89] The Soviet elite were accorded considerable privileges by the regime, but the price they paid for these privileges was the constant danger of sudden arrest on false charges, deportation, or death. During the Great Purge,

---

[86] See Eugene H. Methvin, *Twentieth Century Superkillers*, New Republic, May 31, 1985, at 24.

[87] See Becker, *supra* note 81, at 42; David P. Chandler, The Early Phases of Liberation in Northwest Cambodia: Conversations with Peang Sophi 9 (1976) (Sophi relates, through Chandler, a macabre jingle that circulated through his factory: "The Khmer Rouge kill, but never explain." *("Khmaer krohom somlap, min del prop.")*).

[88] See Becker, *supra* note 81, at 283.

[89] See Quinn, *supra* note 4, at 235.

about two-thirds of the Communist Party Central Committee was liquidated and about half of the officer corps was arrested.[90]

The Party purges in Cambodia in 1977 show a remarkable resemblance to the Stalinist model. Records at Tuol Sleng reveal the swiftness with which Pol Pot moved from a purge of the old government and the intellectual class to a purge of his own party and forces. In 1976, the people executed were members of the old society: 164 factory workers, 112 people from the population at large, sixty-one students, thirty-five professors, twenty doctors and nurses, forty-nine engineers, fifty-five bureaucrats of the old regime, and forty-seven students and dignitaries from overseas. Of the over 750 executions recorded that year at Tuol Slewo more than twelve were Communist party members. The year 1977 signaled a turning point and a change in party directives. The number of recorded executions of party officials jumped to forty-four, and the number imprisoned to sixty-one. By 1978, Communist officials headed the list of Tuol Sleng victims.[91] Not even the members of the Standing Committee of the Central Committee of the CPK were spared. Before the 1978 purges, the committee consisted of eight members: Pol Pot, Nuon Chea, Ta Mok, So Phim, Ieng Sary, Vom Veth, Son Sen, and Tra Keu. By the end of 1978, only five of the eight remained. Tra Keu, Vom Veth, and So Phim had been killed by the orders of their fellow members of the Standing Committee. Cambodians who had helped build the revolution quickly became its victims.[92]

In carrying out these purges, Pol Pot followed the example of Stalin in demanding confessions from the victims. During the Stalin years, the Soviet Union witnessed a succession of trials in which victims would confess in open court to an extraordinary number of crimes, including complicity with Trotsky and/or foreign intelligence agencies in plotting the overthrow of the Soviet regime, the restoration of capitalism, and the dismemberment of the Soviet Union.[93] Before any of the victims at

---

[90] *Id.*

[91] *See* BECKER, *supra* note 81, at 275-76.

[92] *Id.* at 280.

[93] *See* Pereira, *supra* note 84, at 23.

Tuol Sleng were killed, they were forced to write and sign a confession. Those imprisoned at Tuol Sleng were tortured until they signed a confession documenting the networks and subterfuges that were threatening the revolution. These victims were forced to confess of spy networks as well as plots masterminded by the CIA and the Vietnamese.[94]

The final similarity between Cambodia and the Soviet Union was their narrow view of those who could become members of the new society. In China, Mao had an optimistic view of the power of reeducation. He believed that most Chinese citizens had the potential to become good Communists, and he therefore defined the out-group narrowly.[95] Stalin and Pol Pot, on the other hand, had a far narrower view of the in-group, of those who could be trusted, of those who could become good Communists. Pol Pot, for example, thought that those Cambodians who had lived outside of Kampuchea (even those within his own party) were hopelessly corrupted.[96] These Cambodians, who had lived in Vietnam or Europe during the Lon Nol regime, returned to Cambodia only to be immediately seized and imprisoned.[97] In the end, not even Pol Pot's own ambassadors were safe.[98]

French Socialist Thought

Although Maoist goals guided many of Democratic Kampuchea's economic and social transformation schemes, other intellectual antecedents also appear to have had an influence on the development of the uniquely extreme character of the Cambodian revolution. For example, one of the leading theoreticians of the Khmer Rouge, Khieu Samphan, cited the work of the well-known, French-educated Marxist theorist of economic development, Samir Amin, in his dissertation.[99] Amin's work is cited as one of the

---

[94] See BECKER, supra note 81, at 294-97.

[95] See BURGLER, supra note 2, at 245.

[96] Id. at 260.

[97] See BECKER, supra note 81, at 149.

[98] Id. at 284-85.

[99] See Jackson, supra note 7, at 245.

principal sources of many of Khieu Samphan's ideas about the
pernicious effects of integrating Cambodia's precapitalist economy
into the international economic system. Amin argued that in
underdeveloped countries, the traditional economic system has
been gradually destroyed by its integration into the world capitalist
system. "Handicrafts have almost disappeared due to the
competition of manufactured goods, and the system of agricultural
production has deteriorated due to external pressures which have
forced it to adjust to the requirements of the world market."[100] For
Amin, society was divided between those associated with
international capitalism in the towns and the long-suffering rural
peasants whose energies would be liberated if they were only freed
from contact and domination by the forces of international
capitalism.[101] Khmer Rouge practices have another antecedent in
the writings of the French-educated apostle of violent revolution,
Frantz Fanon. Elizabeth Becker cites a senior Chinese diplomat
who was stationed in Cambodia during the reign of the Khmer
Rouge: "The Khmer Rouge came out of the same general
movement as Frantz Fanon, who believed in the cleansing nature
of violent revolution for a people who had been subjugated by
white colonialists."[102] Fanon advocated the morality of class
violence, the rejection of consumption as hedonism, and the
desirability of total revolutionary transformation.[103] He was anti-
proletariat, and anti-intellectual, as well as antibourgeois. He
focused on a division between working peasants and all other
social classes and used geographic location as a most important
criterion for identifying class enemies.[104]

> It cannot be too strongly stressed that in the colonial territories
> the proletariat is the nucleus of the colonized population which
> has been most pampered by the colonial regime. The
> embryonic proletariat of the towns is in a comparatively

---

[100] *Id.* at 245-46.

[101] *Id.*

[102] BECKER, *supra* note 81, at 287-88.

[103] *See* Jackson, *supra* note 7, at 246-47.

[104] *Id.*

privileged position. In capitalist countries the working class has everything to lose; . . . it includes tram conductors, taxi drivers, miners, dockers, interpreters, nurses, and so on [they] constitute . . . the "bourgeois" of the colonized people.[105]

For Fanon, the peasant's only path to redemption, and freedom, was through violence:

> And it is clear that in colonized countries the peasants alone are revolutionary, for they have nothing to lose and everything to gain. The starving peasant, outside the class system, is the first among the exploited to discover that only violence pays.
> For the native, this violence represents the absolute line of action . . . . Violence is thus seen as comparable to a royal pardon. The colonized man finds his freedom in and through violence.[106]

These philosophers provide a clear antecedent for revolutionary policies, which extend beyond any advocated by Marx, Lenin, or Mao. They view whole groups as irredeemable class enemies and see violence as the only desirable path to social transformation.

THE INDIGENOUS ORIGINS OF THE REVOLUTIONARY MOVEMENT; THE VIOLENT NATURE OF CAMBODIA

From an early age Cambodian children learn their culture through the telling of Khmer folk tales. "The world of these fables," according to Elizabeth Becker, "is peopled with all-powerful ministers of the king, greedy crocodiles, wise rabbits, and ordinary Cambodians who allow their violent passions to overrule common sense."[107] Becker provides an example of one of these tales:

---

[105] *Id.* at 247.

[106] *Id.* at 248.

[107] *See* BECKER, *supra* note 81, at 82.

In the Cambodian countryside a childless woman has become dissatisfied with her husband and takes a lover. Every day while her husband is off working, the woman meets her lover for a tryst. Finally, she decides she wants her husband to die. She goes to a tree in the forest that houses a powerful spirit and prays aloud to it asking that the spirit kill her husband so that she may marry her lover. But her husband is working nearby and hears her supplication. He hides behind the tree and, pretending to be the spirit, tells her to return home and prepare chicken soup that he promises will become a magic potion and kill the unwanted husband. She does as he says.

Her husband is waiting for her upon her return. He drinks the soup and feigns an illness. He asks her to help him prepare for his death by boiling water. The husband knows the lover is hiding in a large water urn, the wife does not, and the husband orders her to build a fire under that large water pot. The wife unknowingly boils her lover to death. When she lifts the lid to pour out the water she sees her now dead lover. She says nothing but tries to hide the evidence of her infidelity. When she pushes the lover's body down with her hands, his ears and hair come off. She knows now what her husband has done but says nothing.

Now the woman has one worry—how to dispose of the lover's corpse. After her husband returns to work, she decides on an elaborate ruse that fools four local robbers. They are made to believe the urn holding the corpse is actually filled with fine, rare silks. They carry off the heavy pot to the woods where they discover the trick. They vow to beat up the woman.

The four robbers capture the unfaithful wife but she fools them again. This time she promises to give them half of the money owed to her by a certain riverboat captain. She leads them to the river and tells them to wait on the bank while she collects the money. She then goes to the captain and tells him that the four robbers are her slaves and persuades the captain to buy them from her. The captain sends his men to the riverbank with instructions to tie the robbers in chains, which is done.

The woman heads home with her slave money but night falls suddenly. Afraid to continue her journey, she climbs a tree and goes to sleep in its branches. Meanwhile, the robbers escape. They go off to search for her and end up at the very same tree with the same idea of sleeping in it. Three robbers climb to the lower branches without seeing her and fall asleep. The fourth goes higher, to the same branch with the woman. She silences him by promising to become his Lover and share her money with him. She asks that they seal their pact with a kiss. He complies and she bites off half of his tongue and pushes him to the ground. The robbers on the lower branch hear him fall and they flee, thinking that it is the boat captain returning to fetch his slaves.

The devious woman climbs down from the tree and returns home to her husband.[108]

This folk tale of "The Devious Woman" is ghoulish, belonging to the same general category as those of the Brothers Grimm. What distinguishes the Khmer tale, however, is the nature of the violence and that the cruelty goes unpunished. Becker cites these tales as evidence of a violence that has been a strain of the Cambodian national character since at least the days of the Angkor era.[109]

While Cambodia had seen nothing like the violence unleashed by the Khmer Rouge, violence itself was no stranger to Cambodian society before 1975. The Angkor-era (802-1432) peasant, for example, lived in the shadow of ruthless Cambodian kings who demanded large tithes and forced labor to build monuments to the gods and the royal vanity.[110] The system of justice during this period was often barbaric, as were royal practices. Superstition and animism were constants in the religions of the country, as "there grew a body of primitive magic that . . . required brutal acts. Amputation of parts of the body—the genitals, organs or head— was believed to convey power to the executioner. Rival kings were

---

[108] *Id.* at 82-83.

[109] *Id.* at 83.

[110] *Id.* at 84.

decapitated to show supremacy; there were ritual decapitations of lowly Khmer to start off large construction projects."[111]

The violence that has pervaded Cambodian culture since the demise of the Angkor regime has, in part, been a result of the constant sieges on Cambodian territory and independence over the last five centuries. The neighboring states of Vietnam and Siam (Thailand) waged constant assaults on the country, culminating in the annexation of Battambang and Siemreap by Thailand.[112] These sieges and assaults continued until the arrival of the French in 1864. The period of the French protectorate (1864-1940; 1945-1954) was itself characterized by violence—revolutionary violence and rebellion as Cambodia resisted French rule.[113]

The departure of the French in 1954 brought a return to attacks by Thailand and Vietnam and beginning in the 1960s, internal violence in the form of open resistance to the rule of Prince Norodom Sihanouk. This resistance was crushed by the army with brutal efficiency, as in the peasant revolts of 1967 and 1968.[114] The murder rate in rural areas was sufficiently high during this period, in fact, to warrant government suppression of the homicide statistic.[115] During the aftermath of the coup against Sihanouk in 1970 led by Lon Nol and Sirik Matak, thousands of Vietnamese residents of Cambodia were slaughtered.[116] During that same year in Kampong Chang, two members of parliament were killed by an angry pro-Sihanouk crowd. They were flayed and their livers were grilled and eaten by the crowd.[117] Likewise, the civil war from 1970-1975 was notable for the lack of compassion among combatants; neither side took many prisoners and consumption of human liver took place on both sides.[118]

---

[111] *Id.*

[112] *See* CRAIG ETCHESON, THE RISE AND DEMISE OF DEMOCRATIC KAMPUCHEA 7 (1984).

[113] *Id.*

[114] *See* Marlow Hood & David Ablin, *The Path to Cambodia's Present, in* THE CAMBODIAN AGONY, *supra* note 6, at xviii.

[115] *See* Jackson, *supra* note 1, at 71.

[116] *Id.* at 72.

[117] *Id.*

[118] *Id.*

Despite the common Western perception of the Cambodian people as peaceful, gentle, and primitive,[119] violence was a significant part of the Cambodian culture.[120] In fact, David Chandler has cautioned against overenthusiastic generalizations concerning the alleged tranquillity of antebellum Khmer society:

> We know very little, in quantitative or political terms, about the mass of Cambodian society, many of whom, for most of their history, appear to have been slaves of one sort or another. The frequency of locally-led rebellions in the nineteenth century—against the Thai, the Vietnamese, the French, and local officials—suggests that Cambodian peasants were not as peaceable as their own mythology, reiterated by the French, would have us believe.[121]

Karl Jackson has stated it more strongly: "The fact that massive amounts of blood were shed by the Khmer Rouge diverged from Khmer norms in scope rather than kind."[122]

The National Fear

One of the primary strands of Khmer Rouge thought was the strong belief in total national independence and self-reliance.[123] This led Cambodia to cut off virtually all relations with the outside world in the 1975-1976 period, to deny the influence of any foreign ideological influence, and to refuse any and all humanitarian aid, including medical supplies.[124] The Khmer Rouge repeatedly said that they would not be "beggars" and accept international handouts, regardless of how many Cambodians died. They were also convinced that these offers were simply means for

---

[119] *See* BECKER, *supra* note 81, at 83.
[120] *See* Jackson, *supra* note 1, at 71-72.
[121] ETCHESON, *supra* note 112, at 12.
[122] *See* Jackson, *supra* note 1, at 72.
[123] *Id.* at 39-49.
[124] *Id.* at 48.

foreign powers to manipulate and subvert countries like Cambodia.[125]

The Khmer Rouge cut off international telephone, telegram, and cable communications. There was no international mail service. All regular airline service, save occasional flights from Peking or Hanoi, halted. The borders were closed and mined, the maritime boundaries were patrolled. No one entered or left the country without permission under penalty of death. All foreigners were thrown out and embassies closed.[126]

This extreme concept of national independence and self-reliance is without precedent in the global Communist movement and "springs primarily from the centuries-old Khmer fear of foreign invasion rather than from any twentieth-century foreign ideology."[127] In fact, one characteristic that was common to the very different regimes of Sihanouk, Lon Nol, and Pol Pot was an intense fear of Vietnam incursion.[128]

The long history of the expansionist policies and actions of Thailand and Vietnam left Cambodia under a constant fear of losing their culture and country. The Khmer Rouge began its purification program as early as 1971, and like Lon Nol it struck first at Vietnamese nationals living in eastern Cambodia.[129] Under the pretext that these people were agents of a nebulous Vietnamese plot, they were arrested and killed by the Khmer Rouge. The Khmer Rouge then moved on to those Cambodians who had lived in exile in Vietnam but had returned to help the Khmer Rouge in its fight against Lon Nol. The Communist party led by Pol Pot distrusted these "returnees" and referred to them as "Vietnamese in Cambodian bodies."[130] The Khmer Rouge used these returnees in low-ranking positions in the fight against Lon Nol until it had taken control of the war. By 1975, the vast majority had been slaughtered.[131] Soon the label of "Vietnamese in a Cambodian

---

[125] See BECKER, *supra* note 81, at 184.

[126] *Id.* at 180.

[127] Jackson, *supra* note 7, at 249.

[128] See BECKER, *supra* note 81, at 132.

[129] *Id.* at 149.

[130] *Id.* at 151.

[131] *Id.*

body" became a standard rationale for the elimination of Cambodians who had never been to Vietnam—peasants, cadres, even Central Committee members.[132]

The traditional Cambodian fear of usurpation, as taken to new extremes by the Khmer Rouge leadership, formed the rationale for purge after purge during their reign. The purges eventually extended past a search for Vietnamese insurgents. The Khmer Rouge decided that all of Cambodia's minorities—the Chinese, the Chams, the ethnic Thais, and even the hill tribes people—were a threat to the health and vitality of the Khmer nation.[133] "There is one Kampuchean revolution," the Khmer Rouge decreed. "In Kampuchea there is one nation, and one language, the Khmer language. From now on the various nationalities . . . do not exist any longer in Kampuchea."[134]

The Role of Buddhism

One of the peculiarities of the Communist revolution in Cambodia was the fact that the revolutionaries not only had to fight the political system, but had to displace a religion that was an integral part of Cambodian society and whose beliefs were inherently at odds with theories of revolution and Communism. "Buddhism was so ingrained in the Cambodian culture," according to one scholar, "that it was not properly a separate institution or

---

[132] This paranoid belief of the Khmer Rouge leadership that they were under constant threat of attack from Vietnam and Thailand was not completely unfounded. Thailand and Cambodia were engaged in constant border skirmishes throughout the Khmer Rouge reign. The Khmer Rouge was, at the same time, fighting skirmishes in eastern Cambodia as the Vietnamese were slow to withdraw their troops after their victory over South Vietnam. Moreover, Vietnam made repeated requests to renegotiate the borders between Kampuchea and Vietnam immediately following their victory in the South. In 1975, in fact, Vietnam forcibly captured islands in the Gulf of Siam, which had been within the Cambodian maritime boundary ("the Brevie Line"). Tensions between Cambodia and Vietnam and Thailand continued to escalate until Vietnam launched an all-out offensive against Cambodia on December 22, 1978. *See* BECKER, *supra* note 81, at 300-01.

[133] *Id.* at 253.

[134] *Id.*

faith but an expression of the Cambodian way of life."[135] It infected the language, the yearly calendar, the food, dance, and art, and the people's attitude toward most facets of life. Cambodia was widely believed to be the most Buddhist country in Southeast Asia. To be Cambodian was to be Buddhist.[136]

The most fundamental aspects of Therevada Buddhism are associated with the pursuit of the ultimate goal of nirvana and the more proximate end of attaining a more favorable reincarnation by accumulating karma or merit.[137] The basic teachings of Buddha, as summarized in the Four Noble Truths (Ariya Sacca), advocate withdrawal from the world as the only permanent means of alleviating suffering. All life is inevitably sorrowful; sorrow is due to craving for sensation, satisfaction, and permanence; sorrow can only be stopped through the extinction of craving; and this can be achieved only through the progressive abandonment of individuality attained by carefully disciplined moral conduct culminating in the life of concentration and meditation of a monk.[138] This profoundly pessimistic view of the human condition and man's incapacity for improving his lot in any enduring way is graphically illustrated by the Buddhist affirmation, "Life is a curable disease."[139]

Buddhist doctrine holds that ultimate release from the suffering imposed by the continual cycle of rebirth and death can best be sought by abandoning worldly concerns and becoming a monk.[140] Becoming a monk means becoming a beggar, dependent upon others for food, and thereby allowing others to gain karma through the act of giving. Monks must abstain from labor in the fields, lest they harm any living thing.[141] Furthermore, laboring mightily is merely another example of how the futility of craving is made doubly painful by the obvious impermanence of all such achievements. According to Buddhist thought, setting out to

---

[135] *Id.* at 202.

[136] *See* Jackson, *supra* note 1, at 68.

[137] *Id.* at 69-71.

[138] *Id.*

[139] *Id.*

[140] *Id.*

[141] *Id.*

change the world by transforming society submerges individuals in the hopeless quest for the same illusory permanence.[142]

Clearly, these beliefs contrast sharply with the Khmer Rouge plans for immediate social and economic revolution and its emphasis on mobilizing the entire population for a "great leap forward." The doctrine of karma, for example, is antithetical to the completely equal society sought by the Khmer Rouge. Moreover, the Buddhist concepts of antimaterialism and nonviolence condemn the goals and methods of the revolutionaries.[143] Consequently, Buddhism became an immediate and primary target for annihilation. This goal of eradication of the Buddhist religion can be seen in the Khmer Rouge propaganda, quoted by Francois Ponchaud in 1978:

The Buddhist religion is the cause of our country's weakness.

The bonzes are bloodsuckers, they oppress people, they are imperialists.

Begging for charity like the bonzes do is an offense to the eye and it also maintains the workers in a downtrodden condition.

It is forbidden to give anything to those shaven-asses, it would be pure waste.

If any worker secretly takes rice to the bonzes, we shall set him to planting cabbages. If the cabbages are not full grown in three days, he will dig his own grave.[144]

The Khmer Rouge ideology was driven by many fears, fear of Western influences found in the cities, of the continuing effects of imperialism, of subversive activity sponsored by the Vietnamese or the CIA, of invasion by the Thai or the Vietnamese, and the fear that the centuries-old influence of the Buddhist faith would persist.

---

[142] *Id.*
[143] *Id.*
[144] *Id.* at 68.

The unprecedented scope and ferocity of the violence they unleashed against the Cambodian people was at least in part a response to these fears.

The Khmer Rouge were willing to liquidate the traditional ruling class, empty the cities, and abolish markets, money, and private property all in the name of egalitarian collectivism, rapid economic development, and the dictatorship of the masses. These same goals led them to execute the chief bonzes, defrock ordinary monks, forbid the accumulation of merit through giving, and profane Buddhist temples throughout the country.

CONCLUSION

The extreme character of the Cambodian revolution was the product of an ideology that combined various disparate forms of Marxism with influences and characteristics that were unique to Cambodia. The baseline of this ideology was the thought of Mao Tse-tung; but in order to succeed where Mao failed, the Khmer Rouge drew on the ideas, theories, and actions of a group of very different thinkers and leaders—Lenin, Stalin, and the French socialist school (as represented by Amin and Fanon). This already dangerous mix was made even more so under the unique internal characteristics of Cambodia at the time of the revolution. The result was death and violence on an almost unprecedented scale.

Unfortunately, in the implementation of this ideology, the Cambodian revolution became an example of the futility of trying to force Communism on a nation and of the inevitable violence that results from a revolutionary elite attempting to instill in a nation a Communist ideology as it is implementing it. Hannah Arendt saw this result as inevitable in any non-populist movement for control. "To substitute violence for power can bring victory," she wrote, "but the price is very high . . . [and] the end will be the elimination of all power."[145] She described how a regime that has predicated its rule on violence must first destroy all organized opposition. The people must become "atomized, an outrageously

---

[145] *See* BECKER, *supra* note 81, at 221 (*citing* HANNAH ARENDT, ON VIOLENCE (1969)).

pale, academic word for the horror it implies."[146] They must be separated from each other and forbidden normal ties and relationships, and they must be policed by spies and ubiquitous informers.[147] The result would be a regime where no one could be trusted, a regime of sabotage and subterfuge. And in such an environment, economic progress is doomed because terror produces paralysis in society. Eventually, the regime is consumed by the increasingly inward quest for the mysterious enemies robbing it of progress and power. It must finally turn on itself. The terror "turns not only against its enemies but against its friends and supporters as well, being afraid of all power, even the power of its friends. The climax of terror is reached when the police state begins to devour its own children, when yesterday's executioner becomes today's victims."[148] Written years before the Khmer Rouge took control of Cambodia, it is a startlingly accurate picture of the Cambodian horror from 1975 to 1978. It is also a good description of what the world should be watching for, if we want to prevent such a tragedy from occurring again.

---

[146] *Id.*
[147] *Id.*
[148] *Id.* at 222.

BIBLIOGRAPHY

Arendt, Hannah. *On Violence*. 1969.

Becker, Elizabeth. *When the War Was Over*. 1986.

Burgler, R. A. *The Eyes of the Pineapple: Revolutionary Intellectuals and Terror in Democratic Kampuchea*, volume 3. 1990.

Chandler, David P. "A Revolution in Full Spate." In *The Cambodian Agony*, edited by David Ablin and Marlow Hood, 1987.

———. *Brother Number One: A Political Biography of Pol Pot*. 1992.

———. *The Early Phases of Liberation in Northwest Cambodia: Conversations with Peang Sophi*. 1976.

Dunayevsaya, Raya. *Philosophy and Revolution*. 1973.

Etcheson, Craig. *The Rise and Demise of Democratic Kampuchea*. 1984.

Foreign Broadcast Information Service. Springfield, Virginia. United States Department of Commerce. October 3, 1977.

Harlow, Marlow, and David Ablin. "The Path to Cambodia's Present." In *The Cambodia Agony*.

Jackson, Karl D. "Introduction. The Khmer Rouge in Context." In *Cambodia 1975-1978: Rendezvous with Death*, edited by Karl Jackson, 1989.

———. "The Ideology of Total Revolution." In *Cambodia 1975-1978: Rendezvous with Death* 37, edited by Karl Jackson, 1989.

Kolakowski, Leszek. *Main Currents of Communism: Its Origins, Growth and Dissolution*. 1981.

Marx, Karl. *The Communist Manifesto*, edited by H. L. Laski, 1967.

Medvedev, Roy. *Leninism and Western Socialism*. 1981.

Methvin, Eugene H. "Twentieth Century Superkillers." *New Republic*. May 31, 1985.

Pereira, Norman. "Stalin and the Communist Party in the 1920's." *History Today*, August 1992.

Quinn, Kenneth. "Explaining the Terror." In *Cambodia 1975-1978*, edited by Karl Jackson, 1989.

Shawcross, William. "Paradise Lost." *N.Y. Times*, November 13, 1978.

Westoby, Adam. *The Evolution of Communism*. 1989.

VI

The Third Indochina War: A Case Study on the Vietnamese Invasion of Cambodia

Benjamin E. Kringer

INTRODUCTION

In 1975, Communist forces overthrew the United States-backed governments of both South Vietnam and Cambodia, thus ending years of war and resulting in Communist domination of most of French Indochina. With Communist regimes firmly installed in a now unified Vietnam and Cambodia, there was an expectation that both countries would be occupied by forces supporting these governments and that Communism would continue to expand in the region. Yet a mere three years later, on December 25, 1978, 150,000 Vietnamese troops crossed into Cambodian territory in order to overthrow the existing Communist regime—the Khmer Rouge.[1] Within seventeen days, the army of the Khmer Rouge was overwhelmed and Vietnam had installed a new government (the People's Republic of Kampuchea (PRK)) in the Cambodian capital Phnom Penh.[2] The fact that Vietnam conquered its weaker adversary was not surprising. Vietnam's military was far larger and

---

[1] STEPHEN J. MORRIS, WHY VIETNAM INVADED CAMBODIA: POLITICAL CULTURE AND THE CAUSES OF WAR 111 (1999) (It is impossible to determine exactly when the invasion began, because for two weeks prior to December 25, Vietnamese units began slowly moving into Cambodian territory. However, what is known is that thirteen Vietnamese divisions supported by heavy artillery began driving west in earnest on December 25.).

[2] *Library of Congress: Cambodia, at* http://memory.loc.gov/frd/cs/khtoc.html (Dec. 1987).

more advanced than the army of Cambodia.[3] However, the fact that a Communist country attacked another Communist country just three years after each had defeated governments backed by the United States was surprising. Even more surprising was the fact that the weaker Cambodia had precipitated the invasion through three years of military attacks on the stronger Vietnam.

This chapter analyzes the Vietnamese-Cambodian conflict through the synergy of the theories of the democratic peace and deterrence failure. While discussed in more detail later, the theory of the democratic peace is based on empirical evidence that democracies do not attack non-democracies.[4] Additionally, for a variety of reasons, when democracies are engaged in war, the conflict is almost always caused by the aggression of non-democratic regimes. The conclusion that many have drawn from this empirical research is that if all leaders were democratically elected, there would be little or no war.[5] The other major theory in the study of war avoidance is deterrence failure. Deterrence failure postulates that wars happen when nations do not demonstrate both the ability and the will to adequately defend themselves.[6] In other words, wars happen because nations fail to deter aggressor nations from beginning wars. It is the synergy of these two theories that empirically best explains why war occurred in the past and

---

[3] *Id.*

[4] Jack S. Levy, *The Study of War and Peace, in* HANDBOOK OF INTERNATIONAL RELATIONS (Walter Carlsnaes, Thomas Risse & Beth A. Simmons eds., 2002) (March 2001 Draft) (on file with author). Democracies do not attack each other for a variety of reasons, including that democratic leaders bear much of the risk of war and receive little benefit, while dictators receive all of the benefit and bear little cost of waging war. Bruce Russett, *The Democratic Peace: And Yet it Moves* (draft from author that appeared in 19 INT'L SECURITY 1995) (on file with the University of Virginia School of Law Library).

[5] JAMES L. RAY, DEMOCRACY AND INTERNATIONAL CONFLICT, Ch. 1 (1995).

[6] In addition to demonstrating the ability and will to defend one's country, deterrence also involves alliances, amount of trade, and involvement in the international community—system-wide deterrence. Paul Huth & Bruce Russett, *What Makes Deterrence Work? Cases from 1900 to 1980*, 36 WORLD POL. 496-526 (July 1984); George W. Downs, *The Rational Deterrence Debate*, 41 WORLD POL. 225-37 (Jan. 1989); DONALD KAGAN, ON THE ORIGINS OF WAR AND THE PRESERVATION OF PEACE (1996).

provides a means of avoiding war in the future. Nations must focus on deterring the elites in non-democracies, because they are the people who cause war through aggression. The goal of this chapter is to resolve why the Vietnamese-Cambodian war occurred and to determine how the war fits within the synergy of the democratic peace and deterrence failure.

Obviously, the 1978 invasion of Cambodia perfectly supports the notion that non-democracies are more likely than democracies to be aggressor nations. The war involves two Communist nations led by ideologues who were neither democratically elected nor in any way responsible to the citizens of their countries. Equally obvious is that there was a deterrence failure by Cambodia, which had demonstrated over three years of attacks on Vietnam that its small military was incapable of repelling a Vietnamese invasion.

However, deterrence failure as it has been described above does not explain Cambodia's attacks on Vietnam. Vietnam had a sizeable military advantage over Cambodia, and Cambodia had lost every major battle it fought with Vietnam. In other words, Vietnam displayed both the ability and will to defend itself from attack, so Cambodia should have been deterred. Cambodia's attacks on Vietnam raise two important and intertwined concepts. First, the theory of deterrence failure relies on the generally strong presumption that leaders are rational and will only attack when they think it is in their interest to do so.[7] However, the evidence will demonstrate that the leaders of Cambodia were fanatics whose view of the world was not always rational. Second, when leaders of a country are fanatical in their ideology, the degree of deterrence required to prevent aggression increases.

To demonstrate these points, a background of the historical relationship between Vietnam and Cambodia is provided, the Cambodian aggression toward Vietnam is analyzed, and, finally, the Vietnamese invasion of Cambodia is examined.

---

[7] John N. Moore, Handout on Rationality from the seminar on War and Peace (2001) (on file with author).

A HISTORY OF VIETNAMESE AND CAMBODIAN INTERACTION UNTIL 1975

In order to understand the conflict between Vietnam and Cambodia, it is necessary to understand the historical animosity and mistrust that existed for centuries between the two neighbors. It will be demonstrated that Cambodia's long held fear of Vietnam played a role in the conflict.

Vietnam has long viewed Cambodia as a lesser and dependent nation. Vietnamese emperors thought that they ruled their nation by divine right; thus, kings of other nations were expected to show deference because their claim to rule did not come from higher authority.[8] Further, Vietnam viewed other nations and cultures as inferior to themselves.[9] As a result, Vietnam had historically sought to expand its power and influence over all of Indochina. Although Vietnam was only a moderate regional power, Cambodia was one of the few nations so weak that Vietnam was able to put its foreign policy into practice. Vietnamese emperors expected Cambodia to send periodic gifts and routinely interjected themselves into the internal politics of Cambodia.[10]

Initially, Vietnam only interfered in Cambodia's domestic politics by providing one of the Cambodian factions fighting for the throne with military support.[11] Because Cambodia was weaker than both Vietnam and another regional power, Siam, whoever sat on the Cambodian throne did so only with the support of one nation or the other. It was not until Vietnam was unified in 1802 after a civil war that it was strong enough to overtly take a role in Cambodia.[12] In 1813, Vietnam turned Cambodia into a protectorate and then ruled Cambodia directly in 1834 by making it a

---

[8] MORRIS, *supra* note 1, at 24.

[9] ALEXANDER WOOLSIDE, VIETNAM AND THE CHINESE MODEL: A COMPARISON OF VIETNAMESE AND CHINESE GOVERNMENT IN THE FIRST HALF OF THE NINETEENTH CENTURY 235 (1971).

[10] MORRIS, *supra* note 1, at 24.

[11] WOOLSIDE, *supra* note 9, at 427.

[12] MORRIS, *supra* note 1, at 25.

province.[13] However, in 1863 Cambodia became a French protectorate.[14] Since both Cambodia and Vietnam were under French control, Cambodia was free of Vietnamese intervention for the first time.

Ironically, however, Vietnam continued to benefit at the expense of Cambodia even under French rule. Much of the southern area of Vietnam was originally part of Cambodia, but France allowed Vietnam to colonize the Mekong Delta region.[15] Although both Vietnam and Cambodia were part of French Indochina, France gave Vietnam a large part of the Cambodian province Kampuchea Krom over Cambodia's objection on June 5, 1948.[16] The French also brought Vietnamese citizens into Cambodia to act as administrators for the colonial regime and allowed the Vietnamese to dominate commerce.[17] Vietnamese gains at the expense of Cambodia under French rule contributed to Cambodia's hostility toward Vietnam.

Although Vietnam was only one of many countries that had historically violated Cambodian independence, Vietnam's interference was by far the most egregious and was most feared by the Khmers (Cambodians). In fact, the Siam kingdom (now Thailand), Cambodia's old antagonist, came to Cambodia's aid against the Vietnamese in the latter part of the eighteenth century.[18] The Cambodians' fear of Vietnam grew so great that they came to believe that Vietnam would never rest until it had totally subjugated and conquered Cambodia.[19] Thus, even before

---

[13] *Id.* (The Vietnamese made Cambodia a protectorate when they brought Nak Ong Chan to power in 1813, and then decided to rule Cambodia directly when Nak Ong Chan died in 1834.)

[14] GARY KLINTWORTH, VIETNAM'S INTERVENTION IN CAMBODIA IN INTERNATIONAL LAW 3 (1989).

[15] *Id.*

[16] *Id.* However, when the French redrew Cambodia's border, they did so on all sides. On the border with Siam, France returned some territory to Cambodia that Siam had conquered. *Id.*

[17] MORRIS, *supra* note 1, at 32.

[18] KLINTWORTH, *supra* note 14, at 2.

[19] MICHAEL LEIFER, CAMBODIA, THE SEARCH FOR SECURITY 96 (1967). Leifer also refers to Cambodian news clipping citing Prince Sihanouk (the leader of Cambodia until his overthrow in 1970) as stating that "No Annamite

the Communist insurgencies began in each country, Cambodia feared Vietnam. While logically their joint struggle to install Communist governments should have united them, Cambodian hostility toward Vietnam actually grew worse during their respective insurgencies.

One reason for the increase in hostility was that Vietnam's involvement in Cambodia actually expanded as a result of Communism. Vietnam was the first nation in Indochina to begin a Communist insurgency, due to Nguyen Ai Quoc (Ho Chi Minh). Ho Chi Minh, a native Vietnamese who studied Communism in both France and Russia, became a functionary for Communist International (Comintern), an organization that helped to spread Communism to non-Communist states, in 1923.[20] The Comintern espoused a theory, based on the Soviet Union, that the key to the expansion of Communism was the creation of federations, each run by one country, which would help bring Communism to other countries.[21] Under the Comintern, Ho Chi Minh's mission was to begin a Communist revolution in Vietnam and then lead other countries in Indochina in a revolution. Although originally run under the Communist Party of France, Ho Chi Minh's Indochinese Communist Party (ICP) declared its independence in March 1930.[22] Because neither Cambodia nor Laos had a Communist party at the time, it fell upon Vietnam to lead the ICP and bring about a joint Communist uprising in all three countries.[23]

The first evidence of the Vietnamese Communist forces' (Viet Minh) involvement in Cambodia occurred in 1946 after the French returned to Indochina following Japan's defeat in World War II. A Viet Minh unit entered Cambodia in order to train ethnic Vietnamese already in Cambodia on how to run an insurgency.[24] Although there were already native freedom fighters in Cambodia by that time (the Khmer Issark), they were not Communist and

---

[Vietnamese] will sleep peacefully until he has succeeded in pushing Cambodia towards annihilation, having made it first go through the stage of slavery." *Id.*

[20] MORRIS, *supra* note 1, at 27.

[21] *Id.* at 27.

[22] *Id.* at 28.

[23] *Id.* at 29.

[24] *Id.* at 33.

were not as well armed as the Viet Minh. A Communist party began to form in Cambodia in 1949, but it was established by the Viet Minh and was run by Vietnamese citizens (in fact, Cambodians were not even allowed to join until 1951).[25]

However, once Vietnam began trying to recruit native Cambodians to its cause, it ran into the old enmity between Cambodia and Vietnam. Although the Khmer Issark met with the Viet Minh leaders, Vietnam was having a difficult time persuading Cambodians to join the Communist insurgency.[26] In 1954, when the Viet Minh withdrew from Cambodia per the Geneva Agreement that gave Cambodia freedom from France, the Viet Minh could find only 5,000 Cambodian Communists to take with them into Vietnam for training.[27]

Eventually, an independent Communist party known as the Kampuchean Worker's Party did develop in Cambodia in 1960. In 1966 the Party changed its name to the Kampuchean Communist Party (KCP) and was referred to as the Khmer Rouge.[28] Originally the leaders of the KCP did not fear Vietnam, because they had studied and trained with Vietnamese in France. It was not until the leaders of the KCP began following the doctrine of Mao that Cambodian hostility toward Vietnam began to resurface within the KCP.[29]

The KCP's growing distrust for the Viet Minh resurfaced while Prince Sihanouk (the leader of Cambodia after France granted its independence) was in power. In 1968, the KCP began an open rebellion against Prince Sihanouk's government and requested

---

[25] ROBERT TURNER, VIETNAMESE COMMUNISM, ITS ORIGINS AND DEVELOPMENT 75-77 (1975).

[26] MORRIS, *supra* note 1, at 35.

[27] The hostility of the Cambodians toward the Vietnamese and those that followed the Vietnamese was evident even then, as those who went to Vietnam were dubbed the Khmer Viet Minh. *Id.* at 35.

[28] *Id.* at 37. The Kampuchean Worker's Party came under control of a new breed of Cambodian Communists, young and trained in France. An example is Pol Pot, who became the general secretary of the Kampuchean Worker's Party in 1963 and later ruled Cambodia. *Id.*

[29] *Library of Congress, supra* note 2.

military supplies from the Viet Minh, which Hanoi refused.[30] Although the Viet Minh had long been providing small amounts of aid to the KCP, it refused additional support because Prince Sihanouk allowed the Viet Minh to run part of the Ho Chi Minh Trail through Cambodian territory.[31] The KCP felt betrayed by the Viet Minh. Although the Viet Minh increased its support for the KCP in 1970 following the overthrow of Prince Sihanouk by Lon Nol, relations with the KCP did not improve.[32] However, the limited capabilities and resources of the Khmer Rouge made Viet Minh participation necessary, and by the end of 1970, there were four Viet Minh divisions in Cambodia.[33]

In 1970, there were three different insurgencies in Cambodia working to overthrow the new Lon Nol government: the faction supporting Prince Sihanouk, the Khmer Rouge, and the Viet Minh.[34] For a while, the three worked together to overthrow Lon Nol, using Prince Sihanouk's name. However, the second major rift between the Viet Minh and the Khmer Rouge occurred when the Khmer Rouge began discrediting Prince Sihanouk. The Viet Minh wanted to continue using his name to get the support of the Cambodian people while the Khmer Rouge refused to downplay its ideology for the sake of the cause.[35] This clash led the Khmer

---

[30] MORRIS, *supra* note 1, at 43.

[31] *Id.* at 43 (citing Interrogation Rep. 058/74, Mar. 21, 1974).

[32] Lon Nol commenced a bloodless coup while Prince Sihanouk was out of Cambodia visiting Moscow. He was able to take power by seizing upon the Cambodians' hatred of Vietnam and promising to kick the Vietnamese out of Cambodia. This change from Cambodia being neutral toward Vietnam to it posing a threat to the Ho Chi Minh Trail supply line resulted in Vietnam's newfound support for the Khmer Rouge insurgency. KLINTWORTH, *supra* note 14, at 3.

[33] WILFRED P. DEAC, ROAD TO THE KILLING FIELDS: THE CAMBODIAN WAR OF 1970-1975, at 92 (1997). At the same time, the Vietnamese started infiltrating the Khmer Viet Minh back into Cambodia.

[34] MORRIS, *supra* note 1, at 47-50

[35] Kenneth M. Quinn, *Political Change in Wartime: The Khmer Krahom Revolution in Southern Cambodia*, 28 NAVAL WAR C. REV. 3, 9-10, no. 4 (1976). The refusal of the Khmer Rouge to compromise its values or back away from its doctrine in order to achieve victory foreshadows its strict adherence to the Maoist belief that moral superiority and political faith can overcome a lack of military might. *Id.*

Rouge to take control of the insurgency and decide to exclude Vietnam.

In fact, the Khmer Rouge took control of the insurgency in spite of Vietnam's efforts to command it. Vietnam had been working toward its goal of a Communist federation in Indochina led by Vietnam—especially given how weak the Khmer Rouge was militarily.[36] However, the Khmer Rouge combated the Vietnamese attempt to control the insurgency by preventing Vietnamese trained Communists from obtaining any leadership positions within the insurgency. Eventually, the Khmer Rouge resorted to killing the Khmer Viet Minh and any other person of Vietnamese ancestry involved in the insurgency.[37]

In addition, the Khmer Rouge attacked the Viet Minh forces in Cambodia, despite the fact that at the time the Khmer Rouge could not defeat Lon Nol's forces without substantial assistance from the Viet Minh.[38] The Khmer Rouge had decided that Vietnam was as much its enemy as the Lon Nol government, so although it would take aid from the Viet Minh, it would never trust them.[39] In 1971, the Khmer Rouge made a conscious decision to expel all Vietnamese troops from Cambodia.[40] Khmer Rouge units were involved in kidnapping and assassinating Viet Minh and Viet Cong members.[41] If Vietnamese forces refused to leave voluntarily, the Khmer Rouge would openly attack the Vietnamese to make them leave.[42] The fact that the Khmer Rouge wanted the Viet Minh out

---

[36] MORRIS, *supra* note 1, at 50 (Morris cites a captured Viet Minh document from April 1970 stating: "Although the Cambodian revolutionaries are enthusiastic, they are incapable . . . . Our helping them is one of our international obligations. On the other hand, Cambodia is our staging area. The Cambodian Revolution is weak and its organization loose. We have to strengthen it.").

[37] *Id.* at 53. The purge of the Khmer Viet Minh occurred between 1971 and 1974. The State Security branch of the KCP would lure away members of the Khmer Viet Minh on a pretext and then secretly kill them. *Library of Congress, supra* note 2.

[38] Quinn, *supra* note 35, at 8.

[39] MORRIS, *supra* note 1, at 56.

[40] *Id.*

[41] *Id.* at 57.

[42] *Id.* at 60 (The Viet Minh leaders did not know of either the purges or that the military attacks by the Khmer Rouge were intentional until 1973. By then

of Cambodia when Viet Minh forces comprised three quarters of the Communist troops fighting the Lon Nol government demonstrates how much the Khmer Rouge feared and loathed Vietnam.[43] Vietnam's only response to the Khmer Rouge's attacks on Viet Minh forces was to intermittently cut off supplies going to Cambodia from China.[44] Such retaliation only increased the Khmer Rouge's belief that Vietnam was still Cambodia's enemy.[45]

Thus the stage was set for the third Indochina War, this time between Vietnam and Cambodia. Phnom Penh fell on April 17, 1975, to the Khmer Rouge, two weeks before Saigon fell. Vietnam's hope of controlling Cambodia by turning united Vietnamese forces toward Cambodia and playing a major role in the overthrow of Lon Nol were dashed. Vietnam was unable to have any say in the creation or formulation of the new government. Thus the leaders who came into power in Cambodia in 1975 were the same people who in 1971 had instituted a policy of killing Vietnamese troops and anyone allied with the Vietnamese. Instead of fulfilling its dream of leading a federation of Communist states in Indochina, Vietnam found itself bordering a nation that considered Vietnam its greatest enemy.

THE BEGINNING OF THE THIRD INDOCHINA WAR: CAMBODIAN AGGRESSION TOWARD VIETNAM (1975-1978)

A mere three years after the Khmer Rouge defeated the Lon Nol government, Vietnamese troops crossed into Cambodia, quickly routed the Cambodian army, and defeated the Khmer

---

Vietnam had pulled out most of its fighting forces in Cambodia and what was left was used mainly to protect and supply the Ho Chi Minh Trail. Given its limited supply of troops in the area, Vietnam decided against military reprisals against the Khmer Rouge, as such an offensive would take troops away from the inevitable push toward South Vietnam. *Id.*)

[43] *Library of Congress, supra* note 2. Although, as Vietnamese forces began to withdraw from Cambodia, the strength of the Khmer Rouge's military began to increase. By the end of 1972 the Khmer Rouge military had 50,000 soldiers. *Id.*

[44] MORRIS, *supra* note 1, at 63.

[45] *Id.*

Rouge government. However, as has already been noted, the Vietnamese attack was invited by the Khmer Rouge because of its repeated attacks on Vietnamese villages between 1975 and 1978.[46]

Soon after the Khmer Rouge conquered the Lon Nol government, it began attacking Vietnamese border villages and massacring Vietnamese people.[47] The Khmer Rouge attacked all along the border of the territories that France had given to Vietnam. Yet the attacks were not designed to immediately conquer territory, for the Khmer Rouge members did not attempt to hold the land; they only murdered the inhabitants of the villages.[48] Although at one point an attack managed to reach four miles into Vietnamese territory, the attack was repelled and Cambodian forces withdrew having gained nothing.[49]

At the same time Cambodia was attacking Vietnam, it was also cutting itself off from all foreign trade and investment as a policy of self-reliance (although they ended up taking substantial contributions of aid from China in spite of this policy).[50] Additionally, the atrocities that were committed within the country are now well-known: the purging of anyone associated with the former government, the purging of all the educated and elites, the killing of anyone suspected of being a dissident, and the evacuation of all cities and towns in favor of a forced agrarian society.[51] These policies served only to weaken Cambodia both economically and militarily. The purges killed vast numbers of former Lon Nol military, which could have been used to make the Khmer's army stronger. The agrarian society provided neither the products necessary to train and supply an army nor the money required for their purchase. In addition, a society where people worked fourteen hours a day on a farm and yet were dangerously malnourished will not provide the requisite manpower that a country needs to defend itself. Essentially, almost every action

---

[46] KLINTWORTH, *supra* note 14, at 19.

[47] *Id.*

[48] MORRIS, *supra* note 1, at 98-99.

[49] KLINTWORTH, *supra* note 14, at 19; *Library of Congress, supra* note 2.

[50] MORRIS, *supra* note 1, at 76.

[51] *Library of Congress, supra* note 2.

taken by the Khmer Rouge served only to weaken Cambodia.[52] However, in spite of its inferior and rapidly decaying society, the Khmer Rouge still chose to attack Vietnam. The question is why.

Cambodian Aggression and the Theories of the Democratic Peace and Deterrence Failure

The question of why Cambodia attacked Vietnam must be analyzed under the theories of the democratic peace and deterrence failure. However, it has already been noted that the Cambodian attacks make sense in terms of the democratic peace. The Khmer Rouge was not democratically elected and was not responsible to the Cambodian citizens. In fact, all evidence indicates that not only were the Khmer Rouge not responsible to Cambodian people, but the Khmer Rouge uprooted and purged large segments of the Cambodian populace.[53] This is perhaps the most extreme example of government failure ever. Government failure theory holds that non-democracies engage in war because the elites are able to externalize the costs of war on the third parties, in this case the citizens, while personally getting all of the benefits.[54] The Khmer Rouge, because it did not have to be reelected or even worry about an uprising due to its strong internal security, could attack Vietnam at the expense of countless Cambodian lives without losing power. Further, any benefits from the war would go to the leaders of the Khmer Rouge while the costs of waging the war would be borne by the Cambodian people.

Additionally, one reason why democracies avoid war is that they are transparent in nature.[55] Because democracies require public support to wage war, democratic governments have to be

---

[52] A country cannot expect to raise a sizeable army when it kills off between a quarter and a third of its population. Cambodia even prevented long-term population growth that could have been used to strengthen its military when it discouraged procreation by making extramarital affairs and premarital sex punishable with death, keeping men and women separate, and separating parents from their children.

[53] *Library of Congress, supra* note 2.

[54] Levy, *supra* note 4.

[55] *Id.*

more honest and direct in their public statements in order to persuade the public. However, a dictatorship does not have to be honest in its public statements because it acts with or without the approval of the public. Thus other nations are less likely to trust the public statements of a dictatorship and there are more likely to be misperceptions about the intent of a dictatorship because of a lack of transparency. In this case, although to all outward appearances Vietnam was attempting to befriend Cambodia, the Khmer Rouge leaders refused to believe that Vietnam was no longer a threat. Essentially, they thought Vietnam was their enemy because of a lack of transparency. Since there was no internal check to stop the Khmer Rouge from preemptively attacking Vietnam because of government failure, only an external check (deterrence) could have prevented Cambodian aggression.

Under the theory of deterrence failure, the external check that should have prevented recurring Cambodian attacks was Vietnam's far superior military.[56] Cambodia could not have realistically thought it had a chance of beating Vietnam in a conventional battle.[57] Vietnam's only deterrence failure was that it initially did not retaliate to the border raids commenced by Cambodia.[58] However, although Cambodia's initial raids may have been justified because of Vietnamese restraint, for over a year before Vietnam's invasion in December 1978, Vietnam had engaged in massive retaliation, yet Cambodia continued it raids.[59] Further, in terms of system-wide deterrence, Vietnam was allied to the Soviet Union, a much stronger ally than Cambodia's ally, China. Although Cambodia's decision to raid Vietnamese villages may have been rational when Vietnam was not protecting its border, the decision to continue raiding in the face of strong Vietnamese retaliation did not make sense.

---

[56] MORRIS, *supra* note 1, at 92 (The Khmer Rouge had 230 under strength battalions consisting of a main force of about 60,000 troops and little or no armor or air force. The Vietnamese army consisted of 685,000 army regulars, a 3,000 man navy, and a 12,000 man air force with 268 fighters and bombers.).

[57] *Library of Congress, supra* note 2.

[58] KLINTWORTH, *supra* note 14, at 22.

[59] *Id.* at 23.

Unfortunately, there is no clear explanation for Cambodia's continued aggression toward Vietnam. Many people have tried to explain why a rational leader would instigate and continue a war that it had no hope of winning, yet no single theory provides a complete answer.[60] Any rational person would have known that Cambodia's meager military and decimated population had no chance of defeating a Vietnamese army ten times its size. This leaves only one conclusion—the leaders of Cambodia were not acting rationally.

The problem with calling Pol Pot and the other members of the Khmer Rouge irrational is that it contradicts a basic presumption of deterrence theory—that all leaders are rational and thus can be deterred.[61] The presumption of rational leaders does not hold that a leader will never make a mistake, only that leaders will act in their best interest based on what they perceive that interest to be. When the presumption holds true, an aggressive leader can be deterred by making it evident that the leader's best interest is served by not acting—thus the theory is not so much predictive as it is a necessary assumption. It assumes that leaders are rational because otherwise they could not be influenced and deterred from aggression. If leaders cannot be prevented from pursuing military aggression, the only possible response is to defeat them through

---

[60] The theories were that the attacks were small enough that they were below the scope of what Vietnam would respond to, Vietnam did not effectively deter Cambodia, that Cambodia was attacking preemptively because they feared that Vietnam would eventually attack Cambodia, and that Cambodia was trying to start an uprising in territory that was once Cambodian but was now under Vietnamese control.

[61] Moore, *supra* note 7. The handout is on incentive theory but deals specifically with the presumption of rational actors. The handout provides four reasons to assume that leaders are rational: 1) empirically, leaders who commit aggression are at least rational even if barbaric and ruthless; 2) even if there are exceptions to the rule, the fact that less than 100 percent of leaders are rational does not mean a generally sound concept should be discarded; 3) all theories of war avoidance rely on the ability to influence rational actors; thus any approach to preventing war requires such an assumption; 4) the rare instances of an irrational leader do not change the basic requirement of deterrence, the ability to defend, and the will to do so if attacked.

war. Rationality has to be assumed for the possibility of avoiding war.

However, the assumption of rational leaders becomes more tenuous when the leaders are fanatical. Fanatical leaders filter information they receive through their own skewed perception of the world and thus have a harder time making impartial observations about outcomes and the probability of success.[62] In this case, the Khmer Rouge leaders were rational to the extent that rational means they thought they were acting in their best interest—they honestly thought that they would be better off by attacking Vietnam than by not attacking Vietnam. The problem is that while such a decision might have been "in their best interest" when Vietnam was not protecting its villages and there was nothing to lose, the decision to continue attacking once Vietnam began retaliating was clearly not in their best interest. Further, it was a fundamental defect in the leadership of the Khmer Rouge's perception of reality that caused them to believe that continued aggression toward Vietnam was in their interest. It is not that the Khmer Rouge made a mistake in underestimating Vietnam's willingness to use force or Vietnam's military superiority, the problem was that the Khmer Rouge leaders thought neither factor mattered. The Khmer Rouge's view of the world was so warped that once the Khmer Rouge began attacking, Vietnam had no way of making Cambodia stop attacking short of invasion. As this chapter shall demonstrate, although the decision of the Khmer Rouge to raid Vietnamese villages was not in and of itself irrational, the decision to press the attack against overwhelming odds was.

Vietnam Should Have Been Able to Deter Cambodian Aggression Because Vietnam Had Demonstrated Both the Capacity and the Will to Defend Itself

The fact that Vietnam's military far surpassed that of Cambodia has already been noted several times and does not need to be explored here. Suffice it to say that Vietnam had more than

---

[62] MORRIS, *supra* note 1, at 12.

enough military power to adequately and easily defend itself from
any attacks by Cambodia. But even more importantly, Vietnam
had also already demonstrated to the world its willingness to use
its military by defeating South Vietnam in 1975. However, in May
of 1975, the Khmer Rouge launched a surprise attack on
Vietnamese military bases on islands in the Gulf of Thailand, but
the Vietnamese were still able to defeat the Khmer Rouge forces.[63]
In fact, in response to this unexpected aggression, the Vietnamese
attacked and conquered the Cambodian island of Palo Wai.[64]

Having learned its lesson, Cambodia did not engage in a major
military attack on Vietnam for several years following Palo Wai.
Instead, it engaged in a string of minor raids on Vietnamese
villages in the formerly Cambodian territories.[65] It has been argued
that Vietnam did not properly deter Cambodia from these attacks
because it showed restraint in retaliation. Vietnamese citizens were
being slaughtered and had to flee their villages, yet Vietnam did
not strike back in force.[66] Vietnam had demobilized its army and
did not have many regular troops near the border to begin with,
and those few near the border were ordered to avoid
confrontation.[67] By attempting friendship and not instantly
retaliating to the aggression, Vietnam may have encouraged further
attacks by showing softness to the Khmer Rouge. Thus, from a
deterrence standpoint, the initial raids on Vietnam could rationally
be explained as low grade and thus low risk attacks on relatively
unprotected territory.

However, any doubts about Vietnam's willingness to use force
should have ended by 1977. Vietnam had slowly been building up
its forces near the border and escalating its response to Cambodian
raids. After two Khmer Rouge divisions invaded Vietnam in 1977,
Vietnamese troops forcibly repelled the attack and viciously
counterattacked the Khmer Rouge forces in Cambodia.[68] In

---

[63] MORRIS, *supra* note 1, at 92.

[64] *Id.*

[65] KLINTWORTH, *supra* note 14, at 19.

[66] *Id.* at 20.

[67] *Id.* at 18-21.

[68] MORRIS, *supra* note 1, at 99.

October 1977, Vietnamese troops invaded Cambodia, advancing fifteen miles into Cambodian territory and causing massive destruction to Cambodian forces in the area. Vietnam chose to withdraw its troops only after the point of military superiority had seemingly been made.[69] However, because the Khmer Rouge continued raiding Cambodian villages, the Vietnamese again attacked in December of 1977, this time using tanks, 20,000 troops, and air support.[70] Again the Vietnamese forces willingly withdrew after inflicting massive damage to Khmer Rouge forces in the area.[71] Both attacks should have demonstrated Vietnam's willingness to use force and Vietnam's vast military superiority; Cambodia should have been deterred from further action. Instead, the Khmer Rouge's resolve inexplicably hardened and the attacks continued.[72]

The evidence also demonstrates that Cambodia could not have rationally believed that its attacks were below the threshold of Vietnamese response. Although Vietnam was slow to respond to the raids on its villages, by 1977 Vietnam was moving more forces to the border and was retaliating for attacks on its villages.[73] By the end of 1977, Vietnam had a sizeable force near the border and was retaliating for both raids on its villages and major military attacks. Yet, in spite of the fact that Vietnam was retaliating militarily to the raids on its villages, the raids continued to occur until the Vietnamese invasion in December 1978.[74] In addition, the fact that Cambodia was not engaging only in minor border attacks means

---

[69] KLINTWORTH, *supra* note 14, at 21.

[70] MORRIS, *supra* note 1, at 101. The attack occurred within the province of Svay Rieng, Cambodia, located fifty-five miles from Ho Chi Minh City. *Id.*

[71] DAVID P. CHANDLER, BROTHER NUMBER ONE: A POLITICAL BIOGRAPHY OF POL POT 138 (1999). The Vietnamese army halted before it reached the city of Svay Rieng. Although Vietnamese forces had advanced twenty-four miles into Cambodian territory and could have easily taken the capital of Cambodia, they chose to stop. Upon their return to Vietnam, the army brought back thousands of prisoners after a crushing defeat of the Khmer Rouge army. *Id.*

[72] KLINTWORTH, *supra* note 14, at 26 (not only did the Khmer Rouge continue attacking Vietnamese villages, but it also again attacked Vietnamese-held islands and engaged in further land battles with Vietnamese forces).

[73] MORRIS, *supra* note 1, at 101.

[74] *Library of Congress, supra* note 2.

that it could not have hoped to keep its attacks under Vietnamese radar. Cambodia began its aggression on Vietnam by trying to conquer two Vietnamese islands, and by 1977 it was engaging in attacks consisting of up to two divisions.[75] No country could have ignored such attacks.

Vietnam Did Not Present a Danger to Cambodia Until After Vietnam Was Attacked

It has also been argued that one of the reasons why the Khmer Rouge attacked Vietnam was that it believed Vietnam would eventually attack Cambodia. This goes back to both Cambodia's deep-seated fear of Vietnam and the Khmer Rouge's determination during its insurgency that Vietnam was going to be the long-term enemy of Cambodia.[76] Initially, it must be noted that to a limited extent Cambodian fears were justified—Vietnam had never given up hope of a Communist Indochina led by Vietnam.[77] However Vietnam's wish to guide Cambodia was just that: a wish. As has already been illustrated, Vietnam lost any opportunity it had to control Cambodia when Pol Pot killed all of the Khmer Viet Minh and when Vietnam was not involved in the fall of the Lon Nol government.[78] Even if Vietnam would have liked to control Cambodia, it did not have the means to do so because it had no intention of invading Cambodia—at least not until after three years of Cambodian attacks.[79]

---

[75] KLINTWORTH, *supra* note 14, at 19.

[76] MORRIS, *supra* note 1, at 56. Pol Pot decided in 1971 to expel Vietnamese troops and liquidate Vietnamese supporters in Cambodia, because "Vietnam was the long term acute enemy of Kampuchea." *Id.*

[77] MORRIS, *supra* note 1, at 96.

[78] *Id.* at 55.

[79] KLINTWORTH, *supra* note 14, at 21 (Vietnam did not have troops on the border, Vietnam tried to settle the issue through negotiations, and Vietnam showed restraint in responding.). It was not until early 1978 that Vietnam decided to develop a grassroots movement to overthrow the Khmer Rouge regime. After that plan failed because of the tight security and police forces employed by Pol Pot to prevent any insurgencies, it was not until June 1978 that Vietnam decided to invade and conquer Cambodia. MORRIS, *supra* note 1, at 108.

In fact, even if a less than consistent ally during the insurgency, Vietnam still praised and congratulated the Khmer Rouge after it came to power. The Vietnamese outwardly showed nothing but friendship to Cambodia and the Vietnamese press praised the reforms the Khmer Rouge had installed in turning Cambodia Communist.[80] The Vietnamese invited the leaders of the Khmer Rouge to Hanoi for conferences, and the one-year anniversary of the Khmer Rouge victory over the Lon Nol government was officially celebrated in Vietnam.[81]

In addition to the friendship they offered, the Vietnamese also gave Cambodia little cause for alarm militarily. In 1975, at the request of China, Vietnam withdrew the last of its troops that had been supporting the insurgency and protecting the Ho Chi Minh Trail.[82] Also, as has already been noted, Vietnam did not have many troops along their shared border that could have been perceived as a threat to Cambodia. Even when attacked by Cambodia, Vietnam initially showed incredible restraint in its retaliation.[83] Further, when Vietnam did retaliate to the attack on its islands by taking the Cambodian island of Palo Wai, the island was later returned.[84] Rather than attempting major retaliation against Cambodia, Vietnam instead repeatedly asked for negotiations to mediate the border dispute.[85] This is simply not the kind of threatening action indicative of an aggressive state.

Even more importantly, forgetting for a moment all the evidence to the contrary, assuming Vietnam did plan to conquer Cambodia all along, there is still no justifiable reason for the

---

[80] MORRIS, *supra* note 1, at 92 (Miller cites Vietnamese news articles stating that the "Liberated Cambodia is living in a new and healthy atmosphere.").

[81] *Id.* at 93.

[82] *Id.*

[83] KLINTWORTH, *supra* note 14, at 21.

[84] NAYAN CHANDA, BROTHER ENEMY: THE WAR AFTER THE WAR 195 (1986).

[85] KLINTWORTH, *supra* note 14, at 21. The Vietnamese publicly began requesting negotiations over border disputes and the attacks in April 1977, and there are reports of prior secret appeals to the Khmer Rouge to mediate the dispute that were rebuffed. *Id.*

border attacks instigated by Cambodia.[86] Pol Pot's continuous purging of anyone even suspected of being dissidents by his sizable secret police force prevented Vietnam from fostering a revolution from within.[87] The only way that Vietnam could have posed a threat to the Khmer Rouge was by an actual military invasion of Cambodia. Cambodia's raids and military aggression toward Vietnam gave Vietnam the very excuse it would have needed to justify such an invasion. However, for perhaps the second time in Cambodia's life, Cambodia was free from the risk of an invasion by Vietnam. As a Communist country, Cambodia should have been an ally to Vietnam, as it was to China. The only reason Vietnam allowed three years of Cambodian attacks before invading was that it considered Cambodia a fraternal brother.[88] Although Vietnam may have been opposed to the leaders of the KCP who instigated the raids against Vietnamese villages, Vietnam thought that the Communist organization of the KCP was sound and therefore waited far longer before retaliating than it would have against a non-Communist country.[89] Additionally, Vietnam would not needlessly risk war with China, the largest regional power, by recklessly attacking Cambodia, an ally of China.[90] Vietnam would not undermine Communist unity by attacking another Communist country or risk a war with China without first having a very good reason.[91] The only way Vietnam could ever attack Cambodia again was if it was first provoked in a way that both excused and necessitated invasion. Assuming

---

[86] Again, this is not to argue that Vietnam did not want to control Cambodia or that there was not a history of Vietnamese imperialism and aggression toward Cambodia, but that there is no evidence that after Cambodia was conquered by a Communist insurgency Vietnam intended to militarily invade Cambodia to replace those Communists with its own Communists.

[87] MORRIS, *supra* note 1, at 105.

[88] *Id.* at 106.

[89] *Id.*

[90] Although there was already a rift between the Maoist Communists in China and the revisionist Communists in the Soviet Union, Communist parties would still prefer to show the world a unified front if at all possible. This is demonstrated by the fact that Vietnam maintained relations with both China and the Soviet Union and in fact received aid from both until 1978.

[91] MORRIS, *supra* note 1, at 106-07.

Vietnam wanted to conquer Cambodia, it was the very actions of the Khmer Rouge that allowed it happen.

The fact of the matter is that Vietnam had been friendly with Cambodia up until late 1977 when Cambodia stepped up its border attacks on Vietnam and severed diplomatic relations with Vietnam.[92] It was only after it became obvious to Vietnam that its military superiority to Cambodia and mere shows of force would not deter Pol Pot from attacking Vietnam that Vietnam decided to overthrow the Khmer Rouge regime.[93]

The Khmer Rouge Did Nothing to Aid Its Ostensible Goal of Sparking a Revolution in the Former Cambodian Territories

The reason advanced by the Khmer Rouge for its attacks on Vietnam was a desire to generate an uprising by Cambodians still living in former Cambodian territories given away by the French.[94] However, while such a desire may be valid, there is little or no evidence that the Khmer Rouge did anything to make that desire a reality. There is no evidence that the Khmer Rouge attacked Vietnam with the intent of either training or supplying Cambodian rebels in the captured territories. Rather, the goal of the attacks was to kill Vietnamese citizens and inflict minor military damage.[95] More to the point, there is no evidence either that Cambodian rebels operated in the captured territories or that the Khmer Rouge attempted to create a rebellion.[96] When Vietnam attempted to create a rebellion against the Khmer Rouge in Cambodia, it recruited, trained, and supplied the rebels. When attacking Thailand, even the Khmer Rouge set up an insurgency to try to

---

[92] *Id.* at 102 (the break in relations occurred on December 31 and was supposedly only a temporary reaction to Vietnamese "aggression" against Cambodia).

[93] *Id.* at 108.

[94] WILFRED BURCHETT, THE CHINA-CAMBODIA-VIETNAM TRIANGLE 158 (1981).

[95] KLINTWORTH, *supra* note 14, at 20.

[96] *Id.*

cause a rebellion.[97] Yet, in Vietnam, Cambodia attempted to create a rebellion simply by engaging in raids on border villages. There is no rational way that such minor attacks alone would cause otherwise content farmers of Cambodian descent to take up arms against the Vietnamese government. In fact, rather than causing ethnic Cambodians to take up arms against Vietnam, they fled deeper into Vietnam to take refuge from the fighting and from the atrocities of the Khmer Rouge.[98]

The Khmer Rouge Had a Skewed Perception of Reality

Although this chapter argues that the Khmer Rouge could not correctly perceive reality, in fact the Khmer Rouge was well aware of the military discrepancy between Cambodia and Vietnam. The Khmer Rouge leaders knew all too well that they had a population base of at most eight million and an army of 60,000 in comparison to Vietnam's population of fifty million and an army of 600,000.[99] The Khmer Rouge's problem was not that it was unaware of this huge discrepancy, but that its members thought that the discrepancy did not matter.

Perhaps the best example of the Khmer Rouge's pointed indifference to military odds was provided before it even came to power. While the Khmer Rouge was still trying to overthrow the Lon Nol government, it commenced a major attack on the government about a month before the United States was going to be precluded from intervening in Cambodia by the U.S. Congress.[100] The legislation had already been publicly signed and the date on which the legislation would go into effect was well-known. All the Khmer Rouge had to do was wait until the legislation went into effect, and the U.S. military would be unable to assist the forces of Lon Nol. Nevertheless, the Khmer Rouge

---

[97] MORRIS, *supra* note 1, at 80.

[98] Cambodians on both sides of the border fled to Saigon and other cities in Vietnam. It turned out that the Khmer Rouge were the only people Cambodians feared more than Vietnam. KLINTWORTH, *supra* note 14, at 23.

[99] MORRIS, *supra* note 1, at 103.

[100] *Id.* at 53.

attacked one month before the legislation went into effect. The attack turned into a slaughter of Khmer Rouge forces as U.S. airplanes decimated the Khmer Rouge's poorly equipped ground forces.[101] This was a senseless slaughter that could have been avoided if the Khmer Rouge had waited one month to attack. Yet the concept of military superiority is one that the Khmer Rouge did not understand, and never would.

Essentially, the Khmer Rouge believed that a country with a larger population and military would still be unable to defeat Cambodia—that the Cambodian army would win simply because it had to. This belief stemmed from the Khmer Rouge's fanatical devotion to Maoist Communism.[102] Mao believed that it was human will that made a country great and affected history, not technological superiority.[103] Khmer Rouge members essentially believed that their pure devotion to Communism and their strength of will would lead their people to victory over any "corrupt" foreign invader.[104] The Khmer Rouge's intense dedication to Mao's idiosyncratic view of human will affected their perception of what was militarily feasible and made a realistic calculation of the probability of success impossible.[105] Because the Khmer Rouge leaders followed Mao's teachings so devoutly (in fact, even more than China did), they believed they could overcome any odds.

For example, the Khmer Rouge claimed that one Cambodian fighter was worth thirty Vietnamese fighters, which would more than make up for any discrepancy in technology or numbers.[106] So

---

[101] *Id.*

[102] *Id.* at 104. Morris also cites Cambodian mystical faith movements of the 1800s as a precedent for the belief that weaker forces can overcome stronger ones. Such movements believed that magical power and purity of belief would protect soldiers and guarantee victory. In the case of the Khmer Rouge, the magical power was their pure devotion to Maoist Communism, or hyper-Maoism. *Id.*

[103] SHU GUANG ZHANG, MAO'S MILITARY ROMANTICISM: CHINA AND THE KOREAN WAR (1995).

[104] MORRIS, *supra* note 1, at 12-13.

[105] *Id.* at 12.

[106] *Id.* at 104 (Morris cites a Phnom Penh radio announcement from May 10, 1978. The announcement stated that Cambodia would not need all of its population to defeat Vietnam, because if each troop killed thirty people, then it

long as in every battle each Cambodian fighter killed thirty Vietnamese fighters before he died, Cambodia would only need an army of two million to take on Vietnam's population of fifty million.[107] This is a prime example of the way fanatical leaders filter information. Rather than taking the disparity in military as evidence that an attack should not be made, the unique filtering system of the Khmer Rouge took that information to mean that its soldiers would just have to kill even more of the enemy. Pol Pot did not think Vietnam had a military advantage over Cambodia because of his faulty belief that every single Cambodian soldier could kill thirty Vietnamese, that the Khmer Rouge could take its malnourished and decimated population and raise an army of two million from a population of seven million, and that the Khmer Rouge could accomplish these feats and more simply because it must.

This irrational thinking was actually "put into practice" by the Khmer Rouge during the Vietnamese attack in December of 1977. As has been noted, the Vietnamese army easily marched into Cambodia, smashed the forces of the Khmer Rouge, and took many prisoners. Although the army, only a small fraction of what Vietnam could have used to invade, could have easily marched all the way to the Cambodian capital, it chose to withdraw. However, rather than taking this invasion as a lesson and a warning, the Khmer Rouge called it a victory, claiming that the Vietnamese invaders had been driven from Cambodia at great cost to the Vietnamese.[108] The Khmer Rouge claimed that in defeating Vietnam, it had put into practice with great success its ingenious military tactic of having each Cambodian soldier kill thirty Vietnamese.[109] The belief that a crushing defeat of Cambodia was

---

would "need only 2 million troops to crush the 50 million Vietnamese; and we still would have 6 million people left. We must formulate our combat line in this manner in order to achieve victory.").

[107] *Library of Congress, supra* note 2.

[108] *Id.*

[109] MORRIS, *supra* note 1, at 104 (Morris again cites the Phnom Penh radio broadcast from May 10, 1978, which claimed that the Vietnamese were driven from Cambodian territory at the cost of thirty Vietnamese for every one Cambodian lost.).

in fact a victory and the failure to stop antagonizing Vietnam after such a defeat demonstrates a severely warped view of reality.

Interestingly, Vietnam was not the only country facing attacks by Cambodia. Beginning in 1977, Cambodia was also striving to become entangled in a two-front war by attacking villages in Thailand while also conducting raids in Vietnam.[110] These unprovoked attacks were allegedly over disputed territory but made little sense as Thailand certainly had the military capacity to respond and the attacks were consuming forces needed along Cambodia's border with Vietnam.[111] Although Cambodia ceased its attacks on Thailand in 1978, Cambodia had already wasted precious resources in attacks that did nothing but risk open war on two borders with two larger countries.

Interestingly, the Khmer Rouge blamed its confrontations on Vietnam and Thailand. In Vietnam, the Khmer Rouge was trying to recapture territory, and in Thailand, the Khmer Rouge was attempting to foster a Communist insurgency; yet members of the Khmer Rouge also believed they were defending Cambodia from attacks by its neighbors.[112] This goes back to the overriding paranoia of the Khmer Rouge that it was beset with enemies both from without and from within.[113] The Khmer Rouge believed that both Thailand and Vietnam were attacking Cambodia and that there were both CIA and Vietnamese agents working within Cambodia to overthrow Pol Pot. However, the purges conducted by the Khmer Rouge and the omnipresent internal security forces made the latter unlikely, while undisputable proof demonstrates that Cambodia was the aggressor nation against both Vietnam and Thailand.[114] The Khmer Rouge assertion, without evidence, that it

---

[110] *Id.* at 78.

[111] *Id.* at 81. Although the dispute was claimed to be over land, in fact it was an attempt to foment a Communist revolution. Thais were captured and taken away for training and education and were then re-infiltrated into Thailand so that they could coordinate attacks with the Cambodian army. *Id.*

[112] DAVID P. CHANDLER, DANIEL KIERNAN & CHATHOU BOUA, POL POT PLANS THE FUTURE: CONFIDENTIAL LEADERSHIP DOCUMENTS FROM DEMOCRATIC KAMPUCHEA 126 (1988).

[113] *Id.*

[114] KLINTWORTH, *supra* note 14, at 18-19.

was being attacked on all sides, while in reality it was the Khmer Rouge attacking its neighbors, demonstrates the Khmer Rouge's warped perception of reality.

Rational or Irrational: The Decision to Attack and Continue Attacking Vietnam

It is not enough to state that the Khmer Rouge leaders attacked and continued to attack Vietnam because they were irrational, because they certainly were not insane. Pol Pot and the other leaders of the Khmer Rouge fled Cambodia rather than face the Vietnamese army after Cambodia's army was destroyed during the invasion.[115] The Khmer Rouge even showed certain levels of sophistication in its dealings with other nations. In dealing with Thailand, Cambodia managed to fool the leaders of Thailand into believing that the border attacks were caused by rogue Cambodian generals and was not part of a Cambodian policy, all the while supplying Thai Communists with weapons.[116] Also, the Khmer Rouge was slowly diverging from its policy of self-reliance and seeking greater ties in Southeast Asia.[117] Such a demonstration of growing political sophistication within the Khmer Rouge makes the question of why the Khmer Rouge pressed its attack on Vietnam against such odds even more difficult to answer.

In fact, the only answer left is a combination of deterrence failure and the difficulty of deterring fanatical leaders. Initially, Vietnam did not effectively deter Cambodian aggression. It has been noted that Vietnam did not have many troops on the border with Cambodia and that the commanders of Vietnamese soldiers were ordered to avoid conflicts with Cambodian troops.[118]

---

[115] *Library of Congress, supra* note 2.

[116] MORRIS, *supra* note 1, at 81. The Khmer Rouge engaged in continuous fighting along the border of Thailand. Cambodian soldiers attacked villages and took civilians to Cambodia for education and training. At one point the Khmer Rouge even fired long-range rockets into Thailand. In spite of all this, the Thai prime minister had claimed that the attacks were being waged without the knowledge or approval of Cambodian leadership. *Id.*

[117] *Id.* at 79.

[118] KLINTWORTH, *supra* note 14, at 18-21.

Additionally, when Vietnam did retaliate, such as taking Palo Wai, it gave the territory back to Cambodia.[119] The lesson the Khmer Rouge learned from its early attacks was that the only cost of attacking Vietnam was the lives of Cambodian soldiers, and the Khmer Rouge's indifference to life has already been established.[120]

Additionally, the Khmer Rouge learned the same lesson in Thailand. The Cambodian army had been aggressively attacking Thai villages and military installations on the border, yet Thai leaders did not retaliate and even made excuses for the Khmer Rouge.[121] In its infancy, the Khmer Rouge learned that its aggression toward its neighbors would not be met with force. From attacks on Viet Minh forces in 1972 to attacks on the actual countries of Vietnam and Thailand, the Khmer Rouge never learned the repercussions of aggression.

When the Khmer Rouge first started attacking Vietnam, it also had reason to believe that China would intervene on its behalf if Vietnam retaliated. Although Cambodia was not controlled by China as Vietnam had suspected, China was an ally of Cambodia, and the Khmer Rouge were staunch followers of Mao's ideology.[122] It was China that convinced Cambodia to end its attacks on Thailand in 1978.[123] Further, it was Chinese military supplies that were being used to wage war on Vietnam.[124] Given these ties, the Khmer Rouge had reason to believe that China would aid Cambodia if it were invaded by Vietnam. The possibility of Chinese assistance decreased Vietnam's ability to deter Cambodian aggression because the leaders of the Khmer Rouge thought that China would prevent Vietnam from ever removing them from power.

Thus, from the Khmer Rouge point of view, by attacking Vietnam, it got to attack an enemy and make Vietnamese citizens

---

[119] CHANDA, *supra* note 84, at 195.

[120] *Library of Congress, supra* note 2 (the murder of between a quarter and a third of its population).

[121] MORRIS, *supra* note 1, at 81-82.

[122] Morris even referred to the Khmer Rouge as hyper-Maoists. *Id.* at 12-13.

[123] *Id.* at 81-82.

[124] KLINTWORTH, *supra* note 14, at 24-26. China had military advisors in Cambodia and supplied Cambodia with its weapons. *Id.*

leave territory that Cambodia wanted to control at essentially no risk. In other words, although there was little upside to the attacks (Cambodia could neither hurt Vietnam's military capacity nor lead to the immediate Cambodian control of the disputed territory), there was little downside because there was no risk that the Khmer Rouge would lose power by attacking.

However, even if the initial raids on Vietnam were at least reasonable under this calculation, the attacks cease to make sense in 1977. By that time Vietnam had amassed over 100,000 troops near the border, and it was destroying the Cambodian army at will.[125] Essentially, there was no longer deterrence failure. Vietnam was demonstrating the will and the capacity to use force, and all that Cambodia had to do to stop Vietnamese retaliation was to stop antagonizing Vietnam. It has been argued that Vietnam failed to deter the Khmer Rouge because it willingly withdrew from Cambodia after defeating the Cambodian army.[126] However, that is not really a deterrence failure. If Vietnam had not removed its army from Cambodia and had gone ahead and overthrown the Khmer Rouge, it would no longer have been deterrence but an actual conquering. By 1977 Vietnam had demonstrated that it could crush the Cambodian army and that it could remove the Khmer Rouge from power, but it had stopped short of actually removing the Khmer Rouge in an effort to deter and not occupy. Throughout 1978 Vietnam had troops stationed in Cambodian territory near the border and had amassed an army for invasion at the border.[127] Vietnam had slowly escalated its response to the point where the only option left was all-out invasion.

It has also been asserted that Vietnam failed to deter Cambodian aggression by neglecting to publicly announce that it would actually remove the Khmer Rouge from power. However, by early 1978, the leaders of the Khmer Rouge knew that Vietnam was training insurgents to remove them from power and that Vietnam had assisted those insurgents with air support.[128]

---

[125] KLINTWORTH, *supra* note 14, at 17-20.

[126] *Id.*

[127] MORRIS, *supra* note 1.

[128] *Id.* at 105-07.

Additionally, since the Khmer Rouge had always feared a Vietnamese invasion, such a threat was unnecessary.[129] The problem was not that the leaders of the Khmer Rouge believed that Vietnam would never try to conquer Cambodia; the problem was that they believed that Vietnam could not successfully conquer Cambodia.[130]

In addition, it should have been apparent that Cambodia's ties to China would not deter Vietnam from invading. The fact that the Vietnamese army was inside Cambodia and had systematically demolished the Cambodian army without China attempting to intervene raised serious questions about China's willingness to intercede in the event of full invasion. Although the Khmer Rouge should have expected some minor support from China if Vietnam invaded, it also knew that Chinese assistance would be limited. Relations between China and Cambodia had been strained since Mao's death in 1976—the new government no longer supported the Khmer Rouge's domestic policies.[131] Cambodia could not rely on a Chinese attack to help Cambodia—while they would aid and supply the Khmer Rouge, military intervention was no longer guaranteed. In fact, when China did attack Vietnam to save face, the attack was limited to just teaching Vietnam a lesson and was repelled by Vietnam without even having to use regular army troops.[132]

Thus, even if the Khmer Rouge initially attacked Vietnam because of deterrence failure, by 1977 there was no longer any doubt about Vietnam's ability or will to use force. At almost any point in time before the invasion in December of 1978, the Khmer

---

[129] If the Khmer Rouge thought that Vietnam was its enemy and that Vietnam wanted the Khmer Rouge removed from power, why would the Khmer Rouge think that Vietnam would not try to remove the Khmer Rouge in retaliation for attacks on its border? The leaders of the Khmer Rouge did not need to be threatened with loss of power; they already assumed that Vietnam wanted to take over Cambodia.

[130] The notion that Cambodia would win because it must and because of the strength of will of the Khmer Rouge. *Id.* at 108.

[131] *Id.*

[132] *Id.* at 221. In fact, the invasion was more of an attempt to save face than a credible attempt to force Vietnam to withdraw from Cambodia. *Id.*

Rouge could have prevented the invasion by simply accepting Vietnam's invitation to negotiate and ending its attacks on Vietnam. However, the Khmer Rouge refused to back down even as China's support decreased and Vietnam's retaliation increased. The Khmer Rouge leaders had become so fanatical in their beliefs by 1978 that they were beyond the point of deterrence—or at least beyond the point were Vietnam could deter them. The Khmer Rouge simply refused to believe that Vietnam could defeat Cambodia's army—that Cambodia's strength of will could be defeated. Ultimately, the Khmer Rouge refused to believe that Cambodia could lose when it had to win.

This proves one of the tenets of deterrence failure—the more fanatical a regime is, the harder it is to deter. Fanatical leaders filter information differently, putting a slant on all information that favors their ideology. However, almost any other leader (ideological or otherwise) in the position of Pol Pot would have been deterred from aggression after 1977. Essentially, the Khmer Rouge represents the extreme position of an already extreme group of fanatical leaders. The Khmer Rouge leaders were so bound by their beliefs that it was not just difficult to deter them, it was essentially impossible. Before finally invading, Vietnam fully demonstrated that it could and, if forced to, would remove the Khmer Rouge from power. However, it is impossible to deter leaders who believe that one of their soldiers is worth thirty of their enemies. Because the fanaticism of the Khmer Rouge had reached the point of irrationality, Cambodia could not be made to back down.

Conclusion

The Khmer Rouge leaders made more than a mistake in continuing to antagonize Vietnam—they acted irrationally. Although Cambodia's initial attacks on Vietnam can be written off as a non-democracy attacking when deterrence failed, by early 1978 Vietnam had done everything it could to deter Cambodia except for actually removing the Khmer Rouge from power. Perhaps if Vietnam had responded more authoritatively to

Cambodian aggression in the beginning, Cambodia would have learned its lesson early enough to be deterred. However, by the time Vietnam decided to retaliate, the Khmer Rouge leaders had already reached the conclusion that they could not lose, and therefore they could not be deterred.

THE THIRD INDOCHINA WAR: WHY DID VIETNAM CONQUER CAMBODIA INSTEAD OF JUST REPELLING THE ATTACKS?

The Vietnamese invasion of Cambodia was a complete success in military terms. Initially, the Cambodian army attempted to repel the Vietnamese invasion in a conventional battle, but the Cambodian army was quickly routed and scattered.[133] Within seventeen days the Vietnamese army had destroyed the army of the Khmer Rouge and captured Phnom Penh, which enabled it to install a new government in Cambodia.[134] The leaders of the Khmer Rouge and what was left of their army had to retreat northward and hide near the border.[135] Vietnam had quickly and effectively achieved its goal of ending the threat that the Khmer Rouge posed to its border.

However, the invasion was a failure in almost every measurement besides militarily. The international community never recognized the new government installed by Vietnam.[136] Vietnam was refused aid and trade by almost every country except for Russia during Vietnam's twelve-year occupation of Cambodia.[137] Vietnam's economy floundered under the imposition of international political pressure and economic isolation. Vietnam even suffered a three-week military attack from China in February

---

[133] MORRIS, *supra* note 1, at 220.

[134] KLINTWORTH, *supra* note 14, at 7.

[135] MORRIS, *supra* note 1, at 220. The Khmer Rouge began a guerrilla resistance that never succeeded in regaining power. After Vietnam finally withdrew from Cambodia, the Khmer Rouge dissolved as its atrocities became more public and its support dwindled following UN intervention. *Id.*

[136] *Id.* at 222.

[137] *Id.*

1979 as a result of the invasion.[138] Finally, after Vietnam was forced to withdraw from Cambodia and Cambodia was placed under UN supervision, it was Prince Norodom Sihanouk, the leader of Cambodia who was overthrown in 1970, who returned to power.[139] Given all that Vietnam has suffered as a result of its invasion of Cambodia, it is difficult to determine why Vietnam invaded Cambodia instead of just continuing to repel its attacks.

If Hanoi had chosen to, it could have continued to repel the raids of the Khmer Rouge while occasionally attacking and destroying large segments of the Khmer Rouge's military. However, in spite of the detrimental outcome, the decision to attack made sense at the time. Through an invasion of its weaker neighbor, Vietnam could put a permanent end to Cambodian attacks on Vietnam and develop the Vietnamese dream of a Vietnam-led Indochina federation. Vietnam had to weigh the potential benefits of an invasion against the risk of a two-front war and sanctions by the international community. Nevertheless, even if the decision to invade Cambodia was risky, it was at least rational.

Vietnamese Relations with Cambodia

Having looked at the events of 1975 leading up to the invasion in 1978 from the point of view of the Khmer Rouge, they now must be considered from the point of view of Vietnam. As has been noted, Vietnam did not have any plans to invade Cambodia prior to 1978.[140] However, this does not change the fact that

---

[138] *Id.* at 221.

[139] *Cambodia: Odyssey of the Khmer People*, http://www.mekong.net/cambodia. Cambodia is now a constitutional monarchy. Norodom Sihanouk returned to power as king of Cambodia. A democratically elected prime minister, Norodom Ranariddh, was overthrown in a coup staged by Hun Sen in July 1997. Hun Sen was subsequently elected prime minister in elections in July 1998. There are still elements of the old Vietnamese-sponsored regime in the new government. *Id.*

[140] The section "Vietnam Did Not Present a Danger to Cambodia" addressed this issue already.

Vietnam still wanted Cambodia under its control.[141] From Vietnam's point of view, such a result was demanded not only by Vietnam's historical dominance of Cambodia, but also by Vietnam's role in the Comintern helping to create a Communist Indochina.[142] Historically, Vietnam viewed Cambodia as subservient and had actually ruled Cambodia as a protectorate for a period of time.[143] Then, when Ho Chi Minh initiated a Communist insurgency against the French, he was charged with the duty of formulating and leading a Communist insurgency in Cambodia and Laos as well.[144] It was the goal of the Comintern that Vietnam should lead Indochina in a federalist Communist system, whereby a stronger nation helps the weaker nations in building Communist regimes. Before Ho Chi Minh, there were not any Communists in Cambodia fighting the French; it was the Viet Minh who brought Communism to Cambodia. In fact, for most of the insurgency, the Viet Minh had far more troops in Cambodia than the Khmer Rouge did.[145] Thus, from Vietnam's point of view, it was entitled to a position of leadership and influence in Cambodia.

However, despite Vietnam's belief that it was entitled to lead Cambodia after the joint resolution of the conflicts in Vietnam and Cambodia, at the request of China, Vietnam withdrew its remaining forces from Cambodia. Vietnam had grudgingly accepted the idea that it would be China that would guide Cambodia.[146] Yet, almost immediately after its withdrawal, Vietnam was still attacked by Cambodian forces.[147] Vietnam already thought Cambodia should be run under its direction and guidance, and now the Khmer Rouge's military aggression did little to change that impression. From Vietnam's perspective, the Khmer Rouge was providing Vietnam with an excuse to take what

---

[141] MORRIS, *supra* note 1, at 96.

[142] "A History of Vietnamese and Cambodian Interaction" addressed this issue already.

[143] MORRIS, *supra* note 1, at 25.

[144] *Id.* at 27.

[145] DEAC, *supra* note 33, at 112.

[146] "Vietnam Did Not Present a Danger to Cambodia" discussed this issue.

[147] KLINTWORTH, *supra* note 14, at 22.

Vietnam had thought all along it had a right to—the control of the Indochina area.

Additionally, not only did Vietnam have the means to invade, but an invasion was the only remaining solution for Vietnam that provided protection to its citizens and its territory. It has been established that Vietnam was a much greater power militarily, in terms of sheer number and quality, than Cambodia.[148] The fact that the Khmer Rouge continued to attack Vietnam in spite of Vietnam's strength and in spite of the natural alliance the two Communist countries should have shared indicated that peace with Cambodia would not be easily achieved. [149] Because Cambodia pressed its attack in the face of these facts and in spite of Vietnam's overtures of friendship, Vietnam believed that Cambodia would never stop attacking while the Khmer Rouge was in power. As has been demonstrated, Cambodia refused to stop attacking Vietnam even after the island of Palo Wai was taken, after Vietnam had crushed the Cambodian army in the October and December invasions of 1977, and even after Vietnam began an insurgency against the Khmer Rouge in 1978. Neither the promise of negotiations nor the threat of imminent destruction could persuade the Khmer Rouge to stop its attacks.

In other words, Vietnam was given little reason to believe that the tactic of merely defending its territory and responding to Cambodian aggression in kind would ever convince the Khmer Rouge to stop its attacks. Further, since the Khmer Rouge publicly claimed that the Vietnamese withdrawal from Cambodia (after it had annihilated the Khmer Rouge's army) was a victory for Cambodia that cost Vietnam thirty soldiers for every one Cambodian killed, Vietnam had little reason to believe that Cambodia would voluntarily end its aggression.[150]

---

[148] *Library of Congress, supra* note 2.

[149] It should be noted that although both the countries were Communist and therefore allies against the West, the Khmer Rouge considered the Vietnamese to be "revisionist" Communists, whom they considered to be inferior to Communists who followed the doctrine of Mao as the Khmer Rouge did.

[150] *Library of Congress, supra* note 2.

Cambodia's diplomatic relations with Vietnam also indicated that Cambodia would not stop its attacks. Vietnam had repeatedly asked the Khmer Rouge to meet with Vietnam to negotiate over the border raids, which the Khmer Rouge refused to do.[151] Cambodia wanted all of the land given away by France returned, and because Vietnam refused to just give the territory away, Cambodia felt that there was nothing to negotiate. Vietnam tried many times to bring Cambodia to the negotiating table to end the attacks by the Cambodian army, but the avenue of negotiation had been closed by Cambodia.[152] So long as Vietnam controlled the Mekong Delta region, Vietnam knew that the raids would continue.

Additionally, Vietnam could not appeal to a higher power to resolve the situation. Vietnam made a motion in the United Nations to have UN personnel stationed on the Vietnam-Cambodian border to investigate the attacks with the hope that the United Nations would intercede on its behalf.[153] However, such a motion would have to be passed in the Security Council, where China, Cambodia's ally, had a permanent seat and a veto. The motion did not pass. When the Vietnamese delegation personally appealed to the secretary-general, he replied that the United Nations was powerless to help because of China.[154]

Neither could Vietnam appeal to the Soviet Union, its only ally, for help. During Cambodia's revolution, the Soviet Union had refused to support the Khmer Rouge and had little influence over them.[155] Further, Cambodia was allied to China, which was an enemy of the Soviet Union. The Soviet Union had no leverage in Southeast Asia, which left Vietnam to resolve the situation essentially on its own.

---

[151] KLINTWORTH, *supra* note 14, at 21.

[152] *Id.* Although Vietnam alleges that it made many offers to negotiate its differences with Cambodia in private, there were at least two open proposals for negotiation, in April 1977 and February 1978, that were rejected by Cambodia. *Id.*

[153] BURCHETT, *supra* note 94, at 160.

[154] *Id.*

[155] MORRIS, *supra* note 1, at 198.

Not only did Vietnam realize that the attacks on its border would continue as long as the Khmer Rouge were in power, but it was also becoming clear that Vietnam could not afford to allow the attacks to continue. While it is true that the attacks did little to damage Vietnam militarily, they were taking a toll on Vietnam socially and economically. Although the people in Vietnam were far better off than those living under the Khmer Rouge, they were still very poor and underfed—a situation made worse by Cambodian aggression.[156] The towns and farming villages along the border were emptying as a result of the fighting, which meant Ho Chi Minh City (Saigon) and other southern cities had to take these refugees.[157] Added to the Vietnamese fleeing the fighting were the Cambodian refugees, those fleeing the fighting along the border and those fleeing the oppressive rule of the Khmer Rouge, who further taxed Vietnam's already meager resources.[158] The food shortage already facing Vietnam was compounded by the fact that all the agricultural land in southwestern Vietnam was lying fallow because the farmers had fled.[159] Therefore, Vietnam was facing a food shortage, a refugee crisis, millions of unemployed, and overflowing cities in South Vietnam—a region only recently conquered and not completely purged of former members of the South Vietnamese regime. While an actual revolution was doubtful, Vietnam still knew it was unwise to let such conditions fester in a region already socially divided.

On top of the social crisis caused by the raids, Cambodia posed a unique threat to Vietnam because the area on their border known as Parrot Gap was a mere thirty-three miles from Ho Chi Minh City.[160] Although Vietnam had a much larger military than Cambodia, it was conceivable that a concentrated sneak attack by the Khmer Rouge could reach Ho Chi Minh City before the attack could be repelled. Vietnam could not tolerate the loss of face and

---

[156] KLINTWORTH, *supra* note 14, at 23.

[157] *Id.*

[158] *Id.*

[159] *Id.*

[160] *Id.* (This was an area that Cambodia had attacked through once before. Further, Vietnam already knew of the gap's military significance since it used to run supplies through this same area during the war against South Vietnam.)

the amount of destruction that would occur if Cambodia sacked Ho Chi Minh City. Thus Vietnam, for the safety of its border villages and for its internal security, had a vested interest in ending the Cambodian attacks on Vietnam. Because Vietnam was on its own in stopping the attacks, it was left with three choices: give in to Cambodia and return much of the land now comprising the southwestern part of Vietnam, not return the land and face the prospect of continuous military engagements, or somehow remove the Khmer Rouge from power. Since Vietnam would not give part of its territory to Cambodia and it could not allow its border to be a permanent war zone, Vietnam had to remove the Khmer Rouge from power.

Once Vietnam had decided that the Khmer Rouge had to be overthrown for the security of Vietnam, it also quickly reached the conclusion that a full-scale invasion was the only way to accomplish this goal. From January to April 1978, Vietnam tried to overthrow the Khmer Rouge by creating and supporting an insurgency.[161] Vietnam created camps to train and build a liberation army from the Cambodian refugees who had fled the Khmer Rouge. However, soon after the insurgency began, Vietnam realized it was destined to fail. The Khmer Rouge's internal security force was too powerful to prevent any widespread insurgency, and the Khmer Rouge's military was too strong for the insurgents to defeat in battle, even with Vietnamese air support.[162] Thus, if Vietnam was to remove the Khmer Rouge from power, a full-scale invasion would be required.

Vietnam's Relations with China

The main drawback to Vietnam's plan of invading Cambodia was that Cambodia was closely allied to China, a country more powerful than Vietnam. In fact, the reason that Vietnam first attempted to remove the Khmer Rouge through an insurgency rather than a direct invasion was because of this alliance. Vietnam wanted to avoid involving China in the dispute and providing proof

---

[161] MORRIS, *supra* note 1, at 105.
[162] *Id.* at 107.

for the accusations made by China that Vietnam was trying to create an empire.[163] However, once the insurgency failed, Vietnam had reasons for invading in spite of the risk posed by China.

The first reason was Vietnam's alliance with the Soviet Union. Although Vietnam had alienated China by aligning with the Soviet Union during the ongoing quarrel between the Soviet Union and China, it did ally itself with the stronger of the two countries.[164] The Soviet Union was the major supplier of Vietnamese aid, providing Vietnam with military equipment in exchange for captured U.S. munitions.[165] The countries had also signed agreements of friendship and assistance.[166] Thus Vietnam had reason to believe that were China to attack Vietnam as a result of the invasion, it could expect either direct military assistance or an increase in aid from the Soviet Union to help Vietnam defeat their mutual enemy.[167] It should be noted that Vietnam itself diminished the likelihood of receiving support from the Soviet Union by failing to notify the Soviet Union of the invasion before it happened.[168] However, Vietnam still expected assistance because Vietnam had informed the Soviet Union of its plans to invade

---

[163] *Id.*

[164] *Id.* at 173.

[165] The Soviet Union used these munitions to arm Communist insurgencies in third world countries so that it would not appear that it was the Soviet Union that was supplying them or that the insurgencies were necessarily Communist.

[166] MORRIS, *supra* note 1, at 173.

[167] North Vietnam had received assistance from the Soviet Union in its war against South Vietnam and such assistance would likely continue in a war against China since China and the Soviet Union were now enemies. In fact, although it was often ignored by the western press because of their focus on the Cold War between the East and the West, large segments of China's military and the Soviet Union's military was focused on defending against an attack by a Communist country instead of a democracy.

[168] MORRIS, *supra* note 1, at 215-16. It is impossible to prove that the Soviet Union did not know of the date of the attack (you cannot prove a negative); however there is credible evidence to support the conclusion that although the Soviet Union knew Vietnam was planning an attack, it did not know of the attack before it happened. However, this is not surprising given that Cambodia did not keep China informed and that North Vietnam did not keep the Soviet Union informed of its planned offenses against South Vietnam. *Id.*

Cambodia generally, and the Soviet Union never said it would not get involved if China attacked.[169]

However, with or without the support of the Soviet Union, Vietnam may have felt that a war with China was imminent anyway, so Cambodia's alliance with China was less of a deterrent. Vietnam had always thought that China was behind Cambodia's attacks on Vietnam.[170] Although evidence now indicates that China was not behind the attacks (in fact Cambodia never notified China it was going to attack Vietnam),[171] Vietnam had reason to think that China was behind the attacks.[172] Aside from the fact that Vietnam already felt betrayed by China after China normalized relations with the United States,[173] the old enemy of Vietnam, China had taken further actions that made Vietnam mistrust it. When Vietnam tried to resolve the conflict with Cambodia by seeking the help of the United Nations, China vetoed the action, effectively allowing the attacks to continue.[174] When Vietnam responded to the Cambodian attacks with a limited offensive that was withdrawn, China used that offensive to undermine Vietnam's standing with the Asian community.[175] China was also the major supplier of aid and arms to Cambodia, so it was in effect providing Cambodia with the resources to wage war.[176] Finally, because the Khmer Rouge leaders were Maoists who were tutored and led by the doctrine of Maoist China, the Vietnamese believed that the Khmer acted only with the authority of China.[177] Although

---

[169] *Id.* at 108 (the Soviet Union never revealed in its meetings with Vietnam that it had no intention of going to war with China over Cambodia's dispute with Vietnam).

[170] PAMPHLET, WHO HAS DESTROYED THE VIETNAMESE-CHINESE FRIENDSHIP 16 (1983); ROBERT S. ROSS, THE INDOCHINA TANGLE (1988).

[171] *Id.* at 231.

[172] KLINTWORTH, *supra* note 14, at 24.

[173] The normalizing of relations with the United States is one of the reasons that Vietnam allied itself to the Soviet Union instead of remaining neutral, in spite of the fact that China was at the time a major donor of aid to Vietnam.

[174] BURCHETT, *supra* note 94, at 160.

[175] MORRIS, *supra* note 1, at 107.

[176] KLINTWORTH, *supra* note 14, at 24.

[177] The reality is that the Khmer Rouge stopped following China in 1976 when Mao died. After the death of Mao, China no longer supported the Khmer

evidence indicates that by the time of the invasion the Khmer Rouge was no longer in effect led by China, Vietnam believed that Cambodian policy was formulated by China.

Thus, Vietnam saw itself facing a strong, hostile nation on one side of the country and a weaker hostile nation on the other side. To make matters worse, the weaker nation was attacking Vietnam at the apparent behest of the stronger nation. Vietnam did not have the military to invade China, but it knew it could easily and rapidly defeat Cambodia in its current situation. What Vietnam could not allow was to wait until China had "consolidated itself in Kampuchea."[178] If China was allowed to consolidate in Cambodia, it would take away Vietnam's military advantage over the aggressors and increase the probability that a Cambodian attack would reach Ho Chi Minh City. Further, given Vietnam's view that Cambodia was a "dagger thrust at the heart of Vietnam" wielded by China, Vietnam believed that if it did not attack and conquer Cambodia first, China eventually would invade Vietnam from the north and the west, leaving Vietnam in a two-front war.[179] Whatever China's true intention, Vietnam could not feel secure while surrounded by enemies.

The only solution to Vietnam's predicament was a blitzkrieg-like invasion of Cambodia that quickly ended both the threat of a Cambodian attack and the possibility of a two-front war. If Vietnam successfully invaded and conquered Cambodia before China could respond in force (which it did, capturing Phnom Penh in seventeen days), it could remove the threat from one border and turn its attention to the enemy at the other border.[180] Of course, Vietnam already knew that it could easily defeat the Khmer Rouge

---

Rouge's domestic policies and China's new government was offensive to the hyper-Maoist Khmer Rouge.

[178] MORRIS, *supra* note 1, at 109 (citing Report of a conversation with General Secretary of the CPV Central Committee Le Duan, Sept. 25, 1978).

[179] KLINTWORTH, *supra* note 14, at 24.

[180] MORRIS, *supra* note 1, at 221 (It was not until three months after the invasion that China was finally able to take military action against Vietnam. However, the attack was only designed to "teach Vietnam a lesson" and China was forced to withdraw after three weeks of fighting.).

army, as it had demonstrated in 1977.[181] The worst it would face long-term in Cambodia was guerrilla warfare from those forces that fled before they could be killed. Given that China would now be facing Vietnam (possibly aided by the Soviet Union) without the assistance of Cambodia, there was a good chance that China would do little, if anything, in retaliation. China's incentive to attack would be further reduced given that there would no longer be a Khmer Rouge regime in power for its attack to preserve.[182] Even if China were to force Vietnam to withdraw, there is no guarantee that it would be the Khmer Rouge that would reclaim power.[183]

An additional reason for Vietnam to act was China's own military weakness. Although China had a large army, it was no longer in peak condition and training, whereas Vietnam's was still sharp from its conquest of South Vietnam and its conflict with Cambodia. Although large enough to be feared, there was reason to doubt China's ability to effectively invade another country.[184] In fact, Vietnam had been testing China's military ability through skirmishes on the border with China over disputed territory. By the time Vietnam decided to invade Cambodia, China's military had a reduced deterrent value because it "had not managed to do anything so far in the north."[185] Further, China would be hindered in retaliating against an invasion of Cambodia based on geography.[186] Sending troops to Cambodia would require naval transport through an area controlled by Vietnam, thus putting the troops at risk before they even landed and making supply difficult.

---

[181] KLINTWORTH, *supra* note 14, at 21.

[182] MORRIS, *supra* note 1, at 221 (The Chinese invasion was more of an attempt to save face than an actual invasion to reinstate the Khmer Rouge. Although it aided the Khmer Rouge with supplies for its guerrilla warfare, China never tried to liberate Cambodia by sending troops into Cambodia.).

[183] Prince Sihanouk still claimed that he was the rightful leader of Cambodia and could attempt to seize power. In addition, the Khmer Rouge regime was so oppressive that although it was once popular, its support had dwindled and the people would be more likely to support the prince.

[184] MORRIS, *supra* note 1, at 108-09.

[185] *Id.* (citing Report of a conversation with General Secretary of the CPV Central Committee Le Duan, Sept. 25, 1978).

[186] *Id.*

Meanwhile, a direct invasion of Vietnam on its northern border would prove complex, because the land is unsuitable for military assault. In fact, when China did finally invade, Vietnam was able to repel the Chinese attack after three weeks, without using its main military force.

Essentially, Vietnam was put in a situation where it felt it had no choice but to face China. Vietnam knew that it could not allow Cambodia to continue attacking its border, but it also knew that the attacks would not stop until Vietnam removed the Khmer Rouge from power. Since the only way Vietnam could remove the Khmer Rouge was through an invasion, Vietnam was going to have to risk an attack by China. Yet it had good reason to believe that China would do little or nothing about the invasion. Vietnam was allied to a country stronger than China, the Soviet Union. Vietnam had demonstrated in the Sino-Vietnam border disputes that the Chinese army, while large, was not that effective. Vietnam also had reason to believe that a quick conquest of Cambodia could essentially neutralize China's reason and desire to invade. The only sure repercussion of an invasion was that Vietnam would lose what little aid China was still giving Vietnam. However, this was not much of a deterrent since China had already begun to cut off aid to Vietnam before the invasion even began, and Vietnam got most of its aid and supplies from the Soviet Union anyway.[187] Since Vietnam felt it would face almost no opposition from Cambodia and little repercussion from China, the decision to invade was rational.

Vietnam's Relations with the World

Vietnam knew that an invasion of Cambodia would be controversial in the international community because Vietnam would be using force as a modality of change. Thus, Vietnam had to weigh the possible international repercussions caused by an invasion with the benefits it would derive. However, there were several factors that Vietnam relied on to discount the possible international fallout that an invasion of Cambodia would incur.

---

[187] Morris, *supra* note 1, at 185.

Initially, Vietnam was already something of a rogue state. Having alienated both the French and the United States during its Communist insurgency and then the conquest of South Vietnam, respectively, Vietnam had already put itself on unfriendly terms with two of the major democratic powers in the West. Further, Vietnam had effectively precluded normalization of relations with the United States by demanding war reparations.[188] Until Ho Chi Minh stopped demanding that any U.S. aid be officially called reparation, Vietnam would not be benefiting from major trade or aid from the West. In the East, Vietnam had already cut itself off from one of the major Communist powers (China) by aligning with the Soviet Union.[189] Since Vietnam was getting essentially all of its aid from the Soviet Union already, and since Vietnam knew that the Soviet Union would not cut off relations with Vietnam, the reaction of the international community was less of a deterrent. Thus, from the Vietnamese standpoint, although an attack on Cambodia could make Vietnam slightly more of a pariah internationally than it already was, its situation could not be made much worse.

Secondly, the world had failed to deter Vietnam because it had given indications that it no longer cared about the region. The United States was preempted from intervening in the area because of legislation passed by the U.S. Congress.[190] Further, the United States followed its withdrawal from Southeast Asia by normalizing relations with China. While the United States might still oppose Communism, an attack on the Khmer Rouge would not be a war of Communist expansion. The United Nations had also demonstrated a lack of interest in the affairs of Cambodia by failing to intervene in the dispute when its involvement was requested by Vietnam.[191] There was not great reason for Vietnam to either fear or worry about what the United Nations or the international community

---

[188] *Id.* at 222.

[189] *Id.* at 160.

[190] MORRIS, *supra* note 1, at 53.

[191] BURCHETT, *supra* note 94, at 160.

might do if Vietnam invaded Cambodia given their complete lack of interest prior to December 25, 1978.[192]

Thirdly, Vietnam had reason to hope that it could effectively preempt any international backlash. Although there is a general prohibition on the use of force as a modality of change, the use of force is allowed as a defense to attacks and to prevent human rights atrocities.[193] In the present case, Vietnam could claim both as justifications for the invasion of Cambodia. Vietnam had been attacked by a foreign power for three years and would continue being attacked until the Khmer Rouge was removed from power.[194] Vietnam could realistically claim that its invasion was an appropriate use of force as the only means of stopping the Khmer Rouge attacks that had been butchering Vietnamese civilians and damaging its military.[195] Although it was likely that some in the international community would still criticize the Vietnamese invasion, Vietnam expected that their criticism would be lessened by the fact that the invasion was a reaction to attacks by Cambodia—especially since Vietnam had asked for the United Nations to intervene before it invaded and had not received help.

The human rights atrocities being perpetrated by the Khmer Rouge against its own people also could be used to justify the use of force.[196] A year before the invasion, Vietnam had begun to draw a distinction between Cambodia and the Khmer Rouge and began to criticize the Khmer Rouge for its gross human rights violations.[197] Vietnam was attempting a public relations war to lend credibility to the attack. The extent to which Vietnam actually cared about the oppression of the Cambodians is unknown, especially given Vietnam's own history of eliminating dissidents and purging the educated and wealthy. However, Vietnam could

---

[192] In fact, the United Nations never formally condemned the Vietnamese invasion. Instead, countries individually decided to cut off aid. The worst the United Nations did was pass a resolution calling for the removal of military forces from Cambodia—without mentioning any names.

[193] KLINTWORTH, *supra* note 14, at 14, 51.

[194] *Id.* at 19.

[195] *Id.* at 20.

[196] *Id.* at 53.

[197] MORRIS, *supra* note 1, at 105 (citing Hanoi Radio VNA, June 20, 1978).

still try to justify the invasion as an attempt to end the oppression of the Cambodian people.

Although Vietnam may have been gambling that any negative reaction by the international community would be short-lived, the leaders of Vietnam were confident that Cambodia would be forgotten.[198] After all, the Khmer Rouge was as unpopular as Vietnam. While Vietnam may have alienated the United States when it defeated South Vietnam, the Khmer Rouge also overthrew a U.S.-backed government by defeating Lon Nol's forces. By claiming both self-defense and a desire to end human rights violations, Vietnam had reason to believe that there would not be any long-term condemnation of its invasion.

In fact, this plan might have worked had Vietnam not remained in Cambodia for twelve years, only withdrawing after the Soviet Union collapsed leaving Vietnam unable to afford the cost of remaining in Cambodia.[199] Rather than withdrawing from Cambodia after defeating the Khmer Rouge and setting up a new government (the People's Republic of Kampuchea (PRK)), Vietnam remained in the country and controlled the new regime.[200] Although a slightly prolonged occupation could have been explained as an attempt to firm up the government so that it could face the insurgency by the remnants of the Khmer Rouge, the argument loses credibility when military and political control were maintained for over ten years. If at any time Vietnam had simply withdrawn its troops and aided the new government from the sidelines, the international community's outrage would have died down.[201] In fact, once Vietnam finally withdrew from Cambodia, it was able to develop relations with the United States and the rest of the Western world.

---

[198] Kishore Mahbubani, *The Kampuchean Problem: A Southeast Asian Perception*, 62 FOREIGN AFF. 407 (Winter 1983-84).

[199] MORRIS, *supra* note 1, at 219.

[200] *Id.* at 224.

[201] *Id.* at 223 (The international community would have also settled for a solution where non-Communist Cambodians had a role in government to the exclusion of the Khmer Rouge. Thus Vietnam could have had the sanctions against it lifted and still kept the Khmer Rouge out of power if it had accepted a political solution.).

Vietnam's Invasion Analyzed Through the Theories of a Democratic Peace and Deterrence Failure

The Vietnamese invasion of Cambodia makes perfect sense given what we know from the democratic peace. Vietnam was a Communist country that was not responsible to its citizens, an example of government failure theory.[202] Government failure was also demonstrated by the failure of the sanctions to make Vietnam withdraw from Cambodia. When the international community cut off food aid, it was not the elites who were affected, but the poor and starving masses of Vietnam.[203] Of course, since the leaders of Vietnam were not responsible to the Vietnamese population, Vietnam continued its occupation of Cambodia while the Vietnamese people suffered under crippling international sanctions. Additionally, the lack of transparency between Vietnam, Cambodia, and China prevented Vietnam from trusting China and therefore possibly using it to mediate the dispute.[204]

As for deterrence, given that Cambodia practically invited Vietnam to invade, there was little. On top of the basic difference in numbers between the two armies, Vietnam had also demonstrated over the past three years how easily it could defeat Cambodia in battle.[205] Vietnam knew that it could quickly win a war against Cambodia—one of the keys to deterrence failure.[206] Although Cambodia's alliance with China had some deterrence value, the Soviet Union played a dual role in decreasing its value. First of all, its alliance to Vietnam helped offset the risk that China would enter the war. Secondly, the fact that the Soviet Union

---

[202] Levy, *supra* note 4.

[203] MORRIS, *supra* note 1, at 222.

[204] Levy, *supra* note 4 (China had offered to mediate the dispute between Vietnam and Cambodia, but both nations refused. Vietnam assumed that China was its enemy and therefore could not be trusted, and Cambodia kept China so far out of the loop that it did not notify its ally when it attacked Vietnam in the first place.).

[205] KLINTWORTH, *supra* note 14, at 19-21.

[206] In most instances of aggression, the aggressor nation believes that it will win a war within two weeks, a feat that Vietnam actually managed to do.

shared a border with China and the two countries were enemies meant that China would be limited in how many troops it could withdraw from the Sino-Soviet border to use in an attack on Vietnam. China also diminished its deterrence value when it could not decisively win its border disputes with Vietnam.[207] Vietnam did not believe there was a single credible military threat standing between it and the complete control of Cambodia, which is the very definition of deterrence failure.

Although Vietnam ended up suffering as a result of international pressure and isolation, there was little in the way of systemic deterrence. Vietnam had a legitimate reason to believe its invasion and occupation of Cambodia could be justified under the UN Charter. Because the United Nations recognizes the right of self-defense, and the line on when defense becomes aggression is unclear, it was not irrational for Vietnam to believe that the international community would not condemn Vietnam's invasion, if they paid any attention to it at all. After all, the United Nations' refusal to mediate Vietnam's border dispute indicated that the international community had lost its interest in that region of the world and certainly would have no cause to object to the removal of an aggressive and genocidal regime. Although Vietnam was proven wrong in this belief, the mistake was certainly aided by the failure of the international community to take any actions that would deter such a belief prior to Vietnam's invasion.

Conclusion

The third Indochina War generally supports the synergy between the democratic peace and deterrence in war avoidance. Cambodia's attack on Vietnam and Vietnam's response provides another example of the rule that, empirically, non-democracies cause wars because of government failure. Vietnam's invasion and occupation of Cambodia demonstrates that the deterrence failure is half of the explanation of when a country will go to war. Although Cambodia's attacks on Vietnam are harder to explain in terms of deterrence, the attacks serve to illustrate the very important point

---

[207] MORRIS, *supra* note 1, at 109.

that it is harder to deter the fanatical leaders who are more likely to rise to power in non-democratic nations. Although it was deterrence failure that initially caused Cambodia to attack, it was Cambodia's hyper-Maoist beliefs that made the attacks continue long after deterrence theory indicates they should have stopped. The lesson to be learned is that although deterrence is essential to preventing aggressor nations from attacking, it is simply harder to deter fanatical regimes. Unfortunately, in certain rare cases, it may even prove impossible to deter fanatical regimes, in which case a threatened nation will have to actually defeat the aggressor regime. The fact that some leaders may be harder to deter does not necessitate a change in foreign policy. Rather, it requires the full enforcement of deterrence theory: the ability and will to both adequately defend against aggressor nations and remove those leaders who cannot be deterred.

One objection that might be raised to incentive theory broadly is that it assumes rational actors. That is, if actors are not rational, then a focus on incentives in an effort to alter their behavior would be unavailing. At least four points might be raised in response to what, at first blush, seems a significant objection. First, an examination of historical case studies overwhelmingly suggests that even decisions to commit aggression and other insults to the international community are made by rational actors. Such decisions certainly are ruthless, indeed sometimes barbaric in their inhumanity, and they are frequently mistaken about ultimate consequences. History suggests, however, that the seriously mentally ill are unlikely to assume power, and if they do, they are unlikely to remain in power. Further, in many settings, the decisions of a network of others, relating to financing, political support, etc., may be necessary for maximum effectiveness, and this requirement reduces the likelihood of control by the mentally ill.

Second, as with the evidence of the "democratic peace" itself, or issues of whether non-democracies are principally the aggressors in major interstate conflict, it is a mistake to assume that the concept should be discarded unless it is 100 percent applicable with no counter examples. It may be that some small percentage of actions by national or other powerful leaders are actions of the mentally deranged. This does not, however, take away the utility of the focus on incentives to influence decisions of rational actors, which is the overwhelming reality for most regime members, and other powerful elites, whose control of assets pose the greatest threat. In fact, to develop a counter theory for action based on this non-rational actor objection would be to assume that at least the majority of core war/peace decisions are made by irrational actors. There is no evidence whatsoever suggesting that such a premise is correct.

Third, in that small context of non-rational national leaders, there is no reason to believe that *any* approach would be more effective. *All* present approaches to war avoidance rely on an ability to influence rational actors and, thus, incentive theory, calling for the broadest focus on national and international level incentives certainly should be no less effective than other approaches. Finally, in any setting where the decision for war or democide cannot be influenced for the better before the act, one is inevitably engaged in what might broadly be referred to as "warfighting," meaning a full panoply of diplomatic, economic, military, and other actions to inhibit the major aggression, terrorism, or democide. Such "warfighting" actions, aimed at reducing and controlling capabilities and opportunity for the impermissible action, will frequently resemble the same kinds of measures one would take under incentive theory. In short, this seemingly plausible objection to incentive theory, on closer examination, does not seem persuasive.

BIBLIOGRAPHY

Becker, Elizabeth. *When the War Was Over.* New York: Simon and Schuster, 1986.

Burchett, Wilfred. *The China-Cambodia-Vietnam Triangle.* Vanguard Books, 1981.

Cambodia: Odyssey of the Khmer People, at http://www.mekong.net/cambodia.

Chanda, Nayan. *Brother Enemy: The War After the War.* San Diego: Harcourt Brace Jovanovich, 1986.

Chandler, David P., et al. *Pol Pot Plans the Future: Confidential Leadership Documents from Democratic Kampuchea.* Yale Center for International and Area Studies, 1988.

"The Communist International and the Indochinese Revolution." *Vietnam Courier* (number 2, 1984).

Deac, Wilfred P. *Road to the Killing Fields: The Cambodian War of 1970-1975.* Texas A&M University Press, 1997.

Downs, George W. "The Rational Deterrence Debate." 41 *World Politics* 225-237 (January 1989).

Gledtisch, Nils P. "Geography, Democracy, and Peace." 297 *International Interactions* 20.

Gordon, Bernard K. "The Third Indochina Conflict." *Foreign Affairs* (Fall 1986).

Huth, Paul, and Bruce Russet. "What Makes Deterrence Work? Cases from 1990 to 1980." 36 *World Politics* 496 (July 1984).

Interrogation Report, ARVN no 1635/TTTVHH/BT, August 22, 1972.

Kagan, Donald. *On the Origins of War and the Preservation of Peace.* New York: Anchor Books, 1996.

Klintworth, Gary. *Vietnam's Intervention in Cambodia in International Law.* Australian Government Publishing Service, 1989.

Leifer, Michael. *Cambodia, the Search for Security.* Pall Mall Press, 1967.

Levy, Jack S. "The Study of War and Peace." In *Handbook of International Relations*, edited by Walter Carlsnaes and

Thomas Risse, London: Sage Publications, 2002 (March 2001 draft).

Library of Congress: *Cambodia*, at http://memory.loc.gov/frd/cs/khtoc.html (December 1987).

Mahbubani, Kishore. "The Kampuchean Problem: A Southeast Asian Perception." 62 *Foreign Affairs* 407 (Winter 1983-1984).

Moore, John N. Handout on Rationality from the Seminar on War and Peace (2001) (on file with the author).

———. "The Control of Foreign Intervention in International Conflict." 9 *Journal of International Law* 209 (1969).

Morris, Stephen J. *Why Vietnam Invaded Cambodia: Political Culture and the Causes of War*. Stanford University Press, 1999.

Quinn, Kenneth M. "Political Change in Wartime: The Khmer Krahom Revolution in Southern Cambodia." 28 *Naval War College Review* 3 (number 4, 1976).

Ray, James L. *Democracy and International Conflict*. University of South Carolina Press, 1995.

Report of a Conversation with General Secretary of the CPV Central Committee Le Duan, September 25, 1978.

Ross, Robert S. *The Indochina Tangle*. New York: Columbia Press, 1988.

Russet, Bruce. "The Democratic Peace: And Yet It Moves" (draft from the author that appears in 19 International Security 1995) (on file with the University of Virginia School of Law Library).

Russett, Bruce, and Harvey Starr. "From the Democratic Peace to Kantian Peace: Democracy and Conflict in the International System." In *Handbook of War Studies II* 93, edited by Manus Midlarsky, University of Michigan Press, 2000.

Shawcross, William. *The Quality of Mercy*. London: Andre Deutsch, 1984.

Turner, Robert. *Vietnamese Communism, Its Origins and Development*. Hoover Institution Press: Stanford University, 1975.

Woolside, Alexander. "Nationalism and Poverty in the Breakdown of Sino-Vietnamese Relations." 52 *Pacific Affairs* 3 (1979).

Legal

VII

The Long, Slow Struggle: An Analysis of the Legal Advice at the Beginning of the Vietnam War

*Ronald R. Ratton**

When there is a visible enemy to fight in open combat . . . many serve, all applaud and the tide of patriotism runs high. But when there is a long, slow struggle with no immediate, visible foe, your choice will seem hard indeed.[1]

INTRODUCTION

Before employing U.S. military force abroad, decision makers must make a number of fundamental policy determinations. They must, first of all, clearly identify the vital national interests at stake and articulate objectives based on those interests. They must also consider the legal, political, diplomatic, and economic factors inherent in using force. In particular, the National Command Authority[2] should determine whether there is a clear basis, in both domestic and international law, for the proposed action. Failure to do so will undermine both the government's ability to maintain

---

* The views expressed in this article are those of the author and do not necessarily reflect the official policy or position of the Air Force, the Department of Defense, or the U.S. government.
[1] 27 CONTRAILS, THE AIR FORCE CADET HANDBOOK 109 (1981) (quoting President John F. Kennedy's address to the graduating class, U.S. Naval Academy, June 1961).
[2] The National Command Authority is composed of the president and the secretary of defense.

public support in the United States and international acceptance of any action.

At the time of the Vietnam crisis, there was no direct avenue for providing comprehensive legal advice on national security matters to the president.[3] Two obvious candidates to provide such advice were the Office of the Legal Advisor within the Department of State and the Office of the Attorney General.[4] This chapter examines three instances where these offices attempted to frame and analyze the legal issues involved in deploying U.S. armed forces in Vietnam. These memoranda were written at critical points in the history of the Vietnam War. The first memo was written in November 1961 as the United States was about to introduce the first significant numbers of advisory and support troops to the region. The second memo was written in mid-1964 as the administration contemplated shifting from an advisory to a combat role. When the third memo was written a year later, America was fully committed to a long, slow struggle in the defense of South Vietnam.

HISTORICAL BACKGROUND

The foundation of the Vietnam War was laid in the aftermath of World War II. Prior to that conflict, the French had enjoyed colonial rule over Indochina.[5] During the war, however, Japan occupied Vietnam and faced guerrilla opposition, most notably

---

[3] John Norton Moore, *The Legal Tradition and the Management of National Security, in* TOWARD WORLD ORDER AND HUMAN DIGNITY: ESSAYS IN HONOR OF MYRES S. MCDOUGAL 321, 346 (W. Michael Reisman & Burns H. Weston eds., 1976) (stating that "[t]he Indochina war provides a host of examples in which failure systematically to include an international legal perspective in the national security process has imposed an unnecessary cost").

[4] Another candidate is the Department of Defense General Counsel Office. I have seen a reference to one legal memorandum from that office but have not obtained a copy of it. 2 FOREIGN RELATIONS OF THE UNITED STATES 1964-1968: VIETNAM JANUARY-JUNE 1965, at 759 n.9 (Glenn W. LaFantasie et al. eds., 1996) [hereinafter VIETNAM 1965] (June 10, 1965, memo supporting increased force deployments).

[5] Indochina consisted of Laos, Cambodia, Cochin-China, Amman, and Tonkin. The last three form Vietnam.

from Viet Minh forces led by the Communist leader Ho Chi Minh. After the war, Ho Chi Minh assumed power in the north, but French desires to reassert its colonial power soon interfered with Ho's plans to rule all of Vietnam. Consequently, the first Indochina War began in 1946.

The United States was generally ambivalent about Vietnam at this time. On the one hand, the United States wanted to see colonial peoples achieve independence; on the other hand, it was keen to support France as part of its policy to rebuild Western Europe. The aggressive spread of Communism added further impetus for the United States to assist France in some way.[6]

By 1954, the conflict had grown increasingly unpopular in war-weary France. On May 7 of that year, the Viet Minh forces defeated the French at Dien Bien Phu. While not a major military setback, it was a crushing blow to French morale and set the stage for the disengagement of the French and direct involvement of the United States in Indochina.

The Communist victory at Dien Bien Phu came just as the Geneva Conference formally turned its attention from the situation in Korea to Vietnam.[7] During the two and one-half month negotiations, France recognized the government of Vietnam, the precursor to South Vietnam, as a fully independent and sovereign state.[8] The conference ended on July 21. On the day prior, representatives for the commander-in-chief of the French Union Forces in Indochina and the commander-in-chief of the People's Army of Vietnam signed the Agreement on Cessation of Hostilities

---

[6] In April 1950, NSC-68 was written. This document, though never formally adopted, influenced Washington policy makers to implement a policy of containment to block the further expansion of Soviet power. NSC-68 also recommended that any conflict be limited where possible to avoid global war. In this regard, it quotes *The Federalist No. 28*: "The means to be employed must be proportioned to the extent of the mischief." In June 1950, North Korea invaded South Korea, further evidencing Communist expansion plans. In July, President Truman signed legislation to aid France.

[7] The parties began discussing Vietnam on May 8, 1954.

[8] This occurred on June 4, 1954. JOHN NORTON MOORE, LAW AND THE INDO-CHINA WAR 414 (1972).

in Vietnam.[9] On the final day, the participants released an unsigned Final Declaration of the Geneva Conference.[10] These documents, collectively known as the Geneva Accords, ended the first Indochina War.

The agreement to end hostilities established a provisional military demarcation line at the seventeenth parallel, with French Union Forces to the south and the People's Army of Vietnam to the north.[11] Furthermore, arms, munitions, and other war materiel were to be fixed at the level existing in Vietnam in July 1954, with allowance for piece-for-piece replacement.[12] Article 16 prohibited the introduction into Vietnam of any troop reinforcements and article 18 prohibited the establishment of new military bases. Finally, article 19 sought to limit foreign influences by prohibiting the establishment of foreign military bases or military alliances. Also, neither party was to allow the use of its territory for the renewal of aggression.[13]

The key provisions of the unsigned Final Declaration included paragraph six, which states: "[T]he military demarcation line is provisional and should not in any way be interpreted as constituting a political or territorial boundary."[14] Also, paragraph seven called for general elections in July 1956. The two-year delay was designed to "ensure that sufficient progress in the restoration of peace has been made" and provide time for "all the necessary conditions," including the coordination between the two zones and the supervision of an international elections commission, required for "free expression of the national will . . . ."[15]

---

[9] Agreement on the Cessation of Hostilities in Vietnam (July 20, 1954), *in* 16 FOREIGN RELATIONS OF THE UNITED STATES 1952-1954: THE GENEVA CONFERENCE 1505 (John P. Glennon et al. eds., 1981) [hereinafter Armistice].

[10] The Final Declaration on Indochina (July 21, 1954), *in* 16 FOREIGN RELATIONS OF THE UNITED STATES 1952-1954: THE GENEVA CONFERENCE 1540 (John P. Glennon et al. eds., 1981) [hereinafter Final Declaration].

[11] Armistice, *supra* note 9, art. 1.

[12] Armistice, *supra* note 9, art. 17.

[13] Armistice, *supra* note 9, art. 19.

[14] Final Declaration, *supra* note 10, para. 6.

[15] Final Declaration, *supra* note 10, para. 7.

Unfortunately, the Accords were exceptionally vague on almost all key points. They also suffered from South Vietnam's outright rejection of the concept of partition and elections without UN supervision. The United States issued a unilateral declaration stating that it would refrain from any threat or use of force to disturb the agreements and would "view any renewal of the aggression in violation of the aforesaid agreements with grave concern and as seriously threatening international peace and security."[16]

With the withdrawal of the French Expeditionary Corps, South Vietnam was defenseless except for the forces it could train and equip with U.S. assistance. Between 1954 and 1961, the United States sought to fill the vacuum created by the French withdrawal in order to check Communist expansion in South Vietnam. This policy reflected the dominant belief that if Vietnam fell, so too would other Asian states. On February 12, 1955, the United States assumed full responsibility from the French for training Vietnamese forces.[17]

From 1956 to 1959, Ho Chi Minh was concerned mostly with consolidating his power in the north. Although he had left armed cadres in the south in contravention of the Geneva Accords, the level of guerrilla activity was fairly low.[18] This changed dramatically beginning in 1959. After meeting in Hanoi on May 13, 1959, the Central Committee of the North Vietnamese Communist Party publicly announced its intention to smash the Diem government. Subsequently, North Vietnam significantly increased its infiltration, subversion, assassination, and sabotage,

---

[16] 1 PENTAGON PAPERS: THE DEFENSE DEPARTMENT HISTORY OF UNITED STATES DECISIONMAKING ON VIETNAM (THE SENATOR GRAVEL EDITION) 162 (1971) [hereinafter 1 PENTAGON PAPERS].

[17] *Id.* at 182. *See also* WILLIAM W. MOMYER, AIR POWER IN THREE WARS 247 (1978) (discussing the agreement between General Paul Ely, Commanding General of French forces in Indochina, and General J. Lawton Collins, President Eisenhower's special envoy to Saigon).

[18] It was not, however, *de minimis*. For example, more than 1,000 civilians were murdered or kidnapped from 1957 to 1959.

cloaking its aggression as an insurgency.[19] From 1959 to 1961, North Vietnam infiltrated some 10,000 men into the south.[20] By 1960, the death toll was 1,400 local government officials and 2,200 military personnel, with another 700 persons kidnapped.[21] In 1961, the Vietnamese Communist forces averaged 650 violent incidents per month.[22]

By the end of 1961, the situation was becoming critical in South Vietnam. In January of that year, Soviet leader Khrushchev gave a speech indicating support for wars of national liberation. This underscored the urgency of the U.S. policy of containment and shifted the focus of senior administration officials to counterinsurgency and limited war.[23] Indeed, President Kennedy's military advisor, General Maxwell Taylor, had long been a proponent of low scale, non-nuclear, limited war. From October 15 to November 3, 1961, General Taylor visited Vietnam to get a firsthand look at the situation.[24]

The Taylor Report was submitted to President Kennedy on November 3, 1961.[25] Alluding to a Communist declaration of irregular war, the report recommended a sharp increase in aid to the struggling Saigon government. Taylor also recommended the deployment of U.S. troops for logistical support and military training. Thus began the increase from a few hundred advisors to over 16,000 by the time of the Kennedy assassination two years later.

---

[19] 1 FOREIGN RELATIONS OF THE UNITED STATES 1961-1963, VIETNAM 1961, at 93 (John P. Glennon et al. eds., 1988) [hereinafter VIETNAM 1961].

[20] 12 DIGEST OF INTERNATIONAL LAW 114 (Marjorie M. Whiteman ed., 1971) [hereinafter Whiteman]. An additional 13,000 men would be infiltrated in 1962. By the end of 1964, North Vietnam had infiltrated over 40,000 men. *Id.*

[21] *Id.* at 113.

[22] *Id.*

[23] MOMYER, *supra* note 17, at 9. Strangely, U.S. leaders seemed to lose sight of the fact that the Viet Minh forces had defeated the French using conventional forces in a pitched battle. *Id.* at 10. The year 1961 was turbulent by any measure. Other significant events included the Bay of Pigs fiasco, construction of the Berlin Wall, difficulties in Laos, the Congo Civil War, the Algerian Civil War, and the resumption of nuclear testing by the Soviet Union.

[24] *See generally* VIETNAM 1961, *supra* note 19, at 380-476.

[25] *Id.* at 477-532.

Most of these advisors were U.S. Army Special Forces and other soldiers. The United States Air Force pulled World War II propeller aircraft, primarily the T-28 and B-26, out of storage. In April 1961, the "Air Commando" or JUNGLE JIM unit was formed at Eglin Air Force Base, Florida. A detachment of this unit, code-named FARM GATE, deployed to South Vietnam on October 11, 1961. General Momyer, who served on the Air Staff from 1961 to 1964 and as Commander, Seventh Air Force, in Vietnam from 1966 to 1968, writes:

> The mission of this unit from the outset was ambiguous. The aircraft had VNAF markings, and the unit was not authorized to conduct combat missions without a Vietnamese crew-member. Even then, the missions were training missions although combat weapons were delivered. The missions were designed to train Vietnamese pilots to bomb and shoot, and since there were real targets, the situation provided maximum training.[26]

As the war progressed, USAF crews flew combat missions in response to emergency requests with increasing frequency and defense planners sought to find ways to remove restrictions on its operations.[27]

The United States also initiated a defoliation program to combat ambushes along major roadways[28] and supported South Vietnamese efforts to pacify the countryside with its strategic hamlet program[29] and crop destruction.[30] Even though our forces were sent to teach, it was inevitable that they would become "involved in the fighting at their isolated camps deep in territory

---

[26] MOMYER, *supra* note 17, at 253.

[27] *Id.* at 253-54

[28] 2 FOREIGN RELATIONS OF THE UNITED STATES 1961-1963, VIETNAM 1962, at 144 (John P. Glennon et al. eds., 1990) [hereinafter VIETNAM 1962].

[29] *See generally* 2 THE PENTAGON PAPERS: THE DEFENSE DEPARTMENT HISTORY OF UNITED STATES DECISIONMAKING ON VIETNAM (THE SENATOR GRAVEL EDITION) 128-58 (1971) [hereinafter 2 PENTAGON PAPERS].

[30] VIETNAM 1962, *supra* note 28, at 584.

dominated by the Viet Cong."[31] Vietnam was to be a "laboratory for the development of organizations and procedures for the conduct of sub-limited war."[32] Nonetheless, the administration continued to assert that "[w]e have not sent combat troops in the generally understood sense of the word."[33]

ANALYSIS OF 1961 LEGAL ADVICE

The Department of State Legal Advisor

In 1961, the State Department legal advisor was Abram J. Chayes. Chayes was a noted legal scholar, graduating number one in his class at Harvard Law School in 1949.[34] Prior to coming to the State Department, he had clerked for a Supreme Court justice, practiced law in a private firm, and taught at Harvard Law School.[35] His practice and teaching had been primarily in the domestic arena.[36] After working on President Kennedy's election campaign, however, he took the international law position in the State Department.[37]

In a memorandum dated November 16, 1961, Chayes sought to provide guidance to the secretary of state on future U.S.

---

[31] MOMYER, *supra* note 17, at 10.

[32] *Id.* (quoting Secretary of Defense McNamara).

[33] VIETNAM 1962, *supra* note 28, at 144, 225 (quoting President Kennedy in a February 14, 1962, press conference). *See also* H.R. MCMASTER, DERELICTION OF DUTY 37 (1997) (stating that "[a]lthough U.S. advisers were fighting with South Vietnamese units and U.S. pilots were flying combat missions in South Vietnam, Kennedy denied that Americans were involved in combat, and Vietnam attracted little public or congressional attention").

[34] *Living History Interview with Abram Chayes*, 7 TRANSNAT'L L. & CONTEMP. PROBS. 459, 481 (1997) [hereinafter *Living History*]. Today, Chayes is seen as the founder of the International Legal Process School, which competes with the Policy Science or New Haven School of International Law pioneered by Myres McDougal and Harold Laswell. Harold Hongju Koh, *Why do Nations Obey International Law?* 106 YALE L.J. 2599, 2618 (1997). He is well-known for his representation of Nicaragua against the United States before the International Court of Justice and for opposing the Grenada invasion.

[35] *Id.*

[36] *Id.*

[37] *Id.*

involvement in Vietnam.[38] The memorandum was written in direct response to General Maxwell Taylor's Report on Vietnam.[39] That report recommended immediately sending additional U.S. military personnel and equipment to South Vietnam. The purpose of this augmentation was to provide a U.S. military presence to show "the seriousness of the U.S. intent to resist a Communist takeover."[40] The United States would assist South Vietnam by increasing airlift operations, expanding intelligence operations, implementing naval surveillance activities, and training and equipping South Vietnamese military and civil guard elements.[41] The memorandum went further, however, and also discussed "whether additional United States forces should be introduced even to the extent of a Korea-type operation and whether we may eventually have to attack the source of guerilla aggression in North Viet-Nam . . . ."[42]

Until 1961, the U.S. military presence in Vietnam had remained within the limits of the Geneva Accords.[43] By April of that year, however, the United States was beginning to seriously reconsider its continued support of and adherence to the Geneva Accords since others were openly violating them.[44] The State Department, however, was reluctant to fully disavow the Accords. In a prior memo, Chayes opined that the whole structure of the Indochina partition rested on the Accords.[45] Furthermore, the United States wanted to try to benefit by holding other parties to the terms of the Accords.[46]

---

[38] VIETNAM 1961, *supra* note 19, at 629.

[39] *See supra* notes 24-33 and accompanying text.

[40] VIETNAM 1961, *supra* note 19, at 481.

[41] *Id.* at 480-81.

[42] *Id.*, at 631.

[43] 2 PENTAGON PAPERS, *supra* note 29, at 438.

[44] VIETNAM 1961, *supra* note 19, at 71, 75.

[45] *Id.* at 117. This legal memo has not been found, but the undersecretary of state, George Ball, referred to it in a meeting of the Presidential Task Force in May 1961. *Id.* at 117 n.8.

[46] *Id.* at 121.

Chayes Cover Letter

In all likelihood, Chayes did not draft the actual legal memorandum, though as the legal advisor he would have coordinated and approved the final product.[47] He did, however, include a cover letter to the secretary of state that provides an interesting glimpse into administration feelings on the situation in Vietnam. Pointedly, Chayes viewed the deterioration of the situation in Vietnam as a political problem rather than a military one. In his view, the problem in Vietnam was not primarily one of aggression from North Vietnam, but rather the inability of an unpopular regime to deal with an internal insurrection. Furthermore, Chayes was committed to "the procedures and institutions for peaceful settlement of international problems" as a necessary condition of international rule of law.[48] Consequently, Chayes did not support deeper U.S. military involvement in South Vietnam. Instead, he determined that the United States must "seek to internationalize the problem with a view to a negotiated settlement or a United Nations solution."[49]

---

[47] Although we do not know who actually drafted the memorandum, Chayes' deputy during this time was Leonard Meeker. Interestingly, it was Meeker who provided the legal advice to the administration at the outset of the Cuban Missile Crisis, since Chayes was out of the country. Chayes fully endorsed that advice, which favored the use of quarantine over invasion. That choice was predicated on the conclusion that placing missiles in Cuba did not amount to armed attack as required by Article 51 of the U.N. Charter, thus the right of self-defense was not triggered. Chayes admits that quarantine was the same as blockade, which he considered an act of war. However, the administration chose to use the term quarantine to convey to the Soviet Union that the United States regarded the action as part of the negotiating process rather than an act of war. *Living History*, *supra* note 34, at 468-70. Meeker would later draft a comprehensive legal justification for U.S. actions in Vietnam in a March 6, 1966, memorandum that was released publicly. *The Legality of United States Participation in the Defense of Vietnam*, 60 Am. J. Int'l L. 565 (1966).

[48] Vietnam 1961, *supra* note 19, at 630.

[49] *Id.* at 631. He does make one interesting alternative suggestion. He recommends that if the United States is unable to negotiate a settlement with North Vietnam, it should "seek to establish in the United Nations the facts of foreign intervention in Viet-nam, and to enlist the United Nations' assistance in protecting the independence and integrity of Viet-nam." *Id.* In essence, he was

History has shown Chayes' two premises to be flawed. First, the problem in South Vietnam was always due primarily to aggression from North Vietnam. Indeed, even by the time Chayes wrote his memo, the conflict had taken on many of the characteristics of a conventional, vice guerrilla, war, although senior Department of Defense planners did not generally recognize this change.[50] Second, Chayes' optimistic view of a negotiated settlement evidences a mistake common to international lawyers. Chayes analyzed the conflict using a civil rather than a criminal law paradigm. Rather than seeing the Vietnam War as a civil dispute between two negotiating parties, he should have viewed it as a problem of a criminal state seeking to impose its will on its neighbor. Had he used this criminal law paradigm, he might have seen the potential utility of employing military force to halt and deter North Vietnam's aggression.

The State Department legal memo was divided into two main sections. The first part dealt with the introduction of additional support troops and materiel in light of the Geneva Accords.[51] The second half of the memorandum addressed other potential international legal barriers to U.S. combat action.

The Geneva Accords

With respect to the Geneva Accords, Chayes asserted three bases for finding that South Vietnam was bound by the agreement.[52] First, he stated that even though the South

---

suggesting that the United States should "make its case" before the United Nations as it did during the Cuban Missile Crisis.

[50] MOMYER, *supra* note 17, at 10.

[51] See *supra* text accompanying notes 9-16.

[52] VIETNAM 1961, *supra* note 19, at 632. The assumption that Saigon, and even the United States, was bound by the Accords permeated the thinking of other government officials as well. For example, a May 4, 1961, memo from Robert W. Komer of the National Security Council staff to National Security Advisor McGeorge Bundy states that "[o]ur sending any troops to Vietnam now or later would be violation of Geneva Accords, to which Saigon is a party." The memo goes on to question whether "Pentagon contingency planning . . . is geared too much to sensible military objectives . . . . The purpose of sending forces is *not* to fight guerillas. It would be to establish a U.S. 'presence.'" *Id.* at

Vietnamese representative at the conference refused to sign the Accords and in fact protested certain provisions, it was signed by the French on behalf of the French Union Forces. Since the State of Vietnam was part of the French Union in 1954, it was bound by that signature. Second, Chayes asserted that South Vietnam was bound by the Accords as the Successor State to France. Finally, Chayes relied on policy reasons for treating South Vietnam as bound to the Accords. Specifically, he was concerned that if South Vietnam was not bound, then neither it nor the United States would have a legal basis for demanding compliance by the Viet Minh with its obligations in the agreement, such as respect for the demarcation line and the cease-fire.

Concerning the United States, the memorandum clearly found that the United States was not bound by the Accords since it did not become a party. On the other hand, U.S. policy for the preceding seven years had been to adhere to the troop and equipment limitations in the Accords. This was becoming increasingly difficult to follow.[53] Also, Chayes pointed out that the United States, while not legally bound by the Accords, did issue a unilateral declaration stating that it would refrain from the threat or use of force to disturb the Accords. The United States also declared that it would view any renewal of aggression in violation of the Accords with grave concern and as seriously threatening international peace and security.

After finding that South Vietnam was obliged to adhere to the Accords, Chayes evaluated Taylor's proposed actions in light of the agreement's prohibitions. In general, the Accords prohibited introducing foreign troop reinforcements, additional military personnel, and increased amounts of war materiel into Vietnam.[54]

Unsurprisingly, Chayes found that implementing the recommendations of the Taylor Report would be a prima facie violation of the Accords by South Vietnam. As a non-party, the

---

123-24 (italics in original). *See also id.* at 377 (memo listing possible courses of action stating that "this proposal, if implemented, would be in violation of the Geneva Accord").

[53] *Id.* at 718.

[54] *See supra* text accompanying notes 9-16.

United States would not violate the Accords per se, but would be guilty of "aiding and abetting" South Vietnam's violation. Despite this, U.S. actions would not be inconsistent with the unilateral declaration, since it would not constitute the threat or use of force to upset the Accords.

Having established a prima facie case against South Vietnam (with the United States as an accessory), Chayes then examined the general principles of international law governing treaties to justify the proposed actions. In particular, Chayes stated that under international law, a material breach of a treaty by one party entitles the other either to suspend the operation of the entire agreement or at least to withhold compliance with an equivalent, corresponding or related provision until resumption of observance by the other party. [55]

---

[55] This statement of the law was later codified in the Vienna Convention on the Law of Treaties. Article 60 states in part:

2. A material breach of a multilateral treaty by one of the parties entitles:
    (a) the other parties by unanimous agreement to suspend the operation of the treaty in whole or in part or to terminate it either:
        (ii) in the relations between themselves and the defaulting State, or
        (iii) as between all the parties;
    (b) a party specially affected by the breach to invoke it as a ground for suspending the operation of the treaty in whole or in part in the relations between itself and the defaulting State;
    (c) any party other than the defaulting State to invoke the Breach as a ground for suspending the operation of the treaty in whole or in part with respect to itself if the treaty is of such a character that a material breach of its provisions by one party radically changes the position of every party with respect to the further performance of its obligations under the treaty.
3. A material breach of a treaty, for the purposes of this article, consists in:
    (a) a repudiation of the treaty not sanctioned by the present Convention; or
    (b) the violation of a provision essential to the accomplishment of the object or purpose of the treaty.

Vienna Convention on the Law of Treaties, May 23, 1969, U.N. Doc. A/CONF. 39/27, 8 I.L.M. 679.

Armed with this defense, Chayes opined that introducing troops and materiel into South Vietnam was legally justified under the circumstances. Among the relevant facts, Chayes notes that "[t]he Viet Minh have violated the Geneva Accords by directing, assisting and engaging in active hostilities in South Viet-Nam and presumably by illegal introduction into North Viet-Nam of military personnel and war materials."[56]

Chayes recommended withholding compliance with specific provisions related to the breaches rather than totally suspending the agreement so as to retain the ability to assert the continuing force of other obligations undertaken by the Viet Minh, especially recognition of the demarcation line. Chayes cautioned, however, that this course "imposes upon us some obligation to keep our response appropriately related to the infractions of the other side."[57]

Despite finding this justification, Chayes was still concerned with the impact of the inevitable Communist claims that South Vietnam and the United States were violating the Accords. In order to dampen the persuasive force of such claims, he suggested that U.S. actions be "cast in the form of assistance and training to police and constabulary forces rather than the introduction and training of regular troops . . . ."[58]

Analysis of the Legal Advice Concerning the Geneva Accords

A brief review of State Department documents during this time frame indicates that the United States felt increasingly hemmed in by its policy of observing the Geneva Accords.[59] Chayes provided a narrow legal justification to exceed the troop and materiel limitations of the Accords. His rationale, that South Vietnam was permitted under international law to respond in kind to North Vietnam's non-observance of the Accords, was soon picked up by

---

[56] VIETNAM 1961, *supra* note 19, at 633.

[57] *Id.* One weakness with this approach is that it would hand the military initiative to Hanoi.

[58] VIETNAM 1961, *supra* note 19, at 633-34.

[59] *See supra* note 52.

senior officials arguing in favor of increased U.S. support.[60] Nonetheless, Chayes could have gone further than he did. In particular, he should have found that South Vietnam was not bound by the Accords.

At the time of the signing of the Geneva Accords, South Vietnam was already a separate sovereign entity. This is evidenced by the fact that on June 4, 1954, France had granted the State of Vietnam, the predecessor to South Vietnam, its independence.[61] Indeed, prior to the Geneva settlement, approximately thirty governments had recognized South Vietnam.[62] Furthermore, a French delegate to the conference remarked that the government of the State of Vietnam was independent and solely competent to commit that state.[63] Moreover, South Vietnam's mere presence at the conference as an entity separate from France indicates that it could not be bound by France's signature on the Accords.[64]

---

[60] *See, e.g.,* VIETNAM 1962, *supra* note 28, at 4-5 (memo discussing public affairs program). The United States also considered arguing this case before the International Control Commission (ICC) established to monitor implementation of the Geneva Accords. *Id.* at 117 (telegram from State Department to Embassy in Vietnam outlining proposed response to ICC regarding build-up of U.S. troops and materiel); *Id.* at 184-85 (draft communication to ICC). However, it soon became clear that the Canadian counselor on the ICC did not agree that a breach by one side justified non-observance by the other. *Id.* at 253-54. Consequently, the United States pursued three different approaches with the ICC. First, it argued that the Geneva Accords meant to freeze the military balance and that the introduction of U.S. noncombatants did not violate the Accords. *Id.* at 274-75. Second, the United States sought to reconcile additional military measures with the Accords by asserting that South Vietnam was merely returning to the status that existed before premature withdrawal of French Union Forces. *Id.* at 401-03. Finally, the United States shipped materiel into the country covertly. It appears the United States adopted the latter policy in part because notifying the ICC of the military build-up would be seen as "self-conviction." *Id.* at 456. Of course, by keeping U.S. actions secret, it appeared that it was engaged in unlawful conduct. The United States made this same mistake throughout the war and again during its intervention in Central America during the Reagan administration.

[61] MOORE, *supra* note 8, at 414.

[62] *Id.* at 408.

[63] *Id.* at 414-15.

[64] *Id.* at 415.

Additionally, it appears that South Vietnam satisfied the customary international law test for statehood in 1954. That test, which is substantially the same today,[65] includes the requirement that the entity possess a defined territory and population.[66] Also, the entity must be eligible for recognition and have the capacity to engage in foreign relations. South Vietnam met all of these criteria. Thus, it was a separate sovereign at the time France signed the Geneva Agreement and was not bound by its provisions.

Finally, with respect to the United States' unilateral declaration, Chayes failed to mention that this was not legally binding anyway. Indeed, the only U.S. (and South Vietnamese) obligation at that point was to avoid any use of force inconsistent with the UN Charter.

Other International Law Barriers

Next, Chayes examined whether any other principle of international law barred U.S. military action. At the outset, Chayes stated that the United States was permitted under international law and the UN Charter to send forces to South Vietnam at its invitation in order to assist it in quelling "insurgent activities having substantial external support, inspiration or direction."[67] The key issue, however, was whether those forces could be employed

---

[65] The modern formulation is as follows: "Under international law, a state is an entity that has a defined territory and a permanent population, under the control of its own government, and that engages in, or has the capacity to engage in, formal relations with other such entities." RESTATEMENT (THIRD) OF THE FOREIGN RELATIONS LAW OF THE UNITED STATES § 201 (1995).

[66] When the Chayes memorandum was written, the *Restatement* was still in draft form. The 1960 draft combined statehood and recognition and required an entity to have a defined territory and population to be eligible for recognition and to show a reasonable and substantial promise of being able to establish and maintain its independence as a legal personality under international law. RESTATEMENT OF THE FOREIGN RELATIONS LAW OF THE UNITED STATES § 6 (Tentative Draft No. 4, April 27, 1960). A later draft changed the last requirement to a capacity to engage in foreign relations. RESTATEMENT OF THE FOREIGN RELATIONS LAW OF THE UNITED STATES § 103 (Proposed Final Draft, May 3, 1962).

[67] VIETNAM 1961, *supra* note 19, at 634.

beyond the borders of South Vietnam. Here, Chayes took a curious approach.

First, Chayes examined the legality of immediate cross-border attacks against enemy sanctuaries. In this regard, Chayes stated:

> It would seem justifiable under international law principles relating to hot pursuit to follow the enemy across the border and attempt to destroy his bases of operations adjacent to the border. Such operations would have to be appropriately related to the act provoking them, proportionate in their effects and limited to action necessary to obtain relief.[68]

Second, with respect to strategic attacks against targets deep inside North Vietnam, Chayes concluded that "[i]n the absence of overt aggression by means of armed attack against South Viet-Nam, such action would go beyond permissible self-defense under general international law and would be contrary to the United Nations Charter."[69] Chayes concluded this for the following reason. Such an attack could only be taken if the right of individual or collective self-defense was triggered. Chayes stated that this right could only be invoked under Article 51 of the UN Charter in the event of an "armed attack." He further opined that the term "armed attack" is "generally understood as a direct external attack upon one country by the armed forces of another such as the German invasion of Poland in 1939 or the North Korean attack on South Korea in 1950."[70] Furthermore, it must be a swift action that requires immediate measures to ward off.[71] Consequently, in light of Article 2(4) of the UN Charter, "[I]n cases of aggression that fall short of armed attack . . . it would not be consistent with the purposes of the United Nations for the United States . . . to proceed to the use of armed force to defeat acts which it considers aggressive."[72]

---

[68] *Id.*
[69] *Id.*
[70] *Id.* at 635.
[71] *Id.*
[72] *Id.*

*Analysis of the Legal Advice Concerning Other Barriers to
U.S. Action*

Civil War

The second half of the Chayes memorandum is subdivided into
two sections: "General Intervention" and "Retaliatory Attacks." In
the former, Chayes noted that the United States is permitted to
introduce troops into South Vietnam at that government's request
to help quell insurgent activities. It is interesting to note that in
reaching this conclusion, Chayes seems to imply that there was a
civil war in Vietnam and that the United States could aid one side
in such a struggle. On the other hand, for purposes of evaluating
what he terms "retaliatory attacks," he took for granted that South
and North Vietnam were separate international entities. Thus, in
this instance, he did not raise the "civil war" argument that was
popular in some academic circles.[73]

This latter stance was appropriate, since the use of coercive
force as a modality of change in the modern world should not
depend on legal niceties of statehood recognition. From 1954,
North and South Vietnam had been separate de facto, if not de jure,
entities.[74] They had separate governments, one on each side of the
Cold War ideological fence. Furthermore, the temporary
demarcation line at the seventeenth parallel dictated by the Geneva
Accords was, if nothing else, intended to label as unlawful any use
of force across that boundary. Thus, as John Norton Moore points
out, "[t]o get comfort from the Accords for the proposition that
force by the D.R.V. against the R.V.N. is not unlawful is to stand
the agreements on their head."[75]

---

[73] Moore, *supra* note 8, at 359-66.

[74] *Id.* at 361-62.

[75] *Id.* at 363.

The Right of Hot Pursuit

It is unclear at first blush why Chayes subdivided "retaliatory attacks" between those directed at border sanctuaries in Laos and North Vietnam and those directed at targets further in North Vietnam. Closer examination reveals that implicit in Chayes' approach was a legal distinction between covert and overt aggression. Action in response to the former was limited, according to Chayes, to "hot pursuit." Thus, so long as the enemy limited its actions to supplying forces in country (which Chayes presumably assumed would be wholly indigenous) or to small-scale, guerrilla attacks, South Vietnam could not invoke the right of self-defense. It could only respond when it caught enemy forces in its country. Once it did, it could chase them back to their post or encampment, so long as they were not "deep inside" North Vietnam, and then destroy their bases of operations.

The right of hot pursuit had been vaguely recognized in U.S. history. It dates to May of 1836, when U.S. forces pursued "marauding Indians who had crossed into U.S. territory from Mexico and there committed acts of murder, arson and plunder before fleeing into Mexican territory."[76] Early in the twentieth century, Green Haywood Hackworth described how the United States felt justified in pursuing lawless bands of armed men led by Pancho Villa in raids across the Mexican border.[77] This justification was based on the theory that the arrangement was reciprocal, that the Mexican government did not sponsor the bandits, and that the Mexican government was simply unable to control these armed groups.[78]

---

[76] Whiteman, *supra* note 20, at 75.

[77] 2 DIGEST OF INTERNATIONAL LAW 282-334 (Green Haywood Hackworth ed., 1941) [hereinafter Hackworth].

[78] Bowett writes:

> There are cases of the pursuit of bodies acting without the authority or support of the state whose territory is invaded in hot pursuit, and they presuppose the inadequacy of the territorial state's own measures of prevention. The resultant derogation from the state's territorial sovereignty

This right is distinguished from the right of hot pursuit at sea or in the air. In those cases, the pursuit must end when the ship or aircraft enters the territory of another state.[79] In contrast, the right of hot pursuit on land involves the violation of another state's territorial sovereignty. This response is justified because the neighboring state has allowed its territory to be misused to the detriment of the security of the other state.[80] There is some debate as to whether this right stands on its own or whether it is grounded in the principle of self-defense.[81] The argument for the former is that "in many cases the action of the pursuing state is distinctly punitive in character, and, therefore, since it goes beyond the necessities of protection, is more properly described as reprisals."[82] This would seem untenable under modern international law. Indeed, Bowett concluded in 1958 that "the right of hot pursuit, whatever its conditions in the past, must under present-day international law be subject to those same limitations and conditions which govern any exercise of the right of self-defence."[83]

---

arises directly from that state's inability to secure to its neighbor respect for its territorial integrity.

D.W. BOWETT, SELF-DEFENCE IN INTERNATIONAL LAW 39 (1958).

[79] Whiteman, *supra* note 20, at 76. *See also* Richard J. Erickson, *Use of Armed Force Abroad: An Operational Law Checklist*, REPORTER, June 1988, at 3, 6-7. Erickson lists several conditions that must be satisfied for hot pursuit to be a legitimate use of military force. For example, the hot pursuit must begin within the territory of the pursuing state and continue out onto the high seas or in the air above. The pursuing state must have good reason to believe that the ship or aircraft has violated its laws or regulations while within its territory. Furthermore, the pursuit must be continuous, beginning after a signal to stop has been given and ceasing when the ship or aircraft enters the territory of another state.

[80] Whiteman, *supra* note 20, at 75.

[81] Hackworth, *supra* note 77, at 289 (grounding the cross-border action in self-defense).

[82] BOWETT, *supra* note 78, at 40.

[83] *Id.* at 41. Tellingly, Bowett entitles this section of his book "The So-Called Right of Hot Pursuit." He also notes that while the reasoning appears in principle unobjectionable, all of the incursions involve states with significant power differentials. *Id.* at 40. Perhaps hot pursuit on land would fall into that

Thus, the right of hot pursuit has been effectively collapsed into the right of self-defense. While this is implicit in Chayes' analysis, he still treated hot pursuit as a separate basis for action, perhaps because he concluded that the attackers were "acting without the authority or support" of North Vietnam. In effect, he adopted the concept of hot pursuit in order to justify destroying enemy bases immediately adjacent to the border. He avoided calling these actions self-defense, however, thereby limiting the U.S. military response. By limiting the response to the territory of South Vietnam or border areas during hot pursuit, he left the military advantage with the attacker.

Pointedly, Chayes stated that these guerrilla attacks were not "armed attacks," though surely they were attacks using arms. As noted above, Chayes believed that the term "armed attack" as used in the Charter means an overt attack by conventional armies, such as the German invasion of Poland. Furthermore, it must be a swift blitzkrieg type attack. "Indirect aggression" was excluded from this definition. In the case of acts falling short of the "armed attack" threshold, the aggrieved state was required to absorb the impact and bring the matter to the attention of the United Nations.

A Better Approach

The difficulty with the second part of Chayes' memorandum is that he allowed the scope of possible military action to drive his conclusions rather than deducing the permissible scope of action from the norms of international law. The correct approach would have been to first determine whether there was a basis in international law for U.S. military intervention in Indochina. In general, the UN Charter requires nations to resolve their

---

category of obsolete nineteenth century international law doctrines described by McDougal and Feliciano as reflecting the desire to localize and minimize coercion and violence by permitting quick settlement through superior strength. MYRES S. MCDOUGAL & FLORENTINO P. FELICIANO, LAW AND MINIMUM PUBLIC ORDER 137-38 (1961). It certainly appears to have been an obsolete doctrine at the time of Chayes' memo. Neither Stone nor Greenspan mention it in their treatises. JULIUS STONE, LEGAL CONTROL OF INTERNATIONAL CONFLICT (1959); MORRIS GREENSPAN, THE MODERN LAW OF LAND WARFARE (1959).

international disputes peacefully and refrain from the use of force as a modality of change.[84] All use of force, however, is not proscribed by Article 2(4), only the aggressive use of force. The lawful use of force falls generally into one of four broad categories.[85]

First, states may use force pursuant to a UN Security Council decision under Chapter VII of the UN Charter, which is entitled "Action with Respect to Threats to the Peace, Breaches of the Peace, and Acts of Aggression." Article 42 states that the Security Council "may take such action by air, sea, or land forces as may be necessary to maintain or restore international peace and security." Examples of collective actions authorized by the Security Council include the Korean War and the Persian Gulf War.

Second, Chapter VII of the UN Charter authorizes the creation of various regional organizations "for dealing with such matters relating to the maintenance of international peace and security as are appropriate for regional action . . . ."[86] Article 53 permits enforcement actions to be carried out by a regional organization if sanctioned by the UN Security Council.[87]

Third, some uses of force may be permitted if they fall below the threshold of Article 2(4) of the UN Charter. Any such use of force must therefore not threaten the territorial integrity or political independence of the other state, or be in any manner inconsistent with the purposes of the United Nations.

Finally, states may take actions in individual or collective self-defense pursuant to Article 51 of the UN Charter and customary international law. In the case of Vietnam, the Security Council had not used its authority to sanction the use of force. Indeed, given the

---

[84] The UN Charter states: "All Members shall refrain in their international relations from the threat or use of force against the territorial integrity or political independence of any state, or in any other manner inconsistent with the Purposes of the United Nations." U.N. CHARTER art. 2, para. 4.

[85] NATIONAL SECURITY LAW 86 (John Norton Moore et al. eds., 1990).

[86] U.N. CHARTER art. 52.

[87] U.N. CHARTER art. 53 ("The Security Council shall, where appropriate, utilize such regional arrangements or agencies for enforcement action under its authority. But no enforcement action shall be taken under regional arrangements or by regional agencies without the authorization of the Security Council.").

ideological climate of the time, such authorization would not have been forthcoming had the United States requested it. Thus, we must look to the second broad category of the permissible use of force: the right of a state to act in individual or collective defense.

The first inquiry in this regard is to define the right of self-defense. The appropriate starting point would be Article 51 of the UN Charter, which states:

> Nothing in the present Charter shall impair the inherent right of individual or collective self-defence if an armed attack occurs against a Member of the United Nations, until the Security Council has taken measures necessary to maintain international peace and security. Measures taken by Members in the exercise of this right of self-defence shall be immediately reported to the Security Council and shall not in any way affect the authority and responsibility of the Security Council under the present Charter to take at any time such action as it deems necessary in order to maintain or restore international peace and security.[88]

As an initial matter, it is important to note that the right of self-defense emanates either from customary international law or Article 51 of the UN Charter. Some scholars contend that Article 51 merely reaffirmed the traditional right. Others, however, advocate a "restrictive interpretation" of Article 51.[89] Principally, however, this restrictive interpretation eliminates the traditional right of anticipatory self-defense and thus is not implicated by the situation in Vietnam.[90] Still others use a restrictive interpretation to exclude responses to covert aggression. Chayes apparently fell into this category.[91] Finally, even if one accepts the premise that Article

---

[88] U.N. CHARTER art. 51.

[89] STONE, *supra* note 83, at 244; GREENSPAN, *supra* note 83, at 27.

[90] MOORE, *supra* note 8, at 368 n.18.

[91] Later writings by Chayes would seem to confirm this assessment and place Chayes squarely in the minimalist legal tradition. For example, in *New Sovereignty: Compliance with International Regulatory Agreements*, Chayes opines that states that do not comply with treaty norms do so not because of willful disobedience, but because of deficiencies in the treaty regime. ABRAM

51 states a different, more restrictive right of self-defense, one must decide whether it was meant to displace the broader customary right.[92] If it does not, then the broader customary right is still viable.

As noted above, Chayes falls into to the category of international lawyers who believe that Article 51 displaced the customary right of self-defense with a more restrictive interpretation. This was inappropriate for several reasons.

First, the plain language of the article is that the inherent right of self-defense is triggered by an "armed attack." The phrase is not elsewhere defined as a term of art, nor is it modified by the word "direct." As one diplomat stated,

> Article 51 does not speak of a direct armed attack. It speaks of armed attack. It wishes to cover all cases of attack, direct or indirect, so long as it is an armed attack. Is there any difference from the point of view of the effects between direct armed attack or indirect armed attack if both of them are armed and if both of them are designed to menace the independence of a country?[93]

CHAYES & ANTONIA HANDLER CHAYES, NEW SOVEREIGNTY: COMPLIANCE WITH INTERNATIONAL REGULATORY AGREEMENTS 15 (1995). Concluding that enforcement mechanisms are not useful, he proposes a managerial strategy of discourse and persuasion to induce compliance. *Id.* at 109-11. Thus, he adopts a civil law model for dispute resolution, assuming that all parties will act in good faith and seek settlement to avoid any loss of reputation. *See also* John Norton Moore, *The Secret War in Central America and the Future of the World Order,* 80 AM. J. INT'L L. 43, 107 n.250 (1986) (attacking Chayes' anemic right to defense argument); *International Lawlessness in Grenada,* 78 AM. J. INT'L L. 172 (1984) (signing, along with Richard Falk and seven other scholars, a paper stating in part that "[t]hroughout the 20th century, the U.S. Government has routinely concocted evanescent threats . . . as pretexts to justify armed interventions into sister American states.").

[92] *See, e.g.,* Oscar Schacter, *The Right of States to Use Armed Force,* 82 MICH. L. REV. 1620, 1634 (1984) (reading Article 51 to be limited to overt armed attack, but finding that the customary law right of self-defense was nonetheless undisturbed by adoption of the Charter).

[93] Whiteman, *supra* note 20, at 62 (quoting a Lebanese delegate addressing indirect aggression taken against his country by the United Arab Republic). *See also* Moore, *supra* note 91, at 85.

Thus, the plain meaning of Article 51 encompasses covert insurgency as well as overt aggression.[94]

Second, the French version of the UN Charter, which is equally authoritative, uses the term *agression armee* (armed aggression).[95] This formulation clearly allows a defensive response to a serious covert attack.

Third, the *travaux préparatoires* of the Charter indicate that the inclusion of Article 51 was not intended to narrow the traditional right of self-defense. Rather, the purpose of Article 51 was to accommodate regional security organizations within the Charter's scheme of centralized, global collective security.[96] It was added at the insistence of Latin American states who feared their right of collective defense under the Act of Chapultepec would be frustrated by vetoes cast in the Security Council. Furthermore, in the process of formulating Article 2(4), the drafting committee reported that "[t]he unilateral use of force or similar coercive measures is not authorized or admitted. The use of arms in legitimate self defense remains admitted and unimpaired."[97]

Fourth, the structure of the sentence evidences that Article 51 was intended to reaffirm, not displace, the customary right. The first sentence is written in the negative, stating that "[n]othing in the present Charter shall impair the inherent right of individual or collective self-defense . . . ." Thus, the drafters sought to reassure states that the Charter, an unprecedented document impinging on national sovereignty, would not impact or limit one particular right—the right to self-defense—in any way.

Fifth, there are sound policy reasons to conclude that Article 51 simply reaffirms the customary rule of international law with respect to individual and collective self-defense. The guiding principles of the United Nations as reflected in the UN Charter

---

[94] Moore, *supra* note 91, at 83.

[95] *Id.* at 83. *See* U.N. CHARTER art. 111 (stating that the Chinese, French, Russian, English, and Spanish texts are equally authentic). This principle of treaty interpretation was later codified in the Vienna Convention on the Law of Treaties, *supra* note 55, art. 33.

[96] MCDOUGAL & FELICIANO, *supra* note 83, at 234-35.

[97] *Id.* at 235.

include the maintenance of peace and security,[98] self-determination,[99] territorial integrity, and political independence.[100] Clearly, covert or indirect attacks undermine these principles as effectively as a traditional armed attack. One commentator notes that to argue "that a state may not employ force to combat indirect aggression reveals a considerable lack of understanding of the purposes of the Charter. The drafters meant only to proscribe the unlawful use of force, not coercion in defense of such basic values as political independence or territorial integrity."[101] Any interpretation that prohibits the exercise of self-defense measures in response to secret or indirect armed attacks grants impunity to covert aggressors, a result the drafters of the UN Charter would not have sanctioned. Also, it is unreasonable to conclude that the signatory states in 1945 would have negotiated away a right that protected the most fundamental values of a state.

Thus, it is clear that the right of individual or collective self-defense, whether found in customary international law or in the language of Article 51 of the UN Charter, permits responses to covert as well as overt aggression. Self-defense, however, has two components: necessity and proportionality.[102] The first factual issue, then, is whether North Vietnam was engaged in acts of aggression triggering the right to respond with coercive force. Not all aggressive acts necessarily rise to this level. As Professor John Norton Moore states, "the verbal tests of the Caroline case and Article 51 reflect a community interest in restricting conflict to those cases where fundamental values are seriously threatened by the initiating coercion."[103] Thus, "minor encroachments on sovereignty, political disputes, frontier incidents, the use of non-coercive modalities of interference, and generally aggression which does not threaten fundamental values, such as political and territorial integrity, may not be defended against by major resort to

---

[98] U.N. Charter art. 1, para. 1.

[99] U.N. Charter art. 1, para. 2.

[100] U.N. Charter art. 2, para. 4.

[101] Moore, *supra* note 91, at 84-85 (quoting Roger H. Hull & John C. Novograd, Law and Vietnam 118, 120 (1968)).

[102] McDougal & Feliciano, *supra* note 83, at 217.

[103] Moore, *supra* note 8, at 367.

force against another entity."[104] Whether the initiating coercion rises to the level that permits resorting to the use of responsive force is fact dependent. The initial aggression must be so intense that the target-state has a reasonable expectation that military reaction is necessary to protect its most fundamental values.[105]

In this case, the political stability of South Vietnam was seriously threatened by the North Vietnamese directed aggression, especially assassinations and kidnappings, by the end of 1958.[106] From 1959 to 1961, North Vietnam infiltrated an estimated 10,700 men into South Vietnam.[107] Also, since the end of 1959, well-organized and equipped Viet Cong military units had been attacking South Vietnamese military targets.[108] These armed units had been formed as a result of the Fifteenth Conference of the Central Committee, which met in Hanoi in January 1959.[109] Consequently, there was a necessity for South Vietnam to resort to force.

Having determined that the right of self-defense was triggered, Chayes should have then determined what extent of military action was permissible under international law. In general, the use of responsive force must be proportionate to the threat.[110] Proportionality limits the response to "what is reasonably necessary promptly to secure the permissible objectives of self-defense."[111] Proportionality does not mean matching the aggressor tit for tat. Rather, it means measuring the response against its permissive objectives.[112]

---

[104] *Id.*

[105] *Id.*

[106] 1 PENTAGON PAPERS, *supra* note 16, at 335.

[107] MOORE, *supra* note 8, at 371.

[108] 1 PENTAGON PAPERS, *supra* note 16, at 338.

[109] Gunther Lewy, *Evidence of Aggression from the North and the State Department "White Papers,"* in THE VIETNAM DEBATE, A FRESH LOOK AT THE ARGUMENTS 89, 90-91 (John Norton Moore ed., 1990).

[110] Schacter, *supra* note 92, at 1637 (stating that acts done in self-defense must not exceed in manner or aim the necessity provoking them).

[111] MCDOUGAL & FELICIANO, *supra* note 83, at 242.

[112] Moore, *supra* note 91, at 89.

Here, the permissible objectives of South Vietnam would be protecting its territorial integrity, political independence, and right of self-determination in the face of sustained attacks. These attacks often originated from bases located in Laos or North Vietnam. The insurgent forces in South Vietnam were dependent on supply lines in North Vietnam and Laos. In fact, "[i]n January 1960 General Giap declared that 'the North has become a large rear echelon of our army. The North is the revolutionary base for the whole country.'"[113]

Measured against this threat, Chayes was right to imply that strategic targeting of North Vietnam would have been permissible once the right of self-defense was triggered. The right of defense is a right of effective defense. Effective self-defense may require a counterattack against the source of the attack on a scale that would deter future attacks.[114] Schacter notes, "it does not seem unreasonable, as a rule, to allow a state to retaliate beyond the immediate area of attack, when that state has sufficient reason to expect a continuation of attacks (with substantial military weapons) from the same source."[115] In sum, while the response to unlawful aggression must be proportionate, it need not be anemic.

Lastly, the legal advice should have reminded the decision makers that the United States was required to report any measures it took after the fact to the UN Security Council in accordance with Article 51. Also, collective action was to be promptly terminated should the UN Security Council take effective measures to resolve the situation.

---

[113] Lewy, *supra* note 109, at 91.

[114] Schacter, *supra* note 92, at 1638 (referring to U.S. response to North Vietnamese attacks on naval vessels in the Gulf of Tonkin).

[115] *Id.* Later, Schacter asserts, with no explanation, that proportionality requires an outside intervening state (whose intervention is lawful exercise of collective self-defense) not to introduce higher technology weapons than those used by the aggressor state. In fact, the United States initially avoided deploying sophisticated aircraft in part because of a belief that such aircraft would raise the level of violence and risk widening the war. MOMYER, *supra* note 17, at 10. It is now evident that U.S. restraint was not rewarded and such arbitrary lines, without reference to the factual context, are not useful.

ANALYSIS OF 1964 LEGAL ADVICE

The next major turning point in the Vietnam War came in 1964. American involvement had been gradually and silently deepening.[116] Since 1962, the United States had been involved in various "plausibly deniable" operations as part of the counterinsurgency effort. At the Honolulu conference in early June, General Taylor suppressed the views of his colleagues on the JCS advocating massive military action against the North Vietnamese sanctuary.[117] Instead, the conference adopted Secretary of Defense Robert McNamara's graduated pressure strategy. Relying on quantitative analysis rather than military expertise, McNamara assumed "that the limited application of force would compel the North Vietnamese to the negotiating table and exact from them a favorable diplomatic settlement. There was no need to pursue military victory because negotiations would achieve the same political objectives with only the threat of more severe military action."[118]

Thus, two months before the Gulf of Tonkin incident, the administration was planning on increasing overt U.S. military pressure on North Vietnam in order to "communicate" with Ho Chi Minh. Against this backdrop, the State Department legal advisor once again drafted a legal review for the secretary of state and the president.[119]

Unlike the earlier Chayes memorandum, this document was focused entirely on the domestic legal bases for the use of force abroad. The first section dealt with deploying forces in advisory and noncombatant roles. Of course, the United States already had over 16,000 troops in South Vietnam filling positions of this

---

[116] MCMASTER, *supra* note 33, at 119.

[117] *Id.* at 100-01.

[118] *Id.* at 94.

[119] Memorandum on Legal Basis for Sending American Forces to Viet-Nam, June 26, 1964 (on file with author) [hereinafter 1964 Memo]; 1 FOREIGN RELATIONS OF THE UNITED STATES 1964-1968: VIETNAM 1964, at 532 (John P. Glennon et al. eds., 1992) [hereinafter VIETNAM 1964] (containing Secretary of State Dean Rusk's cover memorandum but not the legal memorandum).

type.[120] The memo affirms that this was lawful pursuant to section 503 of the Foreign Assistance Act of 1961. Furthermore, the memo cites the 1950 Agreement for Mutual Defense Assistance in Indo-China as support for noncombat activities.

The bulk of the legal analysis deals with the president's authority to send U.S. military personnel to Vietnam to engage in combat activities. Predating the War Powers Resolution[121] by ten years, the memo deals solely with the provisions of the U.S. Constitution.

The memo correctly cites Article II, Section 2, of the Constitution as the basis for presidential authority to employ armed forces, which states that "[t]he President shall be Commander in Chief of the Army and Navy of the United States . . . ."[122] The memo also refers indirectly to the executive power of the president found in Section 1 of Article II.[123] The memo alludes to a gray area between the powers of the executive and legislative branches in this area, but concludes that the drafters did not intend the enumerated congressional powers to prejudice the right of the president to repel sudden attacks.[124]

The memorandum next turns to the historical record. In this regard, it notes that there was a long history of the president employing the armed forces without congressional intervention. Many of those cases dealt only with "the general defense of the United States or the protection of some national interest or some concern of American foreign policy."[125]

After noting that the Supreme Court had not considered the issue, the memo addresses congressional interest. Here, the memo concludes that the general view of Congress is that the "President has a right and a duty to take measures which he considers

---

[120] Additionally, many of those advisors were in fact engaged in combat activities. *See supra* notes 26 to 33 and accompanying text.

[121] Pub. L. No. 93-148, § 5, 87 Stat. 555 (1973) (codified at 50 U.S.C. §§ 1541-48 (1982)).

[122] U.S. CONST. art. II, § 2.

[123] "The executive Power shall be vested in a President of the United States of America." *Id.* at § 1.

[124] 1964 Memo, *supra* note 119, at 2.

[125] *Id.* at 3.

necessary for the defense of the United States."[126] The president is to take such measures unilaterally, however, only when the situation is "of such urgency as to brook no delay and to allow no time for seeking the approval of Congress."[127]

Finally, the memorandum concludes by stating that the existence of the Southeast Asia Treaty and its Protocol extending protection to South Vietnam was evidence of U.S. national security interest. The fact that this treaty received the advice and consent of the Senate conferred additional legitimacy to this contention. Interestingly, the memo does not recommend actually invoking the treaty. This would seem to stem from two bases. First, the legislative history of that treaty indicated that invoking the treaty to send U.S. forces into combat would require acting through Congress.[128] Second, the collective defense provisions of the treaty were to be triggered by an "armed attack." The memo opined that it was "difficult to characterize North Vietnamese actions in South Viet-Nam as 'armed attack' within the meaning of the Southeast Asia Treaty and the U.N. Charter."[129]

I have some general observations on this memorandum. First, just as the Chayes memo ignored one half of the picture, so does this one. One would expect that a legal memorandum going to the president from the secretary of state and coordinated with the Department of Justice Office of Legal Counsel would address both the domestic and international legal bases for the use of force abroad. It does not. The only mention of the UN Charter is the flawed conclusion that North Vietnamese aggression to that point did not constitute an armed attack as contemplated in Article 51.[130] Second, the memorandum, including the secretary of state's cover letter, fails to make any recommendations. This failure underscores the vagueness of the memo's contents. For example, the Constitution apparently grants the president the power to repel sudden attacks, but nowhere does the memorandum attempt to

---

[126] *Id.*

[127] *Id.*

[128] *Id.* at 4.

[129] *Id.*

[130] See *supra* notes 88 to 101 and accompanying text.

place this authority in the context of sending armed forces to Vietnam. Furthermore, the desirability or even requirement of seeking congressional approval is not marked with any precision.[131]

Regarding the constitutional analysis, the legal advisor got it about right. Without much elaboration, the memorandum states that the line between the executive and legislative power was not clearly delineated in the Constitution. In fact, the Constitution sets for the legislative powers in limited terms, while the executive power is expressed more generally.[132] Article I, Section 1, provides that "all legislative powers herein granted shall be vested in the Congress of the United States."[133] It then specifies certain national security related powers. They include the power to declare war, raise and support armies, provide and maintain a navy, and make rules for the government and regulation of the land and naval forces.[134]

With respect to the "declare war" clause, it is important to note that "declare war" was a term of art understood by the framers as meaning the initiation of offensive hostilities.[135] Also, it is not synonymous with "make war." The framers consciously chose to change Congress' power from the latter, which it enjoyed under the Articles of Confederation, to the former.[136] Furthermore, the power to declare war, as an enumerated exception to the general executive power, should be construed narrowly.[137] It is intended to be a veto or negative check on the presidential power to initiate an offensive war. To a large degree, this power is obsolete today. By

---

[131] The president would, of course, eventually obtain congressional authorization for his actions via the Gulf of Tonkin Resolution in August 1964.

[132] Robert F. Turner, *War and the Forgotten Executive Power Clause of the Constitution: A Review Essay of John Hart Ely's War and Responsibility*, 34 VA. J. INT'L L. 903, 929-30 (1994).

[133] U.S. CONST. art. I, § 1.

[134] *Id.* § 2.

[135] Turner, *supra* note 132, at 906-07.

[136] *Id.* at 910.

[137] *Id.* at 948.

ratifying the Kellogg-Briand Pact[138] and the UN Charter, the United States effectively gave up its sovereign right to wage aggressive war.[139]

On the other hand, Article II, Section 1, vests the executive power in the president of the United States of America, and Section 2 makes him the commander-in-chief. This clause vests in the president all powers executive in nature unless specifically lodged elsewhere in the Constitution.[140] Essentially, congressional powers in the foreign affairs arena were to be limited, while the president was to have expansive authority. The president needs no special authority to use force to defend against a military threat to the United States or to faithfully execute its laws or treaties.[141]

Consequently, although the memorandum is somewhat vague at points, its general thesis that the executive had been granted broad authority to send forces abroad in the nation's interest was correct.

The brief discussion of the SEATO Treaty[142] is somewhat problematic. Although mainly cited for the proposition that there had been a congressional determination of a vital national security interest in Vietnam, the memorandum seems to imply that the treaty itself would constitute a legal basis for action if invoked. This is not the case, however. The treaty, like other collective defense agreements, does not provide an international legal basis per se. It is simply an agreement between the parties to act together in a certain way in the face of aggression. The actual international legal basis must still be ascertained elsewhere, such as a Security Council resolution authorizing an enforcement action or Article 51 and customary international law sanctioning collective self-defense.

On the other hand, the SEATO Treaty could form part of the domestic legal basis for the use of force. Treaties are part of the

---

[138] General Treaty for the Renunciation of War as an Instrument of National Policy, Aug. 27, 1928, 46 Stat. 2343, 94 L.N.T.S. 57.

[139] Turner, *supra* note 132, at 915.

[140] *Id.* at 929-37.

[141] *Id.* at 914-15.

[142] Southeast Asia Collective Defense Treaty, Sept. 8, 1954, 6 U.S.T. 81.

supreme law of the land,[143] and the president must "take Care that the Laws be faithfully executed . . . ."[144] Article IV of the SEATO Treaty states:

> Each party recognizes that aggression by means of armed attack in the treaty area against any of the Parties or against any State or territory which the Parties by unanimous agreement may hereafter designate, would endanger its own peace and safety, and agrees that it will in that event act to meet the common danger in accordance with its constitutional processes. Measures taken under this paragraph shall be immediately reported to the Security Council of the United Nations.[145]

Thus, under Article IV of the SEATO Treaty, the United States had an obligation to "act to meet the common danger" in the event of an armed attack. Furthermore, the president, under the general grant of executive power in the Constitution, is responsible for fulfilling this duty. Therefore, if the president determined that the United States needed to deploy combat troops to meet this treaty obligation, he was entitled to do so.[146]

ANALYSIS OF 1965 LEGAL ADVICE

In March 1965, the United States began bombing targets in North Vietnam as part of Operation Rolling Thunder. In April of that year, the first ground combat troops waded ashore at Da Nang. On June 10, Attorney General Nicholas deB. Katzenbach advised the president as to whether additional congressional approval was necessary in light of proposed troop increases in South Vietnam.[147]

---

[143] U.S. CONST. art. VI.

[144] U.S. CONST. art. II, § 3.

[145] Southeast Asia Collective Defense Treaty, *supra* note 142, at art. IV.

[146] Similarly, if the president made U.S. forces available to the Security Council under a UN Charter Article 43 agreement, he could do so without the declaration of war since such action would not amount to initiating an offensive war.

[147] VIETNAM 1965, *supra* note 4, at 751-54.

The attorney general was responding to a specific request concerning the proposed increase of 30,000 to 40,000 ground troops in South Vietnam. These would be added to the approximately 50,000 soldiers already stationed there. With this additional force strength, the president also intended to expand the scope of the military mission from an advisory and area security role to offensive operations within South Vietnam.[148]

For much the same reason as expressed in the 1964 memorandum discussed above, Katzenbach concluded that congressional approval was unnecessary. Specifically, the attorney general advised the president that as the commander-in-chief and as the sole organ of the United States in foreign relations, he was empowered to deploy and use the armed forces abroad.[149] Furthermore, he determined that the "declare war" clause was intended to apply to the use of force to conquer and subdue a foreign nation.[150]

Katzenbach further opined that although the president need not ask for congressional authorization, it was sometimes politically wise to do so. However, any such authorization is likely to limit the president's authority.[151] In this case, the president already had congressional authorization in the form of the Tonkin Gulf Resolution.[152] In Katzenbach's judgment, the proposed new measures were still well within the confines of that statute. Seemingly out of an abundance of caution, he noted that the proposed offensive actions were to be carried out by forces in one to two battalion strength. He did this because of the existence of some legislative history "to the effect that the congressional approval did not extend to involvement in large-scale land war in Asia. In this regard, however, there were repeated references to war in 'division strength.'"[153] Thus, he was able to advise the

---

[148] *Id.* at 752.
[149] *Id.*
[150] *Id.*
[151] *Id.* at 753.
[152] Pub. L. No. 93-148, *supra* note 121, at § 5.
[153] VIETNAM 1965, *supra* note 4, at 754.

president that he would not violate any supposed congressional limitations.

While I agree with his conclusion, I have two principal objections to Katzenbach's memorandum. First, he displayed too much lawyerly caution in noting that the Tonkin Gulf Resolution could, in the minds of some, impose some restrictions on presidential action. He need not have been quite so reticent. The legislative history of the statute points much more clearly to a finding that Congress wrote the president a veritable blank check to use military force in Vietnam.[154]

A more serious objection concerns his reasoning about the "declare war" clause. Katzenbach stressed that the commitment was limited in size and that the actions would be confined to South Vietnam and "would be directed against forces claiming to be insurgents rather than the forces of a foreign nation."[155] Thus, the United States would neither be engaging in all-out war nor taking any act of war against a foreign nation. Based on these premises, he found that the congressional power to declare war was not implicated.

Again, Katzenbach was too constraining on the executive power and too generous with the legislative power. As noted above, the congressional power to declare war is a negative on the president's power.[156] Article II, Section 1, of the Constitution granted to the president all of the powers that were executive in nature, with limited exceptions. Those exceptions, such as the authority to declare war, are to be construed narrowly. Consequently, the president did not need congressional authorization to send 50,000 troops to South Vietnam only because they expected to confine their actions to that country. He had the authority to do so under the executive power clause. Congress could not exercise their Article I, Section 2, legislative veto because the president was not taking the country from a state of peace to one of aggressive war.

---

[154] Turner, *supra* note 132, at 960-61.

[155] VIETNAM 1965, *supra* note 4, at 753.

[156] *See supra* notes 135-39 and accompanying text.

CONCLUSION

The Vietnam War effectively began for the United States in 1961 and ended with our withdrawal and abandonment of South Vietnam in 1973. The war has left a deep scar on the American psyche. In an ideal world, things would have gone differently right from the beginning.

Ideally, the president would have identified the political objective in Vietnam, for example, to keep South Vietnam from falling into the Communist camp.[157] His top-level advisors would have given him a range of options. The Joint Chiefs of Staff, in particular, would have prepared a cogent and unified plan based on sound military principles. In general, we know that the United States needed first and foremost to isolate the battlefield. This would have required strategic bombing in North Vietnam to destroy supplies and war-supporting targets, thereby reducing the infiltration flow from north to south.[158] It would also have required the mining of Haiphong Harbor, which was where Hanoi received over 85 percent of its war materiel. Finally, it would have required the physical interdiction of the Ho Chi Minh Trail in Laos. Before making his decision, the president would have had the benefit of sound legal advice. Of course, that is not what happened.

In reality, the political objective was, at best, ambiguous. Vietnam was a microcosm of the Cold War, and U.S. containment policy dictated that it commit resources to defend South Vietnam. Had the president attempted to walk away from Vietnam, he would have been accused of appeasement and "losing" Vietnam. On the

---

[157] President Johnson identified the U.S. objective in 1966 as follows: "Our purpose in Vietnam is to prevent the success of aggression. It is not conquest; it is not empire; it is not foreign bases; it is not domination; it is to prevent the forceful conquest of South Vietnam by North Vietnam." MOMYER, *supra* note 17, at 172 (quoting a speech given by President Johnson on February 23, 1966).

[158] "The [air] campaign, to be effective, had to begin with attacks on the head of the system in North Vietnam. At that point the lines of communications were most vulnerable to an attack, and there the supplies and repair and support facilities for the entire logistics system were located. . . . As the transportation system threaded its way south . . . we found fewer vulnerable segments that could be blocked for any length of time." MOMYER, *supra* note 17, at 174.

other hand, senior administration officials were hesitant to entangle the United States in another large-scale war on the Asian landmass so soon after Korea. Consequently, the United States effectively resolved to avoid defeat rather than attempt victory.[159]

Thus, there was a desire to "control" the war, and Secretary of Defense McNamara professed to be able to do just that with gradual responses to provocation and sophisticated management techniques. Furthermore, under President Kennedy, the Joint Chiefs lost their direct access to the president, and thus any real influence on decision making.[160] Even had they had that access, they were often bitterly divided by service parochialism. All of this played nicely into McNamara's hands. Similarly, the tepid, minimalist legal advice provided by Abram Chayes reinforced the adoption of McNamara's flawed strategy.

National-level decision makers require accurate and comprehensive legal advice prior to employing U.S. armed forces abroad.[161] In 1961, the State Department legal advisor was the best placed official to render this advice before President Kennedy chose to deepen U.S. military involvement in Indochina. The general formula for this advice is fairly simple. First, is there a domestic legal basis for employing U.S. forces abroad? In 1961, this was primarily a question of constitutional law. Second, is there a basis in international law for the proposed action? In this regard, there are four broad categories of permissible use of force: a UN-sanctioned enforcement action, a regional enforcement action, actions falling under the Article 2(4) threshold, and individual or

---

[159] VIETNAM 1962, *supra* note 28, at 301 (memo stating that "there will be neither total victory nor defeat but rather the development of an uneasy fluid stalemate").

[160] MCMASTER, *supra* note 33, at 5. Furthermore, Secretary McNamara, in learning all the wrong lessons from the Cuban Missile Crisis, was "[c]onvinced that military advice based on the objective of achieving victory was outmoded, even dangerous . . . ." *Id.* at 41.

[161] As it turns out, the Chayes memo was five days too late. On November 11, 1961, President Kennedy decided to commit U.S. advisors to South Vietnam in excess of the number permitted in the Geneva Accords. MCMASTER, *supra* note 33, at 37. This fact reinforces the theory that the secretary of state, like the secretary of defense, was merely giving the president the advice he wanted to hear.

collective self-defense pursuant to Article 51 of the UN Charter and customary international law. Measuring the Chayes memorandum against this simple framework, the legal advisor failed to fulfill his responsibility.

Concededly, sound legal analysis, especially in the national security arena, is dependent on availability of accurate facts. Thus, Chayes' legal advice was tainted by misunderstandings about the extent of the external threat to South Vietnam. Nonetheless, even Chayes seemed to recognize that South Vietnam was being victimized by actions directed by North Vietnam. North Vietnam exercised "restraint," however, by cloaking its aggression as an insurgency and delaying a conventional cross-border attack. Because Chayes was unable to conceive of such "indirect aggression" as triggering the right to self-defense, North Vietnam was, in his judgment, free to undermine the state of South Vietnam with relative impunity.

It is difficult to assess the actual impact of the Chayes memorandum on the National Command Authority. Some historians feel that President Kennedy resolved to limit U.S. involvement to "noncombat" roles (FARM GATE and other advisor activities notwithstanding) and then withdraw completely after being reelected.[162] While this may be wishful thinking on the part of Kennedy supporters (and Johnson/Nixon haters), the Chayes memorandum would have provided legal "top cover" for such a withdrawal and reinforced administration impulses to sharply limit the use of military force.

---

[162] RALPH G. MARTIN, A HERO FOR OUR TIME: AN INTIMATE STORY OF THE KENNEDY YEARS 499 (1983). Allegedly, Kennedy was persuaded in part by General Douglas A. MacArthur. Id. at 494 ("The old general was saying, as forcefully as he could, 'Never ever, ever put American soldiers on the mainland of Asia.'"); see also WILLIAM MANCHESTER, REMEMBERING KENNEDY, ONE BRIEF SHINING MOMENT 224 (1983) (recounting an exchange between President Kennedy and Senator Mike Mansfield). Kennedy had started to withdraw 1,000 troops at the end of 1963 and announced that the rest of the troops would be home by 1965. Interestingly, future chairman of the Joint Chiefs of Staff General Colin Powell was transferred back to the United States from Vietnam one month early in November 1961 as part of the 1,000 troops. COLIN POWELL, MY AMERICAN JOURNEY 100 (1995).

The perceived limitations of the Geneva Accords did impact USAF operations somewhat. USAF proposals to modify the T-37 jet trainer into a fighter-bomber for use in Vietnam were rejected, because it would have appeared to violate the Geneva Accords.[163] Jets were finally introduced in early 1965 in response to a rapidly deteriorating military situation.

Also, it is probably fair to conclude that this legal advice reinforced Secretary McNamara's desire to manage the conflict without taking decisive military action. With hindsight, it is clear that such a strategy was doomed to failure. As General Momyer writes, "[w]e prefer to make smaller decisions, win battles, and hope that the enemy will lose heart. . . . But that way leads to a series of Khe Sanhs and eventually in a free society to war-weariness and dissent."[164]

The 1964 and 1965 memoranda are less objectionable. Both correctly conclude that the executive power to deploy troops abroad in the national interest supported presidential plans for Vietnam. Nonetheless, the 1965 memorandum in particular was too limiting, hinting at the necessity to confine the war to South Vietnam. Taken together, all three of these memoranda arguably served to reinforce administration impulses to delay making tough decisions about Vietnam, to sharply limit the use of military force, and to use gradual measures intended to communicate with the enemy rather than attempt to defeat it.

If it is clearer now over thirty years after U.S. forces withdrew, it was nonetheless apparent even in 1961 that one could not fight a "sub-limited" war and win. Though muted, there were military voices recommending stronger action. General Momyer writes, "[b]y mid-1962, many other senior airmen and I were of the opinion that air strikes against the North Vietnamese homeland would be necessary if the war in South Vietnam were to be

---

[163] MOMYER, *supra* note 17, at 250. Also, the administration rejected sending T-33 jets in 1963 for the same reason. 3 FOREIGN RELATIONS OF THE UNITED STATES 1961-1963: VIETNAM 1963, at 197 (John P. Glennon et al. eds., 1991) (Vietnam Working Group memo stating that "[g]iving the Vietnamese jets would be a flat and obvious violation of the Geneva Accords").

[164] MOMYER, *supra* note 17, at 339.

ended."[165] Instead, the United States began a war of attrition in South Vietnam, largely ignoring North Vietnam, Laos, Cambodia, lines of communication, supply routes, and logistics depots. In short, we ignored all of the principles of war. It was a political failure that cost this nation over 58,000 lives and doomed South Vietnam to totalitarian domination. It was also a dereliction of duty by the nation's top legal advisors.

---

[165] MOMYER, *supra* note 17, at 12.

BIBLIOGRAPHY

Bowett, D. W. *Self-Defence in International Law.* Manchester: Manchester University Press, 1958.

Chayes, Abram, and Antonia Handler Chayes. *The New Sovereignty: Compliance with International Regulatory Agreements.* Cambridge: Harvard University Press, 1995.

2 *Digest of International Law*, edited by Green Haywood Hackworth. Washington D.C.: U.S. Government Printing Office, 1941.

12 *Digest of International Law*, edited by Marjorie M. Whiteman. Washington D.C.: U.S. Government Printing Office, 1971.

Erickson, Richard J. "Use of Armed Forces Abroad: An Operational Law Checklist." *The Reporter* (June 1988): 3-9.

16 *Foreign Relations of the United States 1952-1954: The Geneva Conference*, edited by John P. Glennon et al. Washington D.C.: U.S. Government Printing Office, 1981.

1 *Foreign Relations of the United States 1961-1963: Vietnam 1962*, edited by John P. Glennon et al. Washington D.C.: U.S. Government Printing Office, 1988.

2 *Foreign Relations of the United States 1961-1963: Vietnam 1963*, edited by John P. Glennon et al. Washington D.C.: U.S. Government Printing Office, 1990.

3 *Foreign Relations of the United States 1961-1963: Vietnam 1963*, edited by John P. Glennon et al. Washington D.C.: U.S. Government Printing Office, 1981.

1 *Foreign Relations of the United States 1964-1968: Vietnam 1964*, edited by John P. Glennon et al. Washington D.C.: U.S. Government Printing Office, 1992.

2 *Foreign Relations of the United States 1964-1968: Vietnam January-June 1965*, edited by Glenn W. LaFantasie et al. Washington D.C.: U.S. Government Printing Office, 1996.

Greenspan, Morris. *The Modern Law of Land Warfare.* Berkeley: University of California Press, 1959.

Karnow, Stanley. *Vietnam: A History.* New York: Viking Press, 1983.

Koh, Harold Hongju. "Why Do Nations Obey International Law?" 106 *The Yale Law Journal* (1997): 2599-2659.

Lewy, Gunther. "Evidence of Aggression from the North and the State Department White Papers." In *The Vietnam Debate*, edited by John Norton Moore, 89-99. Lanham, MD: University Press of America, 1990.

"Living History Interview with Abram Chayes." 7 *Transnational Law and Contemporary Problems* (Fall 1997): 459-486.

Manchester, William. *Remembering Kennedy, One Brief Shining Moment*. Boston: Little, Brown and Company, 1983.

Martin, Ralph G. *A Hero for our Time: An Intimate Story of the Kennedy Years*. New York: MacMillan, 1983.

McDougal, Myres S., and Florentino P. Feliciano. *Law and Minimum World Public Order*. New Haven: Yale University Press, 1961.

————. *The International Law of War: Transnational Coercion and World Public Order*. New Haven: New Haven Press, 1994.

McMaster, H. R. *Dereliction of Duty: Lyndon Johnson, Robert McNamara, The Joint Chiefs of Staff, and the Lies that Led to Vietnam*. New York: Harper Perennial, 1998.

Momyer, William W. *Air Power in Three Wars*, Washington D.C.: U.S. Government Printing Office, 1978.

Moore, John Norton. *Law and the Indo-China War*. Princeton, NJ: Princeton University Press, 1972.

————. "The Secret War in Central America and the Future of the World Order." 80 *American Journal of International Law* (1984): 43-280.

National Security Law, edited by John Norton Moore et al. Durham, NC: Carolina Academic Press, 1990.

O'Brien, William V. "U.S. Defensive Counterintervention in Collective Self-Defense of the Republic of Vietnam." In *The Vietnam Debate: A Fresh Look at the Argument*, edited by John Norton Moore, 99-142. Lanham, MD.: University Press of America, 1990.

The Pentagon Papers: The Defense Department History of the United States Decisionmaking on Vietnam (The Senator Gravel Edition). 4 volumes. Boston: Beacon Press, 1971.

Pike, Douglas. "The Origins of the War: Competing Perceptions." In *The Vietnam Debate: A Fresh Look at the Argument*, edited by John Norton Moore, 83-89. Lanham, MD: University Press of America, 1990.

Powell, Colin. *My American Journey*. New York: Ballantine Books, 1995.

Restatement of the Foreign Relations Laws of the United States: Tentative Draft No. 4. By the American Law Institute. Philadelphia: 1960.

Restatement of the Foreign Relations Laws of the United States: Proposed Final Draft. By the American Law Institute. Philadelphia: 1962.

Restatement (Third) of the Foreign Relations Laws of the United States. By the American Law Institute. Philadelphia: 1990.

Schacter, Oscar. "The Right of States to Use Armed Force." 82 *Michigan Law Review* (1984): 1620-1646.

Stone, Julius. *Legal Controls of International Conflict*. New York: Rinehart and Company Inc., 1959.

Turner, Robert F. "War and the Forgotten Executive Power Clause of the Constitution: A Review Essay of John Hart Ely's War and Responsibility." 34 *Virginia Journal of International Law* (Summer 1994): 903-979.

Vienna Convention on the Law of Treaties, May 23, 1969, U.N. Doc. A/CONF. 39/27, 8 I.L.M. 679.

VIII

Naval Interception Operations During the Indochina War: Lessons for Naval Interception Operations Today

Jane Gilliland Dalton[1]

INTRODUCTION

> Before we engage in any [war similar to the Indochina War] we must be sure, among other things, that we can use our sea power properly. If for any reason we find that we will be unable to do that, or even are in doubt about it, we owe it to ourselves to find a solution to our problem other than war.[2]

One aspect of the employment of sea power during the Indochina War that merits discussion consists of two naval interception operations: 1) Operation Market Time; and 2) the mining of Haiphong Harbor and other inland and territorial waters of North Vietnam. Though neither operation was identified at the time as a naval blockade, they both bore many characteristics of that traditional naval occupation.

---

[1] This paper was submitted in partial completion of the requirements for the LLM degree at the University of Virginia, Spring 1992. The author is a Captain in the Judge Advocate General's Corps of the United States Navy. She prepared the paper while attending the University of Virginia under the Navy Funded Graduate Education Program. The opinions, conclusions, and recommendations expressed or implied herein are solely those of the author and do not necessarily represent the Department of Defense, the Department of the Navy, or any other government agency.

[2] FRANK UHLIG, JR., VIETNAM: THE NAVAL STORY 8 (1986).

The law of naval blockade has been a frequently discussed and often analyzed topic. Many commentators in the last thirty years have struggled with the changing nature of blockade as states adapt new technologies to a centuries-old concept. One aspect of the law of naval blockade that has survived through the centuries, however, is that blockade is a *belligerent activity*—that is, a blockade legally may be imposed only during time of war.[3] Conversely, a state that imposes a blockade on another state may be deemed to have created, in effect, a state of war between them. At a minimum, the blockading state has "upped the ante" significantly in the threat coercion relationships between the two.

As a result, states have been most reluctant to use the word blockade to identify operations involving the interception of maritime traffic to or from another state, even when a *de facto* state of war exists between them. Rather, states often pick and choose among the various recognized characteristics of traditional blockade to craft an operation specifically tailored to certain goals, and then call the operation by any name other than *blockade*. This practice occurred during the Indochina War of 1965-1973.

The purpose of this chapter is not to conduct a comprehensive review of the law of naval blockade with the intention of defining a new law more applicable to current technology. That task has been conducted frequently and effectively in other studies.[4] Rather, after a review of naval interception operations in the Indochina War, this chapter will analyze three specific aspects of the law of naval blockade to determine what lessons the Indochina operations may have for naval interception operations today.

To avoid confusion, this chapter will use the phrase "naval interception operations" to refer to all situations in which one State attempts to restrict maritime traffic to or from itself or another

---

[3] For example, "[T]he term 'blockade' is a term unknown in the law except as it connotes a belligerent blockade in time of war." William D. Miller, *Belligerency and Limited War*, 62 INTERNATIONAL LAW STUDIES 164 (Richard B. Lillich & John Norton Moore eds., 1980). *See also* MARJORIE M. WHITEMAN, 10 DIGEST OF INTERNATIONAL LAW 869-70 (1968).

[4] *See, e.g.,* Michael G. Fraunces, *The International Law of Blockade: New Guiding Principles in Contemporary State Practice*, 101 YALE L.J. 893 (1992).

state, regardless of whether such actions comply with all the rules or characteristics of a traditional blockade.

NAVAL INTERCEPTION OPERATIONS IN VIETNAM

The United States Navy conducted many different operations during the Indochina War. Perhaps best known are its air attacks into North Vietnam from carriers offshore and its riverine operations, both of which have been extensively documented and analyzed. The navy conducted other traditional maritime tasks, such as naval gunfire support, surface-to-surface operations, transportation of friendly troops, and evacuation of civilians. In addition, the navy was largely involved in the interception of supplies going to North Vietnam, and from North Vietnam to the North Vietnamese and Viet Cong forces in the South. It is this interception effort with which this chapter is concerned.

It has been suggested that the policy makers in Washington never fully appreciated that about 50 percent of the enemy's cargo moved on the internal waterways and that the vast majority of military supplies to the North entered the port of Haiphong by sea.[5] When the United States began sending combat forces to Vietnam in 1964 and 1965, many people, both within and outside the navy, called for the blockade of North Vietnam's ports. Although blockades may not be 100 percent effective in preventing all resupply of an adversary, certainly any supplies that failed to reach the North would only have worked to the advantage of the U.S. and South Vietnamese forces fighting on the other side. Yet the decision was made not to blockade North Vietnam.[6]

Early in the war effort, some international lawyers believed that a blockade of North Vietnam would be illegal.[7] As Professor

---

[5] Vice Admiral Malcolm W. Cagle, USN, *Task Force 77 in Action Off Vietnam*, U.S. NAVAL INST. PROC. 66, 95, 107 (May 1972).

[6] UHLIG, *supra* note 2, at 4-5.

[7] *See, e.g.,* Captain Geoffrey E. Carlisle, USN, *The Interrelationship of International Law and United States Naval Operations in Southeast Asia*, 22 JAG J. 8, 11-12 (1967) (without a legal state of war between the United States and North Vietnam, a blockade would be of doubtful legality). By 1972, the official U.S. position was that a blockade would have been a legitimate measure

D. P. O'Connell pointed out, however, "If naval gunfire directed at bridges and railways is a legitimate exercise of the right of self-defense directed at destroying the logistical support for an 'armed attack', so might be the blockade of a port."[8] Nevertheless, O'Connell posited that the blockade of North Vietnamese ports was excluded on the principles of necessity and proportionality. He stated that under the actual circumstances of the case in 1968, it was not militarily necessary to close Haiphong, and the resulting interference with foreign shipping would not have been proportional to the defense of South Vietnam against armed attack.[9]

Some naval commentators strongly disagree. Rear Admiral John D. Hayes, writing in NAVAL REVIEW 1967, noted that "This decision [not to blockade the North] was an admission by the United States that, in undeclared limited war, it would not avail itself of belligerent rights at sea, and its powerful Navy is, therefore, unable to deny the use of the seas to an enemy."[10]

A naval historian also commented strongly on the decision not to blockade the North:

> In place of the silent, bloodless blockade, conducted by ships far beyond the reach of those they affected, we chose to bomb the enemy's supplies while they were in his towns, on his roads, or piled up under the jungle's triple canopy. The enemy was not helpless to counter that, and knew he was not, for he could see the wreckage of the hundreds of our aircraft he shot down. Indeed, between 1965 and 1968, 421 of the Fleet's fixed-wing aircraft were shot down by the enemy and 450 aviators were lost, many of whom became prisoners of war. . . . Still more serious than the POW issue or any of its aspects is the fact that at a time when the United States had incomparably

---

of self-defense under the traditional laws of war in an international conflict such as the one in Vietnam. *See infra* note 79 and accompanying text.

[8] D.P. O'CONNELL, THE INFLUENCE OF LAW ON SEAPOWER 94 (1975).

[9] *Id.*

[10] Rear Admiral John D. Hayes, *Sea Power, July 1965-June 1966: Commentary*, NAVAL REV. 1967, at 265 (1966).

the most powerful navy in the world, it permitted a foe who in effect had no navy at all to have equal access to the sea and thus both to his own distant forces and to his even more distant sources of arms, ammunition, and the other goods of war.[11]

The decision not to blockade the North Vietnamese ports necessitated the interdiction of coastal and inshore shipping of supplies after they left the North en route to the South. In other words, "[I]f we would not interfere with the shipping of our chosen enemies, we would have to interfere with that of our chosen friends."[12] Market Time, an extensive maritime interception effort, was the result.

Market Time: Coastal Surveillance and Interception

Market Time was, in effect, a defensive self-blockade of the South Vietnamese coast. The basic concepts were developed in March 1965 on the assumption that infiltration into South Vietnam by sea fell into two categories: 1) coastal junk traffic that mingled with over 50,000 civilian craft plying the coastal waters of South Vietnam; and 2) trawler-size or larger vessels, believed to originate in North Vietnam and Communist China, which approached the coast on a generally perpendicular line.[13] To interdict the coastal traffic, the U.S. Navy would assist and train the Vietnamese navy in conducting searches of junk traffic. To interdict the sea-going trawler-size vessels, the U.S. Navy would establish a conventional patrol using U.S. Navy and Coast Guard ships and aircraft and South Vietnamese Navy Sea Force ships. The plan was approved by the Joint Chiefs of Staff on March 16, and the coastal patrol by ships and aircraft began that day.

In April 1965, the Government of South Vietnam declared a Defensive Sea Area within its 3NM territorial sea.[14] Non-innocent

---

[11] UHLIG, *supra* note 2, at 6-8.

[12] *Id.* at 5.

[13] Commander R.L. Schreadley, USN, *The Naval War in Vietnam, 1950-1970, in* UHLIG, *supra* note 2, at 274, 283.

[14] Viet-Nam Decree on Sea Surveillance, April 27, 1965, 4 I.L.M. 461 (1965).

passage, that is, passage prejudicial to the peace, good order, and security of the Republic of Vietnam, was forbidden. Any vessel not clearly engaged in innocent passage was subject to visit and search, arrest, and disposition in accordance with the laws of South Vietnam and accepted principles of international law. The decree listed cargoes that would be subject to seizure unless their legitimate destination could be identified. The list included weapons, ammunition, communications equipment, and explosives, chemicals with military uses, and medical supplies and foodstuffs of North Vietnamese, Chinese Communist, or Soviet-bloc origin. Fiscal, immigration, and customs regulations would be enforced on all ships within the 12NM contiguous zone. Those regulations contained provisions that the entry of all personnel, material, or merchandise was authorized only through recognized routes or ports of entry. Suspicious vessels within the contiguous zone were subject to visit and search, arrest, and disposition as described above.

Beyond the contiguous zone, Vietnam would act to prevent and punish infringements of its laws by its own vessels and by vessels reasonably believed to be South Vietnamese, though flying a foreign flag or refusing to show a flag. If a searched vessel proved to be foreign, the Government of South Vietnam would pay prompt and reasonable compensation for any loss or damage sustained. The decree invoked the doctrine of hot pursuit in the case of vessels within the territory, territorial sea, or contiguous zone and suspected of infringing Vietnamese regulations within the territory or territorial sea of South Vietnam.[15]

On May 11, 1965, the Government of South Vietnam granted formal authorization for U.S. Navy Market Time units to implement the provisions of the April 27 Sea Surveillance Decree.[16]

Four coastal zones were created along the 1200-mile South Vietnamese coast, extending from the seventeenth parallel in the North to the Brevie Line in the Gulf of Thailand. Five coastal

---

[15] *Id.*

[16] Schreadley, *supra* note 13, at 283-85.

surveillance centers coordinated U.S. and Vietnamese navy coastal surveillance units within the four zones. Market Time's primary mission was "to conduct surveillance, gun fire support, visit and search, and other operations . . . along the coast of the Republic of Vietnam in order to assist the Republic of Vietnam in detection and prevention of Communist infiltration from the sea."[17]

A secondary mission of Market Time forces was to improve the Vietnamese navy's counterinsurgency capabilities and to secure the coastal regions and major rivers to defeat the Communist insurgency. The operation was conducted on the "principle that eventually responsibility for all naval operations in Vietnam would be returned to the Vietnamese Navy."[18]

Market Time operations began with completely random patrols, with most attention given to boarding and night operations. Vietnamese navy liaison officers were assigned to U.S. vessels patrolling in areas where junk traffic was heavy. The officers assisted in inspections and boardings and also explained to the population the purpose of the operations. Inspections consisted of checking the papers[19] and looking into a junk or open sampan from

---

[17] *Id.* at 286. Market Time was supplemented by other naval operations with different code names and different missions, but all directed toward interdicting the supply of men and materiel from the North into South Vietnam. For example, an extensive river patrol was established with 120 river patrol craft operating from LSTs anchored off the mouths of the major rivers. The patrols extended twenty-five miles upriver with the objective of controlling traffic through the river mouths. *Id.* In addition, in February 1967, the mining of selected river areas in North Vietnam (not including Haiphong) was authorized to assist in the reduction of North Vietnamese coastal traffic. By mid-April, five river mouths had been sown with air-delivered mines. The North's three main deep water ports, however, were not authorized for mining. It soon became apparent that traffic had virtually dried up in the five mined rivers, and the North stopped moving war supplies by coastal barges in those areas. While apparently accepting defeat in this endeavor, the North simply moved inland, using trucks at night over unpaved roads through the jungle to continue to supply its forces in the South. Cagle, *supra* note 5, at 95.

[18] Schreadley, *supra* note 13, at 286.

[19] The use of identification papers was not particularly helpful in identifying Viet Cong among the local fishermen. An officer involved in Market Time operations in the Gulf of Thailand in 1965 noted:

the deck of the patrol boat. Boardings consisted of an actual search of the boat—entering the after cabin and fish holds to determine what was on board.[20]

The Vietnamese Market Time planners experimented with the use of designated prohibited zones to simplify surveillance. The program was not especially successful since the zones often encompassed the best fishing grounds and fishermen who lived inshore of the zones, in theory, could not pass through them to get to sea. Thus the livelihood of the local fishermen was threatened. In addition, the small junks and sampans had no navigational equipment with which to accurately place their position with respect to the prohibited zones. While the regulation of the zones was a responsibility of the Vietnamese navy, U.S. forces encouraged the establishment of reasonable zones with strict enforcement. Nevertheless, American forces tailored their assistance to the Vietnamese forces to match the degree of enforcement shown by the Vietnamese.[21]

It was difficult to know how effective the interception operations were, largely due to the unreliability of raw statistics. Boarding hundreds of junks that never depart more than two or three miles from their home ports increases the total of junk boardings reported, but decreases effective surveillance of the entire area. Cursory searches took less time and enhanced the statistics but, again, could have a negative effect on the actual effectiveness of the operations.[22] The coastal surveillance operations did appear to be quite successful in discouraging enemy

---

Sample identification papers helped to detect incorrect papers; however, even though the local authorities provided us with long lists of known or suspected Viet Cong, we are not aware of any instance where inspection of papers led to the capture of any Viet Cong during the entire first year of operations in the Gulf. In any event, a government supporter today may be a Viet Cong tomorrow, and in a guerrilla type of operation the use of a rather loose ID card system is of questionable value.

Captain James A. Hodgman, USCG, *Market Time in the Gulf of Thailand, in* UHLIG, *supra* note 2, at 308, 326.

[20] *Id.* at 322-23.

[21] *Id.* at 326-27.

[22] *Id.* at 327.

attempts to "pierce the screen" off the South Vietnamese coast. Those attempts that were made were largely unsuccessful.[23] Yet the massive Tet Offensive of 1968 demonstrated that there existed a major weakness in the interception operations to that date. Obviously great amounts of supplies had been transported to Vietnam to carry out the offensive and had entered and traversed South Vietnam on navigable waters. The failure was blamed on three causes: 1) a major American intelligence failure, which neglected to detect that North Vietnam was freely using Cambodian ports for the supply of its forces in the field;[24] 2) the lack of operational and logistic capability to launch a mobile patrol force along the Cambodian border; and 3) the reluctance of Vietnamese ground force commanders to commit their troops to aggressive river bank patrols in support of naval operations on narrow, restricted waterways.[25] Finally, in late 1968, Operation Sea Lords (Southeast Asia Lake, Ocean, River, and Delta Strategy) was launched to create an inland naval patrol along the Cambodian border to interdict Communist infiltration routes where they crossed or utilized navigable waterways.[26]

The coastal surveillance force did have one major success during the Tet Offensive, when it thwarted an attempt to infiltrate into the South four steel-hulled trawler-type vessels filled with arms. Three vessels were destroyed and the fourth was forced to turn back before entering the contiguous zone.[27] D. P. O'Connell

---

[23] UHLIG, *supra* note 2, at 5; Hodgman, *supra* note 19, at 341. One source describes successful interceptions during 1965-1967, when several trawlers and other steel-hulled vessels were destroyed and military weapons and supplies were recovered. From January 1966 to July 1967, over 700,000 vessels were inspected or boarded by the combined patrol force. No trawler infiltration attempts were detected from July 1967 through the end of the year and from March 1968 to August 1969. EDWARD J. MAROLDA & G. WESLEY PRYCE, III, A SHORT HISTORY OF THE UNITED STATES NAVY AND THE SOUTHEAST ASIAN CONFLICT 1950-1975, at 48-49 (1984).

[24] UHLIG, *supra* note 2, at 5.

[25] Schreadley, *supra* note 13, at 292.

[26] *Id.* at 294-95.

[27] *Id.* at 293. A fifth trawler was spotted by aircraft out to sea, but reversed course and returned north before reaching South Vietnamese waters. MAROLDA & PRYCE, *supra* note 23, at 49.

pointed to this incident as an example of the circumspection employed by the surveillance forces so as not to conflict with international law. Some theories hold that the doctrine of hot pursuit only applies to vessels that have committed offenses in the territorial sea or inland waters. The Vietnamese Decree on Sea Surveillance recognized this limitation and applied the doctrine only to those vessels encountered within the territory, territorial sea, or contiguous zone and suspected of infringing Vietnamese regulations within South Vietnam's territory or territorial sea.[28] Under that doctrine, it would not be appropriate to pursue and punish an incoming vessel for breaches before it enters the coastal state's waters.

Thus, in this case, naval action was taken only against those vessels engaged in the contiguous zone, and those that escaped to the high seas were not subjected to hot pursuit.[29]

Throughout the period of 1965-1968, Market Time resources grew and patrol tactics and operating procedures were developed and refined. The Market Time operations relied on a mixture of small, medium, and large patrol craft and of patrol aircraft to provide maximum coverage, detection, and interception. From the first months of 1965, when fifteen destroyers and minesweepers were assigned to the patrol, the operations expanded to include radar picket escorts to replace the destroyers, twenty-six Coast Guard 82-foot cutters and fifteen Coast Guard high endurance cutters, eighty-four 50-foot Swift boats, and fifty-two other vessels of various sizes and capabilities. Aerial observation was conducted

---

[28] *Supra* notes 14-15 and accompanying text.

[29] D.P. O'Connell, International Law and Contemporary Naval Operations 12 (1971) (unpublished manuscript on file at University of Virginia Law Library). Even this action exceeded the terms of the Vietnamese decree somewhat, by encountering ships as they entered the contiguous zone, before any breaches had occurred in the territory or territorial seas. For a discussion of whether hot pursuit applies to offenses committed within the contiguous zone, *see* D.P. O'CONNELL, 2 THE INTERNATIONAL LAW OF THE SEA 1081-85, 1089 (1984). For a discussion of whether peacetime ocean divisions were appropriately applied in the Indochina conflict, *see infra* section "Extension of Defensive Measures Beyond the Contiguous Zone."

by aircraft flying from carriers, the Philippines, Thailand, and seaplane tenders. Coastal-based surface search radar added to the detection capabilities.[30]

The patrol was divided into three zones: 1) an air surveillance sector farthest out to sea; 2) an outer surface barrier patrolled by the large U.S. ships; and 3) an inner, shallow-water barrier patrolled by U.S. and South Vietnamese craft including coastal junks. In 1966, a fourth zone was created to provide defense and patrol at key South Vietnamese ports.[31]

Success also required reliance on Vietnamese authorities ashore for port security. Smaller patrol vessels were unable to thoroughly search large, over-laden junks. Effectively, the patrol craft were able only to check the junks' manifests for form and substance, spot-check their cargoes, and ensure they were on the trade route between the ports listed on the manifests. Consequently, the patrol forces had to rely on coastal authorities with the responsibility of ensuring that no contraband moved through the government-held villages and towns.[32]

Market Time operations required detailed rules of engagement to permit effective action against the enemy while protecting innocent Vietnamese from victimization by combat operations. The rules demonstrated that limited war in general requires more command judgment than does conventional war, when identification of the enemy is less of a problem. For example, the rules had to provide for positive identification of North Vietnamese vessels, which were considered belligerent in all circumstances, and other foreign vessels, which were only prohibited from delivering certain cargoes as listed in the South Vietnamese Surveillance Decree. They had to delineate the specific circumstances under which vessels were not deemed to be clearly engaged in innocent passage, and they had to distinguish between "immediate pursuit" (pursuit of a vessel that has initiated an attack) and "hot pursuit" (pursuit of a vessel that has breached the law). They required great maturity and judgment by the young

---

[30] MAROLDA & PRYCE, *supra* note 23, at 45-47.

[31] *Id.* at 45.

[32] Hodgman, *supra* note 19, at 328-29.

officers commanding the patrol craft but were generally effective in safeguarding noncombatant Vietnamese and in effectively prosecuting the combat patrols.[33]

A final note on the Market Time Coastal Surveillance operations is that to a large degree they were conducted against an enemy that lacked the normal paraphernalia of naval warfare. The operations would have been much more difficult had the North Vietnamese been able to attack the surveillance forces by air or to infiltrate by submarine.[34] As it happened, by mid-1968 it appears the North was probably deterred from using seaborne infiltration as a major means of supply. Instead, supplies were freely shipped through the Cambodian port of Sihanoukville, and the Ho Chi Minh Trail had become a well-established supply system. Yet the Market Time operation had accomplished its primary mission of limiting the enemy's use of the sea to support his politico-military offensive against South Vietnam.[35]

Mining Haiphong Harbor

Very early on during the Indochina campaign, naval and military experts concluded that the *single military action* that would impact North Vietnam most would be the closing of Haiphong Harbor. At least 85 percent of North Vietnam's military strength entered Haiphong by sea.[36] Yet repeated military proposals to mine the harbor were consistently denied for two reasons: 1) it was feared that mining would escalate the war and

---

[33] O'Connell, unpublished manuscript, *supra* note 29, at 13; Hodgman, *supra* note 19, at 329.

[34] Hodgman, *supra* note 19, at 341.

[35] MAROLDA & PRYCE, *supra* note 23, at 49.

[36] Cagle, *supra* note 5, at 107. Most of the arms and supplies used by North Vietnam's forces in the South were foreign-made, largely from the Soviet Union and China. They entered North Vietnam through its three main ports— Haiphong, Cam Pha, and Hon Gai. Rail and road links between North Vietnam and China also existed but, at least early in the war effort, they carried only 15 percent of the total supplies. Commander (senior grade) Erick Luckow, Royal Danish Navy, *Victory Over Ignorance and Fear: The U.S. Minelaying Attack on North Vietnam*, NAVAL WAR C. REV. 17 (Jan.-Feb. 1982).

risk confrontation with Russia, Communist China, or both; and 2) even if mining succeeded in closing the harbor, it was believed that North Vietnam would find alternative routes by which to resupply.[37]

Finally, however, in 1972, U.S. policy changed. In May of that year, President Nixon ordered the virtual isolation of North Vietnam from external Communist support. His goal, aside from the military objective of interdicting military supply of the North, was to end North Vietnamese intransigence at the Paris peace negotiations. Air-delivered magnetic-acoustic mines were dropped in the river approaches to Haiphong and other major North Vietnamese ports.[38]

The mining was strictly limited to North Vietnam's internal and claimed (12NM) territorial seas. It did not preclude access to neutral ports or coasts and did not interfere in any respect with neutral shipping on the high seas.[39] On May 8, President Nixon announced the mining operations, and ships were given a seventy-two hour period to leave port before the mines were activated. Initial phases of the mining were completed by May 9.[40]

---

[37] Cagle, *supra* note 5, at 107.

[38] MAROLDA & PRYCE, *supra* note 23, at 33.

[39] Lieutenant Commander Frank B. Swayze, USN, *Traditional Principles of Blockade in Modern Practice: United States Mining of Internal and Territorial Waters of North Vietnam*, 29 JAG J. 143, 163 (1977).

[40] Lieutenant Commander J.B. Finkelstein, USN, *Naval and Maritime Events, January 1972-June 1972*, U.S. NAVAL INST. PROC. 45, 58 (May 1973). Even as planning for the mining operations began, U.S. planners anticipated they would also be responsible for clearing the minefields once the interception operations terminated. This fact was taken into account when decisions as to types of mines, settings, and locations were made. In fact, the January 27, 1973, cease-fire agreement included a protocol in which the United States agreed to sweep all mines it had laid. Sweep operations ultimately became a bargaining chip in the post-cease-fire period and were suspended when North Vietnam showed intransigence over the return of U.S. prisoners of war. The use of the sweep operations as a bargaining tool is credited with contributing to the release of the prisoners of war after January 1973. Rear Admiral Brian McCauley, USN, *Operation End Sweep*, U.S. NAVAL INST. PROC. 19 (Mar. 1974). Operation End Sweep, as the mine clearance operation was called, lasted six months. On July 18, 1973, the mission was completed, and the U.S. Seventh Fleet departed North

When they explained the mining campaign, President Nixon and his spokesmen were very careful to emphasize to the Soviets and other nations that their ships would not be harmed so long as they did not attempt to enter the minefields. They implied that the United States retained the option of supplementing the passive minefields with active air strike interdiction if attempts were made to unload the supplies onto lightering craft, but ships themselves would not be stopped or bombed.[41] According to one commentator, the mining of Haiphong and other Vietnamese harbors did not "at that time purport to constitute the establishment of a 'blockade'" of those ports.[42] The naval patrols outside the ports were there to warn incoming merchant vessels of the danger but not to conduct visit and search. If the vessel chose to continue into the harbor through the minefield, it was free to do so. Likewise if a vessel chose to depart Haiphong after the three-day grace period and attempt a minefield transit, it would not be stopped if it successfully reached international waters. Only if it attempted to transfer cargo to a North Vietnamese vessel would the patrolling U.S. Navy craft intervene.[43]

The mining had an immediate effect. On May 10, it was reported that a Soviet ship en route to North Vietnam had changed course; on May 12, reports stated that several merchant ships en route to the North had apparently changed course to avoid the mine fields; and on May 23, the Defense Department asserted that all of the twenty to twenty-five ships en route to North Vietnam when the harbors were mined had changed course and headed elsewhere.[44]

Vietnamese territorial waters for the last time. MAROLDA & PRYCE, *supra* note 23, at 92-93.

[41] Luckow, *supra* note 36, at 19-20.

[42] HOWARD S. LEVIE, MINE WARFARE AT SEA 152-53 (1992).

[43] *Id.*

[44] Finkelstein, *supra* note 40, at 58-60. The fear that mining Haiphong would lead to escalation of the war and the possible involvement of the Soviet Union and/or China proved unfounded. Just seventeen days after President Nixon announced the mining, the United States and the Soviet Union signed an innovative agreement to prevent naval incidents at sea and a day later signed a

From May to December 1972, no large merchant vessels entered or departed North Vietnam's harbors. It has been estimated that North Vietnamese imports were reduced by 30 percent and the supplies available in the combat areas were between 800 and 1,500 tons per day less than they had been previously.[45] There was not a single reported incident of damage or destruction of a foreign merchant vessel during the operation. The only reported casualty was underwater damage to a U.S. vessel, which struck a mine that had broken from its moorings while the vessel was engaged in mine-laying operations.[46] One attempt to lighter cargo to shore from ships anchored outside the minefields was halted when U.S. fleet ships and aircraft did, indeed, intercept and destroy the lightering craft.[47]

ISSUES OF NAVAL INTERCEPTION OPERATIONS THEN AND NOW

Goal Attainment and Legal Justification

The two primary goals of the naval interception operations in the Indochina War were: 1) to prevent the supply of North Vietnamese and Viet Cong forces in the South from the North; and 2) to prevent military supplies from reaching North Vietnam by sea from other countries, primarily China and the Soviet Union. Overriding all was the concern that, whatever actions the United States decided to take, the Soviet Union and Communist China not be provoked into entering the conflict directly with military forces. Whether mining Haiphong Harbor or blockading the North in 1965

---

new arms limitation pact. *Id.* at 60. On June 2, a Russian-speaking American on board *USS McMorris* (DE-1036) used a loudspeaker to warn the Soviet surveillance trawler IZMERITELL away from a mine field near the port of Vinh, North Vietnam. The Russians reportedly thanked the Americans and sailed away. *Id.* at 60.

[45] LEVIE, *supra* note 42, at 148.

[46] Commander Bruce A. Clark, JAGC, USN, *Recent Evolutionary Trends Concerning Naval Interdiction of Seaborne Commerce as a Viable Sanctioning Device*, 27 JAG J. 160, 173 (1973).

[47] MAROLDA & PRYCE, *supra* note 23, at 89.

would have precipitated Soviet or Chinese involvement cannot be known. Less than twenty years earlier, largely due to mistaken estimates of Chinese intentions, U.S. and UN forces suffered dearly when the Chinese actively joined the North Koreans and nearly pushed MacArthur's forces off the Korean Peninsula. Certainly by 1972, however, relations with both China and the Soviets were improving, and the decision to mine Haiphong Harbor resulted only in weak protests from both countries.[48]

Legal Justification: Market Time

There was little need for independent legal justification of the Market Time operations. Customary international law of the time, as reflected in international instruments,[49] permitted such police-type measures. Although aerial surveillance of surface craft occurred beyond the contiguous zone, the actual interception of vessels occurred within South Vietnam's 3NM territorial sea and 12NM contiguous zone. In a peacetime setting, customary law provided for a state to take affirmative actions within its territorial sea to prevent non-innocent passage. Any threat or use of force against the sovereignty, territorial integrity, or political independence of the coastal state by a state transiting the coastal state's territorial sea was *per se* prejudicial to the peace, good order, and security of the coastal state and was, therefore, not innocent passage. Within the contiguous zone, a state could prevent and punish infringement of its customs, fiscal, immigration, and sanitary laws. The measures taken by South Vietnam were legal under the 1958 Geneva Law of the Sea Conventions. They were no more than police measures designed to enforce domestic sanitary, fiscal, and customs laws throughout the

---

[48] Luckow, *supra* note 36, at 20-21; LEVIE, *supra* note 42, at 147-48.

[49] *E.g.,* Convention on the Territorial Sea and the Contiguous Zone, Geneva, Apr. 29, 1958, 15 U.S.T. 1606, T.I.A.S. 5639, 516 U.N.T.S. 205; Convention on the High Seas, Geneva, Apr. 19, 1958, 13 U.S.T. 2312, T.I.A.S. 5200, 450 U.N.T.S. 82.

contiguous zone and on the high seas against ships suspected of being South Vietnamese.[50]

Moreover, and even more importantly, a state always maintains the inherent right of individual and collective self-defense under customary international law as reflected in Article 51 of the UN Charter. The evidence now is uncontroverted that as early as 1959, North Vietnam was engaged in the massive supply of Viet Cong forces in the South and in directing and participating in the destruction of the South Vietnamese regime.[51] The true justification for Market Time was, therefore, to be found in the justification for the overall war effort, that is, to halt armed aggression from the North against the political independence and territorial integrity of the South. The operation was referred to by its code name, Market Time, and was not identified as in any way related to a blockade.

Legal Justification: Mining Operations

The mining of Haiphong and North Vietnamese internal and territorial waters carried different legal implications from those of the Market Time operations. The United States carefully refrained from use of the term *blockade,* referring instead to the *interdiction* of supplies, the *prevention* of access, and the *denial of permission* to land supplies.[52] The mining was justified in two ways: 1)

---

[50] O'Connell, unpublished manuscript, *supra* note 29, at 11-13. One author finds additional justification for the Market Time operations in the right of a state to suspend the right of innocent passage through its territorial waters for security reasons. Carlisle, *supra* note 7, at 12-13. This author disagrees with Carlisle that the right of temporary suspension of innocent passage justified Market Time operations. Innocent passage was never formally suspended by South Vietnam, and the interference with shipping was certainly more than temporary.

[51] *See generally* THE VIETNAM DEBATE: A FRESH LOOK AT THE ARGUMENTS, pts. 2-3 (John Norton Moore ed., 1990). South Vietnam was not a member of the United Nations during this period but could avail itself of the inherent, customary law of self-defense, which was incorporated into Article 51.

[52] *See, e.g.,* Address by President Nixon, *Denying Hanoi the Means to Continue Aggression*, and 66 DEP'T. ST. BULL. 747, 749 (May 29, 1972); *U.N. Notified of New Measures against North Vietnam,* 66 DEP'T. ST. BULL. 750-51

President Nixon announced the "sole purpose" of the action was to protect the 60,000 U.S. troops remaining in South Vietnam from the 1972 Easter offensive onslaught and to prevent the forceful imposition of a Communist government on South Vietnam;[53] and 2) as a measure of collective self-defense under Article 51 of the UN Charter.[54]

Experts in international law disagreed as to whether the operation was a blockade and whether it was legal under international law.[55] Though the United States refrained from using the term *blockade*, the operation was nevertheless tailored to comply with some requirements of a traditional blockade: the action was announced to the world by a competent authority; the geographical limits were specified; and nonbelligerent shipping was given three daylight periods in which to depart before the mines were armed.

In sum, the mining operation apparently was crafted to balance optimum goal attainment with what was perceived at the time would best achieve optimum acceptance by the international community.

> By calling it an interdiction rather than a blockade the President did not open the door for a legal challenge to his authority to order the operation without a formal declaration of war. By confining the measures to internal and territorial waters he could not be accused of interfering with free navigation on the high seas. By complying with some of the rules of blockade, for example, notification of nonbelligerents and providing a period for neutral shipping to evacuate the

---

(May 29, 1972) (U.N. DOC. S/10631); *Secretary of Defense Laird's News Conference*, 66 DEP'T. ST. BULL. 761, 764 (May 29, 1972).

[53] Address by President Nixon, *supra* note 52, at 747, 749.

[54] *U.N. Notified of New Measures Against North Vietnam, supra* note 52, at 750-51.

[55] *See, e.g.,* Abram Chayes, *Mr. Nixon Avoids Use of Blockade*, WASH. POST, May 14, 1972, at B6; Stephen M. Schwebel, *quoted in* Jesse W. Lewis, Jr., *U.S. Tells U.N. Council of Acts Against Hanoi*, WASH. POST, May 9, 1972, at A10; John Norton Moore, *A Professor on the Law of Blockade*, WASH. POST, May 21, 1972, at 21.

ports, he took precautions to minimize the risk of direct confrontation with the U.S.S.R. and China.[56]

Traditional Law of Naval Blockade

Although some early attempts were made to codify the rules relating to blockades,[57] the law of naval blockade has developed almost exclusively as customary international law.[58] Blockade may be defined as "a belligerent operation to prevent vessels and/or aircraft of all nations, enemy as well as neutral, from entering or exiting specified ports, airfields or coastal areas belonging to, occupied by, or under the control of an enemy nation."[59] The focus

---

[56] Luckow, *supra* note 36, at 22.

[57] The Declaration of Paris, April 16, 1856 ("Blockades, in order to be binding, must be effective"), *reprinted in* LEON FRIEDMAN, 1 THE LAW OF WAR: A DOCUMENTARY HISTORY 156-57 (1972) (the United States was not a signatory to the Declaration of Paris); Naval Conference of London, Declaration Concerning the Laws of Naval War, Feb. 26, 1909, Arts. 1-21, *reprinted in id.* at 402-05 (this declaration was not ratified by the United States or the United Kingdom and never entered into force).

[58] W.T. Mallison & Sally Mallison, *A Survey of the International Law of Naval Blockade*, U.S. NAVAL INST. PROC. 44, 45 (Feb. 1976). The *San Remo Manual on International Law Applicable to Armed Conflicts at Sea*, paragraphs 93-104, provides the most recent comprehensive review of the law of blockade. Prepared by a group of international lawyers and naval experts, the *Manual* provides a contemporary restatement of international law applicable to armed conflicts at sea. This author considers the discussion of blockade in the *Manual* to be generally reflective of the current state of customary international law. SAN REMO MANUAL ON INTERNATIONAL LAW APPLICABLE TO ARMED CONFLICTS AT SEA (Louise Doswald-Beck ed., 1995), paras. 93-104 [hereinafter SAN REMO MANUAL].

[59] Office of the Chief of Naval Operations, Department of the Navy, THE COMMANDER'S HANDBOOK ON THE LAW OF NAVAL OPERATIONS 7-7 (NWP 1-14M) [hereinafter COMMANDER'S HANDBOOK]. The *Commander's Handbook* is the definitive work on the law of naval operations for the U.S. Navy. The work is useful as an authoritative description of state practice and, thus, as an indication of customary international law. For a more detailed discussion of the *Commander's Handbook* and its relation to international law, *see* A.V. Lowe, *The Commander's Handbook on the Law of Naval Operations and the Contemporary Law of the Sea*, 64 INTERNATIONAL LAW STUDIES: THE LAW OF NAVAL OPERATIONS 109 (Horace B. Robertson, Jr. ed., 1991).

of a blockade is on ships, not on cargo, although the law of contraband, which focuses on cargo, is closely associated with the law of blockade. Blockades frequently also include restrictions on types of cargo under the contraband rules.

Over the centuries, a number of criteria have been identified as necessary to conduct a legal blockade:

— Blockades must be effective, maintained by a force sufficient to prevent access to the enemy's coast;
— Blockades must be established by an appropriate authority;
— Communication must be given to neutral governments and local authorities of the date the blockade will begin, the geographic limits of the blockade, and the grace period during which neutral vessels may exit;
— The blockade must be applied impartially to the ships of all states; and
— The blockade may not bar access to neutral ports or coasts.[60]

Through the years there has also developed, however, considerable disagreement as to other characteristics that may or may not be necessary for a legal blockade:

— That a blockade must be conducted by surface vessels either alone or in conjunction with other means;[61]
— That a declaration of war must of necessity accompany or presage a blockade;[62]

---

[60] Swayze, *supra* note 39, at 154-55. *See also* COMMANDER'S HANDBOOK, *supra* note 59, at 7-8; Fraunces, *supra* note 4, at 895-99; Naval Conference of London, *supra* note 57, at Arts. 1-21. *But see* Fraunces, *supra* note 4, at 912-17 (suggesting new guiding principles of blockade should be threefold: impartiality, notice, and reasonableness). The five requirements noted above are consistent with the provisions set out in the *San Remo Manual* for the proper conduct of a blockade. SAN REMO MANUAL, *supra* note 58.

[61] LEVIE, *supra* note 42, at 150-51 (discussing various doctrines that require the presence of surface vessels in blockade). For this and the following characteristics, cf. SAN REMO MANUAL, *supra* note 58.

[62] Schwebel, *supra* note 55, at A10. In 1967, the director of the International Law Division of the U.S. Navy also took this position: "If a legal state of war existed between the United States and North Vietnam we could immediately

— That a blockade may only be conducted on the high seas;[63]
— That a blockade may not be conducted from long distances away from the blockaded state;[64]
— That a blockade may not be conducted solely by means of mines;[65] and
— That a blockade must involve the stopping and searching of suspect vessels and their capture and condemnation in prize if found to be violating the terms of the blockade.[66]

With these characteristics in mind, this chapter will turn to an analysis of the Market Time and mining operations.

Nature of the Market Time Operations and Attendant Issues

Even though the purpose of Market Time operations was to blockade or interdict enemy infiltration, the operations did not constitute a traditional blockade. First, the emphasis was on cargo and contraband rather than shipping (with the exception of North Vietnamese vessels, which were hostile in any event). Second, traditional blockade contemplates impeding access to coasts or ports controlled by the adversary, not one's own coasts or ports. One might note, however, that since a belligerent nation is entitled to conduct a blockade in the territorial waters and contiguous zone of an enemy state, it may certainly do so within its own waters to preserve national integrity and security.

---

blockade the port of Hai-Phong as a belligerent right of warfare. Without a state of war, such a blockade would be of doubtful legality. A similar analysis could be made with respect to mining harbors, contraband, neutrality, and the right of visit and search on the high seas." Carlisle, *supra* note 7, at 11-12.

[63] *Secretary of Defense Laird's News Conference of May 10, supra* note 52, at 761, 764; Schwebel, *supra* note 55.

[64] *See* Myres S. McDougal & Florentino P. Feliciano, Law and Minimum World Public Order 491 (1961); O'Connell, *supra* note 29, at 1150.

[65] Castren, The Present Law of War and Neutrality 300-01 (1954), *quoted in* Whiteman, *supra* note 3, at 865; Levie, *supra* note 42, at 151-52.

[66] Daniel Z. Henkin, *quoted in* Terence Smith, *Legal Basis Cited for Nixon Action*, N.Y. Times, May 9, 1972, at 18.

The emerging issue with implications for future naval interception operations is whether such defensive actions should be defined and limited by oceans law terms applicable to peacetime, such as the territorial sea and contiguous zone. It appears clear that the drafters of the South Vietnamese decree were aiming to give precise effect to the 1958 Geneva Convention on the Territorial Sea and Contiguous Zone. In addition, a number of legal and naval scholars at the time couched their writings in such terms. Dr. and Mrs. Mallison, for example, described the Market Time operations as "an invocation of municipal police powers to prevent military infiltration through a state's contiguous zone."[67] In today's terms, such defensive activities would be justified through the provisions relating to the territorial sea and the contiguous zone found in the 1982 United Nations Convention on the Law of the Sea.[68]

In 1971, D. P. O'Connell, using the same peacetime oceans divisions, opined that defensive naval operations should be confined to the territorial sea and contiguous zone.

The experience of the past twenty years tends to verify the hypothesis that, except on occasions when the balance of deterrence which exists between the great powers is threatened, as at the time of the Cuban quarantine operation, hostilities not

---

[67] Mallison & Mallison, *supra* note 58, at 50. A different, but related, form of naval warfare occurs in the defensive mining of one's own coast to thwart a blockade or an invasion. North Korea, North Vietnam, and Iraq have all conducted this type of operation. *See, e.g.,* James J. Hoblitzell, *The Lessons of Mine Warfare*, U.S. NAVAL INST. PROC. 33, 36 (Dec. 1962) (North Korean defensive mining at Wonsan); J.M. Martin, *We Still Haven't Learned*, U.S. NAVAL INST. PROC. 64 (July 1991) (Iraqi defensive mining).

[68] Arts. 19, 21 & 25, United Nations Convention on the Law of the Sea, U.N. A/CONF. 62/122, 21 I.L.M. 1261 (1982). Done at Montego Bay, Jamaica, on Dec. 10, 1982, entered into force Nov. 1994. The United States has signed but not ratified or acceded to the Law of the Sea Convention. In March 1983, however, President Reagan announced that the Convention contained provisions "with respect to traditional uses of the oceans which generally confirm existing maritime law and practice. . . ." He said the United States would accept and act consistently with the provisions of the Convention dealing with navigation, overflight, high seas freedoms, and the exclusive economic zone. Proclamation No. 5030, 48 Fed. Reg. 10,601, 16 U.S.C.A. §1453n (1983).

amounting to war must be confined to the territorial sea, or at least to the contiguous zone. The understanding appears to be that limited war must not escape beyond the territories of the contending parties, so as to threaten the delicate balance of international relations.[69]

One U.S. Navy admiral disagreed with O'Connell. He believed that such actions could be extended beyond the contiguous zone based on the customary practice of asserting a basic right of every State to take such actions at sea as are reasonable and necessary to protect its security interests against the hostile acts of other states.[70]

The real issue, however, is not simply whether such defensive operations can be conducted outside the contiguous zone, but whether, in situations of *de facto* belligerency, the concepts of territorial sea, contiguous zone, etc., have any relevance. In the years since Professor O'Connell wrote the statement quoted above, the world has seen two examples of greatly expanded coastal defensive operations that have encompassed large areas of the high seas, including shipping lanes: the Falklands (Malvinas) War of 1982 and the Iran-Iraq War of 1980-1988.

The Iran-Iraq War is difficult to analyze in the context of this chapter, because the two countries declared exclusion zones with both defensive and offensive characteristics. The zones extended into high seas areas of the Northern Persian Gulf, into highly traveled shipping lanes, and off the coasts of third states, such as Kuwait and the United Arab Emirates.[71]

---

[69] O'Connell, unpublished manuscript, *supra* note 29, at 7.

[70] Miller, *supra* note 3, at 169. Admiral Miller cites three examples: the seizure of the American ship *Virginius* by Spanish authorities in 1873 to prevent the transport of arms to Cuban insurgents; the seizure of the British ship *Deerhound* by Spanish warships for the same reason; and French warships during the Algerian War, which stopped a British ship and a Yugoslav ship suspected of delivering arms to Algerian rebels. *Id.*

[71] For the most thorough and comprehensive discussion of maritime issues during the Iran-Iraq War, *see* PROFESSOR GEORGE K. WALKER, THE TANKER WAR, 1980-88: LAW AND POLICY (2000) (Vol. 74 of the Naval War College's "Blue Book Series on International Law Studies").

Each country's purported objective was to deny its adversary the income from oil exports necessary to support waging the war. The effect, however, was an offensive raiding strategy having only adventitious impact on possible target shipping. Neutral ships became the primary targets even when navigating between two neutral ports or when engaged in fishing activities. Even among those who tentatively accept the establishment of defensive exclusionary zones, some find the zones of the Iran-Iraq War to be merely "an excuse for a raiding strategy directed randomly against . . . shipping found in the Zone without regard to their nationality or to their purpose for being in the Zone."[72]

The Falklands conflict involved the declaration by Great Britain and Argentina of a total of seven exclusion zones. The zones were ostensibly defensive, as they surrounded territory claimed by each side and did not purport to extend to the shores of third parties. Nevertheless the zones encompassed hundreds of square miles of the high seas. They provided for assumptions as to the hostility of vessels, including merchant vessels, found within the zones. Rather than providing for inspections or visit and search, ships and aircraft from other nations were required to obtain prior permission to enter therein.[73]

In neither of these *de facto* belligerent conflicts did either party appear to be particularly constrained by considerations of the territorial sea or contiguous zone regimes.

Nature of the Mining and Attendant Issues

After a detailed review of the conflicting theories about what constitutes a legal blockade,[74] one scholar, with more than a hint of

---

[72] L.F.E. Goldie, *Maritime War Zones and Exclusion Zones, in* 64 International Law Studies: The Law of Naval Operations 156, 176 (Horace B. Robertson, Jr. ed., 1991). Even under the traditional laws of blockade, a violating vessel, if not a belligerent vessel, was subject to capture and condemnation in prize, not to immediate destruction. Robert W. Tucker, 50 International Law Studies: The Law of War and Neutrality at Sea 289 (1955).

[73] Goldie, *supra* note 72, at 171-73.

[74] *See supra* notes 57-66 and accompanying text.

frustration, argued that such legal positions "effectively ignore[ ] the realities of modern naval warfare," "elevate technicalities over substance," and "operate[ ] as a deterrent to rational analysis."[75] As applied to the mining of Haiphong, he continued:

> [S]uch an approach tends to treat law as a static phenomenon, incapable of flexibility or development; and an effort to avoid analyzing the United States action in terms of blockade doctrine, because of purportedly hostile baggage contingent thereto, overlooks the significant components of the doctrine, developed through mutual assessments of their best interests by belligerents and neutrals, which might be brought into play as useful tools for analyzing the actions and persuading others of its legality. . . . [S]o too it may be harmful to eschew a particular word symbol, such as "blockade," when the symbol and the doctrines associated therewith, if recognized and utilized as analytical aids, may assist in the examination of a specified aspect of the coercive process.[76]

Based on state practice in recent years, there simply is no absolute requirement that a blockade be accompanied by a declaration of war, that it be conducted only on the high seas, that it involve of necessity surface vessels and cannot utilize mines, or that ships must be stopped, searched, and condemned in prize. The purpose of the mining of North Vietnamese harbors was to prevent access to North Vietnamese ports and to prevent North Vietnamese naval operations from those ports.[77] That purpose is consistent with the definition of blockade to prevent vessels of all nations from entering or exiting specified ports belonging to an enemy nation. Additionally, the mining operations met all five of the generally recognized criteria for a legal blockade—effective enforcement, proper establishment, adequate notice, impartial application, and respect for neutral rights. Yet, as previously discussed above, President Nixon and his advisors wanted to avoid a traditional

---

[75] Swayze, *supra* note 39, at 159-60.

[76] *Id.* at 160-61.

[77] Address by President Nixon, *supra* note 52, at 747, 749.

blockade of North Vietnam. Henry Kissinger explained to the president that a blockade would produce daily confrontations with the Soviets. Every time a ship was stopped, inspected, or searched, the "drama of the Cuban missile crisis" would be repeated. "Our challenge and the Soviet reaction to it would have to be acted out over and over again, probably on television. The danger of some slip or of a pretext for serious incident would be too great."[78]

By 1972, however, the legal advisor of the Department of State, John R. Stevenson, acknowledged that a blockade would have been a legitimate measure of self-defense under the traditional laws of war applicable in an international armed conflict of the type occurring in Vietnam. But to declare a blockade would have "implied a whole range of actions which would have extended the area of hostilities and risked grave dangers of widening the conflict." To stop, visit, search, and capture vessels would give rise to "challenge and confrontation, threatening expanded conflict." So the United States chose "lesser measures of collective self-defense," which were "more restrictive" than those permissible under the traditional law of blockade.[79]

Nevertheless, it appears that at least some more recent official sources believe the mining of Haiphong was in fact a blockade. Howard S. Levie, in his book *Mine Warfare at Sea*, discusses the U.S. Navy's *Mining Operations* manual published in 1985, which refers to the mine *blockade* of Haiphong Harbor as establishing a legal precedent for blockades established by mines alone.[80] Likewise the *Commander's Handbook* discusses the mining of Haiphong and other Vietnamese ports as conforming to the traditional criteria for a blockade, while recognizing that the term "blockade" was not used at the time.[81] Professor Levie concludes that it would be more accurate to state that, even though the mining of the ports was not intended as a blockade and did not meet all the historical requirements for a blockade, because its overall effect was basically that of an effective traditional blockade and because

---

[78] *Quoted in* Levie, *supra* note 42, at 152-53.
[79] *Quoted in id.* at 153-54.
[80] *Id.* at 155.
[81] Commander's Handbook, *supra* note 59, at 7-9.

of its general acceptance by the world community, it may serve as a precedent for future blockades by mining alone.[82] The emerging issue with implications for future naval interception operations is whether close-in blockades by means of mines will be, or should be, a viable policy alternative.

Blockade as an Act of War and Attendant Issues

This chapter opened with a discussion of the persistent assumption that there is an invariable connection between a blockade and a "state of war." Even when countries are involved in *de facto* hostilities, they are reluctant to use the term *blockade* to describe what appear to be very blockade-like activities. Another persistent notion is that the term *blockade* describes a single type of naval operation, codified by very clear-cut rules. This author agrees with Dr. and Mrs. Mallison that these two assumptions are simply "inconsistent with the juridical doctrines of blockade as they have developed to the present time."[83]

After all, is it not true that the real question is not when war begins, so that certain legal doctrines come into play, but rather whether any particular exercise of coercion is permissible?[84]

It has long been recognized that the old distinction between a state of war and a state of peace no longer reflects the "fluid and complex process of coercion in the contemporary world arena or of the equally complex process of legal authority."[85] Particularly in areas where fast-developing technology leads to "profound and rapid change," as in the establishment and implementation of blockades, "the rate of attrition or obsolescence of particular inherited rules may be accelerated and the emergence of new ones hastened."[86] And to whatever degree the old concepts survive, they will be refashioned by "specific practical interpretations to fit the special conditions and demands of limited wars, with their own

---

[82] LEVIE, *supra* note 42, at 155.

[83] Mallison & Mallison, *supra* note 58, at 52.

[84] Swayze, *supra* note 39, at 161.

[85] MCDOUGAL & FELICIANO, *supra* note 64, at 7.

[86] *Id.* at 51.

peculiar limits or lack of limits."[87] Perhaps it is time the old concepts of blockade be refashioned by specific, practical interpretations to fit the special conditions and demands not only of limited wars, but of deterrence-aggression theory in general.

An argument certainly can be made that it may be desirable to maintain the sharp distinction between a state of war and a state of peace, each with its distinctive set of mutually exclusive prerogatives. Some time ago, one author posited that recognition of a legal state of intermediacy for the purpose of gaining what would otherwise be belligerent rights would unnecessarily abate existing limitations imposed by international law. It would encourage a trend toward greater reliance on the uncontrolled unilateral use of force by reducing the restraints on the improper and illegal use of force presently provided by international law.[88] Yet although it may be desirable to maintain such a distinction, world events, particularly since September 11, 2001, appear to have moved beyond the ability to do so. "The point is that doctrine and practice no longer try to decide what is formally 'war' and what is formally 'peace.' There are simply conflicts between nations which involve the use of force and/or economic sanctions."[89]

The issue then becomes what methods of action will best accomplish a state's objectives with the least loss of life and least chance of escalation of hostilities. Professors Myres McDougal and Florentino Feliciano comment that "the lawfulness of any particular modality of achieving [the objective of embargoing commerce with the enemy] in possible future contexts depends upon appraisal of the relative destructiveness of such modality as compared to any other available alternative modality, rather than upon conformity to practices technologically obsolete."[90]

In other words, if the dichotomy of a law of war and a law of peace provides little utility in a contemporary situation, it should

---

[87] *Id.* at 70.

[88] Lieutenant Commander Bruce Harlow, USN, *The Legal Use of Force . . . Short of War*, U.S. NAVAL INST. PROC. 89, 98 (Nov. 1966).

[89] Mark W. Janis, *Neutrality*, *in* 64 INTERNATIONAL LAW STUDIES: THE LAW OF NAVAL OPERATIONS 148, 148 (Horace B. Robertson, Jr. ed., 1991).

[90] MCDOUGAL & FELICIANO, *supra* note 64, at 494.

perhaps be reconsidered.[91] Perhaps one reason for the persistence of the concept of blockade as a belligerent activity is that one must be prepared to enforce the blockade by force if necessary. This presupposes a willingness to engage in direct, hostile confrontation with vessels that attempt to break the blockade. For example, at a press conference on March 6, 1963, President Kennedy responded to a question about the Castro regime in Cuba as follows:

> To deny the oil would require, of course, a blockade, and a blockade is an act of war . . . [Y]ou should not be under any impression that a blockade is not an act of war, because when a ship refuses to stop, and you then sink the ship, there is usually a military response by the country involved.[92]

Likewise, in the aftermath of the initial overthrow of Haitian President Jean-Bertrand Aristide in 1992, when it appeared the embargo imposed by the Organization of American States (OAS) was becoming increasingly "leaky," some OAS members discussed the imposition of a blockade. An OAS official noted that such a course of action was unlikely: "'A blockade is an act of war and you have to be prepared to take the next step' of military intervention before beginning a blockade."[93]

There have been proposals and historical precedents for a changed perception of the law of naval blockade. The Cuban Quarantine, for example, presented a very close approximation to the belligerent right of contraband under the traditional law of war. The last thing the United States wanted was a state of war between the United States and the Soviet Union, yet the United States exercised a traditional belligerent right. "It certainly seems obvious that a formal state of war should not be required for a state to insist on certain essential protective rights since such would have undoubtedly prejudiced the chances for a peaceful solution of the

---

[91] Miller, *supra* note 3, at 164.

[92] *Quoted in* WHITEMAN, *supra* note 3, at 870.

[93] Al Kamen, *U.S. Seen With Few Good Policy Options on Haiti*, WASH. POST, Jan. 30, 1992, at A15.

matter."[94] Dr. and Mrs. Mallison called the Cuban Quarantine a "limited naval blockade" more along the lines of "a very selective type of contraband control."[95]

Relying on the Cuban Quarantine experience, a U.S. Navy Captain proposed imposing a blockade on North Vietnam that was not declared as an act of war. "The doctrine of blockade is merely part of a larger scheme which is appropriate for application as an instrument of national power in the complex international society of the current century,"[96] he stated. Captain McNulty contended that there was justification for claiming such a blockade as a function of a *de facto* state of belligerency and hence a belligerent right. This state of belligerency might include the right to impose limited restrictions on the freedom of the seas hitherto recognized only in war but falling short of full-scale blockade.[97] But if an armed confrontation could occur between members of the international community under a state other than war (because the participants do not intend to or desire to engage in war) then some legal status should be given to that condition and a body of law developed to apply to it. Such body of law would have to contain rules for the conduct of operations against commerce at sea. "[C]ommerce warfare will always remain as a tool of sea power, and a workable code for its conduct could only benefit all of world society."[98] As a solution, Captain McNulty proposed a naval "quarantine" of the port of Haiphong as a more humane substitute for the aerial bombing campaign and as a means of forcing the modification of the traditional laws associated with blockade.[99] The actual solution, of course, the mining of Haiphong, was far closer to a blockade than to a quarantine.

Perhaps it is time for the old concept of pacific blockade to be revived. Though never well-accepted under international law, and

---

[94] Miller, *supra* note 3, at 170.

[95] Mallison & Mallison, *supra* note 58, at 50.

[96] James F. McNulty, *Blockade: Evolution and Expectation*, in 62 INTERNATIONAL LAW STUDIES 172 (Richard B. Lillich & John Norton Moore eds., 1980).

[97] *Id.* at 187.

[98] *Id.* at 189.

[99] *Id.* at 190.

never actually imposed during the twentieth century, the concept refers to measures of force undertaken by one state against another without necessarily bringing into existence a state of war. It could include a blockade of the ports and harbors of another state, but with the proviso that the blockading state was engaging in forcible actions short of war. Such a state of affairs could exist, however, only so long as the blockaded state consented to view the measures in that light.[100]

Professor D. P. O'Connell has written that under Chapter VII of the UN Charter, the Security Council can institute a form of pacific blockade. That, in fact, occurred during the Rhodesian crisis of 1965. Security Council resolutions, which authorized the United Kingdom to prevent oil delivery to Rhodesia through Portuguese territory and which called upon all members of the United Nations to submit to the blockade, are cited as examples of UN implementation of a pacific blockade.[101]

Similarly, the Maritime Interception Operations of the UN coalition forces during the first Gulf War of 1991 provide examples of a naval action that fell somewhere between pacific and hostile blockade. At least until January 16, 1991, there was no intent to initiate a war. In fact, all efforts were directed toward restoring the peace without an acceleration of hostilities. Yet the Maritime Interception Operations did interfere with the vessels and shipping of third states. These actions were taken pursuant to Security Council resolutions but were not *per se* enforcement actions under Article 42 of the Charter.[102]

This author believes it will be very difficult to avoid the perception of the term *blockade* as a belligerent or hostile activity. For example, the UN General Assembly's "Definition of Aggression" Resolution in Article 3 states: "Any of the following acts, regardless of a declaration of war, shall . . . qualify as an act

---

[100] Pittman B. Potter, *Pacific Blockade or War?* 47 AM. J. INT'L. L. 273-74 (1953). Potter also notes that in a pacific blockade it was a "fairly well-accepted doctrine" that no right to visit, search, or capture the vessels of third parties accrued, even though that limitation did not appear to be strictly logical. *Id.*

[101] O'CONNELL, *supra* note 29, at 1158.

[102] Jane G. Dalton, *The Influence of Law on Sea Power in Desert Shield/Desert Storm*, 41 NAVAL L. REV. 27 (1993).

of aggression: . . . . (c) The blockade of the ports or coasts of a state by the armed forces of another state. . . ."[103]

Yet it is important to develop a law of blockade that will see blockade not as a tension-heightening act, but as a tension-lessening act designed to peacefully deter aggressive action. For that reason, this author proposes the term *blockade* should continue to refer to belligerent or hostile activity, or enforcement actions taken under Article 42 of the UN Charter. *Pacific blockade* may then be reserved for those situations like the Maritime Interception Operations of the first Gulf War, or even the quarantine of the Cuban Missile Crisis, to refer to actions in which there is a determination to halt aggressive action without escalating the conflict into full-blown hostilities. The issue for the future, of course, is whether the international community will be willing to make that distinction.

LESSONS LEARNED FOR NAVAL INTERCEPTION OPERATIONS

Extension of Defensive Measures Beyond the Contiguous Zone

Since the Indochina War, there have been no other examples of the close-in self-blockade type of operation that Market Time represented. Instead there has been a growing tendency to extend defensive operations well beyond one's contiguous zone. The Iran-Iraq War of the 1980s provides an example of an excessive extension of defensive measures. Between 1984 and 1987, Iran attacked 163 ships,[104] thus precipitating the reflagging of Kuwaiti vessels and the escort of shipping by U.S. naval forces. More limited defensive exclusion zones, however, may be more acceptable, and they should not be tied to peacetime concepts of ocean divisions and zones.

Professor L. F. E. Goldie, after an extensive analysis of defensive exclusion zones, concluded that, subject to the tests of proportionality and reasonableness, some such zones may be

---

[103] G.A. Res. 3314, 29 G.A.O.R. Supp. 31 (Aj9631) at 142 (Dec. 14, 1974).

[104] Janis, *supra* note 89, at 150.

moving conditionally into recognition as customary international law.[105] This author proposes that the appropriate baseline is the UN Charter provision in Article 2(4) requiring states to refrain from the threat or use of force against the territorial integrity or political independence of another state.

If "blockading" one's own coast to prevent infiltration and supply of aggressive elements will counter such aggressive action, it should be permissible under Article 51. The criteria for legitimacy is not whether such defensive actions occur only within one's contiguous zone, but whether they contribute effectively to one's defensive efforts. So long as such efforts are necessary and proportional to the aggression, they would have the effect of localizing war, limiting the conduct of war on both land and sea, and lessening the impact of war on international commerce. For these reasons, they should be acceptable under international law, whether or not they extend beyond 24NM from one's coast. Market Time was an early and very limited effort to meet those goals and was probably unnecessarily constrained by peacetime considerations.

Viability of Close-In Blockade by Mining

Some commentators have predicted that the close-in blockade is a thing of the past and is no longer a viable operation. The main reason for this, of course, is that advanced weapons technology makes it difficult to escape the reach of surface-based missiles and missile attacks by submarines and aircraft. The last close-in blockade conducted by U.S. Navy *surface vessels* was during the Korean conflict.[106] United Nations naval forces established command of the sea along the North Korean coast and conducted a

---

[105] Goldie, *supra* note 72, at 184.

[106] On July 6, 1950, the United States informed the secretary general of the United Nations that in support of Security Council Resolutions S/1501 and S/1511 relative to the North Korean attack on the Republic of Korea, the president of the United States had ordered "a naval blockade of the entire North Korean coast." WHITEMAN, *supra* note 3, at 866. The blockade excluded the port city of Rashin, however, which the Soviet navy used as a warm water port throughout the Korean War. Mallison & Mallison, *supra* note 58, at 49.

blockade very much along the traditional lines. It is acknowledged that the operation was possible largely because the Soviet Union, a North Korean ally, chose not to commit any of its submarines and aircraft against the UN forces. Only mines and small and medium caliber guns were furnished to the North Koreans to attempt to resist the blockade.[107] Although they denounced the blockade as illegal, both the Soviet and Chinese governments respected it, and it was successfully maintained for three years.[108]

The mining of Haiphong Harbor, however, demonstrated the viability of mining as a form of close-in blockade. Just as blockade is not always the solution to international confrontations, so mining is not always the optimal way to mount a blockade. Nevertheless, policy planners should not neglect the benefits of mining in appropriate situations. Particularly where it is important to *avoid* "eyeball-to-eyeball" confrontation with the adversary, mining is a valuable weapon. In situations where considerations of "saving face" or national prestige may be at stake, the impersonality of the mine can produce the desired effect in the least confrontational way. The minefield applies force twenty-four hours a day without the necessity of massing naval forces near an antagonist's forces or territory. Likewise, where considerations of proportionality are at stake, a minefield may be the least destructive means of deterrence or counteraction.[109] As one commentator states:

> Of all the weapons at our disposal, only the naval mine can actually be used without killing people and destroying property. This is because the mine when used as a threatening weapon actually performs its mission without even firing, if it denies the enemy the use of a piece of the sea.[110]

And though nonconfrontational, the mine creates a very effective blockade. "In the history of sea warfare, there have been

---

[107] McDougal & Feliciano, *supra* note 64, at 492.

[108] Miller, *supra* note 3, at 169.

[109] Commander J.A. Meacham, USN, *The Mine as a Tool of Limited War*, U.S. Naval Inst. Proc. 51, 53-61; Luckow, *supra* note 36, at 25-26.

[110] *Id.* at 53.

many blockade runners, but precious few minefield runners."[111] The success of the mining of Haiphong Harbor in preventing the resupply of the North by sea is undisputed, and demonstrates that greater expense does not necessarily mean greater effectiveness.[112]

> The blockade of North Vietnamese ports, accomplished by the use of mines, constituted a response limited in area, time and destructive potential, utilizing a minimum amount of effective military power as a response to the massive onslaught of men and armaments employed by North Vietnam in the initiation and perpetuation of its offensive.[113]

Future conflict situations may develop where the use of a blockade by mining is a feasible, inexpensive, and nonconfrontational alternative.

Blockade as an Instrument of Deterrence

To paraphrase a U.S. Navy admiral and representative to the law of the sea negotiations: It is an error of logic to attempt to overlay a centuries-old articulation of rights intended to balance belligerent and neutral interests, as they existed in the days of sail, onto a contemporary and significantly changed set of circumstances. "The question is, then, . . . what are the rules that will preserve the interests of participants and non-participants during armed conflict now and in the future?"[114] The goal, of course, is to allow law to "continue its historic function as a limitation on violence."[115]

---

[111] *Id.* at 61.

[112] Luckow, *supra* note 36, at 27. It was tactically feasible to institute a close-in blockade by use of mines because North Vietnam had little mine counter-measure capability, the range of coastal defense was limited, and the blockading force had air superiority. O'CONNELL, *supra* note 29, at 1156; McCauley, *supra* note 40.

[113] Swayze, *supra* note 39, at 170.

[114] Rear Admiral Bruce A. Harlow, JAGC, USN, *UNCLOS III and Conflict Management in Straits*, 18 L. SEA INST. PROC. 678, 683 (1985).

[115] Mallison & Mallison, *supra* note 58, at 49.

Professor Neill Alford, for example, presciently opined in 1963 that the nature of "future nonbelligerent applications of naval force involving minimum violence" may take the form of selective blockade or pacific contraband aspects of the disused pacific blockade of the last century.[116] Naval interception operations since that time have done exactly that. This author simply suggests that nations dedicated to countering aggression should not hesitate to use measures similar to traditional blockades, with the proviso that there is no intention to engage in hostile activities. United Nations Security Council action may be effective in this area in the future, as it was in the first Gulf War and throughout the ensuing years prior to March 2003, in lending legitimacy and validating the peaceful intentions of such actions. Such non-belligerent blockades could be equally legitimate when taken in self-defense under Article 51 of the UN Charter. In the future, it will remain for state practice to determine how these measures will be implemented and accepted by the international community.

At the same time, however, in situations of *de facto* belligerency, perhaps there should not be so much reluctance to use the actual term *blockade*. South Vietnam could have blockaded North Vietnam to counter its armed aggression consistent with Article 51 concepts of self-defense. And where a third state (Cambodia) was unwilling or unable to prevent its territory from being used as a supply and transhipment point for North Vietnam, its coasts, too, could have been subject to blockade.[117] The failure of a state to adequately defend itself from armed aggression with all available proportionate means can only encourage more aggression.

---

[116] NEILL H. ALFORD, JR., 56 INTERNATIONAL LAW STUDIES: ECONOMIC WARFARE 274-75 (1963).

[117] For a discussion of the legality of the U.S. decision to send combat forces into Cambodia, *see* John Norton Moore, *Decision to Intercede in Cambodia, in* LAW AND THE INDOCHINA WAR 495-513 (1972) (The U.S. and South Vietnamese response was of reasonable scope to promptly achieve permissible defensive objectives).

CONCLUSION

Perhaps the ultimate lesson of naval interception operations during the Indochina War is that it is time to break the linkage between blockade and war so that we are able to acknowledge honestly that blockade is not a single unitary concept; that a blockade can be applied by various methods and with varying degrees of coercion; and that the goal and purpose of blockade is to minimize the use of force and destruction while protecting national values from destruction by outside aggression. Naval interception operations of various types have great potential as effective measures short of war. For the most part, however, it is suggested that an additional lesson of the Indochina War is that such operations should be implemented as soon as reasonably possible.

[O]nce the risks associated with the commencement of such measures during *future* hostilities have been deemed to be acceptable—it is highly commended that the militarily effective and value-conserving instrumentality of a maritime interdiction be implemented *as soon as possible* after the advent of hostilities in order to maximize the flexibility and the impact which this viable and highly selective naval sanctioning device possesses for humanely restoring and maintaining world public order.[118]

---

[118] Clark, *supra* note 46, at 177-78.

BIBLIOGRAPHY

Articles, Books

Alford, Jr., Neill H. 56 *International Law Studies: Modern Economic Warfare*. Washington, DC: Naval War College, U.S. Government Printing Office, 1963.

Cagle, VADM Malcolm W., USN. "Task Force 77 in Action Off Vietnam." *U. S. Naval Institute Proceedings* 66 (May 1972).

Carlisle, CAPT Geoffrey E., USN. "The Interrelationship of International Law and United States Naval Operations in Southeast Asia." 22 *JAG Journal* 8 (1967).

Clark, CDR Bruce A., JAGC, USN. "Recent Evolutionary Trends Concerning Naval Interdiction of Seaborne Commerce as a Viable Sanctioning Device." 27 *JAG Journal* 160 (1973).

Finkelstein, LCDR J. B., USN. "Naval and Maritime Events, January 1972-June 1972." *U.S. Naval Institute Proceedings* 45 (May 1973).

Fraunces, Michael G. "The International Law of Blockade: New Guiding Principles in Contemporary State Practice." 101 Yale Law Journal 893 (1992).

Harlow, RADM Bruce A., USN. "UNCWS III and Conflict Management in Straits, The Developing Order of the Oceans." In 18 *Law of the Sea Institute Proceedings*, edited by Robert B. Krueger and Stefan A. Fiesenfels, Honolulu: The Law of the Sea Institute, University of Hawaii, 1985.

——— (then LCDR Harlow). "The Legal Use of Force . . . Short of War." *U.S. Naval Institute Proceedings* 89 (November 1966).

Hayes, RADM John D. "Sea Power, July 1965-June 1966: A Commentary." *Naval Review 1967*, 265 (1966).

62 *International Law Studies: The Use of Force, Human Rights and General International Legal Issues*, edited by Richard B. Lillich and John Norton Moore, Newport, RI: Naval War College Press, 1980.

64 *International Law Studies: The Law of Naval Operations*, edited by RADM Horace B. Robertson, Jr., Newport, RI: Naval War College Press, 1991.

Levie, Howard S. *Mine Warfare at Sea*. Dordrecht, The Netherlands: Martinus Nijhoff Publishers, 1992.

Luckow, CDR CRD (s.g.) Eric, Royal Danish Navy. "Victory Over Ignorance and Fear: The U.S. Minelaying Attack in North Vietnam." *Naval War College Review* 17 (January-February 1982).

Mallison, W. T., and Sally Mallison. "A Survey of the International Law of Naval Blockade." *U.S. Naval Institute Proceedings* 44 (February 1976).

Marolda, Edward J., and G. Wesley Pryce, III. *A Short History of the United States Navy and the Southeast Asian Conflict 1950-1975*. Washington, DC: Naval Historical Center, Department of the Navy, 1984.

McCauley, RADM Brian, USN. "Operation End Sweep." *U.S. Naval Institute Proceedings* 19 (March 1974).

McDougal, Myres S., and Florentino P. Feliciano. *Law and Minimum World Public Order*. New Haven and London: Yale University Press, 1961.

Meacham, CDR J .A., USN. "The Mine as a Tool of Limited War." *U.S. Naval Institute Proceedings* 50 (February 1967).

Moore, John Norton. *The Vietnam Debate: A Fresh Look at the Arguments*. Lanham, MD: University Press of America, Inc., 1990.

O'Connell, D. P. "International Law and Contemporary Naval Operations (1971) (unpublished manuscript on file in University of Virginia Law Library).

————. *The Influence of Law on Seapower*. Annapolis, MD: The Naval Institute Press, 1975.

————. 2 *The International Law of the Sea*. Oxford: Clarendon Press, 1984.

Office of the Chief of Naval Operations. *The Commander's Handbook on the Law of Naval Operations* (Revision A).

Potter, Pittman B. "Pacific Blockade or War?" 47 *American Journal of International Law* 273 (1953).

San Remo Manual on International Law Applicable to Armed Conflicts at Sea, edited by Louise Doswald-Beck, 1995.

Swayze, LCDR Frank B., USN. "Traditional Principles of Blockade in Modern Practice: United States Mining of Internal and Territorial Waters of North Vietnam," 29 *JAG Journal* 143 (1977).

Tucker, Robert W. 50 *International Law Studies: The Law of War and Neutrality at Sea.* Washington, DC: Naval War College, U.S. Government Printing Office, 1955.

Vietnam: The Naval Story, edited by Frank Uhlig, Jr., Annapolis, MD: Naval Institute Press, 1986.

Walker, Professor George K. 74 *International Law Studies: The Tanker War, 1980-88: Law and Policy.* Newport, RI: Naval War College Press, 2000.

Whiteman, Marjorie M. 10 *Digest of International Law.* Washington, DC: Department of State Publication 8367, U.S. Government Printing Office, 1968.

Periodicals

American Journal of International Law. Washington, DC: American Society of International Law.

Department of State Bulletin. Washington, DC: Department of State, U.S. Government Printing Office.

JAG Journal. Washington, DC: Office of the Judge Advocate General of the Navy, U.S. Government Printing Office.

Naval War College Review. Newport, RI: Naval War College.

New York Times. New York, NY: The New York Times Company.

United States Naval Institute Proceedings. Annapolis, MD: U.S. Naval Institute Press.

Washington Post. Washington, DC: The Washington Post Company.

Conventions, Statutes, Treaties

Convention on the High Seas, Geneva, April 29, 1958, 13 U.S.T. 2312; T.I.A.S. 5200, 450 U.N.T.S. 82.

Convention on the Territorial Sea and Contiguous Zone, Geneva, April 29, 1958, 15 U.S.T. 1606, T.I.A.S. 5639, 516 U.N.T.S. 205.

Declaration of Paris, April 16, 1856, reprinted in Leon Friedman. 1 *The Law of War: A Documentary History* 156-57 (1972).

Definition of Aggression Resolution, G.A. Res. 3314, 29 G.A.O.R. Supp. 31 (A/9631) at 142 (December 14, 1972).

Naval Conference of London, Declaration Concerning the Laws of Naval War, February 26, 1909, reprinted in Leon Friedman. 1 *The Law of War: A Documentary History* 402-05 (1972).

President Reagan, Proclamation No. 5030, 48 Fed. Reg. 10,601, 16 U.S.C.A. §1453n (1983).

United Nations Convention on the Law of the Sea, U.N. A/CONF. 62/122, 21 I.L.M. 1261 (1982).

Viet-Nam Decree on Sea Surveillance, April 27, 1965, 4 I.L.M. 461 (1965).

IX

No More My Lais: Reshaping the Law of Command Responsibility

Hiren P. Patel

INTRODUCTION

In 1967, U.S. military intelligence feared that the Quang Ngai Province was a stronghold for Viet Cong soldiers.[1] As a result, the United States instituted fierce bombing and artillery campaigns in the area, which was declared a "free-fire zone." By the end of 1967, almost 140,000 civilians had been left homeless and most of the dwellings in the zone were leveled. Limited instruction on the laws of war and a MACV card entitled "The Enemy in Your Hands" did little to stop commanders from providing positive incentives for their soldiers to produce kills. These kills could be used to inflate body counts and demonstrate progress. Some GIs stated that "anything that's dead and isn't white is a VC" and began calling the native population "gooks."

---

[1] *See* Douglas Linder, *An Introduction to the My Lai Courts-Martial*, *available at* http://www.law.umkc.edu/faculty/projects/ftrials/mylai/Myl_intro. html; William G. Eckhardt, *My Lai: An American Tragedy*, 68 UMKC L. REV. 671 (2000); Jeffrey F. Addicott & William A. Hudson, Jr., *The Twenty-Fifth Anniversary of My Lai: A Time to Inculcate the Lessons*, 139 MIL. L. REV. 153, 156-59 (1993). The account of My Lai included in this chapter consists primarily of the facts presented by Linder, Eckhardt, and Addicott. Many of the facts surrounding My Lai may be disputed, but certain consistencies do exist. The purpose of this chapter is not to give a thorough, indisputable account of what happened, but to merely use My Lai as a springing point of reference for the discussion of the law of command responsibility.

In the midst of this backdrop, Charlie Company, commanded by Capt. Ernest Medina, arrived in Quang Ngai in January of 1968. Charlie Company was one of the three companies assigned to Task Force Barker, a unit led by Lt. Col. Frank Barker, Jr., to combat the Viet Cong in a discrete area of Quang Ngai known as "Pinkville."

In Pinkville, just two days before the My Lai massacre, Charlie Company fell victim to a booby trap, which claimed the life of a sergeant and wounded others. This event may well have given the soldiers of Charlie Company extra motivation to exact vengeance.

Prior to the mission on March 16, Capt. Medina brought the company together for a motivational talk and a briefing on the mission. Medina laid out the plan of attack against the 48th Battalion of the Viet Cong in the little hamlet of My Lai 4. The mission called for Charlie Company to seek out the Viet Cong (VC), engage the enemy, and destroy the village, which was thought to be a safe haven for VC soldiers. Medina informed his company that the only people who would be left in the hamlet would be enemy soldiers and that all the noncombatant civilians would have already left the area. All told, the Americans would have approximately seventy-five soldiers supported by a number of aerial gunships.

In the aftermath of My Lai, one of the disputed facts pertains to the exact instructions given by Medina to his soldiers. Some soldiers recall Medina providing explicit instructions to kill all the people in the area, including women and children. Other soldiers do not recall such instructions. Medina himself maintained that he simply did not address women and children.

On the morning of March 16, nine helicopters carrying Charlie Company touched down about 150 yards from My Lai. Assault helicopters had already attacked the area in order to clear a space for landing the troops. The plan of attack primarily involved two platoons from Charlie Company, one led by Lt. William Calley and the other by Lt. Stephen Brooks. These two platoons were to take the lead on the assault of the hamlet, while Medina and a third platoon would wait near the landing site and serve as an auxiliary force. Throughout the ensuing events, Lt. Col. Barker was observing the actions of Charlie Company from an altitude of about 1,000 feet.

By 8:00 a.m., the assault had begun in earnest. Calley's platoon entered the village from its southern side and began the standard operating procedure of searching and destroying VC forces. People were removed from their homes and interrogated about the VC. At one point, an individual man was stabbed with a bayonet, another was dropped down a well, and a group of women were killed execution style with bullets through the back of their heads. The massacre had begun. Even while many of the native population proclaimed that they were not VC soldiers, Calley's platoon began killing and torturing the inhabitants. At one point, about eighty elderly men, women, and children were brought to a drainage ditch, thrown inside, and shot.

When investigators came to the scene more than a year and a half later, they found mass graves containing at least 500 victims.

The extent of Medina's knowledge of the massacre is in dispute. Certain witnesses place Medina on the scene at 10:00 a.m., when much of the killing had already taken place. Others place Medina on the scene around 9:00 a.m., which would be during the commission of a fair number of these war crimes.

In any event, there is much evidence that Medina aided in a vast cover-up of the incident in question. The official army report detailed a victorious battle with 128 enemy dead and only one American wounded. However, certain individuals on the scene (including a helicopter pilot named Hugh Thomson, who rescued certain civilians) filed complaints after hearing the official reports. In response, Maj. Charles Calhoun ordered Medina to return to the scene and conduct a thorough body count to determine what actually happened on March 16. This order was countermanded by Maj. Gen. Samuel Koster, who felt satisfied by directly asking Medina about the number of civilian casualties. Medina informed Koster that about twenty to twenty-eight civilians had been killed. Thereafter, certain GIs were interviewed, but no one thought to interview native Vietnamese witnesses. Michael Bernhart, a GI in Charlie Company, expressed an interest in writing his congressman about My Lai, but was dissuaded by Medina himself.

My Lai was all but forgotten for about a year. In March 1969, Ronald Ridenhour, a former member of a reconnaissance unit who heard about My Lai, wrote a letter to numerous officials in the government urging them to investigate this incident. Congressman Morris Udall took the forefront in the movement to assess the allegations contained in Ridenhour's letter. General Westmoreland ordered the inspector general to conduct a thorough investigation, which ended up lasting months and resulted in the interviews of many witnesses. Once the atrocities committed in My Lai had been officially uncovered, the next move was to bring charges against some of the military personnel at the scene. On September 5, 1969, formal charges were brought against Lt. William Calley.

Pursuant to a directive from the Nixon administration, General William Peers conducted another closed-door investigation that involved the interviewing of 398 witnesses. More than 20,000 pages of direct testimony of personnel ranging from the top to the bottom of the command structure were gathered. The Peers Report recommended that criminal sanctions be instituted against numerous individuals involved in My Lai for a host of different war crimes.[2]

Including Calley and Capt. Medina, a total of twenty-five military personnel were charged with crimes relating to the My Lai incident. The prosecution of Capt. Medina proceeded under the theory of command responsibility. The theory of command responsibility pursued by the prosecutors came from Article 77 of the Uniform Code of Military Justice (UCMJ), which dealt with aiding and abetting. The mens rea requirement of this article mandated that the officer possessed actual knowledge of the underlying crimes and took no action to prevent or punish those actions. This standard turned out to be the prosecution's downfall, and Medina's defense successfully argued against actual

---

[2] Some have suggested that the killing of civilians at My Lai did not constitute a war crime according to the precise legal definition because the victims were not enemy civilians. *See* Eckhardt, *supra* note 1, at 677-78. Regardless of the specific technical use of the term, this chapter will refer to war crimes as inclusive of both the legal category of war crimes as well as other serious battlefield crimes committed against friendly noncombatants.

knowledge of the My Lai war crimes. It took the jury only fifty-seven minutes to reach a verdict of not guilty.

Under the facts of the My Lai massacre, a different approach might have enabled prosecutors to convict more individuals in the command structure. Instead, the UCMJ approach eventually adopted made it difficult for any individual (aside from Lt. Calley) to face charges.

The morning of March 16, 1968, should never become a mere footnote in history. On that fateful day and the days thereafter, the United States committed two atrocious acts. First, American soldiers massacred upwards of 500 unarmed elderly people, women, and children in the small hamlet of My Lai. Second, the United States failed to bring to justice many of those responsible for this grave breach of international law.

The failure to bring Capt. Ernest Medina and others in the army command structure to justice for their involvement in the My Lai massacre raises many questions about the application of the law of command responsibility. Command responsibility generally refers to the responsibility commanding officers incur for the actions of their subordinates. Unfortunately, the doctrine of command responsibility suffers from a disconnect between the international standard found in customary international law and the domestic standard found in the UCMJ.

This chapter will explore the history of the law of command responsibility.[3] First, the chapter will outline the history of the doctrine of command responsibility found in the international law of war. Special emphasis will be placed on certain key eras of development of command responsibility in order to fully capture the various ideas, goals, and methods employed. Second, the chapter will discuss the salient differences between the international law of command responsibility and the available

---

[3] The main focus of this chapter will be the issue of command responsibility for the crimes of subordinates. Generally, crimes committed during combat will meet the technical definition of war crimes, but the overall rules of command responsibility should apply to situations where serious combat offenses are committed against friendly civilians or others to whom the legal definition of a war crime might not apply.

mechanisms for punishing commanders for the crimes of subordinates available in the UCMJ. Finally, the chapter will attempt to draw on the historical evolution of command responsibility, both internationally and domestically, to suggest a new policy better equipped to achieve the humanitarian goals of the law of war without reaching too far. The overall goal, after all, in developing a workable and sensible doctrine of command responsibility is to ensure that future My Lais never occur in combat.

THE EVOLUTION OF THE LAW OF COMMAND RESPONSIBILITY

The doctrine of command responsibility purports to provide the proper incentives to military commanders and civilian officials to prevent and punish violations of the law of war.[4] This aspect of the law of war interjects certain humanitarian goals into the harsh milieu of armed conflict.[5] Since infractions of the law of war occur mostly during war, the majority of legal decisions defining the contours of the doctrine of command responsibility have arisen in postwar prosecutions. Due to the political environment surrounding these postwar cases, the presiding courts and tribunals often have not had the desire or opportunity to conduct sufficient reasoned deliberation to draw detailed distinctions.[6] The twentieth century evolution of the law of command responsibility is thus best understood in the context of the major armed conflicts giving rise to the criminal prosecutions of commanders for the acts of subordinates.

---

[4] *See* Matthew Lippman, *Humanitarian Law: The Uncertain Contours of Command Responsibility*, 9 TULSA J. COMP. & INT'L L. 1 (2001).

[5] *Id.*

[6] *See Comment, Command Responsibility for War Crimes*, 82 YALE L.J. 1274 (1973).

World War I

In the aftermath of World War I, the Preliminary Peace Conference at Versailles created a Commission on the Responsibility of the Authors of the War and on Enforcement of Penalties. The Commission developed a report detailing the Central Powers' responsibility for the war and the various violations of international law.[7] The Commission determined that the Central Powers committed "outrages of every description . . . on land, at sea, and in the air, against the laws and customs of war and the laws of humanity," including "the most cruel practices."[8] The Commission proposed that the traditional immunity guaranteed to high-ranking civilian and military officials had no place in international law, and those responsible for the violations of the laws of war should be subject to criminal prosecution.[9] Otherwise, "the greatest outrages against the laws and customs of war and the laws of humanity . . . could in no circumstances be punished. Such a conclusion would shock the conscience of civilized mankind."[10] The Commission recommended holding individuals accountable for a direct act or a failure to intervene and terminate an ongoing war crime.[11] The reasoning behind punishing individuals for the failure to intervene applied to officials in the command structure who could have mitigated the effects of their subordinates' actions. "[A] word from them would have brought about a different method in the action of their subordinates on land, at sea and in the air."[12]

In light of allegations and evidence of war crimes, the allies established various mechanisms to try individuals based on a combination of the knowledge of war crimes committed by

---

[7] *See Commission on the Responsibility of the Authors of the War and on Enforcement of Penalties (March 29, 1919)*, 14 AM. J. INT'L L. 95 (1920). The Central Powers were comprised of Germany and its allies during World War I.

[8] *Id.* at 113.

[9] *Id.* at 116.

[10] *Id.*

[11] *Id.* at 117.

[12] *Id.*

subordinates and the ability and failure to act in their prevention.[13]
As the legal infrastructure for prosecuting post-World War I war
criminals   was   being   erected,   American   and   Japanese
representatives launched reasoned dissents, especially with respect
to the Commission's formulation of command responsibility. In
particular, American representatives Robert Lansing and James
Brown Scott voiced American disagreement with the notion that a
civilian or military commander could be held liable for a failure to
prevent war crimes.[14] Lansing and Scott thought direct knowledge
of the criminal acts should be proven in order to impose criminal
liability.[15]   Furthermore,   Lansing   and   Scott   denounced   the
abrogation of sovereign immunity with respect to the heads of
states under the traditional rule in international law that a head of
state cannot be subject to foreign control.[16]

Overriding the dissent of the United States and Japan, the
German Supreme Court in Leipzig recognized certain affirmative

---

[13] Report Presented to the Preliminary Peace Conference, Versailles, Mar. 29,
1919, *reprinted in* 14 AM J. INT'L. L. 95 (1920). The Treaty of Peace with
Germany amended the traditional sovereign immunity due to the ex-Kaiser by
allowing his prosecution before a five-judge international tribunal. *See* Arts.
227-28, Treaty of Peace with Germany, 13 AM. J. INT'L L. 151 (Doc. Supp.)
(1919). As for other persons accused of violating the laws of war, the criminal
prosecutions would be based on the victim of the crimes. If a person was
accused of committing a crime affecting the interests of only one of the Allied
Powers, then that nation would have the right to use its own military tribunal. If
a person was accused of committing a crime affecting the interests of multiple
states, then a multinational military tribunal would be convened. *See id.*
However, upon further consideration, the Allied Powers determined that
establishing international tribunals could undermine the Weimar regime, and
thus allowed the Germans to conduct the appropriate prosecutions. *See* JAMES F.
WILLIS, PROLOGUE TO NUREMBERG, THE POLITICS AND DIPLOMACY OF
PUNISHING WAR CRIMINALS OF THE FIRST WORLD WAR 124-28 (1982). The
Germans eventually prosecuted forty-five individuals, most of whom were
relatively low on the command chain. *See id.* at 130-31; *Judgment in the Case of
Karl Heynen (May 26, 1921)*, 16 AM. J. INT'L L. 674 (1922).

[14] *See* Memorandum of Reservations Presented by the Representatives of the
United States to the Report of the Commission on Responsibilities, annex II,
127.

[15] *Id.* at 143.

[16] *Id.* at 148.

duties held by commanding officers. The *Trial of Emil Muller* focused on potential culpability of a camp commander for the conditions in his camp. Muller commanded a prison camp housing mainly English prisoners of war.[17] The camp was maintained in an unsanitary, disease-producing marsh and lacked adequate food and water.[18] Muller attempted to remedy the camp's deficiencies by demanding more supplies and improving some substandard conditions.[19] The Court found Muller not guilty of willful neglect because "he had perceived the danger in good time and had done everything to prevent it."[20] The failure to completely remedy the situation was due to "circumstances which were beyond both him and also his immediate superiors."[21]

Muller had also been charged with mistreatment of prisoners. In at least two documented instances, internees had been bound and fastened in a position forcing them to stare directly at the sun.[22] The Court did not hold Muller liable for these actions due to a lack of evidence of actual knowledge. However, in one instance, Muller witnessed one of his subordinates callously reprimanding a prisoner and then knocking the prisoner out with a severe physical blow.[23] The Court used this evidence to determine that Muller "at least tolerated and approved of this brutal treatment, even if it was not done on his orders."[24] As such, the Court sentenced Muller to six months in prison for the mistreatment of prisoners in his camp.[25]

The aftermath of World War I brought to the forefront of legal discussion the issue of command responsibility. The postwar political atmosphere produced a strong inclination to hold civilian

---

[17] *See Judgment in the Case of Emil Muller (May 30, 1921)*, 16 AM. J. INT'L L. 684 (1922).

[18] *Id.* at 685-86.

[19] *Id.* at 686.

[20] *Id.* at 687.

[21] *Id.*

[22] *Id.* at 689.

[23] *Id.* at 691.

[24] *Id.*

[25] *Id.* at 685.

and military officials responsible for the failure to prevent or remedy the commission of war crimes by subordinates. In the *Trial of Emil Muller*, the one leading case of the era applying a theory of command responsibility, the Court required a demonstration of knowledge, position, power, and capacity to halt the crime.[26] Further, while commanders assume the responsibility to implement remedies, a commander need not fully correct a problem not created by his own doing.[27] The post-World War II era drastically altered the *Muller* rules of command responsibility.

World War II

The post-World War II developments in the law of command responsibility originate from a number of different sources. Specifically, command responsibility played an important role in the *Yamashita* prosecution, the Nuremberg Tribunal, the Tokyo Tribunal, and the Control Council No. 10 prosecutions.

The Yamashita Prosecution

The U.S. war crimes commission convicted General Tomoyuki Yamashita for a failure to control his troops stationed in the Philippines.[28] The American Army Command and the U.S. Supreme Court affirmed Yamashita's conviction and sentence of death.[29] The story of Yamashita provides quite telling information about the way the power of the law of command responsibility began to grow out of its World War I cocoon.

---

[26] *See generally id.*

[27] *See id.*

[28] *See Trial of General Tomoyuki Yamashita*, 1948 L. REP. WAR CRIM. 1, 35-37 (Oct. 8-Dec. 17, 1945).

[29] *See* General Headquarters United States Army Forces, Pacific Office of the Theater Judge Advocate, Review of the Record of Trial by a Military Commission of Tomoyuki Yamashita, General Japanese Army (Dec. 26, 1945), *reprinted in* COURTNEY WHITNEY, THE CASE OF GENERAL YAMASHITA: A MEMORANDUM 60 (1950) [hereinafter Review of the Record]; In re Yamashita, 327 U.S. 1 (1945); A.F. REEL, THE CASE OF GENERAL YAMASHITA (1949).

The indictment of Yamashita contained detailed and graphic allegations of the commission of numerous war crimes by Yamashita's troops.[30] When American forces invaded the Japanese-controlled Philippine Islands, Yamashita's forces began an uncontrolled and rapid retreat. The crimes committed by Japanese soldiers included:

> the execution and massacre without trial of civilian internees and prisoners of war; the torture, rape, and killing of women, children and members of religious orders through starvation, beheading, bayoneting, clubbing, hanging, immolation and the use of explosives; and the demolition without military necessity of large numbers of homes, businesses, places of religious worship, hospitals and educational institutions.[31]

Between October 1944 and May 1, 1945, upwards of 25,000 civilians lost their lives in the Batangas Province of Luzon Island.[32] Hundreds of civilians were squashed with heavy weights after being forced to leap down a well; hundreds more women were raped and made to suffer through the mutilation of their breasts and sexual organs; individuals were burned and blinded; and prisoners of war were starved and brought to dementia.[33]

In response to the accumulating evidence of war crimes at trial, Yamashita claimed in his defense that he had lost all communications with the 240,000 troops under his direct control.[34] Further, Yamashita argued that the intervening naval units not under his direct command demonstrated a lack of willingness to follow his orders and exacerbated the situation.[35] These naval forces committed a large portion of the war crimes by destroying large sections of Manila and killing or torturing at least 15,000

---

[30] *Trial of General Tomoyuki Yamashita, supra* note 28, at 5.

[31] Lippman, *supra* note 4, at 10-11. *See also Trial of General Tomoyuki Yamashita, supra* note 28, at 4.

[32] *Trial of General Tomoyuki Yamashita, supra* note 28, at 5.

[33] Review of the Record, *supra* note 29, at 63-69.

[34] *Id.* at 72-73.

[35] *Id.*

civilians.[36] Yamashita maintained innocence by claiming he did not order, tacitly accept, or know of any of the war crimes alleged in the indictment.[37] The prosecution relied on the widespread nature of the war crimes to contend that Yamashita must have known of the crimes and that any ignorance resulted from "affirmative action not to know."[38]

In its decision, the American military commission conceded the unfairness of holding an officer culpable for every single crime committed by a subordinate.[39] Nonetheless, because commanders had the authority and responsibility to maintain order and discipline, officers could be held criminally liable when the crimes of subordinates were rampant and the commander did not make an "effective attempt" to "discover and control" the unlawful conduct.[40] Since the Japanese soldiers under Yamashita's command had committed widespread atrocities in the Philippine Islands and Yamashita failed to exercise any sort of control, Yamashita was convicted and sentenced to death.[41]

General Douglas MacArthur convened a review board that pronounced a related, but slightly distinct reasoning in support of affirming the conviction. The board determined that the unrelenting nature of the crimes being committed led to the conclusion that "the accused knew about them and either gave his tacit approval to them or at least failed to do anything either to prevent them or to punish their perpetrators."[42]

The U.S. Supreme Court then reviewed the decision and also affirmed the conviction.[43] The majority opinion stressed the role of a commanding officer to protect civilians and wounded individuals.[44] Violations of the law of war are "to be avoided

---

[36] *Id.* at 62.

[37] *Trial of General Tomoyuki Yamashita, supra* note 28, at 18.

[38] *Id.* at 17.

[39] *Id.* at 35.

[40] *Id.*

[41] *Id.*

[42] Review of the Record, *supra* note 29, at 60.

[43] *In re* Yamashita, 327 U.S. 1, 15 (1946).

[44] *Id.*

through the control of the operations of war by commanders who are . . . responsible for their subordinates."[45] A commanding officer assumes an "affirmative duty to take such measures as were within his power and appropriate in the circumstances to protect prisoners of war and the civilian population."[46] The Court sidestepped the issue of knowledge and affirmatively imposed on every commander the duty to take reasonable measures to prevent war crimes.[47] The purpose behind the humanitarian underpinnings of the law of war "would largely be defeated if the commander of an invading army could with impunity neglect to take reasonable measures" to protect innocent civilians and prisoners of war.[48] The majority's position, therefore, did not require any showing of either knowledge or constructive knowledge.

Justice Frank Murphy opined in his dissent that imposing criminal liability on Yamashita for the actions of his subordinates greatly abrogated the traditional notions of individual responsibility. Since no evidence had been presented to prove any direct involvement or knowledge of the atrocities on the part of Yamashita, the only way to impose criminal liability would be through an unprecedented charge of disregarding a duty to control subordinates.[49] Justice Murphy noted a real danger of such a standard being used against the entirety of the U.S. military command chain, including the president and his advisors.[50] Apart from pointing to a lack of legal precedent for the majority's position, Justice Murphy also found the context of many of the war crimes relevant. The United States had lodged a massive assault on the Philippine Islands and endeavored to disrupt Japanese communications, which in turn made it more difficult for Yamashita to control his troops. Further, Yamashita's forces lacked proper equipment, training, morale, and a host of other

---

[45] *Id.* at 16.
[46] *Id.*
[47] *Id.* at 15.
[48] *Id.*
[49] *Id.* at 28.
[50] *Id.*

elements of a disciplined army.[51] According to Murphy, the standard used by the majority would provide an avenue for future postwar prosecutions to be based on retribution and revenge against a defeated commander rather than on principles of justice.[52]

As a result of the *Yamashita* case, the U.S. Supreme Court imposed an affirmative duty on all commanders to pursue measures to prevent and punish violations of the laws of war. In imposing this obligation, the Court used facts specific to Yamashita's particular situation, and thus created a rule based on facts not likely to reoccur in substantially the same way. In response to incredibly widespread and rampant war crimes, the Court essentially ignored any mens rea requirement and held Yamashita strictly liable for his failure to prevent and punish the actions of his subordinates in the Philippine Islands. Certainly, in light of the rules of command responsibility from the post-World War I era, this new rule revolutionized the set of obligations assumed by military commanders.

The Nuremberg Trials

The International Military Tribunal at Nuremberg focused on potential criminal action of twenty-two Nazi officials.[53] In order to provide some legal legitimacy to the proceedings, the Court truncated the protective power of sovereign immunity in cases where the state "in authorizing action, moves outside its competence under international law."[54] Consequently, the individuals being prosecuted could not hide beneath the veil of sovereign immunity for the commission of crimes under international law.

The Tribunal invoked the doctrine of command responsibility in numerous cases, including cases against civilian officials.

---

[51] *Id.* at 34-35.

[52] *Id.* at 34.

[53] *See* United States v.Hermann Goring, *in* TRIAL OF THE MAJOR WAR CRIMINALS BEFORE THE INTERNATIONAL MILITARY TRIBUNAL, XXII, at 411 (1948).

[54] *Id.* at 466.

Wilhelm Frick, the minister of the interior during World War II, had jurisdiction over many health care facilities actively participating in the practice of euthanasia.[55] The Tribunal found that Frick had knowledge of the euthanasia practice occurring at the facilities under his control and consequently deemed Frick to have violated international law.[56] Ernst Kaltenbrunner, the Chief of Security Police, retained authority over concentration camps and their detainees. Kaltenbrunner argued before the Tribunal that the extermination of the Jews and the general conditions of the concentration camps reflected policies in place prior to his appointment as chief and that he generally had no knowledge of these activities.[57] Despite his claims, the Tribunal found him responsible for the actions of those directly involved in the killing and torture due both to his broad control over the camps and evidence of his knowledge of, and possible participation in, crimes against humanity.[58] Fritz Saukel, as plenipotentiary general for the utilization of labor, assumed "overall responsibility for the slave labor program" and "was aware of [the] ruthless methods being taken to obtain laborers and vigorously supported them on the ground that they were necessary to fill the quotas."[59]

Consequently, the Nuremberg Tribunal's application of the doctrine of command responsibility resulted in the attribution of numerous war crimes and crimes against humanity to a select group of individuals. However, in so applying the notion of command responsibility, the Tribunal also elucidated some key limitations. The Tribunal relied upon evidence of knowledge of the acts as well as some sort of authority vested in the individual to prevent or punish.[60] Some defendants were found to have taken no measures to prevent crimes even when the commission of the crimes could have been reasonably anticipated. Further, the Tribunal also made note of every instance where evidence existed

---

[55] *Id.* at 546.
[56] *Id.* at 546-47.
[57] *Id.* at 538.
[58] *Id.* at 566.
[59] *Id.* at 566-67.
[60] *Id.* at 546-47.

linking directly the civilian or military official to the underlying crimes, thus removing the need to rely on the derivative nature of command responsibility.

The lesson, then, of the Nuremberg Tribunal is that the *Yamashita* strict liability standard had been implicitly rejected. In order to rely upon command responsibility to convict an individual, evidence of knowledge and control had to be presented. This departure from the strict liability standard seems especially intriguing considering the temporal proximity of Nuremberg to the *Yamashita* trial.

The Tokyo Tribunal

While the Nuremberg trials focused on criminal liability on the part of German officials, a separate tribunal for the Far East convicted Pacific theater military personnel for their failure to prevent or appropriately punish war crimes. The upper echelons of the military had both a duty to comply with the laws of war and a duty to ensure compliance on the part of subordinate military personnel. A failure to uphold this latter duty in cases of treatment of prisoners of war and noncombatant civilians resulted in numerous convictions.[61]

The Tokyo Tribunal primarily focused on the treatment of prisoners of war. The Tribunal imposed affirmative duties on all military and civilian officials who either possessed knowledge of war crimes against prisoners or would have possessed such knowledge but for their own negligence.[62] The affirmative duties included taking "such steps as were within their power to prevent

---

[61] *See The Hirota Case*, 3 JUDGMENTS OF THE INTERNATIONAL MILITARY TRIBUNAL FOR THE FAR EAST 1 (1948); 20 Record of Proceedings of the International Military Tribunal for the Far East (1946-1949) (Lib. of Cong. Microfilm, reel 37 of 37) 49, 816 *reprinted in* THE TOKYO WAR CRIMES TRIAL (John R. Pritchard et. al. eds., 1981).

[62] *See* International Military Tribunal for the Far East, The Tokyo War Crimes Trial (Nov. 1948), *reprinted in* THE LAW OF WAR: A DOCUMENTARY HISTORY II 1029, 1039 (Leon Friedman ed., 1972).

the commission of such crimes."[63] The key wrinkle in the law of command responsibility exposed by the Tokyo Tribunal involved the imposition of criminal liability in cases where negligence caused the lack of knowledge. In determining whether knowledge should be imputed, the Tribunal determined whether the underlying crimes were "notorious, numerous and widespread as to time and place."[64]

In order to prevent violations of the laws of war, the Tribunal noted that military and civilian figures with the appropriate authority must anticipate the commission of crimes and take "adequate steps" to prevent such crimes.[65] The definition of "adequate steps" was not clearly established, but the Tribunal did indicate that individuals must use their formal and informal powers to prevent and remedy the commission of war crimes.[66] Consequently, the time at which the evidence indicates that the individual either had knowledge or would have had knowledge but for negligence serves as the point from which the individual is held responsible for all subsequent war crimes if "adequate steps" had not been taken.[67] For example, the Tribunal held criminally culpable numerous Cabinet level officials and other administrators for maintaining their positions in lieu of resignation despite knowing of the unlawful mistreatment of prisoners.[68]

In the trial of Kuniaki Koiso, the 1944 prime minister appointee, the Tribunal imputed knowledge based on the notion that Japanese war crimes in every theatre of the war were "notorious" to the point that Koiso probably knew about them through their reputation or inter-departmental communications.[69] Evidence also demonstrated receipt of reports regarding the mistreatment of prisoners, but Koiso chose to remain in office and

---

[63] *Id.*

[64] *Id.*

[65] *Id.*

[66] *Id.*

[67] *Id.*

[68] *Id.* at 1039-40.

[69] *Id.* at 1141.

take no remedial measures.[70] The Tribunal found this to be a "deliberate disregard of his duty."[71]

In the trial of Hidecki Tojo, prime minister until 1944, the Tribunal found a lack of "adequate steps" to punish offenders, especially with regard to the 1942 Bataan Death March.[72] Tojo, aware of such atrocities, did not demand a thorough investigation and failed to prosecute or punish any of the soldiers involved.[73] Even though Tojo claimed his soldiers failed to follow specific orders from him and his office in Tokyo, the Tribunal determined that the "head of the Government of Japan knowingly and willfully refused to perform the duty which lay upon that Government of enforcing performance of the Laws of War."[74] Further, Tojo authorized the use of prisoners of war in a railway construction project without providing the necessary provisions for food and hygiene.[75] When reports came in regarding the grotesque conditions of the workers on the project, Tojo assigned an officer to investigate and subjected one company commander to trial.[76] The Tribunal viewed these meager actions as indifference giving rise to criminal liability.[77]

In the trial of Koki Hirota, the foreign minister, the Tribunal imposed criminal sanctions because Hirota had failed to take notice of ongoing atrocities in Nanking. In 1937, Japanese troops created a death toll of over 200,000 civilians over a period of six weeks.[78] When Hirota learned of the crimes against humanity, he asked for and received assurances of future curtailment of these

---

[70] *Id.*

[71] *Id.*

[72] *Id.* at 1153-54. The Bataan Death March consisted of the forced marching of upwards of 70,000 starved and sick American and Filipino prisoners of war. Over the course of the sixty plus mile march, over 10,000 of the prisoners died. *See* The Britannica Concise, *available at* http://education.yahoo.com/search/be?lb=t&p=url%3Ab/bataan_death_march.

[73] International Military Tribunal for the Far East, *supra* note 62, at 1154.

[74] *Id.*

[75] *Id.*

[76] *Id.* at 1154-55.

[77] *Id.* at 1155.

[78] *Id.* at 1061-62, 1132.

actions.[79] However, reports of the crimes continued to trickle in over the next month, and Hirota took no "immediate action" to cause the Japanese military to control the situation.[80] Even though Hirota had no direct authority over the military, the Tribunal believed he should have exercised his influence instead of relying on the assurances of the military, which he knew to be false.[81] The Tribunal did indeed punish this "criminal negligence."[82]

The Tokyo Tribunal used the doctrine of command responsibility more than ever before. In order to establish criminal liability under the theory, the Tribunal required only knowledge or constructive knowledge using a negligence standard and either formal authority or informal influence.

Control Council Law No. 10

In subsequent European tribunals, the law of command responsibility as understood at the time was applied in a variety of circumstances. Officers in the German High Command were charged with violating this responsibility when subordinates implemented Hitler's plan to exterminate unfriendly civilians.[83] Officers were convicted for allowing the execution of hostages in the Balkans area, an act committed by subordinates in reaction to guerrilla attacks against German forces.[84]

The Allies, in Control Council No. 10, devised a system to promote uniformity and appropriate procedure for the prosecution

---

[79] *Id.* at 1134.

[80] *Id.*

[81] *Id.* at 1132-33.

[82] *Id.*

[83] *United States v. Von Leeb*, 11 TRIALS OF WAR CRIMINALS BEFORE THE NUREMBERG MILITARY TRIBUNALS UNDER CONTROL COUNCIL LAW NO. 10, at 1, 462 (1950).

[84] *United States v. List, et. al.*, 11 TRIALS OF WAR CRIMINALS BEFORE THE NUREMBERG MILITARY TRIBUNALS UNDER CONTROL COUNCIL LAW NO. 10, at 1230 (1951).

of Nazis.[85] While numerous cases were prosecuted, two cases hold considerable importance for the development of the doctrine of command responsibility: the *Hostage* case[86] and the *High Command* case.[87]

In the *Hostage* case, an American Tribunal acting under Control Council No. 10 adjudicated a case involving territorial commanders in charge of both executive and military functions.[88] The conceptual difference between military commanders and territorial commanders rests in the scope of authority. Military commanders possess authority over those below them in the command chain. Territorial commanders possess authority over a specific geographic area.[89] The territorial commanders in the *Hostage* case failed to prevent and punish atrocities occurring within their own geographic sphere of influence. One of the main crimes against humanity involved the order from Field Marshal Wilhelm List to execute 100 hostages in Greece and Yugoslavia in retribution for the killing of a single German soldier.[90] While the Tribunal found List directly culpable for the killing of the hostages, List's subordinates exceeded his orders and continued to execute civilians within his territorial command.[91] The Tribunal found List responsible for all the additional killings, because he failed to prevent and punish the individuals responsible, even after receiving reports describing his subordinates' crimes.[92] In addition to List, many of List's immediate subordinates were also found liable.[93]

---

[85] Control Council Law No. 10, *reprinted in* VI TRIALS OF WAR CRIMINALS BEFORE THE NUREMBERG MILITARY TRIBUNALS UNDER CONTROL COUNCIL LAW NO. 10, XVIII (1952).

[86] *See United States v. List, supra* note 84.

[87] *See United States v. Von Leeb, supra* note 83.

[88] *United States v. List, supra* note 84, at 1256.

[89] *Id.* at 1260.

[90] *Id.* at 1262-63.

[91] *Id.* at 1271.

[92] *Id.*

[93] *Id.* at 1274-1311.

The *Hostage* case established liability for territorial commanders for failing to prevent and punish the commission of crimes both within their direct chain of command and without their chain of command, so long as the crimes occurred within their geographic spheres of influence.[94] The Tribunal also made findings of constructive knowledge based on the evidence that reports of the criminal conduct were received by the territorial commander.[95]

In the *High Command* case, the Tribunal considered similar facts, but established some important parameters to liability through command responsibility. While the Tribunal reiterated the responsibility of a territorial commander to maintain security throughout the particular geographic sphere of influence, the Tribunal did not presume knowledge of notorious or systematic war crimes within the territory.[96] Furthermore, territorial commanders could legally assume that their subordinates and others within the territorial sphere were acting in accordance with all applicable laws.[97] As a corollary, the territorial commanders did not have an affirmative duty to constantly keep tabs on their subordinates. Such a duty would only arise upon direct or constructive knowledge of war crimes. The evidence required to prove constructive knowledge would necessarily involve the receipt of reports or other similar means of providing notice.[98]

The combination of the *Hostage* case and the *High Command* case seriously questioned the strict liability standard imposed in *Yamashita*. Considering the temporal proximity of the decisions, the post-World War II trials brought little clarity to the doctrine of command responsibility. Nonetheless, the period is important for the evolution of the law, because it cast to the forefront numerous different rules to which military and civilian commanders could be held.

---

[94] *Id.* at 1256.

[95] *Id.* at 1271.

[96] *United States v. Von Leeb, supra* note 83, at 544.

[97] *Id.* at 543.

[98] *Id.* at 567.

The Codification of Command Responsibility

Despite the numerous applications of the doctrine at the time, the 1949 Geneva Conventions contained no express provision regarding command responsibility.[99] Because of the lack of an expressly codified duty during the ensuing thirty years, nations remained reluctant to apply the established standards of command responsibility for actions of subordinates.[100] In 1977, the status of the doctrine received a significant boost with its inclusion in Articles 86 and 87 of Geneva Protocol I.[101] This inclusion started a trend, wherein today the doctrine of command responsibility appears in numerous international agreements and documents: Article 6 of the International Law Commission's Draft Code of Crimes Against the Peace and Security of Mankind,[102] Article 7(3) of the Statute of the International Criminal Tribunal for the Former Yugoslavia (ICTY),[103] Article 6(3) of the Statute of the International Criminal Tribunal for Rwanda (ICTR),[104] and Article 28(2) of the Statute of the International Criminal Court (ICC).[105]

---

[99] Convention for the Amelioration of the Condition of the Wounded and Sick in Armed Forces in the Field (Geneva Convention No. I), Aug. 12, 1949, 75 U.N.T.S. 31; Convention for the Amelioration of the Condition of the Wounded, Sick, and Shipwrecked Members of the Armed Forces at Sea (Geneva Convention No. II), Aug. 12, 1949, 75 U.N.T.S. 85; Convention Relative to the Treatment of Prisoners of War (Geneva Convention No. III), Aug. 12, 1949, 75 U.N.T.S. 135; Convention Relative to the Protection of Civilian Persons in Time of War (Geneva Convention No. IV), Aug. 12, 1949, 75 U.N.T.S. 287.

[100] Ilias Bantekas, *The Contemporary Law of Superior Responsibility*, 93 AM. J. INT'L L. 573, 574 (July 1999).

[101] Protocol Additional to the Geneva Conventions of 12 August 1949, and Relating to the Protection of Victims of International Armed Conflicts, June 8, 1977, 1125 U.N.T.S. 3 [hereinafter Protocol I].

[102] ILC Draft Code Art. 6.

[103] International Tribunal for the Prosecution of Persons Responsible for Serious Violations of International Humanitarian Law Committed in the Territory of the Former Yugoslavia since 1991, Statute, U.N. Doc. S/25704, annex (1993), *reprinted in* 32 ILM 1192 (1993).

[104] International Criminal Tribunal for the Prosecution of Persons Responsible for Genocide and Other Serious Violations of International Humanitarian Law Committed in the Territory of Rwanda and Rwandan Citizens Responsible for

Article 86(2) of Geneva Protocol I provides the actual codification of command responsibility reflected in the customary international law of 1977. Article 86(2) holds superiors responsible for violations of the Geneva Conventions committed by subordinates when the superiors "knew, or had information which should have enabled them to conclude in the circumstances at the time" that a subordinate was "committing or was going to commit [a breach]."[106] The Protocol crystallizes the requirements for secondary criminal liability for commanders into three basic elements: authority, intent, and failure to exercise the appropriate duty.

The Geneva Protocol only imposed liability on superiors for the violations of their subordinates. In order to qualify as a superior, an individual must have direct authority over the perpetrators of the underlying criminal acts, including those civilian officials with control over the military.[107] The Protocol retained the applicability of the doctrine of command responsibility to territorial commanders with direct or indirect control of military forces in their geographic spheres of influence.[108] Under Article 87(1), military officials must terminate and report breaches of the Convention executed by "armed forces under their command" and "other persons under their control."[109] This sort of secondary

---

Genocide and other such Violations Committed in the Territory of Neighboring States, between 1 January 1994 and 31 December 1994, S.C. Res. 955, annex U.N. SCOR, 49th Sess., Res. & Dec., at 15, U.N. Doc. S/INF/50 (1994), *reprinted in* 33 ILM 1602 (1994).

[105] The Rome Statute of the International Criminal Court, July 17, 1998, Art. 28, U.N. Doc. A/CONF. 183/9, *available at* http://www.un.org/icc, *reprinted in* 37 ILM 999 (1998).

[106] Protocol I, *supra* note 101, at art. 86(2).

[107] *See* COMMENTARY ON THE ADDITIONAL PROTOCOLS OF 8 JUNE 1977 TO THE GENEVA CONVENTIONS OF 12 AUGUST 1949, at 1013 (Yves Sandoz et al. eds., 1987) [hereinafter COMMENTARY].

[108] *Id.* at 1020, 1023.

[109] Protocol I, *supra* note 101, at art. 87(1). One important question with regard to command responsibility involves the duty to report war crimes. This is an especially important consideration when applied to low-level field commanders who may not possess the power to prevent or punish other soldiers.

criminal liability can be imposed upon all officials and commanders, ranging from the commander-in-chief to the lowest levels in the command structure.[110]

The commentary on Article 86(2) of the Protocol describes the mens rea requirement as including both a specific intent and a gross negligence standard.[111] Evidence of negligence must be quite strong and persuasive to be sufficient.[112] Because of the perceived difficulty in most cases of establishing actual knowledge, the Protocol included its "should have enabled them to conclude" language allowing multiple means of fulfilling the mens rea requirement.[113] According to the commentary, a superior is automatically deemed to be aware of notorious breaches and, in any case, cannot claim ignorance of any reports directly addressed to him.[114] This mens rea requirement represents essentially a compromise among the various standards applied in the post-World War II era.

If authority and intent can be proven, the final element to be considered is the violation of a particular legal duty or obligation. The Protocol imposes two such obligations: the duty to prevent and the duty to punish.[115] Article 87(3) establishes a requirement for military officials who are aware of the possibility or actuality of war crimes committed by subordinates to take preventive measures and "initiate disciplinary or penal action."[116] Article 86(2) tempers this requirement by only mandating "feasible" measures with the

---

Nonetheless, no application of the doctrine of command responsibility requires a commander to exceed the authority he possesses. In many cases, the duty to prevent or punish can only be met if a commander reports the war crime to a superior. Therefore, the best understanding of a duty to report would still be under the current rubric, for reporting the crime does help prevent future crimes and aids in the punishment of the present crimes.

[110] See COMMENTARY, *supra* note 107, at 1019.

[111] *Id.* at 1012.

[112] *Id.*

[113] Bantekas, *supra* note 100, at 589.

[114] See COMMENTARY, *supra* note 107, at 1014.

[115] *Id.* at 1015.

[116] Protocol I, *supra* note 101, at art. 87(1).

commander's powers.[117] While the Protocol does compel the military to combat aggressively the commission of war crimes, the Protocol does not require the exhaustion of every possible method of addressing breaches.[118]

The Geneva Protocol provided one of the first codifications of the law of command responsibility. The International Law Commission's Draft Code of Crimes Against the Peace and Security of Mankind contains essentially the same set of requirements as the Geneva Protocol.[119] Command responsibility rules have been codified in the statutes of the ICTY and ICTR as well, and it is those institutions that provide an understanding of the modern day contours of this seemingly fluctuating set of standards.

Recent Developments

In response to the events in the former Yugoslavia and Rwanda, the United Nations has created two separate criminal tribunals to investigate and prosecute the commission of war crimes. The decisions of these two tribunals add much to the current understanding of the doctrine of command responsibility.

The International Criminal Tribunal for the Former Yugoslavia

The ICTY was formulated with the express power to punish individuals under the doctrine of command responsibility.[120] The commentary published by the UN Commission to create the ICTY specifically states that a crime committed by a subordinate

> does not relieve his superior of criminal responsibility if he knew or had reason to know that the subordinate was about to

---

[117] See COMMENTARY, *supra* note 107, at 1015.

[118] *Id.* at 1020-22.

[119] ILC Draft Code Art. 6.

[120] See Final Report of the United Nations Commission of Experts Established Pursuant to Security Council Resolution 780, PP 55-60 (1992), U.N. Doc. S/1994/674 (1994).

commit such acts or had done so and the superior failed to take
the necessary and reasonable measures to prevent such acts or
to punish the perpetrators thereof.[121]

This language was transferred almost verbatim into the statute of
the ICTY and, later, into the statute of the ICTR.

The ICTY has adjudicated numerous cases applying the
doctrine of command responsibility.[122] The Appellate Chamber in
the *Delalic*, a case involving the commander of the Celebici prison
camp, has summarized most of the resulting jurisprudence. The
ICTY also crystallized the doctrine of command responsibility into
the three elements of authority, mens rea, and the violation of an
affirmative duty. However, the ICTY significantly altered the
understanding of each of these elements.

In describing the requisite authority under the doctrine of
command responsibility, the ICTY determined that Article 7(3) of
its statute called for a dual understanding of the word "superior."
Both civilians and military officials could be superiors by
possessing either de jure authority or de facto authority.[123]
Essentially, the determination of whether an individual is
responsible for a criminal act through command responsibility rests
on whether the individual wielded effective control over the
primary perpetrators.[124] De jure command involves official grants
of power to an individual over others, while de facto command
involves no formal status. De jure command can be ascertained
through an examination of the accused's position "in the overall

---

[121] *Id.* at 55.

[122] *See generally* Prosecutor v. Delalic, Case No. 96-21-T, PP 4-10 (Int'l
Crim. Trib. for the Former Yugoslavia 1998), *available at* http://www.un.
org/icty; Prosecutor v. Blaskic, Judgment, Case No. IT-95-14, PP 9 (Int'l Crim.
Trib. for the Former Yugoslavia 2000), *available at* http://www.un.org/icty;
Prosecutor v. Aleksovski, Case No. IT-95-14/1-T, PP 1 (Int'l Crim. Trib. for the
Former Yugoslavia 1999), *available at* http://www.un.org/icty; Prosecutor v.
Kordic, Case No. IT-95-14/2-T (Int'l Crim. Trib. for the Former Yugoslavia
2001), *available at* http://www.un.org/icty.

[123] Prosecutor v. Delalic, *supra* note 122, at para. 192; Bantekas, *supra* note
100, at 578.

[124] Prosecutor v. Delalic, *supra* note 122, at paras. 197-98.

organization, with a view to determining his/her institutional functions."[125] This examination must first determine the nature of the organization and its capacity to transfer power and authority. A court can generally assume an individual with official status has the power and authority ordinarily given to that position.[126]

De jure command has definite boundaries established by the governmental authority delegating the power; consequently, the separate concept of de facto command had to be developed to capture those people wielding effective control over others without an official grant of governmental authority. A de facto commander must exercise "substantially similar powers of control over subordinates" as de jure commanders.[127] Therefore, the primary criminal need not be a subordinate in an established chain of command.[128] The question is whether the purported superior is "senior" in "some sort of formal or informal hierarchy to the perpetrator."[129] The Appellate Chamber specifically pointed to the possibility of situations where one individual has de facto control over another who is of equal rank in the formal chain of command.[130] However, the facts must demonstrate de facto superior authority in order for the doctrine of command responsibility to apply; an individual with the same authority cannot be convicted for derivative criminal liability.[131]

In discussing the element of authority, the Appellate Chamber rejected the position of some of the tribunals in the post-World War II era by excluding "substantial influence" from the parameters of command responsibility. If an individual has merely

---

[125] Prosecutor v. Karadzic and Mladic, Review of the Indictment Pursuant to Rule 61 of the Rules of Procedure and Evidence, Nos. IT-95-5-R61 and IT-95-18-R61 (July 11, 1996), *reprinted in* 108 ILR 86, para. 66 (1998) [hereinafter Karadzic and Mladic].

[126] Prosecutor v. Delalic, *supra* note 122, at para. 197.

[127] *Id.*

[128] *Id.* at para. 251.

[129] *Id.* at para. 303.

[130] *Id.*

[131] *Id.*

the power to influence the activities of others, but lacks effective control, then no criminal liability can be imposed.[132]

In terms of mens rea, the ICTY seems to require either direct knowledge or reason to know.[133] "Knowledge" refers to the awareness as to the existence of a circumstance or awareness that it is occurring.[134] "Actual knowledge" for the purposes of Article 7(3) of the ICTY statute can be proven through both direct and circumstantial evidence.[135] The reason to know standard applies when the superior has "some general information" placing "him on notice of possible unlawful acts by his subordinates."[136] This standard applies when a commander had "in his possession information of a nature, which at the least, would put him on notice of the risk of such offenses by indicating the need for additional investigation in order to ascertain whether such crimes were committed or were about to be committed by his subordinates."[137] The type of information could potentially be in the form of oral or written reports detailing criminal activity, but it is not required to be.[138] Other types of information could include general knowledge of deficiencies in training, violent tendencies on the part of particular subordinates, and even perhaps information regarding substance abuse.[139] A UN Commission of Experts determined that commanders "must have known" of the subordinates' criminal activities based on the

> number, type and scope of illegal acts; the time during which they occurred; the number and type of troops involved; the logistics involved, if any; the geographical location of the acts; their widespread occurrence; the tactical tempo of operations;

---

[132] *Id.* at para. 257.

[133] *Id.* at para. 234.

[134] ICC Prep-Com, 11-21 Feb. 1997, Decisions Taken by the Preparatory Committee, U.N. Doc. A/AC.249/1997/L.5 Art. H (Mar. 12, 1997).

[135] Prosecutor v. Delalic, *supra* note 122, at para. 383.

[136] *Id.* at para. 238.

[137] *Id.* at para. 383.

[138] *Id.*

[139] *Id.*

the *modus operandi* of similar illegal acts; the offenders and staff involved and the location of the commander at the time.[140]

In *Karadzic*, statements were used to prove Karadzic's direct knowledge of hostage taking.[141] Constructive knowledge was also imputed due to the numerous UN resolutions issued about the problem of hostage taking.[142] This information must be provided or made available to the superior to be sufficient, but the commander need not have "actually acquainted himself with the information."[143] Contrary to earlier decisions by different tribunals, knowledge cannot be imputed to the commander based solely on the authority the commander possesses; the Appellate Chamber described such imputations as tantamount to strict liability.[144] Essentially, the ICTY has adopted a totality of the circumstances approach to determine whether a superior had reason to know of any illicit conduct.

In terms of the specific duties and obligations of superiors, the ICTY has generally held that a commander with authority and knowledge has the duty to prevent and punish criminal conduct.[145] The ICTY has refrained from enunciating more specific jurisprudence and instead has left the determinations of whether such duties have been met to the specifics of each individual case.[146] This totality of the circumstances approach avoids the necessity of pursuing the unrealistic goal of establishing uniform prerequisites of prevention and punishment.[147] However, it is important to note that the Appellate Chamber has rejected the position of the Trial Chamber that the doctrine of command

---

[140] *See* Final Report of the Commission of Experts, Established pursuant to Security Council Resolution 780 (1992), U.N. SCOR, Annex, U.N. Doc. S/1994/674, para. 58 (May 27, 1994).

[141] Karadzic and Mladic, *supra* note 125, at para. 72.

[142] *Id.*

[143] Prosecutor v. Delalic, *supra* note 122, at para. 238.

[144] *Id.* at para. 239.

[145] *Id.* at para. 394.

[146] *Id.*

[147] *Id.*

responsibility imposes an affirmative obligation to exercise active due diligence.[148] The duty to prevent crimes and the duty to punish crimes are independent obligations under international law.[149]

The International Criminal Tribunal for Rwanda

The ICTR has applied the doctrine of command responsibility more sparingly than its Yugoslavia counterpart. In accepting a plea agreement from Jean Kambanda, the ICTR documented several key factors giving rise to command responsibility.[150] Kambanda, the former prime minister of the Interim Government of Rwanda, conceded that he had been present at a government meeting where many massacres perpetrated by the government were being discussed.[151] Kambanda conceded his failure to perform "his duty to ensure the safety of the children and the population of Rwanda."[152] The Kambanda plea illustrated the ICTR's overt acceptance of essentially the same formulation of command responsibility as the ICTY. In *Akayesu*, the ICTR applied the three elements of command responsibility in the trial of the head of the Taba Commune for genocide and crimes against humanity.[153] The ICTR found that under Rwandan law, Akayesu's position made him the head of the communal administration, the *officier de l'etat*, and the individual responsible for maintaining and restoring peace.[154] However, Akayesu only had effective control over members of the Hutu militia resident in his headquarters and, thus, did not have effective control of the individuals actually

---

[148] Prosecutor v. Blaskic, *supra* note 122, at para. 332.

[149] *See* Prosecutor v. Blaskic, Decision on the Defence Motion to Strike Portions of the Amended Indictment Alleging "Failure to Punish" Liability, paras. 12-16 (Apr. 4, 1997).

[150] Prosecutor v. Kambanda, No. ICTR 97-23-8, para. 39 (Int'l Crim. Trib. Rwanda 1998), *available at* http://www.un.org/ictr.

[151] *Id.* at para. 39.

[152] *Id.*

[153] Prosecutor v. Akayesu, No. ICTR 96-4-T, para. 139 (Int'l Crim. Trib. Rwanda 1998), *available at* http://www.un.org/ictr.

[154] *Id.* at para. 21.

committing the crimes.[155] Thus, even though Akayesu in fact knew of the crimes being committed by other members of the Hutu militia in the Taba Commune and took no measures to prevent further occurrences or punish those directly responsible, the ICTR decided not to apply the doctrine of command responsibility.[156] Instead, the ICTR drew on other facts demonstrating active encouragement of the crimes against humanity to hold Akayesu liable under an aiding and abetting theory.[157]

The current international law doctrine of command responsibility as enunciated in the ICTY and applied in the ICTR provides a three-element approach to imputing liability upon commanding officers. First, the actual commander-subordinate relationship must be established, through either de jure or de facto evidence. Second, it must be established that the commander either knew or had reason to know of the underlying war crime. Third, it must be proven that the commander failed to meet the duty to prevent or punish the war crime. While these elements provide the same cogent systematic way of analyzing command responsibility as the Geneva Protocol, the ICTY's use of the totality of the circumstances approach represents a significant addition to the current law.

THE U.S. LAW OF COMMAND RESPONSIBILITY

The United States has an interesting dichotomy of law and policy with regard to command responsibility. In 1956, after the repeated use of the international doctrine of command responsibility in the aftermath of World War II, the U.S. Army published *Field Manual 27-10*, entitled "The Law of Land Warfare."[158] Paragraph 501 of the manual essentially incorporates

---

[155] *Id.* at para. 96.

[156] *Id.* at para. 132.

[157] *Id.* at para. 132-33.

[158] U.S. DEP'T OF THE ARMY, FIELD MANUAL 27-10, THE LAW OF LAND WARFARE (July 1956) [hereinafter FM 27-10].

the international law standard of command responsibility as understood at the time. It states:

> In some cases, military commanders may be responsible for war crimes committed by subordinate members of the armed forces, or other person subject to their control. Thus, for instance, when troops commit massacres and atrocities against the civilian population of occupied territory or against prisoners of war, the responsibility may rest not only with the actual perpetrators but also with the commander. Such a responsibility arises directly when the acts in question have been committed in pursuance of an order of the commander . . . . The commander is also responsible if he has actual knowledge, or should have knowledge, through reports received by him or through other means, that troops or other persons subject to his control are about to commit or have committed a war crime and he fails to take the necessary and reasonable steps to insure compliance with the law of war or to punish violators thereof.[159]

Although many commentators consider this statement to be a direct adoption of the standard from the *Yamashita* case, this field manual's articulation of the law of command responsibility more closely adheres to the rulings of the Nuremberg, Tokyo, and Control Council No. 10 Tribunals.[160]

Running counter to this policy declaration is the general policy to prosecute military personnel under the UCMJ instead of the international law of war. This policy, as described in *FM 27-10* is as follows:

> The United States normally punishes war crimes as such only if they are committed by enemy nationals or by persons serving

---

[159] *Id.* at para. 501.

[160] *See* Kenneth A Howard, *Command Responsibility for War Crimes*, 21 J. PUB. L. 7, 16 (1972); Roger S. Clark, *Medina: An Essay on the Principles of Criminal Liability for Homicide*, 5 RUTGERS-CAM. L.J. 59, 71 (1973).

the interests of the enemy state. Violations of the law of war committed by persons subject to the military law of the United States will usually constitute violations of the Uniform Code of Military Justice, and, if so, will be prosecuted within the United States under that code. . . . [161]

For instances of command responsibility, the UCMJ contains an aiding and abetting provision in Article 77,[162] which seeks to classify aiding and abetting as being equivalent to the principal crime for the purposes of prosecution. The article requires a direct knowledge requirement of the underlying war crimes, if used in the war crimes context. This difference in the mens rea requirement marks the first instance of disparate effects between the international doctrine of command responsibility and its UCMJ equivalent.

The second major departure applies to the existence of duties to intervene in the face of criminal activity. The *Manual for Courts-Martial* indicates that a limited duty to intervene in the face of criminal activity does exist but that a failure to intervene only gives rise to criminal liability if it can be proven that the failure to act was intended to support the subordinates in violating the law.[163] Essentially, in order to impose criminal liability based on an omission, the prosecution would have to prove: 1) the existence of an affirmative legal duty; 2) that the omission intended to serve as encouragement for the underlying criminal activity; and 3) that this encouragement in fact aided the criminal activity.[164] It is sufficient to say that these elements are significantly more difficult to prove than the corresponding omission requirements in the international doctrine.

The UCMJ makes it distinctly more difficult to impose criminal liability on commanders for the actions of their subordinates. In the case of Capt. Medina, the heightened standards

---

[161] FM 27-10, *supra* note 158, at para. 507.

[162] UCMJ, Art. 77.

[163] 1969 MANUAL FOR COURTS-MARTIAL.

[164] *See* UCMJ, *supra* note 162, at art. 77.

used by the court may have affected the overall outcome. Recognition of this disparity between the international standard and the domestic law seems to provide the impetus for a change of U.S. policy—especially if the goal of the criminal justice system in this regard is to provide officers and commanders with more incentive to proactively prevent war crimes.

TOWARD A BETTER APPROACH TO COMMAND RESPONSIBILITY

None of the existing approaches to command responsibility are perfect.[165] The history of the international law rules of command responsibility reveals divergent opinions on how best to deal with secondary criminal liability. Under international law, command responsibility has changed from a strict liability offense to one that now seems to rely heavily on the circumstances of each individual incident. The UCMJ approach requires actual knowledge and, of course, only applies to military officials. Developing a synthesis of all the conflicting ideas and methods is of vital importance in order give clear guidance to military and civilian officials involved in combat.

To pursue a sensible approach to command responsibility for the United States, My Lai serves as an appropriate case study. The massacre involved field level crimes akin to many of the atrocities committed in the other major conflicts of the century. Subsequently, individuals may have attempted to cover up the incident and, certainly, the judicial response to My Lai hardly seemed appropriate given the gravity of the incident.

A discussion of what the law of command responsibility should be, in light of what it was and has now become, must begin first with the goals of establishing any standards of command

---

[165] Up to this point, the chapter has provided a descriptive account of the historical applications of command responsibility. The following sections represent a normative perspective. The primary importance of understanding the history of command responsibility is its ability to guide how the nations of the world can best apply a doctrine in the future.

responsibility. A consideration of the facts of My Lai would certainly aid in the process of formulating an appropriate set of goals. Thereafter, the specific shortcomings of the major approaches must be revealed. Finally, a compromise must be reached in order to best achieve the goals set out.

The Goals of an Effective Doctrine of Command Responsibility

The doctrine of command responsibility can, obviously, have multiple goals. The best approach to command responsibility, then, would consist of a careful balance of any and all of the conflicting goals. The following discussion will highlight some of the most important goals of an effective doctrine of command responsibility.

Preventing War Crimes

The countless horrific and grave war crimes committed by military officials need not be reiterated here. Suffice to say, war crimes tend to occur in every major military altercation and have occurred numerous times in the major wars of the twentieth century. War crimes can be perpetrated under orders of high-level military commanders and civilian officials, as in the case of Hitler in World War II, or they can be committed by rank and file soldiers without an adequate understanding of the bounds of professional military conduct, as in My Lai. Pursuing criminal prosecutions of the direct participants certainly results in appropriate retribution for the crime and some deterrence for future criminal acts.

However, in most military situations, the existence of a defined command structure can provide a valuable method of preventing war crimes. Soldiers are trained to obey orders from superiors, but in the absence of orders, they may engage in illicit conduct. Command responsibility gives the superior officers an incentive to affirmatively police the individuals under their control to prevent them from committing war crimes. Whether such policing includes constant supervision, as in the case of platoon commanders, or effective training and education, as in the case of other commanders, the result is the same—war crimes will be less likely to occur. No one can say whether My Lai would have occurred if someone in the army chain of command had an appropriate grasp of how Lt. Calley might react. No one can say whether My Lai would have occurred if Capt. Medina or Lt. Col. Barker had taken a more proactive role in preventing war crimes. In any event, the chances of future My Lais will decrease if commanders are given appropriate incentives to proactively police their subordinates.

The reason to impose derivative liability upon commanders mirrors one reason to impose liability on the primary criminals—to alter an individual's decision making process. Without a doctrine of command responsibility, two situations exist. First, commanders have less incentive to ensure their subordinates' compliance with the laws of war. Second, soldiers have a smaller chance of being brought to justice, because their commanders have less incentive to control them effectively. The doctrine of command responsibility provides the necessary incentive for commanders, which in turn bolsters the deterrence of subordinates committing war crimes.

Discovering War Crimes

One of the central problems with war crimes being committed by field soldiers involves their discovery. In certain cases, war crimes are so widespread and notorious that knowledge of them is commonplace. However, in other cases, war crimes can occur on a smaller order of magnitude and be relatively simple to cover up. Even evidence of the My Lai massacre took a substantial amount of time to uncover. In order to address war crimes on a small scale, sufficient incentive must be given to commanders to adopt proactive measures encouraging soldiers to report evidence of ongoing war crimes. Furthermore, an active cover-up by a low-level commander not directly involved in the commission of the war crime should be punishable. Developing a sensible command responsibility doctrine must provide these appropriate incentives in order to increase the likelihood of discovering and subsequently addressing the war crimes to which higher-level commanders, civilian authorities, and the international community would otherwise not be privy.

Punishing War Crimes

The doctrine of command responsibility should not be confused with the punishment of the actual offenders. Certainly, direct criminal liability can and should be imposed on war criminals when appropriate. However, the doctrine of command responsibility can provide commanders with the incentive to punish and discipline their subordinates and, therefore, deter future criminal behavior.

Without an effective doctrine of command responsibility, the punishment of war crimes might likely decrease. Liability from a failure to punish individuals in certain situations essentially polices the individuals who are in the best position to control the soldiers in combat, especially in situations where war crimes are committed against enemy prisoners of war or enemy civilians. Given the "us versus them" mentality likely to arise in combat situations, a code of conduct under which commanders have no tolerance for war crimes, even when committed against the enemy, is essential to punish war crimes not likely to be punished otherwise.

Clarity

One of the essential goals of a sensible doctrine of command responsibility should be clarity. Ideally, commanders should be fully apprised of their obligations under international law. In order for these obligations to be properly understood, clarity and simplicity are important. A convoluted doctrine of command responsibility might result in mere confusion on the part of the military and civilian officials who comprise the doctrine's primary target.

Consistency

As a corollary to clarity, a doctrine of command responsibility also ought to be consistent in its application. The history of this doctrine illustrates an utter lack of consistency. Yamashita was held responsible for the actions of soldiers with whom he may not have been able to communicate, while Medina faced no repercussions for the actions of his immediate subordinates at My Lai, which took place less than a mile from his field position.

Consistency might be difficult to achieve with an overly fact-based inquiry that is heavily reliant on amorphous standards instead of specific rules. Furthermore, consistency in a doctrine of command responsibility would entail fair and equal application, regardless of the nationality of the victim, the nationality of the perpetrator, or the identity of the victor in combat. While most of the problems of inconsistency are inherent in any sort of criminal justice system administered by people, the development of a doctrine of command responsibility should at least factor into the equation and attempt to diminish the effects of inconsistent application.

Evidentiary Issues

A doctrine of command responsibility must consider how and what kind of evidence must be presented. During war, collecting and maintaining evidence of war crimes might be difficult given the circumstances of an ongoing conflict, the possibility of key witnesses being killed in battle, and the likelihood of physical records being lost. Consequently, a doctrine of command responsibility must be tailored to address the specific limitations of collecting evidence in the context of war.

Furthermore, with spoliation of evidence a real concern, a system of law should provide an incentive to preserve key evidence of war crimes, especially in a situation where it might be easier for such evidence to be "lost." Consequently, an appropriate balance must be reached between the interest of collecting and preserving evidence and the interest of keeping the commander's primary focus on actual combat.

Practicality

Finally, a doctrine of command responsibility must be practical in its administration. The interest of practicality is multifaceted. On the first level, practicality requires relatively quick and efficient administration with a minimization of burdensome costs, both monetary and other. On the second level, the specific rules of command responsibility must actually target the appropriate people. In doing so, the doctrine must neither be over- nor under-inclusive. For any given war crime, the argument can be made that the doctrine of command responsibility should require criminal culpability to attach to every superior on the command chain. Such a focus ignores the realities of command structures and bureaucracies. Developing a doctrine requiring criminal liability to attach to the entirety of the command chain would be over-inclusive, as it would not significantly enhance any of the goals of prevention, discovery, and punishment of war crimes.

However, adopting a doctrine of command responsibility, which makes it increasingly difficult to hold higher-level commanders responsible for the actions of the rank and file might be under-inclusive. The higher-ranking commanders are sometimes in the unique position to adequately prevent war crimes by implementing better training and harsher disciplinary programs. Ignoring their influence on military actions certainly does not enhance the goals of prevention, discovery, and punishment of war crimes.

The Status Quo Falls Short

Having highlighted some of the more important goals of a doctrine of command responsibility, the next step is to isolate the specific shortcomings in all of the historical formulations of command responsibility.

Yamashita Strict Liability

The tribunals and courts interpreting *Yamashita* have classified its command responsibility standard as strict liability. Strict liability was perhaps not the intent of the tribunals in *Yamashita*, but certainly the argument can be made that the decision did, indeed, employ a strict liability standard. While the "notorious" nature of the crimes being committed in the Philippines seemed to have played a part in the *Yamashita* decision, the fact is, it did not matter to the tribunal whether Yamashita actually knew or should have known of those crimes. Furthermore, in many war crimes contexts, ex post investigation can uncover many facts that a tribunal can later consider to have rendered the war crimes "notorious," whether or not the war crimes were widely known at the time of commission. In any case, one possible approach to the doctrine of command responsibility is strict liability.

The strict liability standard set attributed to *Yamashita* certainly has strengths, but those strengths are far outweighed by its disadvantages. In terms of preventing, discovering, and punishing war crimes, the strict liability standard provides perhaps the most incentive for commanders to take proactive measures to ensure discipline among their subordinates. This discipline would not only serve to prevent the war crimes to begin with, but would encourage soldiers to report crimes committed by their equals. With cooperation from a disciplined group of subordinates, the entire system would operate with greater efficiency in the investigation of war crimes allegations. Finally, faced with strict liability, a commander would be encouraged to vigorously punish the crimes occurring under his command or in his territory.

The strict liability standard is also quite clear; no commander would be confused as to whether potential criminal liability would attach if a subordinate commits a crime. This clarity would give commanders perfect notice of the law and the implications of subordinate acts. The standard would also be remarkably consistent, as no convening tribunal would have to make a decision under the more amorphous and arbitrary legal standards involving "reasonableness" or other similar concepts. No convening tribunal would have to make the difficult decision of whether a commander actually knew or should have known of the actions of his subordinates. Furthermore, the standard requires only evidence of the underlying crimes and the superior/subordinate relationship of the actual perpetrators and the accused commander. Concerns about cover-ups and the possibility of key physical and documentary evidence establishing knowledge do not arise.

Unfortunately, the standard is not preferable because it is highly impractical. All the advantages of strict liability in the command responsibility context mirror the advantages of strict liability in other criminal contexts. Yet, strict liability is rarely used in most legal systems. Aside from strict liability's theoretical conflict with the notion that criminal sanctions ought to require some sort of malicious intent requirement, strict liability in the context of command responsibility can be highly over-inclusive. Under such a standard, every single commander above the actual criminal would face secondary liability, including civilian leaders in charge of the military. If war crimes, no matter how serious, create criminal liability for the entire command structure, the rule would ignore the realities of war. Those on the upper echelons of the command structure have responsibilities over hundreds of thousands of military personnel. Imposing liabilities on these people will not likely provide any marginal benefit to the prevention of war crimes and would simply punish more people for crimes concerning which they had no knowledge or intent.

Additionally, one practical consideration of adopting a sensible approach to command responsibility is having governments accept the policy. No government is likely to seriously consider a strict liability standard, which could result in such widespread criminal liability and contravene the mens rea element essential in most criminal law. Given these important practical limitations, the strict liability standard should clearly be rejected. It seems that the *Yamashita* case is an example of a postwar prosecution based more on retribution and revenge than on a pursuit of appropriate criminal liability using a sensible legal theory.

*Knowledge or Constructive Knowledge (Negligence) + Duty to
Prevent or Punish*

The remainder of the post-World War II decisions generally
adopted an approach to command responsibility requiring
knowledge or constructive knowledge and a duty to prevent or
punish. The constructive knowledge concept entailed an
examination of whether the commander would have known of the
underlying crimes but for his own negligence. Under this
formulation, the duty to prevent or punish was predicated upon
authority or power to do so, including the indirect power of
influence. This approach to command responsibility is much less
severe than the strict liability approach while offering many of the
same advantages. Nonetheless, as formulated in the post-World
War II era, this conception of command responsibility is not
perfect.

In terms of the prevention, discovery, and punishment of
criminal acts, this standard serves as an analog to the U.S. system
of tort law, which is primarily based on negligence. Imposing
criminal liability for negligence gives commanding officers
appropriate incentives to train their men effectively, proactively
prevent war crimes, conduct efficient investigations of any
allegations of war crimes, and punish those responsible. However,
the incentive to take prophylactic measures is not as strong as with
strict liability, because the commander is not automatically liable
for the actions of his subordinates.

This approach cannot be as clear and consistent as the strict
liability approach given the inherent limitations of proving
negligence, especially in the context of war crimes. Proving what
an ordinary reasonable individual under the circumstances would
have done will largely depend on what a tribunal thinks of the
circumstances of the case. In certain situations, for example, in the
middle of coordinating a complicated offensive, a commander
might not be negligent for failing to investigate some incoming
reports of war crimes. Determining the reasonableness of the
commander's actions will often be done ex post, essentially
eliminating the advantages of giving commanders clear directives

ex ante. This problem is also exacerbated by the relative dearth of case law to which future tribunals may make comparisons or draw analogies to further define the boundaries of "reasonableness." Nonetheless, systems based on a negligence standard have somewhat successfully advanced their overall goals.

In terms of proof, the need for additional evidence describing the war crimes and the situations surrounding the commander's notice of war crimes is much greater than with the strict liability standard. The problems of collecting evidence in a combat situation will affect the accuracy of decisions made under this standard. Usually, however, the absence of evidence will favor the defendant leading to perhaps more acquittals than appropriate, especially under the "beyond a reasonable doubt" burden in criminal law. A significant concern would, of course, be the destruction of evidence of knowledge or a tendency not to report war crimes to superiors. This tendency, however, is likely to exist in all systems and would simply require more safeguards inherent in the military justice system.

The one area where this system greatly surpasses strict liability is in practicality. A system based on negligence is more likely to be accepted by different governments to police their own militaries. While trials may be more extensive and costly, this system is far less likely to be overinclusive. Tribunals applying this standard would have to consider the relative position of the commander in the overall command chain, thus allowing the tribunal to factor in the limitations of upper echelon commanders to police the battlefield actions of the rank and file.

However, imposing a duty to influence the actions of others without actual control seems over-inclusive, for it may include people obviously not the target of the command responsibility rules. Infusing within this standard a requirement of de facto or de jure authority seems necessary for it to be a viable option. Overall, however, the knowledge or constructive knowledge formulation does more carefully balance the goals of the doctrine of command responsibility than the strict liability standard.

Knowledge or Constructive Knowledge (gross negligence) + Duty to Prevent or Punish

Protocol I of the Geneva Conventions essentially adopted a knowledge or constructive knowledge standard along with the pendent duties to prevent or punish. This constructive knowledge standard, however, required proving that the commander would have known of the criminal acts but for his gross negligence. This set of standards closely resembles the set developed in post-World War II tribunals; however, the gross negligence standard detracts from its overall effectiveness. In terms of prevention, discovery, and punishment of war crimes, a requirement of gross negligence gives commanders less incentive to tightly control the actions of their subordinates. Gross negligence is inherently more difficult to prove, and therefore, the likelihood of being convicted for the actions of subordinates is diminished. With a lower likelihood of conviction, commanders will be less likely to prevent, investigate, or punish war crimes.

The lower deterrent effect of this standard is not outweighed by any other advantage. The gross negligence standard suffers from the same, if not worse, lack of clarity and consistency as the negligence standard. While this standard might be much less likely to be over-inclusive, it runs a significant risk of being under-inclusive. Some field commanders might indeed be negligent in their duties, and their negligence might allow war crimes to continue unpunished. Consequently, the gross negligence standard adopted by Protocol I does not adequately balance the interests of having a command responsibility paradigm and provides no other advantages to the negligence standard.

Effective Control + Totality of the Circumstances

The ICTY and ICTR have recently adopted an effective control and totality of the circumstances approach to command responsibility. In order to be responsible for the actions of others, a commander must have possessed effective control either through de jure or de facto authority. Furthermore, it must be proven that a commander either knew or had reason to know of the war crimes considering the totality of the circumstances. If these two elements are met, then the commander must prevent and punish.

The totality of the circumstances approach retains the concept that a commander might be held criminally responsible without direct knowledge; however, with the amorphous totality of the circumstances standard, this formulation leaves much to be desired. Certainly, the ICTY and ICTR have adopted their three element approach in order to provide the appropriate incentives for commanders to prevent, discover, and punish war crimes. However, this approach significantly lacks any clear ex ante operational directive; it gives commanders no idea of what to do in certain situations. Furthermore, the approach will probably lead to inconsistent results given the relative lack of jurisprudence. For example, a totality of the circumstances approach in Fourth Amendment reasonable suspicion jurisprudence is aided by the relatively high number of cases from which a subsequent court can draw comparisons and reach a decision in accord with precedent. In terms of command responsibility, the opportunity for judicial bodies to fully develop a totality of the circumstances approach does not exist to the same degree. Additionally, a totality of the circumstances approach would require significant amounts of evidence in order to fully flesh out the circumstances.

Despite these disadvantages, a totality of the circumstances approach might be more likely to avoid over- and under-inclusion. The tribunal might be more willing and able to consider the relative position and capabilities of the commander to curb the war crimes in question.

Actual Knowledge

The actual knowledge requirement used against Medina is the current standard used by the United States in prosecuting aiding and abetting cases. When applied in the context of command responsibility, this standard is quite lacking. The actual knowledge standard is the most difficult to prove and therefore provides the least incentive for commanders to take proactive steps to prevent, discover, and punish crimes. If turning a blind eye can relieve a commander of responsibility, many commanders might be inclined to do so.

While the actual knowledge requirement is remarkably clear, the clarity merely exacerbates the improper incentive system. Further, the application of this standard might not even lead to consistent results. The evidentiary requirements of proving actual knowledge, absent a confession from the accused, are likely to be extreme. Consequently, the criminal liability of two commanders in similar circumstances will be more dependent on the quantity of evidence gathered. While the quantity of evidence is always an issue under any standard, the requirements under an actual knowledge standard make it more likely that inconsistent results will follow.

The actual knowledge standard will also be under-inclusive. For example, a person in Medina's position is the type of person who can take proactive action to prevent or at least stop atrocious crimes as they are occurring. Without imposing liability on these types of commanders, a doctrine of command responsibility will not fully address the problems of crimes committed during combat.

Toward a Sensible Solution

Each of the standards that have been applied in the context of command responsibility has its advantages and disadvantages. None are perfect, and a better solution can be devised. An appropriate set of standards for command responsibility must attempt to address the prevention and punishment of war crimes, while at the same time creating a practical and consistent system under which commanders will be absolutely clear on their obligations.

Of the available options, the strict liability standard created the greatest incentives for commanders to proactively address criminal acts committed by subordinates. It further created a consistent, clear, and efficient system of administration. However, the over-inclusion problem clearly renders strict liability unworkable and undesirable. The negligence-oriented standard, however, achieves nearly the same advantages in prevention and punishment, but loses the clarity and consistency. At the same time, the negligence standard more accurately focuses on the appropriate individuals without overreaching in the command chain. The gross negligence and totality of the circumstances standards provide no real additional advantages and actually provide less incentive for commanders to prevent and punish crimes. Finally, the actual knowledge standard suffers from under-inclusion and a lack of any real incentive to prevent and punish war crimes.

Thus far, then, it seems that the negligence standard best balances the competing interests at the heart of command responsibility. However, some important modifications need to be made. In order to address the problems of clarity and consistency, a more coordinated legal and policy system must be adopted. Each commander should be held to the knowledge or constructive knowledge (negligence) standard, but must be given a series of directives to serve as a resource when making decisions. Thus, in order to prevent the ex post problem of inconsistent results, every nation must make important ex ante decisions on appropriate command conduct. This series of directives must require commanders to routinely inform and educate subordinates about war crimes, to effectively deter the commission of war crimes through repeated statements of the consequences of such actions, to better equip commanders to identify those who might be more likely to commit crimes in the heat of battle, to develop a system of reporting to ensure no war crimes are covered up, to implement a disciplinary procedure, and to adopt other measures designed for the proactive prevention of war crimes. The following may be used in carrying out these responsibilities:

- A series of standard operating procedures for investigation and punishment in light of an oral or written report of a war crime or grave breach committed by a subordinate;
- A series of standard disciplinary procedures; and
- A series of proactive measures, such as proper motivational techniques and any other measures deemed fit, to prevent the commission of war crimes.

A field manual tailored to each command level in the command chain addressing these issues will provide ex ante directives upon which commanders will rely only if total compliance makes a commander presumptively not negligent for the purposes of criminal liability. Essentially, a complex system of prevention and punishment requirements can act as a uniform standard of negligence. Failure to comply with any provision does not make a commander negligent per se, but full compliance defeats any charges. If an accused commander raises compliance with this field manual as a defense, the prosecution must prove beyond a reasonable doubt that full compliance was not met in order to convict. In the case where a commander has not fully complied, the tribunal can independently judge the negligence of the commander based on a reasonableness standard, basically judging whether the commander's noncompliance, given the situation, was reasonable.

A system such as this would retain the benefits of a negligence standard, because it would give commanders the incentive to proactively prevent and punish war crimes using methods and procedures determined ex ante by professionals well acquainted with combat situations. The set of procedures also serves as a clear directive on the obligations of a commander and shields the commander from being railroaded at trial. Obviously, for this system to work, the field manual must be specific, clear, and tailored to the responsibilities of each particular command level. The costs of developing such a system might be significant, but would be start-up costs only. Thereafter, an effective system would exist for the prevention and punishment of war crimes.

Certainly, many nations already employ field manuals apprising soldiers of their obligations under international and domestic law. Some of these field manuals may already contain most of the information necessary; nonetheless, they must be reviewed with an eye toward the prevention of such crimes.

In order to be fully effective, the requirement of a system of procedures must be imposed on all nations as a matter of international law. Of course, this would require the development of a new treaty or an amendment to an existing treaty. In order to provide the compliance defense to a commander of any nationality if prosecuted under international law in an international tribunal, other nations must adopt virtually identical field manuals. Of course, uniform adoption of general guidelines for the prevention and punishment of war crimes can only serve to decrease their occurrence worldwide, which is definitely a desirable goal.

Currently, the United States has a policy to prosecute its military personnel under the UCMJ's aiding and abetting provision. In order to best incorporate this policy, the UCMJ ought to be amended to contain a separate provision for command responsibility for war crimes and a list of other serious crimes, such as murder or torture of friendly civilians. This provision should explicitly allow the affirmative defense of compliance with a command responsibility field manual. Furthermore, the United States must also adopt a twin provision in the Federal Criminal Code to deal with the civilians who exercise control over the armed forces.

Had this policy been in place at the time of My Lai, the various commanders of Lt. William Calley may have recognized the danger posed by sending him to combat. Medina may have actually complied with a series of procedures specifically designed to punish those responsible for My Lai (assuming he, in fact, had no knowledge of the events at the time they occurred). Any failure to adhere to the procedures would have allowed prosecution of Medina and certain other superiors under a negligence standard, a standard that might have resulted in conviction.

CONCLUSION

The My Lai massacre resulted in one conviction, though many more should have been held responsible. The inadequacies of the system allowed escape from responsibility. Yet, adopting a harsher standard of command responsibility to punish individuals like Medina must be done with caution. Drawing on the inconsistent and often arbitrary historical applications of the doctrine of command responsibility, a new system can be designed. Command responsibility for war crimes seeks to provide commanders with the proper incentives to prevent, discover, and punish war crimes, for commanders are in a position of authority to do so. In setting incentives through criminal liability, appropriate attention must be given to notions of clarity, consistency, and evidentiary efficiency. Given these conflicting interests, the best system must involve a careful balance, driven not by ex post decisions, which might become arbitrary or retributive, but by reasoned ex ante decisions.

Those best able to determine an appropriate code of conduct for commanders in light of the potential for war crimes and other serious crimes to be committed must develop a new field manual tailored to each level on the command chain. This field manual must provide a system of procedures all commanders must follow, and total compliance must defeat criminal liability in order to ensure clarity and consistency. At the same time, when compliance does not occur, a knowledge or constructive knowledge, through negligence, standard must be used to judge the responsibility of the commander. Such a standard appropriately sets the correct incentives and punishes commanders for turning a blind eye.

In order for this system to be successful, the procedures in the field manual must be appropriate to the goal of preventing serious war crimes. Furthermore, the system must be adopted universally, either through treaty or custom, so as to ensure the same treatment for military and civilian commanders from any nation employing professional armed forces. In the United States, this begins with an amendment to the UCMJ creating criminal liability through command responsibility, but including the affirmative defense of compliance. The United States must also develop corollary provisions in the criminal code for civilians exercising authority over the armed forces.

This policy is a product of the weighing of a century's worth of command responsibility jurisprudence, and it is important to ensure that the mistakes of the past can guide the decisions of the future. Hopefully, in the future, there will be no more My Lais.

BIBLIOGRAPHY

Cases

In re Yamashita. 327 U.S. 1 (1945).

"Judgment in the Case of Emil Muller (May 30, 1921)." 16 *American Journal of International Law* 684 (1922).

"Judgment in the Case of Karl Heynen (May 26, 1921)." 16 *American Journal of International Law* 674 (1922).

Prosecutor v. Akayesu. No. ICTR 96-4-T, P 139 (International Criminal Tribunal for Rwanda 1998). Available at http://www.un.org/ictr.

Prosecutor v. Aleksovski. Case No. IT-95-14/1-T, PP 1 (International Criminal Tribunal for the Former Yugoslavia 1999). Available at http://www.un.org/icty.

Prosecutor v. Blaskic. Decision on the Defence Motion to Strike Portions of the Amended Indictment Alleging "Failure to Punish" Liability (April 4, 1997).

Prosecutor v. Blaskic. Judgment, Case No. IT-95-14, PP 9 (International Criminal Tribunal for the Former Yugoslavia 2000). Available at http://www.un.org/icty.

Prosecutor v. Delalic. Case No. 96-21-T, PP 4-10 (International Criminal Tribunal for the Former Yugoslavia 1998). Available at http://www.un.org/icty.

Prosecutor v. Kambanda. No. ICTR 97-23-8, P 39 (International Criminal Tribunal for Rwanda 1998). Available at http://www.un.org/ictr.

Prosecutor v. Karadzic and Mladic. Review of the Indictment Pursuant to Rule 61 of the Rules of Procedure and Evidence, Nos. IT-95-5-R61 and IT-95-18-R61 (July 11, 1996). Reprinted in 108 *ILR* 86 (1998).

Prosecutor v. Kordic. Case No. IT-95-14/2-T (International Criminal Tribunal for the Former Yugoslavia 2001). Available at http://www.un.org/icty.

"The Hirota Case." 3 *Judgments of the International Military Tribunal for the Far East* 1 (1948).

"Trial of General Tomoyuki Yamashita." *1948 Law Reports on War Criminals* 1 (October 8-December 17, 1945).

"United States v. Hermann Goring." In *Trial of the Major War Criminals Before the International Military Tribunal, XXII* 411 (1948).

"United States v. List, et. al." *11 Trials of War Criminals Before the Nuremberg Military Tribunals Under Control Council Law No. 10*, at 1230 (1951).

"United States v. Von Leeb." *11 Trials of War Criminals Before the Nuremberg Military Tribunals Under Control Council Law No. 10*, at 1 (1950).

Treaties and International Legal Materials

"Commission on the Responsibility of the Authors of the War and on Enforcement of Penalties (March 29, 1919)." 14 *American Journal of International Law* 95 (1920).

"Control Council Law No. 10." Reprinted in *VI Trials of War Criminals Before the Nuremberg Military Tribunals Under Control Council Law No. 10, XVIII* (1952).

Convention for the Amelioration of the Condition of the Wounded, Sick, and Shipwrecked Members of the Armed Forces at Sea (Geneva Convention No. II). August 12, 1949. 75 U.N.T.S. 85.

Convention for the Amelioration of the Condition of the Wounded and Sick in Armed Forces in the Field (Geneva Convention No. I). August 12, 1949. 75 U.N.T.S. 31.

Convention Relative to the Protection of Civilian Persons in Time of War (Geneva Convention No. IV). August 12, 1949. 75 U.N.T.S. 287.

Convention Relative to the Treatment of Prisoners of War (Geneva Convention No. III). August 12, 1949. 75 U.N.T.S. 135.

Final Report of the United Nations Commission of Experts Established Pursuant to Security Council Resolution 780, PP 55-60 (1992). U.N. Doc. S/1994/674 (1994).

ICC Prep-Com, 11-21 February 1997, Decisions Taken by the Preparatory Committee. U.N. Doc. A/AC.249/1997/L.5 Art. H (March 12, 1997).

International Criminal Tribunal for the Prosecution of Persons Responsible for Genocide and Other Serious Violations of International Humanitarian Law Committed in the Territory of Rwanda and Rwandan Citizens Responsible for Genocide and Other such Violations Committed in the Territory of Neighboring States, between 1 January 1994 and 31 December 1994. S.C. Res. 955, annex U.N. SCOR, 49th Sess., Res. & Dec., at 15. U.N. Doc. S/INF/50 (1994). Reprinted in 33 *ILM* 1602 (1994).

International Law Commission's Draft Articles on Crimes Against Humanity.

International Military Tribunal for the Far East, The Tokyo War Crimes Trial (November 1948). Reprinted in *The Law of War: A Documentary History II* 1029, 1039, edited by Leon Friedman, 1972.

International Tribunal for the Prosecution of Persons Responsible for Serious Violations of International Humanitarian Law Committed in the Territory of the Former Yugoslavia since 1991, Statute. U.N. Doc. S/25704, annex (1993). Reprinted in 32 *ILM* 1192 (1993).

Memorandum of Reservations Presented by the Representatives of the United States to the Report of the Commission on Responsibilities, annex II.

Protocol Additional to the Geneva Conventions of 12 August 1949, and Relating to the Protection of Victims of International Armed Conflicts. June 8, 1977. 1125 U.N.T.S. 3.

20 "Record of Proceedings of the International Military Tribunal for the Far East (1946-1949)" (Lib. of Cong. Microfilm, reel 37 of 37) 49, 816. Reprinted in *The Tokyo War Crimes Trial*, edited by John R. Pritchard et. al., 1981.

Report Presented to the Preliminary Peace Conference, Versailles. March 29, 1919. Reprinted in 14 *American Journal of International Law* 95 (1920).

The Rome Statute of the International Criminal Court, July 17, 1998, Art. 28. U.N. Doc. A/CONF. 183/9. Available at http://www.un.org/icc. Reprinted in 37 *ILM* 999 (1998).

"Treaty of Peace with Germany." 13 *American Journal of International Law* 151 (Doc. Supp.) (1919).

Secondary Legal Materials

Addicott, Jeffrey F., and William A. Hudson, Jr. "The Twenty-Fifth Anniversary of My Lai: A Time to Inculcate the Lessons." 139 *Military Law Review* 153 (1993).

Bantekas, Ilias. "The Contemporary Law of Superior Responsibility." 93 *American Journal of International Law* 573, 574, July 1999.

Clark, Roger S. "Medina: An Essay on the Principles of Criminal Liability for Homicide." 5 *Rutgers-Camden Law Journal* 59, 71 (1973).

"Comment, Command Responsibility for War Crimes." 82 *Yale Law Journal* 1274 (1973).

Commentary on the Additional Protocols of 8 June 1977 to the Geneva Conventions of 12 August 1949, edited by Yves Sandoz et al., 1987.

Eckhardt, William G. "My Lai: An American Tragedy." 68 *UMKC Law Review* 671 (2000).

Howard, Kenneth A. "Command Responsibility for War Crimes." 21 *Journal of Public Law* 7 (1972).

Linder, Douglas. "An Introduction to the My Lai Courts-Martial." Available at http://www.law.umkc.edu/faculty/projects/ftrials/mylai/Myl_intro.html.

Lippman, Matthew. "Humanitarian Law: The Uncertain Contours of Command Responsibility." 9 *Tulsa Journal of Comparative and International Law* 1 (2001).

Reel, A. F. *The Case of General Yamashita* (1949).

The Britannica Concise. Available at http://education.yahoo.com/search/be?lb=t&p=url%3Ab/bataan_death_march.

Willis, James F. *Prologue to Nuremberg, the Politics and Diplomacy of Punishing War Criminals of the First World War* (1982).

Military Materials

General Headquarters United States Army Forces, Pacific Office of the Theater Judge Advocate. *Review of the Record of Trial by a Military Commission of Tomoyuki Yamashita, General Japanese Army (Dec. 26, 1945)*. Reprinted in Courtney Whitney, *The Case of General Yamashita: A Memorandum* 60 (1950).

Manual for Courts-Martial (1969).

Uniform Code of Military Justice. Available at http://www.military -network.com/main_ucmj/main_ucmj.htm.

U.S. Dep't of Army. *Field Manual 27-10, The Law of Land Warfare* (July 1956).

Contemporary

X

Anatomy of a Failure: The Silencing of the Joint Chiefs of Staff and the Adoption of Gradualism

Gary R. Lawson, II

STATUTORY RESPONSIBILITIES IN THE DEFENSE ESTABLISHMENT

The National Security Act of 1947

Any investigation regarding the relationship between Lyndon B. Johnson (LBJ), his senior appointed civilian advisors, and the Joint Chiefs of Staff (JCS) must begin with a brief review of the statutory provisions that establish the basic framework for the interactions among these parties. The National Security Act of 1947 (NSA of 1947) established the fundamental framework for the national security apparatus that existed at the time and that continues to provide the basic structure of those functions today. The NSA of 1947 formally created the National Security Council, the Central Intelligence Agency, and the Office of the Secretary of Defense (OSD). Moreover, it provided statutory guidance regarding the roles and responsibilities each of these institutions would have vis-à-vis each other and with regard to the president. Specifically, as it pertains to the OSD, the NSA of 1947 created the positions of the secretary of defense and the Joint Chiefs of Staff, while also institutionalizing the four branches of the armed forces (by adding the air force).

The objectives of the NSA of 1947 were manifold. The need for increased integration and cooperation of the armed services was voiced during General Dwight D. Eisenhower's testimony before Congress in November 1945. Describing his own personal transformation he stated, "at one time I was an infantryman, but I have long since forgotten that fact, under the responsibility of commanding combined arms." General Eisenhower, alluding to what he would later refer to as parochialism between the various branches, added that "competition is like some of the habits we have—in small amounts they are very desirable; carried too far they are ruinous." Furthermore, the general recognized the need to have the capability to "root out empire builders with a sledgehammer."[1] Thus, the victorious general presented the case for greater centralization in the defense establishment through a strong secretary who would compel harmony through the exercise of concentrated authority and control. The NSA of 1947 was designed to accomplish that directive.

The NSA of 1947 gave the secretary of defense statutory authority over the national military establishment. This was a substantial modification of the previous arrangement, which included co-equal positions for the secretary of war and the secretary of the navy. Thus, by centralizing the authority in one individual, power within the defense establishment was considerably more concentrated. It also created the potential that the individual occupying the position would have significantly enhanced abilities to influence the direction of deliberations regarding national military strategy vis-à-vis the senior uniformed military advisors who had previously enjoyed prominence in this realm, particularly during the Second World War. This was true because after the NSA of 1947, no longer did the competing voices of the secretary of war and the secretary of the navy, supported by the technical and experiential judgments of the senior uniformed military, present their ideas directly to the president of the United States on an equal basis. Thus, it can be seen that the senior appointed civilian defense official's ability to exert influence on presidential decision-making prospered at the expense of the uniformed military, since the latter's views were no longer

---

[1] Herman Wolk, *American Chieftains*, A.F. MAG. ONLINE (Sept. 2002), *at* http://www.afa.org/magazine/Sept2002/0902chiefs.asp.

necessarily presented directly to the president as they were when General George C. Marshall and Admiral Ernest King were advising President Franklin D. Roosevelt (FDR).

Additionally, the NSA of 1947 established the Office of the Joint Chiefs of Staff. This office comprised the most senior uniformed officers representing the army, navy, air force, and the Marine Corps.[2] According to the NSA of 1947, the JCS were to serve as "the principal military advisors to the president." A literal interpretation of this statutory decree would indicate that the JCS were to have responsibility to advise the president in a direct, unfiltered manner on all matters involving the derivation of national military strategy, considerations of when and whether to use military force, and the manner in which force was to be applied in the event that it was necessary to do so.

Moreover, as "principal" advisors, it would seem that the legislative intent was that these advisors were to be treated as the primary experts in rendering their judgments in this arena and thereby enjoy a certain degree of primacy in those assessments. In fact, it seems that the Congress intended to create a body comparable to a board of directors that could give the president a range of professional military views from which he could make executive decisions based upon their input. This design seemed to address the concern articulated by the first secretary of defense, James Forrestal, who stated that reliance on "a single military genius" would risk "mistakes of judgment." However, when assembled together, the competition between various viewpoints would elucidate issues and corresponding potential solutions, which could then be vetted through vigorous deliberations. Additionally, the designation of the JCS as the principal advisors to the president concerning military affairs seemed not to contemplate a potential situation where the secretary of defense would interpose himself between this body and the president in

---

[2] The Marine Corps was to participate in meetings of the JCS at the discretion of the commandant of the Marine Corps where the interests of the service were deemed to be affected.

deliberations of this nature. Any attempt to do so would seem to be in contravention to the legislative intent.

The Defense Reorganization Act of 1958

The next major legislative act affecting the relationships among the key actors within the defense establishment was the Defense Reorganization Act of 1958. The act significantly modified the operational lines of authority by providing that operational control of U.S. combat forces flowed from the president, to the secretary of defense, to the Unified Commanders, and through to the Specified Commanders, thus removing the military departments from the chain of command. The law gave the secretary of defense a number of other powers that helped to centralize authority in his office, such as the creation of a director of defense research, answerable to the secretary, who would control and direct military research and development.

While designed to streamline decision-making in the operational chain of command, an imperative necessitated in large part by the dawning of the nuclear age, it clearly had the effect of marginalizing the JCS in operational matters. Moreover, this act significantly added to the effects of the NSA of 1947 by further diluting the influence of the JCS while strengthening the voice of the secretary of defense in all matters pertaining to defense policy.[3] In advocating the passage of this law, President Eisenhower declared that "in all elements, with all services, as one single concentrated effort . . . strategic and tactical planning must be completely unified" and that the unified command structure would "go far toward realigning our operational plans, weapons systems, and force levels," which would provide "maximum security at minimum cost."[4]

---

[3] *Ibid.*
[4] *Ibid.*

THE KENNEDY ADMINISTRATION'S IMPACT ON CIVIL-MILITARY RELATIONS

Reform of the Structure and Function of the NSC

The Kennedy administration's redefinition of the role of the uniformed military advisors in devising and executing national military strategy set the stage for the state of affairs that would exist within President Johnson's administration. Therefore, it is important to consider the major events and decisions during John F. Kennedy's tenure to understand the relationships that existed and developed during LBJ's presidency.

John F. Kennedy (JFK) was elected to the Office of the President of the United States from his seat in the U.S. Senate after fourteen years in the Congress. The new president was unaccustomed to the executive's role, unlike his predecessor, who had been groomed for the presidency during a successful military career. Unsurprisingly, JFK's approach to the position was much different from Eisenhower's, for not only was JFK not accustomed to the executive role, he tended to view as cumbersome the rigid hierarchy within the national security apparatus that was bequeathed to him.[5] Therefore, upon assuming responsibilities as president, he significantly altered the structure of the National Security Council by abolishing the Planning Board and the Operations Coordinating Board, which served to coordinate policy making by reviewing policies in a systematic way before they were passed on to the president. JFK intended to abolish what he perceived to be an inefficient process and implement policy making through ad hoc executive committees designed to analyze and formulate policies. In the process, the NSC's influence was dramatically diminished.

Moreover, while the NSC maintained its voice in policy making, the JCS's voice was quieted through another modification of President Eisenhower's organizational structure. President

---

[5] H.R. McMaster, Dereliction of Duty 4 (1997).

Eisenhower included all of the service chiefs in NSC meetings. Additionally, the Planning Board and the Operations Coordinating Board included a significant military presence, which allowed the services to insert items on the NSC agenda. President Kennedy's structural modifications eliminated this formal participation of his military advisors and muted the uniformed advisors on two fronts—influencing the agenda and offering inputs directly to the president. President Johnson maintained Kennedy's organizational method and therefore also maintained the severely diminished JCS access to the president in influencing strategic military policy and execution decisions.

The Bay of Pigs and the Cuban Missile Crisis

Two major events highlight the effects of this revised policy making structure. These events also offer insight into the ways in which relationships among senior administration officials and the uniformed military were established during the early years of JFK's presidency and how they developed in the ensuing years. The first major incident was the Bay of Pigs debacle. JFK's dismantlement of the Operations Coordinating Board, and the intelligence office within, impeded his staff's ability to familiarize themselves with the plan. Additionally, since the forum for effective coordination between the various agencies was crippled, planning for the operation was concentrated within the CIA. Since JFK relied on an ad hoc decision-making apparatus, the operation had not received a thorough review by all parties; therefore, the president was not given a full critique, which would have allowed him to consider comprehensively the consequences that might follow. By the time that the Department of Defense became aware of the operation's existence on April 15, 1961, planning was too far along for any meaningful impact by the military advisors.[6] Although the Chiefs voiced skepticism over the plan's chances for success without a simultaneous uprising in Cuba, the operation

---

[6] MAXWELL TAYLOR, SWORDS AND PLOUGHSHARES 186 (1972).

went ahead nonetheless. Of course, the operation quickly fell apart once execution began. The president then turned to his military advisors for solutions that might save the operation. The Chiefs insisted that the operation could only succeed if it received U.S. air support. JFK refused to take that step and the operation turned into a disaster with all of the Cuban forces being either killed or captured. Shortly after the failed adventure, President Kennedy addressed the nation in a press conference where he accepted full responsibility for the failure.[7] Privately, however, JFK blamed the JCS and vowed to never be "overawed by professional military advice again."[8]

The experience convinced JFK that it was necessary for him to obtain an independent military advisor of high rank and high stature in whom he could seek counsel. JFK immediately sought out the retired four-star general, Maxwell Taylor, to lead the Cuba Study Group in investigating the failed operation. After Taylor's group had interviewed more than fifty witnesses who had significant roles in the operation, Taylor submitted his conclusions to Kennedy.[9] Despite his admission that the JCS did not see the CIA's final plan until April 15, 1961, and despite their reservations concerning the plan's viability before the operation was launched, Taylor stated:

> Piecing all of the evidence together, we concluded that whatever reservations the Chiefs had about the plan, about the propriety of having the CIA continue to conduct a military operation of growing complexity, or about the erosion of military requirements by political considerations, they never expressed their concern to the president in such a way as to consider seriously a cancellation of the enterprise or the alternative of backing it up with U.S. forces . . . [They] had been insufficiently forthright in expressing their reservations.[10]

---

[7] ARTHUR SCHLESINGER, A THOUSAND DAYS 290 (1965).

[8] *Ibid.*

[9] MARK PERRY, FOUR STARS 114 (1989).

[10] *Ibid.*, 113-15.

Taylor's report reinforced JFK's initial perception following the botched plan—the JCS had let him down and were largely responsible for the debacle. JFK approved of Taylor's conclusions, as he naturally might considering that they were identical to his own, and his personal interaction with Taylor convinced him that the retired general would be a valuable member of the administration. JFK offered him the role of CIA director after completing his report, but Taylor turned down the offer by claiming to be unqualified for the position. However, JFK was determined to make Taylor a member of his close circle of advisors in an official capacity. The president soon thereafter created the post of "military advisor to the president" and appointed Taylor to serve in that role.

Kennedy's decision to create this new post deserves attention. A matter of first priority is the statutory role of the JCS as delineated in the NSA of 1947. As stated previously, this legislation provided that the JCS were to be the principal military advisors to the president. JFK's decision to appoint a retired officer to a position that seemed to encroach upon the role that Congress intended for the JCS is noteworthy. Secondly, JFK was appointing a military advisor outside the chain of command and without any formal relationships, coordinating Taylor's consultations with those of his legally designated military advisors. Unquestionably, this formula created enormous potential for strained relations with his senior uniformed officers, who would presumably consider their new status as peripheral to the internal White House discussions on matters of military policy. Thirdly, JFK's move was a clear indication of his dissatisfaction with the advice provided by his military advisors, despite statements to the contrary. As such, it is difficult to imagine that this move would have been interpreted in any other way than as an affront to the professional military judgment of the service chiefs. Lastly, appointing Taylor to this post after his stinging rebuke of the JCS's role during the Bay of Pigs blunder seemed to communicate that Kennedy had brought in a military professional who could guide the president in ensuring that the JCS would never again "fail" the commander in chief.

The Cuban Missile Crisis of October 1962 was the second major incident during the Kennedy administration that engendered consequential effects on the relationships between senior civilian advisors and the Joint Chiefs, and it foretold the essential nature of those associations during the following six years. A detailed description of that episode is unnecessary; however, several key insights are provided by an inquiry into a few salient issues that arose in that context. As had become routine in the Kennedy White House, the president established an ad hoc committee to handle the crisis. Known as the EXCOMM (Executive Committee), the panel of advisors was assembled on an exclusive basis to analyze events and to counsel the president. The entire composition of the EXCOMM is worth noting: Robert Kennedy, attorney general; Dean Rusk, secretary of state; Robert McNamara, secretary of defense; John McCone, director of central intelligence; Douglas Dillon, treasury secretary; McGeorge Bundy, special assistant for national security affairs; Theodore Sorenson, special counsel to the president; George Ball, under secretary of state; U. Alexis Johnson, under secretary of state for political affairs; Edward Martin, assistant secretary of state for Inter-American affairs; Llewellyn Thompson, Soviet expert; Roswell Gilpatric, deputy secretary of defense; and General Maxwell Taylor, who had been brought back to active duty the same month to assume responsibilities as the Chairman of the JCS after General Lyman Lemnitzer stepped down to become NATO commander.[11] Most notable among this group of advisors is that while this crisis represented the closest that the United States had come, before or since, to the brink of nuclear armed conflict with the Soviet Union, only one uniformed military advisor was included in the committee that provided advice on a nearly exclusive basis to the president. Indeed, the one professional advisor who was included was one who had been retrieved from retirement a few years prior due to his political alignment with Kennedy. The committee's lack of any meaningful military representation is even more striking when the other

---

[11] SCHLESINGER, *supra* note 7, at 802.

personnel who comprised the Cabinet are considered. It is hard to discern why personnel who had little expertise in the matter were included in deliberations while those who could provide critical military judgment were consciously excluded.

As the crisis deepened, so did skepticism among the members of the JCS that Taylor was adequately representing the views of the Chiefs. As LeMay said later, "we in the military felt that we were not in the decision-making process at all . . . we didn't agree with Taylor in most cases, so we felt that the president was not getting . . . unfiltered military advice."[12] The distrust between the chairman and his Chiefs culminated on October 18 when the Chiefs insisted that General Taylor schedule a meeting with Kennedy so that they could be certain that their undiluted views reached him. The tension between Taylor and the rest of the Joint Chiefs is evident in his recollections recorded in his memoirs:

> Following each EXCOMM meeting, I returned to the Pentagon, reported to the Chiefs the events of the meeting, and . . . the decisions taken. When these decisions did not accord with the Chiefs' views, I was always cross-examined to see whether I had been sufficiently vigorous in defending their position. Occasionally, in the face of obvious skepticism as to the quality of my efforts . . . .[13]

Clearly, the relationship between the Chiefs and their newly-assigned chairman was not established on bedrock of mutual trust. The Chiefs were being left out of the critical discussions regarding a military crisis of herculean proportions; moreover, their sole representative in these deliberations seemingly lacked the fidelity required to present their views to the president and his advisors.

Another significant by-product of this crisis, which would have a lasting impact on decision-making as the war in Vietnam escalated, was the rise of McNamara's influence within the

---

[12] THOMAS COFFEY, IRON EAGLE: THE TURBULENT LIFE OF GENERAL CURTIS LEMAY 393.

[13] TAYLOR, *supra* note 6, 269.

administration. It was his idea to institute a naval "quarantine" to deal with the prospect that the Soviets would attempt to deliver more missiles to Cuba, and it was this concept that many, including JFK, accepted as the reason why full-scale conflict was averted.[14] A blockade by another name, the "quarantine" was designed to intercept Soviet ships believed to be laden with nuclear missiles and destined for Cuba. Several aspects related to the idea for, and implementation of, the "quarantine" are illuminating. First, the measure was McNamara's idea alone and was not borne of consultation with the JCS. Secondly, the Chiefs were presented with the quarantine decision on October 19, 1962, without ever even having been directly consulted before the EXCOMM and the president arrived at the decision.[15]

A telling incident from this crisis also provides insight into the Kennedy administration's conception of the appropriate relationship between civilian and military leadership. During the execution of the quarantine on shipping into Cuba, McNamara closely supervised every aspect of the operation. He feared that the military might not understand that "this was a communication exercise, not a military operation," so he remained in the Pentagon for nearly the entire duration of the crisis. The "Flag Plot" in the Pentagon was the nerve center during the operation and, as such, the secretary naturally gravitated there so that he might be better able to control events. The specific details of what transpired in the Flag Plot have been disputed, but all agree that a confrontation occurred between Admiral Anderson, the chief of naval operations, and McNamara. Apparently weary of what he deemed to be the secretary's intrusive micromanagement of operational details, the admiral communicated to McNamara that the navy had been conducting blockades since the days of John Paul Jones and suggested that the secretary of defense return to his office and let the navy run the operation. After brief retort, McNamara did indeed leave the Flag Plot. However, that incident marked the end of Admiral Anderson's naval career as it represented the

---

[14] SCHLESINGER, *supra* note 7, at 804, 831-33.
[15] PERRY, *supra* note 9, at 124-27.

culmination of previous run-ins with McNamara regarding the TFX fighter, among other issues. A few months later, he stepped down as CNO after his first two-year term to become ambassador to Portugal.[16]

The Cuban Missile Crisis demonstrates the decision-making process under President Kennedy, especially the relative unimportance attached to the perspectives of the JCS. Additionally, it also indicates a willingness on the part of senior civilian advisors to infringe upon areas where discretion had traditionally been left to the military. Lastly, the crisis presented the context in which notions concerning the use of military force primarily for the purposes of "signaling" or "communicating" acquired not only credibility but substantial popularity. While many inside observers, and many more historians looking back in later years, attributed the peaceful resolution of the crisis to skillful tradeoffs involving American missiles in Turkey, most members of the president's closest circle of advisors viewed the "signaling" achieved by the quarantine as the decisive factor.[17] All indications seem to support the view that McNamara came away from the incident convinced of the power of "signaling" by using the instruments of military power. Ultimately, these elements foreshadowed the way in which subsequent policy decisions in Vietnam would evolve under the direction of President Lyndon Johnson.

LYNDON JOHNSON AND THE BREAKDOWN OF CIVILIAN-MILITARY RELATIONS

Lyndon Johnson Assumes Presidency

By the time President Kennedy was assassinated on November 22, 1963, civil-military relations had deteriorated tremendously. Nearly three years of constant strain and distrust had produced a highly dysfunctional system where the chief executive not only did not actively seek the views of his senior uniformed advisors, either

---

[16] McMaster, *supra* note 5, at 28.

[17] Perry, *supra* note 9, at 126.

through formal organizational channels or informally, but in many cases the president showed a palpable distrust of the advice provided by them. LBJ's ascension to the role of commander in chief would precede an even more dramatic rift between the civilian and uniformed leadership, which would engender enormous consequences as America's role in the Indochina conflict deepened significantly.

President Johnson issued National Security Memorandum 273 (NSAM 273) on November 26, 1963, the day following the fallen president's funeral. NSAM 273 affirmed LBJ's commitment to continuing the American policy of assisting the South Vietnamese in winning "their contest against the externally directed and supported Communist conspiracy." The memorandum also called for a timely submission of plans for covert, cross-border operations against North Vietnam.[18] Furthermore, at approximately the same time, LBJ contacted the U.S. ambassador to South Vietnam, Henry Cabot Lodge, to bid him to "tell those generals in Saigon that Lyndon Johnson intends to stand by our word."[19] Seemingly, LBJ was determined to vigorously pursue policies designed to defeat the Communist aggression in South Vietnam.

Three days later, LBJ met with the JCS for the first time. Tellingly, he primarily emphasized his desire to find ways to cut defense spending and encouraged the Chiefs to find ways to shave expenses from the defense budget. A few days later, he conducted extensive discussions with senior senators and representatives explaining his desires to slash spending on defense dramatically in order to free resources for his domestic agenda. LBJ explained to Representative Carl Vinson (D-GA) that he "was not going to have any fat" in the defense budget, and he extended phone calls to other key legislators echoing that same theme. The newly-seated president eagerly pointed to McNamara's reforms that had achieved cost savings in the Pentagon and he affirmed his desire to further emphasize those efforts.[20] Already, it was becoming clear

---

[18] MCMASTER, *supra* note 5, at 49.

[19] STANLEY KARNOW, VIETNAM: A HISTORY 339 (2d ed. 1991).

[20] MCMASTER, *supra* note 5, at 53.

that LBJ's priorities would require subordination of military needs to his designs for domestic social policy. The extent to which this realization would hold true, however, could not have been anticipated yet.

LBJ's Perception of Defense and Military Issues

Although Lyndon Johnson became president of the United States in an instant as the result of an assassin's bullet, his rise to a position that allowed him to take that step was a long one. LBJ's ascent from high school teacher in Texas, to congressman's assistant, to his own election to the House of Representatives, to the Senate, where by 1955 he had achieved the station of Senate Democratic Majority Leader, was a rise marked by his mastery of the art of close political combat and skillful maneuvering. When his own failed attempt at the Democratic nomination brought him an offer to serve as JFK's vice-presidential running mate, he accepted. Then, on that fateful November morning in Dallas, Texas, LBJ's political ascent reached its pinnacle.[21]

LBJ's initial interaction with the Chiefs revealed much of his political nature. His political instincts and sensibilities were primarily forged during FDR's presidency, and it was his ambition to vigorously expand the social welfare programs initiated during the New Deal. Yet, he also observed the ramifications suffered by Democratic presidents who failed to aggressively counter the spread of Communism. From his vantage in the U.S. Senate, he was able to witness Senator Joseph McCartney's exploitation of the "Red Scare" following the fall of China to Mao Zedong and the Chinese Communists. Therefore, he was keenly aware that his dreams for a greatly expanded welfare state would be mortally imperiled should another domino in Asia fall to the Communists. As he confided to his biographer, Doris Kearns Goodwin:

---

[21] KARNOW, *supra* note 19, at 336

I knew from the start that I was bound to be crucified either way I moved. If I left the woman I really loved—the Great Society—in order to get involved with that bitch of a war on the other side of the world, then I would lose everything at home. All my programs. All my hopes to feed the hungry and shelter the homeless. All my dreams to provide educational and medical care to the browns and blacks and the lame and the poor. But if I left that war and the Communists take over South Vietnam, then I would be seen as a coward and my nation would be seen as an appeaser, and we would both find it impossible to accomplish anything for anybody anywhere on the globe.[22]

LBJ's sense of international politics was chiefly informed by the same experiences that shaped the sensibilities of the majority of his generation—the Munich Pact and the dangers of appeasement. As he characterized it, "If you let a bully come into your front yard one day, the next day he'll be up on your porch, and the day after that he'll rape your wife in your own bed."[23] This quote is revealing in a number of ways. Indeed, while this sort of homespun wisdom laced with graphic metaphors was common for LBJ, it typically masked his own deep insecurity, for he himself was a notorious bully who had used those abilities to great effect in his long career on Capitol Hill. Additionally, it also reveals the extent to which LBJ relied upon crude assessments based on questionable assumptions in arriving at an elementary sense of the workings of international affairs. One could hardly allege that LBJ attempted a learned approach to understanding the complexities of geo-strategic issues.

LBJ's first real involvement with military affairs came during his first campaign for the Senate in 1941. He advocated stronger military preparedness efforts in an attempt to make his platform more conservative and balance his longtime support of FDR's New

---

[22] *Ibid.*

[23] *Ibid.*, at 337.

Deal policies.[24] After LBJ's campaign for the Senate failed, he took a five-week leave of absence from his seat in the House of Representatives to fulfill a campaign promise to volunteer for military service.[25] LBJ secured a commission from FDR as a lieutenant commander in the navy and an assignment to the Pacific theater as a part of a three-man observation team where he sought action in a danger zone to garnish his political resume.

While serving in this assignment, he was able to hitch a ride during a B-26 bombing raid. As the plane approached the target area it experienced mechanical difficulty, which the pilot was able to overcome as he carefully guided the aircraft back to its home base. LBJ returned to the United States the following day. During a stopover in Australia on his way home, General Douglas MacArthur informed Johnson that he was to be awarded the Silver Star for gallantry in connection with his ride as an observer on the B-26. No other member of the crew, not even the pilot of the endangered aircraft, received any award.[26] Within a few weeks, LBJ was safely back in his seat in Congress where he received several inquiries by journalists regarding the incident. In Johnson's accounts, the plane's engine was knocked out by enemy fire; even more striking was his recollection that the men in the 22nd Bomber Group had given him the sobriquet "Raider" Johnson. Although he had told a journalist that he did not really deserve the award, he arranged to have the medal presented to him in public on several different occasions.[27] Johnson's false bravado and propensity to bend the truth for political effect would be qualities that would undermine his relationship with his Joint Chiefs and compromise his leadership abilities as commander in chief.

---

[24] McMaster, *supra* note 5, at 50.

[25] Rowland Evans & Robert Novak, Lyndon Johnson: The Exercise of Power, A Political Biography 16, 47, 191 (1966), *quoted in* McMaster, *supra* note 5, at 50.

[26] Robert Caro, The Years of Lyndon Johnson, Vol. 2, Means of Ascent 30-55 (1990).

[27] McMaster, *supra* note 5, at 51.

LBJ subsequently would selectively engage on discrete defense issues, particularly those that he perceived would bolster his credentials and balance a liberal political philosophy, which might otherwise leave him vulnerable to attacks back in his home state of Texas. A recurring theme, however, is the level to which his positions on these issues were attributable to domestic political posturing as opposed to a thorough grasp of the geopolitical and strategic issues concerned. For example, days after the outbreak of war on the Korean Peninsula, LBJ arranged for the chairman of the Senate Armed Services Committee, Richard Russell, to create a subcommittee charged with overseeing the American conduct of the war. Of course, LBJ also ensured that Senator Russell appointed him as chairman of the subcommittee so that he could properly enjoy the publicity that accompanied such a high profile position. LBJ was able to use this position to great advantage and further enhanced his defense "credentials" through his criticisms of Truman's rejection of JCS requests for increased U.S. air power.[28] LBJ fundamentally was a politician who viewed every issue through the lens of domestic electoral politics; it was a characteristic that would follow him into the White House and mold decision-making with respect to Vietnam.

LBJ's view of senior uniformed leaders differed little from his view of other political actors in Washington; in essence, they were just one more constituency that was to be appeased so that he could advance those social issues most important to him. His tragically simplistic, even juvenile, remarks reveal his measurement of the sort of men who made careers as officers in the armed forces. According to LBJ, "wars are too serious to be trusted to generals" because, among other reasons, they "need battles and bombs and bullets in order to be heroic."[29] Of course, to LBJ, who had sought his badge of military valor during his five-week stint as a lieutenant commander in order to enhance his political resume, there could be no other reason for the generals to seek a life of service in uniform. Indeed, at a White House reception on

---

[28] *Ibid.*
[29] KARNOW, *supra* note 19, at 342.

Christmas Eve 1963, he told the Joint Chiefs, "Just let me get elected, and then you can have your war."[30] LBJ's cartoonish views concerning the motivations of his senior military advisors and his view that they merely represented another constituency to be placated polluted the relationship and eroded any possibility that a coherent policy regarding Vietnam could emerge under his direction.

LBJ's years of political intrigue on Capitol Hill had imbued him with a chronic distrust of nearly everyone and a concomitant obsession with loyalty. This fixation with loyalty was evident from his earliest days as president and would have dire consequences for the prosecution of the military effort in Vietnam. As McGeorge Bundy articulated, "Johnson was worried about the unknown . . . . He knew that the only way to avoid failure was to put yourself on guard against it, and he was, in that sense, the wariest man about whom to trust that I have ever encountered."[31]

JCS Memorandum 46-64

The Joint Chiefs of Staff responded promptly to the presidential directive issued in NSAM 273. In January 1964, the Chiefs submitted JCS Memorandum 46-64 (JCSM 46-64) to McNamara outlining their proposals for the successful achievement of America's strategic objectives in Vietnam. As it was the first formal communication from the JCS regarding Vietnam policy since President Johnson's assumption of responsibilities as president, it set the foundation for the way in which the Pentagon viewed the challenge. Although its diagnoses and prescriptions were clear, the JCS spent the next four years attempting to implement the recommendations contained therein against the steady opposition of those advocating a gradualist approach to the application of military force in Vietnam.

---

[30] *Ibid.*
[31] McGeorge Bundy, *quoted in* MERLE MILLER, LYNDON: AN ORAL BIOGRAPHY 386 (1980).

In the memorandum, the Chiefs begin by declaring that they "are of the opinion that the United States must be prepared to put aside many of the self-imposed restrictions which now limit our efforts, and to undertake bolder actions which may embody greater risks."[32] After acknowledging the strategic stakes as they were enunciated in NSAM 273, namely that "a loss of South Vietnam to the communists will presage an early erosion of the remainder of our position in that subcontinent," the JCS went on to suggest a number of specific recommendations. First, JCSM 46-64 defined the problem as one that was not limited to Vietnam alone, nor was it simply a military problem; rather it was a dilemma affecting all of Indochina in economic, military, and political dimensions. As such, it required an integrated approach that acknowledged the interconnectedness of the geographical and strategic issues. Second, the JCS stated that fulfillment of the president's guidance in NSAM 273 would require the United States to be prepared "for whatever level may be required and, being prepared, must then proceed to take actions necessary to achieve our purposes surely and promptly."

JCSM 46-64 delivered a stark assessment of the measures currently in application as of January 1964.

Currently we and the South Vietnamese are fighting the war on the enemy's terms. He has determined the locale, the timing, and the tactics of the battle while our actions are essentially reactive. One reason for this is the fact that we have obliged ourselves to labor under self-imposed restrictions with respect to impeding external aid to the Viet Cong . . . . These restrictions, while they may make our international position more readily defensible, all tend to make the task in Vietnam more complex, time consuming, and in the end, more costly.[33]

---

[32] 3 Pentagon Papers: The Defense Department History of the Vietnam War 496 (Senator Mike Gravel ed., 1971).

[33] *Ibid.*

The memorandum then turned to problems South Vietnam was facing in preserving its independence. Foremost among these challenges was the "aid now coming to the Viet Cong from outside the country in men, resources, advice, and direction." The Chiefs articulated their conviction that the character of the conflict in South Vietnam could be markedly transformed if the interference from North Vietnam could be halted. While the JCS endorsed the covert operations that were currently being contemplated, the memorandum issued the following warning: "we believe, however, that it would be idle to conclude that these efforts will have a decisive effect on the communist determination to support the insurgency."[34]

JCSM 46-64 made the following specific recommendations, *inter alia*: assign to the U.S. commander responsibilities for the total U.S. program in Vietnam, including complete tactical direction of the war; induce the Government of Vietnam to undertake ground operations in Laos to impede the flow of personnel and materiel to the Viet Cong; aerial bombing of critical targets in North Vietnam and mining the sea approaches to that country; large-scale commando raids against critical targets in North Vietnam; and commit additional U.S. forces, as necessary, in support of South Vietnam.[35]

McNamara and Taylor's Recommendations to the President

McNamara received JCSM 46-64 from the Joint Chiefs and subsequently submitted his own recommendations to LBJ. McNamara's memorandum followed only days after his return from a trip to Vietnam, where he was joined by General Taylor. In it he evaluated a variety of options for further prosecution of American objectives, ranging from a total withdrawal of U.S. support as implied by de Gaulle's "Neutralization Plan" to direct military action against North Vietnam. The secretary contemplated various forms of assistance to South Vietnam, including limited

---

[34] *Ibid.*, at 498.
[35] *Ibid.*, at 498-99.

aims such as border control actions to limited direct military action against North Vietnam. Ultimately, McNamara's recommendations to LBJ focused on preparations to begin "Graduated Overt Military Pressure" against North Vietnam. Noticeably missing from McNamara's recommendations to the president were the bold initiatives contained in the recommendations the JCS had conveyed to McNamara in JCSM 46-64.[36]

The Joint Chiefs were given a copy of McNamara's memorandum prior to its submission to the president. On March 14, 1964, it served as the focal point of discussion for the JCS led by General Taylor. Although Taylor seemed sympathetic to McNamara's views, the other Chiefs were unanimous in their assessment that the measures the secretary of defense proposed were inadequate to achieve the aims articulated in NSAM 273. The Chiefs emphasized the critical need for authority to pursue Viet Cong guerrillas into Cambodia, strengthen efforts in South Vietnam, and conduct reconnaissance of Viet Cong sanctuaries in Cambodia and supply routes through Laos; and General Wallace M. Greene, Jr., commandant of the Marine Corps, issued the call as he had done previously for the introduction of U.S. Marines into enclaves into South Vietnam. LeMay, disenchanted with the positions assumed by McNamara and Taylor, insisted that since the views of the JCS were not being represented by the two men the service chiefs' concerns should go directly to LBJ.[37] Indeed, later that month General Greene protested to Major General Chester Clifton, the military aide to the president, concerning the "insulation, or walling away, of President Johnson from the Joint Chiefs."[38]

When the NSC met with the president three days later, Taylor was the only military representative included, and the JCS had not been given the opportunity to submit a separate point paper as

---

[36] *Ibid.*, at 499-10.

[37] Harold K. Johnson, Notes on JCS Meeting, 14 Mar.—11:00 AM, Box 126, Notes on Meetings of the JCS Jan.-Apr. 1964, H.K. Johnson Papers, *quoted in* MCMASTER, *supra* note 5, at 77.

[38] LEWIS SORLEY, HONORABLE WARRIOR 149 (1998).

sought by LeMay. In that meeting, McNamara largely disregarded the views of the JCS and continued to assert the positions he had constructed in his memorandum. Taylor chimed in by stating, falsely, that the Chiefs "supported the McNamara report" and later qualified that support by stating that the JCS believed that intensified action against North Vietnam "might be necessary."[39] Of course, the JCS not only thought such action might be necessary, the Chiefs had insisted in JCSM 46-64, and again during deliberations days before, that anything less than that would be insufficient to ensure the goals articulated in NSAM 273.

In truth, the Chiefs were not unified in their positions regarding specific courses of action in Vietnam. As had been the case so often in the past, service rivalries and parochialism between the Joint Chiefs, as well as legitimate differences of opinion, plagued their efforts at forming a consensus. Although, as General Clifton stated in a talking paper on the topic, the "Chiefs were badly split on this one," it is clear that they viewed the loss of South Vietnam as a disastrous outcome and that the measures advocated by McNamara and Taylor were inadequate.[40] The Chiefs' inability to set aside service competition to forge some position that had the strength of appearing as a form of consensus undermined their ability to have their voices heard in an organizational structure that did not allow them frequent direct access to the president.

The initial deliberations following LBJ's first few months in office established the paradigm within which the president would view options in Vietnam for the remainder of his presidency. The reluctance to take bold steps to cut off the flow of supplies from North Vietnam, the refusal to deal conclusively with the threat posed by the supply routes through Laos and the sanctuaries in Cambodia, and the unwillingness to apply meaningful pressure against North Vietnam were the hallmarks of all future decisions that emerged from the Johnson administration pertaining to the

---

[39] Bromley Smith, Summary Record of the National Security Council Meeting No. 524, 17 Mar. 1964, NSF, NSC Meetings, vol. 1, tab 5 item #2, LBJ Library, *quoted in* MCMASTER, *supra* note 5, at 78.

[40] SORLEY, *supra* note 38, at 149.

Indochina War. The course of the war throughout 1964, and indeed through 1968, followed the path laid down in the first few months of 1964. Likewise, the inability of the JCS to shape presidential decision-making in any tangible way was undercut in ways similar to those employed in the debates of early 1964.

Tuesday Lunches and Presidential Decision-Making

LBJ began a routine in early 1964 that would have a deep and indelible impact upon military policy formulation and execution during the Vietnam War. On February 4, 1964, the president held the first of the "Tuesday Lunches." These lunches were sessions where the highest priority issues of strategy and defense were discussed and, frequently, momentous decisions were made. Vietnam was a regular topic of discussion and in later years, the president would use these sessions to consider and select specific targets that would be authorized for attack. Revealingly, no military officer, not even General Taylor, was a regular member of this group, which typically included just Secretary of State Rusk, National Security Advisor McGeorge Bundy, and McNamara, who at times would be joined by some of his "Whiz Kids," such as the former Harvard Law School Professor turned defense "expert," John McNaughton. The rationale for these tightly-closed meetings was summed up by Michael Forrestal:

> There was a bad thing in this period. The government was extremely scared of itself. There was a tremendous nervousness that if you expressed an opinion it might somehow leak out . . . and the president would be furious and everyone's head would be cut off . . . . It inhibited an exchange of information and prevented the president himself from getting a lot of the facts that he should have had.[41]

---

[41] Michael Forrestal, Oral History Transcript, 29 July 1969, LBJ Library, sec. 2, at 19-20, *quoted in* MCMASTER, *supra* note 5, at 89.

Again, LBJ's obsession with loyalty and the appearance of harmony served as the primary driver determining the manner in which he would organize his deliberative process. LBJ addressed these concerns in a way that would minimize debate and the potential for political vulnerability arising from leaks. And, as JFK had done before him, he processed information and made decisions in an ad hoc method rather than through a systematic analysis that allowed a complete airing of views from the relevant top advisors. Thus, in the absence of adequate organizational systems and with an utter lack of interest in the military judgment of his senior military advisors, LBJ excluded the JCS from the forums where their advice would have been most necessary and he further marginalized their influence.

SIGMA I-64 and SIGMA II-64

The military decided to test the assumptions underlying the theory of "graduated response," the military theory of "signaling" that McNamara believed had been effective in defusing the Cuban Missile Crisis and had asserted in justifying his recommendations on Vietnam. The JCS conducted a war game in April 1964, which would simulate what might occur if North Vietnam and the United States undertook programs of gradually increasing pressures. The results of SIGMA I-64 were prescient in the conclusions they compelled. The participants who were assigned the task of role-playing the North Vietnamese response relied upon a lack of U.S. resolve to maintain the level of commitment required. In response to increased U.S. pressure, the opposition force escalated the rate of attacks in the south and launched terrorist attacks against U.S. personnel and installations (as occurred later that year at Bien Hoa and the Brink's Hotel in Saigon). The game indicated that the end result of the gradualism approach would be a sizeable, protracted American commitment, as North Vietnam was capable of responding to American escalation and its resolve to do so was high.[42] SIGMA I-64 indicated that the assumptions upon which "gradualism" rested were flawed and would not achieve an acceptable outcome in Vietnam. Since no effective deliberation medium existed between the Chiefs and the commander in chief, the president never received the results of this war game.[43]

In September 1964, the JCS conducted SIGMA II-64 to specifically test the "Rostow thesis," which stated:

By applying limited, graduated military actions, reinforced by political and economic pressures, against a nation providing external support for an insurgency, we could cause that nation to decide to reduce greatly, or eliminate altogether, its support for the insurgency. The objective of the attacks and pressures is not to destroy the nation's ability to provide support but rather to affect its calculation of interests.[44]

The Rostow thesis was the theoretical justification for the limited reprisal strikes taken in the aftermath of the Gulf of Tonkin incident. The American response to the attack on the USS *Maddox*, and the alleged attack on the USS *C. Turner Joy*, was sharply limited, as it was thought that this action would be a sufficient "signal" to Hanoi of American resolve. Additionally, the 1964 presidential election campaign was in full swing and the president's assurances that the American response was limited helped assuage fears of the wider war that LBJ had committed to avoid.

The results of SIGMA II-64 did not bode well for the Rostow thesis. Adhering to the principle that for every action there is an equal and opposite reaction, the war game predicted that each escalation by the United States would be matched by an escalation by the North Vietnamese. "Both sides felt that they were making

---

[42] KARNOW, *supra* note 19, at 415.

[43] MCMASTER, *supra* note 5, at 89.

[44] Draft "Summary" of the Rostow Thesis prepared by OSD/ISA, 3 Aug. 1964, Rostow Papers, Box 13, Southeast Asia, item #30, LBJ Library, *quoted in* MCMASTER, *supra* note 5, at 156.

themselves clear to the opposition in a way that indicated the futility of the opponent's action"; however, each side failed to "read" this message and the war continued to escalate. The war game led to the commitment of U.S. ground forces, which irrevocably committed the country to success at nearly any cost. SIGMA II-64 predicted that American public support would deteriorate in this process and that eventually they would make the decision to pull out rather than continue to endure high levels of casualties. According to William Bundy, "the United States was faced with the decision whether to send in major ground forces in support of a weak South Vietnamese government."[45] Despite the prescient nature of this exercise, its impact on the course of future decision-making was entirely muted as the key civilian decision-makers had already accepted the correctness of their thesis and were unwilling to consult with the JCS to further consider their judgments.

CONCLUSION

An Extension of Politics by Other Means

The groundwork for the future prosecution of the Vietnam War during the Johnson administration was already established in the late days of 1963 and the early months of 1964. The dynamics that altered the national security apparatus before and during the Kennedy administration had a large role in shaping the evolution of events during the early days of Johnson's presidency. As 1964 wore on, the president became fixated upon the election campaign and sought to keep attention away from the situation in Vietnam. Even when the nation was confronted with overt aggression in the Gulf of Tonkin and at Bien Hoa air base before the election, LBJ responded in a way primarily designed to affect domestic politics, not in a manner calculated to materially affect the situation in

---

[45] Donald V. Bennett, Oral History Transcript, U.S. Army Institute for Military History, 1976, interview #7, at 26-27, *quoted in* McMaster, *supra* note 5, at 158.

Vietnam. After his election, his attentions then shifted to the Great Society agenda—the embodiment of his lifelong ambition in politics and his opportunity to rival his icon, FDR, in the annals of progressivism.

LBJ was committed to fighting the war as an extension of domestic politics. This approach had several practical ramifications. First, no discernible "strategy" for prosecuting the war ever emerged. Of course, this result is intuitive since the whims of domestic politics change rapidly and long-term strategy requires adherence to deliberately instituted objectives. Instead, all military measures were largely designed as a reaction to domestic political criticism or the possibility of such criticism. Although LBJ and some of his civilian advisors would cite fear of Chinese or Soviet intervention, LBJ's real fear was of criticism from "hawks" who would accuse him of being soft on Communism. The political toll suffered by Truman after the fall of China in 1949 was a lesson clearly imprinted in LBJ's memory, and he knew that a similar political failure would have the effect of severely undermining his Great Society ambitions. Ironically, escalation also posed threats to that most coveted ambition. First, the money to pay for the escalation and political resources required to muster support on Capitol Hill would threaten the Great Society programs by diffusing his political capital and siphoning funds from the domestic agenda to the war front. Furthermore, LBJ feared attacks from the "doves" on the university campuses. Ultimately, in a perverted misapplication of Carl von Clausewitz's well-known dictum, LBJ conceived of the Vietnam War as an extension of politics by other means; however, instead of the war being an extension of geopolitics shaped by strategic considerations, LBJ made the war an extension of domestic politics. In so doing, he spoiled any real possibility of forging a long-term view of the specific objectives for Vietnam and developing goals and assigning appropriately apportioned resources to achieve those objectives. LBJ therefore, and perhaps unwittingly, decided to pursue a middle course, which merely limited criticism from his political rivals without achieving conclusive results.

Disdain for "Military Judgment"

LBJ and his civilian advisors also had little appreciation for the advice of his senior military leaders. According to the president, "The generals only know two words—spend and bomb."[46] McNamara and the Whiz Kids came into office intent upon sweeping out the ossified methods of the "establishment" military, so they viewed military leaders with suspicion and skepticism. Furthermore, the senior level civilian advisors harbored deeply-seated misperceptions borne of the major events during JFK's presidency with them through the duration of their tenures. They simply regarded military leaders as inept and thirsty for war, and they treated them with a caustic mix of arrogance and disdain. Lieutenant General James Woolnough, deputy chief of staff for army personnel under General Harold Johnson, remarked, "Military judgment was just a term you never even mentioned because military judgment just didn't mean anything to any of those people."[47] The infrequency with which the JCS interacted with LBJ on a one-on-one basis is telling. During a House subcommittee hearing in August 1967, General Wallace Greene was asked when he had last met with the president to discuss Vietnam; General Greene's response—fourteen months.[48] General Johnson recalled that he had the opportunity to speak with LBJ about the war—once in 1964, five times in 1965, once in 1966, and twice in 1968.[149] The JCS were all but completely excluded from the decision-making that led to the gradual American buildup in Vietnam and the years of idle effort that produced few substantial gains.

---

[46] Sorley, *supra* note 38, at 221.

[47] *Ibid.*

[48] *Ibid.*, at 226.

[49] *Ibid.*

Military Operations as a "Signaling" Device

McNamara, arguably LBJ's foremost civilian advisor regarding Vietnam policy, also shared his boss's view of war strategy, because he was mostly concerned with ensuring the president's success in the terms by which LBJ defined success. McNamara, however, viewed military measures in another way also. He viewed military strategy as a way of "communicating" or "signaling" one's intent to the enemy. According to this paradigm, the goal of military force is to demonstrate to the enemy the steadfastness of one's resolve and "convince" them that they cannot succeed. Therefore, destruction of the enemy's will and capability are not necessary; it is only necessary for the enemy to "realize" that it cannot succeed. Since McNamara and his collection of academics assumed that the enemy would respond as would that creation of tort law known as "the reasonable man," mere demonstration of superior resolve and capability would cause the enemy to capitulate. Thus, a policy of "graduated pressure" would most effectively convey this message, and once it was effectively "communicated" to the North Vietnamese, victory would be won. As a result, a decisive, overwhelming application of military force designed to compel victory in a timely manner was unnecessary and even dangerous, since it might cause an uncontrollable escalation. McNamara placed great faith in this theory; the fact that it conveniently permitted the president to prosecute the war in a way that did not compromise his goals of keeping the war from interfering with the campaigns for election and passage of the Great Society was, to the uncritical eye, merely a fortunate coincidence.

LBJ's and his chief civilian advisors' conceptions of war strategy stood in stark contrast to that of his most senior uniformed military advisors. These men viewed war as a battle of wills and capabilities. In order to win, these men believed that the enemy's capability and will to do battle in the pursuit of its political aims had to be destroyed. Of course, their view of victory was not framed within the paradigm of domestic political calculations pertaining to social welfare programs. Rather, their view of success was that laid out *by the president* in NSAM 273—the continued viability of a free and independent South Vietnam. Thus, since the president and his closest senior civilian advisors had a distinctly different view of the objectives in Vietnam from those articulated in NSAM 273 and other official pronouncements, and also different from those declared by previous administrations and held by the JCS, it is unsurprising that civil-military relations would have been strained. When these philosophical differences regarding the prosecution of war objectives in Vietnam were combined with deep-seated tensions arising from the way in which the secretary of defense managed affairs in the Pentagon, it became even more difficult for the members of the JCS to influence decision-making regarding the war.

Organizational Structure Shortcomings

Exacerbating the situation further was LBJ's inherent distaste for foreign policy and military affairs in general; he viewed them as distractions from his most important responsibility—the domestic agenda. Further compounding all of these issues was LBJ's insistence on internal harmony amongst his advisors, which manifested itself in multifarious ways, including relentless efforts to suppress leaks and stifle dissent. First among the methods to accomplish this end was the use of ad hoc groups. These were mostly devoid of significant representation by uniformed advisors, to wit, the "Tuesday Lunch" sessions, which became the primary forum where the most important decisions were made regarding Vietnam policy and detailed specifics on the application of force in the theater. Thus, the president's insecurity and his concomitant desire for secrecy resulted in his dependence upon the deliberations of a small group of civilian advisors in making the most pivotal wartime decisions. These factors further removed senior military advisors from their statutory roles as principal military advisors to the president.

Final Result

The relationships between LBJ, McNamara, and the JCS were unmistakably strained due to a confluence of factors that reinforced each other. In addition, the inability of the JCS to manage its own internal divisions wrought by parochialism, which have long characterized the relationship between the services, further complicated this caustic mix. The result was a disempowered JCS, which played an anemic role in formulating strategic objectives in Vietnam and proposing the means, methods, and resources required to achieve those objectives.

RECOMMENDATIONS

Diagnosis

The systematic and intentional elimination of any meaningful role for the Joint Chiefs of Staff did not persist to the same degree following the conclusion of the Johnson presidency. However, the role of the JCS in contributing to the formulation of American strategic objectives and its primacy in advising the president on military matters has experienced an ebb and flow depending upon the constitution of the chief executive. Depending upon each president's, and his respective defense chief's, own confidence in the uniformed leadership of the U.S. military, the relative influence of the JCS has risen or fallen accordingly. The fact that the JCS's ability to fulfill its statutory responsibility as the "primary military advisors to the president" is so dependent upon the personalities of the president and the secretary is seemingly a cause for concern. Likewise, the potential that an imperious secretary of defense may interpose himself between the senior uniformed military and the president, thereby diluting or obscuring their views, is also troublesome. Since he is in the chain of command between the president and the Unified Commanders, it is reasonable that the secretary would insist upon such a relationship. However, considering that the secretary may or may not have significant military experience, the necessity of the current structure is questionable. In essence, why should the president not hear the views of his military commanders directly from them and then weigh that advice with the other inputs into the interagency process? What compelling justification exists for interposing a civilian intermediary between the president and his "primary military advisors"? If an intermediary does exist, is it really possible for the JCS to be "primary" in advising the president on these issues?

An important issue to consider is the subtle, and not so subtle, pressure that a secretary of defense can exert on the senior uniformed leaders. First, it is the secretary who presents the president with the nominees for the most important senior level assignments. Thus, there is a screening process wherein the secretary can ensure that the only officers who advance are those who share views sympathetic to his own. Since the secretary is a political appointee, it is not inconceivable that he might employ politically motivated considerations in determining which officers should advance, despite their professional qualifications. Additionally, this arrangement also introduces the possibility that the secretary might nominate only those senior officers who will quietly accept the administration's, or his own, prerogatives while ensuring that any officers who might not are either placed outside the circle of influence via marginalized assignments or are retired. Such a result is hardly far-fetched—McNamara ensured that General Lemnitzer was reassigned while going so far as to bring another general out of retirement to assume responsibilities as the chairman of the JCS. Of course, General Taylor was an officer in whom the administration knew they could trust, because he would stifle dissenting views from within the JCS and minimize the possibility of adverse publicity.

Thus, the current structure allows for the secretary of defense to employ a screening function in determining which officers have the opportunity to advance and to receive influential assignments, and which will ultimately determine whether their strategic and military views are heard. Furthermore, this power also results in a pre-emptive ability to shape advice before it is even received. An agenda-driven secretary, who seems unwilling to consider views different from his own and makes his views unmistakably clear to his subordinates, is unlikely to receive advice that dramatically deviates from his own views. Therefore, the secretary possesses enormous potential to stifle legitimate alternative views. Where dissenting views do not reach the president, as was the case during the Kennedy and Johnson administrations, the potential for grave errors in judgment is multiplied substantially.

The solution to this predicament is one that must be consistent with the notion of civilian control of the military. However, it seems appropriate to consider what the actual notion of "control" ought to mean. Civilian leaders risk woeful errors when they attempt to micromanage military affairs by substituting their own tactical and operational "judgment" for that of seasoned professionals. The Vietnam lesson highlights the folly of such efforts. Properly understanding the optimal relationship between the uniformed military and the civilian leadership is central to any recommendations in improving the current one.

Possible Solutions

The most radical recommendation is the elimination of the position of secretary of defense. This alternative is the most controversial and, therefore, probably the most difficult to implement. This approach would result in relationships among the service chiefs and secretaries nearly identical to that which existed before the National Security Act of 1947 and most notably observed during the Second World War. The ability of General Marshall and Admiral King to consult directly with President Roosevelt increased their influence enormously. Since their experience, wisdom, and insight was not obfuscated nor in any other way filtered before it reached the president, FDR was able to formulate an informed strategy. Interestingly, he did not always decide to accede to the assertions of his chief military advisors. Most notably, while they were advocating a delay in entering the European theater in order to save America's strength for an invasion of the continent, FDR favored an earlier entry to the theater with landings in Africa. This decision delayed the

Normandy invasion by at least a year, maybe more. The important lesson in that instance is that allowing the most senior military advisors to advise the president in a direct manner will not always mean that the president will follow their recommendations. However, when the president does make a consequential decision related to military force, he does so in an informed manner.

The strengths of removing the position of secretary of defense from its current status interposing him between the JCS and the president would include the ability for the president to hear competing views on military strategy. Also, since there would be less centralization with the Department of Defense, it would be more difficult to stifle opposing views within any of the services.

The modification described above might permit some of the same shortcomings currently existing, namely, the politicization of the military through the civilian secretary's primacy in selecting personnel for promotion to the highest ranks and assignments in the most influential billets. This might persist through the actions of the individual service secretaries, although, by the nature of their diffused power vis-à-vis the power enjoyed by a secretary of defense, it would be less difficult to achieve. Nevertheless, this proposal should also include a feature that gives the uniformed military much greater deference in making appointments to operational command assignments, subject to the veto of the service secretary, the president, and, for the highest assignments, the Congress, which already provides that oversight function.

The weakness of such a proposal is the likelihood of increased service rivalry and parochialism that might take root without a strong defense secretary to rein in such impulses. Additionally, some critics might claim that the secretary's role in streamlining the advice that reaches the president helps economize the efforts the president must exert on defense-related issues. Of course, the persuasiveness of that argument depends upon one's view of the importance of military and strategic issues among the president's many responsibilities. For those who view that responsibility as paramount, it may provide little comfort knowing that the defense secretary can define the agenda for the president on matters of such import.

Less drastic alterations in the current structure would include amplifying language that further articulates the JCS role in the formulation of military strategy at the presidential level. Perhaps it would be appropriate to include language that requires a president to include all members of the JCS, not just the chairman, along with the Unified Commanders in appropriate circumstances, in meetings where military options are being contemplated. This language would enunciate a formalized role for the military in these deliberations. As a result, the military's enhanced status could give them the ability to have their views heard and would convey a markedly improved ability to draw attention to severe neglect of military counsel when necessary. In this arrangement, when another senior general or admiral faces a situation like the one faced by General Harold Johnson during the Vietnam War, he or she can have the confidence of knowing that his or her resignation might receive enough attention to actually affect the public dialogue. This enhanced visibility could help the country avert another tragically inept application of military power as the one observed during the Vietnam War.

The structural modifications suggested here would improve the flow of information to the president and allow him to hear a wider variety of views. Additionally, it would require him to hear directly from his military leadership in all significant, relevant matters. One cannot help but wonder how differently the Vietnam War might have developed if these recommended changes had been in place then. Moreover, one wonders if America's current involvement in Iraq might have been materially different if the views of General Eric Shinseki had been heeded, or if the commanders in the theater had been given direct access to the president at all stages of the planning, especially early in the process with regard to force levels, without the interposition of the secretary of defense. Now, the question is: how many more times must we re-learn the same lessons?

XI

U.S. Intervention in Somalia: A Reprise of America's Failure in Vietnam

Major Brian Allan Hughes

A mission worth doing is a mission worth doing right.

The U.S. intervention in Somalia from 1991 to 1995 highlighted shortcomings in American foreign policy that mirror those the nation encountered a quarter of a century earlier in Vietnam. In both cases, the United States faced a challenging problem where success could not be guaranteed. In both cases, success was denied because the nation's leadership failed to precisely define its objectives and then commit the resources necessary to achieve those aims. America's leadership misunderstood the strategic calculus of the enemy and underestimated its resources and its will to succeed. In satisfying the political desire for a quick, negotiated settlement, U.S. leaders abandoned the application of military power necessary for capitulation of the immediate enemy and for strategic deterrence of other adversaries. And in abandoning worthy efforts on behalf of human rights and democracy, America's leadership drew the wrong lessons from their self-defined failure, perpetuating the disaster in Rwanda, Haiti, the Balkans, and an unforeseen number of other failed states around the globe.

Like the political and military debacle of Vietnam, the tragedy in Somalia extended beyond the confines of U.S. engagement in that country. As the United States struggled to account for its own failures in the aftermath of the Somalia mission, many American policy makers unfairly impugned the United Nations for expanding

the mission from humanitarian intervention into nation-building—
it was, after all, an expansion backed by the United States in the
UN Security Council. According to these critics, the problem was
not in our execution of the UN-sanctioned mission, but in the
particularly nasty and foolhardy mission we had been somehow
tricked into by the United Nations. Hence was born one of the
most persistent bogeymen of American foreign policy in the post-
Cold War era. "Nation-building" became understood as a dreaded
tar baby with high political risks and the potential for long-term,
low-intensity conflict, rather than a noble exercise of American
power on behalf of human rights and democracy.

The tragedy in this misunderstanding of America's ultimate
failure in Somalia was that it condemned millions of lives to
continuing hardship. In truth, Operation Provide Relief and
Operation Restore Hope were shining examples of humanitarian
missions in which American power saved 300,000 human lives.
And yet, one month after the United States abandoned Somalia,
fearing the shibboleth of nation-building, America failed to
intervene in Rwanda at the eventual expense of 500,000 human
lives. It is now too late to redress the failure of the UN mission in
Somalia or the international community's shameful dereliction in
Rwanda, but an accurate identification of where U.S. policy went
wrong in Somalia can help ensure that a post-Cold War slogan of
"No More Vietnams" is properly understood. The reality is that in
the post-Cold War world, the United States must address the "root
causes" of instability created by failed states. The United States, its
allies, and the United Nations must work together to stabilize these
countries by ridding these nations of entrenched and criminal elites
and by fostering the spread of democratic institutions.

ORIGIN OF CRISIS: SOMALIA'S FAILED STATE

On January 26, 1991, President Siad Barre fled the Somali
capital of Mogadishu and took refuge with the remnants of his
loyal forces as his twenty-one year dictatorship collapsed violently
after three years of bloodshed, which cost 50,000 Somali lives. The
civil war displaced an estimated one-fifth of the total population of

8.5 million, internally displacing 500,000 Somalis, and creating over 700,000 refugees.[1] Already one of the world's poorest nations, the civil war devastated the nation's agricultural resources and livestock, plunging Somalia into political and economic chaos. With no central government to maintain law and order, citizens relocated to their traditional clan-held areas for safety, but found none as rival militias fought for control of towns and regions. Barre exploited this chaos during the following two years, launching two attacks to regain power. Although both attacks were repulsed, the battles resulted in the spoliation of Somalia's principal food-producing regions. During the fighting, Barre plundered the countryside for food, and then scorched the earth to deny food to his opponents. Barre's ruination of the land and displacement of the farming population was the single greatest cause of the famine that followed in 1992-1993.[2] As ever, war and not weather was the "root cause" of famine. The severe drought merely exacerbated the damage already wrought by violence. Somalia's ability to provide for its own people was never adequate, even in the best of times.

In 1992, its gross domestic product was only $106 per person. The country was never self-sufficient in food, and it is estimated that the average Somali's daily caloric supply was only 81 percent of the minimum required to avoid malnourishment. Only 27 percent of the population had access to even rudimentary health services, compared to an average of 81 percent for all developing countries. Only 60 percent had access to safe drinking water, and only 17 percent had access to sanitation.[3] Given its meager natural resources and extreme poverty, the protracted civil war left the state of Somalia in utter collapse.

Barre's abdication left rival factions of the United Somali Congress (USC) struggling for power over the decimated country. The two leading contenders for control of Somalia's clan-based

---

[1] THE UNITED NATIONS AND SOMALIA 1992-1996, U.N. Blue Books Series, Vol. VIII, at 13, U.N. Sales No. E.96.I.8 (1996) [hereinafter U.N. AND SOMALIA].

[2] Id.

[3] Id.

society were Ali Mahdi Mohamed, a Mogadishu businessman, and General Mohamed Farah Aideed, the leader of the USC militia that had driven Barre from power. During the summer of 1991, the second of two conferences sponsored by the Italians and Egyptians resulted in an uneasy power-sharing arrangement. On July 5, 1991, the Third United Somali Congress overwhelmingly elected Aideed as its chair with 72 percent of the vote. A month later, the USC then recognized Mahdi as the nation's interim president until general elections could be held two years later. Aideed, meanwhile, was named commander in chief of the new national army.[4] As the two leaders set about consolidating their respective holds on power, tensions flared and finally erupted in new conflict amid mutual recriminations. In the fall of 1991, full-scale war broke out between Aideed and Mahdi in the capital city and main port of Mogadishu, already swollen with more than 250,000 internally displaced civilians from the fighting with Siad Barre. The warlords pounded areas of the city populated by rival clansmen with artillery, tanks, and "technicals"—light vehicles mounted with heavy weapons. It is estimated that 25,000 Somali civilians and 5,000 militiamen of both sides were killed or wounded during the brutal fighting. The clash left the city of Mogadishu divided into two zones by a "Green Line," and the suffering people of Mogadishu without basic services.[5]

INITIAL UN INTERVENTION: A CEASE-FIRE AND UNOSOM I (JANUARY 1992-DECEMBER 1992)

During the worst fighting of the civil war against Barre, the United Nations had evacuated its personnel from Somalia, but the destruction and loss of life in Mogadishu prompted the United Nations to reenter the Somali crisis in an attempt at reconciliation between the warring factions. As one of his first acts upon assuming office, UN Secretary-General Boutros Boutros-Ghali

---

[4] John Drysdale, *Foreign Military Intervention in Somalia: The Root Cause of the Shift from Peacekeeping to Peacemaking and Its Consequences, in* Learning From Somalia 77, 84 (Walter Clarke & Jeffrey Herbst eds., 1997).

[5] U.N. and Somalia, *supra* note 1, at 12.

tasked UN Undersecretary-General James Jonah with brokering a cease-fire. On January 23, 1992, the UN Security Council, "gravely alarmed at the rapid deterioration of the situation in Somalia and the heavy loss of life and widespread material damage resulting from the conflict in the country and aware of its consequences on stability and peace in the region," unanimously passed Resolution 733.[6] Utilizing the regional arrangements encouraged under Chapter VIII of the UN Charter, the Security Council requested increased humanitarian assistance from its members to the people of Somalia. The Security Council also requested the secretary-general, in cooperation with the Organization of African Unity and the League of Arab States, to "contact all parties involved in the conflict, to seek their commitment to the cessation of hostilities in order to permit the humanitarian assistance to be distributed, to promote a cease-fire and compliance therewith, and to assist in the process of a political settlement of the conflict."[7] Furthermore, using its Chapter VII powers authorizing enforcement action for breaches of peace, the Security Council imposed a "general and complete embargo on all deliveries of weapons and military equipment."[8] The United Nations' diplomatic efforts were successful and, after talks personally held by Secretary-General Boutros-Ghali, the two Somali factions agreed to an immediate cessation of hostilities and negotiations for implementing a cease-fire in Mogadishu on February 14, 1992. Mahdi, however, insisted the cease-fire agreement include provisions for international military observers to supervise the pact.[9] On March 3, 1992, the parties worked out an agreement to implement the cease-fire. Both factions promised to refrain from hostilities or action to extend the territory under their

---

[6] S.C. Res. 733, U.N. SCOR, 47th Sess., 3039th mtg. at 2, U.N. Doc. S/RES/733 (1992).

[7] *Id.*

[8] *Id.*

[9] Joint Communique dated 14 February 1992 issued at the conclusion of discussions between United Nations Officials and representatives of the League of Arab States, the Organization of African Unity, and the Organization of the Islamic Conference with representatives of the Somali factions in the conflict in Mogadishu, U.N. Press Release IHA/434 (1992).

control, to allow the unimpeded delivery of humanitarian aid, to accept military observers to monitor security arrangements at the ports, and to organize a national reconciliation conference.[10]

While UN intervention did stop the fighting, the agreement uncovered Aideed's unwillingness to have a political settlement imposed by the international community. The cease-fire had cemented Aideed's recent gains in Mogadishu, and as the leader of the better-armed faction, Aideed felt he had the power in the long run to consolidate rule over the entire nation. Peacekeepers would eventually constrict his ability to apply force to reach his goals. For that very reason, his nemesis Mahdi quickly and publicly agreed to the deployment of UN military observers and furthermore called for the deployment of peacekeeping troops to Somalia, which Aideed continued to fiercely resist.

Further complicating the UN's peace efforts, Aideed believed that his key role in defeating Barre's military during the civil war entitled him not only to power, but to legitimate sovereignty as well. He was extremely sensitive, therefore, to any perceived grant of legitimacy to the Mahdi faction, a fear that even an objectively neutral UN diplomacy could do little to assuage.[11] Aideed's sense of entitlement was reinforced that April when he defeated the second attempt in less than a year by ex-President Barre to reestablish his power in southern Somalia. Aideed probably felt much like Ho Chi Minh at the 1954 Geneva Conference. His arms had won the war of revolution, but international actors were conspiring to deny him the fruits of victory and granting legitimacy to a weaker rival.

Despite the March cease-fire, problems in Somalia continued. Perhaps uncritically, the United Nations noted that armed elements "beyond the control" of Mahdi and Aideed were responsible for

---

[10] *The Situation in Somalia: Report of the Secretary-General*, U.N. SCOR, 47th Sess. at 4, U.N. Doc. S/23693 (1992) [hereinafter *Report of the Secretary-General*].

[11] As an example of Aideed's concern that UN diplomacy was biased toward Mahdi and his resistance to the outside interference, Aideed delivered an expulsion notice to the UN observer's headquarters the day after they arrived in-country, claiming that a UN World Food Program flight illegally delivered hard currency and military equipment to Mahdi's faction the week before. *Id.* at 1-2.

the "banditry, looting, and reckless firing [that has] complicated all efforts to bring humanitarian assistance to the people of Somalia, particularly the hundreds of thousands of displaced people."[12] According to some estimates, 70 percent to 80 percent of all food aid was being stolen before it could be distributed.[13] In response, the Security Council passed Resolution 746 on March 17, 1992, which expressed its deep regret "that factions have not yet abided by their commitment to implement the cease-fire." The Council stated that it was "deeply disturbed by the magnitude of the human suffering caused by the conflict and concerned that the continuation of the situation in Somalia constitute[d] a threat to international peace and security." As a result, the Security Council urged "all the Somali factions to cooperate with the U.N.'s efforts to deliver humanitarian assistance" and approved the dispatch of a technical team to "develop a high-priority plan to establish mechanisms to ensure the unimpeded delivery of humanitarian assistance."[14] On April 24, 1992, the United Nations followed that resolution with Resolution 751, which authorized the immediate deployment of fifty military observers to supervise the cease-fire and agreed "in principle" to the establishment of a UN security force to safeguard humanitarian relief operations.[15] Aideed's hard bargaining and the UN's determination to reach an agreement of some kind, however, undermined the effectiveness of this peacekeeping force. Aideed was successful in limiting the number of observers to fifty. He also prevailed in ensuring that the observers would be unarmed. To further undermine the prestige of the observers, Aideed even went so far as insisting they wear only civilian attire with UN insignia. While Aideed lost that particular demand, he retained control over the size and mission of the deployment by insisting on a proviso that the observers and the

---

[12] *Id.* at 4.

[13] Don Oberdorfer & Trevor Rowe, *U.S. Offers Ground Troops for Intervention in Somalia; U.N. Moves toward Sending Armed Force to Deliver Food*, WASH. POST, Nov. 26, 1992, at A1.

[14] S.C. Res. 746, U.N. SCOR, 47th Sess., 3060th mtg., U.N. Doc. S/RES/746 (1992).

[15] S.C. Res. 751, U.N. SCOR, 47th Sess., 3069th mtg., U.N. Doc. S/RES/751 (1992).

peacekeeping force would be deployed only "in consultation with the parties."[16]

Aideed adopted delaying tactics to frustrate the introduction of the observers and peacekeeping force while he continued to consolidate his power. After difficult negotiations with UN Ambassador Mohamed Sahnoun, the secretary-general's special representative to Somalia, Aideed eventually allowed seven UN observers under the supervision of a Pakistani general into Mogadishu in July 1992, three months after Resolution 751 called for their deployment. Negotiations for the peacekeeping force, which was to be termed UNOSOM I (United Nations Operation in Somalia), dragged on into mid-August, and the 500-man contingent of the Pakistani army did not reach Mogadishu until September 14, 1992, five months after the passage of Security Council Resolution 751. The Pakistani battalion, consisting only of an unsupported light infantry force, was hopelessly outgunned and over-tasked, and Aideed was able to keep the peacekeepers bottled up in the Mogadishu Airport.[17] The secretary-general, meanwhile, grew more concerned that even this force would not be sufficient to contain the deepening humanitarian crisis. Even as his special representative was attempting to get the hostile Aideed to agree to the token UN force, Boutros-Ghali was advocating a larger UN role before the Security Council. In his July 22, 1992, Report of the Secretary-General on the Situation in Somalia, Boutros-Ghali painted a bleak picture. "Somalia is today a country without central, regional, or local administration, and without services: no electricity, no communications, no transport, no schools, and no health services."[18] The Report also stated that the food situation was critical, threatening widespread famine. One million children were malnourished and 4.5 million needed food assistance.[19] To prevent an immediate disaster, on July 27, 1992, the UN Security Council issued Resolution 767, authorizing the airlift of food

---

[16] Id.

[17] Todd Shields, *Troops in Somalia: Frustration Every Day; Pakistanis Only Hold Mogadishu Airport*, WASH. POST, Dec. 3, 1992, at A1.

[18] *Report of the Secretary-General, supra* note 10, U.N. Doc. S/23693 (1992).

[19] Id.

supplies to accelerate the provision of humanitarian assistance and to prevent mass starvation.[20] While concerned that resources pledged by the international community were inadequate, Boutros-Ghali identified the security of both personnel and relief supplies as the main obstacle to the humanitarian operation.

> The United Nations and its partners are ready and have the capacity to provide substantially increased assistance, but they have been prevented from doing so by the lawlessness and lack of security that prevails throughout Somalia. . . . Current security conditions do not permit the assured delivery of humanitarian assistance by overland transport and are thus the main cause of the current food crisis in Somalia.[21]

Realizing that the Pakistani force could not possibly extend its influence over the areas worst affected by the famine, Boutros-Ghali proposed expanding UNOSOM I by deploying 3,000 additional forces to provide escort and protection for humanitarian aid activities and personnel throughout the country. Boutros-Ghali believed this more aggressive intervention was necessary to break the "vicious cycle of insecurity and hunger" that had developed in Somalia. "Lack of security prevents the delivery of food, while food shortages contribute significantly to the level of violence and insecurity."[22] But the severity of the developing famine and the introduction of the food aid had the unintended consequence of making control of the food the principal military objective of competing warlords. As a result, aid workers were continually threatened and even killed as food convoys, rather than rival clans, became the targets of the warring factions.

On August 28, 1992, the UN Security Council approved Resolution 775 calling for the expansion of UNOSOM I by 3,000

---

[20] S.C. Res. 767, U.N. SCOR, 47th Sess., 3101st mtg., U.N. Doc. S/RES/767 (1992).

[21] *The Situation in Somalia: Report of the Secretary-General*, U.N. SCOR, 47th Sess. at 6, U.N. Doc. S/24480 (1992) [hereinafter *Report of the Secretary-General*].

[22] *Id.*

troops. The mission would divide the nation into four operational zones to carry out humanitarian programs, monitor the cease-fire, provide security, and promote national reconciliation.[23] Boutros-Ghali envisioned the UN effort as "comprehensive and multifaceted," consisting of measures to demobilize regular and irregular forces, to establish law and order by constituting a unified local police force, and to educate and vocationally train the militiamen in order to reintegrate them into Somali society.[24]

The contemplated expansion of UNOSOM I never occurred. Aideed, who had been resisting Sahnoun's efforts to negotiate the introduction of the token UN military observers and security personnel, was more certain than ever after the passage of Resolution 755 that the UN intervention represented a threat to his bid for power. He was determined to defy the UN mission. On October 28, 1992, Aideed made his intentions clear when he:

(a) Declared that the Pakistani battalion, which had been carrying [on] peace-keeping patrols, would no longer be tolerated on the streets of Mogadishu;

(b) Ordered the expulsion of UNOSOM's coordinator for Humanitarian Assistance, Mr. [David] Bassiouni, on the grounds that his activities went counter to the interests of the Somali people and his security could no longer be guaranteed; and

(c) Warned that any forcible UNOSOM deployment would be met by violence and that the deployment of United Nations troops . . . was no longer acceptable.[25]

Events over the next two weeks reinforced the message that UNOSOM was no longer welcome. On November 6, 1992, armed militia hijacked two UNOSOM patrol vehicles manned by

---

[23] S.C. Res. 775, U.N. SCOR, 47th Sess., 3110th mtg., U.N. Doc. S/RES/775 (1992).

[24] *Report of the Secretary-General, supra* note 21.

[25] *Letter Dated 24 November 1992 From the Secretary-General Addressed to the President of the Security Council*, U.N. SCOR, 47th Sess., U.N. Doc. S/24859 (1992).

unarmed military observers along the "Green Line." On November 10, 1992, the Pakistani battalion was engaged with heavy machine-gun, rocket, and mortar fire.[26] Once again the warring factions brought the humanitarian relief efforts to a standstill in both Mogadishu and the countryside.

By the end of November, Boutros-Ghali felt compelled to report to the Security Council that the situation in Somalia was no longer improving and that it was now "exceedingly difficult for the United Nations' operation to achieve [its] objectives." The secretary-general argued that it was now "necessary to review the basic premises and principles of the United Nations effort in Somalia."[27] The Security Council agreed and asked Boutros-Ghali to examine the UN's options and present recommendations to the Council for further action. On November 29, 1992, the secretary-general presented the UN Security Council with five distinct options in three categories: continuation, withdrawal, or vigorous expansion of the UN mission.[28] Under Boutros-Ghali's first option, the United Nations would continue its plan to implement Resolution 775 and send the 3,500 peacekeeping troops to Somalia. The force would abide by the "existing principles and practices of United Nations peace-keeping operations," which meant that they would not deploy without the agreement of Aideed and Mahdi and that they would use force only in self-defense. The secretary-general dismissed this option as inadequate, however, given the fact that neither Aideed nor Mahdi would agree to the deployment of forces outside of Mogadishu, where security for the relief effort was most critical. Furthermore, Boutros-Ghali acknowledged that elements, which he uncritically termed "outside the control of the two warlords," virtually guaranteed that the introduction of UN forces into the four proposed zones would result in attacks on the peacekeepers.

---

[26] *Id.*

[27] *Id.*

[28] *Letter Dated 29 November 1992 From the Secretary-General Addressed to the President of the Security Council*, U.N. SCOR, 47th Sess., U.N. Doc. S/24868 (1992) [hereinafter *Letter Dated 29 November 1992 to the S.C.*].

A second option proposed by Boutros-Ghali was to withdraw UNOSOM and abandon international military efforts to safeguard the humanitarian relief efforts of the NGOs, leaving those organizations to negotiate alone and at the mercy of the warlords. In some areas, agencies had been able to "hire" militiamen for protection, but the end result was that less aid reached those in need.[29] Boutros-Ghali rejected this option as "encourag[ing] further fragmentation and destroy[ing] hopes of national reconciliation." In his judgment, "the difficulties being experienced in Somalia were attributable not to the presence of international military personnel but to the fact that not enough of them were there and that they did not have the right mandate."[30]

Judging that continuing the current policy was inadequate and withdrawal was unwise, the secretary-general turned to proposals to substantially increase UN intervention in Somalia by utilizing Chapter VII peace-enforcement measures. Under Article 39 of the UN Charter, if the Security Council determined that a threat to the peace or a breach of peace existed, it could decide what measures should be taken in accordance with Article 42 to maintain or restore international peace and security.[31] Article 42, in turn, authorized such use of force as might be necessary to restore international peace and security should the Security Council determine that measures not involving the use of armed force were inadequate.[32] In Boutros-Ghali's view,

> The purpose of each of the three options involving the possible use of force would be to ensure, on a lasting basis, that the current violence against the international relief effort was brought to an end. To achieve this, it would be necessary for at least the heavy weapons of the organized factions to be neutralized and brought under international control and for the

---

[29] "The International Committee of the Red Cross was reported to have 15,000 to 20,000 armed guards on its staff at the height of the anarchy." Andrew Natsios, *Humanitarian Relief Intervention in Somalia, in* LEARNING FROM SOMALIA 77, 84 (Walter Clarke & Jeffrey Herbst eds., 1997).

[30] U.N. AND SOMALIA, *supra* note 1, at 31.

[31] U.N. Charter art. 39.

[32] U.N. Charter art. 42.

irregular forces and gangs to be disarmed. It is to be noted that this action would help de facto to bring about a cease-fire between the factions and that this would be a positive factor in the context of national reconciliation.[33]

The third option Boutros-Ghali presented to the Security Council involved a local show of force by UNOSOM in Mogadishu in hopes that the action would bolster the credibility of the United Nations in carrying out its previous resolutions concerning protection of the relief effort. But, even if large maneuvers in the city itself were successful, Boutros-Ghali doubted whether it would carry much weight with factions in the countryside, where it was imperative that the humanitarian relief effort operate and the greatest problems were occurring. Boutros-Ghali then turned to country-wide options.

In his fourth option, Boutros-Ghali resurrected the concept of a UN standing army under UN command and control. Although authorized by Article 43, the concept of a standing UN army was sidelined by the Cold War and a general lack of interest in the international community. Boutros-Ghali reiterated his arguments for such a force in *Agenda for Peace*, wherein he advocated an expansion of the UN role, given the historic opportunity presented by the end of the debilitating Cold War divisions of the Security Council.[34] The secretary-general preferred this option, but did not shy from acknowledging that the Secretariat did not at that time have the resources or the institutional expertise for such an undertaking. The proposal was, as Boutros-Ghali well recognized, a non-starter given the reluctance of member states—especially the United States—to accept that their forces would "take their orders from the United Nations and not from their national authorities."[35]

This left only the fifth option: "a country-wide enforcement operation undertaken by a group of Member-States authorized to

---

[33] *Letter dated 29 November 1992 to the S.C., supra* note 28.

[34] Boutros Boutros-Ghali, *An Agenda for Peace: Report of the Secretary-General on the Work of the Organization*, U.N. Doc. A/47/277, S/24111 U.N. Sales No. E.95.I.15 (1992).

[35] *Letter dated 29 November 1992 to the S.C., supra* note 28.

do so by the Security Council."[36] Boutros-Ghali was concerned, however, that the Security Council maintain control of the UN mission by ensuring that participating member states recognized the fact that the operation "had been authorized by the Security Council and that the Security Council therefore had a legitimate interest in the manner in which it was carried out."[37] If this option were selected, Boutros-Ghali argued, the enabling resolution should make clear that "the military operation [was] being authorized in support of the wider mandate entrusted to the Secretary-General to provide humanitarian relief and promote national reconciliation and reconstruction in Somalia."[38] Furthermore, the enabling resolution should stipulate that "the purpose of the operation was to resolve the immediate security problem and that it would be replaced by a United Nations peace-keeping operation, organized along conventional lines, as soon as the irregular groups had been disarmed and the heavy weapons of the organized factions brought under international control."[39]

On December 3, 1992, the Security Council chose the fifth option and passed Resolution 794, which "shared the Secretary-General's assessment that the situation in Somalia [was] intolerable," and "endorse[d] his recommendation . . . to the President of the Security Council that action under Chapter VII of the Charter of the United Nations should be undertaken to establish a secure environment for humanitarian relief operations in Somalia as soon as possible."[40] The Security Council determined that "the magnitude of the human tragedy caused by the conflict in Somalia, further exacerbated by the obstacles being created to the distribution of humanitarian assistance, constitute[d] a threat to international peace and security." Although the enabling resolution made no specific reference to disarmament of irregulars or demobilization of heavy weapons, the resolution did cite Chapter

---

[36] *Id.*

[37] *Id.*

[38] *Id.*

[39] *Id.*

[40] S.C. Res. 794, U.N. SCOR, 47th Sess., 3145th mtg., U.N. Doc. S/RES/794 (1992). *See* John M. Goshko, *U.N. Orders U.S.-Led Force into Somalia*, Wash. Post, Dec. 4, 1992, at A1.

VII in authorizing member states to use "all necessary means to establish as soon as possible a secure environment for humanitarian relief operations in Somalia."[41] Resolution 794 marked only the fifth time that the Security Council had authorized member states to take military action, and the first time that Chapter VII had been invoked in the context of a humanitarian intervention into a failed state.[42] The adoption of Resolution 794, while nominally a UN action, was in reality the result of a decision by the United States to commit itself directly in the international effort to provide relief and restore hope to Somalia.

U.S. INTERVENTION: OPERATIONS PROVIDE RELIEF AND RESTORE HOPE (AUGUST 1992-DECEMBER 1993)

Up to this point, U.S. involvement in Somalia was largely limited to supporting efforts by nongovernmental organizations (NGOs) to provide humanitarian relief and its general support in the Security Council for the policies outlined by the secretary-general. The United States had closed its Embassy in Somalia in January 1991, and it was looted during the civil war. In the post-Cold War world, the Horn of Africa had dropped off the list of American national security interests, and American attention focused on the breakup of the Soviet Union, the Balkans, and Iraq.[43] More than a dozen UN peacekeeping operations had been authorized since 1990, and the cost to American taxpayers of providing support and troops for the missions was mounting. The highest priority was given to the deteriorating situation in the former Yugoslavia and calls for a peacekeeping mission in Bosnia.

---

[41] *Letter dated 8 December 1992 from the Secretary-General to President Bush of the United States discussing the establishment of a secure environment in Somalia and the need for continuous consultations, in* U.N. and Somalia, *supra* note 1, at 216.

[42] The other occasions were in response to the invasion of South Korea in 1950, to enforce an embargo against Southern Rhodesia in 1966, and twice during the 1990-1991 Iraqi invasion of Kuwait. *Id.* at 33.

[43] James L. Woods, *U.S. Government Decisionmaking Processes During Humanitarian Operations in Somalia, in* LEARNING FROM SOMALIA 151, 151-52 (Walter Clarke & Jeffrey Herbst eds., 1997).

However, as the situation worsened in Somalia in the first part of 1992, momentum began to build on several domestic fronts for greater U.S. involvement.

As the media began to expose the impact that the fighting and the famine were having on the Somali people, leaders in Congress and the executive branch began to examine the crisis. Senator Nancy Kassebaum (R-KS) took a personal interest in Somalia and in April 1991 introduced Senate Resolution 115, which called upon the president of the United States to "lead a world-wide humanitarian effort in Somalia to relieve the suffering."[44] In presenting the resolution, Kassebaum stated, "Two things are clear: First, that the United States has a moral humanitarian obligation to lead worldwide relief efforts in Somalia, and second, that an active United States role strongly supporting—and possibly leading— efforts to reconcile the conflicting factions would improve the prospects for peace and stability in Somalia."[45] In 1992, Congress called State Department and Agency for International Development (AID) officials to testify before House and Senate committees seven times. These hearings "were influential in publicizing the Somalia crisis, pressuring the U.N. and the executive branch toward action, and articulating the basis of a policy of intervention for the United States."[46] The House Select Hunger Committee hearing on July 22, 1992, made clear that Congress would support forceful intervention in Somalia for

---

[44] S. Res. 115, 102nd Cong., 137 Cong. Rec. S5311-01 (1991). S. Res. 115 was approved on June 28, 1991.

[45] *Id.*

[46] Harry Johnston & Ted Dange, *Congress and the Somalia Crisis, in* Learning from Somalia 191, 193 (Walter Clarke & Jeffrey Herbst eds., 1997). *See generally The Horn of Africa: Changing Realities and the U.S. Response: Hearing Before the Subcomm. on African Affairs of the Senate Comm. on Foreign Relations,* 102nd Cong. (1992); *Somalia: The Case for Action: Hearing Before the House Select Committee on Hunger, supra* note 47; *U.N. Peacekeeping in Africa: The Western Sahara and Somalia: Hearing Before the Subcomm. on Africa of the Senate Comm. on Foreign Relations,* 102nd Cong. (1992); *Operation Restore Hope, The Military Operations in Somalia: Hearing Before the Senate Committee on Armed Services,* 102nd Cong. (1992); *The Crisis in Somalia: Hearing Before the House Comm. on Foreign Affairs,* 102nd Cong. (1992).

humanitarian purposes. Senator Kassebaum, who had just returned from a weeklong fact-finding delegation to the Horn of Africa, testified that "the situation had reached the point where the United Nations should go forward with the security force with or without General Aideed or Ali Mahdi's consent."[47] As the Security Council considered passage of UN resolution 775 expanding the UNOSOM force to 3,500, Congress continued to press for greater U.S. involvement. Senate Concurrent Resolution 132 approved of the administration's support within the United Nations to deploy UNOSOM, and "urge[d] the President to work with the United Nations Security Council to deploy these security guards immediately, with or without the consent of the Somalia factions, in order to assure that humanitarian relief gets to those most in need."[48]

The Bush administration had not entirely ignored the situation in Somalia. The United States rallied to the UN's call for increased humanitarian assistance in Resolution 733, quickly becoming the largest donor of humanitarian assistance to Somalia and remaining so throughout its involvement. In March 1992, the United States reached an agreement to supply 24,000 tons of food aid through the International Committee of the Red Cross. The following month, the United States promised an additional 20,000 tons of food through the World Food Program.[49] By the end of July 1992, the United States had pledged over $85 million in humanitarian relief.[50] In July 1992, President Bush set in motion interagency efforts to establish a more comprehensive plan for U.S. aid to Somalia. Like Senator Kassebaum, President Bush also had experienced famine firsthand, visiting the Sudan while vice-president.[51] But it was the combination of a cable from U.S. Ambassador Smith Hempstone entitled "A Day in Hell" and an

---

[47] *Somalia: The Case for Action: Hearing Before the House Select Committee on Hunger*, 102nd Cong. 6 (1992);

[48] S. Con. Res. 132, 102nd Cong., 138 Cong. Rec. H7829-02 (1992) (enacted).

[49] Woods, *supra* note 43, at 153.

[50] Don Oberdorfer, *U.S. Took Slow Approach to Somali Crisis; Delay in Action Attributed to Civil War, Other Global Problems, Lack of Media Attention*, WASH. POST, Aug. 24, 1992, at A1.

[51] Natsios, *supra* note 29, at 84.

article published in the *New York Times* that firmly fixed the president's attention on Somalia.[52]

On August 14, 1992, President Bush announced his plan for dealing with the crisis. First, he offered to provide U.S. airlift capabilities to the United Nations to transport the Pakistani peacekeepers to Mogadishu. Second, he announced U.S. support for a donor's conference on the Somali crisis that would also include representatives of the major Somali factions. Third, he declared that the United States would make an additional 145,000 tons of food aid available. Finally, the president unveiled what was code-named Operation Provide Relief, an emergency airlift of tons of food aid to Somalia and refugee camps in Kenya, bypassing the warlords and delivering the food directly to the International Red Cross and private voluntary organizations at four airfields in the Somali interior. Between August 1992 and its termination in February 1993, Operation Provide Relief flew over 2,500 missions, carrying over 28,000 tons of supplies into the areas worst hit by the famine.[53] The United States delivered another 338,000 tons of relief supplies to Somalia by sea.

However, the problem in Somalia was only tangentially the lack of adequate food. Andrew Natsios, President Bush's special coordinator for the Somali relief effort, described the situation succinctly: "The problem here is not resources or food. It is security. It is the clan war. It is the anarchy."[54] Indeed, the United States was forced to suspend the airlift in October 1992, after C-

---

[52] Oberdorfer, *supra* note 50. *See* Smith Hempstone, *Dispatch From a Place Near Hell; The Killing Drought in Kenya, As Witnessed by the U.S. Ambassador*, WASH. POST, Aug. 23, 1992, at C1; Jane Perlez, *Food Relief Grows but So Do Somalia's Dead*, N.Y. TIMES, July 19, 1992, at A2.

[53] Don Oberdorfer, *Bush Orders Food Airlift to Combat Somali Famine; Deliveries to Interior to Begin Within Days*, WASH. POST, Aug. 15, 1992, at A1.

[54] Keith B. Richburg, *Solutions for Somalia Complicated by Chaos; Authority Is Absent and Food Is Power*, WASH. POST, Aug. 30, 1992, at A1. On the very day that the first U.S. aircraft arrived, Somali gunmen fired on a UN-marked vehicle, wounding two unarmed UN observers. The bandits then stole twenty-five trucks, 300 tons of food, and 200 barrels of fuel, the UN World Food Program's entire supply for emergency operations in Somalia. Keith B. Richburg, *U.S. Starts Relief Effort in Somalia; 4 Planes Bring Tons of Food, Equipment*, WASH. POST, Aug. 29, 1992, at A1.

130s drew fire on two separate occasions while landing at rural airstrips.[55] Food deliveries to the port of Mogadishu stopped after November 14, 1992, when a relief ship was shelled while entering the harbor.[56] Even as the Somali factions attacked UN observers and the Pakistani peacekeepers, the administration was at work preparing plans for the direct commitment of U.S. troops in Somalia to ensure that the relief effort would succeed. According to James L. Woods, deputy assistant secretary of defense for African affairs and chair of the office of the secretary of defense interagency Somalia task force, the Bush administration had reached several conclusions:

1. The expanded humanitarian effort was failing. Interference from the warlords at Mogadishu port and on the highways was preventing food from getting through in quantities adequate to turn the corner. The airlift, even with Department of Defense planes flying ten or twelve missions a day, would never in itself be able to bring starvation under control.

2. The U.N. emergency intervention had essentially failed. The Pakistani battalion remained at the airport, endless debate continued in New York about augmentation forces, Mohamed Sahnoun had resigned in disgust, and it was obvious— whatever the longer-term possibilities—the U.N. offered no immediate solutions to Somalia's crisis.

3. An effective short-term solution, one that would bring dramatic improvement in a matter of weeks, could be mounted only by the United States, alone or leading a coalition (the success of Desert Storm being very much in mind). But this would heavily involve the U.S. military and in general give the United States a broad overall responsibility; and many in the executive branch and in Congress remained very uncomfortable with this approach.

---

[55] Keith B. Richburg, *U.S. Suspends Relief Flights to Somali Town*, WASH. POST, Oct. 26, 1992, at A12.

[56] Kevin M. Kennedy, *The Relationship Between the Military and Humanitarian Organizations in Operation Restore Hope, in* LEARNING FROM SOMALIA 99, 102 (Walter Clarke & Jeffrey Herbst eds., 1997).

4. If the United States were nevertheless to leap into the fray, the operation would perforce be a very "heavy" one, probably a "2-division plus" force, heavily armed and inevitably with huge logistics requirements. This meant that the locus of the main effort would be Mogadishu, and the operation would necessarily be heavily involved in getting the ports open and working, as well as the road network into the countryside.[57]

By mid-November, a national consensus had emerged that the United States should step forward and act. U.S. relief organizations met at the UN and publicly issued an appeal to the Bush administration for more protection, declaring that the "humanitarian agencies cannot work effectively in Somalia without greater security."[58] The American Somali, Muslim, and African-American community favored extending greater American help.[59] Representative John Lewis (D-GA), a member of the congressional Black Caucus who had just returned from a congressional delegation to Somalia, introduced a resolution asking the president to "express to the United Nations Security Council the desire and willingness of the United States to participate, consistent with applicable United States legal requirements, in the deployment of armed United Nations guards, as authorized by the Security Council, in order to secure emergency relief activities."[60] Less than a month earlier, Senator Paul Simon (D-IL) had proposed a measure that authorized the Department of Defense, rather than the Department of State, to spend up to $300 million for any UN peacekeeping efforts. This accounting legerdemain removed the budgetary constraints

---

[57] Woods, *supra* note 43, at 157. Woods also notes that a plan to introduce a smaller, more flexible force operating outside of Mogadishu was rejected. While favored by some in both the NGO and the Special Operations community, the military believed that heliborne and amphibious operations could not move enough supplies and it insisted on applying the doctrine of massive, overwhelming force.

[58] Don Oberdorfer, *The Path to Intervention; A Massive Tragedy 'We Could Do Something About,'* WASH. POST, Dec. 6, 1992, at A1.

[59] *Id.*

[60] H.R. Con. Res. 370, 102nd Cong. (1992) (enacted).

hindering greater U.S. involvement.[61] Assistant Secretary of State Bob Gallucci, chief of political-military affairs, recommended to acting Secretary of State Lawrence Eagleburger that the United States should seek a UN Security Council authorization to use "all necessary means," including armed force, to address the humanitarian crisis.

On November 21, 1992, Admiral David Jeremiah, deputy chairman of the Joint Chiefs, presented three options to the president: 1) increased support for the existing efforts to augment UNOSOM to 3,500 troops by securing the cooperation of Aideed and Mahdi; 2) a U.S.-organized coalition effort under the United Nations and with American forces supplying logistics and a Quick Reaction Force (QRF); or 3) a major U.S. effort to lead a multinational force in which U.S. ground troops took the leading role.[62] Admiral Jeremiah told the president, "If you think U.S. forces are needed, we can do the job."[63] On November 25, 1992, the day before Thanksgiving, President Bush met with the Deputies Committee, a National Security Council panel of officials just below the Cabinet level, and announced, "I like it. We'll do it."[64] President Bush decided that, if the Security Council authorized Chapter VII peace enforcement, the United States would organize and lead an international force to Somalia. It was with this offer in hand that Secretary-General Boutros-Ghali submitted his aforementioned letter of November 29, 1992, to the Security Council. On December 3, 1992, the Security Council authorized Resolution 794, which was drafted in a large and unprecedented measure by the United States Department of Defense.[65]

The next day, President Bush announced his decision in a national statement.

---

[61] *U.N. Peacekeeping in Africa: The Western Sahara and Somalia: Hearing Before the Subcomm. on Africa of the Senate Comm. on Foreign Relations, supra* note 46.

[62] Woods, *supra* note 43, at 157.

[63] Oberdorfer, *supra* note 58, at A1.

[64] COLIN POWELL, MY AMERICAN JOURNEY 564 (1995).

[65] Walter Clarke, *Failed Visions and Uncertain Mandates in Somalia, in* LEARNING FROM SOMALIA 3, 9 (Walter Clarke & Jeffrey Herbst eds., 1997).

The United States alone cannot right the world's wrongs, but we also know that some crises in the world cannot be resolved without American involvement, that American action is often necessary as a catalyst for broader involvement in the community of nations. Only the United States has the global reach to place a large security force on the ground in such a distant place quickly and efficiently and, thus, save thousands of innocents from death. . . . Once we have created that secure environment, we will withdraw our troops, handing the security mission back to a regular U.N. peacekeeping force. Our mission has a limited objective—to open the supply routes, to get the food moving, and to prepare the way for a U.N. peacekeeping force to keep it moving. This operation is not open-ended. We will not stay one day longer than is absolutely necessary. And let me be very clear. Our mission is humanitarian, but we will not tolerate armed gangs ripping off their own people, condemning them to death by starvation. The outlaw elements in Somalia must understand this is serious business. We will accomplish our mission. We have no intent to remain in Somalia with fighting forces, but we are determined to do it right, to secure an environment that will allow food to get to the starving people of Somalia. [Our] troops have the authority to take whatever military action is necessary to safeguard the lives of our troops and the lives of Somalia's people. To the people of Somalia I promise this: We do not plan to dictate political outcomes. We respect your sovereignty and independence. Based on my conversations with other coalition leaders, I can state with confidence we come to your country for one reason only: to enable the starving to be fed.[66]

---

[66] George Bush, *'The People of Somalia . . . the Children . . . Need Our Help,'* WASH. POST, Dec. 5, 1992, at A16 [hereinafter Bush address]. Unfortunately. Bush's recently released memoirs do not shed any more light on his fateful decision. Somalia is mentioned but once and only in praise of General Powell's thoroughness and concern for American troops. GEORGE BUSH & BRENT SCOWCROFT, A WORLD TRANSFORMED (1998).

Opinion polls showed that 84 percent of the American public approved the president's decision.[67] President-elect Clinton also supported the U.S. operation and praised President Bush for his leadership "on this important humanitarian effort." The great majority of voices in Congress approved of the president's decision as well. The Speaker of the House, Thomas Foley (D-WA), expressed that "the overall judgment of congressional leaders . . . was that 'the president has acted wisely, and in circumstances where he had very little choice without grave humanitarian consequences resulting.'" [68] The sweeping rhetoric of presidential speeches have an unfortunate tendency to make the most difficult issues seem perfectly clear, rallying the troops for a good cause. The United States had decided to commit itself to a great undertaking, whose outcome, however, was anything but clear. The president had given the green light, and now it was time to hit the ground.

---

[67] Carolyn J. Logan, *U.S. Public Opinion and the Intervention in Somalia: Lessons for the Future of Military-Humanitarian Interventions*, FALL FLETCHER F. WORLD AFF. 155, 156 (1996).

[68] Don Oberdorfer, *Bush Sends Forces To Help Somalia; 'America Must Act,' President Says*, WASH. POST, Dec. 5, 1992, at A1. In contrast, Senator Hank Brown (R-CO), though acknowledging that he was in the clear minority on Capitol Hill, compared the U.S. intervention in Somalia to the failed operations in Vietnam and Lebanon. Brown expressed concern that "Bush had committed U.S. forces 'without clear, precise military objectives,' a stated date to end the operation, a limit to U.S. involvement and well-defined rules governing their authority." *Id.* Representative John Murtha (D-PA), chairman of the Appropriations Subcommittee on Defense, also opposed the action for reasons including "the impact on the national budget deficit, a lack of congressional consultations and uncertainty about the military mission [which] represent[ed] . . . 'a basic change in direction of our policy' because 'no national interest from the standpoint of defending the United States from some outside threat' exists in Somalia." Ann Devroy & Kenneth Cooper, *Bush Calls Foreign Leaders for Support on Somalia Force*, WASH. POST, Dec. 3, 1992, at A32.

U.S. INVOLVEMENT IN TRANSITION: UNITAF TO UNOSOM II (DECEMBER 1992-MARCH 1993)

On December 9, 1992, within a week of the passage of UN Resolution 794, the U.S. Marine Corps splashed ashore on the beaches of Mogadishu. The media was already waiting to broadcast the U.S. "invasion," just as it had twenty-seven years earlier in Danang.[69] U.S. Ambassador-at-large Robert Oakley was given the diplomatic mission of dealing with the warlords, and U.S. Central Command drew the task of putting the broad pronouncements of President Bush into operation.[70] The mission statement CENTCOM gave to Lieutenant General Robert B. Johnston, commander of the Unified Task Force (UNITAF), had four principal elements:

- Secure Mogadishu port, airfield, and other key objectives in the capital
- Secure lines of communication to the interior by placing coalition security detachments at regional hubs in the Somali interior
- Provide security escorts for relief supply convoys and relief organizations' operations
- Assist United Nations nongovernmental organizations in providing humanitarian relief under U.N. auspices.[71]

---

[69] *Compare* Photographs of the Danang landing in STANLEY KARNOW, VIETNAM: A HISTORY 403 (1983), *with* John Lancaster, *Hitting the Beach in Glare of the Night; TV Turns Stealthy Moment into Shining One, Angering Pentagon Aides*, WASH. POST, Dec. 9, 1992, at A1, *and* Tom Shales, *Television's Beachhead in Somalia*, WASH. POST, Dec. 9, 1992, at C1.

[70] Oakley was known to the Somalis, having been the U.S. ambassador to Somalia from 1983 to 1984. Don Oberdorfer, *Oakley Is Called from Retirement to Head Political Side of Operation in Somalia*, WASH. POST, Dec. 9, 1992, at A27. Oakley was also a political officer in the Saigon Embassy in the early days of the Vietnam War. Keith B. Richburg, *Broader U.S. Role Developing in Somalia*, WASH. POST, Dec. 31, 1992, at A16.

[71] Kennedy, *supra* note 56, at 100.

The United States deployed over 28,000 troops in support of the UN mandate and was in operational command of major troop contributions by France, Italy, and Canada in addition to the Pakistanis already in place.[72] A total of twenty countries contributed forces to the effort. Total UNITAF strength reached a peak of 37,000 troops, including the 8,000 marines and sailors stationed offshore.[73] Oakley worked independently of UNOSOM and established the acquiescence of both Aideed and Mahdi to the introduction of UNITAF, arranging a public meeting of the two to sign another cease-fire.[74] Despite the agreement, U.S. forces became engaged in violent firefights within the first few weeks of the intervention.[75]

From December 1992 until April 1993, UNITAF executed 154 long-haul food convoys carrying 100,000 tons from the ports of Mogadishu and Kismayu in the south to the displaced civilian camps and cities in the Somali interior. Each convoy carried 600 metric tons of relief supplies and averaged twenty trucks. The Mogadishu food distribution system itself delivered 350 tons per day, six days a week, at thirty-five feeding centers across the city. In addition, UNITAF performed hundreds of security escort missions for humanitarian fieldworkers (237 from Mogadishu alone). In order to move the supplies by convoy, UNITAF engineers either repaired or improved 1,800 kilometers of roads and nine airfields. UNITAF engineers also dug fourteen municipal

---

[72] Non-U.S. forces totaled around 10,000: France (2,783), Morocco (1,356), Canada (1,262), Saudi Arabia (643), Belgium (572), Turkey (309), Botswana (303), Egypt (270), United Kingdom (90), Germany (60), Kuwait (43), and New Zealand (42). Australia, Nigeria, Zimbabwe, India, Tunisia, and Sweden also participated. *Letter dated 19 January 1993 from the United States to the President of the Security Council transmitting a report on the progress made by UNITAF*, U.N. Doc. S/25126 (1993), *in* U.N. AND SOMALIA, *supra* note 1, at 216.

[73] *Report by the United States Pursuant to Security Council Resolution 794*, U.N. SCOR, 47th Sess., Annex, U.N. Doc. S/24976 (1992).

[74] William Claiborne, *Rival Warlords Sign Peace Pact in Somalia*, WASH. POST, Dec. 12, 1992, at A1.

[75] Barton Gellman, *Marines Fight Gunmen, Deliver Food in Somalia*, WASH. POST, Dec. 13, 1992, at A1.

wells.[76] Ambassador Oakley was justifiably proud of the work that UNITAF accomplished. "Within six weeks after the first U.S. Marines landed on December 9, 1992, clan warfare had practically ceased and mass famine and disease had been brought under control."[77]

It was beyond question that the deployment of UNITAF was vanquishing starvation in Somalia in the short-term, saving 300,000 lives. The long-term solution, however, required a sustained commitment of resources to Somalia and no guarantee of quick success. The United States had made it clear that it saw its intervention as an immediate response to the Somali famine and that it was unwilling to shoulder the burden of reconstituting the failed state of Somalia. President Bush initially hoped that American troops could be removed before the January 20, 1993, inauguration of Bill Clinton to avoid saddling the incoming president with the problem of extrication. While disabusing President Bush of the idea that the intervention could succeed that quickly, both General Powell and National Security Advisor Brent Scowcroft believed that the U.S. mission could be accomplished in three months.[78]

President Bush made U.S. policy clear in his statement to the American people announcing Operation Restore Hope. The address emphasized that, once the humanitarian effort was secure, U.S. troops would withdraw, handing the security mission back to a regular UN peacekeeping force. The president's statement declared that the U.S. mission had only a limited objective—to enable the starving to be fed—and that U.S. forces would not stay any longer than absolutely necessary to accomplish that goal.[79] "Our job is strictly limited," stated Scowcroft at the deployment's

---

[76] Kennedy, *supra* note 56, at 107.

[77] Robert B. Oakley, *What We Learned In Somalia*, WASH. POST, Mar. 20, 1994, at C7.

[78] POWELL, *supra* note 64, at 565. Fifteen hundred American troops were withdrawn the week before the inauguration, perhaps providing the first hint of military maneuver as an adjunct to political maneuvering.

[79] Bush address, *supra* note 66.

outset. "It is not to solve all of the problems of Somalia."[80] Secretary of Defense Dick Cheney echoed the policy that the military's mission was only to ensure the delivery of humanitarian relief. "If you are looking for the U.S. to stay until all the problems are solved in Somalia, that is not going to happen."[81]

The devil is in the details, however, and there was some official confusion on whether official policy included disarmament. Secretary Cheney acknowledged that the mission could include disarming the factions and gangs, stating, "We may well want to go in and round up troops or weapons."[82] U.S. troops did conduct limited disarmament of local Somali factions in Mogadishu where possible and to further its security mission.[83] Furthermore, under the cease-fire agreements of January 8, 1993, and January 15, 1993, signed in Addis Ababa, the militias began to implement the cease-fire by storing their heavy weapons in declared cantonment sites subject to routine UNITAF inspections, but still under Somali control.[84] "When challenged by the warlords, the UNITAF forces showed no hesitation in using measured force to destroy technicals and illegal weapons caches."[85] U.S. forces dealt with problems on an ad hoc basis, taking steps to disarm Somalis carrying weapons openly, while leaving others, those not presenting immediate threats, to go on about their business. In January 1993, UNITAF confiscated sixteen

---

[80] Kathy Sawyer, *U.S. Officials Estimate Cost, Length of Somalia Mission; Humanitarian Operation Seen Taking 2 to 3 Months*, WASH. POST, Dec. 7, 1992, at A27.

[81] *Id.*

[82] *Compare* Sawyer, *id.*, *with* John Lancaster, *Powell Says Mission Duration Is Flexible; Operation Could Take 3 Months, General Says*, WASH. POST, Dec. 5, 1992 ("We are not in the business of rounding up every AK-47 in the country," Cheney said. "We're not in the business of disarming every teenager who's running loose in the streets of Mogadishu.").

[83] Richburg, *supra* note 70, at A16.

[84] *Report of the Commission of Inquiry Established Pursuant to Security Council Resolution 885 (1993) to Investigate Armed Attacks on UNOSOM II Personnel which led to Casualties Among Them*, U.N. SCOR, 49th Sess., Annex 5, U.N. Doc. S/1994/653 (1994) [hereinafter *Report of the Commission of Inquiry*].

[85] Woods, *supra* note 43, at 157.

truckloads of weapons and ammunition, including 265 rifles and assault guns and fifty-five machine guns from gunmen in Mogadishu.[86]

U.S. CENTCOM commander, Marine General Joseph Hoar, however, announced that the question of disarming Somalia's clan fighters essentially is "a political issue, one that needs to be settled first and foremost by the Somalis."[87] One journalist put it this way:

> The fear of "getting sucked in"—the fear of another Vietnam— explains American public wariness about moving more aggressively into disarming Somalia's warring factions, getting involved in policing actions to quell looting and violence, and highlighting U.S. efforts to broker a political solution. When U.S. officials insist publicly that American troops should not be allowed to become "Somalia's police force," they say privately that they recall the painful lesson of how U.S. troops came to play just that role in Saigon. And when they say they have no interest in drawing up a constitution and helping select new leaders for Somalia, they recall the failure and frustration of earlier American efforts to do just that for South Vietnam.[88]

At this juncture, a growing schism was exposed between what the United States was willing to do and what the United Nations— and Boutros-Ghali in particular—thought necessary. From the beginning, both the United States and the United Nations intended that UNITAF be replaced by a follow-on UN force. The main difference in opinion concerned the conditions under which UNITAF would hand responsibility back to a UN-controlled

---

[86] Kenneth B. Noble, *400 U.S. Marines Attack Compound of Somali Gunmen*, N.Y. TIMES, Jan. 8, 1993, at A1. The first U.S. fatality was a U.S. Army civilian employee, killed by a land mine on December 23, 1992. The first service member was killed in action on January 13, 1993. George Esper, *U.S. Marine Killed in Somali Firefight; First Military Casualty of Relief Effort Dies During Patrol*, WASH. POST, Jan. 13, 1993, at A15.

[87] John Lancaster, *General Bars Disarming Somali Clans; Marine Commander's Comments Add to Confusion Over U.S. Mission*, WASH. POST, Feb. 15, 1993, at A1.

[88] Richburg, *supra* note 70, at A16.

peacekeeping force. Secretary Boutros-Ghali believed that there were three essential elements that had to be addressed in order to solve the Somali crisis in the long term. First, Boutros-Ghali argued, "any forceful action by the international community must have the objective of ensuring that at least the heavy weapons of the warring factions are neutralized and brought under international control and that the irregular forces and gangs are disarmed."[89] The secretary-general concluded that de-fanging the warlords was necessary not only to promote national reconciliation, but also to reduce the threat to the humanitarian relief effort to a size that a conventional UN force could manage. Second, Boutros-Ghali maintained that the foreign military presence had to be extended across the entire nation. Although the areas worst affected by the famine were under UNITAF control, the warlords could (and did) move their weapons and operations to areas not secured by UNITAF, waiting to emerge after the United States had withdrawn. Finally, Boutros-Ghali saw the need for "close and continuous consultations" concerning the "division of labor," whereby "the United States has undertaken to take the lead in creating a secure environment which is an inescapable condition for the United Nations to provide humanitarian relief and promote national reconciliation and economic reconstruction" and in "planning for the eventual transfer of responsibilities from the Unified Command to a United Nations peacekeeping operation in the form of an enlarged UNOSOM [to be called UNOSOM II]."[90]

It was the issue of disarmament especially that required close and continuous consultations, and it was there that differences proved irreconcilable. The secretary-general rightly saw that there could be no peace without disarmament. The United States realistically saw that inevitable and unacceptable bloodshed would accompany any organized effort to disarm militia fighters who

---

[89] *Letter dated 08 December 1992 from the Secretary-General to President Bush, supra. See also The Situation in Somalia: Report of the Secretary-General Submitted in Pursuance of Paragraphs 18 and 19 of Security Council Resolution 794*, U.N. SCOR, 47th Sess., 7, U.N. Doc. S/24992 (1992) [hereinafter *The Situation in Somalia*]. Boutros-Ghali also called on UNITAF to begin clearance of the estimated one million land mines in Somalia. *Id.*

[90] *Id.*

were not truly at peace. Boutros-Ghali refused to acknowledge that the two views were incompatible, claiming that this "minor difference in point of view" with the United States was "not a real problem" and could be resolved through "shared consultation."[91] As James Woods observed, the divergence between the views of the United States and the United Nations became manifest in spring 1993:

- UNITAF refused to take on the expanded tasks [of extending the areas of operation and engaging in general disarmament], despite the urgings of the Secretary-General to make UNOSOM's follow-on job more manageable [and]
- U.N. slowness verged on foot-dragging in mounting [UNOSOM II] and the critical associated activities in the civil, police, and justice sectors. [92]

This unresolved disagreement would portend failure for the UNOSOM II operation to follow. The United States, however, had the strategic upper hand in negotiating with the secretary-general. Just as Senator George Aiken (R-VT) had proposed at the height of the Vietnam War, the United States began to "declare victory, and get out."[93] The humanitarian crisis had been averted, and the United Nations had a paper agreement disarming the warlords and committing them to a peaceful transition to a national government. To spur the United Nations into action, the United States began to

---

[91] Lancaster, *supra* note 87. The United States was also unwilling to publicly speak candidly to Boutros-Ghali. U.S. Ambassador Edward J. Perkins said, "use of the word 'differences' [was] a 'misnomer,' stating that Secretary [Eagleburger] and the secretary general are in complete accord on how this is going and that there will be issues that must continue to be discussed." Barton Gellman, *U.S., U.N. Differ over Best Way to Silence Somalia's Many Guns; Americans Focus on Heavy Arms; World Body Targets Individuals*, WASH. POST, Dec. 23, 1992, at A19.

[92] Woods, *supra* note 43, at 160.

[93] Charles Krauthammer, *Enough of Sideshows*, WASH. POST, Mar. 12, 1993, at A23.

withdraw troops, forcing the secretary-general to fill the gap.[94] In time for the inauguration, the United States under President Bill Clinton had an exit strategy in place and was beginning to execute it.

UNOSOM II AND THE EXPANDED MANDATE (MARCH 1993-OCTOBER 1993)

On March 3, 1993, Secretary-General Boutros-Ghali submitted his assessment of the situation in Somalia and outlined his proposal for the UNOSOM II force that would assume UNITAF's responsibilities. While acknowledging the "positive impact of UNITAF on the security situation in Somalia and on the effective delivery of humanitarian assistance," Boutros-Ghali stressed that the situation could not yet be "regarded as irreversible and conditions [were] still volatile."[95] "It is clear," he declared, "that the effort undertaken by UNITAF to establish a secure environment in Somalia is far from complete. . . . Moreover, there have been, especially recently, some disheartening reverses. . . . Accordingly, the threat to international peace and security . . . is still in existence."[96] Boutros-Ghali stated that "the Council will now have to consider whether to authorize an enlargement of UNOSOM and redefine its mandate to include operations under Chapter VII of the Charter. The consequences of such a decision [would] be far-reaching for political, legal, and logistical reasons and would entail a major financial commitment," he warned.[97]

---

[94] John Lancaster, *U.S. Beginning Pullout From Somalia; Slow Withdrawal Aimed Partly at Forcing U.N. to Take Responsibility*, WASH. POST, Jan. 19, 1993, at A1.

[95] *Further Report of the Secretary-General Submitted in Pursuance of Para. 18 of Resolution 814*, U.N. SCOR, 48th Sess. at 7-11, U.N. Doc. S/26317 (1993).

[96] *Id.* Boutros-Ghali was referring to the skirmishes in Kismayo instigated by former Defense Minister General Mohamed "Morgan," son-in-law to ex-President Barre, against Aideed's ally, Colonel Omar Jess. UNITAF neutrality in the conflict drew the ire of General Aideed and resulted in confrontations between UNITAF and gangs in Mogadishu. Drysdale, *supra* note 4, at 130.

[97] *Further Report of the Secretary-General Submitted in Pursuance of Para. 18 of Resolution 814*, *supra* note 95.

Specifically, Boutros-Ghali proposed that UNOSOM II extend its mandate beyond the 40 percent of Somalia already under UNITAF control to include the entire country and undertake the following military tasks:

1) Monitor the Addis Ababa cease-fire agreement;
2) Prevent any resumption of violence, and, if necessary, take appropriate action against any faction violating the cease-fire;
3) Maintain control of the heavy weapons already corralled in the cantonment areas until destroyed or turned over to a Somali national army;
4) Seize small arms from irregular forces;
5) Continue to protect the relief workers and maintain the supply lines of the humanitarian assistance;
6) Clear mines; and
7) Assist in repatriating both internal refugees and those exiled abroad.[98]

Boutros-Ghali recognized that this mandate significantly expanded that of both Resolutions 751 and 794. In his view, "the strength of the forces required to implement such a mandate would have to be substantial in the early stage in order to minimize the risk of any deterioration in the security conditions and to ensure a secure environment as quickly as possible," so the secretary-general requested a force of 28,000 troops.[99] In essence, Boutros-Ghali was asking the Security Council to authorize its first-ever UN-commanded peace enforcement operation, which he had argued for in his *Agenda for Peace*, as his recommended course of action to the Security Council.[100] Boutros-Ghali's proposal was a blueprint for nation-building.

On March 26, 1993, the Security Council unanimously adopted Resolution 814, authorizing the secretary-general to establish

---

[98] *Id.*

[99] *Id.*

[100] Boutros-Ghali, *supra* note 34; *Letter Dated 29 November 1992 to the S.C.*, *supra* note 28.

UNOSOM II with its expanded mandate through October 31, 1993.[101] Again, the U.S. Department of Defense provided the resolution's first draft. The cost of the operation was estimated to be $1.5 billion annually, or one-half of all UN expenditures on active peacekeeping missions.[102] Thirty countries made contributions to UNOSOM II, commanded by Turkish General Cevik Bir, which reached a peak strength of about 21,000 troops. President Clinton placed 2,700 logistical troops under the operational command of UNOSOM II, kept a Joint Task Force stationed off the Somali coast, and maintained a Quick Reaction Force of 1,200 under the command of Major General Thomas Montgomery (U.S. Army), who was "dual-hatted" as the deputy commander of UNOSOM II in order to maintain some unity of command.[103]

UNOSOM II faced major difficulties from the outset. The United Nations did not have the competency to command or control such a large number of diverse troops in the short time before the United States pulled out its UNITAF forces. Some states were unable to deploy their troops in a timely manner. Other states could not provide their forces with adequate weapons and equipment on their own and required arrangements with third states. The weaknesses, claimed Boutros-Ghali, "emboldened certain elements who seemed intent on undermining the efforts of the United Nations to bring stability, rehabilitation, and political reconciliation to Somalia."[104]

On June 5, 1993, twenty-four Pakistani UN troops were killed and fifty-six wounded in fighting that erupted across the city of Mogadishu. Attacks occurred in Aideed's sector during an

---

[101] S.C. Res. 814, U.N. SCOR, 48th Sess., 3188th mtg. at 5, U.N. Doc. S/RES/814 (1993); Clarke, *supra* note 65, at 9.

[102] Paul Lewis, *U.N. Will Increase Troops in Somalia*, N.Y. TIMES, Mar. 27, 1993, at A3.

[103] *Further Report of the Secretary-General Submitted in Pursuance of Para. 18 of Resolution 814, supra* note 95.

[104] *Id.* On May 7, 1993, a Belgian officer was wounded in the Kismayo fighting between Colonel Jess and General Morgan. On May 13, 1993, A Moroccan soldier was killed at a checkpoint in Baryweine. *Report of the Commission of Inquiry, supra* note 84.

authorized inspection of a weapons cantonment site co-located with the general's anti-UN, propaganda-blasting radio station, RADIO Mogadishu. Another separate attack occurred at a food distribution center, and reinforcements from the Pakistani Brigade Headquarters were ambushed on their way to that engagement.[105] Although he was not violently provoked, Aideed rightly suspected that the weapons inspection was merely a pretext, albeit lawful, for a reconnaissance mission by U.S. Special Forces as a prelude to taking the station.[106] Furthermore, Aideed's old fears of being shunted aside in the reconciliation process made it only a matter of time before he struck out against the foreign intervention. "He expected to be anointed president of Somalia and discovered that was not in the cards," a State Department official said, acknowledging that U.S. goals were designed to marginalize the warlords in favor of other national groups, including Aideed's nemesis Mahdi.[107]

The United Nations responded immediately with Resolution 837, expressing international outrage at the "criminal attacks." The Security Council reaffirmed the secretary-general's authority under Resolution 814 to "take all measures necessary against all those responsible for the armed attack . . . . including their arrest and detention for prosecution, trial, and punishment."[108] Resolution 837 amounted to a declaration of all-out war between UNOSOM II and General Aideed. On June 12, 1993, UNOSOM II, with the participation of American combat forces, began a campaign of air and ground military actions designed to destroy the warlord's weapons stored in the cantonments. To drive the point home, AC-130 SPECTRE gunships destroyed RADIO Mogadishu and the Pakistani ambush site, as well as other militia targets.

---

[105] *Report Pursuant to Para. 5 of Security Council Resolution 837 (1993) on the Investigation into the 5 June 1993 Attack on United Nations Forces in Somalia Conducted on Behalf of the Secretary-General,* U.N. SCOR, 48th Sess., Annex at 2, U.N. Doc. S/26351 (1993).

[106] *Report of the Commission of Inquiry, supra* note 84.

[107] Daniel Williams, *Raid on Warlord Designed to Oust Him From Somali Power Struggle,* WASH. POST, June 15, 1993, at A17.

[108] S.C. Res. 837, U.N. SCOR, 48th Sess., 3229 plen. mtg. at 4, U.N. Doc. S/RES/837 (1993).

In addition to attacking General Aideed's forces, the United Nations, using U.S. combat forces, undertook extensive efforts to capture him personally.[109] Admiral Howe distributed wanted posters, offering a $25,000 reward for Aideed "Dead or Alive," and Secretary-General Boutros-Ghali declared that Aideed's "physical elimination" would help the situation.[110] On June 17, 1993, AC-130s attacked the residences of Aideed and Jess, while a combined UN force of Pakistanis, Moroccans, Italians, and French captured 100 of General Aideed's militia, narrowly missing Aideed himself.[111] American casualties continued to mount as soldiers were wounded weekly by civilian riots, mortar attacks, and sniper fire. The death of four U.S. soldiers conducting a vehicle patrol by a command detonated land mine prompted the decision in August 1993 to deploy a special operations force, Task Force Ranger, to provide increased firepower in support of UNOSOM II's mandate and to capture General Aideed.[112] The Clinton administration had finally awakened to the fact that the United States was now involved in a serious conflict with a determined and resourceful enemy. To the balance of men and materiel would have to be added the strength of will to see the conflict through to its end.

THE BATTLE OF MOGADISHU (3 OCTOBER 1993)

The 1968 Tet Offensive was actually a massive military defeat for the North Vietnamese under Ho Chi Minh and the Viet Cong guerrillas who executed his plans. Confident of a popular uprising,

---

[109] After an interview with the president, Jim Hoagland wrote, "[President Clinton's] remarks left no doubt that he was intently involved in the effort to run Aideed to ground and would not be satisfied until the Somali clan leader was jailed. Decision-making on air strikes targeting Aideed's lieutenants and the warlord himself has been entirely in American hands." Jim Hoagland, *Beware 'Mission Creep' In Somalia*, WASH. POST, July, 20, 1993, at A17.

[110] Gerard Prunier, *The Experience of European Armies in Operation Restore Hope*, in LEARNING FROM SOMALIA 135, 147 n.31 (Walter Clarke & Jeffrey Herbst eds., 1997).

[111] *Report of the Commission of Inquiry, supra* note 84.

[112] POWELL, *supra* note 64, at 584.

the Viet Cong attacked cities across South Vietnam. Once fixed, American superior firepower cost them thousands of casualties. The attack exposed the clandestine North Vietnamese leadership and decimated the Viet Cong guerrilla infrastructure in South Vietnam. The Tet Offensive was, however, an enormous political victory for the Communists, causing Americans to lose confidence in their leaders, their optimistic pronouncements, and their rationale for fighting the war. On October 3, 1993, General Aideed scored the Somali equivalent of the Tet Offensive when he counterattacked Task Force Ranger, killing eighteen Americans, wounding seventy-eight more, and capturing one American pilot, while costing the Somalis 312 killed and 814 wounded. Task Force Ranger fired almost 60,000 rounds of ammunition and took 70 percent casualties, the most intense combat involving U.S. soldiers since the Vietnam War, causing some military officers to compare it to the 1965 massacre in the Ia Drang Valley.[113] Stung by battle, America's leaders executed a remarkable about-face. Far from arresting and trying Aideed as a war criminal, within a month, U.S. aircraft flew Aideed to national reconciliation talks with the imprimatur of legitimacy, while the Clinton administration negotiated with Congress over the best strategy to extricate the United States from Somalia completely.

Contrary to a popular myth, U.S. combat forces in Somalia were, at all times, under the operational control of National Command authorities; only the logistics forces supporting UNOSOM II and the humanitarian relief effort were under the operational control of General Cevik Bir's UN command. American combat forces in Somalia were under the strategic control of U.S. Central Command (CENTCOM) under Marine Corps General Joseph Hoar. Major General Thomas Montgomery provided the link to UNOSOM II as its deputy commander, while

---

[113] John Heilprin, *Air Force Veteran Remembers Colleagues Who Died in Utah Crash and in Somalia; Weekend marks the fifth anniversary of bloody battle in streets of Mogadishu*, Salt Lake Trib. Oct. 5, 1998, at D3; Rick Atkinson, *Firefight in Mogadishu: The Last Mission of Task Force Ranger*, Wash. Post, Jan. 31, 1994, at A1. *Compare* Harold Moore & Joseph Galloway, We Were Soldiers Once and Young (1989).

also serving as commander of U.S. forces in Somalia, including operational command of the 1,200 soldiers in the Quick Reaction Force (QRF) from the 10th Mountain Division. Major General William F. Garrison commanded the Joint Special Operations Command in Somalia, which included Task Force Ranger, composed of a reinforced Ranger company, Delta Force, and a special operations aviation squadron.

Upon arrival in Mogadishu in the last week of August, Task Force (TF) Ranger planned a three-phase mission: phase one was to get the force up and running; phase two would concentrate exclusively on finding and capturing Aideed; and phase three would target Aideed's command structure.[114] Task Force Ranger went straight to work and conducted four successful and two unsuccessful raids, not a surprising score given the scarcity of hard intelligence about its objective. The CIA's "humint" assets in Mogadishu consisted of around twenty principal Somali agents and a wider array of informants. Because Aideed had not been seen publicly since July 28, 1993, TF Ranger shifted almost immediately to phase three.[115] TF Ranger conducted six raids snaring fifty-six detainees, including a major prize, Osman Atto, one of Aideed's largest financial backers and arms suppliers.[116]

On October 3, 1993, at about 1 p.m., a Somali agent reported that two of Aideed's chief lieutenants, Omar Salad Elmi and Mohamed Hassan Awale, would meet that afternoon near the Olympic Hotel, only three miles from Task Force Ranger's base at the airport.[117] By 3:30 p.m., forty-six special operations troops

---

[114] Mark Bowden, *A Wrong Turn in Somalia: An Ill-Conceived Copter Raid Turned Many Somalis against U.S. Forces*, SEATTLE TIMES, Feb. 9, 1998, at A1.

[115] Rick Atkinson, *The Raid That Went Wrong; How an Elite U.S. Force Failed in Somalia*, WASH. POST, Jan. 30, 1994, at A1.

[116] *Report of the Commission of Inquiry, supra* note 84.

[117] Details from the battle are drawn from a number of sources. *Report of the Commission of Inquiry, supra* note 84; Bowden, *supra* note 114; Atkinson, *supra* note 115; DAVID HACKWORTH, HAZARDOUS DUTY (1996); *U.S. Military Operations in Somalia: Hearings Before the Senate Comm. on Armed Services*, 103d Cong. (1994); Briefing by Daniel McKnight, COL, USA, Commander, 3d Bn, 75th Ranger Regt. to officers of the 1st Bn, 3d Inf. Regt. (The Old Guard) at Fort Myer, Va. (Nov. 1995); Interview with Timothy Ryan, CPT, USA, Platoon Leader, 2d Bn, 14th Regt. 10th Mountain Division at Fort McNair (Oct. 1998).

from Delta Force's C Squadron and sixty Rangers, commanded by Colonel McKnight, were heliborne with the mission to capture Aideed's men. The units, already highly trained, were operating in a compressed planning cycle, using standard operating procedures and "audibles" to minimize reaction time. Ten UH-60 Black Hawk helicopters airlifted the assault force while a ground convoy of eight lightly-armored HMMWVs (High-Mobility, Multi-Wheeled Vehicles) and three 5-ton trucks would link up with them to extract the force along with the prisoners and any casualties. Four additional AH-6 helicopters provided air support, while General Garrison controlled the entire operation from the air. A search and rescue squad aboard a Black Hawk was held in reserve, along with a flight of Cobra gunships standing by at the airfield for additional firepower. Less than ten minutes later, the four MH-6 Little Birds of Delta Force were hovering over the target, disgorging the elite unit, while the Rangers fast-roped from Black Hawks around the target's perimeter to establish blocking positions.

Private First Class Todd Blackburn became the first casualty of the operation, falling three stories to the street below. He suffered internal injuries, head wounds, and a broken hip and leg, requiring immediate evacuation by the ground convoy. The assault itself went exactly as planned, netting twenty-four detainees, including Aideed's two lieutenants. Unfortunately, Aideed's militia was also operating to minimize reaction time, and they had discerned the American's operational tactics. Reinforcements were quickly rushed to the sector armed with cached RPGs (rocket-propelled grenades).

Having studied under Soviet tutelage, Aideed's militia leaders had absorbed the guerrilla warfare tactics of General Vo Nguyen Giap in Vietnam, and their application in Latin America and Afghanistan, and they had practiced them against their countrymen and neighbors for a decade. Although the RPG is not a guided weapon, in volley fire it can be effective against heliborne targets. As the evacuation of the prisoners began, the Somalis succeeded in downing a Black Hawk helicopter, killing the pilot, Chief Warrant

---

The After-Action Review of Task-Force Ranger Action in Mogadishu is classified Top-Secret/ Special Category.

Officer Wolcott, and his co-pilot around 4:10 p.m. Two snipers in the aircraft's rear survived the crash and were about 300 to 500 meters from the ground convoy. TF Ranger had prepared for this contingency, and a fragmentary order was issued to secure the aircraft from the air and ground and to alert the Quick Reaction Force from the 10th Mountain Division for back-up. As the ground convoy maneuvered through the labyrinth toward the crash site, it took fire from every direction, as squad after squad of Somali militiamen trained RPGs and automatic fire on the column. Because of mounting casualties, the ground convoy from TF Ranger was unable to consolidate and reorganize at the crash site. It was forced, instead, to fight its way through Somali roadblocks back to its base at the airfield. Two platoons of Rangers from the security detail did make it to the crash site, just as another squad of Rangers rappelled from the designated search and rescue chopper.

A heroic team from another special ops MH-6 Little Bird had already evacuated the two badly wounded snipers under heavy fire by landing their miniature helicopter in an alleyway with just feet between the rotors and the buildings on either side. The thirty-three Rangers on the ground forced their way into a nearby building, carrying eleven wounded and one dead into the strongpoint. Meanwhile, a second Black Hawk pulling security over Wolcott's downed chopper was hit and tried to limp back to base as well. Chief Warrant Officer Michael Durant was forced, however, to crash-land the helicopter more than 800 meters away from the site of the first crash at 4:50 p.m. Master Sergeant Gary Gordon and Sergeant First-Class Randall Shugart fast-roped down to the wreckage to defend Durant, the sole survivor. As they moved toward the crash site, the helicopter they had just dismounted was hit, knocking the co-pilot unconscious and severing the leg of the remaining Delta Force sniper. The pilot just managed to nurse his aircraft back to base, but that left Gordon and Shugart without any air support. After a tremendous fight, the helicopter was overrun. The Somalis captured CWO Durant alive, and mutilated the five dead Americans, dragging three of their bodies through the streets of Mogadishu as television cameras broadcast the desecration. Congress posthumously awarded Master Sergeant Gary Gordon and Sergeant First-Class Randall Shugart the Medal of Honor for their selfless gallantry.[118]

Back at the airbase, a small relief column held in reserve by Task Force Ranger immediately rushed out, only to be beaten back by heavy fire. When news of the crash reached the 10th Mountain's Quick Reaction Force, it moved from its compound at the Somali National University to stage at the airfield. As Durant's bird went down, the Quick Reaction Force dispatched a company-sized convoy of nine 5-ton trucks and twelve HMMWVs with 150 troops. The relief column was ambushed on Via Lenin and had to retreat, revealing the intricate battle plan laid by Aideed's militia. General Montgomery then began coordination with Pakistani and Malaysian commanders tasked to UNOSOM II, alerting them to standby in case their help was necessary. He also contacted an adjacent Italian commander and asked him to dispatch an armored force to Mogadishu from its base, thirty miles away.

The UNOSOM II rescue column slowly mustered at the New Port with four Pakistani M-48 tanks and twenty-eight Malaysian armored personnel carriers; language barriers, lack of prior coordination, and the absence of unity of command under fire added to the frictions of war. Six hours later, at 11:15 p.m., the convoy of seventy vehicles, loaded with two light infantry companies from the 10th Mountain Division and fifty more Rangers, moved out, only to be attacked repeatedly en route. It took almost three hours for the relief column to fight its way through the Somali roadblocks to reach the area of the city near the two downed aircraft. The column then split in half: Alpha Company, 2d Battalion, 14th Infantry Regiment, linked up with the Ranger strongpoint and Charlie Company, 2/14th Infantry, secured CWO Durant's now stripped and empty Black Hawk. The Rangers had been resupplied by air with ammunition and medical supplies, and spent the night defending their position by calling in air support to within fifteen meters of their position. When the relief section arrived, the Rangers began to load their casualties and

---

[118] These American heroes are buried in Arlington National Cemetery and honored with an annual wreath-laying ceremony sponsored by the "No Greater Love" Society.

mount up while still taking fire. At dawn, the two sections linked up again at their rendezvous point and fought their way through intense resistance back to the airbase. The relief column itself suffered many casualties. Three U.S. soldiers were killed and thirty-six wounded. The other forces also suffered heavily. One Malaysian and one Moroccan were killed, and ten Malaysians, ten Moroccans, three Pakistanis, and an Italian were wounded.

Many tactical lessons have been drawn from the Battle of Mogadishu, not all of them fair, especially so removed from the battlefield. First, General Garrison was criticized for relying on the same tactics used in the prior six raids, and for executing a daylight raid when American special operations forces can best use their superior equipment at night. The operational situation, however, usually allowed less than an hour to react. For every raid that was executed, six were planned but not executed because of insufficient intelligence or because the operational window closed. Targets of opportunity had to be quickly evaluated and the missions executed as they occurred. Task Force Ranger's advantage was tactical surprise, not creativity, and there was no guarantee that the target would wait until darkness fell. Second, Colonel McKnight was criticized because the soldiers did not wear full body-armor, carry night vision devices, or carry more than the standard load of ammunition; Colonel McKnight made a tactical decision to sacrifice equipment for speed. McKnight was also criticized for expending so many more lives in pursuit of the Ranger Creed—"I will never leave a fallen comrade to fall into the hands of the enemy." The warrior ethic may be difficult for some to understand, but that is the code of the U.S. Army Ranger.

Tactical decisions have to be made at the tactical level. More cutting criticisms allege that inter- and intra-service rivalries and a breakdown in unity of command caused more casualties than necessary. General Montgomery may have created other problems by violating the rule of unity of command. General Montgomery commanded the QRF while General Garrison commanded Task Force Ranger, and both micromanaged Colonel McKnight, the leader on the ground, as so frequently happened in Vietnam. General Garrison, a special operations warrior, never called for the additional fire support available from the Cobra gunships belonging to the "straight leg" 10th Mountain Division, nor did his contingency plan call for more than the TF Ranger relief column held in reserve. As a result, the QRF relief column had to be improvised as the situation rapidly deteriorated. Furthermore, the AC-130 SPECTRE crew was allowed to go to Italy on R&R, depriving TF Ranger of the aircraft's cannon and howitzer support.

The United States clearly underestimated Aideed as an opponent. In the politicians' desire to portray Aideed and his militia as gangsters and unorganized thugs, commanders may have forgotten that Aideed was in fact a formally-trained general in charge of an army that had ousted Barre and twice defeated his return. When Operation Restore Hope began, intelligence reports indicated that Aideed controlled the "largest army in Somalia, with as many as 10,000 armed men at his disposal."[119] Yet, as UNOSOM II took over, Admiral Howe estimated that his forces numbered no more than 200 gunmen.[120] The strong inference is that, as in Vietnam, U.S. leaders manipulated the picture of the enemy to suit its political purposes. The much lower figure better supported the political strategy of downplaying Aideed's legitimacy and at the same time diminished the perception that American forces faced significant risk.

It was fatal to underestimate the Somali warlord. Aideed had already displayed his militia's tactical proficiency in his attack on the Pakistani peacekeepers on June 5, 1993, revealing his own favorite tactic of pinning one unit while ambushing its reinforcements. Brigadier General Ikram ul-Hassan, the Pakistani commander, described the battle on that date:

> The Pakistanis managed to inflict heavy casualties as [we] fought back for two hours while waiting for reinforcements. . . . Italian tanks backed by helicopters from a U.S. 'quick-reaction force' did not arrive for more than an hour, as the

---

[119] John Lancaster, *Stabilizing Riven Somalia a Monumental Task*, WASH. POST, Dec. 3, 1992, at A34.

[120] Keith B. Richburg, *Aideed's Forces May Have Been Underestimated, Officials Concede*, WASH. POST, Oct. 8, 1993, at A18.

Somalis kept up the assault with grenades, rockets and antitank weapons. . . .

We were totally surprised by the Somalis, . . . They were sitting on the dominant ground. They had taken up position.

. . . This was a proper, organized ambush. They probably went there overnight. These were trained people.[121]

Aideed also had an effective command and control system that divided his home turf in Mogadishu into eighteen sectors linked by short-range radios and messengers that evaded American high tech collection assets. Urban warfare also negated the advantage of American superior firepower. The most effective fire support for U.S. forces was provided by helicopter gunships. But only one week prior to the October 3 raid, Aideed's forces had shot down an American helicopter with RPGs, killing all three crewmembers. In the week of punishing raids aimed at destroying Aideed following his attack on the Pakistanis, Aideed refused to commit his forces to open battle where they could be crushed by superior firepower, showing his patience in seeking fights only on his terms, while avoiding American strengths.

These critiques are important because they may have had an impact on the number of casualties sustained on October 3 and 4. Some problems were indeed fixable. None of these issues, however, would have prevented the battle that occurred on October 3. In combat operations, the enemy also has a vote. Once the United States had determined to treat Aideed as a hostile force, the United States should have expected a thinking enemy to seize the initiative where possible and attack at a time and place of his choosing. More consequential criticisms, however, go to the heart of the internal contradictions in U.S. policy itself.

One question that the House Armed Services Committee focused intently upon was the role U.S. armor could have played in the battle. Several issues need to be addressed on that point. First, why did the United States not have armored forces of its own deployed in Somalia? And to what extent was that a function of the

---

[121] Keith B. Richburg, *Aid Staffs Pull Out of Mogadishu; Violence That Killed 22 Soldiers Called 'Organized Ambush,'* WASH. POST, June 7, 1993, at A1.

U.S. military still being unable to conduct truly joint operations as envisioned under the Goldwater-Nichols Act. CENTCOM did have *Marine* armored units available pre-positioned at Diego Garcia, a four-day sail away from the *army*'s QRF and Task Force Ranger. Organic mechanized units from the 10th Mountain's base at Fort Drum, New York, could have reached Somalia within a week. From the beginning, General Garrison requested that both the AC-130 and armored vehicles be available in reserve for his mission. General Montgomery had relayed that request to CENTCOM's General Hoar, and the chairman of the Joint Chiefs, General Powell, endorsed the demand. The president himself had approved AC-130s for use after the attacks on the Pakistani peacekeepers. But on September 14, 1993, Secretary of Defense Les Aspin refused the request for M1A1 Abrams tanks and Bradley Fighting Vehicles, because he saw "no great sense of urgency" and was sensitive to the likelihood of backlash in Congress to any military escalation.[122] Aspin accepted full responsibility for the error in judgment and resigned two months later.

If the politicization of war-fighting that occurred at the level of the Office of the Secretary of Defense was reminiscent of Vietnam, so was the response of the military high command. None of the generals involved—not Powell, Hoar, Montgomery, or Garrison—publicly challenged the decision. Instead, they pressed ahead with missions that in their best professional military judgment they knew had inadequate resources to accomplish the assigned objective. They, too, were as guilty as their predecessors of "dereliction of duty," to use H. R. McMaster's thesis. In extenuation, both Generals Montgomery and Garrison testified that the introduction of armored forces would not have made a difference. They would not have been assigned to the initial raid, and most of the casualties occurred before any relief column could have extracted Task Force Ranger. It is true, however, that the poorly armored UNOSOM II rescue column sustained significant

---

[122] Barton Gellman, *Somalia Options Reviewed as Discontent in Congress Grows; U.S. Lacked Strong Plan To Aid Besieged Troops*, WASH. POST, Oct. 6, 1993, at A1.

casualties en route and that as many as thirty-six casualties, including six deaths might have been avoided.

The tactical debate over the effect U.S. armor might have had at the engagement, however, is academic to the real impact of the Battle of Mogadishu, which needs to be recognized most importantly as a key battle in a political struggle, rather than a tactical skirmish between hostile forces. The United States has failed to make this leap and, as in Vietnam, we have drawn the wrong lessons as a result. First, as in Vietnam, U.S. leaders allowed politics to drive the military assets available, rather than the tactical situation on the ground. Second, armored vehicles were not the decisive weapon in the larger battle. Aideed's objective was to win a political victory, by influencing the battle raging in the U.S. Congress caused by political opportunism over the first U.S. casualties. The addition of an armored task force would not have deterred Aideed from executing the attack. Unlike Tet's North Vietnamese planners, Aideed never believed that his offensive would be a military success. Furthermore, armored forces could not have prevented Somali militiamen from inflicting some number of casualties on Task Force Ranger, nor the overrunning of the downed and isolated helicopters. It was the pilot's capture and the televised spectacle of the dead Americans being dragged through the streets that inflamed public opinion. Considering the daily mortar attacks and land mines that Americans faced, it was only a matter of time before a significant and unlucky incident caused major American casualties that would force U.S. leadership to acknowledge that it faced a real war for which it had not prepared the American people.

A second issue that surfaced was the alleged poor performance of UNOSOM II, both in mounting the rescue effort and in the larger sense that it was not successfully pursuing its expanded nation-building mandate. Although the UNOSOM II relief column was delayed, that could certainly be expected regardless of its international composition. The UN report of the incident accurately described the inherently complex operation as "one where a heavy joint and combined multi-national task force alerted, moved at night, deployed at night, and successfully executed, at night, under complex combat conditions, their rescue plan to extract 70 soldiers with wounded in approximately eight hours."[123] To be sure, the allies' equipment did not measure to American standards: the 1958 Pakistani tanks needed to be refueled en route, the Malaysian APCs were not heavily enough armored to withstand RPGs, and neither nation's forces had night vision devices. But at least they were on the battlefield.

The American commanders' key tactical failure was in not coordinating mutually supporting roles with UNOSOM II forces, despite General Montgomery's ostensible role as UNOSOM II deputy commander to facilitate international teamwork. The congressional investigation focused on this lack of prior coordination as an American failure. Others, in an effort to undermine any further U.S. cooperation with UN peacekeeping specifically or the supranational institution in general, indicted the UN force as inherently unable to professionally conduct multinational operations. The question often asked is: why were the other national commanders not informed prior to the operation?

The simplest answer was that commanders at Task Force Ranger did not share their operations with other nations because they suspected that sensitive information was being leaked to Aideed. There was general distrust of UN officials and peacekeeping forces, but specific, though unarticulated, suspicion fell on the Italian unit, led by Brigadier General Bruno Loi. The Italians opposed the transformation of UNOSOM II from a humanitarian effort at nation-building into a man-hunt for Aideed, because in their view, it closed off options for a negotiated settlement. The Italians understood, from the beginning, that taking on Aideed would result in a long and costly guerrilla war.[124]

The damning part was that the Clinton administration had decided in secret that the Italians were correct, at least two weeks

---

[123] *Report of the Commission of Inquiry, supra* note 84.

[124] Keith B. Richburg, *Italy, in Rebuke to U.N., to Pull Troops Out of Mogadishu; General Refuses to 'Use Same Means That Guerrillas Use,'* WASH. POST, Aug. 14, 1993, at A15; *Italian Minister Denounces 'Rambo' U.N. Commanders,* WASH. POST, Aug. 14, 1993, at A17; *U.S. Military Operations in Somalia: Hearings Before the Senate Comm. on Armed Services, supra* note 117, at 75.

prior to the Battle of Mogadishu. Like previous administrations in Vietnam, the Clinton administration secretly decided to change course in a fight it secretly decided it could not win. After the mine-attack that killed four American soldiers and drew the deployment of Task Force Ranger, Aideed initiated contact with the U.S. government through former President Jimmy Carter, suggesting renewal of the cease-fire and the reconciliation process. The official U.S. position remained that "Aideed must submit to the authority of the international community" by turning himself in to UN forces. But an anonymous State Department official stated that "there is no reason *not* to negotiate if some other channel appears promising, and [that] Aideed's proposal [was] under discussion."[125] On the same day, moreover, after several hours of consultations with *Italian* Prime Minister Carlo Ciampi, President Clinton stated that "The United States cannot continue to pursue a military solution or be obsessed with Aideed" and pledged to "develop a 'political initiative' to restore government in Somalia and establish conditions for the withdrawal of United States peace-keeping troops."[126] In fact, under President Clinton's direction, former President Carter had been in contact with Aideed to negotiate a diplomatic outcome.[127] As in Vietnam, once the United States signaled a willingness to settle for a negotiated exit, the enemy's incentive was to meet conciliatory acts with greater violence to strengthen their position at the bargaining table. Once American resolve weakened, greater casualties translated into greater political gains in the negotiations. Yet, the administration had told neither the chairman of the Joint Chiefs nor Task Force Ranger. "With or without U.N. consent, Clinton had sole power to stop the track-and-snatch operation against Aideed. He did not. 'We never had a change of mission. As far as we're concerned the

---

[125] Thomas W. Lippman, *U.S. Studies Somali's Note Seeking U.N. Investigation; Aideed Says He Would Abide by Conclusion*, WASH. POST, Sept. 17, 1993, at A29 (emphasis added).

[126] Ann Devroy & Daniel Williams, *Clinton Vows to Find Political Solution for Somalia*, WASH. POST, Sept. 18, 1993, at A18.

[127] *U.S. Military Operations in Somalia: Hearings Before the Senate Comm. on Armed Services, supra* note 117, at 67.

mission to detain Aideed [was] still valid,' said Army Major David Stockwell."[128]

Congress was also steadily turning against the continuing American involvement in Somalia, despite its earlier passage of Joint Resolution 45 approving of the deployment of UNITAF retroactively and UNOSOM II as well.[129] Although there had been many earlier voices against any U.S. intervention in Somalia, including Senator Brown and Representative Murtha, Senator Robert Byrd (D-WV) was the first really powerful congressional leader to renew questions about the Clinton administration's policy in Somalia after the expansion of UNOSOM II's mission into "nation-building."[130] If Aideed was as conscious of political warfare as the Vietnamese Communists were, then statements like those coming from Senator Dan Coats (R-IN) must have been revealing and particularly heartening. "When our objectives are

---

[128] Barton Gellman, *U.S. Rhetoric Changed, but Hunt Persisted; Clinton Had Power to Stop Operation Against Aideed*, WASH. POST, Oct. 7, 1993, at A37.

[129] The application of the War Powers Resolution was gingerly sidestepped by both administrations and many members of Congress. But others, including Representative Lee Hamilton (D-IN), felt strongly about Congress' role in shaping foreign policy and felt bound by the law to follow the mechanism found in the War Powers Resolution. "Congress set no terms or conditions on that deployment until U.S. Army Rangers were killed in October 1993 in the streets of Mogadishu—and then it tried to cut-off funding. Here you had a major military intervention by the United States—involving 25,000 U.S. troops at its peak, with frequent combat engagements—and Congress never authorized or approved it." Lee Hamilton, Address at Georgetown University (Nov. 18, 1998). The Senate quickly passed Joint Resolution 45, "Authorizing the Use of Force in Somalia" on February 4, 1993, but the House version was more controversial because an amendment adopted a more expansive objective that suggested "nation-building." Attempting to squarely straddle the fence, the House compromised by including the language approving the broader mandate, but limited the troop deployment to one year. The House version passed on May 25, 1993, two months after the Pentagon-drafted "nation-building" Resolution 814 was approved by the Security Council. Johnston & Dange, *supra* note 46, at 198-99; *The Crisis in Somalia: Hearing Before the House Comm. on Foreign Affairs, supra* note 46.

[130] Keith B. Richburg, *Criticism Mounts Over Somali Raid; 'Pack Up, Go Home,' U.S. Troops Urged*, WASH. POST, July 15, 1993, at A21.

unclear, one death is too many."[131] On September 9, 1993, the U.S. Senate, 90 to 7, passed a nonbinding resolution calling on the president to consult with Congress on the goals and objectives of U.S. policy toward Somalia by October 15 and receive congressional authorization by November 15 for the U.S. deployment in Somalia to continue.[132] "Expanding the peace-keeping mission in Somalia was a mistake, and it is time for Congress to narrow the U.S. role there so it has a definite ending point," declared Senator Sam Nunn (D-GA), the chairman of the Senate Armed Services Committee.[133]

After the Battle of Mogadishu, President Clinton's policy in Somalia had no credibility or support whatsoever, and the debate was reduced to how quickly the United States could retreat, consistent with not appearing to have surrendered or deserted our partners in the United Nations. "We expect our troops in Somalia to remain calm and collected under fire, and we owe them nothing less than equal composure back here in Washington," cautioned Senator Nunn.[134] But Representative Ronald Dellums (D-CA), chairman of the House Armed Services Committee, was more typical of congressional sentiment in "calling upon the administration and the United Nations to seek an immediate cease-fire in Somalia, abandon the hunt for Aideed and expand the effort to find a political solution among the various factions in

---

[131] Helen Dewar, *Senate Debates U.S. Role in Somalia; Lawmakers Seek Clarification of Administration's Objectives*, WASH. POST, Sept. 9, 1993, at A35. With masterful timing rivaling Dienbienphu, Aideed attacked TF Ranger three weeks later, only ten days before the administration's request for continued deployment of the troops was expected by Congress.

[132] Dewar, *supra* note 131; Barton Gellman, *Senate Asks Clinton to Get Approval for Continued Troop Deployment*, WASH. POST, Sept. 10, 1993, at A31.

[133] *Nunn: Congress Should Narrow U.S. Somalia Role*, WASH. POST, Sept. 27, 1993, at A16.

[134] Helen Dewar, *Senate Vote on Pullout Delayed; Opponents of Immediate Withdrawal Warn Against Precipitous Action*, WASH. POST, Oct. 7, 1993, at A39.

Somalia."[135] Sixty-five House Republicans, including Minority Leader Robert Michel (R-IL), wrote President Clinton demanding a plan for withdrawal of U.S. forces from Somalia, calling the administration's policy a "failure," and asserting that America could not afford an "indecisive and naive approach to foreign policy."[136]

As in Vietnam, however, the American public seemed to digest the tragedy more maturely than their leaders. A poll conducted on October 15, 1993, found that only 28 percent of the public favored immediate withdrawal. Forty-three percent favored withdrawal in six months, while 27 percent did not want to withdraw until "we have stabilized the country, even if this takes longer than six months."[137] The *Washington Post* reported that "lawmakers are receiving a large number of telephone calls on Somalia from constituents, nearly all urging withdrawal *or*, as one aide put it, a policy of '*get tough or get out.*'"[138]

Just as the 1968 New Hampshire primary was misinterpreted as a vote against Vietnam, rather than a vote against American leadership, Congress and the president apparently believed the American people wanted out of Somalia. Actually, a majority of 70 percent of Americans continued to support the goals of American intervention. The American people were not unwilling to make sacrifices, but they were unwilling to accept those sacrifices without specific and articulated reasons from their leaders. Rather than communicate the purposes of American intervention in support of UNOSOM II, the Clinton administration attempted to bury it. "What happens is what the Clinton administration wants to happen—it goes away," said Linda Mathews, foreign editor of ABC's "World News Tonight."[139] As the number of U.S. troops

---

[135] Ann Devroy, *Somalia Options Reviewed as Discontent in Congress Grows; New Deployment Raises Confusion on U.S. Goals*, WASH. POST, Oct. 6, 1993, at A1.

[136] Dewar, *supra* note 134.

[137] Steven Kull, *What New Isolationism? Wrong, Pundits. We Still Feel a Global Duty, Even in Somalia*, WASH. POST, Oct. 24, 1993, at C2.

[138] Dewar, *supra* note 134 (emphasis added).

[139] Howard Kurtz, *Deaths Spur Media Retreat From Somalia*, WASH. POST, July 17, 1993, at A11.

dropped from 25,000 to 4,000, media coverage gradually diminished, a pattern familiar from the U.S. disengagements from Vietnam, Grenada, and Panama. "Most of the media assumes that American interest is driven by American presence," Mathews said. "When the Marines pull back, we're all not that interested."[140] When the media shocked the American people with the reality and costs of American intervention abroad, the turmoil prevented any principled, unemotional presentation of the rationale for supporting the UN mandate in Somalia. The visceral response in both Congress and the administration was to get out. "Television in particular has an ability to set the foreign policy agenda through the power of its images. That certainly happened in Somalia: television drove us into Somalia and television drove us out."[141]

RETREAT AND WITHDRAWAL (OCTOBER 1993-MARCH 1995)

On October 7, 1993, President Clinton addressed the American people in a belated attempt to explain America's continued presence in Somalia, promising "straight answers." President Clinton explained that the reason American troops were in Somalia in the first place was to "help stop one of the great human tragedies of this time. A third of a million people had died of starvation and disease. Twice that many were at risk of dying," and the American-led intervention had "saved close to 1 million lives."[142] President Clinton also told the American people that an immediate withdrawal would cause the other nations involved in UNOSOM II to evacuate in a rout.

Chaos would resume. The relief effort would stop. And starvation would return. . . . Within months, Somali children

---

[140] *Id.*

[141] Hamilton, *supra* note 129; Rick Atkinson, *Deliverance from Warlord's Fury*, WASH. POST, Oct. 7, 1993, at A1.

[142] *Remarks of President William J. Clinton on U.S. Policy in Somalia, October 7, 1993, in* NATIONAL SECURITY LAW 327 (John Norton Moore ed., Spring 1998).

again would be dying in the streets. Our credibility with friends
and allies would be severely damaged. Our leadership in world
affairs would be undermined at the very time when people are
looking at America to help promote peace and freedom in the
post-Cold War world. All around the world, aggressors, thugs,
and terrorists will conclude that the best way to get us to
change our policies is to kill our people. It would be open
season on Americans.[143]

It is clear that President Clinton recognized the stakes involved
in deciding the next step for the United States in Somalia.
President Clinton quoted General Powell as saying, "because
things get difficult, you don't cut and run. You work the problem
and try to find a correct solution." In the end, however, President
Clinton could not provide straight answers to the fundamental
questions of U.S. intervention in Somalia. If it is in the American
national interest to intervene to ameliorate a massive human
tragedy, is it not also critical to address the conditions that created
the famine to begin with? If the United States as the world's only
superpower is unwilling to commit the resources and forces
necessary to ensure a long-term solution to the problem, why
would or should any other nation? The president refused to
candidly address the obvious fact that peace would not be restored
to Somalia by the March 31, 1994, date he set for the withdrawal
of American forces. He must have realized that his slow surrender
would not salvage the credibility he feared the United States would
lose if it were to pull out immediately. President Clinton promised
the American people straight answers on American policy in
Somalia, but he certainly did not deliver.

In Congress, the Clinton administration also prevaricated. It
quickly disassociated itself from the "nation-building" mandate it
had earlier endorsed in supporting UN Resolution 814. Its report to
Congress on October 13, 1993, claimed that "at no time have U.S.
forces been tasked with such missions as nation-building," an

---

[143] *Id.* at 327-29.

absurd statement.[144] The administration did recognize, however, that

> an immediate withdrawal of U.S. forces would have significant and far-reaching consequences, because it would force many other nations that [were] dependent on U.S. logistical support and force protection to leave Somalia . . . . The result would be the collapse of UNOSOM, the probable return of anarchy and civil war and with it famine, and a loss of the significant gains achieved to date.[145]

There are not many graceful ways to sound the retreat, but in the short run, the administration sought to stabilize the situation with a number of policy changes. First, the president augmented the Quick Reaction Force with 3,000 additional personnel, including the previously denied armor, in order to return Mogadishu to a secure environment. Second, the president ordered all U.S. troops in Somalia to "bunker down," abandoning their limited disarmament and escort duties in order to maximize force protection. Third, the president ended the manhunt for Aideed to "depersonalize" the conflict and announced the withdrawal of Task Force Ranger. Fourth, the president reappointed Ambassador Oakley as his special envoy to negotiate a political settlement with

---

[144] The "Report to Congress on U.S. Policy in Somalia" states that "the U.S. goal is humanitarian. . . . in support of the overall U.N. effort to assist the Somali people so that civil war, with its attendant anarchy and famine, does not return when the international presence departs." *Report to Congress on U.S. Policy in Somalia, in* NATIONAL SECURITY LAW 327 (John Norton Moore ed., Spring 1998) (emphasis added). The Report also correctly states that UNOSOM II's mandate was "nation-building"—"to provide security, help implement the Addis Ababa agreements, assist in political reconciliation, and support relief activities. The mandate also authorized U.N. agencies to facilitate refugee repatriation, reestablish the police and judiciary systems, and create a demining program." Less than two weeks earlier, the United States had voted to pass UN Resolution 865, which commended "all personnel of the United Nations in Somalia II for their achievements in greatly improving the conditions of the Somali people and beginning the process of nation-building." S.C. Res. 865, U.N. SCOR, 48th Sess., 3280th mtg., U.N. Doc. S/RES/865 (1993).

[145] *Id.*

Aideed, who would be accorded status as a legitimate clan and military leader. Finally, the president established a fixed date, March 31, 1994, to withdraw American combat forces and hand off its logistical support mission to other nations or civilian contractors. The president believed that the six months of breathing space would "afford the U.N. operation sufficient time and opportunity to complete the transition to an effective operation without U.S. military units [and give] . . . the Somali people a reasonable opportunity to overcome the barriers to a peaceful process of national political reconciliation." At the same time, he made clear that "this drawdown of U.S. military personnel is not conditioned upon the successful completion of any steps by the Somali people or the U.N."[146]

Despite President Clinton's disingenuous suggestion that the American reinforcements would forestall the withdrawal of other nations' commitments, more than 9,000 UNOSOM II troops were withdrawn by their respective nations over the next six months. The United Nations was, therefore, forced to retreat from the broad nation-building mandate of Resolution 814, which was set to expire on October 29, 1993. That day, the Security Council passed Resolution 878, extending the mandate for an interim period of three weeks in which to consider its course. On November 16, 1993, the Security Council passed Resolution 885, which established an independent commission to reinvestigate the June 5, 1993, attack on the Pakistani forces (a previous investigation, of course, had found conclusively that they were the responsibility of Aideed) and suspended its order authorizing the arrest of Aideed.[147]

On November 18, 1993, the Security Council again renewed UNOSOM II's mandate, passing Resolution 886, which extended the mission until May 31, 1994, with a midterm review by February 1, 1994. Resolution 886 expressed the same goals as the nation-building Resolution of 814 but dropped confrontational language about "demanding" peace and "requiring" security, in

---

[146] *Id.*

[147] S.C. Res. 885, U.N. SCOR, 48th Sess., 3315th mtg., U.N. Doc. S/RES/885 (1993).

favor of "urging," "reminding," and "underscoring" a commitment to a political settlement of the conflict.[148] On January 6, 1994, the secretary-general submitted a report on options for the future mandate of UNOSOM II, finding that the political national reconciliation process was blocked, that malnutrition levels were on the rise aggravated by the insecurity of the humanitarian relief effort, and that any disarmament policy was impracticable because Somali cooperation was not forthcoming.[149] Despite that pessimistic report, on February 4, 1994, the Security Council passed Resolution 897, reducing the level of UNOSOM II forces to an authorized strength of 22,000 and altering UNOSOM II's mandate to protection of humanitarian aid deliveries, by omission revoking its authority to "use all necessary means" to prevent resumption of violence or undertake disarmament activities. Further, UNOSOM II would only "encourage and assist" in the national reconciliation process, which "should culminate in the installation of a democratically elected government." Although previous resolutions had always "recognized that the people of Somalia bear the ultimate responsibility for setting up viable national political institutions and for reconstructing their country," Resolution 897 transferred the primary responsibility for nation-building to the Somali factions themselves.[150]

The United States kept its commitment to withdraw its troops from Somalia by March 1994 and was followed by other major powers, including Belgium, France, and Italy, leaving a UN force of 19,000. Only the Pakistanis responded to the UN's call for reinforcements, sending an additional 2,000 troops.[151] After considering further reports from the secretary-general and a

---

[148] S.C. Res. 886, U.N. SCOR, 48th Sess., 3315th mtg., U.N. Doc. S/RES/886 (1993).

[149] *Further Report of the Secretary-General Submitted in Pursuance of Paragraph 4 of Resolution 886*, U.N. Doc. S/1994/12 (1994), *in* U.N. AND SOMALIA, *supra* note 1, at 345.

[150] S.C. Res. 897, U.N. SCOR, 49th Sess., 3334th mtg., U.N. Doc. S/RES/897 (1994).

[151] *Further Report of the Secretary-General on UNOSOM, submitted in pursuance of paragraph 14 of Resolution 897* (1994), U.N. Doc. S/1994/614 (1994), *in* U.N. AND SOMALIA, *supra* note 1, at 355.

Security Council mission to Somalia about the lack of progress toward national reconciliation in Somalia, the Security Council, in Resolution 954, decided to proceed with a secure and orderly withdrawal of all UNOSOM II military forces from Somalia by March 31, 1995.[152] On February 28, 1995, the United States made its last foray into Somalia, Operation United Shield, commanding 14,000 troops from seven nations to cover the withdrawal of the remaining 2,400 UNOSOM II troops from Somalia.[153]

LESSONS AND CONCLUSIONS

The conventional wisdom assessing the U.S. intervention in Somalia is that the initial success of the U.S.-led Operation Provide Relief and Operation Restore Hope for the limited purpose of humanitarian relief gave way to the abysmal failure of the UN-led UNOSOM II operation because of "mission creep" toward "nation-building." The problem with the conventional wisdom, however, is that it conveniently forgets that the United States, as the world's only superpower, was the architect behind both endeavors.

As already noted, both UN Resolution 794 establishing UNITAF and UN Resolution 814 establishing UNOSOM II were drafted in the Pentagon, accepted by congressional resolution, and passed the Security Council with U.S. support. The initial reason for the intervention was the collapse of the Somali state and its inability to provide for the common welfare of the Somali people. The famine was not an act of nature, but a product of political chaos. Food was not the answer, security and order were. By

---

[152] *Report of the Secretary-General to the Security Council on Somalia*, U.N. SCOR, 49th Sess., 977th mtg., U.N. Doc. S/1994/977 (1994); *Report by the Secretary-General Concerning the Situation in Somalia*, U.N. SCOR, 49th Sess., 1068th mtg., U.N. Doc. S/1994/1068 (1994); *Report of the Secretary-General Concerning the Situation in Somalia*, U.N. SCOR, 49th Sess., U.N. Doc. S/1994/1166 (1994); *Report of the Security Council Mission to Somalia (26 and 27 October 1994)*, U.N. SCOR, 49th Sess., U.N. Doc. S/1994/1245 (1994); S.C. Res. 954, U.N. SCOR, 49th Sess., 3451st mtg., U.N. Doc. S/RES/954 (1994).

[153] Rick Atkinson, *Marines Launch Final Phase of Somalia Pullout*, WASH. POST, Feb. 28, 1995, at A12.

championing Resolution 794, and then brilliantly executing Operation Restore Hope, the United States began to do those things for the Somali people that their failed state was unable to accomplish. By "using all necessary means to establish as soon as possible a secure environment for humanitarian relief operations in Somalia," the United States was "nation-building" from the start.[154] As much as the United States might have hoped otherwise, the Somali crisis required an integrated "humanitarian-political-security strategy"[155] that responded to the immediate humanitarian crisis as well as the underlying failure of the political reconciliation process to form a viable state. U.S. policy had to address root causes—not solely poverty, but political instability. The determined use of military power would have created the foundation for the solution to the problem of a failed state, and treated its symptom, the famine. The reason that UNITAF was successful at both aspects of the problem, for its short duration at any rate, is that the United States applied all of the resources necessary to accomplish its objective. The humanitarian crisis was averted because the foodstocks that were always available were delivered without interference from the warlords, and the political situation stabilized because UNITAF was too powerful to oppose.

> During the U.S.-led operation, Aideed occasionally tried to pose a military challenge—and each time, the warlord and his militia were slapped down hard. "We suppressed it because we intimidated them," said a senior U.S. Marine officer in Somalia during the U.S.-led intervention. "They knew what kind of a response they would get from us. And it wouldn't be proportional." Aideed, said this officer, "walked a line. He pushed us as close as he could, but he never went to the point of killing people."[156]

---

[154] S.C. Res. 794, *supra* note 40.

[155] Walter Clarke, *supra* note 65, at 3, 13.

[156] Keith B. Richburg, *American Casualties in Somalia: A Policy Time Bomb Explodes*, WASH. POST, Aug. 12, 1993, at A01.

With 28,000 American troops controlling Somalia, Aideed didn't dare confront UNITAF, but when the United States withdrew and turned the mission over to UNOSOM II on May 4, the situation rapidly deteriorated. UNOSOM II held a more ambitious Security Council mandate, yet its effective military power was reduced to the 1,200-man Quick Reaction Force. Within a month, Aideed attacked the UN forces in an effort to drive them out. The conclusion is plain. The U.S.-led UNITAF had the power to be an effective deterrent; the weakening of combat power in UNOSOM II resulted in classic deterrence failure. The actions and statements of Ambassador Oakley and General Johnston convinced Aideed that they were no threat to his power so long as he did not provoke them, so Aideed simply waited patiently for the promised troop withdrawals to occur and he was left to face the weak and divided UNOSOM II force.

> Indeed, one of the fundamental mistakes of attributing success to the United States and failure to the U.N. is that the American forces made it so clear that they would not challenge the warlords and would be in Somalia for such a short period of time that it was in the interest of the warlords not to hinder the Americans and speed their departure.[157]

While the United States failed to resource the security mission adequately for the long-term, it also failed to support the necessary political process required to cement the gains of Operation Restore Hope. As a result, Professor Clarke maintains, time, money, and U.S. domestic commitment to multilateral action were squandered. The lesson is not that "[we] intervened smartly in a limited humanitarian mission while the U.N. bumbled because it chose to do nation building. Rather the two missions differed fundamentally

---

[157] Walter Clarke & Jeffrey Herbst, *Somalia and the Future of Humanitarian Intervention*, in LEARNING FROM SOMALIA 239, 243 (Walter Clarke & Jeffrey Herbst eds., 1997). Predictably, as the date of American departure neared, attacks on UNITAF did increase somewhat, as if to hurry the United States out the door. The United States chose to ignore the provocations at that point because it was fixated on the seamless transfer and its sacred exit strategy.

because U.S. leadership simply ducked the problems that logically followed from the decision to intervene and then get out as quickly as possible."[158]

The United Nations inherited the problems raised by the UN-sponsored, U.S.-led intervention under Resolution 794, but did not receive the resources to solve the problems from the world community or its most powerful citizen, the United States. Furthermore, when the United States realized that the United Nations did not have the capability to handle the situation, it deployed Task Force Ranger for a specific and limited military purpose (itself denied all of the resources necessary for its mission to protect political appearances to Congress and the American public), but it made no greater effort to engage other parties in a political settlement. In a bewildering contradictory policy, it was declaring Aideed a "thug" and hunting him as a war criminal, while simultaneously conducting negotiations to secure his agreement to a political settlement. Yet, it was not committing any resources to settling the conflict without Aideed, if its plan to capture him succeeded.

Operation Restore Hope was a military operation planned by military personnel who were influenced by their decisions in Vietnam. The military learned from that conflict that overwhelming power must be applied decisively, not in graduated doses, and it also learned that public support of the mission must be generated and sustained. The military applied these lessons well. On the other hand, the military also learned in Vietnam that nation-building was a difficult and costly mission without guaranteed success, so it worked to avoid any possibility that Somalia would become a long-term commitment.[159] Unfortunately,

---

[158] *Id.*

[159] For example, the U.S. military has a tremendous civil affairs and military police capability that would have been extremely useful in Somalia. In a little over two months, the Civil Affairs Task Force successfully assisted the Kuwaitis in reconstituting their judiciary and police after the Iraqi occupiers were forced out. One thousand civil affairs officers were deployed to Panama with Operation Just Cause. Ronald Smith, the chief of that task force, estimated that 200 civil affairs reservists could have accomplished the same task in Somalia in ninety

many in the Department of State and elsewhere in the administration had also been through the Vietnam War and were themselves opposed to entangling engagements. The problem, however, was that facilitating a political solution for Somalia was their responsibility and that *necessitated* a long-term involvement both in Somalia and in building support among the American people for the goals it sought to accomplish. All of the later tragedy might have been avoided if the political leadership had employed UNITAF's "overwhelming advantages in military force, command and control, logistics, and communications to support the political agenda" of rehabilitating Somali political institutions, civil administration, and police.[160] In the words of Admiral Howe, "the need to rebuild the police and restore a system of justice was clear. . . . It was our ticket out of Somalia. For UNOSOM II to succeed, it had to rebuild and leave behind a force capable of preventing Somalia from descending again into the chaos of civil war."[161]

In the end, the leadership of the United States tried to purchase a cheap ticket out of Somalia. By failing to pursue its worthwhile goals while it had overwhelming force on the ground in Somalia, the United States prolonged, rather than diminished, its intervention and may well have incurred greater costs. More disturbing, however, is the fact that the failure of U.S. leadership provided lessons not only for us, but, as in Vietnam, for our adversaries as well. The American surrender of Vietnam encouraged Soviet adventurism and the exportation of the Communist revolution in the Third World from Latin America to Africa. Similarly, the pusillanimity of the Clinton administration in the application of force has endangered American interests and lives. After Somalia, the Clinton administration directed a national security study on the policy of U.S. intervention. The resulting policy, Presidential Decision Directive 25 (PDD-25) adopted in

---

days. The reservists were never activated, however, because the military planned Operation Restore Hope as a six-week mission. Clarke, *supra* note 65.

[160] *Id.*

[161] REFUGEE POLICY GROUP, HOPE RESTORED? HUMANITARIAN AID IN SOMALIA, 1990-1994, at 47 (1994).

May 1994, prescribes seventeen conditions to be met prior to committing U.S. forces to a UN-sponsored operation that might result in hostilities.[162] Although the questions it forces policy makers to answer are important and should have been asked in every intervention in the past and future, the checklist response itself shows weak leadership and flagging moral courage. The question has now become whether the proper procedure was followed in checking each block toward intervention and that is a pale substitute for leadership. It simply mirrors the current trend toward substituting a date of withdrawal for an articulated end state. It is McNamara all over again. And the result has real-world consequences beyond the ethereal policy debates.

—In Rwanda: "It was almost as if the Hutus had read [PDD-25]. The new restrictive guidelines made it not only possible for the United States to remain on the sidelines, but also to prevent others from getting involved while genocide proceeded apace."[163] In his public address, President Clinton recognized that "American leadership and America's troops" were indispensable to saving one million Somali lives, but less than six months later, the United States applied neither as 500,000 Rwandans were slaughtered in April 1994.

—In Haiti, the United States was a laughing-stock as warships were turned away from docks by a rock-throwing mob.

In November 1998, the United States indicted Osama bin Laden for the Embassy bombings in Kenya and Tanzania that killed 224 and wounded 5,500 and for his involvement in Somalia. Bin Laden declared "open season on Americans:"[164]

---

[162] James Terry, *A Legal Review of U.S. Military Involvement in Peacekeeping and Peace Enforcement Operations*, 42 NAVAL L. REV. 79 (1995).

[163] Thomas Weiss, *Rekindling Hope in U.N. Humanitarian Intervention*, in LEARNING FROM SOMALIA 207, 208 (Walter Clarke & Jeffrey Herbst eds., 1997).

[164] *Remarks of President William J. Clinton on U.S. Policy in Somalia*, *supra* note 142.

We have seen, in the last decade, the decline of the American government and the weakness of the American soldier who is ready to wage Cold Wars and unprepared to fight long wars. This was proven in Beirut, when the marines fled after two explosions. It also proves they can run in less than 24 hours, and this was also repeated in Somalia.[165]

The world is a dangerous place, but without resolute leadership that is willing to utilize overwhelming power effectively in the interests of the nation and what is morally right, the world can be even more deadly. Freedom isn't free. If our mission in Somalia was worth saving 300,000 lives, it was a mission worth doing, and we could have and should have done it right.

---

[165] G.E. Willis, *Analysts say Somalia's Legacy is Confusion about U.S. Resolve*, DEF. NEWS, Oct. 12, 1998, at 92. The author also asserts that the 1995 terrorist bombing at the Khobar towers "can be traced to the decision to pull out of Somalia after a handful of casualties."

BIBLIOGRAPHY

Atkinson, Rick. "Deliverance from Warlord's Fury." *Washington Post*, October 7, 1993, at A1.
———. "Firefight in Mogadishu: The Last Mission of Task Force Ranger." *Washington Post*, January 31, 1994, at A1.
———. "Marines Launch Final Phase of Somalia Pullout." *Washington Post*, February 28, 1995, at A12.
———. "The Raid That Went Wrong; How an Elite U.S. Force Failed in Somalia." *Washington Post*, January 30, 1994, at A1.
Boutros-Ghali, Boutros. An Agenda For Peace: Report of the Secretary-General on the Work of the Organization. U.N. Doc. A/47/277, S/24111, U.N. Sales No. E.95.I.15 (1992).
Bowden, Mark. "A Wrong Turn in Somalia: An Ill-Conceived Copter Raid Turned Many Somalis against U.S. Forces." *Seattle Times*, February 9, 1998, at A1.
Bush, George. "The People of Somalia . . . the Children . . . Need Our Help," *Washington Post*, December 5, 1992, at A16.
Bush, George, and Brent Scowcroft, *A World Transformed* (1998).
Claiborne, William. "Rival Warlords Sign Peace Pact in Somalia." *Washington Post*, December 12, 1992, at A1.
Clarke, Walter. "Failed Visions and Uncertain Mandates." In *Learning from Somalia* 3, edited by Walter Clarke and Jeffrey Herbst, 1997.
Clarke, Walter, and Jeffrey Herbst. "Somalia and the Future of Humanitarian Intervention." In *Learning from Somalia* 243, edited by Walter Clarke and Jeffrey Herbst, 1997.
Devroy, Ann. "Somalia Options Reviewed as Discontent in Congress Grows; New Deployment Raises Confusion on U.S. Goals." *Washington Post*, October 6, 1993, at A1.
Devroy, Ann, and Daniel Williams. "Clinton Vows to Find Political Solution for Somalia." *Washington Post*, September 18, 1993, at A18.
Devroy, Ann, and Kenneth Cooper. "Bush Calls Foreign Leaders for Support on Somalia Force." *Washington Post*, December 3, 1992, at A32.

Dewar, Helen. "Senate Vote on Pullout Delayed; Opponents of Immediate Withdrawal Warn Against Precipitous Action." *Washington Post*, October 7, 1993, at A39.

Dewar, Helen, and Barton Gellman. "Senate Asks Clinton to Get Approval for Continued Troop Deployment." *Washington Post*, September 10, 1993, at A31.

———. "Senate Debates U.S. Role in Somalia; Lawmakers Seek Clarification of Administration's Objectives." *Washington Post*, September 9, 1993, at A35.

Drysdale, John. "Foreign Military Intervention in Somalia: The Root Cause of the Shift from Peacekeeping to Peacemaking and Its Consequences." In *Learning from Somalia* 118, edited by Walter Clarke et al., 1997.

Esper, George. "U.S. Marine Killed in Somali Firefight; First Military Casualty of Relief Effort Dies During Patrol." *Washington Post*, January 13, 1993, at A15.

Further Report of the Secretary-General on UNOSOM, submitted in pursuance of paragraph 14 of Resolution 897 (1994). U.N. Doc. S/1994/614 (1994).

Further Report of the Secretary-General Submitted in Pursuance of Paragraph 18 of Resolution 814. U.N. SCOR, 48th Sess., U.N. Doc. S/26317 (1993).

Further Report of the Secretary-General Submitted in Pursuance of Paragraph 4 of Resolution 886. U.N. Doc. S/1994/12 (1994).

Gellman, Barton. "Marines Fight Gunmen, Deliver Food in Somalia." *Washington Post*, December 13, 1992, at A1.

———. "Somalia Options Reviewed as Discontent in Congress Grows; U.S. Lacked Strong Plan To Aid Besieged Troops." *Washington Post*, October 6, 1993, at A1.

———. "U.S. Rhetoric Changed, but Hunt Persisted; Clinton Had Power to Stop Operation Against Aideed." *Washington Post*, October 7, 1993, at A37.

———. "U.S., U.N. Differ over Best Way to Silence Somalia's Many Guns; Americans Focus on Heavy Arms; World Body Targets Individuals." *Washington Post*, December 23, 1992, at A19.

Goshko, John. "U.N. Orders U.S.-Led Force into Somalia." *Washington Post*, December 4, 1992, at A1.

Hackworth, David. *Hazardous Duty* (1996).

Heilprin, John. "Air Force Veteran Remembers Colleagues Who Died in Utah Crash and in Somalia; Weekend marks the fifth anniversary of bloody battle in streets of Mogadishu." *Salt Lake Tribune*, October 5, 1998, at D3.

Hempstone, Smith. "Dispatch From a Place Near Hell; The Killing Drought in Kenya, As Witnessed by the U.S. Ambassador." *Washington Post*, August 23, 1992, at C1.

Hoagland, Jim. "Beware 'Mission Creep' In Somalia." *Washington Post*, July, 20, 1993, at A17.

———. "Bluster and Blink." *Washington Post*, October 22, 1998, at A25.

House of Representatives Concurrent Resolution 370. 102nd Cong. (1992) (enacted).

"Italian Minister Denounces 'Rambo' U.N. Commanders." *Washington Post*, August 14, 1993, at A17.

Johnston, Harry, and Ted Dange. "Congress and the Somalia Crisis." In *Learning from Somalia* 191, edited by Walter Clarke and Jeffrey Herbst, 1997.

Joint Communique dated 14 February 1992 issued at the conclusion of discussions between United Nations Officials and representatives of the League of Arab States, the Organization of African Unity, and the Organization of the Islamic Conference with representatives of the Somali factions in the conflict in Mogadishu. U.N. Press Release IHA/434, 14 February 1992.

Karnow, Stanley. *Vietnam: A History* (1983).

Kennedy, Kevin. "The Relationship Between the Military and Humanitarian Organizations in Operation Restore Hope." In *Learning from Somalia* 99, edited by Walter Clarke and Jeffrey Herbst, 1997.

Krauthammer, Charles. "Enough of Sideshows." *Washington Post*, March 12, 1993, at A23.

Kull, Steven. "What New Isolationism? Wrong, Pundits. We Still Feel a Global Duty, Even in Somalia." *Washington Post*, October 24, 1993, at C2.

Kurtz, Howard. "Deaths Spur Media Retreat From Somalia." *Washington Post*, July 17, 1993, at A11.

Lancaster, John. "General Bars Disarming Somali Clans; Marine Commander's Comments Add to Confusion over U.S. Mission." *Washington Post*, February 15, 1993, at A1.

Lancaster, John. "Hitting the Beach in Glare of the Night; TV Turns Stealthy Moment into Shining One, Angering Pentagon Aides." *Washington Post*, December 9, 1992, at A1.

———. "Powell Says Mission Duration Is Flexible; Operation Could Take 3 Months, General Says." *Washington Post*, December 5, 1992.

———. "Stabilizing Riven Somalia a Monumental Task." *Washington Post*, December 3, 1992, at A34.

———. "U.S. Beginning Pullout from Somalia; Slow Withdrawal Aimed Partly at Forcing U.N. to Take Responsibility." *Washington Post*, January 19, 1993, at A1.

"Letter dated 08 December 1992 from the Secretary-General to President Bush of the United States discussing the establishment of a secure environment in Somalia and the need for continuous consultations." In *The United Nations and Somalia 1992-1996*. U.N. Blue Books Series, Volume VIII, U.N. Sales No. E.96.I.8 (1996).

Letter Dated 24 November 1992 From the Secretary-General Addressed to the President of the Security Council. U.N. SCOR, 47th Sess., U.N. Doc. S/24859 (1992).

Letter Dated 29 November 1992 From the Secretary-General Addressed to the President of the Security Council. U.N. SCOR, 47th Sess., U.N. Doc. S/24868 (1992).

Lewis, Paul. "U.N. Will Increase Troops in Somalia." *New York Times*, March 27, 1993, at A3.

Lippman, Thomas. "U.S. Studies Somali's Note Seeking U.N. Investigation; Aideed Says He Would Abide by Conclusion." *Washington Post*, September 17, 1993, at A29.

Logan, Carolyn, "U.S. Public Opinion and the Intervention in Somalia: Lessons for the Future of Military-Humanitarian Interventions." *Fall Fletcher Forum on World Affairs* 155 (1996).

Moore, Harold, and Joseph Galloway. *We Were Soldiers Once . . . and Young* (1989).

Natsios, Andrew. "Humanitarian Relief Intervention in Somalia." In *Learning from Somalia* 77, edited by Walter Clarke and Jeffrey Herbst, 1997.

Noble, Kenneth. "400 U.S. Marines Attack Compound of Somali Gunmen." *New York Times*, January 8, 1993, at A1.

"Nunn: Congress Should Narrow U.S. Somalia Role." *Washington Post*, September 27, 1993, at A16.

Oakley, Robert. "What We Learned in Somalia." *Washington Post*, March 20, 1994, at C7.

Oberdorfer, Don. "Bush Orders Food Airlift to Combat Somali Famine; Deliveries to Interior to Begin Within Days." *Washington Post*, August 15, 1992, at A1.

———. "Bush Sends Forces To Help Somalia; 'America Must Act,' President Says." *Washington Post*, December 5, 1992, at A1.

———. "Oakley Is Called from Retirement to Head Political Side of Operation in Somalia." *Washington Post*, December 9, 1992, at A27.

———. "The Path to Intervention; A Massive Tragedy 'We Could Do Something About.'" *Washington Post*, December 6, 1992, at A1.

———. "U.S. Took Slow Approach to Somali Crisis; Delay in Action Attributed to Civil War, Other Global Problems, Lack of Media Attention." *Washington Post*, August 24, 1992, at A1.

Oberdorfer, Don, and Trevor Rowe. "U.S. Offers Ground Troops for Intervention in Somalia; U.N. Moves toward Sending Armed Force to Deliver Food." *Washington Post*, November 26, 1992, at A1.

Operation Restore Hope, The Military Operations in Somalia: Hearing Before the Senate Committee on Armed Services. 102nd Cong. (1992).

Perlez, Jane. "Food Relief Grows but So Do Somalia's Dead." *New York Times,* July 19, 1992, at A2.

Powell, Colin. *My American Journey* (1995).

Prunier, Gerard. "The Experience of European Armies in Operation Restore Hope." In *Learning from Somalia* 135, edited by Walter Clarke and Jeffrey Herbst, 1997.

Refugee Policy Group. *Hope Restored? Humanitarian Aid in Somalia, 1990-1994* (1994).

Report by the Secretary-General Concerning the Situation in Somalia. U.N. SCOR, 49th Sess., 1068th mtg., U.N. Doc. S/1994/1068 (1994).

Report by the United States Pursuant to Security Council Resolution 794. U.N. SCOR, 47th Sess., Annex, U.N. Doc. S/24976 (1992).

Report of the Commission of Inquiry Established Pursuant to Security Council Resolution 885 (1993) to Investigate Armed Attacks on UNOSOM II Personnel which led to Casualties among Them. U.N. SCOR, 49th Sess., Annex 5, U.N. Doc. S/1994/653 (1994).

Report of the Secretary-General Concerning the Situation in Somalia. U.N. SCOR, 49th Sess., U.N. Doc. S/1994/1166 (1994).

Report of the Secretary-General on the Situation in Somalia. U.N. SCOR, 47th Sess., U.N. Doc. S/24343 (1992).

Report of the Secretary-General to the Security Council on Somalia. U.N. SCOR, 49th Sess., 977th mtg., U.N. Doc. S/1994/977 (1994).

Report of the Security Council Mission to Somalia (26 and 27 October 1994). U.N. SCOR, 49th Sess., U.N. Doc. S/1994/1245 (1994).

Report Pursuant to Paragraph 5 of Security Council Resolution 837 (1993) on the Investigation into the 5 June 1993 Attack on United Nations Forces in Somalia Conducted on Behalf of the Secretary-General. U.N. SCOR, 48th Sess., Annex, U.N. Doc. S/26351 (1993).

Richburg, Keith. "Aid Staffs Pull Out of Mogadishu; Violence That Killed 22 Soldiers Called 'Organized Ambush.'" *Washington Post*, June 7, 1993, at A1.

———. "Aideed's Forces May Have Been Underestimated, Officials Concede." *Washington Post*, October 8, 1993, at A18.

———. "American Casualties in Somalia: A Policy Time Bomb Explodes." *Washington Post*, August 12, 1993, at A1.

———. "Broader U.S. Role Developing in Somalia; Americans Move beyond 'Narrow Focus' to Take on Some Tasks of Civil Rehabilitation." *Washington Post*, December 31, 1992, at A16.

———. "Criticism Mounts over Somali Raid; 'Pack Up, Go Home,' U.S. Troops Urged." *Washington Post*, July 15, 1993, at A21.

———. "Italy, in Rebuke to U.N., to Pull Troops Out of Mogadishu; General Refuses to 'Use Same Means That Guerrillas Use.'" *Washington Post*, August 14, 1993, at A15.

———. "Solutions for Somalia Complicated by Chaos; Authority Is Absent and Food Is Power." *Washington Post*, August 30, 1992, at A1.

———. "U.S. Starts Relief Effort in Somalia; 4 Planes Bring Tons of Food, Equipment." *Washington Post*, August 29, 1992, at A1.

———. "U.S. Suspends Relief Flights to Somali Town." *Washington Post*, October 26, 1992, at A12.

Sawyer, Kathy. "U.S. Officials Estimate Cost, Length of Somalia Mission; Humanitarian Operation Seen Taking 2 to 3 Months." *Washington Post*, December 7, 1992, at A27.

Security Council Resolution 733. U.N. SCOR, 47th Sess., 3039th mtg., U.N. Doc. S/RES/733 (1992).

Security Council Resolution 746. U.N. SCOR, 47th Sess., 3060th mtg., U.N. Doc. S/RES/746 (1992).

Security Council Resolution 751. U.N. SCOR, 47th Sess., 3069th mtg., U.N. Doc. S/RES/751 (1992).

Security Council Resolution 767. U.N. SCOR, 47th Sess., 3101st mtg., U.N. Doc. S/RES/767 (1992).

Security Council Resolution 775. U.N. SCOR, 47th Sess., 3110th mtg., U.N. Doc. S/RES/775 (1992).

Security Council Resolution 794. U.N. SCOR, 47th Sess., 3145th mtg., U.N. Doc. S/RES/794 (1992).

Security Council Resolution 814. U.N. SCOR, 48th Sess., 3188th mtg., U.N. Doc. S/RES/814 (1993).

Security Council Resolution 837. U.N. SCOR, 48th Sess., 3229th mtg., U.N. Doc. S/RES/837 (1993).

Security Council Resolution 865. U.N. SCOR, 48th Sess., 3280th mtg., U.N. Doc. S/RES/865 (1993).

Security Council Resolution 885. U.N. SCOR, 48th Sess., 3315th mtg., U.N. Doc. S/RES/885 (1993).

Security Council Resolution 886. U.N. SCOR, 48th Sess., 3315th mtg., U.N. Doc. S/RES/886 (1993).

Security Council Resolution 897. U.N. SCOR, 49th Sess., 3334th mtg., U.N. Doc. S/RES/897 (1994).

Security Council Resolution 954. U.N. SCOR, 49th Sess., 3451st mtg., U.N. Doc. S/RES/954 (1994).

Senate Concurrent Resolution 132. 102nd Cong., 138 Cong. Rec. H7829-02 (1992) (enacted).

Senate Resolution 115. 102nd Cong., 137 Cong. Rec. S5311-01 (1991).

Shales, Tom. "Television's Beachhead in Somalia." *Washington Post*, December 9, 1992, at C1.

Shields, Todd. "Troops in Somalia: Frustration Every Day; Pakistanis Only Hold Mogadishu Airport." *Washington Post*, December 3, 1992, at A1.

The Crisis in Somalia: Hearing Before the House Comm. on Foreign Affairs. 102nd Cong. (1992).

The Horn of Africa: Changing Realities and the U.S. Response: Hearing Before the Subcommittee on African Affairs of the Senate Committee on Foreign Relations. 102nd Cong. (1992).

The Situation in Somalia: Report of the Secretary-General. U.N. SCOR, 47th Sess., U.N. Doc. S/23693 (1992).

The Situation in Somalia: Report of the Secretary-General. U.N. SCOR, 47th Sess., U.N. Doc. S/24480 (1992).

The Situation in Somalia: Report of the Secretary-General Submitted in Pursuance of Paragraphs 18 and 19 of Security

Council Resolution 794. U.N. SCOR, 47th Sess., U.N. Doc. S/24992 (1992).

Somalia: The Case for Action: Hearing Before the House Select Committee on Hunger. 102nd Cong. (1992).

Terry, James. "A Legal Review of U.S. Military Involvement in Peacekeeping and Peace Enforcement Operations." 42 *Naval Law Review* 79 (1995).

The United Nations and Somalia 1992-1996. U.N. Blue Books Series, Volume VIII, U.N. Sales No. E.96.I.8 (1996).

U.N. Peacekeeping in Africa: The Western Sahara and Somalia: Hearing Before the Subcommittee on Africa of the Senate Committee on Foreign Relations. 102nd Cong. (1992).

U.S. Military Operations in Somalia: Hearings Before the Senate Committee on Armed Services. 103d Cong. (1994).

Weiss, Thomas. "Rekindling Hope in U.N. Humanitarian Intervention." In *Learning from Somalia* 207, edited by Walter Clarke and Jeffrey Herbst, 1997.

Williams, Daniel. "Raid on Warlord Designed to Oust Him from Somali Power Struggle." *Washington Post*, June 15, 1993, at A17.

Willis, G. E. "Analysts say Somalia's Legacy is Confusion about U.S. Resolve." *Defense News*, October 12, 1998, at 92.

Woods, James L. "U.S. Government Decisionmaking Processes During Humanitarian Operations in Somalia." In *Learning from Somalia*, edited by Walter Clarke and Jeffrey Herbst, 1997.

Index

Index